This book is dedicated to

Helen and Donald White

and

Clare and Harry Matlin

Cognitive
Psychology

SEVENTH EDITION
INTERNATIONAL STUDENT VERSION

MARGARET W. MATLIN
SUNY Geneseo

WILEY

John Wiley & Sons, Inc.

ISBN: 978-0-470-40947-3

Printed in Asia

10 9 8 7 6 5 4 3 2 1

I started to write this preface in May, 2008, just after I had finished grading the final exams of the students in my Cognitive Psychology class. I then began thinking how much the discipline of Cognitive Psychology had changed since I was the same age as my students. As an undergraduate at Stanford University, we had no course in Cognitive Psychology. Yes, I had enjoyed Albert Hastorf's course, which had emphasized cognitive approaches to social psychology. Leonard Horowitz, my undergraduate mentor, had kindly allowed me to audit his graduate course in human memory, clearly a forerunner of contemporary Cognitive Psychology.

I also completed a psychology course taught by Gordon Bower. In 2005, Bower won the prestigious National Medal of Science. The citation that accompanied this award praised him "for his unparalleled contributions to cognitive and mathematical psychology, for his lucid analyses of remembering and reasoning, and for his important service to psychology and American science." The course that Bower taught during the 1960s was called "Learning." Each student was given a rat, and we learned about schedules of reinforcement, shaping, and numerous other behaviorist concepts . . . but I don't recall any mention about topics such as imagery, schemas, or mnemonics.

Just three years after Bower's course, I was walking along a hallway in the Human Performance Center at the University of Michigan. A young man suddenly rushed past me, shouting, "Hey, everybody, I just got a copy of Neisser's *Cognitive Psychology*!" As my flashbulb memory suggests, many psychologists enthusiastically welcomed the emerging cognitive perspective. They were intrigued that the mind could be viewed as an information-processing system, rather than the mechanical switchboard endorsed by the behaviorists (Treisman, 2003). I had the good fortune to watch the discipline of cognitive psychology develop during its infancy, with interesting early research on such topics as short-term memory, knowledge representation, and language comprehension.

More than 25 years ago, I began writing the first edition of my textbook, *Cognitive Psychology*. That first edition, which was published in 1983, included 382 pages of text. It featured only one chapter on memory and one on language—and a mere 23 pages of references.

Now, in the year 2008, cognitive psychology has passed through childhood, and even adolescence. Our relatively mature discipline now features dozens of journals, hundreds of professional books, and numerous handbooks. In fact, I found it challenging to limit this seventh edition of *Cognitive Psychology* to 480 pages of text and 74 pages of references.

As I write this preface for the current edition of *Cognitive Psychology*, I'm reminded of the impressive advances in our discipline since that first edition was published. Cognitive psychologists have explored topics that were not even mentioned in the first edition—topics such as thought suppression, metamemory, and bilingualism.

Researchers have also developed new theoretical approaches. For example, Baddeley's sophisticated working-memory model has replaced the fixed capacity view of short-term memory. Furthermore, the first edition of *Cognitive Psychology* barely alluded to individual differences in cognitive processes. This edition now includes 12 special features on individual variation, as well as many briefer discussions throughout the book.

Innovative research techniques have also opened new pathways. For example, neuroscience research allows us to investigate the biological basis of cognitive processes such as attention, memory, mental imagery, and language comprehension. Many of the new research methods provide helpful information about cognitive mechanisms, so it's exciting to contemplate how the field of Cognitive Psychology will expand during future decades!

This research continues to emphasize the impressive competence of our cognitive processes. For instance, most adults can read at the rate of 250 to 300 words per minute. Even infants are cognitively competent. Research shows that newborns can discriminate between two languages that have different rhythms, such as English and Italian. Cognitive skills increase rapidly during childhood. Furthermore, 6-year-olds know approximately 12,000 words, which they use to construct grammatically accurate sentences that no human has previously uttered.

Still, many cognitive psychology textbooks are written in such a dry, academic style that they fail to capture these inherently interesting capabilities. Over the years, I've received letters and comments from hundreds of students and professors, telling me how much they enjoyed reading this textbook. Using their feedback, I have tried to write this seventh edition with these readers in mind. This task is especially challenging because the research has become increasingly specialized since I wrote the first edition of *Cognitive Psychology*.

FEATURES OF THIS TEXTBOOK

I have now taught the cognitive psychology course at SUNY Geneseo more than 40 times. Each time I revise *Cognitive Psychology*, I try to think about students like those in my classes. This vigilance keeps me honest, because I must continually ask myself, "Would my own students really understand this, or would they simply give me a blank stare?"

Here are some of the ways in which I consider this textbook to be student-oriented:

1. The writing style is clear and interesting, with frequent examples to make the information more concrete.

2. The text demonstrates how our cognitive processes are relevant to our everyday, real-world experiences.

3. The book frequently examines how Cognitive Psychology can be applied to other disciplines, such as clinical psychology, social psychology, consumer psychology, education, communication, business, medicine, and law.

4. The first chapter introduces five major themes that I emphasize throughout the book. Because the research in cognitive psychology is now so extensive, students need a sense of continuity that helps them appreciate connections among many diverse topics.

5. An outline and a preview introduce each chapter, providing an appropriate framework for new material.

6. Each new term is presented in **boldface print.** Every term is also accompanied by a concise definition that appears in the same sentence. In addition, I include pronunciation guides for new terms with potentially ambiguous pronunciation. Students who are hesitant about the pronunciation of terms such as *schema* and *saccadic* will be reluctant to use these words or ask questions about them.

7. Many easy-to-perform demonstrations illustrate important experiments in Cognitive Psychology, and they clarify central concepts in the discipline. I designed these demonstrations so that they would require equipment that most undergraduate students would have on hand.

8. Each major section within a chapter concludes with a summary. This feature enables students to review and consolidate material before moving to the next section, rather than wait until the chapter's end for a single, lengthy summary.

9. Each chapter includes comprehensive review questions and a list of new terms.

10. Each chapter concludes with a list of recommended readings, along with a brief description of each resource.

11. A glossary at the end of the book provides a definition of every new term. I tried to include additional contextual information wherever it might be useful, in order to clarify the terms as much as possible.

THE TEXTBOOK'S ORGANIZATION

A textbook needs to be interesting and helpful. It must also reflect current developments in the discipline, and it must allow instructors to adapt its structure to their own teaching plans. The following features should therefore be useful for professors:

1. The seventh edition of *Cognitive Psychology* offers a comprehensive overview of the field, including chapters on perceptual processes, memory, imagery, general knowledge, language, problem solving and creativity, reasoning and decision making, and cognitive development.

2. Each chapter is a self-contained unit. For example, a term such as *heuristics* or *top-down processing* is defined in every chapter in which it is used. This feature allows professors considerable flexibility in the sequence of chapter coverage. Some professors may wish to discuss the topic of imagery (Chapter 7) prior to the three chapters on memory. Others might want to assign the chapter on general knowledge (Chapter 8) during an earlier part of the academic term.

3. Each section within a chapter can stand as a discrete unit, especially because every section concludes with a section summary. Professors may choose to cover individual sections in a different order. For example, one professor may want students to read the section on schemas prior to the chapter on long-term memory. Another professor might prefer to subdivide Chapter 13, on cognitive development, so that the first section of this chapter (on memory) follows

Chapter 5, the second section (on metacognition) follows Chapter 6, and the third section (on language) follows Chapter 10.

4. Chapters 2 through 13 each include an "In Depth" feature, which focuses on recent research about a selected topic in cognitive psychology and provides details on research methods. Four of these features are new to this seventh edition, and the remaining seven have been substantially updated and revised.

5. In all, the bibliography contains 2,064 references; 806 of them are new to the seventh edition. Furthermore, 1227 (62%) have been published since the year 2000. As a result, the textbook provides a very current overview of the discipline.

6. This seventh edition includes a new feature called "Individual Differences"; this feature is described in detail in Chapter 1 on pages 25 and 26.

HIGHLIGHTS OF THE SEVENTH EDITION

The field of cognitive psychology has made impressive advances since the sixth edition of this textbook was published in 2005. Research in the areas of perception, memory, language, and cognitive development has been especially ambitious. In addition, researchers have provided more details about theoretical approaches to the field. Other researchers have employed neuroscience techniques to provide information about cognitive topics as diverse as face recognition, language comprehension, and memory development during childhood.

I have made two types of changes in the current edition of *Cognitive Psychology*. Specifically, I added a new feature to the textbook, and I also updated the discussions about the cognitive psychology research.

The Individual Differences Feature

While organizing the material for this seventh edition of *Cognitive Psychology*, I noticed a substantial increase in the number of research articles that focused on individual differences in cognitive performance. Furthermore, I discovered that my own students' literature-review papers frequently addressed topics such as "The Relationship between Major Depression and Working-Memory Performance."

As you will see, Chapters 2 through 13 in this seventh edition now include an "Individual Differences Feature." Some of these focus on psychological disorders such as schizophrenia and depression. Others focus on demographic variables—such as gender, profession, and culture—that could potentially be related to cognitive performance. In Chapter 1 (pages 25–26), you can read more details about this new feature.

Updated Coverage of Research in Cognitive Psychology

In preparing this seventh edition, I carefully reviewed each chapter. In fact, every page of this textbook has been updated and rewritten. Some of the more substantial changes include the following:

- Chapter 1 includes a new demonstration about non-psychologists' knowledge about cognitive psychology. I also expanded the discussion of cognitive neuroscience.

- Chapter 2 examines new research about the neuroscience research on face recognition. It also explores people's errors in object recognition.

- Chapter 3 now features more coverage about divided attention during driving and about neuroscience research on attention networks.

- Chapter 4 examines new neuroscience research about the phonological loop and the visuospatial sketchpad.

- Chapter 5 explores new research on encoding specificity, as well as reorganized and updated coverage of autobiographical memory.

- Chapter 6 includes new information about the testing effect, prospective memory, and the regulation of study strategies.

- Chapter 7 has been restructured so that the sections on mental imagery and on cognitive maps now address similar topics in the same order. Furthermore, the in-depth section on creating cognitive maps now includes more information on the importance of inferences.

- Chapter 8 is somewhat shorter, and it includes new information about semantic memory, expertise, and inferences based on schemas.

- Chapter 9 includes new studies about ambiguity, neurolinguistics, and meta-comprehension.

- Chapter 10 examines new information about lexical entrainment, metacognitive components of writing, and bilingualism.

- Chapter 11 features expanded coverage of situated Cognitive Psychology, functional fixedness, and stereotype threat.

- Chapter 12 is now somewhat shorter, and it includes new information about the heuristic-analytical approach to reasoning, Gigerenzer's critiques of the heuristics approach to decision making, and overconfidence.

- Chapter 13 discusses new research on the own-race bias in babies, prospective memory in elderly adults, and infants' speech-perception skills.

In preparing this new edition, I made every possible effort to emphasize current research. I searched for relevant articles in seven cognitive psychology journals and five general psychology journals. This investigation was supplemented by numerous specific *PsycINFO* searches. Furthermore, I systematically searched through the new-book lists from eight publishers that specialize in cognitive psychology. I also wrote to more than 200 prominent researchers, requesting reprints and preprints. The research on Cognitive Psychology is expanding at an ever-increasing rate, and I want this textbook to capture the excitement of the current research.

ACKNOWLEDGMENTS

I want to thank many individuals at John Wiley & Sons for their substantial contributions to the development and the production of the seventh edition of *Cognitive Psychology*. I have been extremely fortunate to work with two superb Associate Editors, in preparing this edition. Maureen Clendenny and Eileen McKeever were very conscientious about responding quickly to my questions and providing information about new developments that were relevant to this textbook. They were also especially skilled in seeking out excellent reviewers who provided feedback about the chapters in the seventh edition. I would also like to acknowledge Jay O'Callaghan (Vice-President and Publisher, Higher Education) and Chris Johnson (Executive Editor) for their editorial guidance throughout the planning and writing phases of this textbook.

The Production Department at Wiley is also wonderful! Valerie A. Vargas is a top-notch Senior Production Editor, and she managed all aspects of production with intelligence and efficiency. Madelyn Lesure created an elegant and user-friendly design for this seventh edition.

During the production phase of the seventh edition, I was extremely pleased with Patty Donovan, who was my Project Coordinator at Pine Tree Composition. She was masterful in thinking flexibly, answering questions quickly, and resolving puzzling issues about production. She also skillfully negotiated the complex flow of edited material between Lewiston, Maine, and my home in Linwood. The seventh edition of *Cognitive Psychology* is the 22nd book I have written, so I know how important a good editor can be to the success of a textbook!

Once more, Linda Webster compiled both the subject index and the author index, and she also prepared the glossary. Linda has worked on all my recent textbooks, and I continue to be impressed with her intelligent and careful work on these important components of the textbook.

In addition, I would like to thank Danielle Torio and Rachel Cirone, the marketing managers at Wiley, for their creativity, positive feedback, and excellent organizational skills. Thanks are also due to the Wiley sales representatives for their excellent work and enthusiastic support!

During my undergraduate and graduate training, many professors encouraged my enthusiasm for the growing field of Cognitive Psychology. I would like to thank Gordon Bower, Albert Hastorf, Leonard Horowitz, and Eleanor Maccoby of Stanford University, and Edwin Martin, Arthur Melton, Richard Pew, and Robert Zajonc of the University of Michigan.

Many other people have contributed in important ways to this book. My student assistants on this edition of *Cognitive Psychology* were Kristina Condidorio, Catherine Burke, Catherine Urban, and Abigail Hammond. These four superb students helped to locate and order references. They also checked to make sure that the chapter citations agreed with the entries in the reference section, and they handled numerous other details connected with writing a textbook. Also, Carolyn Emmert and Connie Ellis kept other aspects of my life running smoothly, allowing me more time to work on this writing project.

In addition, I want to acknowledge the helpfulness of Harriet Sleggs and Bill Baker. These two individuals coordinate the Information Delivery Service at Milne Library, SUNY Geneseo. They efficiently ordered several hundred books and articles for this seventh edition of *Cognitive Psychology*. It's difficult to imagine how I could have completed this book without their intelligent and timely assistance!

In addition, a number of students contributed to the book and provided useful suggestions after reading various editions of *Cognitive Psychology:* Jennifer Balus, Mary Jane Brennan, A. Eleanor Chand, Miriam Dowd, Elizabeth Einemann, Michelle Fischer, Sarah Gonnella, Laurie Guarino, Benjamin Griffin, Jessica Hosey, Don Hudson, Jay Kleinman, Jessica Krager, Mary Kroll, Eun Jung Lim, Pamela Mead, Pamela Mino, Kaveh Moghbeli, Jacquilyn Moran, Michelle Morante, Jennifer Niemczyk, Danielle Palermo, Alison Repel, Judith Rickey, Mary Riley, Margery Schemmel, Richard Slocum, John Tanchak, Brenna Terry, Sherri Tkachuk, Dan Vance, Heather Wallach, and Rachelle Yablin. Several students at Stanford University's Casa Zapata provided insights about bilingualism: Laura Aizpuru, Sven Halstenburg, Rodrigo Liong, Jean Lu, Edwardo Martinez, Sally Matlin, Dorin Parasca, and Laura Uribarri.

Other students provided information about useful cognitive psychology articles: Ned Abbott, Angela Capria, Stacey Canavan, Elizabeth Carey, Lindsay Ciancetta, Melissa Conway, Amanda Crandall, Moises Gonzales, Katie Griffin, Hideaki Imai, Peter Kang, Becky Keegan, Maria Korogodsky, Patricia Kramer, Leslie Lauer, Sally Matlin, Kristen Merkle, Bill Monteith, Jill Papke, Christopher Piersante, Heather Quayle, Brooke Schurr, Laura Segovia, Nancy Tomassino, Sara Vonhold, Melissa Waterman, and Lauren Whaley.

Thanks also to colleagues Drew Appleby, Ganie DeHart, Thomas Donnan, K. Anders Ericsson, Beverly Evans, Hugh Foley, Mark Graber, Elliot D. Hammer, Douglas Herrmann, Eve Higby, Ken Kallio, Colin M. MacLeod, Lisbet Nielsen, Paul Norris, Bennett L. Schwartz, Douglas Vipond, Lori Van Wallendael, Julia Wagner, and Alan Welsh for making suggestions about references and improved wording for passages in the text.

Special thanks are due to Lucinda DeWitt, who created the PowerPoint slides for this seventh edition. In addition, Lucinda provided careful and intelligent feedback on the chapters, and she assisted with the Test Item File for *Cognitive Psychology* 7th edition. Lucinda was also a superb reviewer on earlier editions of this textbook, and her contributions continue to influence this textbook!

Three psychology professors have provided excellent ancillaries for this seventh edition of *Cognitive Psychology*, as well as the previous edition. Thanks to Ami Spears (web activities), Lise Abrams (web links), and Richard Block (self quizzes). [name of PowerPoint author to be added.]

I would also like to express my continuing appreciation to the textbook's reviewers. The reviewers who helped on the first edition included: Mark Ashcraft, Cleveland State University; Randolph Easton, Boston College; Barbara Goldman, University of Michigan, Dearborn; Harold Hawkins, University of Oregon; Joseph Hellige, University of Southern California; Richard High, Lehigh University; James Juola, University of Kansas; Richard Kasschau, University of Houston; and R. A. Kinchla, Princeton University.

The reviewers who provided assistance on the second edition were: Harriett Amster, University of Texas, Arlington; Francis T. Durso, University of Oklahoma; Susan E. Dutch, Westfield State College; Sallie Gordon, University of Utah; Richard Gottwald, University of Indiana, South Bend; Kenneth R. Graham, Muhlenberg College; Morton A. Heller, Winston-Salem State University; Michael W. O'Boyle, Iowa State University; David G. Payne, SUNY Binghamton; Louisa M. Slowiaczek, Loyola University, Chicago; Donald A. Smith, Northern Illinois University; Patricia Snyder, Albright College; and Richard K. Wagner, Florida State University.

The third-edition reviewers included: Ira Fischler, University of Florida; John Flowers, University of Nebraska; Nancy Franklin, SUNY Stony Brook; Joanne Gallivan, University College of Cape Breton; Margaret Intons-Peterson, Indiana University; Christine Lofgren, University of California, Irvine; Bill McKeachie, University of Michigan; William Oliver, Florida State University; Andrea Richards, University of California, Los Angeles; Jonathan Schooler, University of Pittsburgh; and Jyotsna Vaid, Texas A & M University.

The reviewers of the fourth edition included: Lucinda DeWitt, Concordia College; Susan Dutch, Westfield State College; Kathleen Flannery, Saint Anselm College; Linda Gerard, Michigan State University; Catherine Hale, University of Puget Sound; Timothy Jay, North Adams State College; W. Daniel Phillips, Trenton State College; Dana Plude, University of Maryland; Jonathan Schooler, University of Pittsburgh; Matthew Sharps, California State University, Fresno; Greg Simpson, University of Kansas; Margaret Thompson, University of Central Florida; and Paul Zelhart, East Texas State University.

The reviewers for the fifth edition included: Lise Abrams, University of Florida; Tom Alley, Clemson University; Kurt Baker, Emporia State University; Richard Block, Montana State University; Kyle Cave, University of Southampton (United Kingdom); Lucinda DeWitt, University of Minnesota; Susan Dutch, Westfield State College; James Enns, University of British Columbia; Philip Higham, University of Northern British Columbia; Mark Hoyert, Indiana University Northwest; Anita Meehan, Kutztown University of Pennsylvania; Joan Piroch, Coastal Carolina University; David Pittenger, Marietta College; and Matthew Sharps, California State University, Fresno. The excellent advice from the reviewers of these five earlier editions continued to guide me as I prepared this most recent version of the book.

The reviewers of the sixth edition included Lise Abrams, University of Florida; Thomas R. Alley, Clemson University; Tim Curran, University of Colorado; Susan E. Dutch, Westfield State College; Ira Fischler, University of Florida; Kathy E. Johnson, Indiana University-Purdue University Indianapolis; Gretchen Kambe, University of

Nevada, Las Vegas; James P. Van Overschelde, University of Maryland; and Thomas B. Ward, University of Alabama.

Last—but certainly not least—I want to praise the reviewers of this seventh edition of *Cognitive Psychology*. These individuals provided advice about organizing the chapters in this textbook. They also suggested sections that could be shortened, advice that reviewers are typically reluctant to supply! They were also skilled in reviewing my manuscript from their own perspectives—as well-informed professors—and also from the perspective of fairly naïve psychology students. Enthusiastic thanks go to: Heather Bartfeld, Texas A&M University; James Bartlett, University of Texas at Dallas; Nancy Franklin, SUNY Stony Brook; Robert J. Hines, University of Arkansas, Little Rock; Joseph Lao, Teachers College, Columbia University; Susan Lima, University of Wisconsin, Milwaukee; Janet Nicol, University of Arizona; Catherine Plowright, University of Ottawa; Sara Ransdell, Nova Southeastern University; Tony Ro, Rice University; Michael Root, Ohio University; and David Somers, Boston University.

The final words of thanks belong to my family members. My husband, Arnie Matlin, encouraged me to write the first edition of this book during the early 1980s. His continuing enthusiasm, superb sense of humor, and loving support always bring joy to my writing, and certainly to my life! Our daughters now live in other parts of the United States. I'd like to thank Sally Matlin, who now lives in the San Francisco Bay area. Thanks also to Beth Matlin-Heiger and Neil Matlin-Heiger (and our grandchildren, Jacob and Joshua Matlin-Heiger), who live in the Boston area. Their continuing pride in my accomplishments makes it even more rewarding to be an author! Last, I would like to express my gratitude to four other important people who have shaped my life, my parents by birth and my parents by marriage: Helen and Donald White, and Clare and Harry Matlin.

Margaret W. Matlin
Geneseo, New York

◎ Table of Contents

CHAPTER 2   Recognizing Visual and Auditory Stimuli   **31**

CHAPTER 6   Using Memory Strategies and Metacognition   **163**

CHAPTER 1

Introducing Cognitive Psychology

Introduction

A Brief History of Cognitive Psychology

The Origins of Cognitive Psychology
The Emergence of Modern Cognitive Psychology

Current Issues in Cognitive Psychology

Cognitive Neuroscience
Artificial Intelligence
Cognitive Science

An Overview of Your Textbook

Preview of the Chapters
Themes in the Book
How to Use Your Book

PREVIEW

Cognition is an area within psychology that describes how we acquire, store, transform, and use knowledge. Human thought processes have intrigued theorists for more than 2,000 years. The contemporary study of cognition can be traced to Wundt's contributions in creating the discipline of psychology, the early research in memory, and William James's theories about cognitive processes. In the early twentieth century, the behaviorists emphasized observable behavior, rather than mental processes. New research in areas such as memory and language produced disenchantment with behaviorism, and the cognitive approach gained popularity during the 1960s.

Cognitive psychology is influenced by research in cognitive neuroscience and artificial intelligence. Cognitive psychology is also part of an active interdisciplinary area known as cognitive science.

This introductory chapter also gives you a preview of the chapters in this book and an overview of five themes in cognitive psychology. The chapter concludes with some tips on how to make the best use of your textbook's special features.

INTRODUCTION

At this exact moment, you are actively performing several cognitive tasks. In order to reach this second sentence of the first paragraph, you used pattern recognition to create words from an assortment of squiggles and lines that form the letters on this page. You also consulted your memory and your knowledge about language to search for word meanings and to link together the ideas in this paragraph. Right now, as you think about those cognitive accomplishments, you are engaging in another cognitive task called *metacognition*, or thinking about your thought processes. You may also have used decision making—yet another cognitive process—if you were debating whether to begin reading this textbook or to send an e-mail to a friend.

Cognition, or mental activity, describes the acquisition, storage, transformation, and use of knowledge. If cognition operates every time you acquire some information, place it in storage, transform that information, and use it . . . then cognition definitely includes a wide range of mental processes! This textbook will explore mental processes such as perception, memory, imagery, language, problem solving, reasoning, and decision making.

A related term, **cognitive psychology**, has two meanings: (1) Sometimes it is a synonym for the word *cognition*, and so it refers to the variety of mental activities we just listed. (2) Sometimes it refers to a particular theoretical approach to psychology. Specifically, the **cognitive approach** is a theoretical orientation that emphasizes people's mental processes and their knowledge. For example, a cognitive explanation of ethnic stereotypes would emphasize topics such as the influence of these stereotypes on the judgments we make about people from different ethnic groups (Whitley & Kite, 2006).

Psychologists often contrast the cognitive approach with several other current theoretical approaches. For example, the behaviorist approach emphasizes our observable behaviors, and the psychodynamic approach focuses on our unconscious emotions. To explain ethnic stereotypes, these two approaches would describe our behaviors or our emotions, rather than our cognitive processes.

Why should you and other students learn about cognition? One reason is that cognition occupies a major portion of human psychology. Think about this: Almost everything you have done in the past hour required you to perceive, remember, use language, or think. As you'll soon see, psychologists have discovered some impressive information about every topic in cognitive psychology. Even though cognitive psychology is extraordinarily central in every human's daily life, many college students cannot define this term accurately (Maynard, 2006; Maynard et al., 2004). To demonstrate this point, try Demonstration 1.1.

A second reason to study cognition is that the cognitive approach has widespread influence on other areas of psychology, such as clinical psychology, educational psychology, and social psychology. Let's consider one example from clinical psychology. One cognitive task asks people to recall a specific memory from their past. People who are depressed tend to provide a general summary, such as "visiting my grandmother." In contrast, people who are not depressed tend to describe an extended memory that lasts more than one day, such as "the summer I drove across the country" (Wenzel, 2005). Cognitive psychology also influences interdisciplinary areas. For example, a journal called *Political Psychology* emphasizes how cognitive factors can influence political situations. In summary, your understanding of cognitive psychology will help you appreciate many other areas of psychology, as well as disciplines outside psychology.

ⓖ Demonstration 1.1

Awareness About Cognitive Psychology

Locate several friends at your university or college who have not enrolled in any psychology courses. Ask each person the following questions:

1. How would you define the term "cognitive psychology"?
2. Can you list some of the topics that would be included in a course in cognitive psychology?

When Amanda Maynard and her coauthors (2004) asked introductory psychologists to define "cognitive psychology," only 29% provided appropriate definitions. How adequate were the responses that your own friends provided?

The final reason for studying cognition is more personal. Your mind is an impressively sophisticated piece of equipment, and you use this equipment every minute of the day. If you purchase a cell phone, you typically receive a brochure that describes its functions. However, no one issued a brochure for your mind when you were born. In a sense, this book is like a brochure or owner's manual, describing information about how your mind works. This book—like some owner's manuals—also includes hints on how to improve performance.

This introductory chapter focuses on three topics. First, we'll briefly consider the history of cognitive psychology, and then we'll outline some important current issues. The final part of the chapter describes this textbook, including its content and major themes; it also provides suggestions for using the book effectively.

A BRIEF HISTORY OF COGNITIVE PSYCHOLOGY

The cognitive approach to psychology traces its origins to the classical Greek philosophers and to developments in nineteenth- and twentieth-century psychology. As we will also see in this section, however, the contemporary version of cognitive psychology emerged within the last fifty years.

The Origins of Cognitive Psychology

Philosophers and other theorists have speculated about human thought processes for more than twenty-three centuries. For example, the Greek philosopher Aristotle (384–322 BC) examined topics such as perception, memory, and mental imagery. He also discussed how humans acquire knowledge through experience and observation (Barnes, 2004; Sternberg, 1999). Aristotle emphasized the importance of **empirical evidence**, or scientific evidence obtained by careful observation and experimentation. His emphasis on empirical evidence and many of the topics he studied are consistent with twenty-first-century cognitive psychology. In fact, Leahey (2003) suggests that Aristotle could reasonably be called the first cognitive psychologist. However, psychology as a discipline did not emerge until the late 1800s.

Wilhelm Wundt. A central researcher in the history of psychology is Wilhelm Wundt (pronounced "Voont"), who lived in Leipzig, Germany between 1832 and 1920. Historians often give credit to Wundt for creating the new discipline of psychology—a discipline that was separate from philosophy and physiology. Within several years, students journeyed from around the world to study with Wundt, who taught about 28,000 students during the course of his lifetime (Bechtel et al., 1998; Fuchs & Milar, 2003).

Wundt proposed that psychology should study mental processes, using a technique called introspection. **Introspection**, in this case, meant that carefully trained observers would systematically analyze their own sensations and report them as objectively as possible (Fuchs & Milar, 2003; Zangwill, 2004b). For example, observers might be asked to objectively report their reactions to a specific musical chord, without relying on their previous knowledge about music.

Wundt's introspection technique sounds subjective to most current cognitive psychologists (Sternberg, 1999; Zangwill, 2004b). As you'll see throughout this textbook, our introspections are sometimes inaccurate. For example, you may introspect that your eyes are moving smoothly across this page. However, cognitive psychologists have determined that your eyes actually move in small jumps—as you'll learn in Chapter 3.

Early Memory Researchers. Another important German psychologist, named Hermann Ebbinghaus (1850–1909), focused on factors that influence human memory. He constructed more than 2,000 nonsense syllables (for instance, DAK) and tested his own ability to learn these stimuli. Ebbinghaus examined a variety of factors that might influence performance, such as the amount of time between list presentations. He specifically chose nonsense syllables—rather than actual words—to reduce the influence of previous experience with the material (Fuchs & Milar, 2003; Zangwill, 2004a).

Meanwhile, in the United States, similar research was being conducted by psychologists such as Mary Whiton Calkins (1863–1930). For example, Calkins reported a memory phenomenon called the recency effect (Madigan & O'Hara, 1992). The **recency effect** refers to the observation that our recall is especially accurate for the final items in a series of stimuli. Calkins was the first woman to be president of the American Psychological Association. In connection with that role, she developed guidelines for teaching college courses in introductory psychology (Calkins, 1910; McGovern & Brewer, 2003).

Ebbinghaus, Calkins, and other pioneers inspired hundreds of researchers to examine how selected variables influenced memory. These early researchers typically used nonsense stimuli. As a result, it's difficult to apply their results to the strategies that people adopt when they try to recall meaningful material.

William James. Another crucial figure in the history of cognitive psychology was an American named William James (1842–1910). James was not impressed with Wundt's introspection technique or Ebbinghaus's research with nonsense syllables. Instead, James preferred to theorize about our everyday psychological experiences (Fuchs & Milar, 2003; Hunter, 2004a). He is best known for his textbook *Principles of Psychology*, published in 1890. (Incidentally, try Demonstration 1.2 on page 6 before you read further.)

Principles of Psychology provides detailed descriptions about people's everyday experience. It also emphasizes that the human mind is active and inquiring. The book foreshadows numerous topics that fascinate twenty-first-century cognitive psychologists, such as perception, attention, memory, reasoning, and the tip-of-the-tongue phenomenon. Consider, for example, James's vivid description of the tip-of-the-tongue experience:

> Suppose we try to recall a forgotten name. The state of our consciousness is peculiar. There is a gap therein but no mere gap. It is a gap that is intensely active. A sort of wraith of the name is in it, beckoning us in a given direction, making us at moments tingle with the sense of our closeness and then letting us sink back without the longed-for term. (1890, p. 251)

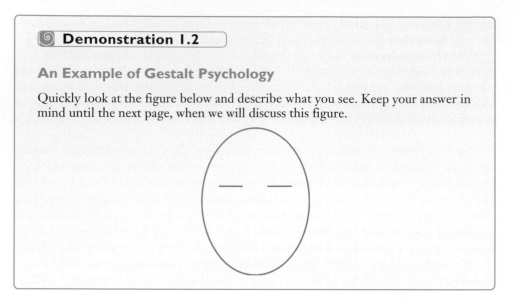

Demonstration 1.2

An Example of Gestalt Psychology

Quickly look at the figure below and describe what you see. Keep your answer in mind until the next page, when we will discuss this figure.

Behaviorism. During the first half of the twentieth century, behaviorism was the most prominent theoretical perspective in the United States. According to the **behaviorist approach**, psychology must focus on objective, observable reactions to stimuli in the environment (Pear, 2001). The most prominent early behaviorist was the U.S. psychologist John B. Watson (1913), who lived from 1878–1958.

Because Watson and other behaviorists emphasized observable behavior, they completely rejected Wundt's introspection approach (Bargh & Ferguson, 2000; Epstein, 2004). They also avoided terms that referred to mental events, such as *image*, *idea*, or *thought* (Fuchs & Milar, 2003).

Behaviorists argued that researchers could not objectively study mental processes (Epstein, 2004; Skinner, 2004). Although they did not conduct research in cognitive psychology, they did contribute significantly to contemporary research methods. For example, behaviorists emphasized the importance of the **operational definition**, a precise definition that specifics exactly how a concept is to be measured. Similarly, cognitive psychologists in the twenty-first-century need to specify exactly how memory, perception, and other cognitive processes will be measured in an experiment. Behaviorists also valued carefully controlled research, a tradition that is maintained in current cognitive research (Fuchs & Milar, 2003)

We must also acknowledge the important contribution of behaviorists to contemporary applied psychology. Their learning principles are extensively used in psychotherapy, business, and education (Rachlin, 2002; Staddon, 2001).

The Gestalt Approach. Behaviorism thrived in the United States for several decades, but it had less influence on European psychology. An important development in Europe at the beginning of the twentieth century was gestalt (pronounced "*gehshtahlt*") psychology. **Gestalt psychology** emphasizes that we humans have basic tendencies to actively organize what we see; furthermore, the whole is greater than the sum of its parts (Coren, 2003). Consider, for example, the figure in Demonstration 1.2. You probably saw a human face, rather than simply an oval and two straight lines. This figure seems to have unity and organization. It has a **gestalt**, or overall quality that transcends the individual elements (Fuchs & Milar, 2003).

Because gestalt psychologists valued the unity of psychological phenomena, they strongly objected to Wundt's introspective technique of analyzing experiences into separate components. They also criticized the behaviorists' emphasis on breaking behavior into individual stimulus-response units and ignoring the context of behavior (Sharps & Wertheimer, 2000; Sternberg, 1999). Gestalt psychologists constructed a number of laws that explain why certain components of a pattern seem to belong together. We'll consider some of these laws in Chapter 2.

Gestalt psychologists also emphasized the importance of insight in problem solving (Fuchs & Milar, 2003; Sharps & Wertheimer, 2000; Viney & King, 2003). When you are trying to solve a problem, the parts of the problem initially seem unrelated to each other. However, with a sudden flash of insight, the parts fit together into a solution. Gestalt psychologists conducted most of the early research in problem solving. We will examine their concept of insight—as well as more recent developments—in Chapter 11 of this textbook.

Frederic C. Bartlett. In the early 1900s, the behaviorists were dominant in the United States, and the gestalt psychologists were influential in continental Europe. Meanwhile in England, a British psychologist named Frederic C. Bartlett (1886–1969) conducted his research on human memory. His important book *Remembering: An Experimental and Social Study* (Bartlett, 1932) rejected the carefully controlled research of Ebbinghaus (Pickford & Gregory, 2004). Instead, Bartlett used meaningful materials, such as lengthy stories. He discovered that people made systematic errors when trying to recall these stories. Bartlett proposed that human memory is an active, constructive process, in which we interpret and transform the information we encounter. We search for meaning, trying to integrate this new information so that it is more consistent with our own personal experiences (Pickford & Gregory, 2004).

Bartlett's work was largely ignored in the United States during the 1930s, because most U.S. research psychologists were committed to behaviorism. However, about half a century later, U.S. cognitive psychologists discovered Bartlett's work and appreciated his use of naturalistic material, in contrast to Ebbinghaus's artificial nonsense syllables. Bartlett's emphasis on a schema-based approach to memory foreshadowed some of the research we will explore in Chapters 5 and 8 (Pickford & Gregory, 2004).

The Emergence of Modern Cognitive Psychology

We have briefly traced the historical roots of cognitive psychology, but when was this new approach actually "born"? Cognitive psychologists generally agree that the birth of cognitive psychology should be listed as 1956 (Thagard, 2005; Viney & King, 2003). During this prolific year, researchers published numerous influential books and articles on attention, memory, language, concept formation, and problem solving. Many researchers also attended an important symposium at the Massachusetts Institute of Technology (Miller, 1979).

Enthusiasm for the cognitive approach grew rapidly, so that by about 1960, the methodology, approach, and attitudes had changed substantially (Mandler, 1985). Another important turning point was the publication of Ulric Neisser's (1967) book *Cognitive Psychology* (Leahey, 2003; Palmer, 1999).

In fact, the growing support for the cognitive approach has sometimes been called the "cognitive revolution" (Bruner, 1997). Let's examine some of the factors that contributed to the increased popularity of cognitive psychology. Then we'll consider the information-processing approach, one of the most influential forces in the early development of cognitive psychology.

Factors Contributing to the Rise of Cognitive Psychology. The emerging popularity of the cognitive approach can be traced to psychologists' disenchantment with behaviorism, as well as to new developments in linguistics, memory, and developmental psychology. By the late 1960s, psychologists were becoming increasingly disappointed with the behaviorist outlook that had dominated U.S. psychology. Complex human behavior could not readily be explained using only the concepts from traditional behaviorist theory, such as observable stimuli, responses, and reinforcement. This approach tells us nothing about psychologically interesting processes, such as the thoughts and strategies people use when they try to solve a problem (Bechtel et al., 1998).

New developments in linguistics also increased psychologists' dissatisfaction with behaviorism (Bargh & Ferguson, 2000). The most important contributions came from the linguist Noam Chomsky (1957), who emphasized that the structure of language was too complex to be explained in behaviorist terms (Pinker, 2002; Leahey, 2003). Chomsky and other linguists argued that humans have an inborn ability to master all the complicated and varied aspects of language (Chomsky, 2004). This perspective clearly contradicted the behaviorist perspective that language acquisition can be entirely explained by learning principles.

Research in human memory began to blossom at the end of the 1950s, further increasing the disenchantment with behaviorism. Psychologists examined the organization of memory, and they proposed memory models. They frequently found that material was altered during memory by people's previous knowledge. Behaviorist principles such as "reinforcement" could not explain these alterations (Bargh & Ferguson, 2000).

Another influential force came from research on children's thought processes. Jean Piaget (pronounced "Pea-ah-*zhay*") was a Swiss theorist who lived from 1896 to 1980. His perspectives continue to shape developmental psychology (Feist, 2006). According to Piaget, children actively explore their world in order to understand important concepts (Gregory, 2004b). Furthermore, children's cognitive strategies change as they mature. During infancy, for example, babies master **object permanence**, the knowledge that an object exists, even when it is temporarily out of sight. In contrast, an adolescent often uses sophisticated strategies in order to conduct experiments about scientific principles. Piaget's books began to attract the attention of U.S. psychologists and educators toward the end of the 1950s.

We have seen that the growth of the cognitive approach was encouraged by research in linguistics, memory, and developmental psychology. By the mid-1970s, the cognitive approach had replaced the behavioral approach as the dominant theory in psychological research (Robins et al., 1999). Let's now consider an additional factor contributing to that growth, which was the enthusiasm about the information-processing approach. For many years, the information-processing approach was the most popular theory within the cognitive approach.

The Information-Processing Approach. During the 1950s, communication science and computer science began to develop and gain popularity. Researchers then began speculating that human thought processes could be analyzed from a similar perspective (Leahey, 2003; MacKay, 2004). Two important components of the **information-processing approach** are that (a) a mental process can be compared with the operations of a computer, and (b) a mental process can be interpreted as information progressing through the system in a series of stages, one step at a time.

Researchers proposed a number of information-processing models to explain human memory. For example, Richard Atkinson and Richard Shiffrin (1968) developed a model that became tremendously popular within the emerging field of cognitive psychology (Rose, 2004). Because the Atkinson-Shiffrin theory quickly became the standard model, it is often called the "modal model." The **Atkinson-Shiffrin model** proposed that memory can be understood as a sequence of discrete steps, in which information is transferred from one storage area to another. Let's look more closely at this model because it was so influential in persuading research psychologists to adopt the cognitive psychology perspective.

Figure 1.1 shows one version of the Atkinson-Shiffrin model, with arrows indicating the transfer of information. External stimuli from the environment first enter sensory memory. **Sensory memory** is a storage system that records information from each of the senses with reasonable accuracy. During the 1960s and 1970s, psychologists frequently studied either iconic memory (visual sensory memory) or echoic memory (auditory sensory memory) (e.g., Darwin et al., 1972; Parks, 2004; Sperling, 1960). The model proposed that information is stored in sensory memory for 2 seconds or less, and then most of it is forgotten. For example, your echoic memory briefly stores the last words of a sentence spoken by your professor, but the "echo" of those words disappears within 2 seconds.

Atkinson and Shiffrin's model proposed that some material from sensory memory then passes on to short-term memory. **Short-term memory** (now called **working memory**) contains only the small amount of information that we are actively using. Memories in short-term memory are fragile—though not as fragile as those in sensory memory (J. Brown, 2004). These memories can be lost within about 30 seconds unless they are somehow repeated.

According to the model, only a fraction of the information in short-term memory passes on to long-term memory (Leahey, 2003). **Long-term memory** has an enormous capacity because it contains memories that are decades old, in addition to memories that arrived several minutes ago. Atkinson and Shiffrin proposed that information stored in long-term memory is relatively permanent and not likely to be lost.

FIGURE 1.1

Atkinson and Shiffrin's Model of Memory.

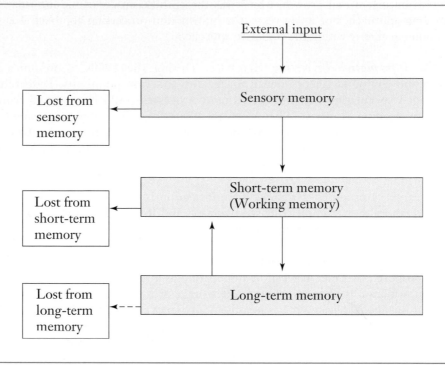

Source: Based on Atkinson & Shiffrin, 1968.

Let's see how the Atkinson-Shiffrin model could account for the task you are working on right now. For instance, the sentences in the previous paragraph served as "external input," and they entered into your iconic memory. Only a fraction of that material passed into your short-term memory, and then only a fraction passed from short-term memory to long-term memory. In fact, without glancing back, can you recall the exact words of any sentence in that previous paragraph?

Atkinson and Shiffrin's (1968) information-processing model dominated memory research for many years. However, its influence is now diminished. For instance, most cognitive psychologists now consider sensory memory to be the very brief storage process that is part of perception (Baddeley, 1995).

Many researchers also question Atkinson and Shiffrin's (1968) clear-cut distinction between short-term memory and long-term memory (Baddeley, 1995; J. Brown, 2004). Still, cognitive psychologists typically divide the huge topic of memory into two parts, more for the sake of convenience than a conviction that we have two entirely different kinds of memory. In this textbook, for instance, Chapter 4 examines short-term memory, although I use the current, more descriptive term "working memory" as the chapter title. Chapters 5, 6, 7, and 8 examine various components of long-term memory.

We have been discussing the Atkinson-Shiffrin (1968) model of memory because it is the best-known example of the information-processing approach. In general, enthusiasm for this kind of information-processing model has declined. Although many cognitive psychologists still favor the computer metaphor, they now acknowledge that we need more complex models to account for human thinking (Leahey, 2003).

Instead, some emphasize either a neuroscience approach or the parallel distributed processing approach; we'll introduce both of these in the next section. Still others do not support any theoretical framework. As many noted researchers in the field have remarked, the discipline has been experiencing an identity crisis for at least the last decade. Cognitive psychology lacks a unified theoretical direction for the future (Leahey, 2003; Neisser, 1994). Throughout this book, however, we will consider a number of small-scale theoretical viewpoints that guide the current research in cognitive psychology.

◎ Section Summary: *A Brief History of Cognitive Psychology*

1. The term *cognition* refers to the acquisition, storage, transformation, and use of knowledge; *cognitive psychology* is sometimes used as a synonym for cognition, and sometimes it refers to a theoretical approach to psychology.

2. Many historians argue that Wilhelm Wundt is responsible for creating the discipline of psychology; Wundt also developed the introspection technique.

3. Hermann Ebbinghaus and Mary Whiton Calkins conducted early research on human memory.

4. William James examined everyday psychological processes, and he emphasized the active nature of the human mind.

5. Beginning in the early twentieth century, behaviorists such as John B. Watson rejected the study of mental processes; the behaviorists helped to develop the research methods used by current cognitive psychologists.

6. Gestalt psychology emphasized organization in pattern perception and insight in problem solving.

7. Frederick C. Bartlett conducted memory research using long stories and other meaningful material.

8. Cognitive psychology began to emerge in the mid-1950s. This new approach was stimulated by disenchantment with behaviorism and also by a growth of interest in linguistics, human memory, developmental psychology, and the information-processing approach.

9. According to the information-processing approach, mental processes operates like a computer, with information flowing through a series of storage areas.

10. The best-known example of the information-processing approach is the Atkinson-Shiffrin (1968) model, which proposes three different memory-storage systems. Enthusiasm has declined for both this model and for the general information-processing approach.

CURRENT ISSUES IN COGNITIVE PSYCHOLOGY

Cognitive psychology has had an enormous influence on the discipline of psychology. For example, almost all psychologists now recognize the importance of mental representations, a term that behaviorists would have rejected in the 1950s. In fact, examples of "pure behaviorism" are now difficult to locate. For instance, the Association of Behavioral Therapy is now known as the Association for Behavioral and Cognitive Therapies. Recent articles in their journal, *Cognitive and Behavioral Practice*, focused on using cognitive behavioral therapy for a variety of clients, including refugees from Cambodia with post-traumatic stress disorder, adolescents experiencing pain, and urban residents experiencing panic disorder.

The cognitive approach has also permeated most areas of psychology that had not previously emphasized thought processes. Demonstration 1.3 illustrates this point.

Cognitive psychology has its critics, however. One common complaint concerns the issue of ecological validity. Studies are high in **ecological validity** if the conditions in which the research is conducted are similar to the natural setting where the results will be applied. Consider an experiment in which participants must memorize pairs of unrelated English words, presented at 10-second intervals on a white screen in a barren laboratory room. The results of this experiment might tell us something about the way memory operates. However, this task is probably low in ecological validity, because it cannot be applied to the way people learn in the real world (Sharps & Wertheimer, 2000). How often do you try to memorize pairs of unrelated words in this fashion, when you study for an upcoming psychology exam?

Most cognitive psychologists prior to the 1980s did indeed conduct research in artificial laboratory environments, often using tasks that differed from daily cognitive activities. However, current researchers are much more likely to study everyday issues in natural settings (Herrmann et al., 2006; Woll, 2002). For instance, cognitive psychologists are currently studying real-life issues such as college students' strategies for generating and remembering their passwords (Brown et al., 2004), people's decreased recall for a radio advertisement when the ad includes background music (Oakes & North, 2006), and the benefits of practice when learning a surgical skill (Keehner et al., 2006). Psychologists are also studying how cognitive processes

---

> ### Demonstration 1.3
>
> #### The Widespread Influence of Cognitive Psychology
>
> Locate a psychology textbook used in some other class. An introductory textbook is ideal, but textbooks in developmental psychology, social psychology, abnormal psychology, etc., are all suitable. Glance through the subject index for words related to *cognition* or *cognitive*, and locate the relevant pages. Depending on the nature of the textbook, you may also find entries under terms such as *memory*, *language*, and *perception*.

operate in our everyday social interactions (e.g., Cacioppo & Berntson, 2005a; Easton & Emery, 2005). In general, most cognitive psychologists acknowledge that the discipline must advance by conducting both ecologically valid and laboratory-based research.

Several topics are important to our overview of current cognitive psychology. First, we will look at two areas within cognitive science that have contributed most to cognitive psychology: cognitive neuroscience and artificial intelligence. Then we will consider cognitive science. This interdisciplinary approach includes all of these topics, as well as contributions from other research-based disciplines.

Cognitive Neuroscience

Cognitive neuroscience combines the research techniques of cognitive psychology with various methods for assessing the structure and function of the brain. In the last few years, researchers have discovered which structures in the brain are activated when people perform a variety of cognitive tasks. Furthermore, psychologists now use neuroscience techniques to explore the kind of cognitive processes that we use in our interactions with other people; this new discipline is called **social cognitive neuroscience** (Cacioppo & Berntson, 2005a; Easton & Emery, 2005). For example, researchers have identified a variety of brain structures that are active when people look at a photograph of a face and judge whether the person is trustworthy (Winston et al., 2005).

However, neurological explanations for many cognitive processes are often elusive. For example, take several seconds to stand up and walk around the room in which you are reading. As you walk, notice what you see in your environment. This visual activity is actually extremely complicated, requiring billions of neurons and more than fifty regions of the surface of your brain (Emery & Easton, 2005).

Because the brain is so complex, you need to be cautious when you read summaries of cognitive neuroscience research in the popular media. For example, I discovered a newspaper article that claimed "Scientists Find Humor Spot in the Brain." In reality, numerous parts of the brain work together to master the complicated task of appreciating humor.

Let's examine several neuroscience techniques that have provided particularly useful information for cognitive psychologists. We will begin with a method that examines individuals who have experienced brain damage. We'll next consider three methods used with normal humans: positron emission tomography, functional magnetic resonance imaging, and the event-related potential technique. Finally, we will discuss the single-cell recording technique, which is used only with animals.

Brain Lesions. The term **brain lesions** refers to the destruction of tissue in the brain, most often by strokes, tumors, or accidents. The formal research on lesions began in the 1860s, but major advances came after World War II, when researchers examined the relationship between damaged regions of the brain and cognitive deficits (Farah, 2004). The study of brain lesions has definitely helped us understand the organization of the brain. However, the results are often difficult to interpret. For example, people with brain lesions seldom have the damage limited to a specific area. As a result, researchers cannot associate a cognitive deficit with a specific brain structure (Gazzaniga et al., 2002; Kalat, 2007). In this textbook, we will occasionally discuss research on people with lesions. However, the following neuroscience techniques provide better-controlled information (Hernandez-García et al., 2002). Let's first examine two brain-imaging techniques.

Positron Emission Tomography. When you perform a cognitive task, your brain needs oxygen to support the neural activity. The brain does not store oxygen. Instead, the blood flow increases in the activated part of the brain in order to carry oxygen to that site. Brain-imaging techniques measure brain activity indirectly. These techniques are based on the following logic: By measuring certain properties of the blood in different regions of the brain while people perform a cognitive task, we can determine which brain regions are responsible for that cognitive task (Buckner & Logan, 2001; Coren et al., 2004). Let's first examine a brain-imaging technique called positron emission tomography (PET) scans; we'll discuss functional magnetic resonance imaging (fMRI) in the following section. Both of these methods can detect activity in a region of the brain that is no larger than the period at the end of this sentence (Posner & DiGirolamo, 2000b).

In a **positron emission tomography (PET scan)**, researchers measure blood flow by injecting the participant with a radioactive chemical just before this person performs a task. The chemical travels through the bloodstream to the parts of the brain that are activated during the task. A special camera makes an image of the accumulated radioactive chemical throughout the brain. By examining this image, researchers can determine which parts of the brain are activated when the participant works on the task (Coren et al., 2004; Raichle, 2001). PET scans can be used to study such cognitive processes as attention, memory, and language (Binder & Price, 2001; Nyberg & McIntosh, 2001).

PET scans require several seconds to produce data, so this method is not very precise. If the activity in a specific brain region increases and then decreases within this period, the PET scan will record an average of this activity level (Hernandez-García et al., 2002). For example, you can scan an entire room in 2 or 3 seconds, so an average activity level for this entire scene would not be meaningful. Furthermore, in the current era, PET scans are used less often than some other imaging techniques, because they are expensive and they expose people to radioactive chemicals (Kalat, 2007)

Functional Magnetic Resonance Imaging. We have just seen that PET scans measure the blood flow to various brain areas. In contrast, fMRIs measure the amount of oxygen in the blood in various brain areas. More specifically, **functional magnetic resonance imaging (fMRI)** is based on the principle that oxygen-rich blood is an index of brain activity (Cacioppo & Berntson, 2005b; Kalat, 2007). The research participant reclines with his or her head surrounded by a large, doughnut-shaped magnet. This magnetic field produces changes in the oxygen atoms. A scanning device takes a "photo" of these oxygen atoms while the participant performs a cognitive task. For example, researchers have used the fMRI method to examine regions of the brain that process visual information. They found that specific locations in the brain respond more to letters than to numbers (Polk et al., 2002).

The fMRI technique was developed during the 1990s, based on the magnetic resonance imaging (MRI) used in medical settings. In general, an fMRI is preferable to a PET scan because it is less invasive, with no injections and no radioactive material. In addition, an fMRI can measure brain activity that occurs fairly quickly—in about 1 second (Frith & Rees, 2004; Huettel et al., 2004; Kalat, 2007). The fMRI technique is relatively precise in identifying the exact time sequence of cognitive tasks, compared to the PET scan, which requires several seconds. The fMRI technique can also detect subtle differences in the way that the brain processes language. For example, Gernsbacher and Robertson (2005) used this technique to discover a different pattern of brain activation when students read sentences like, "The young child played in a backyard," as opposed to "A young child played in a backyard."

However, even the fMRI technique is not precise enough to study the sequence of events in the cognitive tasks that we perform very quickly (Fuster, 2003). For example, you can read the average word in this sentence out loud in about half a second. If a researcher gathered fMRI measures while you were reading that word, the image would show simultaneous neural activity in both the visual and the motor parts of your brain (Buckner & Petersen, 1998). Specifically, the fMRI cannot identify that you actually looked at the word (a visual task) before you pronounced the word (a motor task).

In addition, neither PET scans nor fMRIs can provide precise information about a person's thoughts. For instance, some commentators have suggested using brain scans to identify terrorists. However, the current technology for this precise kind of identification is clearly inadequate (Farah, 2002).

Event-Related Potential Technique. As we've seen, PET scans and the fMRI technique are too slow to provide precise information about the timing of brain activity. In contrast, the **event-related potential (ERP) technique** records the brief fluctuations (lasting just a fraction of a second) in the brain's electrical activity, in response to a stimulus (Huettel et al., 2004).

To use the event-related potential technique, researchers place electrodes on a person's scalp. Each electrode records the electrical activity generated by a group of neurons located directly underneath the skull (Gazzaniga et al., 2002). The ERP technique cannot identify the response of a single neuron. However, it can identify electrical changes over a very brief period in a specific region of the brain (Fuster, 2003).

For example, suppose that you are participating in a study that examines how humans respond to facial movement. Specifically, you have been instructed to watch a brief video showing a woman either opening her mouth or closing her mouth. The electrodes are fastened to your scalp, and you watch numerous presentations of each facial movement. Later, the researchers will average the signal for each of the two conditions, to eliminate random activity in the brain waves.

The ERP technique provides a reasonably precise picture about changes in the brain's electrical potential during a cognitive task. Consider the research on facial movement, for example. If you were to participate in this study, your brain would show a change in electrical potential about half of a second after you saw each mouth movement. However, your brain would respond more dramatically when you watch her mouth *open* than when you watch a mouth *close* (Puce & Perrett, 2005). Why does this fine-grained ERP analysis show that your brain responds differently to these two situations? Puce and Perret propose that a mouth-opening movement is important, because it signals that a person is about to say something. You therefore need to be attentive, and this exaggerated ERP reflects this attentiveness. In contrast, it's less important to notice that someone has finished talking.

Single-Cell Recording Technique. So far, we have examined four techniques that neuroscientists can use to study humans. In contrast, the single-cell recording technique cannot safely be used on humans. Specifically, in the **single-cell recording technique**, researchers study characteristics of an animal's brain and nervous system by inserting a thin electrode into or next to a single neuron (Gazzaniga et al., 2002). (A **neuron** is the basic cell in the nervous system.) Researchers then measure the electric activity generated by that cell. A neuroscientist repeats this process in many other regions of the brain in order to test hypotheses about how our cognitive processes operate (Fuster, 2003).

The major goal of the single-cell recording technique is to identify which variations in a stimulus produce a consistent change in a single cell's electrical activity. For example, Hubel and Wiesel (1965, 1979, 2005) inserted an electrode next to a neuron in the visual cortex, at the back of a cat's brain. They found that some kinds of cells in the visual cortex responded vigorously only when a line was presented in a particular orientation. These same cells responded at a much lower level when the line was rotated only a few degrees. More details on this technique can be found elsewhere (e.g., Coren et al., 2004; Farah, 2000a; Hubel & Wiesel, 2005). Clearly, this research has important implications for visual pattern recognition: The cells provide a mechanism for recognizing specific patterns, such as letters of the alphabet. We will examine this research further in Chapter 2.

A detailed investigation of cognitive neuroscience techniques is beyond the scope of this book. However, these techniques will be mentioned further in the chapters on perception, memory, and language. You can also obtain more information from other resources (e.g., Cacioppo & Berntson, 2005a; Easton & Emery, 2005; Fuster, 2003; Kalat, 2007).

Artificial Intelligence

Artificial intelligence (AI), a branch of computer science, seeks to explore human cognitive processes by creating computer models that accomplish the same tasks that humans do (Boden, 2004; Chrisley, 2004). Researchers in artificial intelligence have tried to explain how you recognize a face, create a mental image, write a poem, as well as hundreds of additional cognitive accomplishments (Boden, 2004; Farah, 2004;

Thagard, 2005). In this textbook, you'll read about research on artificial intelligence in Chapter 7 (mental maps), Chapter 9 (language comprehension), and Chapter 11 (problem solving). Let's consider several important topics within the domain of artificial intelligence: (1) the computer metaphor, (2) pure AI, (3) computer simulation, and (4) the parallel distributed processing approach.

The Computer Metaphor. Throughout the history of cognitive psychology, the computer has been a popular metaphor for the human mind. According to the **computer metaphor**, our cognitive processes work like a computer, that is, a complex, multipurpose machine that processes information quickly and accurately.

Of course, researchers acknowledge obvious differences in physical structure between the computer and the human brain that manages our cognitive processes. However, both may operate according to similar general principles. For example, both computers and humans can compare symbols and can make choices according to the results of the comparison. Furthermore, computers have a processing mechanism with a limited capacity. Humans also have a limited attention capacity. As we'll discuss in Chapter 3, we cannot pay attention to everything at once.

Computer models need to describe both the relevant *structures* and the *processes* that operate on these structures. Thagard (2005) suggests that we can compare a computer model with a recipe in cooking. A recipe has two parts: (1) the ingredients, which are somewhat like the structures; and (2) the cooking instructions for working with those ingredients, which are somewhat like the processes.

Researchers who favor the computer approach try to design the appropriate "software." With the right computer program and sufficient mathematical detail, researchers hope to mimic the flexibility and the efficiency of human cognitive processes (Boden, 2004).

AI researchers favor the analogy between the human mind and the computer because computer programs must be detailed, precise, unambiguous, and logical (Boden, 2004). Researchers can represent the functions of a computer with a flowchart that shows the sequence of stages in processing information. (Figure 1.1 on page 10 shows a simplified flowchart.) Suppose that the computer and the human show equivalent performance on a particular task. Then the researchers can speculate that the computer program represents an appropriate theory for describing the human's cognitive processes (Carpenter & Just, 1999).

Every metaphor has its limitations, and the computer cannot precisely duplicate human cognitive processes. For example, no artificial-intelligence system can speak and understand language as well as you do, because your background knowledge is so much more extensive (Boden, 2004). Furthermore, humans have more complex and fluid goals. If you play a game of chess, you may be concerned about how long the game lasts, whether you are planning to meet a friend for dinner, and how you will interact socially with your opponent. In contrast, the computer's goals are simple and rigid; the computer deals only with the outcome of the chess game.

Pure AI. We need to draw a distinction between "pure AI" and computer simulation. **Pure AI** is an approach that seeks to accomplish a task as efficiently as possible, even if the computer's processes are completely different from the processes used by humans. For example, the most high-powered computer programs for chess will evaluate as many potential moves as possible in as little time as possible (Michie, 2004). Chess is an extremely complex game, in which both players together can make about 10^{128} possible different moves—more than the total number of atoms contained in our universe. Consider a computer chess program named "Hydra." The top chess players in the world make a slight error about every ten moves. Hydra can identify this error—even though chess experts cannot—and it therefore wins the game (Mueller, 2005).

Researchers have designed pure AI systems that can play chess, speak English, or diagnose an illness. However, as one researcher points out,

> AI systems typically confine themselves to a narrow domain; for example, chess-playing programs don't usually speak English. They tend to be brittle, and thus break easily near the edges of their domain, and to be utterly ignorant outside it. I wouldn't want a chess-playing program speculating as to the cause of my chest pain. (Franklin, 1995, p. 11)

Computer Simulation. As we have seen, pure AI tries to achieve the best possible performance. In contrast, **computer simulation** or **computer modeling** attempts to take human limitations into account. The goal of computer simulation is to design a system that resembles the way humans actually perform a specific cognitive task. A computer simulation must produce the same number of errors—as well as correct responses—that a human produces (Carpenter & Just, 1999; Thagard, 2005).

Computer-simulation research has been most active in such areas as language processing, problem solving, and logical reasoning (Eysenck & Keane, 2005; Thagard, 2005). For example, Carpenter and Just (1999) created a computer-simulation model for reading sentences. This model was based on the assumption that humans have a limited capacity to process information. As a result, humans will read a difficult section of a sentence more slowly. Consider the following sentence:

> The reporter that the senator attacked admitted the error.

Carpenter and Just (1999) designed their computer simulation so that it took into account the relevant linguistic information contained in sentences like this one. The model predicted that processing speed should be fast for the words at the beginning and the end of the sentence. However, the processing should be slow for the two verbs, *attacked* and *admitted*. In fact, Carpenter and Just demonstrated that the human data matched the computer simulation quite accurately.

Interestingly, some tasks that humans accomplish quite easily seem to defy computer simulation. For example, a 10-year-old girl can search a messy bedroom for her watch, find it in her sweatshirt pocket, read the pattern on the face of the watch, and then announce the time. However, a computer cannot yet simulate this task. Computers also cannot match humans' sophistication in learning language, identifying objects in everyday scenes, or solving problems creatively (Jackendoff, 1997; Sobel, 2001).

The Parallel Distributed Processing Approach. In 1986, James McClelland, David Rumelhart, and their colleagues at the University of California, San Diego, published an influential two-volume book called *Parallel Distributed Processing* (McClelland & Rumelhart, 1986; Rumelhart et al., 1986). This approach contrasted sharply with the traditional information-processing approach. As we discussed on pages 9 to 11, the information-processing approach emphasizes that a mental process can be represented as information progressing through the system in a series of stages, one step at a time.

In contrast, the **parallel distributed processing** (or **PDP**) approach argues that cognitive processes can be understood in terms of networks that link together neuron-like units; in addition, many operations can proceed simultaneously—rather than one step at a time (Fuster, 2003; O'Reilly & Munakata, 2000). Two other names that are often used interchangeably with the PDP approach are **connectionism** and **neural networks**.

The PDP approach grew out of developments in both neuroscience and artificial intelligence—the two topics we have just discussed. During the 1970s, neuroscientists developed research techniques that could explore the structure of the **cerebral cortex**, the outer layer of the brain that is responsible for cognitive processes. One important discovery was the numerous connections among neurons, a pattern that resembles many elaborate networks (Rolls, 2004; Thagard, 2005).

This network pattern suggests that an item stored in your brain cannot be localized in a specific pinpoint-sized region of your cortex (Fuster, 2003; Woll, 2002). Instead, the neural activity for that item seems to be *distributed* throughout a section of the brain. For example, we cannot pinpoint one small portion of your brain in which the name of your cognitive psychology professor is stored. Instead, that information is probably distributed throughout thousands of neurons in a region of your cerebral cortex.

The researchers who developed the PDP approach proposed a model that simulates many important features of the brain (Levine, 2002; Woll, 2002). Naturally, the model captures only a fraction of the brain's complexity. However, like the brain, the model includes simplified neuron-like units, numerous interconnections, and neural activity distributed throughout the system.

During the time that some researchers were learning about features of the human brain, other researchers were discovering the limitations of the classical artificial intelligence approach. This classical approach viewed processing as a series of separate operations; in other words, processing would be serial. During **serial processing**, the system handles only one item at a given time; furthermore, the system must complete one step before it can proceed to the next step in the flowchart.

This one-step-at-a-time approach may capture the leisurely series of operations you conduct when you are thinking about every step in the process. For example, a classical AI model would be appropriate when you are solving a long-division problem (Leahey, 2003).

In contrast, it is difficult to use classical AI models to explain the kinds of cognitive tasks that humans do very quickly, accurately, and without conscious thought. For example, these AI models cannot explain how you can instantly perceive a visual scene (Leahey, 2003). Glance up from your book, and then immediately return to this paragraph. When you looked at this visual scene, your retina presented about one million signals to your cortex—all at the same time. If your visual system had used serial processing in order to interpret these one million signals, you would still be processing that visual scene, rather than reading this sentence! Many cognitive activities seem to use **parallel processing**, with many signals handled at the same time, rather than serial processing. On these tasks, processing seems to be both parallel and distributed, explaining the name *parallel distributed processing approach*.

Many psychologists welcomed the PDP approach as a groundbreaking new framework. They have developed models in areas as unrelated to one another as reading disabilities (Welbourne & Ralph, 2007), consciousness (Kashima et al., 2007), and interpersonal attachment (Fraley, 2007). Researchers continue to explore whether the PDP approach can adequately account for the broad range of skills represented by our cognitive processes.

Keep in mind that the PDP approach uses the human brain—rather than the serial-computer—as the basic model (Woll, 2002). This more sophisticated design allows the PDP approach to achieve greater complexity, flexibility, and accuracy as it attempts to account for human cognitive processes.

Cognitive Science

Cognitive psychology is part of a broader field known as cognitive science. **Cognitive science** is a contemporary field that tries to answer questions about the mind. As a result, cognitive science includes three disciplines we've discussed so far—cognitive psychology, neuroscience, and artificial intelligence. It also includes philosophy, linguistics, anthropology, sociology, and economics (Sobel, 2001; Thagard, 2005).

According to cognitive scientists, thinking requires us to manipulate our internal representations of the external world. Cognitive scientists focus on these internal representations. In contrast, you'll recall, the behaviorists focused only on observable stimuli and responses in the external world.

Cognitive scientists value interdisciplinary studies. For example, according to Carolyn Sobel (2001), both the theory and the research in cognitive science are so extensive that no one person can possibly master everything. However, if all these different fields remain separate, then cognitive scientists won't achieve important insights and relevant connections. Therefore, cognitive science tries to coordinate the information that researchers have gathered throughout the relevant disciplines.

◎ Section Summary: *Current Issues in Cognitive Psychology*

1. Cognitive psychology has a major influence on the field of psychology. In the current era, cognitive psychologists are more concerned about ecological validity than in previous decades.

2. Cognitive neuroscientists search for brain-based explanations for cognitive processes. Their research is based on brain-lesion studies, positron emission tomography (PET) scans, functional magnetic resonance imaging (fMRI), event-related potentials (ERPs), and single-cell recording.

3. Theorists who are interested in artificial intelligence (AI) approaches to cognition typically design computer programs that accomplish tasks as efficiently as possible (pure AI) or programs that accomplish these tasks in a human-like fashion (computer simulation).

4. According to the parallel distributed processing (PDP) approach, cognitive processes operate in a parallel fashion, and neural activity is distributed throughout a relatively broad region of the cortex.

5. Cognitive science examines questions about the mind; it includes disciplines such as cognitive psychology, neuroscience, artificial intelligence, philosophy, linguistics, anthropology, sociology, and economics.

AN OVERVIEW OF YOUR TEXTBOOK

This textbook examines many different kinds of mental processes. We'll begin with perception and memory—two processes that contribute to all of the other cognitive tasks. We'll then consider language, which is probably the most challenging cognitive task that humans need to master. Later chapters discuss "higher-order" processes. As the name suggests, these higher-order cognitive processes depend upon the more basic processes introduced at the beginning of the book. The final chapter examines cognition across the life span. Let's preview Chapters 2 through 13. Then we'll explore five themes that can help you appreciate some general characteristics of cognitive processes. Our final section provides hints on how you can use your book more effectively.

Preview of the Chapters

Visual and auditory recognition (**Chapter 2**) are perceptual processes that use our previous knowledge to interpret the stimuli that are registered by our senses. For example, visual recognition allows you to recognize each letter on this page, whereas auditory recognition allows you to recognize the words you are hearing on the radio.

Another perceptual process is attention (**Chapter 3**). The last time you tried to follow a friend's story—while simultaneously reading a book—you probably noticed the limits of your attention. This chapter also examines a related topic, **consciousness**, or your awareness of the external world, as well as your thoughts and emotions about your internal world.

Memory—the process of maintaining information over time—is such an important part of cognition that it requires several chapters. **Chapter 4** describes working memory (short-term memory). You're certainly aware of the limits of working memory when you forget someone's name that you heard just 30 seconds ago!

Chapter 5, the second of the memory chapters, focuses on long-term memory. We'll examine several factors, such as mood and expertise, that are related to people's ability to remember material for a long period of time. We'll also explore memory for everyday life events. For example, eyewitnesses who are not very confident about their memory accuracy are usually almost as accurate as more confident eyewitnesses.

Chapter 6, the last of the general memory chapters, provides suggestions for memory improvement. This chapter also considers **metacognition**, which is your knowledge about your own cognitive processes. For instance, do you know whether you could remember the definition for *metacognition* if you were to be tested tomorrow morning?

Chapter 7 examines **imagery**, which is the mental representation of things that are not physically present. One important controversy in the research on imagery is whether mental images truly resemble perceptual images. Another important topic concerns the mental images we have for physical settings. For example, the cognitive map you developed for your college campus is likely to show several buildings lined up in a straight row, even though an accurate map would show a much more random pattern.

Chapter 8 concerns general knowledge. One area of general knowledge is **semantic memory,** which includes factual knowledge about the world as well as knowledge about word meanings. General knowledge also includes **schemas,** which are generalized kinds of information about situations. For example, you have a schema for the sequence of events during a visit to your dentist.

Chapter 9 is the first of two chapters on language, and it examines language comprehension. One component of language comprehension is perceiving spoken language. A friend can mumble a sentence, yet you can easily perceive the speech sounds. A second component of language comprehension is reading; you easily recognize familiar words and can figure out the meaning of unfamiliar words. You can also understand **discourse,** which is a long passage of spoken or written language.

Chapter 10, the second language chapter, investigates how we produce language. One component of speaking is its social context. For example, when you are describing an event to a friend, you probably check to make certain that he or she has the appropriate background knowledge. Writing requires many cognitive processes that are different from speaking, but psychologists have not yet studied writing in detail. Our final language topic is bilingualism; even though learning a single language is challenging, many people can speak two or more languages fluently.

Chapter 11 considers problem solving. Suppose you want to solve a problem, such as how to contact a friend who has no cell phone. You'll need to represent the problem, perhaps in terms of a mental image or symbols. You can then solve the problem by several strategies, such as dividing the problem into several smaller problems. Chapter 11 also explores creativity. We'll see, for example, that people are often less creative if they have been told that they will be rewarded for their creative efforts.

Chapter 12 addresses deductive reasoning and decision making. Reasoning tasks require you to draw conclusions from several known facts. In many cases, our background knowledge interferes with drawing accurate conclusions on these problems. When we make decisions, we supply judgments about uncertain events. For example, people often cancel an airplane trip after reading about a recent terrorist attack, even though statistics usually show that driving is more dangerous.

Chapter 13 examines cognitive processes in infants, children, and elderly adults. People in these three age groups are more competent than you might guess. For example, 6-month-old infants can recall an event that occurred two weeks earlier. Young children are also very accurate in remembering events from a medical procedure in a doctor's office. Finally, elderly people are competent on many memory tasks, such as remembering whether an advertisement is familiar or unfamiliar. Chapter 13 also encourages you to review your knowledge about three important topics in cognitive psychology: memory, metamemory (or your thoughts about your memory), and language.

Themes in the Book

This book emphasizes certain themes and consistencies in cognitive processes. The themes are designed to guide you and offer you a framework for understanding many of the complexities of our mental abilities. These themes are also listed in abbreviated form inside the front cover; you can consult the list as you read later chapters. The themes are as follows:

Theme 1: *The cognitive processes are active, rather than passive.* The behaviorists viewed humans as passive organisms, who wait until a stimulus arrives from the environment before they respond. In contrast, the cognitive approach proposes that people seek out information. In addition, memory is a lively process that requires you to actively synthesize and transform information. When you read, you actively draw inferences that were never directly stated. In summary, your mind is not a sponge that passively absorbs information leaking out from the environment. Instead, you continually search and synthesize.

Theme 2: *The cognitive processes are remarkably efficient and accurate.* For example, the amount of material in your memory is awe-inspiring. Language development is similarly impressive, yet preschoolers can master thousands of new words, in addition to complex language structure. Naturally, humans make mistakes. However, these mistakes can often be traced to the use of a rational strategy. For instance, people frequently base their decisions on how easily they can recall relevant examples. This strategy often leads to a correct decision, but it can occasionally produce an error.

Furthermore, many of the limitations in human information processing may actually be helpful. You may wish that you could remember more accurately. However, if you retained all information forever, your memory would be hopelessly cluttered with facts that are no longer useful. Before you read further, try Demonstration 1.4, which is based on a demonstration by Hearst (1991).

Demonstration 1.4

Looking at Unusual Paragraphs

How fast can you spot what is unusual about this paragraph? It looks so ordinary that you might think nothing is wrong with it at all, and, in fact, nothing is. But it is atypical. Why? Study its various parts, think about its curious wording, and you may hit upon a solution. But you must do it without aid; my plan is not to allow any scandalous misconduct in this psychological study. No doubt, if you work hard on this possibly frustrating task, its abnormality will soon dawn upon you. You cannot know until you try. But it is commonly a hard nut to crack. So, good luck!

I trust a solution is conspicuous now. Was it dramatic and fair, although odd? *Author's hint:* I cannot add my autograph to this communication and maintain its basic harmony.

Theme 3: *The cognitive processes handle positive information better than negative information.* We understand sentences better if they are worded in the affirmative—for example, "Mary is honest," rather than the negative wording, "Mary is not dishonest." In addition, we have trouble noticing when something is missing, as illustrated in Demonstration 1.4 (Hearst, 1991). (If you are still puzzled, check page 29 at the end of this chapter for the answer to this demonstration.) We also tend to perform better on a variety of different tasks if the information is emotionally positive (that is, pleasant), rather than emotionally negative (unpleasant). In short, our cognitive processes are designed to handle what is, rather than what is not (Hearst,1991; Matlin, 2004).

Theme 4: *The cognitive processes are interrelated with one another; they do not operate in isolation.* This textbook discusses each cognitive process in one or more separate chapters. However, this organizational plan does not imply that every process can function by itself, without input from other processes. For example, decision making requires perception, memory, general knowledge, and language. In fact, all higher mental processes require careful integration of the more basic cognitive processes. Consequently, such tasks as problem solving, logical reasoning, and decision making are impressively complex.

Theme 5: *Many cognitive processes rely on both bottom-up and top-down processing.* **Bottom-up processing** emphasizes the importance of information from the stimuli registered on your sensory receptors. Bottom-up processing uses only a low-level sensory analysis of the stimulus. In contrast, **top-down processing** emphasizes the influence of concepts, expectations, and memory upon the cognitive processes. This top-down processing requires higher-level cognition—the kind we will emphasize in Chapters 5 and 8 of this textbook. Both of these mechanisms work simultaneously to ensure that our cognitive processes are typically fast and accurate.

Consider pattern recognition. You recognize your aunt partly because of the specific information from the stimulus—information about your aunt's face, height, shape, and so forth. This bottom-up processing is important. At the same time, top-down processing would operate if you drove to her house, and you were expecting to see her in this location.

How to Use Your Book

Your textbook includes several features that are specifically designed to help you understand and remember the material. As you read the list that follows, figure out how to use each features most effectively. In addition, Chapter 6 focuses on memory-improvement techniques. Turn to Table 6.1 on page 180 to 181. This table summarizes many memory strategies, and they are explored in more detail throughout Chapters 5 and 6. However, you may discover some hints to help you right now!

Chapter Outline. Notice that each chapter begins with an outline. When you start to read a new chapter, first examine the outline so that you can appreciate the general structure of a topic. For example, you can see that Chapter 2 has four major sections labeled (1) Background on Visual Object Recognition, (2) Top-Down Processing and Visual Object Recognition, (3) Face Perception, and (4) Speech Perception.

Chapter Preview. Another feature is the chapter preview, which is a short description of the material to be covered. This preview builds upon the framework provided in each chapter outline, and it also introduces some important new terms.

Opening Paragraph. Each chapter begins with a paragraph that encourages you to think how your own cognitive experiences are related to the material in the chapter. By combining the material from the outline, the preview, and the opening paragraph, you'll be well prepared for the specific information about the research and theories in each chapter.

Demonstrations. I designed the demonstration in this book to make the research more meaningful. The informal experiments in these demonstrations require little or no equipment, and you can perform most of them by yourself. Students have told me that these demonstrations help make the material more memorable.

Individual Differences Feature. In this new feature, Chapters 2 through 13 each discuss one study that focuses on individual differences in cognitive performance. Prior to about 1995, cognitive psychologists rarely examined whether there might be systematic differences in the way that groups of individuals perform on the same cognitive task.

For example, people with major depression feel sad, discouraged, and hopeless. In an earlier era, psychologists seldom tested whether depressed individuals differed from other individuals when performing cognitive tasks. Fortunately, many contemporary psychologists now conduct research on the relationship between psychological disorders and cognitive performance. This research is important, from both practical and theoretical perspectives. As you know, Theme 4 emphasizes that our cognitive processes are interrelated. Therefore, cognitive aspects of psychological problems—such as major depression—could certainly be related to attention, memory, and other cognitive processes (Collins, 2008).

Other researchers who investigate individual differences choose to compare groups of people who differ on a demographic characteristic. In Chapter 7, for example, we'll see that women and men are similar in most kinds of spatial abilities.

Here is the list of individual differences that we will explore in this textbook:

Chapter 2 (Recognizing Visual and Auditory Stimuli):
    Face Identification in People with Schizophrenia

Chapter 3 (Paying Attention):
    Thought Suppression and Obsessive-Compulsive Disorder

Chapter 4: (Using Working Memory)
    Major Depression and Working Memory

Chapter 5: (Using Long-Term Memory):
   Social Goals and Long-Term Memory

Chapter 6: (Using Memory Strategies and Metacognition)
   Metamemory and Adults with Attention-Deficit/Hyperactivity Disorder

Chapter 7: (Using Mental Imagery and Cognitive Maps)
   Gender Comparisons in Spatial Ability

Chapter 8: (Using General Knowledge)
   Expertise and Prototypes

Chapter 9: (Comprehending Language)
   Test Anxiety and Reading Comprehension

Chapter 10 (Producing Language)
   Simultaneous Interpreters and Working Memory

Chapter 11 (Using Problem Solving and Creativity)
   Cross-Cultural Comparisons in Problem-Solving Strategies

Chapter 12 (Using Reasoning and Decision Making)
   Decision-Making Style and Psychological Well-Being

Chapter 13 (Developing Cognitive Abilities)
   Children's Intelligence and Eyewitness Testimony

Applications. As you read the actual chapters, notice the numerous applications of cognitive psychology. The recent emphasis on ecological validity has inspired many studies that are relevant for our everyday cognitive activity. In addition, research in cognition has important applications in such areas as education, medicine, business, and clinical psychology. These applications provide concrete illustrations of psychological principles.

These examples should also facilitate your understanding because research on memory demonstrates that people recall information better if it is concrete, rather than abstract, and if they try to determine whether the information applies to themselves (Paivio, 1995; Rogers et al., 1977; Symons & Johnson, 1997).

New Terms. Notice that each new term in this book appears in boldface type (for example, **cognition**) when it is first discussed. I have included the definition in the same sentence as the term, so you do not need to search an entire paragraph to discover the term's meaning. Also notice that phonetic pronunciation is provided for a small number of words that are often mispronounced. Students tell me that they feel more comfortable using a word in class discussion if they are confident that their pronunciation is correct. (I also included pronunciation guides for the names of several prominent theorists and researchers, such as Wundt and Piaget.)

Also, some important terms appear in several different chapters. I will define these terms the first time they occur in each chapter, so that you can read the chapters in any order.

In-Depth Feature. Chapters 2 through 13 each contain an "In Depth" feature, which examines research on an important topic relevant to the chapter. These features focus on the research methodology and the outcome of the studies.

Section Summaries. A special component of this textbook is a summary at the end of each major section in a chapter, rather than at the end of the entire chapter. For example, Chapter 2 includes four section summaries. These summaries allow you to review the material more frequently and to master small, manageable segments before you move on to new material. When you reach the end of a section, cover the section summary and see which important points you remember. Then read the section summary and notice which items you omitted or remembered incorrectly. Finally, test yourself again and recheck your accuracy. Also, you may learn the material more efficiently if you read only one section at a time, rather than an entire chapter.

End-of-Chapter Review. You will find a set of review questions and a list of new terms at the end of each chapter. Many review questions ask you to apply your knowledge to an everyday problem. Other review questions encourage you to integrate information from several parts of the chapter.

New Terms List. At the end of each chapter, a new terms list shows these terms in order of their appearance in the chapter. Check each item to see whether you can supply a definition and an example. You can consult the chapter for a discussion of the term; the glossary also has a brief definition for each of the terms.

Recommended Readings. Each chapter features a list of recommended readings. This list can supply you with resources if you want to write a paper on a particular topic or if an area is personally interesting. In general, I tried to locate books, chapters, and articles that provide more than an overview of the subject but are not overly technical.

Glossary. Your textbook includes a glossary at the end of the book. The glossary will be helpful when you need a precise definition for a technical term. It will also be useful when you want to check your accuracy while reviewing the list of new terms in each chapter.

One unusual aspect of cognitive psychology is that you are actually using cognition to learn about cognition! These learning aids, combined with the material on memory improvement in Chapter 6, should help you use your cognitive processes even more efficiently.

CHAPTER REVIEW QUESTIONS

1. Define the terms *cognition* and *cognitive psychology*. Now think about your ideal career, and suggest several ways in which the information from cognitive psychology would be relevant to this career.
2. Compare the following approaches to psychology, with respect to their emphasis on thinking: (a) William James's approach, (b) behaviorism, (c) gestalt psychology, (d) Frederic Bartlett's approach, and (e) the cognitive approach.

3. This chapter addressed the tradeoff between ecological validity and experimental control. Define these two concepts. Then compare the following approaches in terms of their emphasis on each concept: (a) Ebbinghaus's approach to memory, (b) James's approach to psychological processes, (c) Bartlett's approach to memory, (d) the behaviorist approach, (e) the cognitive psychology approach from several decades ago, and (f) current cognitive psychology research.

4. List several reasons for the increased interest in cognitive psychology and the decline of the behaviorist approach. In addition, describe the field of cognitive science, noting the disciplines that are included in this field.

5. The section on cognitive neuroscience described five different research techniques. Answer the following questions for each technique: (a) Can it be used with humans? (b) How precise is the information it yields? (c) What kind of research questions can it answer?

6. What is artificial intelligence, and how is the information-processing approach relevant to this topic? Select three specific cognitive processes that might interest researchers in artificial intelligence. Then provide examples of how pure AI and the computer-simulation investigations of these cognitive process might differ in their focus.

7. How does parallel distributed processing (PDP) differ from the classical artificial intelligence approach? List three characteristics of the PDP approach. In what way is this approach based on discoveries in cognitive neuroscience?

8. Theme 4 emphasizes that your cognitive processes are interrelated. Think about a problem you have solved recently, and point out how the solution to this problem depended upon perceptual processes, memory, and other cognitive activities. Use the description of chapter topics (see pp. 21–23) to help you answer this question.

9. As you'll see in Chapter 6, your long-term memory is more accurate if you carefully think about the material you are reading; it is especially accurate if you try to relate the material to your own life. Review the section called "How to Use Your Book" (pp. 24–27), and point out how you can use each feature to increase your memory for the material in the remaining chapters of this book.

10. Review each of the five themes of this book. Which of them seem consistent with your own experiences, and which seem surprising? From your own life, think of an example of each theme.

KEYWORDS

cognition
cognitive psychology
cognitive approach

empirical evidence
introspection
recency effect

behaviorist approach
operational definition
gestalt psychology

gestalt
object permanence
information-processing
  approach
Atkinson-Shiffrin model
sensory memory
short-term memory
working memory
long-term memory
ecological validity
cognitive neuroscience
social cognitive neuroscience
brain lesions
positron emission tomography
  (PET scan)
functional magnetic resonance
  imaging (fMRI)

event-related potential (ERP)
  technique
single-cell recording
  technique
neuron
artificial intelligence (AI)
computer metaphor
pure AI
computer simulation
  (computer modeling)
parallel distributed processing
  (PDP)
connectionism
neural networks
cerebral cortex
serial processing
parallel processing

cognitive science
consciousness
memory
metacognition
imagery
semantic memory
schemas
discourse
Theme 1
Theme 2
Theme 3
Theme 4
Theme 5
bottom-up processing
top-down processing

RECOMMENDED READINGS

Kalat, J. W. (2007). *Biological psychology* (9th ed.) Belmont, CA: Thomson Wadsworth. Kalat's textbook provides a clear description of biopsychology/neuropsychology; the illustrations are especially helpful.

Freedheim, D. F. (Ed.). (2003). *Handbook of psychology* (*Vol. 1: The history of psychology*, pp. 465–481). Hoboken, NJ: Wiley. I recommend this well-written volume for people interested in the history of

psychology. The chapters on perception, cognition, and education are especially relevant to cognitive psychology.

Pashler, H., & Wixted, J. (Eds.). (2002). *Stevens' handbook of experimental psychology* (3rd ed., Vol. 4, pp. 223–269), New York: Wiley. Here's an advanced-level resource that provides a sophisticated discussion of topics such as neuroscience methods and connectionism.

ANSWER TO DEMONSTRATION 1.4

The letter *e* is missing from this entire passage. The letter *e* is the most frequent letter in the English language. Therefore, a long passage—without any use of the letter *e*—is highly unusual. The exercise demonstrates the difficulty of searching for something that is not there (Theme 3).

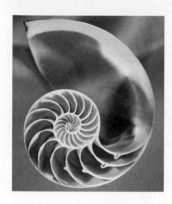

CHAPTER 2
Recognizing Visual and Auditory Stimuli

PREVIEW

During perception, you use your previous knowledge to gather and interpret the stimuli that your senses register. Chapter 2 explores visual and auditory recognition, which are especially relevant for cognitive psychology. (Chapter 3 will examine another equally relevant perceptual process, paying attention.)

When you recognize a visual object, you identify a complex arrangement of sensory stimuli, such as a letter of the alphabet or a human face. We will briefly discuss the visual system, and then explore how the visual system organizes our visual world. Then we will consider three theories that try to explain how we recognize objects.

The principle of top-down processing emphasizes that our concepts, expectations, and memory influence perceptual processing. We will explore how top-down processing aids reading. Then an in-depth discussion examines how overactive top-down processing can lead to errors in object recognition.

Face perception is vitally important in our social interactions, and we seem to process human faces differently from other visual stimuli. Neuroscience research helps to clarify the biological processes that explain face perception. The section on face perception also explores the challenges of recognizing faces from identification cards and from security surveillance systems. Then we'll consider how people with schizophrenia often encounter difficulties in face recognition.

Speech perception is more complicated than it initially appears. For example, people need to create boundaries between words. People also vary in the way they pronounce the basic speech sounds. However, we use context to fill in missing sounds. We also use visual cues to help us interpret ambiguous sounds. Researchers have proposed two theories to account for speech perception.

INTRODUCTION

Take a minute to appreciate your perceptual abilities. For instance, hold your hand directly in front of your eyes. You clearly perceive a solid object that includes distinctive characteristics. For example, you can easily identify its size, shape, and color. You also notice that your hand is a unified object, clearly located in front of a more distant and less clearly defined background.

As you shift your gaze back to this textbook, your eyes perceive a series of squiggles on this page. However, it doesn't seem surprising that you can identify each squiggle as a letter of the alphabet. If a friend walks by, you can instantly recognize this person's face. Your auditory abilities are equally impressive; you can recognize spoken words, music, squeaking chairs, and footsteps.

Most of us take perception for granted (Jain & Duin, 2004). *Of course* we can see and hear! Chapters 2 and 3 should persuade you that perception is actually a remarkably complex human ability. Perception may seem to be far easier than other cognitive skills, such as playing chess. However, as we noted in Chapter 1, a computer program can be designed that can beat a chess master. In contrast, you cannot buy a vision machine that will beat the visual skills of a preschool child. Perceptual processes provide clear evidence for Theme 2 of this textbook, because our visual and auditory achievements are impressively efficient and accurate (Grill-Spector & Kanwisher, 2005; Lappin & Craft, 2000).

In Chapters 2 and 3, we'll explore perception. **Perception** uses previous knowledge to gather and interpret the stimuli registered by the senses. For example, you use perception to interpret each of the letters on this page. Consider how you managed to perceive the letter *n* at the end of the word *perception*. You combined (1) information registered by your eyes, (2) your previous knowledge about the shape of the letters of the alphabet, and (3) your previous knowledge about what to expect when your visual system has already processed the fragment *perceptio-*.

Notice that perception combines aspects of both the outside world (the visual stimuli) and your own inner world (your previous knowledge). You'll notice that this process of pattern recognition is a good example of Theme 5 of this book, because it combines bottom-up and top-down processing.

Many colleges offer an entire course on the topic of perception, so we cannot do justice to this discipline in just two chapters. Other resources can provide information about basic sensory processes, such as the nature of the receptors in the eye and the ear (Gallagher & Nelson, 2003; Goldstein, 2007; Greenberg & Ainsworth, 2006). You can find more details about perception in other books (e.g., Coren et al, 2004; Matlin & Foley, 1997; Wolfe et al., 2006). These books examine how we perceive important characteristics of visual objects, such as shape, size, color, texture, and depth. These resources also investigate other perceptual systems—audition, touch, taste, and smell.

Our current chapter will explore several aspects of perceptual processing. We will begin with some background information on visual object recognition. Then we'll examine two important topics in vision: top-down processing and face perception. Finally, we will shift to the perceptual world of audition as we consider speech perception. These perceptual processes are vitally important because they prepare the "raw" sensory information so that it can be used in the more complex mental processes—such as reading—which are discussed in later chapters of this book.

This textbook includes two chapters about perceptual processes. Chapter 2 examines how we recognize visual and auditory stimuli. Chapter 3 discusses attention. For example, if you are paying close attention to the sentence you are reading, can you simultaneously perceive a nearby conversation?

BACKGROUND ON VISUAL OBJECT RECOGNITION

During **object recognition** or **pattern recognition**, you identify a complex arrangement of sensory stimuli, and you perceive that this pattern is separate from its background. When you recognize an object, your sensory processes transform and organize the raw information provided by your sensory receptors. You also compare the sensory stimuli with information in other memory storage. Consistent with Theme 2, we recognize objects quickly and accurately (Kersten et al., 2004; Kubovy et al., 2003). Let's briefly consider the visual system, how organization operates in visual perception, and three theories about object recognition.

The Visual System

Psychologists have developed two terms to refer to perceptual stimuli. The **distal stimulus** is the actual object that is "out there" in the environment—for example, the cell phone over on your desk. The **proximal stimulus** is the information registered on your sensory receptors—for example, the image that your cell phone creates on your retina. The **retina** lines the inside back portion of your eye; it contains millions of different kinds of neurons that register and transmit visual information from the outside world.

When we recognize an object, we manage to figure out the identity of the distal stimulus, even when the information available in the proximal stimulus is far from perfect (Kersten et al., 2004; Pasternak et al., 2003; Vecera & O'Reilly, 1998). For example, you can recognize your cell phone, even when you view it from an unusual angle and even when it is partly hidden by your book bag (Palmer, 2003). Try Demonstration 2.1 to illustrate your skill in identifying the distal stimulus.

Demonstration 2.1 notes that you can recognize objects in a new scene that has been presented for about 1/10 of a second (Biederman, 1995). Does this mean that your visual system manages to take the proximal stimulus, representing perhaps a dozen objects, and recognize all of these objects within 1/10 of a second? Fortunately, your visual system has some assistance from one of its other components (Gregory, 2004a). As we noted in Chapter 1 (p. 9), your **sensory memory** is a large-capacity storage system that records information from each of the senses with reasonable accuracy. To be specific, **iconic memory,** or visual sensory memory, preserves an image of a visual stimulus for a brief period after the stimulus has disappeared (Hollingworth, 2006b; Parks, 2004; Sperling, 1960).

⊚ Demonstration 2.1

The Immediate Recognition of Objects

Turn on a television set and adjust the sound to "mute." Now change the channels with your eyes closed. Open your eyes and then immediately shut them. Repeat this exercise several times. Notice how you can instantly identify and interpret the image on the TV screen, even though you did not expect that image and have never previously seen it in that exact form. In less than a second—and without major effort—you can identify colors, textures, contours, objects, and people.

This demonstration was originally suggested by Irving Biederman (1995), who noted that people can usually interpret the meaning of a new scene in 1/10 of a second. Incidentally, you can also recognize the rapidly presented images on MTV even though they may be shown at a rate of five per second. Consistent with Theme 2, humans are impressively efficient in recognizing patterns.

Visual information that is registered on the retina (the proximal stimulus) must make its way through the visual pathway, a set of neurons between the retina and the primary visual cortex. The **primary visual cortex** is located in the occipital lobe of the brain; it is the portion of your cerebral cortex that is concerned with basic processing of visual stimuli. (See Figure 2.1.) If you place your hand at the back of your head, just above your neck, the primary visual cortex lies just beneath your skull at that location.

The primary visual cortex is only the first stop within the cortex. For instance, researchers have identified at least thirty additional areas of the cortex that play a role in visual perception (Bruce et al., 2003; Frishman, 2001; Sillito, 2004). These regions beyond the primary visual cortex are activated when we recognize complex objects. Researchers are currently studying the functions of these regions. However, they have not yet discovered which brain region is paired with each component of object recognition (Farah, 2000a; Pasternak et al., 2003; Purves & Lotto, 2003). Our examination of face recognition, later in this chapter, will emphasize these more "sophisticated" regions of the cortex.

FIGURE 2.1

A Schematic Drawing of the Cerebral Cortex, as Seen from the Left Side, Showing the Four Lobes of the Brain. Notice the primary visual cortex (discussed in this section). The inferotemporal cortex (discussed on p. 52) plays an important role in recognizing complex objects such as faces.

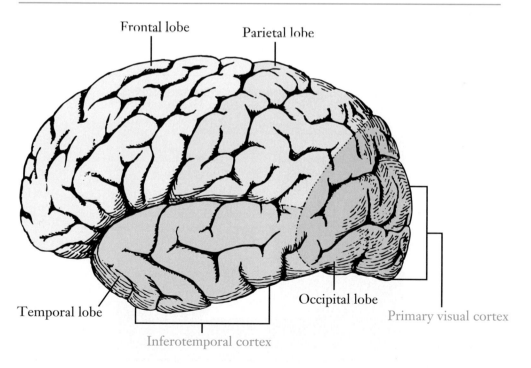

Organization in Visual Perception

At the beginning of this chapter, we emphasized that object recognition is a remarkable human achievement. As it happens, our visual system is designed to impose organization on the richly complicated visual world (Geisler & Super, 2000; Palmer, 2003).

In Chapter 1, we introduced a historical approach to psychology called gestalt psychology. One important principle in **gestalt psychology** is that humans have basic tendencies to organize what they see; without any effort, we see patterns, rather than random arrangements (Gordon, 2004). For example, when two areas share a common boundary, the **figure** has a distinct shape with clearly defined edges. In contrast, the **ground** is the region that is left over, forming the background. As gestalt psychologists pointed out, the figure has a definite shape, whereas the ground simply continues behind the figure. The figure also seems closer to us and more dominant than the ground (Kelly & Grossberg, 2000; Palmer, 2003; Rubin, 1915/1958). Even young infants demonstrate some of the gestalt principles of organization (Quinn et al., 2002).

In an **ambiguous figure-ground relationship**, the figure and the ground reverse from time to time, so that the figure becomes the ground and then becomes the figure again. Figure 2.2 illustrates the well-known vase-faces effect. At first, you see a white vase against a blue background, but a moment later, you see two faces against a white background. Even in this ambiguous situation, our perceptual system imposes organization on a stimulus, so that one portion stands out and the remainder recedes into the background.

FIGURE 2.2

The Vase-Faces Effect: An Example of an Ambiguous Figure-Ground Relationship.

The explanation for these figure-ground reversals has two components: (1) The neurons in the visual cortex become adapted to one figure, such as the "faces" version of Figure 2.2, so you are more likely to see the alternative or "vase" version; and (2) Furthermore, people try to solve the visual paradox by alternating between two reasonable solutions (Gregory, 2004a; Long & Toppino, 2004; Toppino & Long, 2005).

Surprisingly, we can even perceive a figure-ground relationship when a scene has no clear-cut boundary between the figure and the ground. One category of visual illusions is known as illusory contours. In **illusory contours** (also called **subjective contours**), we see edges even though they are not physically present in the stimulus (Palmer, 2003). In the illusory contour in Figure 2.3, for example, people report that an inverted white triangle seems to loom in front of the outline of a second triangle and three small blue circles. Furthermore, the triangle appears to be brighter than any other part of the stimulus (Grossberg, 2000; Palmer, 2002).

Two factors help to explain how we perceive these illusory contours:

1. During the early stages of visual processing, some cells in the visual system respond to these illusory contours (Grossberg, 2003a); and

2. During the later stages, the visual system tries to make sense of this disorderly jumble. For example, an efficient explanation for the jumble in Figure 2.3 is that a white triangle is located in front of the other figures. Illusory contours can therefore help us organize our visual perception (Gillam & Chan, 2002; Palmer, 2003).

FIGURE 2.3

An Example of Illusory Contours.

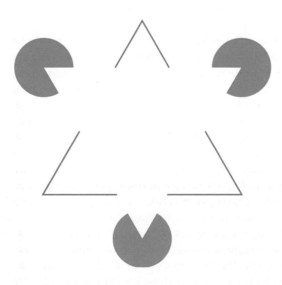

In our everyday life, we typically perceive scenes more accurately if we "fill in the blanks." However, in the case of illusory contours, this rational strategy leads to a perceptual error (Mendola, 2003; Purves & Lotto, 2003).

Theories of Visual Object Recognition

Researchers have proposed many different theories of object recognition, and we will consider three of them. Our discussion begins with the template-matching approach because it was the first modern explanation for object recognition. The two other theories—feature analysis and recognition-by-components—are more sophisticated. As you read about these two current theories, keep in mind that we don't need to decide that one theory is correct and the other is wrong. Humans are flexible creatures, and we may use different approaches for different object-recognition tasks (Mather, 2006; Riddoch & Humphreys, 2001).

Template-Matching Theory. You look at a letter P and you immediately recognize it. According to the **template-matching theory**, you compare a stimulus with a set of **templates**, or specific patterns that you have stored in memory. After comparing the stimulus to a number of templates, you note the template that matches the stimulus. You've probably had the experience of trying to find a piece of a jigsaw puzzle that will complete part of the puzzle. The piece must fit precisely, or else it won't work. Similarly, the stimulus must fit the template precisely. Thus, the letter Q will not fit the template for the letter O because of the extra line on the bottom.

Some machine recognition systems are based on templates. For example, if you have a checking account, look at the numbers at the bottom of a check. These numbers are specially designed to be recognized by check-sorting computers. Each number has a constant, standardized shape. Each number is also distinctly different from the others, so the computer will not make a recognition error when comparing the number with the templates.

A template system may work well for computers that process a standardized set of numbers. But notice why templates are totally inadequate for explaining the complex process of object recognition in humans. One problem with the template-matching theory is that it is extremely inflexible. If a letter differs from the appropriate template even slightly, the pattern cannot be recognized. However, every day you succeed in recognizing letters that differ substantially from the classic version of a letter. Notice in Figure 2.4 how all the P's in *Pattern* differ from one another in both style and size. Some P's are more slanted or more curved than others. Still, you can recognize each of those letters, even if you view the letters from a different perspective (Palmer, 2003). Your perceptual processes must therefore employ a more flexible system than matching a pattern against a specific template (Biederman, 1995: Gordon, 2004; Jain & Duin, 2004).

Furthermore, template models work only for isolated letters, numbers, and other simple two-dimensional objects presented in their complete form (Palmer, 2003). Look up from your textbook right now and notice the complex array of fragmented objects registered on your retina. Perhaps these include a lower edge of a lamp, a corner of a desk, and a portion of a book. Nonetheless, you can sort out this jumble and recognize the shapes. Your visual system could not possibly include templates for the lower edges

FIGURE 2.4

An example of variability in the shape of letters. Notice specifically the difference in the shape of the letter *P* in *Pattern*.

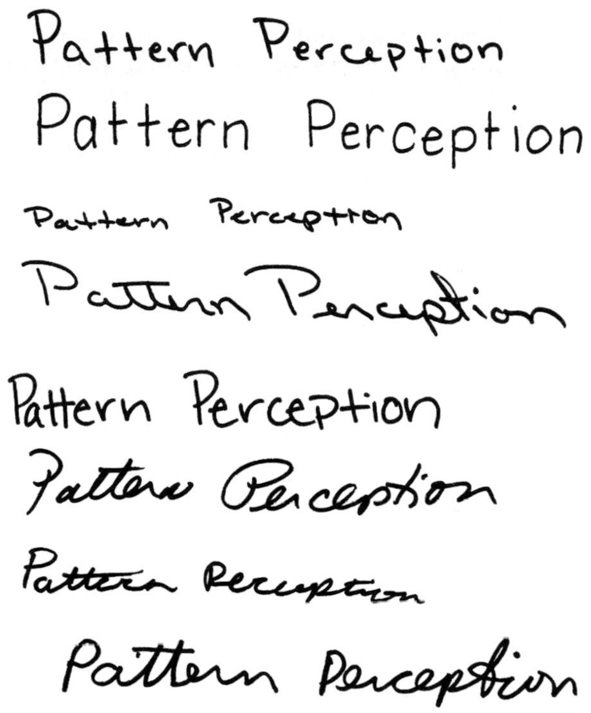

of lamps and other fragments. Clearly, the template-matching theory cannot account for the complexity of human visual processing.

Feature-Analysis Theory.   Several **feature-analysis theories** propose a more flexible approach, in which a visual stimulus is composed of a small number of characteristics or components (Gordon, 2004). Each characteristic is called a **distinctive feature**. Consider, for example, how feature-analysis theorists might explain the way we recognize letters of the alphabet. They argue that we store a list of distinctive features for each letter. For example, the distinctive features for the letter R include a curved component, a vertical line, and a diagonal line. When you look at a new letter, your visual system notes the presence or absence of the various features. It then compares this list with the features stored in memory for each letter of the alphabet. People's handwriting may differ, but each of their printed R's will include these three features.

Try Demonstration 2.2, which is based on a chart developed by Eleanor Gibson (1969). The feature-analysis theories propose that the distinctive features for each alphabet letters remain constant, whether the letter is handwritten, printed, or typed. These models can also explain how we perceive a wide variety of two-dimensional patterns,

Demonstration 2.2

A Feature-Analysis Approach

Eleanor Gibson proposed that letters differ from each other with respect to their distinctive features. The demonstration below includes an abbreviated version of a table she proposed. Notice that the table shows whether a letter of the alphabet contains any of the following features: four kinds of straight lines, a closed curve, an intersection of two lines, and symmetry. As you can see, the P and R share many features. However, W and O share only one feature. Compare the following pairs of letters to determine which distinctive features they share: A and B; E and F; X and Y; I and L.

Features	A	E	F	H	I	L	V	W	X	Y	Z	B	C	D	G	J	O	P	R	Q
Straight																				
horizontal	+	+	+	+		+					+				+					
vertical		+	+	+	+	+				+		+		+				+	+	
diagonal/	+						+	+	+	+	+									
diagonal\	+						+	+	+	+									+	+
Closed Curve												+		+			+	+	+	+
Intersection	+	+	+	+					+			+						+	+	+
Symmetry	+	+		+	+		+	+	+	+		+	+	+			+			

Source: Based on Gibson, 1969.

such as figures in a painting, designs on fabric, and illustrations in books. However, most research on this topic focuses on our ability to recognize letters and numbers.

Feature-analysis theories are consistent with both psychological and neuroscience research. For example, the psychological research by Eleanor Gibson (1969) demonstrated that people require a relatively long time to decide whether one letter is different from a second letter when those two letters share a large number of critical features. According to the table in Demonstration 2.2, the letters P and R share many critical features; Gibson's research participants made slow decisions about whether these two letters were different. In contrast, O and L do not share any critical features; in the research, people decided relatively quickly whether letter pairs like these were different from each other.

Other psychological research analyzes the letters and numbers in the addresses that people write on envelopes (Jain & Duin, 2004). For example, Larsen and Bundesen (1996) designed a model based on feature analysis that correctly recognized an impressive 95% of the numbers written in street addresses and zip codes.

The feature-analysis theories are also compatible with evidence from neuroscience (Gordon, 2004; Palmer, 2002). As described in Chapter 1, the research team of Hubel and Wiesel used the single-cell recording technique to insert small wires into the visual cortex of anesthetized animals (Hubel, 1982; Hubel & Wiesel, 1965, 1979, 2005). Next, they presented a simple visual stimulus—such as a vertical bar of light—directly in front of each animal's eyes. Hubel and Wiesel then recorded how a particular neuron responded to that visual stimulus. In this fashion, they tested how a variety of neurons in the primary visual cortex responded to visual stimuli.

Hubel and Wiesel's results showed that each neuron responded especially vigorously when a bar was presented to a specific retinal region and when the bar had a particular orientation. For example, suppose that a bar of light is presented to a particular location on the animal's retina. One neuron might respond strongly when the bar has a vertical orientation. Another neuron, just a hairbreadth away within the visual cortex, might respond most vigorously when the bar is rotated about 10 degrees from the vertical.

Furthermore, one small patch of the primary visual cortex could contain a variety of neurons, some especially responsive to vertical lines, some to horizontal lines, and some to specific diagonal lines. In fact, the visual system contains feature detectors that are present when we are born (Gordon, 2004). These detectors help us recognize certain features of letters and simple patterns.

However, the feature-analysis approach has several problems. First, a theory of object recognition should not simply list the features contained in a stimulus; it must also describe the physical relationship among those features (Groome, 1999). For example, in the letter T, the vertical line *supports* the horizontal line. In contrast, the letter L consists of a vertical line resting at the side of the horizontal line.

In addition, bear in mind that the feature-analysis theories were constructed to explain the relatively simple recognition of letters. In contrast, the shapes that occur in nature are much more complex (Kersten et al., 2004). How can you recognize a horse? Do you analyze the stimulus into features such as its mane, its head, and its hooves? Wouldn't any important perceptual features be distorted as soon as the horse moved— or as soon as *you* moved? Horses and other objects in our environment contain far too many lines and curved segments, and the task is far more complicated than letter recognition (Palmer, 2003; Vecera, 1998). The final approach to object recognition, which we discuss next, specifically addresses how people recognize these more complex kinds of stimuli found in everyday life.

The Recognition-by-Components Theory. Irving Biederman and his colleagues have developed a theory to explain how humans recognize three-dimensional shapes (Biederman, 1990, 1995; Hayworth & Biederman, 2006; Kayaert et al., 2003). The basic assumption of their **recognition-by-components theory** (also called the **structural theory**) is that a specific view of an object can be represented as an arrangement of simple 3-D shapes called *geons*. Just as the letters of the alphabet can be combined into words, geons can be combined to form meaningful objects.

FIGURE 2.5

Five of the Basic Geons (A) and Representative Objects that can be Constructed from the Geons (B).

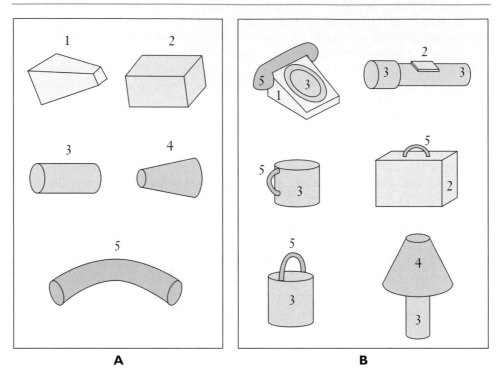

A   B

Source: Biederman, 1990.

You can see five of the proposed geons in Part A of Figure 2.5. Part B of this figure shows six of the objects that can be constructed from the geons. As you know, letters of the alphabet can be combined to form words with different meanings, depending upon the specific arrangements of the letters. For example, *no* has a different meaning from *on*. Similarly, geons 3 and 5 from Figure 2.5 can be combined to form different meaningful objects. A cup is different from a pail, and the recognition-by-components theory emphasizes the specific way in which these two geons are combined.

In general, an arrangement of three geons gives people enough information to classify an object. Notice, then, that Biederman's recognition-by-components theory is essentially a feature-analysis theory for the recognition of three-dimensional objects.

Biederman and his colleagues have conducted fMRI research with humans and single-cell recording studies with monkeys. Their findings show that areas of the cortex beyond the primary visual cortex respond to geons like those in Figure 2.5A (Hayworth & Biederman, 2006; Kayaert et al., 2003).

However, the recognition-by-components theory requires an important modification because people recognize objects more quickly when those objects are seen from a standard viewpoint, rather than a much different viewpoint (Friedman et al., 2005; Graf et al., 2005; O'Reilly & Munakata, 2000). Notice, for instance, how your own hand would be somewhat difficult to recognize if you look at it from an unusual perspective.

One modification of the recognition-by-components theory is called the **viewer-centered approach**; this approach proposes that we store a small number of views of three-dimensional objects, rather than just one view (Mather, 2006). Suppose that we see an object from an unusual angle, and this object does not match any object shape we have stored in memory. We must then mentally rotate the image of that object until it matches one of the views that *is* stored in memory (Dickinson, 1999; Tarr & Vuong, 2002; Vecera, 1998). This mental rotation may require a second or two, and we may not even recognize the object. (Chapter 7 discusses mental rotation in more detail.)

At present, both the feature-analysis theory and the recognition-by-components theory (modified to include the viewer-centered approach) can explain some portion of our remarkable skill in recognizing objects. In addition, researchers must explore whether these theories can account for our ability to recognize objects that are more complicated than isolated cups and pails. For example, how were you able to immediately identify numerous complex objects in the scene you viewed on your television screen in Demonstration 2.1? The theoretical explanations will become more detailed, as researchers continue to explore how we recognize real-world objects and scenes, using increasingly sophisticated research methods (Gordon, 2004; Henderson, 2005; Hollingworth, 2006a, 2006b; Tarr & Vuong, 2002).

Section Summary: *Background on Visual Object Recognition*

1. Perception uses previous knowledge to gather and interpret the stimuli registered by the senses; in object recognition, we identify a complex arrangement of sensory stimuli.

2. Visual information from the retina is transmitted to the primary visual cortex; other regions of the cortex are active when we recognize complex objects.

3. According to gestalt principles, people tend to organize their perceptions, even when they encounter ambiguous figure-ground stimuli and even in illusory-contour stimuli, when no boundary actually separates the figure from the background.

4. Researchers have proposed several theories of object recognition. The oldest of these, the template-matching theory, can be rejected because it cannot account for the complexity and flexibility of object recognition.

5. Feature-analysis theory is supported by research showing that people require more time to make decisions about letters of the alphabet when those letters share many critical features. This theory is also supported by neuroscience research using the single-cell recording technique.

6. The recognition-by-components theory argues that objects are represented in terms of an arrangement of simple 3-D shapes called geons. Furthermore, according to the viewer-centered approach, we also store several alternate views of these 3-D shapes, as viewed from different angles.

TOP-DOWN PROCESSING AND VISUAL OBJECT RECOGNITION

Our discussion so far has emphasized how people recognize isolated objects. We have not yet considered how our knowledge and expectations can aid recognition. In real life, when you try to decipher a hastily written letter of the alphabet, the surrounding letters of the word might be helpful. Similarly, the context of a coffee shop is useful when you try to identify an object that consists of a narrow, curved geon that is attached to the side of a wider, cylindrical geon.

Theme 5 emphasizes the difference between two kinds of processing. Let's first review that distinction. Then we'll see how these two processes work together in a complementary fashion to help us recognize words during the reading process. Finally, we'll see how we can sometimes make mistakes if our top-down processing is overly active.

The Distinction Between Bottom-Up Processing and Top-Down Processing

So far, this chapter has focused on bottom-up processing. **Bottom-up processing** emphasizes the importance of the stimulus in object recognition. Specifically, the physical stimuli from the environment are registered on the sensory receptors. This information is then passed on to higher, more sophisticated levels in the perceptual system (Gordon, 2004).

For example, a moment ago, the sensory receptors in the retina of my left eye registered information about a shape that streaked passed my window. This information included characteristics such as the object's shape (vaguely oval, with a long, narrow structure on one end), its color (pale brown, with two narrow, darker stripes), and its speed (rapid). The arrival of this information started the object-recognition process. This information started from the most basic (or *bottom*) level, and it worked its way *up* until it reached the more sophisticated cognitive processes beyond the primary visual cortex. The combination of simple, bottom-level features allows us to recognize more complex, whole objects.

The very first part of visual processing may be bottom-up (Palmer, 2002). However, an instant later, the second process begins. This second process in object recognition is top-down processing. **Top-down processing** emphasizes how a person's concepts and higher-level mental processes influence object recognition. Specifically, our concepts, expectations, and memory help in identifying objects. We expect certain shapes to be found in certain locations, and we expect to encounter these shapes because of past experiences. These expectations help us recognize objects very rapidly. In other words, our expectations at the higher (or *top*) level of visual processing will work their way *down* and guide our early processing of the visual stimulus (Donderi, 2006; Gregory, 2004a).

Here is a likely explanation for the perceptual experience that I just described. My house is located in a woodland setting. An occasional deer, wild turkey, or coyote may wander past my window, but chipmunks and squirrels are much more common. My top-down processing (in terms of my expectations and memory) combined together with specific information about the stimulus from bottom-up processing. As a result, I quickly concluded that the blurry shape must have been a chipmunk.

Top-down processing is especially strong when stimuli are incomplete or ambiguous. Top-down processing is also strong when a stimulus is registered for just a fraction of a second (Groome, 1999).

⊚ **Demonstration 2.3**

Context and Pattern Recognition

Can you read the following sentence?

THE MAN RAN.

How does top-down processing operate in vision? Some researchers propose that specific structures along the route between the retina and the visual cortex may play a role. These structures may store information about the relative likelihood of seeing various visual stimuli in a specific context (Kersten et al., 2004).

Cognitive psychologists propose that both bottom-up and top-down processing are necessary to explain the complexities of object recognition (Riddoch & Humphreys, 2001). We cannot ask whether perceivers interpret just the whole or just the parts, because both processes are required. For example, you recognize a coffee cup because of two almost simultaneous processes: (1) Bottom-up processing forces you to register the component features, such as the curve of the cup's handle; and (2) the context of a coffee shop encourages you to recognize the handle on the cup more quickly, because of top-down processing. Let's now consider how this top-down processing facilitates reading.

Top-Down Processing and Reading

Before you read further, try Demonstration 2.3. As you can see, the same shape—an ambiguous letter—is sometimes perceived as an *H* and sometimes as an *A*. In this demonstration, you began to identify the whole word *THE*, and your tentative knowledge of that word helped to identify the second letter as an *H*. Similarly, your knowledge of the words *MAN* and *RAN* helped you identify that same ambiguous letter as an *A* in this different context.

Researchers have demonstrated that top-down processing can influence our ability to recognize a variety of objects (e.g., Gregory, 2004a; Henderson & Hollingworth, 2003; Hollingworth & Henderson, 2004; Kersten et al., 2004; Riddoch & Humphreys, 2001; Tanaka & Curran, 2001). Most of the research on this topic examines how context helps us recognize letters of the alphabet during reading.

Psychologists who study reading have realized for decades that a theory of recognition must include some factor (or factors) other than the information in the stimulus. When you read, suppose that you do identify each letter by analyzing its features. In addition, suppose that each letter contains four distinctive features, a conservative guess. Taking into account the number of letters in an average word—and the average reading rate—this would mean that you would need to analyze about 5,000 features every minute. This estimate is ridiculously high; your perceptual processes couldn't handle that kind of workload!

Furthermore, we can still manage to read a sentence, even if some of the middle letters in a word have been rearranged. For example, Rayner and his colleagues (2006) found that college students could read normal sentences at the rate of about 255 words per minute. They could still read jumbled sentences such as, "The boy cuold not slove the probelm so he aksed for help." However, their reading rate dropped to 227 words per minute.

One of the most widely demonstrated phenomena in the research on recognition is the word superiority effect. According to the **word superiority effect**, we can identify a single letter more accurately and more rapidly when it appears in a meaningful word than when it appears alone by itself or else in a meaningless string of unrelated letters (Palmer, 2002).

For example, Reicher (1969) demonstrated that people's recognition accuracy was significantly higher when a letter appeared in a word such as *work*, rather than in a non-word such as *orwk*. Since then, dozens of studies have confirmed the importance of top-down processing in letter recognition (e.g., Grainger & Jacobs, 2005; Jordan & Bevan, 1994; Palmer, 1999; Williams et al., 2006). For example, the letter *s* is quickly recognized in the word *island*, even though the *s* is not pronounced in this word (Krueger, 1992).

Researchers have also shown that the context of a sentence facilitates the recognition of a word in a sentence. For example, people easily recognize the word *juice* in the sentence, "Mary drank her orange juice" (Forster, 1981; Stanovich & West, 1981, 1983).

Let's discuss a classic study that explored this word-in-a-sentence effect. Rueckl and Oden (1986) demonstrated that both the features of the stimulus and the nature of the context influence word recognition. That is, both bottom-up and top-down processing operate in a coordinated fashion. These researchers used stimuli that were either letters or letter-like characters. For example, one set of stimuli consisted of a perfectly formed letter *n*, a perfectly formed letter *r*, and three symbols that were intermediate between those two letters. Notice these stimuli arranged along the bottom of Figure 2.6. In each case, the letter pattern was embedded in the letter sequence "bea-s." As a result, the study included five stimuli that ranged between "beans" and "bears." (In other words, this variable tested the effects of bottom-up processing.)

The nature of the context was also varied by using the sentence frame, "The _____ raised (bears/beans) to supplement his income." The researchers constructed four sentences by filling the blank with a carefully selected term: "lion tamer," "zookeeper," "botanist," and "dairy farmer." You'll notice that a lion tamer and a zookeeper are more likely to raise bears, whereas the botanist and the dairy farmer are more likely to raise beans. Other similar ambiguous letters and sentence frames were also constructed, each using four different nouns or noun phrases. (In other words, this variable tested the effects of top-down processing.)

Figure 2.6 shows the results. As you can see, people were definitely more likely to choose the "bears" response when the line segment on the right side of the letter was short, rather than long: The features of the stimulus are extremely important because word recognition operates in a bottom-up fashion. However, you'll also notice that people were somewhat more likely to choose the "bears" response in the lion tamer and zookeeper sentences than in the botanist and dairy farmer sentences: The context is important because word recognition also operates in a top-down fashion. Specifically, our knowledge about the world leads us to expect that lion tamers and zookeepers would be more likely to raise bears than beans.

FIGURE 2.6

The Influence of Stimulus Features and Sentence Context on Word Identification.

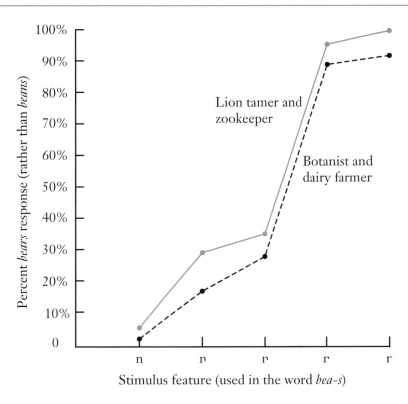

Stimulus feature (used in the word *bea-s*)

Source: Based on Rueckl & Oden, 1986

Think about how these context effects can influence your reading speed. The previous letters in a word help you identify the remaining letters more quickly. Furthermore, the other words in a sentence help you identify the individual words more quickly. Without context to help you read faster, you might still be reading the introduction to this chapter!

Overactive Top-Down Processing and Occasional Errors in Object Recognition

According to Theme 2, our cognitive processes are remarkably efficient and accurate. However, when we occasionally *do* make a mistake, that mistake can often be traced to a "smart mistake," such as overusing the strategy of top-down processing. Because we overuse top-down processing, we sometimes demonstrate **change blindness**; we fail to detect a change in an object or a scene. Overusing top-down processing can also lead us to demonstrate **inattentional blindness;** when we are paying attention to some events in a scene, we may fail to notice when an unexpected but completely visible object suddenly appears (Most et al., 2005). Let's consider these two kinds of visual-processing errors.

Change Blindness. Imagine that you are walking along a sidewalk near your college campus. Then, as in Part A of Figure 2.7, a stranger asks you for directions to a particular building. Right in the middle of this interaction, two workers—who are carrying a wooden door—walk between you and the stranger. (See Part B of Figure 2.7.) When they have passed by, the original stranger has been replaced by a different stranger. Would you notice that you are no longer talking with the same individual? You may be tempted to reply, "Of course!"

When Daniel Simons and Daniel Levin (1997a; 1997b; 1998) tried this stranger-and-the-door study, only half of the bystanders reported that one stranger had been

Figure 2.7

A Study on Change Blindness. These photos are four frames from a video of a study on change blindness. Frames A through C show the sequence of the shift, and Frame D shows the original stranger and the "substitute stranger," standing side by side.

Source: Simons & Levin, 1998

---

⑨ **Demonstration 2.4**

Detecting the Difference Between Two Pictures

Turn to the front of this book, on the right-hand side, where you'll see two color photos of children in a park. Look back and forth between these two scenes until you have detected which feature is different. The answer is at the end of the chapter, on p. 63.

---

replaced by a different stranger. Many were still "clueless" when they were explicitly asked, "Did you notice that I'm not the same person who approached you to ask for directions?" (Simons & Levin, 1998, p. 646). Take a moment to try Demonstration 2.4. How quickly can you detect the difference between these two similar scenes?

This chapter examines how we see objects. When perceiving an entire scene, our top-down processing encourages us to assume that the basic meaning of the scene will remain stable. This assumption is rational, and the mistaken perception makes sense (Saylor & Baldwin, 2004). In the real world, one person does not suddenly morph into a different person!

Laboratory research provides other examples of change blindness. For instance, Rensink and his colleagues (1997) asked participants to look at a photo, which was briefly presented twice. Then a slightly different version of the photo was briefly presented twice. This sequence of alternations was repeated until the participant detected the change.

This result showed that people quickly identified the change when the change was important. For example, when a view of a pilot flying a plane showed a helicopter either nearby or far away, participants required only 4.0 alternations to report the change. In contrast, they required 16.2 alternations to report a change that was unimportant, such as the height of a railing behind two people seated at a table. Again, these results make sense (Saylor & Baldwin, 2004). The basic meaning of the scene with the pilot is drastically different if the helicopter is nearby, rather than distant. In contrast, the height of the railing doesn't change the meaning of the scene at the table.

Furthermore, people are somewhat likely to notice an improbable change, such as a window in one picture that is entirely missing in the next picture. In contrast, they seldom notice a probable change, such as a window in one picture that is covered with a curtain in the next picture (Beck et al., 2004).

Additional studies confirm that people are surprisingly blind to fairly obvious changes in the objects that they are perceiving (e.g., Rensink, 2002; Saylor & Baldwin, 2004; Scholl et al., 2004; Simons et al., 2002). In general, then, when we look at a scene with many objects, most people do not store a detailed representation of that scene.

However, Heather Pringle and her coauthors (2004) have discovered individual differences in this skill. People who are accurate in detecting changes are typically more skilled in paying attention to a large visual scene, and they are also more skilled in storing an accurate image of a geometric shape.

Inattentional Blindness. As we noted on page 48, inattentional blindness occurs when you are paying attention to something, and you fail to notice an unexpected but completely visible object. In general, psychologists use the term *change blindness* when people fail to notice a change in some part of the stimulus. In contrast, they use the term *inattentional blindness* when people fail to notice that a new object has appeared. In both cases, however, people are using top-down processing as they concentrate on some objects in a scene. As a result, when an object appears that is not consistent with their concepts, expectations, and memory, people often fail to recognize this changed object (change blindness) or this new object (inattentional blindness).

Let's now consider a dramatic study about inattentional blindness. Simons and Chabris (1999) asked participants to watch a videotape of people playing basketball. They were instructed to mentally tally the number of times that members of a specified group made either a bounce pass or an aerial pass. Shortly after the video began, a person dressed in a gorilla suit wandered into the scene and remained there for 5 seconds. Amazingly, 46% of the participants failed to notice the gorilla! Other research confirms that people often fail to notice a new object, if they are paying close attention to something else (Intraub, 1999; Most et al., 2001; Most et al., 2005). Incidentally, Daniel Simons's Web site contains some interesting demonstrations of his research: http://viscog.beckman.uiuc.edu/djs_lab/demos.html

Theme 2 of this textbook states that our cognitive processes are remarkably efficient and accurate. How can we reconcile the data on change blindness with this theme? One important point is that many of the visual stimuli that people fail to see are *not* high in ecological validity (Rachlinski, 2004). Studies are high in **ecological validity** if the conditions in which the research is conducted are similar to the natural setting where the results will be applied. Frankly, I doubt if anyone reading this book has seen someone in a gorilla suit strolling through a basketball game!

Simons and Levin (1997a) emphasize that we actually function very well in our normal visual environment. If you are walking along a busy city street, a variety of perceptual representations will rapidly change from one glance to the next. People move their legs, shift a bag to another arm, and move behind traffic signs. If you precisely tracked each detail, your visual system would rapidly be overwhelmed by the trivial changes. Instead, your visual system is accurate in integrating the gist or general interpretation of a scene. You focus only on the information that appears to be important, such as the distance of an approaching bus as you cross the street, and you ignore unimportant details. Change blindness and inattentional blindness illustrate a point we made in connection with Theme 2: Our cognitive errors can often be traced to the use of a rational strategy.

We have been discussing research that illustrates how we make errors in object recognition if we are not paying close attention to the object. In Chapter 3 (Perceptual Processes II: Attention and Consciousness), we will examine attention in more detail.

So far, we have discussed the visual system, perceptual organization, and theories of object recognition. We have also emphasized the importance of top-down processing in perception. Now let's consider another topic in some detail. One of the most active areas of research on object recognition is the challenging topic of face perception.

⊚ Section Summary: *Top-Down Processing and Visual Object Recognition*

1. Bottom-up processing emphasizes the importance of the stimulus in object recognition; in contrast, top-down processing emphasizes how a person's concepts, expectations, and memory influence object recognition. Both processes work together to allow us to recognize objects.

2. Context can facilitate recognition; for example, the word superiority effect shows that we can identify a single letter more accurately and more rapidly when it appears in a meaningful word than when it appears by itself or in a meaningless string of letters.

3. Overactive top-down processing can also encourage us to make two kinds of errors: (a) change blindness, or errors in recognizing that an object has changed, and (b) inattentional blindness, or failing to notice that a new object has appeared.

FACE PERCEPTION

So far, our exploration of visual recognition has emphasized how we perceive letters of the alphabet and geometric objects. Now let's consider the most socially significant kind of recognition: How do you manage to recognize a friend, by simply looking at this person's face? The task *should* be challenging because all faces have generally the same shape.

A further complication is that you can recognize the face of your friend Monica—even when you see her face from a different angle, in an unusual setting, and wearing an unexpected frowning expression. Impressively, you manage to overcome all these sources of variation (Esgate & Groome, 2005; McKone, 2004; Styles, 2005). Almost instantly, you perceive that this person is indeed Monica.

We'll consider four areas of research in this section of the chapter. First, we'll examine some laboratory-based research showing that our perceptual system processes human faces differently from other visual stimuli. Next, we'll consider the neuroscience research on face perception. Then we'll explore some applied research on face perception. Our final topic focuses on individual differences, and it demonstrates that people with schizophrenia tend to have difficulty in recognizing faces, as well as facial expression.

Recognizing Faces Versus Recognizing Other Objects

Some psychologists argue that most people perceive faces in a different fashion from other stimuli; in other words, face perception is somehow "special" (Farah, 2004; McKone, 2004). For example, young infants track the movement of a photographed human face more than other similar stimuli (Bruce et al., 2003; Johnson & Bolhuis, 2000).

Similarly, Tanaka and Farah (1993) found that people were significantly more accurate in recognizing facial features when they appeared within the context of a whole face, rather than in isolation. That is, they could recognize a whole face much more accurately than, say, an isolated nose. In contrast, when they judged houses, they were just as accurate in recognizing an isolated house feature (such as a window) as in recognizing house features within the context of a complete house.

We recognize most objects—such as houses—by identifying the individualized features that combine together to create these objects. In contrast, faces apparently have a special, privileged status in our perceptual system. We recognize faces on a **holistic** basis—that is, in terms of their overall shape and structure. In other words, we perceive a face in terms of its **gestalt**, or overall quality that transcends its individual elements. It makes sense that face perception has a special status, given the importance of faces in our social interactions (Farah, 2004; Fox, 2005; Styles, 2005).

Neuroscience Research on Face Recognition

Much of the research on face recognition comes from people with brain lesions. In humans, the term **brain lesions** refers to the destruction of tissue, most often by strokes, tumors, or accidents. For example, McNeil and Warrington (1993) studied a professional man who lost his ability to recognize human faces after he had experienced several strokes. He then decided on a dramatic career change, and he began to raise sheep. Amazingly, he could recognize many of his sheep's faces, even though he still could not recognize human faces! In contrast, most people—even those who routinely work with sheep—are much more accurate in recognizing people's faces. This man has prosopagnosia (pronounced "pro-soap-ag-*know*-zhia"). **Prosopagnosia** is a condition in which people cannot recognize human faces visually, though they perceive other objects relatively normally (Farah, 2004).

Many neuroscience case studies show that individuals with prosopagnosia can easily recognize common objects. For example, a man with prosopagnosia may quickly identify a chair, a coffee cup, or a sweater. He may even look at a woman's smiling face and report that she looks happy. However, he may fail to recognize that this woman is his own wife (Farah, 2004; Palmer, 1999). Furthermore, people with prosopagnosia often report that the various parts of a person's face seem independent of one another, instead of forming a unified, complete face (Farah, 2004).

Earlier, we mentioned that the occipital lobe, at the back of your brain, is the location in the cortex that is responsible for the initial, most basic visual processing. Information then travels from that location to numerous other locations throughout the brain. The location most responsible for face recognition is the temporal cortex, at the side of your brain (Bentin et al., 2002; Farah, 2004). The specific location is known as the *inferotemporal cortex*, in the lower portion of the temporal cortex. (See Figure 2.1 on p. 35.) Researchers have tested monkeys, using the single-cell recording technique. They report that certain cells in the inferotemporal cortex respond especially vigorously to a photo of another monkey's face (Rolls & Tovee, 1995; Wang et al., 1996).

Chapter 1 also mentioned the **fMRI** technique, a technique for obtaining images of human brain activity. The fMRI studies have shown that the brain responds more quickly to faces presented in the normal, upright position, in comparison to faces presented upside-down (D'Esposito et al., 1999). Other related research shows that people are also much more accurate in identifying upright faces, compared to upside-down faces (McKone, 2004).

The neuroscience research demonstrates that specific cells in the inferotemporal cortex are responsible for perceiving faces (Farah, 2004; Kanwisher et al., 2001). The research is far from complete. However, these cells may help to explain why face perception seems to follow different rules, emphasizing holistic processing rather than isolated components.

Applied Research on Face Recognition

As we have noted, many cognitive psychologists now emphasize the importance of ecological validity. The applied research on face recognition focuses on real-life situations that assess our ability to recognize people's faces.

Kemp and his coauthors (1997) studied the accuracy of supermarket cashiers who had been instructed to make judgments about ID photos. Specifically, undergraduate students were given credit cards that showed a 1" × 1" color photo. Each student was told to select some items at a supermarket and then present his or her credit card to the cashier. The cashier could then decide whether to accept or reject the credit card.

When students carried a credit card that showed their own photo, the cashiers correctly accepted the card 93% of the time. However, when students carried a card that showed a photo of another person—who looked fairly similar—they correctly *rejected* the photo only 36% of the time. In other words, they let someone with an incorrect photo ID slip past them 64% of the time!

Another applied study on face recognition focused on security surveillance systems. Many banks, businesses, and institutions use a video security system, typically recording people who walk through a door. Burton and his coauthors (1999) asked people to look at video clips of psychology professors walking through the entrance of the department of psychology at the University of Glasgow in Scotland. The participants in the study saw a series of video clips of ten professors. Then they saw a series of high-quality photos of twenty professors; ten of these professors had appeared in a video, and ten had not. The participants were instructed to rate each photo, using a scale from 1 (indicating certainty that the person in the photo had not appeared in a video) to 7 (indicating certainty that the person in the photo had appeared in a video).

Burton and his colleagues (1999) also tested three categories of participants. Twenty of the participants had been taught by all twenty professors in the video clips. Twenty were other students who had never been taught by any of these professors, and twenty were experienced police officers.

Figure 2.8 shows the ratings provided by the three categories of participants. As you can see, the students who were familiar with the professors had highly accurate recognition. These students were very confident in identifying the ten professors who had actually appeared in the videos, and they were also very confident that the other 10 professors had not appeared in the videos.

However, the students who were unfamiliar with the professors were only slightly more confident about the professors they had actually seen, compared to the professors they had not seen. Unfortunately, the experienced police officers were no more accurate than the second group of students. Additional research confirmed that people are accurate in identifying familiar faces and inaccurate in identifying unfamiliar faces

FIGURE 2.8

Participants' Confidence About Having Seen a Target Person in an Earlier Video, as a Function of Kind of Observers and Whether the Target Had Been Seen or Not Seen.

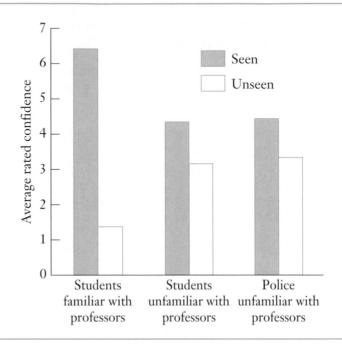

(Bruce et al., 2001; Henderson et al., 2001). These results are alarming, because robberies are more likely to be committed by strangers than by people we know!

Individual Differences: Face Identification in People with Schizophrenia

Schizophrenia is one of the most serious psychological disorders. People with **schizophrenia** typically do not show intense emotions, and they may have hallucinations. For students studying cognitive psychology, an especially important facet is disordered thinking. For example, individuals with schizophrenia are less likely than control-group individuals to use top-down processing in visual perception (Holden, 2003; Uhlhaas & Silverstein, 2005).

Another common characteristic in schizophrenia is difficulty in perceiving faces (Bediou et al., 2005; Hall et al., 2004). Let's consider a study by Flavie Martin and her coauthors (2005). These researchers made color photographs of five young-adult males. Five photos were made of each man, each photo representing a different emotion (happiness, fear, sadness, anger, and disgust).

The researchers then identified twenty hospitalized individuals with schizophrenia. They also selected twenty control-group individuals who were similar in age and gender, but they had no psychiatric problems. During one session, people in both groups were instructed to look at two photos, one after another, and classify these photos as representing either the same person or two different people. The individuals with schizophrenia responded more slowly than those in the control group, and they also made more errors in face recognition.

During a second session, the participants again looked at two photos, one after another. However, this time they were instructed to classify the photos as representing either the same emotion or two different emotions. Once again, the individuals with schizophrenia responded more slowly than those in the control group. However, they made even more errors in recognizing facial expressions than they had made on the face-recognition task during the first session. Furthermore, those individuals with schizophrenia who showed the least variation in their own expression of emotions tended to make the most errors in recognizing facial expressions in other people. In fact, Martin and her colleagues (2005) speculate that people who cannot express their own emotions are likely to have difficulty recognizing emotions in other individuals.

Section Summary: *Face Perception*

1. People can quickly recognize the faces of people they know; we seem to process a face in terms of its gestalt, or its overall shape and structure.

2. A variety of neuroscience techniques—including research with people who have prosopagnosia, the single-cell recording technique, and the fMRI technique—have demonstrated that cells in the inferotemporal cortex play an important role in perceiving faces.

3. Applied research suggests that people are not very accurate in judging whether a photo matches the face of the cardholder. Furthermore, people are not very accurate in judging whether a photo of an unfamiliar person matches a person in a video that they saw earlier.

4. Individuals with schizophrenia are likely to have difficulty identifying people's faces, as well as their facial expressions.

SPEECH PERCEPTION

Speech perception seems perfectly easy and straightforward . . . until you begin to think about the relevant components. During **speech perception**, your auditory system must record the sound vibrations generated by someone talking; then the system must translate these vibrations into a sequence of sounds that you perceive to be speech. Adults who speak English produce about 15 sounds every second (Kuhl, 1994). Therefore, you must somehow perceive about 900 sounds each minute!

In order to perceive a word, you must distinguish the sound pattern of one word from the tens of thousands of irrelevant words that are stored in your memory. And—as if these tasks are not challenging enough—you must separate the voice of the speaker from a noisy background that typically includes other, simultaneous conversations as well as a wide variety of nonspeech sounds (Brown & Sinnott, 2006; Grossberg et al., 2004; Plack, 2005). In fact, it's astonishing that we ever manage to perceive spoken language!

Speech perception is extremely complex, and you can locate more details in other books (Coren et al., 2004; Goldstein, 2007; Matlin & Foley, 1997; Pisoni & Remez, 2005). We'll consider two aspects of speech perception in this section: (1) characteristics of speech perception and (2) theories of speech perception.

Characteristics of Speech Perception

The next time you listen to a radio announcer, pay attention to the sounds you are hearing, rather than the meaning of the words. When describing these speech sounds, psychologists and linguists use the term *phoneme* (pronounced "*foe*-neem"). A **phoneme** is the basic unit of spoken language, such as the sounds *a*, *k*, and *th*. The English language uses about forty-five phonemes, a number that includes both vowels and consonants. When you listen to spoken English, you may hear brief quiet periods throughout this string of sounds. However, most of the words are simply run together in a continuous series.

Let's consider several important characteristics of speech perception:

1. Listeners can impose boundaries between words, even when these words are not separated by silence.
2. Phoneme pronunciation varies tremendously.
3. Context allows listeners to fill in missing sounds.
4. Visual cues from the speaker's mouth help us interpret ambiguous sounds.

All these characteristics provide further evidence for the Theme 2 of this book. Despite a less-than-perfect speech stimulus, we perceive speech with remarkable accuracy and efficiency.

Word Boundaries. Have you ever heard a conversation in an unfamiliar language? The words seem to run together in a continuous stream, with no boundaries of silence to separate them. You may think that the boundaries between words seem much more distinct in English—almost as clear-cut as the white spaces that identify the boundaries between the words in this textbook. In most cases, however, the actual acoustical stimulus of spoken language shows no clear-cut pauses to mark the boundaries. An actual physical event—such as a pause—marks a word boundary less than 40% of the time (Davis et al., 2002; Flores d'Arcais, 1988; McQueen, 2005).

Impressively, we are rarely conscious of the difficulty of resolving ambiguities concerning word boundaries. The research shows that our speech recognition system initially considers several different hypotheses about how to divide a phrase into words. This system immediately and effortlessly uses our knowledge about language in order to place the boundaries in appropriate locations (Grossberg et al., 2004; McQueen, 2005; Vroomen & de Gelder, 1997). Most of the time—fortunately—this knowledge leads us to the correct conclusions.

Variability in Phoneme Pronunciation. Perceiving phonemes does not initially seem like a challenging task. After all, don't we simply hear a phoneme and instantly perceive it? Actually, phoneme perception is not that easy. For example, speakers vary tremendously in the pitch and tone of their voices, as well as their rate of producing phonemes (Jusczyk & Luce, 2002; McQueen, 2005; Plack, 2005; Uchanski, 2005).

A second source of variability is that speakers often fail to produce phonemes in a precise fashion (Plack, 2005). Try Demonstration 2.5 to appreciate the problem of sloppy pronunciation that listeners must decode.

A third source of variability is called **coarticulation**; when you are pronouncing a particular phoneme, your mouth remains somewhat the same shape as it was in pronouncing the *previous* phoneme; furthermore, your mouth is also preparing to pronounce the *next* phoneme—all at the same time. As a result, the phoneme you produce varies slightly from time to time, depending upon the surrounding phonemes (Diehl et al., 2004; Jusczyk & Luce, 2002; McQueen, 2005). For example, notice that the *d* in *idle* sounds different from the *d* in *don't.*

Despite this remarkable variability in phoneme pronunciation, we still manage to understand the speaker's intended phoneme. Factors such as word boundaries, context, and visual cues help us achieve this goal.

Context and Speech Perception. People are active listeners, consistent with Theme 1. Instead of passively receiving speech sounds, they can use context as a cue to help them figure out a sound or a word (Cleary & Pisoni, 2001; Warren, 2006). We saw earlier in this chapter that context and other top-down factors influence visual perception. Top-down factors also influence speech perception (Theme 5), because we use our vast knowledge about language to help us perceive ambiguous words.

For example, when you are listening to your professors' lectures, extraneous noises will sometimes mask a phoneme. People knock books off desks, cough, turn pages, and whisper. Still, without much effort, you can usually reconstruct the missing sound. People tend to show **phonemic restoration**: They can fill in a missing phoneme, using contextual meaning as a cue (Grossberg, 2003b).

⊚ **Demonstration 2.5**

Variability in Phoneme Pronunciation

Turn on the radio and locate a station on which you hear someone talking. After hearing one or two sentences, turn the radio off, and write down the two sentences. Try to determine whether the speaker produced each phoneme in a precise fashion. For instance, did the speaker omit some portion of a word (e.g., *sposed* instead of *supposed)*? Did he or she pronounce consonants such as *k* or *p* precisely? Now try pronouncing the words in each sentence very carefully, so that every phoneme can be clearly identified.

In a classic study, Warren and Warren (1970) showed that people are skilled at using the meaning of a sentence to select the correct word from several options. They played tape recordings of several sentences for their research participants:

1. It was found that the *eel was on the axle.
2. It was found that the *eel was on the shoe.
3. It was found that the *eel was on the orange.

A coughing sound was inserted in the location indicated by the asterisk. The spoken sentences were identical with one exception: A different word was spliced onto the end of each sentence. The results showed that people typically heard the "word" *eel as *wheel* in the first sentence, *heel* in the second sentence, and *peel* in the third. In this study, then, people were able to reconstruct the missing word on the basis of a context cue at the end of the sentence, which occurred four words later!

Notice that phonemic restoration is a kind of illusion. People think they hear a phoneme, even though the correct sound vibrations never reach their ears. Phonemic restoration is a well-documented phenomenon, and it has been demonstrated in numerous studies (Samuel & Ressler, 1986; Warren, 2006). Our ability to perceive a word on the basis of context also allows us to handle sloppy pronunciations, the problem we mentioned earlier.

Because we are so tolerant of mispronunciations in sentences, we often fail to notice startling mispronunciations that people make, for instance, when children sing a song (Bond, 2005). One of my students recalled singing a Christmas carol in which the shepherds "washed their socks by night," rather than "watched their flocks by night." Many songs that children learn are never explained, and so they make up versions that make sense to them. Furthermore, as experienced listeners, adults have well-developed top-down processing, and the context encourages them to ignore these mispronunciations (Bond, 2005).

One likely explanation for the influence of context on perception is top-down processing, although researchers have also offered other explanations (Carroll, 2004; Grossberg et al., 2004; Plack, 2005). The top-down processing approach argues that we use our knowledge about language to facilitate recognition, whether we are looking at objects or listening to speech. Understanding language is not merely a passive process in which words flow into our ears, providing data for bottom-up processing. Instead, we actively use our knowledge about language to create expectations about what we might hear. Consistent with Theme 5 of this textbook, top-down processing influences our cognitive activities.

Visual Cues as an Aid to Speech Perception. Try Demonstration 2.6 when you have the opportunity. This simple exercise illustrates how visual cues contribute to speech perception (Smyth et al., 1987). Information from the speaker's lips and face helps resolve ambiguities from the speech signal, much as linguistic cues help us choose between *wheel* and *heel* (Dodd & Campbell, 1986). Similarly, you can hear conversation more accurately when you closely watch a speaker's lips, instead of listening to a conversation over the telephone (Massaro & Stork, 1998). Even with a superb telephone connection, you miss the lip cues that would inform you whether the speaker was discussing *Harry* or *Mary*.

⊚ Demonstration 2.6

Visual Cues and Speech Perception

The next time you are in a room with both a television and a radio, try this exercise. Switch the TV set to the news or some other program where some-one is talking straight to the camera; keep the volume low. Now turn on your radio and tune it between two stations, so that it produces a hissing noise. Turn the radio's volume up until you have difficulty understanding what the person on television is saying. The radio's "white noise" should nearly mask the speaker's voice. Face the TV screen and close your eyes; try to understand the spoken words. Then open your eyes. Do you find that speech perception is now much easier?

Source: Based on Smyth et al., 1987.

Adults with normal hearing seldom notice or take full advantage of these visual cues. In fact, we are likely to appreciate visual cues only in unusual circumstances. For example, you may notice a poorly dubbed movie, perhaps one that was filmed in French with U.S. actors' voices substituted afterward. The actors' lips often move independently of the sounds presumably coming from those lips.

However, researchers have demonstrated that we do integrate visual cues with auditory cues during speech perception—even if we don't recognize the usefulness of these visual cues (Nicholls et al., 2004). These results have been replicated for speakers of English, Spanish, Japanese, and Dutch (Massaro, 1998; Massaro et al., 1995).

Research by McGurk and McDonald (1976) provides a classic illustration of the contribution of visual cues to speech perception. These researchers showed participants a video of a woman whose lips were producing simple syllables, such as "gag." Meanwhile, the researchers presented different auditory information (coming from the same machine), such as "bab."

When the observers were asked to report what they perceived, their responses usually reflected a compromise between these two discrepant sources of information. In this case, the listeners typically reported hearing the word "dad." The **McGurk effect** refers to the influence of visual information on speech perception, when individuals must integrate both visual and auditory information (Massaro, 1999; Rosenblum, 2005). Fortunately, however, a speaker's lips usually move in a manner that is consistent with the speaker's auditory message, therefore improving the listener's accuracy.

In summary, then, we manage to perceive speech by overcoming the problems of a less-than-ideal speech stimulus. We do so by carving out boundaries between words, overcoming the variability in phoneme pronunciation, and using context to resolve ambiguous phonemes. If we can watch the speaker who is producing the stream of speech, the visual information from the speaker's lips provides additional helpful clues.

Theories of Speech Perception

Most current theoretical approaches to speech perception fall into two categories. Some theorists believe that we humans must have a special mechanism in our nervous system that explains our impressive skill in speech perception. Others admire humans' skill in speech perception, but they argue that the same general mechanism that handles other cognitive processes also handles speech perception.

Earlier in this chapter, we examined three theories of visual pattern perception. Unfortunately, researchers have not developed such detailed theories for speech perception. One reason for this problem is that humans are the only species who can understand spoken language. As a result, cognitive neuroscientists have a limited choice of research techniques.

The Special Mechanism Approach. According to the **special mechanism approach** (also called the **speech-is-special approach**), humans are born with a specialized device that allows us to decode speech stimuli. As a result, we process speech sounds more quickly and accurately than other auditory stimuli, such as instrumental music. Supporters of this approach argue that humans possess a **phonetic module** (or **speech module**), a special-purpose neural mechanism that specifically handles all aspects of speech perception; it cannot handle other kinds of auditory perception. This phonetic module would presumably enable listeners to perceive ambiguous phonemes accurately. It would also help listeners to segment the blurred stream of auditory information that reaches their ears, so that they can perceive distinct phonemes and words (Liberman, 1996; Liberman & Mattingly, 1989; Todd et al., 2006).

Notice that the special mechanism approach to speech perception suggests that the brain is organized in a special way. Specifically, the module that handles speech perception does *not* rely on the general cognitive functions discussed throughout this book—functions such as recognizing objects, remembering events, and solving problems (Trout, 2001). Incidentally, this modular approach is not consistent with Theme 4 of this textbook, which argues that the cognitive processes are interrelated and dependent upon one another.

One argument in favor of the phonetic module was thought to be categorical perception. Early researchers asked people to listen to a series of ambiguous sounds, such as a sound halfway between a *b* and a *p*. People who heard these sounds typically showed **categorical perception**; they heard either a clear-cut *b* or a clear-cut *p*, rather than a sound partway between a *b* and a *p* (Liberman & Mattingly, 1989).

When the special mechanism approach was originally proposed, supporters argued that people show categorical perception for speech sounds, but they hear nonspeech sounds as a smooth continuum. However, more recent research has shown that humans also exhibit categorical perception for some complex nonspeech sounds (Esgate & Groome, 2005; Pastore et al., 1990).

The General Mechanism Approaches. Although some still favor the special mechanism approach (Trout, 2001), most theorists now favor one of the general mechanism approaches (e.g., Cleary & Pisoni, 2001; Massaro & Cole, 2000). The **general mechanism approaches** argue that we can explain speech perception without proposing any special phonetic module. People who favor these approaches believe that humans use the same neural mechanisms to process both speech sounds and nonspeech sounds. Speech perception is therefore a learned ability—indeed, a very impressive learned ability—but it is not really "special."

Current research seems to favor the general mechanism approach. As we already noted, humans exhibit categorical perception for complex nonspeech sounds (Pastore et al., 1990). Other research supporting the general mechanism viewpoint uses event-related potentials (ERPs), which we discussed in Chapter 1. This research demonstrates that adults show the same sequence of shifts in the brain's electrical potential, whether they are listening to speech or to music (Patel et al., 1998).

Other evidence against the phonetic module is that people's judgments about phonemes are definitely influenced by visual cues, as we saw in the discussion of the McGurk effect (Cleary & Pisoni, 2001; Massaro, 1998). If speech perception can be influenced by visual information, then we cannot argue that a special phonetic module handles all aspects of speech perception.

Several different general mechanism theories of speech perception have been developed (e.g., Cleary & Pisoni, 2001; Fowler & Galantucci, 2005; Jusczyk & Luce, 2002; McQueen, 2005; Todd et al., 2006). These theories tend to argue that speech perception proceeds in stages and that it depends upon familiar cognitive processes such as feature recognition, learning, and decision making.

In summary, our ability to perceive speech sounds is impressive. However, this ability can probably be explained by our general perceptual skill—combined with our other cognitive abilities—rather than any special, inborn speech mechanism. We learn to distinguish speech sounds in the same way we learn other cognitive skills.

Section Summary: *Speech Perception*

1. Speech perception is an extremely complex process; it demonstrates that humans can quickly perform impressively complex cognitive tasks.

2. Even when the acoustical stimulus contains no clear-cut pauses, people are able to determine the boundaries between words with impressive accuracy.

3. The pronunciation of a specific phoneme varies greatly, depending upon vocal characteristics of the speaker, imprecise pronunciation, and variability caused by coarticulation.

4. When a sound is missing from speech, listeners demonstrate phonemic restoration, using context to help them perceive the missing sound.

5. People also use visual cues to facilitate speech perception, as illustrated by the McGurk effect.

6. According to the special mechanism approach to speech perception, humans have a special brain device (or module) that allows us to perceive phonemes more quickly and accurately than nonspeech sounds.

7. The current evidence supports a general mechanism approach to speech perception; research suggests that humans perceive speech sounds in the same way we perceive nonspeech sounds.

CHAPTER REVIEW QUESTIONS

1. Think of a person whom you know well, who has never had a course in cognitive psychology. How would you describe perception to this person? Using details from this chapter, describe how this person accomplishes two visual tasks and two auditory tasks that he or she performs frequently.

2. Imagine that you are trying to read a sloppily written number that appears in a friend's class notes. You conclude that it is an *8*, rather than a *6* or a *3*. Explain how you recognized that number, using the template-matching and feature-analysis theories.

3. Look up from your book and notice two nearby objects. Describe the characteristics of each "figure" in contrast to the "ground." How would Biederman's recognition-by-components theory describe how you recognize these objects?

4. Distinguish between bottom-up and top-down processing. Explain how top-down processing can help you recognize the letters of the alphabet in the word "alphabet." How would the word superiority effect operate if you tried to identify one letter in the word "alphabet" if it were presented very quickly?

5. This chapter emphasized visual and auditory object recognition. How does top-down processing (e.g., prior knowledge) operate when you smell a certain fragrance and try to identify it? Then answer this question for both taste and touch.

6. According to the material in this chapter, face recognition seems to be "special," and it probably differs from other recognition tasks. Discuss this statement, mentioning research on the comparison between faces and other visual stimuli. Be sure to describe material from neuroscience research on this topic, as well as difficulties encountered by people with schizophrenia.

7. Our visual world and our auditory world are both richly complicated. Describe several ways in which the complexity of the proximal stimuli presents challenges when we try to determine the "true" distal stimuli.

8. Both our visual system and our auditory system are designed to impose organization on our perceptual world. How does the gestalt approach help in visual perception? What factors help us overcome the difficulties in recognizing speech?

9. What kinds of evidence supports the general mechanism approach to speech perception? Contrast this approach with the special mechanism approach. How is the special mechanism approach to speech similar to the findings about perceiving faces?

10. Throughout this book, we will emphasize that the research from cognitive psychology can be applied to numerous everyday situations. For example, you learned some practical applications of the research on face perception. Skim through this chapter and describe at least five other practical applications of the research on visual and auditory recognition.

KEYWORDS

perception
object recognition
pattern recognition
distal stimulus
proximal stimulus
retina
sensory memory
iconic memory
primary visual cortex
gestalt psychology
figure
ground
ambiguous figure-ground
  relationship
illusory contours
subjective contours
template-matching theory

templates
feature-analysis theories
distinctive feature
recognition-by-components
  theory
structural theory
geons
viewer-centered approach
bottom-up processing
top-down processing
word superiority effect
change blindness
inattentional blindness
ecological validity
holistic (recognition)
gestalt
brain lesions

prosopagnosia
fMRI
schizophrenia
speech perception
phoneme
coarticulation
phonemic restoration
McGurk effect
special mechanism approach
speech-is-special approach
phonetic module
speech module
categorical perception
general mechanism
  approaches

RECOMMENDED READINGS

Coren, S., Ward, L. M., & Enns, J. T. (2004). *Sensation and perception* (6th ed.). Hoboken, NJ: Wiley. Coren and his colleagues' mid-level textbook emphasizes vision and hearing; however, other chapters provide information on taste, smell, the skin senses, and the perception of time.

Farah, M. J. (2004*). Visual agnosia* (2nd ed.). Cambridge, MA: MIT Press. I strongly recommend Martha Farah's book for anyone interested in neuroscience; the book is both informative and well written.

Greenberg, S., & Ainsworth, W. A. (Eds.). (2006). *Listening to speech: An auditory perspective.* Mahwah, NJ: Erlbaum. Here is a current advanced-level exploration of speech perception, speech processing, and auditory scene analysis.

Henderson, J. M. (Ed.). (2005). *Real-world scene perception.* Hove, UK: Psychology Press. Most of the current chapter focused on how we perceive isolated objects. This interesting book addresses more complicated questions about how we perceive scenes in the everyday world.

Levin, D. T. (Ed.). (2004b). *Thinking and seeing: Visual metacognition in adults and children.* Cambridge, MA: MIT Press. Here's a book that examines change blindness and inattentional blindness. Many of the chapters in this book also discuss whether we are aware of these kinds of deficits.

ANSWER TO DEMONSTRATION 2.4

Look to the left of the teacher's head. The two bushes are slightly further apart in the figure on the bottom.

CHAPTER 3
Paying Attention

PREVIEW

If you've ever tried to study while someone is shouting into a cell phone, you know that attention can be limited. Research confirms that performance usually suffers on *divided-attention tasks*, where you must perform two or more tasks simultaneously. Research also shows that we have difficulty on three kinds of *selective-attention tasks:* (1) If you are paying close attention to one conversation, you usually notice little about another simultaneous conversation; (2) On a Stroop task, ink of one color—such as blue—is used for printing the name of a different color—such as *red*—people have trouble saying the color of the ink; (3) People have trouble searching quickly for visual stimuli when the task is difficult. The third category is *saccadic eye movements*, which regulate our visual attention during tasks such as reading.

This chapter also discusses neuroscience and theoretical explanations of attention. According to neuroscience research, one kind of attention network is responsible for visual search. A different attention network is responsible for handling conflicting messages and for acquiring academic skills. An early theoretical explanation of attention proposed that the brain resembles a bottleneck in the way it limits our attention. A current theoretical explanation proposes that we can register some visual features automatically via distributed attention, but more challenging tasks require focused attention and serial processing.

One issue related to consciousness is that people are sometimes unaware of the way their cognitive processes operate. In addition, they may have difficulty eliminating some thoughts from consciousness, and this difficulty is intensified in people with obsessive-compulsive disorders. Finally, in a rare condition called "blindsight," people with a damaged visual cortex can detect an object, even though they believe that they cannot see it.

INTRODUCTION

Take a few minutes to pay attention to your attention processes. First, look around you and try to take in as many visual objects as possible. If you are reading this book in a room, for instance, try to notice all the objects that surround you. Be sure to notice their shape, size, location, and color. If your room is typical, you'll have the sensation that your visual attention is overworked, far beyond its limits, even after a single minute.

Now continue this same exercise, but also try to notice every sound in your environment, such as the hum of your computer, the noise of a clock ticking, and a distant automobile. Next, try to maintain all these visual and auditory stimuli, but also notice your skin senses. Can you feel the pressure that your watch creates on your wrist, and can you sense a slight itch or a subtle pain? If you somehow manage to pay simultaneous attention to your vision, hearing, and skin senses, try expanding your attention to include smell and taste. You'll easily discover that you cannot attend to everything at once (Cowan, 2005).

Interestingly, though, we seldom give much thought to our attention. Instead, attention just "happens," and it seems as natural to us as breathing (LaBerge, 1995).

Attention is a concentration of mental activity that allows you to take in a limited portion of the vast stream of information available from both your sensory world and your memory (Fernandez-Duque & Johnson, 2002; Styles, 2006; Ward, 2004). Meanwhile the *unattended* items lose out, and they are not processed in detail. Attention has always been an important topic in cognitive psychology, from the beginning of the cognitive revolution and continuing to the present (Cowan, 2005; Logan, 2004; Posner & Rothbart, 2007b).

Consistent with Theme 4, many of the concepts in this chapter are related to concepts in the previous chapter on perceptual recognition. As you will see, attention tasks use both top-down and bottom-up processing (Chun & Marois, 2002). Specifically, we sometimes concentrate our mental activity because an interesting stimulus in the environment has captured our attention (bottom-up processing). For example, an object in your peripheral vision might suddenly move. Other times we concentrate our mental activity because we want to pay attention to some specific stimulus (top-down processing). For example, you might be searching for the face of a particular friend in a crowded cafeteria.

Chapter 2 also discussed several visual phenomena that illustrate how shape perception and attention work cooperatively. Consider, for example, ambiguous figure-ground relationships (see Figure 2.2 on p. 36). When you pay attention to the central white form, you see a vase; when you shift your attention to the two outer blue forms, you see two faces. Other relevant concepts from Chapter 2 include change blindness (when you fail to notice a change in an object) and inattentional blindness (when you fail to notice that a new object has entered a scene).

Attention also has implications for many of the chapters in the remaining part of this book. For example, attention plays a major role in regulating how many items we can process in working memory (Chapter 4). Attention is also intertwined with our long-term memory (Chapter 5), concepts (Chapter 8; Logan, 2002), and reading (Chapter 9; Henderson & Ferreira, 2004a). Furthermore, as Chapter 11 describes, when we attempt to solve a problem, we need to pay attention to relevant information, while ignoring trivial details (Anderson et al., 2005). Also, Chapter 12 explains how we make incorrect decisions when we pay too much attention to relatively unimportant information.

We will begin our discussion by considering three interrelated cognitive tasks: divided attention, selective attention, and saccadic eye movements. Our second section examines both biological and theoretical explanations for attention. Our final topic, consciousness, focuses on our awareness about the external world, as well as our cognitive processes.

THREE KINDS OF ATTENTION PROCESSES

Before you finish reading this chapter, you are likely to perform three kinds of attention processes. For example, you may momentarily try to use divided attention, concentrating on a nearby conversation, as well as the words in your cognition textbook. You'll easily discover, though, that you cannot accurately attend to both categories of stimuli. As a result, you will try to use selective attention, focusing on just one category of stimuli; let's be optimistic and presume that your selective attention is directed toward your textbook. Selective attention will not allow you to take in much information about the unattended conversation. Finally, as you read your textbook, you will make saccadic movements; your eyes will move systematically to the right to take in an appropriate amount of new information.

Divided Attention

In a **divided-attention task,** you try to pay attention to two or more simultaneous messages, responding to each as needed. In most cases, your accuracy decreases, especially if the tasks are challenging (Ward, 2004).

In the laboratory, researchers typically study divided attention by instructing participants to perform two tasks at the same time. Many researchers study driving performance (Fisher & Pollatsek, 2007; Strayer & Drews, 2007). For example, Levy and his coauthors (2006) asked moderately experienced drivers to perform a simulated-driving task. Specifically, each person sat in a "driver's seat" and used a steering wheel, following a car in front (the "lead car"), which was shown on a large screen. One task required the participant to quickly press the brake pedal when the lead car braked suddenly. The second task required the participant to make a simple choice. For instance, a tone was presented either once or twice, and the participant responded either "one" or "two."

The results showed that the drivers used their brakes much more quickly if the choice task occurred just a fraction of a second *before* the lead car braked, rather than at the same time. If you are an experienced driver, you may think you can use your car brakes automatically, no matter what else you are doing at the same time. Unfortunately, Levy and his colleagues would disagree.

This research on divided attention also has important implications for people who use cell phones while driving. Many U.S. states and Canadian provinces have passed a law prohibiting the use of hand-held cell phones during driving. Still, some people carry on distracting conversations by using their hands-free cell phones. The research shows that people make more driving errors when they are either talking or listening, compared to driving without conversation (Kubose et al., 2006; Strayer & Drews, 2007).

David Strayer and his colleagues (2003) used a simulated-driving task to determine whether the hands-free cell phone interferes with driving. From time to time, the lead car would brake unexpectedly, and the researchers measured the time required to press the brake. The participants in the control group simply drove the simulated car. In contrast, the participants in the experimental group conversed on a hands-free cell phone with a lab assistant.

When the traffic was light, the people in the cell-phone group took slightly longer to apply the brake than those in the control group. During heavy-traffic conditions, however, the people in the cell-phone group took significantly longer than those in the control group.

With further testing, Strayer and his colleagues discovered that the participants who used cell phones showed a form of inattentional blindness (see pp. 49–50 of Chapter 2). For example, their attention had been reduced for information that appeared in the center of their visual field. Even if you use a hands-free cell phone, your attention may wander away from a dangerous situation right in front of you!

In some cases, people can perform divided attention tasks more competently if they have had time to practice these tasks. For example, Wikman and her colleagues (1998) compared experienced drivers with novice (inexperienced) drivers. The researchers instructed all the participants to drive as they normally would, while performing several routine, secondary tasks: changing an audiocassette, dialing a cell phone, and tuning the radio.

The novices in this study divided their attention ineffectively. Specifically, they frequently glanced away from the highway for longer than 3 seconds. More worrisome still, their cars often swung to the side as they glanced away. The experienced drivers managed to complete each task quickly and efficiently, glancing away from the road for less than 3 seconds for each task. Still, can't you imagine road conditions that could create an accident in less than 3 seconds?

Selective Attention

Selective attention is closely related to divided attention. In a divided-attention task, people try to pay equal attention to two or more sources of information. In a **selective-attention task,** people are instructed to respond selectively to certain kinds of information, while ignoring other information (Fuster, 2003; Milliken et al., 1998). Selective-attention studies often show that people notice little about the irrelevant tasks (McAdams & Drake, 2002). Perhaps you've noticed that you can usually follow closely only one conversation at a noisy party; in contrast, you typically cannot process the content of the other conversations.

At times, you might wish that attention were not so selective. Wouldn't it be wonderful to notice the details of all the other conversations going on around you? On the other hand, think how confusing this would be. Perhaps you would be in the midst of talking with a friend about a new job prospect, and then you might suddenly start talking about baseball—the topic of a neighboring conversation.

Furthermore, imagine the chaos you would experience if you simultaneously paid attention to all the information your senses register. As we discussed earlier, you would notice hundreds of sights, sounds, smells, tastes, and touch sensations. You could not focus your mental activity enough to respond appropriately to just a few of these sensations. Fortunately, then, selective attention simplifies our lives. As Theme 2 suggests, our cognitive apparatus is impressively well designed. Features such as selective attention—which may initially seem to be drawbacks—may actually be beneficial.

Let's consider three basic categories of selective attention: (1) an auditory task called dichotic listening, (2) a visual task called the Stroop effect, and (3) visual search.

Dichotic Listening. Have you ever held a phone to one ear, while your other ear registers a message from a nearby radio? If so, you have created a situation known as dichotic listening (pronounced "die-*kot*-ick"). In the laboratory, **dichotic listening** is studied by asking people to wear earphones; one message is presented to the left ear and a different message is presented to the right ear. Typically, the research participants are asked to **shadow** the message in one ear; that is, they listen to that message and repeat it after the speaker. If the listener makes mistakes in shadowing, then the researcher knows that the listener is not paying selective attention to that message (Styles, 2005).

In the classic research, people noticed very little about the unattended, second message (Cherry, 1953). For example, people didn't even notice that the second message was sometimes switched from English words to German words. People did notice, however, when the voice of the unattended message was switched from male to female.

When do people notice the meaning of the unattended message in a dichotic-listening situation? In general, we can process only one message at a time (Cowan, 2005). However, people are likely to process the unattended message when (1) both messages are presented slowly, (2) the task is not challenging, and (3) the meaning of the unattended message is relevant (e.g., Cowan & Wood, 1997; Duncan, 1999; Harris & Pashler, 2004). For example, they may process the unattended message if it focuses on something they intend to do in the future (Marsh et al., 2007).

In addition, when people perform a dichotic listening task, they sometimes notice when their name is inserted in the unattended message (Clump, 2006; Moray, 1959; Wood & Cowan, 1995). Have you ever attended a social gathering, when you are surrounded by many simultaneous conversations? Even if you are paying close attention to one conversation, you may notice if your name is mentioned in a nearby conversation; this phenomenon is sometimes called the **cocktail party effect.** Wood and Cowan (1995), for example, found that 35% of the participants reported that they had heard their name in the message that they were supposed to ignore. But why did the participants *ignore* their own name about two-thirds of the time? One possible explanation for why people did not report hearing their names more frequently is that the Wood and Cowan study was conducted in a laboratory, so this research may not have high ecological validity (Baker, 1999). Most social gatherings are much less structured, and our attention may easily wander to other intriguing conversations.

Furthermore, the capacity of a person's working memory could help to explain why some people hear their name, but others do not. As we'll see in Chapter 4, **working memory** is the brief, immediate memory for material we are currently processing. Conway and his coauthors (2001) found that students who had a high working-memory capacity noticed their name only 20% of the time. In contrast, students with a low working-memory capacity noticed their name 65% of the time in a dichotic-listening task. Apparently, these people with a relatively low capacity have difficulty blocking out the irrelevant information about their name (Cowan, 2005). In other words, they are easily distracted from the task they are supposed to be completing.

In summary, when people's auditory attention is divided, they can notice some characteristics of the unattended message—such as the gender of the speaker and whether their own name is mentioned. On the other hand, under more challenging conditions, they may not even notice whether the unattended message is in English or in a foreign language.

The Stroop Effect. So far, we have examined selective attention on auditory tasks. In these tasks, people are instructed to shadow the message presented to one ear and ignore the message presented to the other ear. Researchers have also conducted extensive research on selective visual attention (Cox et al., 2006).

Try Demonstration 3.1, which illustrates the famous Stroop effect. After reading these instructions, turn to Color Figure 3, inside the back cover. Notice the word in the

(turn to Color Figure 3 inside the back cover.)

---

⑨ Demonstration 3.1

The Stroop Effect

For this demonstration, you will need a watch with a second hand. Turn to Color Figure 3 inside the back cover. First, measure how long it takes to name the colors in Part A. Your task is to say out loud the names of the ink colors, ignoring the meaning of the words. Measure the amount of time it takes to go through this list *five* times. (Keep a tally of the number of repetitions.) Record that time.

   Now you will try a second color-naming task. Measure how long it takes to name the colors in the rectangular patches in Part B. Measure the amount of time it takes to go through this list five times. (Again, keep a tally of the number of repetitions.) Record the time.

   Does the Stroop effect operate for you? Are your response times similar to those obtained in Stroop's original study?

---

upper-left corner of Part A. Here, the word RED is printed in yellow ink. You'll probably find that it's much more difficult to name the color of the ink (YELLOW) than to name the color of the ink in any of the yellow rectangles in Part B.

   The Stroop effect is named after James R. Stroop (1935), who created this well-known task. According to the **Stroop effect,** people take a long time to name the ink color when that color is used in printing an incongruent word; in contrast, they can quickly name that same ink color when it appears as a solid patch of color.

   In a typical study on the Stroop effect, people may require about 100 seconds to name the ink color of 100 words that are incongruent color names (for example, blue ink used in printing the word YELLOW). In contrast, they require only about 60 seconds to name the ink colors for 100 colored patches (C. M. MacLeod, 2005). Notice why the Stroop effect demonstrates selective attention: People take longer to name a color when they are distracted by another feature of the stimulus, namely, the meaning of the words themselves (Styles, 2006).

   Since the original research, hundreds of additional studies have examined variations of the Stroop effect. For example, Elliot and Cowan (2001) demonstrated that practice can improve people's selective attention, as measured by the Stroop task. Furthermore, clinical psychologists have created a related technique called the emotional Stroop task (C. MacLeod, 2005; MacLeod & MacLeod, 2005; C. M. MacLeod, 2005). On the **emotional Stroop task,** people are instructed to name the ink color of words that are related to a possible psychological disorder.

   For example, suppose that someone appears to have a **phobic disorder,** which is an excessive fear of a specific object. A person with a fear of spiders would be instructed to name the ink colors of printed words such as *hairy* and *crawl.* People with phobias are significantly slower on these anxiety-related words than on control words. In contrast, people without phobias show no difference between the two kinds of words

(Williams et al., 1996). These results suggest that people who have a phobic disorder are hyper-alert to words related to their phobia, and they show an attentional bias to the meaning of these stimuli. As a result, they pay relatively little attention to the ink color of the words.

Other research shows that people who are depressed take a long time to report the color of words related to sadness and despair. In addition, people with eating disorders take a long time to report the ink color of words related to food or body weight (C. MacLeod, 2005). Furthermore, the Stroop test can be used to assess addiction to alcohol and cigarettes (Cox et al., 2006).

Researchers have examined a variety of explanations for the Stroop effect. Some have suggested that it can be explained by the parallel distributed processing (PDP) approach (e.g., Cohen et al., 1998; C. M. MacLeod, 2005). According to this explanation, the Stroop task activates two pathways at the same time. One pathway is activated by the task of naming the ink color, and the other pathway is activated by the task of reading the word. Interference occurs when two competing pathways are active at the same time. As a result, task performance suffers.

Furthermore, adults have had much more practice in reading words than in naming colors (T. L. Brown et al., 2002; Cox et al., 2006; Luck & Vecera, 2002). The more automatic process (reading the word) interferes with the less automatic process (naming the color of the ink). As a result, we automatically—and involuntarily—read the words that are printed in Part A of Color Figure 3. In fact, it's difficult to prevent ourselves from reading those words—even if we want to! For instance, right now, stop reading this paragraph! Were you successful?

Let's review what we have discussed so far in this section on selective attention. According to the research on dichotic listening, people usually have trouble picking up much information about the auditory message that they were instructed to ignore. The research on the Stroop effect shows that people have trouble naming the color of a stimulus when the letters of the stimulus are used to spell the name of a different color. Because we read words quite automatically, it's difficult to pay attention to the less automatic part of the message on the Stroop task. Let's now consider visual search, a third kind of selective-attention task.

Visual Search. You've probably conducted several visual searches within the last hour, perhaps a notebook, a sweater, or a yellow marking pen. In some cases, our lives may depend on accurate visual searches. For instance, airport security officers search travelers' luggage for possible weapons, and radiologists search a mammogram to detect a tumor that could indicate breast cancer (Wolfe et al., 2005).

Researchers have identified an impressive number of variables that influence visual searches. For example, Jeremy Wolfe and his colleagues (2005) found that people are much more accurate in identifying a target if it appears frequently. If the target appears—in a visually complex background—on 50% of the trials, participants missed the target 7% of the time. When the same target appeared in this same complex background on only 1% of the trials, participants missed the target 30% of the time.

Let's examine two stimulus variables in more detail: (1) whether we are searching for a single, isolated feature or a combined set of features; and (2) whether we are

---

⊚ Demonstration 3.2

The Isolated-Feature/Combined-Feature Effect

After reading this paragraph, turn to Color Figure 4 inside the back cover. First, look at the two figures marked Part A. In each case, search for a blue *X*. Notice whether you take about the same amount of time on these two tasks. After trying Part A, return to this page and read the additional instructions.

Additional instructions: For the second part of this demonstration, return to Part B inside the back cover. Look for the blue *X* in each of the two figures in Part B. Notice whether you take the same amount of time on these two tasks or whether one takes slightly longer.

---

searching for a target for which a particular feature is present or a target for which this feature is absent. As you'll see, two researchers—Anne Treisman and Jeremy Wolfe—have been especially active in studying visual search. Before you read further, however, try Demonstration 3.2.

1. *The isolated-feature/combined-feature effect.* Demonstration 3.2 is based on classic research by Treisman and Gelade (1980). According to their research, if the target differed from the irrelevant items in the display with respect to a simple feature such as color, observers could quickly detect the target. In fact, they could detect this target just as fast when it was presented in an array of 24 items as when it was presented in an array of only 3 items (Geng & Behrmann, 2003; Styles, 2006; Treisman, 1993; Treisman & Gelade, 1980). If you tried Part A of Demonstration 3.2, you probably found that the blue *X* seemed to "pop out," whether the display contains 2 or 23 irrelevant items.

In contrast, Part B of Demonstration 3.2 required you to search for a target that is a combination (or conjunction) of two properties. When you searched for a blue *X* among red *X*'s, red *O*'s, and blue *O*'s, you probably found that you had to pay attention to one item at a time, using serial processing. You were distracted by stimuli that resembled the target because they had either a blue color or an *X* shape (Serences et al., 2005). This second task is more complex, and the time taken to find the target increases dramatically as the number of distracters increases (Wolfe, 2000, 2001). As a result, Figure B2 required a more time-consuming search than Figure B1 did. Now try Demonstration 3.3 before you read further.

2. *The feature-present/feature-absent effect.* Theme 3 of this book states that our cognitive processes handle positive information better than negative information. Turn back to Demonstration 1.3 on page 24 to remind yourself about this theme. The research of Treisman and Souther (1985) provides additional support for that theme, as you can see from Demonstration 3.3.

Notice in Part A of this demonstration that the circle with the line seems to "pop out" from the display. The search is rapid when we are looking for a particular feature that is *present*. Treisman and Souther (1985) found that people performed rapid searches

ⓢ Demonstration 3.3

Searching for Features That Are Present or Absent

In Part A, search for the circle with the line. Then, in Part B, search for the circle *without* the line.

A

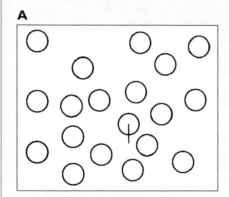

B

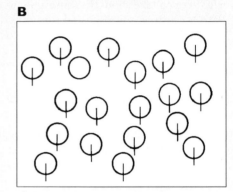

Source: Based on Treisman & Souther, 1985.

for a feature that was present (like the circle with the line in Part A), whether the display contained zero irrelevant items or numerous irrelevant items. When people are searching for a feature that is *present*, the target item in the display usually captures their attention automatically (Franconeri et al., 2005; Wolfe, 2000, 2001). In fact, this "pop-out" effect is automatic, and researchers emphasize that locating the target is strictly a bottom-up process (Boot et al., 2005).

In contrast, notice what happens when you are searching for a feature that is *absent* (like the circle *without* the line in Part B). Treisman and Souther (1985) found that the search time increased dramatically as the number of irrelevant items increased. People who are searching for a feature that is *absent* must use focused attention, emphasizing both bottom-up processing and top-down processing. This task is substantially more challenging, as Wolfe (1998, 2000, 2001) has also found in his extensive research on the feature-present/feature-absent effect.

Another example of the feature-present/feature-absent effect was discovered by Royden and her coauthors (2001). According to their research, people can quickly locate one moving target when it appears in a group of stationary distracters. In contrast, they take much longer to locate one stationary target when it appears in a group of moving distracters. In other words, it's easier to spot a movement-present object than a movement-absent object.

As we have seen in this discussion of visual search, we search more quickly for an isolated feature, as opposed to a combination of two features. Furthermore, we search more quickly for a feature that is present (as opposed to a feature that is absent).

IN DEPTH

Saccadic Eye Movements

In this first section of Chapter 3, we began by considering divided attention, in which we pay attention to two or more simultaneous messages. Then we discussed three kinds of selective attention: (a) dichotic listening, (b) the Stroop effect, and (c) visual search. Now let's consider a third kind of attention task that you are performing right now. You are moving your eyes forward so that you can read the next words on this page.

Our eye movements provide important information about the way our minds operate when we perform a number of everyday cognitive tasks (Engbert et al., 2005; Radach et al., 2004b; Yang & McConkie, 2004). For example, researchers have studied how our eyes move when we are looking at a scene (e.g., Findlay & Gilchrist, 2001; Henderson & Ferreira, 2004b; Irwin & Zelinsky, 2002) and when we are driving (Fisher & Pollatsek, 2007; Recarte & Nunes, 2000). Researchers have also discovered that our eyes move when we are speaking (Griffin, 2004; Meyer, 2004). However, this in-depth section focuses on eye movements during reading.

We have already considered one perceptual process that is central to reading. In Chapter 2, on object recognition (pp. 39–41), we considered how people recognize letters of the alphabet. In that section, we also discussed how context facilitates the recognition of both letters and words.

Eye movement is a second perceptual process that is central to reading. For a moment, pay attention to the way your eyes are moving as you read this paragraph. Your eyes actually make a series of little jumps as they move across the page. This very rapid movement of the eyes from one spot to the next is known as saccadic (pronounced "suh-*cod*-dik") eye movement. The purpose of a **saccadic eye movement** is to bring the center of the retina into position over the words you want to read. A very small region in the center of the retina, known as the **fovea,** has better acuity than other retinal regions. Therefore, saccadic movement is essential in order to move the eye so that new words can be registered on the fovea (Irwin, 2003, 2004; Starr & Inhoff, 2004). Saccadic eye movement is another example of Theme 1 (active cognitive processes); we actively search for new information, including the material we will be reading (Findlay & Gilchrist, 2001; Radach & Kennedy, 2004).

When you read, each saccade moves your eye forward by about 7 to 9 letters. Researchers have estimated that people make between 150,000 and 200,000 saccadic movements every day (Irwin, 2003; Rayner & Johnson, 2005). We do not process much visual information when the eye is moving (Irwin, 2003; Radach & Kennedy, 2004). However, fixations occur during the period between these saccadic movements. During each **fixation,** your visual system pauses for about 50 to 500 milli seconds in order to acquire information that is useful for reading (Rayner et al., 2006; Wright & Ward, 2008). Incidentally, you may think that you have a smooth, continuous view of the material you are processing, even though your eyes are actually alternating between jumps and pauses (Rayner & Liversedge, 2004; Reichle & Laurent, 2006).

The term **perceptual span** refers to the number of letters and spaces that we perceive during a fixation (Rayner, 1998; Rayner & Liversedge, 2004). Researchers have found large individual differences in the size of the perceptual span (Irwin, 2004). When you read English, this perceptual span normally includes letters lying about 4 positions to the left of the letter you are directly looking at, and the letters about 15 positions to the right of that central letter. Notice that the perceptual span is definitely lopsided. After all, when we read English, we are looking for reading cues in the text that lies to the right, and these cues provide some general information (Findlay & Gilchrist, 2001; Findlay & Walker, 1999; Starr & Inhoff, 2004). For instance, the material in the extreme right side of the perceptual span is useful for spotting the white spaces between words, which provide information about word length. However, we usually cannot actually identify a word that lies more than 8 spaces to the right of the fixation point (Rayner, 1998).

Other research has demonstrated that saccadic eye movements show several predictable patterns. For example, when the eye jumps forward in a saccadic movement, it rarely moves to a blank space between sentences or between words. The eye usually jumps past short words, words that appear frequently in a language, and words that are highly predictable in a sentence (Drieghe et al., 2004; Kliegl et al., 2004; White & Liversedge, 2004). In contrast, the size of the saccadic movement is small if the next word in a sentence is misspelled or if it is unusual (Pynte et al., 2004; Rayner et al., 2004; White & Liversedge, 2004). All these strategies make sense, because a large saccadic movement would be unwise if the material is puzzling or challenging.

Good readers differ from poor readers with respect to their saccadic eye movements. Figure 3.1 shows how two such readers might differ. The good reader makes larger jumps and is also less likely to make **regressions,** by moving backward to earlier material in the sentence. People often make regressions when they realize that they have not understood the passage they are reading (White & Liversedge, 2004).

Furthermore, the good reader pauses for a shorter time before making the next saccadic movement. (Figure 3.1 does not show this pause.) A typical good reader might pause for 1/5 second each time, whereas a poor reader might pause for 1/2 second (Liversedge & Findlay, 2000; Rayner, 1998). Thus, good and poor readers differ with respect to the size of the saccadic movement, the number of regressions, and the duration of the fixation pause.

Our saccadic movements are also sensitive to thematic aspects of the material we are reading (Deubel et al., 2000; Liversedge & Findlay, 2000). We'll be discussing these more sophisticated aspects of reading in more detail in Chapter 9. However, if

FIGURE 3.1

Eye Movement Patterns and Fixations for a Good Reader (top numbers) and a Poor Reader (bottom numbers).

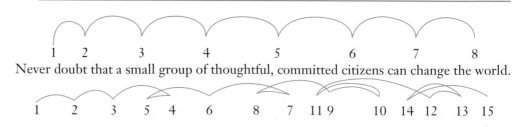

we read a paragraph with a surprise ending, we make a larger number of regression movements as we reread the puzzling passage (Underwood & Batt, 1996). In summary, the research shows that a wide variety of cognitive factors have an important influence on the pattern and speed of our saccadic eye movements (McDonald & Shillcock, 2003; Reichle et al., 1998). Saccadic eye movements clearly help us become more active, flexible readers (Findlay & Gilchrist, 2001).

⊚ Section Summary: *Three Kinds of Attention Processes*

1. Attention is a concentration of mental activity, and it allows our cognitive processes to take in limited portions of our environment and our memory.

2. The first kind of attention process discussed in this chapter is divided attention. Research on divided attention shows that performance often suffers when people must attend to several stimuli simultaneously. For example, we cannot talk on a hands-free cell phone and drive carefully at the same time. However, with extensive practice, people's performance on some divided-attention tasks can improve.

3. The second kind of attention process is selective attention, and the chapter inspects three different examples of selective attention.

    a. The first example of selective attention is the dichotic listening technique, which shows that we typically notice little about an irrelevant message. Occasionally, however, we may notice the gender of the speaker, our own name, or some semantic aspects of the irrelevant message.

    b. A second example of a selective-attention task is the Stroop effect. A variant called the "emotional Stroop task" demonstrates that people with certain disorders have difficulty identifying the ink color of words relevant to their disorder; for example, people with eating disorders take longer than other people to report the ink color of words related to food.

    c. A third example of selected-attention findings is visual search. For example, we can locate a target faster if it appears frequently, if it differs from irrelevant objects on only one dimension (e.g., color), and if a specific feature of a stimulus (e.g., a line) is present rather than absent.

4. The final kind of attention process is saccadic eye movements, which our visual system makes during reading. Saccadic-movement patterns depend on factors such as the predictability of the text, individual differences in reading skill, and the more general meaning of the text.

EXPLANATIONS FOR ATTENTION

So far, this chapter has examined three attention processes that help us regulate how much information we take in from our visual and auditory environment. Specifically, we have difficulty paying attention to two or more messages at one time (divided attention). In addition, when we are paying attention to one message, we have difficulty noticing information about irrelevant messages (selective attention). Furthermore, our saccadic eye movements regulate the way our eyes move in order to acquire information. Researchers have tried to account for these components of attention by conducting neuroscience studies and by devising theories to explain the characteristics of attention.

Neuroscience Research on Attention

During recent decades, researchers have developed a variety of sophisticated techniques for examining the biological basis of behavior; we introduced many of these approaches in Chapter 1. Research using these techniques has identified a network of areas throughout the brain that accomplish various attention tasks (Farah, 2000a; Posner & Rothbart, 2007b).

Several regions of the brain are responsible for attention, including some structures that are below the surface of the cerebral cortex (Just et al., 2001; Posner & Rothbart, 2007b). For example, several brain structures beneath your own cortex are now coordinating their actions so that your eye can leap forward in saccadic movements until you reach the end of this sentence (Schall, 2004). In this discussion, however, we'll focus on structures in the cerebral cortex, as shown in Figure 3.2. Take a moment to compare Figure 3.2 with Figure 2.1 (p. 35), which showed the regions of the cortex that are most relevant in object recognition.

FIGURE 3.2

A Schematic Drawing of the Cerebral Cortex, as Seen from the Left Side, Showing the Four Lobes of the Brain and the Regions That Are Most Important on Attention Tasks.

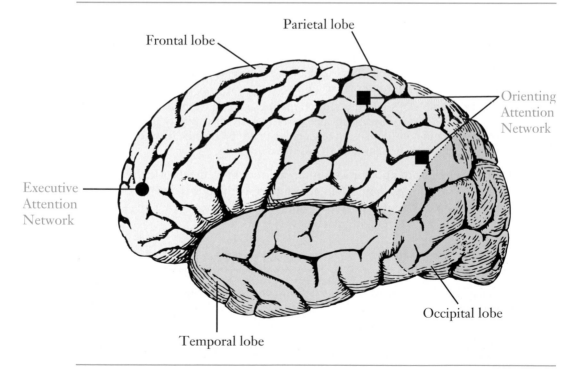

Michael Posner and Mary Rothbart (2007a, 2007b) propose that three systems in the cortex manage different aspects of attention: (1) the orienting attention network, (2) the executive attention network, and (3) the alerting attention network. This third system, the **alerting attention network,** is responsible for making you sensitive and alert to new stimuli; it also helps to keep you alert and vigilant for long periods of time (Posner & Rothbart, 2007a, 2007b). Because this chapter has not examined the alerting component of attention, we will focus instead on the other two systems, the orienting attention network and the executive attention network.

The Orienting Attention Network. Imagine that you are searching the area around a bathroom sink for a lost contact lens. When you are selecting information from sensory input, your orienting attention network is activated. The **orienting attention network** is responsible for the kind of attention required for visual search, in which you must shift your attention around to various spatial locations (Chun & Wolfe, 2001; Luck & Vecera, 2002; Posner & Rothbart, 2007b). According to Posner and Rothbart (2007a), the orienting network develops during the first year of life. Figure 3.2 shows that two important components of the orienting attention network are located in the parietal lobe of the cortex.

How did researchers identify the parietal cortex as the region of the brain used in attention tasks related to visual searches? Several decades ago, the only clue to the organization of the brain was provided by people with brain lesions (Posner, 2004). The term **brain lesion** refers to specific brain damage caused by strokes, accidents, or other traumas. People who have brain damage in the parietal region of the right hemisphere of the brain have trouble noticing a visual stimulus that appears on the left side of their visual field. In contrast, people with damage in the left parietal region have trouble noticing a visual stimulus on the right side (Luck & Vecera, 2002; Posner & DiGirolamo, 2000a; Styles, 2005).

The lesions produce unusual deficits. For instance, a woman with a lesion in the left parietal region may have trouble noticing the food on the right side of her plate. She may eat only the food on the left side of her plate, and she might even complain that she didn't receive enough food (Farah, 2000a; Humphreys & Riddoch, 2001). Amazingly, however, she may not seem to be aware of her deficit.

Part A of Figure 3.3 shows a simple figure—a clock—that was presented to a man with a lesion in the right parietal lobe. He was asked to copy this sketch, and Part B shows the figure he drew. Notice that the left part of the drawing is almost completely missing. The drawing demonstrates that this man is experiencing **unilateral neglect**, defined as a spatial deficit for one half of the visual field.

Much of the more recent research on the orienting attention network has used **positron emission tomography (PET scan),** in which researchers measure blood flow in the brain by injecting the participant with a radioactive chemical just before he or she performs a cognitive task. As discussed in Chapter 1, this chemical travels through the blood to the parts of the brain that are active during the cognitive task. A special camera makes an image of the accumulated chemical. According to PET-scan research, the parietal cortex shows increased blood flow when people perform visual searches and pay attention to spatial locations (e.g., Palmer, 1999; Posner & Rothbart, 2007b).

FIGURE 3.3

The Original Figure (A) Presented to a Man with a Lesion in the Right Parietal Lobe, and the Figure He Drew (B).

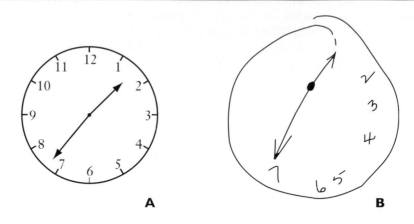

A   **B**

Source: Bloom & Lazerson, 1988.

The Executive Attention Network. The Stroop task that you tried in Demonstration 3.1 relied primarily on your executive attention network. The **executive attention network** handles the kind of attention we use when a task features conflict (Posner & Rothbart, 2007a, 2007b). On the Stroop task, for example, you need to inhibit your automatic response of reading a word, in order to name the color of the ink (Fan et al., 2002). The executive attention network is responsible for inhibiting your automatic responses to stimuli (Stuss et al., 2002). As you can see in Figure 3.2, the prefrontal portion of the cortex is the region of your brain where the executive attention network is especially active.

The executive attention network also operates when people are asked to listen to a list of nouns and to state the use of each word, such as listening to the word *needle* and responding "sew" (Posner & DiGirolamo, 2000a). Furthermore, the executive attention network is active for top-down control of attention (Farah, 2000a). The executive attention network begins to develop at about age 2, much later than the orienting attention network (Posner & Rothbart, 2007a).

Posner and Rothbart (2007b) argue that the executive attention network is extremely important when you acquire academic skills in school, for example, when you learned to read. Executive attention also helps you learn new ideas (Posner & Rothbart, 2007a). For example, as you are reading this passage, your executive attention network has been actively taking in new information and—ideally—comparing this network with the orienting attention network. This process of reading and understanding a college-level textbook is challenging. Not surprisingly, the location of the executive attention network overlaps with the areas of your brain that are related to general intelligence (Duncan et al., 2000; Posner & Rothbart, 2007b).

In summary, PET scans and other neuroscience techniques have identified one brain region that is active when we are searching for objects (the orienting attention network). These techniques also show that a different brain region is active when we must inhibit an automatic response and produce a less obvious response (the executive attention network); this second network is also active in academic learning.

Theories of Attention

Let us first summarize an approach to attention that was proposed several decades ago, when cognitive psychology was in its infancy. Then we will discuss Anne Treisman's feature-integration theory, which is probably the most influential contemporary explanation of attention (Styles, 2005).

Early Theories of Attention. The first approaches to attention emphasized that people are extremely limited in the amount of information that they can process at any given time. A common metaphor in these theories was the concept of a bottleneck. This metaphor was especially appealing because it matches our introspections about attention. The narrow neck of a bottle restricts the flow into or out of the bottle.

Bottleneck theories proposed a similar narrow passageway in human information processing. In other words, this bottleneck limits the quantity of information to which we can pay attention. Thus, when one message is currently flowing through a bottleneck, the other messages must be left behind. Researchers proposed many variations of this bottleneck theory (e.g., Broadbent, 1958; Treisman, 1964). Furthermore, some aspects of these early theories still hold true in contemporary research. For example, Lachter and his colleagues (2004) confirmed Broadbent's (1958) observation that people cannot identify a visual stimulus unless they actually pay attention to it.

However, you may recall from the discussion of the theories of object recognition (Chapter 2) that researchers rejected the template theory because it was not flexible enough. Similarly, researchers rejected the bottleneck theories because those theories underestimate the flexibility of human attention (Luck & Vecera, 2002; Pashler & Johnston, 1998; Tsang, 2007).

As Chapter 1 pointed out, no metaphor based on a simple machine or a simple structure can successfully account for the sophistication of human cognitive processes. A bottleneck is far too simple (Schneider & Shiffrin, 1977; Shiffrin & Schneider, 1977). For example, current neuroscience research demonstrates that information is not lost at just one phase of the attention process, as the bottleneck theories suggest. Instead, information is lost throughout many phases of attention, from the beginning through later processing (Kanwisher et al., 2001; Posner & DiGirolamo, 2000a). As Luck and Vecera (2002) conclude,

> The term *attention* applies to many separable processes, each of which operates within a different cognitive subsystem and in a manner that reflects the . . . structure and processing demands of that cognitive subsystem. (p. 261)

Feature-Integration Theory. Anne Treisman has developed an elaborate theory of attention and perceptual processing. Her original theory, proposed in 1980, was elegantly simple (Treisman & Gelade, 1980). As you might expect, the current version is more complex. Let's consider (1) the basic elements of feature-integration theory, (2) research on the theory, and (3) the current status of the theory.

1. *The basic elements*: According to Treisman's **feature-integration theory,** we sometimes look at a scene using distributed attention,* with all parts of the scene processed at the same time; on other occasions, we use focused attention, with each item in the scene processed one at a time. Furthermore, distributed attention and focused attention form a continuum, so that you frequently use a kind of attention that is somewhere between those two extremes.

Let's examine these two kinds of processing in more detail before considering other components of Treisman's theory (Treisman & Gelade, 1980; Treisman, 1993). One kind of processing uses distributed attention. **Distributed attention** allows you to register features automatically; you use parallel processing across the field, registering all the features simultaneously. Distributed attention is a relatively low-level kind of processing. In fact, this kind of processing is so effortless that you are not even aware that you're using it.

The second kind of processing in Triesman's theory is called focused attention. **Focused attention** requires serial processing, and you identify one object at a time. This more demanding kind of processing is necessary when the objects are more complex. Focused attention identifies which features belong together—for example, which shape goes with which color.

2. *Research on the theory*: Treisman and Gelade (1980) examined distributed attention and focused attention by studying two different stimulus situations. One situation used isolated features (and therefore it used distributed attention). In contrast, the other situation used combinations of features (and therefore it used focused attention).

Let's first consider the details of the research on distributed attention. According to Treisman and Gelade, if you processed isolated features in distributed attention, then you should be able to rapidly locate a target among its neighboring, irrelevant items. That target should seem to "pop out" of the display automatically, no matter how many items are in the display.

To test their hypothesis about distributed attention, Treisman and Gelade conducted a series of studies. You already tried Demonstration 3.2 (p. 73), which illustrated part of their study. Remember the results of that demonstration: If the target differed from all the irrelevant items in the display with respect to one simple feature such as color, you could quickly detect this target. In fact, you could detect it just as fast when it appeared in an array of 23 items as when it appeared in an array of only 3 items (Treisman, 1986; Treisman & Gelade, 1980). Distributed attention can be accomplished in a parallel fashion and relatively automatically; the target seemed to pop out in Demonstration 3.2A.

---

*In some of her research, Treisman uses the phrase "divided attention," rather than "distributed attention." However, I will use "distributed attention" in this textbook, in order to avoid confusing this concept with the research on divided attention discussed on pages 68–69.

In contrast, consider the details of the research on focused attention. Demonstration 3.2B required you to search for a target that was an object—that is, a conjunction (or combination) of properties. When you searched for a blue *X* buried among red *X*'s, red *O*'s, and blue *O*'s, you needed to use focused attention. In other words, you were forced to focus your attention on one item at a time, using serial processing. You searched at the object level, rather than at the feature level. This task is more complex. Treisman and Gelade (1980) as well as current researchers have found that people need more time to find the target when there are a large number of distracters (Parasuraman & Greenwood, 2007).

Earlier in this chapter, we discussed another important component of feature-integration theory, in connection with Demonstration 3.3. As you learned, the feature-present/feature-absent effect tells us that people search much more rapidly for a feature that is present—as in Part A—compared to searching for a feature that is absent—as in Part B (Treisman & Souther, 1985).

So far, we have reviewed the isolated-feature/combined-feature effect and the feature-present/feature-absent effect. A third effect related to feature-integration theory is called an *illusory conjunction*. Specifically, when we are overwhelmed with too many simultaneous visual tasks, we may form an illusory conjunction (Treisman & Schmidt, 1982; Treisman & Souther, 1986). An **illusory conjunction** is an inappropriate combination of features, perhaps combining one object's shape with a nearby object's color. Many studies by other researchers have demonstrated, for example, that a blue *N* and a green *T* can produce an illusory conjunction in which the viewer actually perceives a blue *T* (e.g., Ashby et al., 1996; Hazeltine et al., 1997).

This research on illusory conjunctions confirms a conclusion demonstrated in other perception research. Contrary to our common-sense intuitions, the visual system actually processes an object's features independently. For example, when you look at a red apple, your visual system actually analyzes its red color separately from its round shape (Goldstein, 2007; Hazeltine et al., 1997). In other words, the human visual system sometimes has a **binding problem** because your visual system does not represent the important features of an object as a unified whole (Wheeler & Treisman, 2002; Wolfe & Cave, 1999).

When you use focused attention to look at the apple, you will accurately perceive an integrated figure—a red, round object. Attention allows the binding process to operate. To use a metaphor, focused attention seems to act like a form of glue, so that an object's color and shape can stick together.

In contrast, suppose that a researcher presents two arbitrary figures, for example, a blue *N* and a green *T*. Suppose also that your attention is overloaded or distracted, so that you must use distributed attention. In this situation, the blue color from one figure may combine with the *T* shape from the other figure. As a result, you may perceive the illusory conjunction of a blue *T*.

Other research shows that our visual system can create an illusory conjunction from verbal material (Treisman, 1990; Wolfe, 2000). For example, an observer whose attention is distracted might be presented with two nonsense words, *dax* and *kay*. This observer may report seeing the English word *day*. When nonsense words do not receive focused attention, we form illusory conjunctions that are consistent with our expectations. As we emphasized in Chapter 2, top-down processing helps us screen out inappropriate combinations (Treisman, 1990).

3. *Current status of the theory*: The basic elements of feature-integration theory were proposed more than twenty-five years ago. Since that time, researchers have conducted dozens of additional studies, and the original, straightforward theory has been modified. For example, researchers have found that people can search very quickly for conjunction targets (like a blue *X*), if they have had extensive practice (Coren et al., 2004; Treisman et al., 1992).

As we will see throughout this textbook, researchers often propose a theory that initially draws a clear-cut distinction between two or more psychological processes. With extensive research, however, theorists frequently conclude that reality is much more complex. Rather than two clear-cut categories, we find that—in some conditions—distributed attention can occasionally resemble focused attention (Bundesen & Habekost, 2005).

Researchers are currently examining how some of the components of feature-integration theory can be explained at the cellular level (Bundesen et al., 2005). The theory will probably be modified after additional cognitive and neuropsychology research has been conducted. However, feature-integration theory still provides an important framework for understanding visual attention (Müller & Krummenacher, 2006; Palmer, 1999; Quinlan, 2003b).

Section Summary: *Explanations for Attention*

1. Neuroscience research on attention has used the PET scan to establish that the posterior attention network—located in the parietal cortex—is active during visual search. In addition, when people have a lesion in the parietal cortex, they cannot notice visual objects in the opposite visual field.

2. Neuroscience research has also used PET scans to establish that the anterior attention network—located in the frontal lobe—is active during the Stroop task and other tasks focusing on word meaning.

3. Early theories of attention emphasized a "bottleneck" that limits attention at a particular part of processing, but this perspective is too simplistic.

4. Treisman proposed a feature-integration theory that contains two components: (a) distributed attention, which can be used to register single features automatically, and (b) focused attention, which is used to search for combinations of features and for a feature that is missing. Illusory conjunctions may arise when attention is overloaded. With some modifications, feature-integration theory accounts for many important aspects of visual attention.

CONSCIOUSNESS

Our final topic in this chapter—consciousness—is a controversial subject. One reason for the controversy is the variety of different definitions for the term (Coward & Sun, 2004; Dehaene et al., 2006; Zeman, 2004). I prefer a broad definition: **Consciousness** means the awareness that people have about the outside world and about their perceptions, images, thoughts, memories, and feelings (Chalmers, 2007; Davies, 1999; Zeman, 2004). The contents of consciousness can therefore include your perceptions of the world around you, your visual imagery, the comments you make silently to yourself, the memory of events in your life, your beliefs about the world, your plans for activities later today, and your attitudes toward other people (Baars, 1997; Coward & Sun, 2004). As David Barash (2006) writes,

> Thus, consciousness is not only an unfolding story that we tell ourselves, moment by moment, about what we are doing, feeling, and thinking. It also includes our efforts to interpret what other individuals are doing, feeling, and thinking, as well as how those others are likely to perceive one's self. (p. B10)

Consciousness is closely related to attention, but the processes are not identical (Lavie, 2007). After all, we are frequently not aware or conscious of the tasks we are performing with the automatic, distributed form of attention. For example, when you are driving, you may automatically put your foot on the brake in response to a red light. However, you may not be at all *conscious* that you performed this motor action. In general, consciousness is associated with the kind of controlled, focused attention that is not automatic (Cohen & Schooler, 1997; Dehaene & Naccache, 2001).

As Chapter 1 noted, the behaviorists considered topics such as consciousness to be inappropriate for scientific study. However, consciousness edged back into favor as psychologists began to adopt cognitive approaches (Dehaene & Naccache, 2001; Jacoby et al., 1997) Since the 1990s, consciousness has become a popular topic for numerous books (e.g., Baars & Newman, 2002; Baruss, 2003; Dehaene, 2001; Edelman, 2005; Hassin et al., 2005; Velmans & Schneider, 2007; Wegner, 2002; Zeman, 2004).

In recent years, cognitive psychologists have been especially interested in three interrelated issues concerned with consciousness: (1) our ability to bring thoughts into consciousness; (2) our inability to let thoughts escape from consciousness; and (3) blindsight, which reveals that people can perform quite accurately on a cognitive task, even when they are not conscious of their accuracy. Before you read further, however, try Demonstration 3.4.

⟳ Demonstration 3.4

Thought Suppression

This demonstration requires you to take a break from your reading and just relax for 5 minutes. Take a sheet of paper and a pen or pencil to record your thoughts as you simply let your mind wander. Your thoughts can include cognitive psychology, but they do not need to. Just jot down a brief note about each topic you think about as your mind wanders. One final instruction:

During this exercise, do not think about a white bear!

Consciousness About Our Higher Mental Processes

To what extent do we have access to our higher mental processes? For example, answer the following question: "What is your mother's maiden name?" Now answer this second question: "How did you arrive at the answer to the first question?" If you are like most people, the answer to the first question appeared swiftly in your consciousness, but you probably cannot explain your thought process. Instead, the name simply seemed to pop into your memory.

In a classic article, Richard Nisbett and Timothy Wilson (1977) argued that we often have little direct access to our thought processes. As they pointed out, you may be fully conscious of the *products* of your thought processes (such as your mother's maiden name). However, you are usually not conscious of the *processes* that created these products (such as the memory mechanisms that produced her maiden name). Similarly, people may solve a problem correctly; however, when asked to explain how they reached the solution, they may reply, "It just dawned on me" (Maier, 1931; Nisbett & Wilson, 1977). We'll discuss this topic further in Chapter 11 on problem solving.

Psychologists currently believe that our verbal reports are somewhat accurate reflections of our cognitive processes (Ericsson, 2003c; Johansson et al., 2006; Nelson, 1996; Wilson, 1997). As we'll see in Chapter 6, we do have relatively complete access to some thought processes (e.g., judgments about how well you will perform on a simple memory task). However, we have only limited access to other thought processes, such as: (1) whether your attention is drifting when you are listening to a lecture; (2) how well you understand the information in an essay; and (3) your awareness about the step-by-step procedures in a motor activity that has become automatic (Diana & Reder, 2004; Levin, 2004a).

We need to raise this topic of consciousness about thought processes, because it emphasizes that cognitive psychologists should not rely on people's introspections (Johansson et al., 2006; Nisbett & Wilson, 1977; Wegner, 2002). For example, when several people are talking to me at once, it genuinely *feels* like I am experiencing an "attention bottleneck." However, as we saw earlier in this section, humans actually have fairly flexible attention patterns; we really do not experience a rigid bottleneck. Throughout this book, we'll see that the research findings sometimes do not match our commonsense introspections. This discrepancy emphasizes that objective research is absolutely essential in cognitive psychology.

Thought Suppression

I have a friend who decided to quit smoking, so he tried valiantly to get rid of every idea associated with cigarettes. As soon as he thought of anything remotely associated with smoking, he immediately tried to push that thought out of his consciousness. Ironically, however, this strategy backfired, and he was haunted by numerous ideas related to cigarettes. Basically, he could not eliminate these undesirable thoughts. How successful were you in suppressing your thoughts in Demonstration 3.4? Did you have any difficulty carrying out the instructions?

The original source for the white bear study is literary, rather than scientific. Apparently, when the Russian novelist Tolstoy was young, his older brother tormented him by instructing him to stand in a corner and *not* think about a white bear (Wegner, 1996; Wegner et al., 1987). Similarly, if you have ever tried to avoid thinking about food when on a diet, you know that it's difficult to chase these undesired thoughts out of consciousness.

Wegner (1997b, 2002) uses the phrase **ironic effects of mental control** to describe how our efforts can backfire when we attempt to control the contents of our consciousness. Suppose that you try valiantly to banish a particular thought. Ironically, that same thought is *especially* likely to continue to creep back into consciousness.

Wegner and his coauthors (1987) decided to test Tolstoy's "white bear" task scientifically. They instructed one group of students *not* to think about a white bear during a 5-minute period, and then they were allowed to think about a white bear during a second 5-minute period. The participants in this group were very likely to think about a white bear during the second period, even more so than students in a control group who were instructed to think freely about a white bear—without any previous thought-suppression session. In other words, initial suppression of specific thoughts can produce a rebound effect.

Many studies have replicated the rebound effect following thought suppression (e.g., Purdon, 2005; Tolin et al., 2002; Wegner, 2002). Furthermore, this rebound effect is not limited to suppressing thoughts about white bears and other relatively trivial ideas. For example, when people are instructed not to notice a painful stimulus, they are likely to become even more aware of the pain. Similar ironic effects—which occur when we try to suppress our thoughts—have been documented when people try to concentrate, avoid movement, or fall asleep (Harvey, 2005; Wegner, 1994).

Individual Differences: Thought Suppression and Obsessive-Compulsive Disorder

The topic of thought suppression is highly relevant for clinical psychologists (Clark, 2005; Wegner, 1997a). For example, suppose that a client has severe depression, and the therapist encourages this person to stop thinking about depressing topics. Ironically, this advice may produce an even greater number of depressing thoughts (Wenzlaff, 2005). Thought suppression is also relevant for individuals who experience posttraumatic stress disorder, generalized anxiety disorder, and psychosis (Falsetti et al., 2005; Morrison, 2005; Wells, 2005).

Thought suppression should be especially difficult for people with obsessive-compulsive disorder (Purdon, 2005; Purdon et al., 2005). When people experience an **obsession,** they have a persistent thought or image that is intrusive or inappropriate, and this obsession makes them feel extremely anxious. When people experience a **compulsion,** they engage in repetitive behaviors that are designed to reduce that anxiety. Therefore, people with **obsessive-compulsive disorder (OCD)** have recurrent obsessions or compulsions that they recognize are excessive, uncontrollable, and time consuming (American Psychiatric Association, 2000; Clark & O'Connor, 2005).

Let's consider a study by David Tolin and his colleagues (2002), who studied three groups of individuals. Two groups consisted of individuals who were seeking outpatient treatment for psychological disorders. People in one group had high scores on a measure of obsessive-compulsive disorder. People in the second group had received a diagnosis of another anxiety disorder, but none of them had OCD. A third group consisted of people in the community who had not been diagnosed with any psychological disorder. The second and third groups therefore served as controls.

The participants in all three groups were tested, one at a time, on the same task, a variant of Wegner's "white bear" study. During the first 5-minute period, people were told to say aloud whatever came to mind, including—if they wished—"white bear." In the second 5-minute period, they were instructed to try *not* to think of a white bear. The third 5-minute period was like the first period; they could think of anything they wanted. Throughout all three periods, they were instructed to press a space bar whenever they thought about a white bear.

For our purposes, the most interesting results were the number of times that the people in each group pressed the space bar during the second period, when they had been instructed not to think about a white bear. The people with OCD pressed the bar an average of 20 times; in other words, they could not push the white bear out of consciousness. In contrast, the people in both of the control groups pressed the bar an average of only 6 times. However, none of the groups showed the "ironic effects of mental control" that Wegner had described—a rebound effect in which people would press the bar significantly more often in the third period than in the first period. Still, we need to emphasize the large number of times that people with OCD pressed the bar during the second period; people with this disorder have difficulty inhibiting their obsession with an idea they are trying to ignore.

Blindsight

The first topic in this discussion on consciousness illustrated that we often have difficulty bringing some information about our cognitive processes into consciousness. The discussion of thought suppression suggested another concern: We often have difficulty *eliminating* some information from consciousness.

The research on a visual condition called blindsight reveals a third point about consciousness: In some cases, people can perform a cognitive task quite accurately, with no conscious awareness that their performance is accurate (Rasmussen, 2006; Weiskrantz, 2007). **Blindsight** refers to an unusual kind of vision without awareness. In more detail, blindsight is a condition in which an individual with a damaged visual cortex (e.g., from a stroke) claims not to be able to see an object. Nevertheless, he or she can accurately report some characteristics of that object, such as its location (Farah, 2001; Weiskrantz, 2007; Zeman, 2004).

Individuals with blindsight believe that they are truly blind in part or all of their visual field. In other words, their consciousness contains the thought, "I cannot see." In a typical study, the researchers present a stimulus in a region of the visual field that had previously been represented by the damaged cortex. For example, a spot of light might be flashed at a location 10 degrees to the right of center. People with blindsight are then asked to point to the light. Typically, these individuals report that they did not even see the light, so they could only make a guess about its location. Surprisingly, however, researchers have discovered that the participants' performance is significantly better than chance—and often nearly perfect (Weiskrantz, 1997, 2007). People with blindsight can report visual attributes such as color, shape, and motion (Zeman, 2004).

Additional research has eliminated several obvious explanations. Furthermore, the individuals do have genuine, complete damage to the primary visual cortex (Farah, 2001; Weiskrantz, 2007).

Here is the most likely current explanation. Most of the information that is registered on the retina travels to the visual cortex. However, a portion of the information from the retina travels to other locations on the cerebral cortex, outside the visual cortex (Weiskrantz, 2007; Zeman, 2004). A person with blindsight can therefore identify some characteristics of the visual stimulus—even with a damaged primary visual cortex—based on information registered in those other cortical locations.

The research on blindsight is especially relevant to the topic of consciousness. In particular, it suggests that visual information must pass through the primary visual cortex in order to be registered in consciousness. However, if that information takes a detour and bypasses the primary visual cortex, it is possible that the individual will not be conscious of the visual experience (Baars et al., 1998; Farah, 2001; Zeman, 2004). In Chapter 5, we will consider a related phenomenon in our discussion of implicit memory; people can often remember some information, even when they are not aware of this memory.

In summary, this discussion has demonstrated that consciousness is a challenging topic. Our consciousness is not a perfect mirror of our cognitive processes; that is, we often cannot explain how these processes operate. It is also not a blackboard; we cannot simply erase unwanted thoughts from our consciousness. Consciousness is not even an accurate reporter, as the research on blindsight demonstrates. As Wegner (2002) concludes, we usually assume that "How things seem is how they are" (p. 243). However, this convergence between our consciousness and reality is often an illusion.

◎ Section Summary: *Consciousness*

1. Consciousness, or awareness, is currently a popular topic. Research suggests that people are sometimes unaware of their higher mental processes. For instance, they may solve a problem but not be conscious of how they actually reached the solution.

2. Research on thought suppression illustrates the difficulty of eliminating some thoughts from consciousness; ironically, if you try to avoid thinking about an issue, you may actually think about it more frequently. People with obsessive-compulsive disorder have trouble suppressing intrusive thoughts or images.

3. Individuals with blindsight can identify characteristics of an object, even when their visual cortex is destroyed and they have no conscious awareness of that object.

CHAPTER REVIEW QUESTIONS

1. What is divided attention? Give several examples of divided-attention tasks you have performed within the past 24 hours. What does the research show about the effects of practice on divided attention? Can you think of some examples of your own experience with practice and divided-attention performance?

2. What is selective attention? Give several examples of selective-attention tasks—both auditory and visual—that you have performed within the past 24 hours. In what kind of circumstances were you able to pick up information about the message you were supposed to ignore? Does this pattern match the research?

3. This chapter discussed the Stroop effect in some detail. Can you think of other tasks that you routinely work on, where you also need to suppress the most obvious answer in order to provide the correct response? What attentional system in your cortex is especially active during these tasks?

4. Imagine that you are trying to carry on a conversation with a friend at the same time you are reading an interesting article in a magazine. Describe how the bottleneck theories and automatic versus controlled processing would explain your performance. Then describe Treisman's feature-integration theory and think of an example of this theory, based on your previous experiences.

5. Imagine that you are searching the previous pages of this chapter for the term "dichotic listening." What part of your brain is activated during this task? Now suppose that you are trying to learn the meaning of the phrase *dichotic listening*. What part of your brain is activated during this task? Describe how research has clarified the biological basis of attention.

6. Summarize the two theoretical approaches to attention that we discussed in this chapter: the bottleneck approach and Treisman's feature-integration approach. Then for each approach, think of a situation you have recently experienced and apply the approach to this situation.

7. Define the word *consciousness*. Based on the information in this chapter, do people have complete control over the information stored in consciousness? Does this information provide an accurate account of your cognitive processes? How is consciousness different from attention?

8. Cognitive psychology has many practical applications. Based on what you have read in this chapter, what applications can you suggest for driving and highway safety? Describe the research described in this chapter, and then list three or four additional applications.

9. Cognitive psychology can also be applied to clinical psychology. Discuss some applications of the Stroop effect and thought suppression to the area of psychological problems and their treatment.

10. Chapters 2 and 3 both examine perception. To help you synthesize part of this information, describe as completely as possible how you are able to perceive the letters in a word, using both bottom-up and top-down processing. Describe how your attention would operate in both a selective-attention situation and a divided-attention situation. How are saccadic eye movements relevant?

KEYWORDS

attention
divided-attention task
selective-attention task
dichotic listening
shadow
cocktail party effect
working memory
Stroop effect
emotional Stroop task
phobic disorder
saccadic eye movement
fovea

fixation
perceptual span
regressions
alerting attention network
orienting attention network
brain lesion
unilateral neglect
positron emission tomography
   (PET scan)
executive attention network
bottleneck theories
feature-integration theory

distributed attention
focused attention
illusory conjunction
binding problem
consciousness
ironic effects of mental
   control
obsession
compulsion
obsessive-compulsive disorder
   (OCD)
blindsight

RECOMMENDED READINGS

Clark, D. A. (2005). *Intrusive thoughts in clinical disorders: Theory, research, and treatment.* New York: Guilford Press. Here is an ideal book for people who are interested in the connections between cognitive psychology and clinical psychology. It examines how people with a variety of clinical disorders have difficulty suppressing their thoughts.

Posner, M. I., & Rothbart, M. K. (2007b). Research on attention networks as a model for the integration of psychological science. *Annual Review of Psychology, 58,* 1–23. This chapter emphasizes the neuroscience research on attention, and it argues that attention plays a major role in cognitive development and in psychological disorders.

Radach, R., Kennedy, A., & Rayner, K. (Eds.). (2004a). *Eye movements and information processing during reading.* Hove, UK: Psychology Press. This book contains ten articles that examine how our saccadic eye movements are influenced by characteristics of the material we are reading.

Styles, E. A. (2006). *The psychology of attention* (2nd ed.). New York: Psychology Press. Elizabeth Styles's book provides an excellent overview of attention, including such topics as auditory and visual attention, divided attention, and consciousness.

Wright, R. D., & Ward, L. M. (2008). *Orienting of attention.* New York: Oxford University Press. Students who are interested in an in-depth examination of attention will especially enjoy reading this book. It explores how we shift attention from one location to another, even without observable body movements.

CHAPTER 4

Using Working Memory

PREVIEW

Our topic in this chapter is working memory. At this moment, you are using your working memory to remember the beginning of this sentence until you reach the final word in this sentence. On other occasions, your working memory helps you remember visual and spatial information. In addition, working memory coordinates your cognitive activities, and it plans strategies.

We'll begin this chapter by examining some influential milestones in the history of working-memory research. The first section starts with George Miller's classic view that our immediate memory can hold approximately seven items. We'll also explore other early research and theories. For example, your working memory holds many more items with one-syllable names than items with three-syllable names.

The second part of this chapter explores the working-memory approach originally proposed by Alan Baddeley. His research showed that people can perform a verbal task and a spatial task at the same time, with little loss of speed or accuracy. This research led Baddeley to propose that working memory has two separate components—the phonological loop and the visuospatial sketchpad—which have independent capacities. We'll examine these two components as well as the central executive, the component that coordinates our ongoing cognitive activities. We'll also consider the episodic buffer, a temporary storehouse where information from the phonological loop and the visuospatial sketchpad is combined with information from long-term memory. The chapter ends with an individual-differences feature, which shows that people with major depression experience working-memory problems in several areas.

INTRODUCTION

You can probably recall a recent experience like this: Your friend Chris introduces you to a young man whom you do not know, and Chris pronounces his first and last name very clearly. The two of them leave less than a minute later, and you find yourself saying, "Now what was his name? How could I possibly forget it?" Some memories are so fragile that they evaporate before you can begin to use them. As you'll soon see, research confirms that your memory is limited in both its duration and its capacity when you must remember new information, even after a delay of less than 1 minute (Cowan, 2005; Paas & Kester, 2006; Rose, 2004).

You may also become aware of these limits when you try mental arithmetic, read a complex sentence, work on a reasoning task, or solve a complex problem (Gathercole et al., 2006; Morrison, 2005). Demonstration 4.1 illustrates the limits of our immediate memory for two of these tasks; try each task before reading further.

In Demonstration 4.1, you probably had no difficulty with the first mathematics task and the first reading task. The second math and reading tasks were more challenging,

---

◎ **Demonstration 4.1**

The Limits of Short-Term Memory

A. Try each of the following mental multiplication tasks. Be sure not to write down any of your calculations. Do them entirely "in your head."

1. $7 \times 9 =$
2. $74 \times 9 =$
3. $74 \times 96 =$

B. Now read each of the following sentences, and construct a mental image of the action that is being described. *(Note: Sentence 3 is technically correct, though it is confusing.)*

1. The repairman departed.
2. The librarian that the secretary met departed.
3. The salesperson that the doctor that the nurse despised met departed.

---

but you could still manage. The third tasks probably seemed beyond the limits of your immediate memory.

In the preceding chapter, we saw that attention is limited. Specifically, you have difficulty dividing your attention between two simultaneous tasks. Furthermore, if you are paying selective attention to one task, you typically notice very little about the unattended task. Therefore, these attention processes limit the amount of information that can be passed on to your memory.

The current chapter also emphasizes the limited capacity of cognitive processes. However, it focuses on limited *memory* instead of limited *attention*. Specifically, this chapter examines working memory. **Working memory** is the brief, immediate memory for material that you are currently processing; a portion of working memory also actively coordinates your ongoing mental activities. In other words, working memory lets you keep information active and accessible, so that you can use it in a wide variety of cognitive tasks (Cowan, 2003, 2005; Hassin, 2005; Pickering, 2006b). (The term *working memory* is currently more popular than a similar but older term, **short-term memory.**) In contrast to this chapter on working memory, Chapters 5, 6, 7, and 8 will explore long-term memory. **Long-term memory** has a large capacity and contains our memory for experiences and information that have accumulated over a lifetime.

In discussing working memory, we need to repeat a point we made in connection with the Atkinson-Shiffrin model of memory in Chapter 1. According to some psychologists, the research evidence supports the proposal that working memory and long-term memory are basically the same (e.g., Davelaar et al., 2005; Nairne, 2002; Winkler & Cowan, 2005). Another important point is that those who *do* believe in two different systems may not all share the same theoretical explanations (e.g., Atkinson & Shiffrin, 1968; Baddeley, 2006; Cowan, 2005; Engle & Kane, 2004; Miyake & Shah,1999a; Paas & Kester, 2006).

In this discussion, we also need to repeat a different point we made in Chapter 1: Your performance on everyday tasks is often different from your performance on tasks in the psychology laboratory. In everyday life, for instance, your memory is often much more impressive, especially because you are working on a variety of complex tasks within a short period of time (Miyake & Shah, 1999b). Your working memory must decide what kind of information is useful to you right now, and it selects this material out of an enormous wealth of information you possess (Brown, 2004; Cowan, 2005; Goldberg, 2001). At this moment, for example, your working-memory system is rapidly inspecting your vast knowledge of words, grammar, and concepts, so that you can understand the meaning of this sentence. However, you may soon shift to a completely different memory task; for example, you might contemplate whether you can make a decent meal from the food in your refrigerator.

So let's begin by inspecting some of the classic research on working memory. As you'll notice, the concept of limited memory capacity is an important feature of this research (Cowan, 2005; Cowan et al., 2005). Then we'll explore the multicomponent model—originally proposed by Alan Baddeley—which is currently the most widely accepted theoretical explanation of working memory (Neath et al., 2005; Pickering, 2006b). As you'll see, this theory is more flexible than earlier explanations, and it also emphasizes that your memory is active, rather than passive. However, Baddeley's model still emphasizes that each of the major components of working memory has a limited capacity.

THE CLASSIC RESEARCH ON WORKING MEMORY (SHORT-TERM MEMORY)

We'll start by discussing George Miller's perspective on the limitations of memory, as well as some early studies that attempted to measure these limitations. Our next topic in this section is the Atkinson-Shiffrin model, and we'll end by considering two factors that affect the capacity of working memory.

George Miller's "Magical Number Seven"

In 1956, George Miller wrote a famous article titled "The Magical Number Seven, Plus or Minus Two: Some Limits on Our Capacity for Processing Information." Miller proposed that we can hold only a limited number of items in short-term memory (as this brief memory was called at the time). Specifically, he suggested that people can remember about seven items (give or take two), that is, between five and nine items.

Miller used the term *chunk* to describe the basic unit in short-term memory. According to the current definition, a **chunk** is a memory unit that consists of several components that are strongly associated with one another (Cowan et al., 2004). Miller suggests, therefore, that short-term memory holds approximately seven chunks.

A chunk can be a single numeral or a single letter, because people can remember a random sequence of about seven numerals or letters. However, you can organize several numbers or letters so that they form a single chunk. For example, suppose that your area code is 617, and all the phone numbers at your college begin with the same digits, 346. If 617 forms one chunk and 346 forms another chunk, then the phone number 617-346-3421 really contains only six chunks (that is, 1 + 1 + 4). The entire number may be within your memory span. Miller's (1956) article received major attention, and the magical number 7±2 became a prominent concept known to almost all psychology students.*

Miller's article was unusual because it was written at a time when behaviorism was very popular. As you know, behaviorism emphasized observable *external events*. In contrast, Miller's article proposed that people engage in *internal mental processes* in order to convert stimuli into a manageable number of chunks. This article emphasized that our cognitive processes are active—consistent with Theme 1—rather than focusing only on the visible stimuli and the visible responses (Baddeley, 1994). Miller's work also helped to inspire some of the classic research on short-term memory.

Other Early Research on Short-Term-Memory Capacity

During the late 1950s and the 1970s, researchers frequently used two methods to assess how much information our short-term memory could hold. Two especially popular measures were the Brown/Peterson & Peterson Technique and a measure derived from the serial position effect. (Incidentally, here we will use "short-term memory"—the term used during that era—rather than the more current "working memory.")

The Brown/Peterson & Peterson Technique. Demonstration 4.2 shows a modified version of the Brown/Peterson & Peterson Technique, a method that provided much of our original information about short-term memory. John Brown (1958, 2004), a British psychologist, and Lloyd Peterson and Margaret Peterson (1959), two U.S. psychologists, independently demonstrated that material held in memory for less than a minute is frequently forgotten. The technique therefore bears the names of all three researchers.

---

*In more recent research, Nelson Cowan (2005) argues that the magical number is really in the range of four, when we consider the "pure capacity" of short-term memory—without the possibility of chunking.

Demonstration 4.2

A Modified Version of the Brown/Peterson & Peterson Technique

Take out six index cards. On one side of each card, write one of the following groups of three words, one underneath another. On the back of the card, write the three-digit number. Set the cards aside for a few minutes and practice counting backward by threes from the number 792. Then show yourself the first card, with the side containing the words toward you, for about 2 seconds. Then immediately turn over the card and count backward by threes from the three-digit number shown. Go as fast as possible for 20 seconds. (Use a watch with a second hand to keep track of the time.) Then write down as many of the three words as you can remember. Continue this process with the remaining five cards.

1. appeal		4. flower	
simple	687	classic	573
burden		predict	
2. sober		5. silken	
persuade	254	idle	433
content		approve	
3. descend		6. begin	
neglect	869	pillow	376
elsewhere		carton	

Peterson and Peterson (1959), for example, asked people to study three letters. The participants then saw a three-digit number and counted backward by threes from this number for a short period. This counting activity prevented them from rehearsing the stimuli during the delay. (**Rehearsal** means repeating the items silently.) Finally, the participants tried to recall the letters they had originally seen. On the first few trials, people recalled most of the letters. However, after several trials, the previous letters produced interference, and recall was poor. After a mere 5-second delay—as you can see from Figure 4.1—people forgot approximately half of what they had seen.

The early research using the Brown/Peterson & Peterson Technique provided important information about the fragility of memory for material stored for just a few seconds. This technique also inspired hundreds of studies on short-term memory, and it played an important role in increasing the support for the cognitive approach (Bower, 2000; Kintsch et al., 1999).

The Recency Effect.   Researchers have also used the serial position effect to examine short-term memory. The term **serial position effect** refers to the U-shaped relationship

FIGURE 4.1

Typical Results for Percentage Recalled with the Brown/Peterson & Peterson Technique.

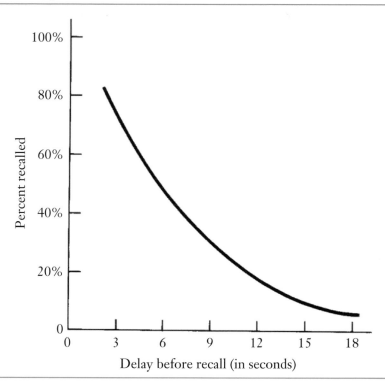

between a word's position in a list and its probability of recall. Figure 4.2 shows a classic illustration of the serial position effect in research (Rundus, 1971). The U-shaped curve is very common, and it continues to be found in more recent research (e.g., Hulme et al., 2004; Thompson & Madigan, 2005; Ward et al., 2005).

As you can see, the curve shows a strong **recency effect**, with better recall for items at the end of the list. Many researchers have argued that this relatively accurate memory for the final words in a list means that these items were still in short-term memory at the time of recall. Thus, one way of measuring the size of short-term memory is to count the number of accurately recalled items at the end of the list (Davelaar et al., 2005; Davelaar et al., 2006; R. G. Morrison, 2005).

Typically, the size of short-term memory is estimated to be two to seven items when the serial-position curve method is used. (Notice that the serial-position curve also shows a strong **primacy effect,** with better recall for items at the beginning of the list, presumably because people rehearse these early items more frequently.) The information gathered from these two research methods was useful in constructing Atkinson and Shiffrin's (1968) influential approach to human memory.

FIGURE 4.2

The Relationship Between an Item's Serial Position and the Probability That It Will Be Recalled.

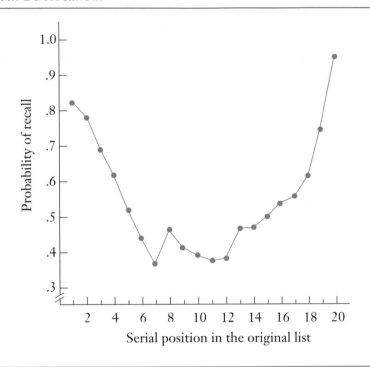

Serial position in the original list

Source: Based on Rundus, 1971.

Atkinson and Shiffrin's Model

Richard Atkinson and Richard Shiffrin (1968) proposed the classic information-processing model that we presented in Chapter 1. Turn back to this model, shown in Figure 1.1 on page 10. As you can see, short-term memory (as it was then called) is distinctly separate from long-term memory in this diagram. Atkinson and Shiffrin argued that memories in short-term memory are fragile, and they could be lost within about 30 seconds unless they are repeated.

In addition, Atkinson and Shiffrin proposed **control processes,** or intentional strategies—such as rehearsal—that people may use to improve their memory (Hassin, 2005; Raaijmakers & Shiffrin, 2002). The original form of this model focused on the role of short-term memory in learning and memory. The model did not explore how short-term memory is central when we perform other cognitive tasks (Roediger et al., 2002).

The Atkinson-Shiffrin model played a central role in the growing appeal of the cognitive approach to psychology. For instance, researchers conducted numerous studies to determine whether short-term memory really is distinctly different from long-term memory; this question still does not have a clear-cut answer. Research on this topic declined during the mid-1970s, partly because Alan Baddeley's new approach did not emphasize this distinction. Before we consider Baddeley's approach, however, let's examine two factors that have an important effect on working memory.

Other Factors Affecting Working Memory's Capacity

We have already considered one important factor that influences the capacity of working memory. As Miller's (1956) work demonstrated, we can increase the number of items in memory by using the chunking strategy. Let's focus on two other influential variables: (1) pronunciation time, and (2) the semantic similarity of the items.

Pronunciation Time. The research shows that pronunciation time strongly influences the number of items that we can store in working memory (Hulme et al., 2004; Hulme et al., 2006; Tolan & Tehan, 2005). Try Demonstration 4.3, which is a modification of a study by Baddeley and his colleagues (1975). These researchers found that people could accurately recall an average of 4.2 words from the list of countries with short names. In contrast, they recalled an average of only 2.8 words from the list of countries with long names.

One of the most systematic studies about pronunciation time focused on the recall of numbers in four different languages. Naveh-Benjamin and Ayres (1986) tested memory spans for people who spoke English, Spanish, Hebrew, or Arabic. The names for English numbers between 1 and 10 are almost all one-syllable words. As you can see from the dotted line in Figure 4.3, these words can be pronounced quickly. Notice that the memory span for English numbers is about seven numbers. The names for Spanish and Hebrew numbers have a greater number of syllables, and the memory span for these numbers is lower. Arabic numbers have even more syllables, and the memory span for these numbers is still lower. Clearly, pronunciation rate—as well as number of chunks—needs to be considered when discussing the capacity of working memory.

ⓖ Demonstration 4.3

Pronunciation Time and Memory Span

Read the following words. When you have finished, look away from the page and try to recall them.

Burma, Greece, Tibet, Iceland, Malta, Laos

Now try the task again with a different list of words. Again, read the words, look away, and recall them.

Switzerland, Nicaragua, Botswana,
Venezuela, Philippines, Madagascar

FIGURE 4.3

Memory Span and Pronunciation Rate for Numbers in Four Different Languages.

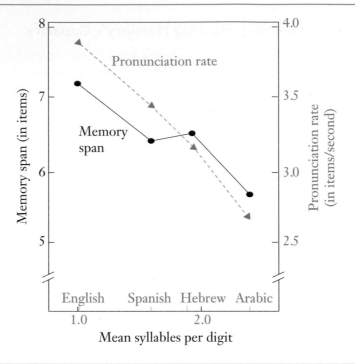

Source: Naveh-Benjamin & Ayres, 1986.

Semantic Similarity of the Items in Working Memory. The research on pronunciation time emphasized the importance of the acoustic properties of stimuli—that is, the *sound* of words. Now let's focus on **semantics,** that is, the meaning of words and sentences. The research shows that the *meaning* of words can also have an important effect on the number of items that you can store in working memory.

For example, consider a classic study by Wickens and his colleagues (1976). Their technique uses an important concept from memory research called proactive interference. **Proactive interference (PI)** means that people have trouble learning new material because previously learned material keeps interfering with new learning. Suppose you had previously learned three items—XCJ, HBR, and TSV—in a Brown/Peterson & Peterson test of memory. You will then have trouble remembering a fourth item, KRN, because the three previous items keep interfering. However, if the experimenter shifts the category of the fourth item from letters to, say, numbers, your memory will improve. You will experience a **release from proactive interference;** performance on a new, different item (say, 529) will be almost as high as it had been on the first item, XCJ.

Many experiments have demonstrated release from PI when the category of items is shifted, for example, from letters to numbers. However, Wickens and his coauthors (1976) demonstrated that release from PI could also be obtained when they shifted the

FIGURE 4.4

Release from Proactive Interference, as a Function of Semantic Similarity. On Trials 1, 2, and 3, each group saw words belonging to the specified category (e.g., occupations). On Trial 4, everyone saw the same list of three fruits.

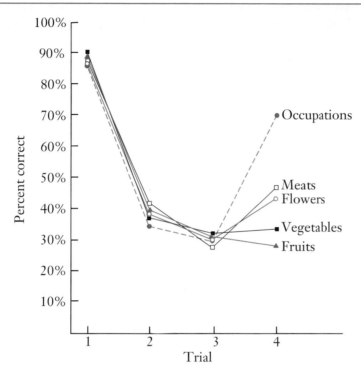

Source: Based on Wickens et al., 1976.

semantic category of the items. Their study employed five semantic categories, which you can see in Figure 4.4. Wickens and his colleagues initially gave people three trials on the Brown/Peterson & Peterson test. In other words, on each trial they saw a list of three words, followed by a three-digit number. After counting backward from this number for 18 seconds, they tried to recall the three words.

On each trial in this study, participants saw three related words. For example, participants in the Occupations condition might begin with "lawyer, firefighter, teacher" on the Trial 1. On Trials 2 and 3, the people in this condition saw lists of additional occupations. Then on Trial 4, they saw a list of three fruits—such as "orange, cherry, pineapple"—as did the people in the other four conditions.

Look through the five conditions shown at the right side of Figure 4.4. Wouldn't you expect the buildup of proactive interference on Trial 4 to be the greatest for those in the fruits (control) condition? After all, people's memories should be filled with the names of other fruits that would be interfering with the three new fruits.

How should the people in the other four conditions perform? If meaning is important in working memory, then their recall in these conditions should depend upon the semantic similarity between these items and fruit. For example, people who had seen vegetables on Trials 1 through 3 should do rather poorly on the fruit items, because vegetables and fruit are similar—they are edible and they are produced by plants. People who had seen either flowers or meats should do somewhat better, because flowers and meats each share only one attribute with fruits. However, people who had seen occupations should do the best of all, because occupations are not edible and they are not produced by plants.

Figure 4.4 is an example of the kind of results every researcher hopes to find. Note that the results match the predictions perfectly. In summary, semantic factors influence the number of items that we can store in working memory. Specifically, words that we have previously stored can interfere with the recall of new words that are similar in meaning. Furthermore, the degree of semantic similarity is related to the amount of interference. The importance of semantic factors in working memory has also been confirmed by other researchers (Cain, 2006; Potter, 1999; Walker & Hulme, 1999). We know, then, that the number of items stored in working memory depends on chunking strategies, word length, and word meaning. Let's summarize the information in this section and then examine Baddeley's approach to working memory.

◎ Section Summary: *The Classic Research on Working Memory (Short-Term Memory)*

1. Working memory is the very brief, immediate memory for material that we are currently processing.
2. In 1956, George Miller proposed that we can hold about seven chunks of information in short-term memory.
3. The Brown/Peterson & Peterson Technique, which prevents rehearsal, shows that people have only limited recall for items after a brief delay. The recency effect in a serial-position curve has also been interpreted as a measure of the limited capacity of short-term memory.
4. The Atkinson-Shiffrin model proposed that short-term memories can be lost from memory within about 30 seconds unless they are repeated.
5. Pronunciation time has an important effect on the number of items that can be stored in working memory. This effect has been confirmed with a variety of stimuli, such as the names of countries and the names of numbers.
6. Word meaning can also influence the recall of items that we store in working memory; when the semantic category changes between adjacent trials, our recall increases.

THE WORKING-MEMORY APPROACH

For several years, researchers eagerly explored the characteristics of short-term memory. However, no one developed a comprehensive theory for this brief kind of memory until Alan Baddeley and his colleagues proposed the working-memory approach.

Now that you are familiar with several factors that influence working-memory capacity, we can explore this approach in some detail.

During the early 1970s, Alan Baddeley and Graham Hitch were examining the wealth of research on short-term memory. They soon realized that researchers had ignored one very important question: What does short-term memory actually accomplish for our cognitive processes? Eventually, they agreed that its major function is to hold several interrelated bits of information in our mind, all at the same time, so that this information can be worked with and then used appropriately (Baddeley & Hitch, 1974).

For example, if you are trying to comprehend the sentence that you are reading right now, you need to keep the beginning words in mind until you know how the sentence is going to end. (Think about it: Did you in fact keep those initial words in your memory until you reached the word *end*?) Baddeley and Hitch (1974) also realized that this kind of working memory would be necessary for a wide range of cognitive tasks, such as language comprehension, mental arithmetic, reasoning, and problem solving.

According to the **working-memory approach** proposed by Baddeley, our immediate memory is a multipart system that temporarily holds and manipulates information as we perform cognitive tasks. Figure 4.5 illustrates the current design of the model, featuring the phonological loop, the visuospatial sketchpad, the central executive, and the episodic buffer—which was added more recently (Baddeley, 2000a, 2000b, 2001, 2006).

Baddeley's approach emphasizes that working memory is not simply a passive storehouse with a number of shelves to hold partially processed information until it moves on to another location, presumably long-term memory. Instead, Baddeley's emphasis

FIGURE 4.5

A Simplified Version of Alan Baddeley's (2000b) Model of Working Memory.

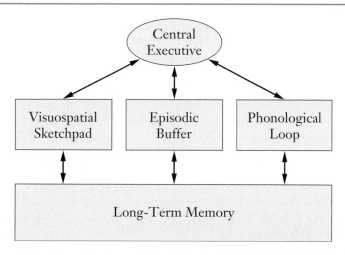

Note: This diagram shows the phonological loop, the visuospatial sketchpad, the central executive, and the episodic buffer—as well as their interactions with long-term memory.

Source: Based on Baddeley (2000b).

on the manipulation of information means that working memory is more like a work-bench where material is constantly being handled, combined, and transformed. Fur-thermore, this workbench holds both new material and old material that you have retrieved from storage (long-term memory). In Figure 4.5, notice that several compo-nents of working memory have access to long-term memory.

Let's begin our analysis of the research by first considering why Baddeley felt com-pelled to conclude that working memory is not unitary. Next we'll consider each of the four components. The first component—the phonological loop—will be considered in depth, and then we'll look at the three other components: the visuospatial sketchpad, the central executive, and the episodic buffer. Then the individual-differences feature will focus on the relationship between psychological depression and the components of working memory.

Evidence for Components with Independent Capacities

An important study by Baddeley and Hitch (1974) provided convincing evidence that working memory is not unitary. These researchers presented a string of random num-bers to participants, who were instructed to rehearse them in order. The string of num-bers varied in length from zero to eight items. In other words, the longer list approached the upper limit of short-term memory, according to Miller's (1956) 7 ± 2 proposal. At the same time, the participants also performed a spatial reasoning task. The reasoning task required them to judge whether certain statements about letter order were correct or incorrect. For example, suppose that the participants see the two letters *BA*. If they also see the statement, "*A* follows *B*," they should respond by pressing a "yes" button. In contrast, suppose that they see the two letters *BA*, accompanied by the statement, "*B* follows *A*." In this case, the participants should press the "no" button.

Imagine yourself performing this task. Wouldn't you think you would take longer and make more errors on the reasoning task if you had to keep rehearsing eight numerals, instead of only one? To the surprise of everyone—including the participants in the study—people performed remarkably quickly and accurately on these two simultaneous tasks. For example, Baddeley and Hitch (1974) discovered that these participants required less than a second longer on the reasoning task when instructed to rehearse eight numerals, in contrast to a task that required no rehearsal. Even more impressive, the error rate remained at about 5%, no matter how many numerals the participants rehearsed!

The data from Baddeley and Hitch's (1974) study clearly contradicted the view that temporary storage has only about seven slots, as Miller (1956) had proposed. Specif-ically, this study suggested that people can indeed perform two tasks simultaneously—for instance, one task that requires verbal rehearsal and another task that requires visual or spatial judgments. Some research does suggest that verbal and visual tasks can inter-fere with each other (Morey & Cowan, 2004, 2005). However, most memory theorists believe that working memory seems to have several components, which can operate somewhat independently of each other (Baddeley, 2006; Davelaar et al., 2005; Miyake & Shah, 1999b).

As we've already described, Baddeley and his colleagues proposed four compo-nents for working memory: a phonological loop, a visuospatial sketchpad, a central executive, and—more recently—an integrative component that Baddeley calls an "episodic buffer" (Baddeley, 2000a, 2000b, 2001, 2006; Gathercole & Baddeley, 1993; Logie, 1995). We'll examine the phonological loop in detail, and then we'll consider the other three components.

IN DEPTH

Phonological Loop

According to the working-memory model, the **phonological loop** processes a limited number of sounds for a short period of time. Theorists argue that the pronunciation-time research you learned about in Demonstration 4.3 (p. 101) can be explained by the limited storage space in the phonological loop (Baddeley, 2003, 2006; Lobley et al., 2005). You can pronounce country names such as *Burma* and *Greece* fairly quickly, so you can rehearse a large number of them quickly. In contrast, you can pronounce only a limited number of longer names, such as *Switzerland* and *Nicaragua*. When you need to rehearse a large number of these long names, some will inevitably be lost from the phonological loop. Researchers also report that the relationship between pronunciation time and recall accuracy holds true, whether you actually pronounce the words aloud or use **subvocalization,** pronouncing the words silently.

Research on Acoustic Confusions. We emphasized earlier that the phonological loop stores information in terms of sounds. Therefore, we would expect to find that people's memory errors can often be traced to **acoustic confusions;** that is, people are likely to confuse similar-sounding stimuli (Baddeley, 2003; Wickelgren, 1965).

For example, a classic study by Conrad and Hull (1964) showed participants two kinds of lists of letters of the English alphabet. Some lists featured letters that had similar-sounding names, such as the sequence *C, T, D, G, V, B*. Other lists featured letters with different-sounding names, such as the sequence *C, W, Q, K, R, and X*. The participants correctly recalled more letters from the second list, where the sounds were different.

Notice an important point: In studies such as Conrad and Hull's, the letters were presented visually. However, people must have been "translating" these visual stimuli into a format based on the acoustic properties of the letters. Other related research examined recall for words. When the words sounded different from one another, people recalled more items than when the words sounded similar (Kintsch & Buschke, 1969).

A recent study by Dylan Jones and his colleagues (2004) proposes a different explanation for these acoustic confusions. These researchers suggest that people confuse acoustically similar sounds with one another when they are rehearsing the items, not when these items are simply stored in the phonological loop. Suppose, for example, that you want to remember the sequence of letters mentioned above: *C, T, D, G, V, B*. Dylan and his colleagues (2004) suggest that you try to pronounce these letters in order to repeat them silently to yourself. You may stumble and silently pronounce the wrong sound, just as you might stumble on a rhyming tongue twister such as "She sells seashells." We'll examine this kind of speech-production error in more detail in Chapter 10.

Other Uses for the Phonological Loop.   The phonological loop plays a crucial role in our daily lives, beyond its obvious role in working memory (Baddeley, 2003, 2006; Morrison, 2005). For example, we use it on simple counting tasks. Try counting the number of words in the previous sentence, for example. Can you hear your "inner voice" saying the numbers silently? Now try counting the number of words in that same sentence, but rapidly say the word *the* while you are counting. When your phonological loop is preoccupied with saying *the*, you cannot perform even a simple counting task!

Theme 4 of this textbook states that our cognitive processes are interrelated with one another; they do not operate in isolation. The multiple uses for the phonological loop illustrate this theme. For example, the phonological loop plays an important role in reading, as we'll see in Chapter 9. (Be honest: The first time you see a long word, such as *phonological*, can you read that word without silently pronouncing it?) In addition, the phonological loop is active when we acquire new vocabulary words in our first language (de Jong, 2006; Knott & Marslen-Wilson, 2001) and also in a foreign language (Masoura & Gathercole, 2005).

Furthermore, mathematical calculations and problem-solving tasks require the phonological loop in order to keep track of numbers and other information (Bull & Espy, 2006). In fact, the phonological loop is important whenever you are working on a complex task that requires you to remember the task instructions for an extended period of time (Gathercole et al., 2006).

Neuroscience Research on the Phonological Loop.   Researchers have also used brain-imaging techniques to explore the phonological loop. In general, these studies have shown that phonological tasks activate parts of the frontal lobe and the temporal lobe in the left hemisphere of the brain (Baddeley, 2006; Gazzaniga et al., 2002; Lustig et al., 2005). This finding makes sense, as you may recall from other psychology courses. Compared to the right hemisphere of the brain, the left hemisphere is more likely to process information related to language. (We will explore this topic in more detail in Chapter 9.)

More fine-grained brain-imaging research reveals that the phonological loop stores auditory information in the parietal lobe of the cortex (Thompson & Madigan, 2005). Figure 2.1, on page 35, shows a diagram of the cortex. Furthermore, the regions of your frontal lobe that handle speech are activated when you rehearse verbal material (Newman et al., 2002; Thompson & Madigan, 2005).

Visuospatial Sketchpad

A second component of Baddeley's model of working memory is the **visuospatial sketchpad**, which processes both visual and spatial information. This sketchpad allows you to look at a complex scene and gather visual information about objects and landmarks. It also allows you to navigate from one location to another (Logie & Della Sala,

2005). Incidentally, the visuospatial sketchpad has been known by a variety of different names, such as *visuo-spatial scratchpad*, *visuo-spatial working memory*, and *short-term visual memory* (Cornoldi & Vecchi, 2003; Hollingworth, 2004). You may encounter these alternate terms in other discussions of working memory.

The visuospatial sketchpad allows you to store a coherent picture of both the visual appearance of the objects and their relative positions in a scene (Cornoldi & Vecchi, 2003; Hollingworth, 2004, 2006; Logie & Della Salla, 2005). The visuospatial sketchpad also stores visual information that you encode from verbal stimuli (Baddeley, 2006; Pickering, 2006a). For example, when a friend tells a story, you may find yourself visualizing the scene.

As you begin reading about the visuospatial sketchpad, keep in mind the research by Baddeley and Hitch (1974) that we discussed earlier. People can work simultaneously on one verbal task (rehearsing a number) and one spatial task (making judgments about the spatial location of the letters *A* and *B*)—without much alteration in their performance.

However, like the phonological loop, the capacity of the visuospatial sketchpad is limited (Alvarez & Cavanagh, 2004; Baddeley, 2006; Hollingworth, 2004; Wheeler & Treisman, 2002). I remember tutoring a high school student in geometry. When working on her own, she often tried to solve her geometry problems on a small scrap of paper. As you might imagine, the restricted space caused her to make many errors. Similarly, when too many items enter your visuospatial working memory, you cannot represent them accurately enough to recover them successfully.

Alan Baddeley (1999, 2006) describes a personal experience that made him appreciate how one visuospatial task can interfere with another. As a British citizen, he became very intrigued with U.S. football while spending a year in the United States. On one occasion, he decided to listen to a football game while driving along a California freeway. In order to understand the game, he tried to form clear, detailed images of the scene and the action. While creating these images, however, he discovered that his car began drifting out of its lane!

Apparently, Baddeley found it impossible to perform one task requiring a mental image—with both visual and spatial components—at the same time that he performed a visuospatial task that required him to keep his car within specified boundaries. In fact, Baddeley found that he had to switch the radio to music in order to drive safely.

Let's consider some research on visual coding, as well as some other applications of the visuospatial sketchpad. We'll also briefly consider some relevant brain-imaging research.

Research on the Visuospatial Sketchpad. Baddeley's dual-task experience during driving inspired him to conduct some laboratory studies. This research confirmed the difficulty of performing two visuospatial tasks simultaneously (Baddeley, 1999, 2006; Baddeley et al., 1973).

In general, however, psychologists have conducted less research on the visuospatial sketchpad than on the phonological loop (Baddeley, 2006; Engle & Oransky, 1999). One problem is that we do not have a standardized set of visual stimuli that would be comparable to the words processed by the phonological loop.

Another problem is that research participants (at least in Western cultures) tend to provide names for stimuli presented in a visual form. Beginning at about age 8, participants look at a shape and provide a name such as "It's a circle inside a square" (Pickering, 2006a). This kind of verbal coding then requires the phonological loop—instead of the visuospatial sketchpad—for further processing.

Can researchers encourage participants to use the visuospatial sketchpad? Brandimonte and her colleagues (1992) instructed participants to repeat an irrelevant syllable ("la-la-la") while looking at a complex visual stimulus. When the phonological loop was occupied with this repetition task, the participants usually did not provide names for the stimuli. Instead, they were more likely to use visuospatial coding.

Other Uses for the Visuospatial Sketchpad. It's probably safe to say that students in psychology and other social sciences use the phonological loop more often than the visuospatial sketchpad. However, students in disciplines such as engineering, art, and architecture frequently use visual coding and the visuospatial sketchpad in their academic studies.

You also use your visuospatial sketchpad in your everyday life. For example, look at several objects that are within your reach. Now close your eyes and try to touch one of these objects. Your sketchpad allowed you to retain a brief image of that scene while your eyes were closed (Logie, 2003). In addition, your visuospatial sketchpad is activated when you try to find your way from one location to another (Logie, 2003). Your sketchpad is also useful in many leisure activities, such as videogames, jigsaw puzzles, and games involving a maze (Pickering, 2006a).

Furthermore, your visuospatial sketchpad is active when you watch television. For example, Toms and her colleagues (1994) found that people had trouble working on a task requiring spatial imagery if they were required to simultaneously view a shifting design on a television screen. Notice that this kind of task has both spatial and visual components (Baddeley, 2001).

We will examine other uses for visual and spatial memory in Chapter 7. In particular, that chapter explores the mental manipulations we perform on visuospatial information.

Neuroscience Research on the Visuospatial Sketchpad. In general, the neuroscience research suggests that visual and spatial tasks are especially likely to activate the right hemisphere of the cortex, rather than the left hemisphere (Gazzaniga et al., 2002; Logie, 2003; Thompson & Madigan, 2005). Again, these studies are consistent with information you probably learned in other courses; the right hemisphere is generally more responsible for processing visual and spatial tasks.

Visual and spatial tasks often activate a variety of regions of the cortex. For example, working-memory tasks with a strong visual component typically activate the occipital region, a part of the brain that is responsible for visual perception (Baddeley, 2001). (Refer again to Figure 2.1, p. 35.) However, the specific location of brain activity depends on the specific characteristics such as task difficulty (Logie & Della Sala, 2005).

In addition, various regions of the frontal cortex are active when people work on visual and spatial tasks (Logie & Della Sala, 2005; E.E. Smith, 2000; Smith & Jonides, 1998). Research on spatial working memory also suggests that people mentally rehearse this material by shifting their selective attention from one location to another in their mental image (Awh et al., 1999). As a result, this mental rehearsal activates areas in the frontal and parietal lobes (Diwadkar et al., 2000; Olesen et al., 2004; Posner & Rothbart, 2007b). These are the same areas of the cortex that are associated with attention, as we discussed in Chapter 3.

Central Executive

According to the working-memory model, the **central executive** integrates information from the phonological loop, the visuospatial sketchpad, the episodic buffer, and from long-term memory. The central executive also plays a major role in focusing attention, planning strategies, transforming information, and coordinating behavior (Baddeley, 2001; Reuter-Lorenz & Jonides, 2007). The central executive is therefore extremely important and complex. However, it is also the least understood component of working memory (Baddeley, 2006; Bull & Espy, 2006).

In addition, the central executive is responsible for suppressing *irrelevant* information (Baddeley, 2006; Engle & Conway, 1998; Hasher et al., 2007). In your everyday activities, your central executive helps you decide what to do next. It also helps you decide what *not* to do, so that you do not become sidetracked from your primary goal.

Characteristics of the Central Executive. Most researchers emphasize that the central executive plans and coordinates, but it does not store information (Baddeley, 2000b, 2006; Logie, 2003; Richardson, 1996a, 1996b). As you know, the phonological loop and the visuospatial sketchpad both have specialized storage systems.

Compared to the two systems we've discussed, the central executive is more difficult to study using controlled research techniques. However, the central executive plays a critical role in the overall functions of working memory. As Baddeley (1986) points out, if we concentrate on, say, the phonological loop, the situation would resemble a critical analysis of Shakespeare's play *Hamlet* that focuses on Polonius—a minor character—and completely ignores the prince of Denmark!

Baddeley (1999, 2006) proposes that the central executive works like an executive supervisor in an organization. According to this metaphor, an executive decides which issues deserve attention and which should be ignored. An executive also selects strategies, figuring out how to tackle a problem. Similarly, the central executive plays an important role when we try to solve mathematical problems (Bull & Espy, 2006). We will examine this issue of strategy selection more completely in Chapter 6 (metacognition) and in Chapter 11 (problem solving).

A good executive also knows not to keep repeating a strategy that doesn't work (Baddeley, 2001). Furthermore, like any executive in an organization, the central executive has a limited ability to perform simultaneous tasks. Our cognitive executive cannot make numerous decisions at the same time, and it cannot work effectively on two simultaneous projects.

> ### 🌀 Demonstration 4.4
>
> #### A Task That Requires Central-Executive Resources
>
> Your assignment for this demonstration is to generate a sequence of random numbers. In particular, make sure that your list contains a roughly equal proportion of the numbers 1 through 10. Also, be sure that your list does not show any systematic repetition in the sequence. For example, the number 4 should be followed equally often by each of the numbers 1 through 10.
>
> As quickly as you can, write a series of digits on a piece of paper (at the rate of approximately one digit per second). Keep performing this task for about 5 minutes. If you find yourself daydreaming, check back at the numbers you have generated. During these periods, you'll probably find that your numbers do not form a truly random sequence.

The Central Executive and Daydreaming. Let's look at a representative study about the central executive. At this very moment, you may be engaging in the slightly embarrassing activity we typically call "daydreaming." For example, right now you may be thinking about a TV show you saw last night or what you will be doing next weekend, rather than the words that your sensory receptors are currently registering.

Interestingly, daydreaming requires the active participation of your central executive. Consider part of a study by Teasdale and his colleagues (1995), which you tried in Demonstration 4.4. These researchers examined a task that should compete for your central executive's limited resources. This task, called the *random-number generation task*, requires the research participants to supply one digit every second, in a random sequence described in this demonstration. As Demonstration 4.4 illustrates, the task is challenging. Approximately every 2 minutes, the researcher interrupted the task and asked the participants to write down any thoughts.

The researchers then inspected the trials on which the participants reported that they had been thinking about the numbers. On those trials, the results showed that the participants had been able to successfully generate a random sequence of numbers. In contrast, when the participants reported daydreaming, their number sequences were far from random. Apparently, their daydreaming occupied such a large portion of the resources of the central executive that they could not create a truly random sequence of numbers.

Neuroscience Research on the Central Executive. In general, researchers know less about the biological underpinnings of the central executive than they know about the phonological loop or the visuospatial sketchpad. However, neuroscientists have gathered data from people with frontal-lobe lesions, as well as from neuroimaging research. This research clearly shows that the frontal lobe of the cortex is the most active portion of the brain when people work on a variety of central-executive tasks (Baddeley, 2006; Han & Kim, 2004; Smith & Jonides, 1997). However, the executive processes do not seem to be confined to any particular locations within the frontal lobe (Beardsley, 1997; Carpenter et al., 2000).

To some extent, this uncertainty about frontal-lobe activity is due to the fact that the central executive actually handles a large number of distinctive tasks (Baddeley, 2000a, 2006; Smith & Jonides, 1999). For example, suppose you are writing a paper for your cognitive psychology course. While you are working on the paper, your central executive may inhibit you from paying attention to some research articles that would distract you from your topic. The central executive may also help you plan the order of topics in your outline. In addition, it guides you as you make decisions about your time frame for writing the paper. Each of these central-executive tasks seems qualitatively different, though all are clearly challenging. Perhaps we'll have more definitive answers about the biological correlates of the central executive once we have a more clear-cut classification of the kinds of tasks that the central executive performs.

Episodic Buffer

Approximately twenty-five years after Alan Baddeley proposed his original model of working memory, he proposed a fourth component of working memory called the *episodic buffer* (Baddeley, 2000a, 2000b, 2006). You can locate this component in Figure 4.5 on page 105. The **episodic buffer** serves as a temporary storehouse where we can gather and combine information from the phonological loop, the visuospatial sketchpad, and long-term memory. (As Chapter 5 will explain, the term "episodic" refers to your memories about events that happened to you; these memories describe episodes in your life.)

Why did Baddeley feel compelled to propose the episodic buffer? As Baddeley (2006) explains, his original theory had proposed that the central executive plans and coordinates various cognitive activities. However, the theory had also stated that the central executive did not actually *store* any information. Baddeley therefore proposed the episodic buffer as the component of working memory where auditory, visual, and spatial information can be combined with the information from long-term memory. This arrangement helps to solve the theoretical problem of how working memory integrates information from different modalities (Morrison, 2005).

This episodic buffer actively manipulates information so that you can interpret an earlier experience, solve new problems, and plan future activities. For instance, suppose that you are thinking about an unfortunate experience that occurred yesterday, when you unintentionally said something rude to a friend. You might review this event and try to figure out whether your friend seemed offended; naturally, you'll need to access some information from your long-term memory about your friend's customary behavior. You'll also need to decide whether you do have a problem, and, if so, how you can plan to resolve the problem.

Because the episodic buffer is new, we do not have details about how it works and how it differs from the central executive. However, Baddeley (2000a, 2006) proposes that it has a limited capacity—just as the capacities of the phonological loop and the visuospatial sketchpad are limited.

Furthermore, this episodic buffer is just a temporary memory system, unlike the relatively permanent long-term memory system. Some of the material in the episodic buffer is verbal (e.g., the specific words you used) and some is visuospatial (e.g., your friend's facial expression and how far apart you were standing). The episodic buffer therefore allows you to temporarily store and integrate information from both the phonological loop and the visuospatial sketchpad (Gathercole et al., 2006; Styles, 2006; Towse & Hitch, 2007). This episodic buffer allows us to create a richer, more complex representation of an event. This complex representation can then be stored in our long-term memory.

We have examined four components of the working-memory model, as proposed by Alan Baddeley. Although this model is widely supported, other psychologists have devised somewhat different theories about working memory (e.g., Conway et al., 2007; Cornoldi & Vecchi, 2003; Cowan, 2005; Izawa, 1999; Miyake & Shah, 1999a; Morrison, 2005). However, the theories consistently argue that working memory is complex, flexible, and strategic. The current perspective is certainly different from the view held during the 1950s and 1960s that short-term memory was relatively rigid and had a fixed capacity.

Meanwhile, other psychologists are focusing on individual differences in working memory. This aspect of working memory has become especially productive during the last decade. Working-memory performance is related to numerous important cognitive skills. It's worthwhile to note several individual differences before we begin the individual-differences feature, which examines the relationship between depression and the components of working memory.

1. Scores on working-memory tasks are correlated with overall intelligence and grades in school (Cowan et al., 2007; Gathercole et al., 2004; Oberauer et al., 2007).

2. Scores on central-executive tasks are correlated with verbal fluency, reading comprehension, reasoning ability, and note-taking skills (Daneman & Hannon, 2001; Engle, 2002; Jarrold & Bayliss, 2007; Oberauer et al., 2007; Rosen & Engle, 1997).

3. Scores on tests of working memory—especially the phonological loop—are usually correlated with reading ability (Bayliss et al., 2005; Swanson, 2005).

4. **Attention-deficit/hyperactivity disorder (ADHD)** is a psychological disorder characterized by inattention, hyperactivity, and impulsivity (American Psychiatric Association, 2000). Children with ADHD often have more difficulty than other children on many central-executive tasks, especially when they must inhibit a response, plan a project, or work on two tasks at the same time (Karatekin, 2004; Martinussen et al., 2005; Willcutt et al., 2005).

Individual Differences: Major Depression and Working Memory

For this chapter's individual-differences feature, we will focus on the relationship between psychological depression and working memory. An individual who experiences **major depression** feels sad, discouraged, and hopeless; he or she typically reports feeling fatigued, with little interest in leisure activities (American Psychiatric Association, 2000). Between 10 and 15% of U.S. residents will experience major depression at some point during their lifetime (American Psychiatric Association, 2000). Because major depression is relatively common, it's important to consider how this disorder is related to working memory.

Let's consider a representative study by Gary Christopher and John MacDonald (2005), which compared the working-memory performance of individuals who were either depressed or nondepressed. These researchers tested 35 hospital inpatients who met the criteria for major depression, as well as 29 assistants who worked at the same hospital. The average ages were comparable, 38 for the individuals with depression and 37 for the individuals without depression. The two groups were also comparable in terms of vocabulary skills.

Christopher and MacDonald examined the three major components of Baddeley's model of working memory. For instance, they administered two tests that assessed the phonological loop. One task, for example, asked people to look at a series of similar-sounding letters (such as CDP), while simultaneously repeating the word "the." Then they were instructed to remember the letters in the correct order. The individuals with depression correctly repeated 3.4 letters in a row, in contrast to 5.3 letters for individuals without depression. This difference was statistically significant.

The researchers also administered one test that assessed the visuospatial sketchpad. First, the participants saw a series of visual patterns. Each pattern was arranged in a 3 × 3 display of black and white squares. Each pattern was displayed for 1 second, beginning with 2 patterns and working up to a longer series. The participants then saw a "probe pattern," and they reported whether this pattern matched one of the original patterns. The individuals with depression had an average span of 6.7, in contrast to 7.8 for individuals without depression. Although the difference between the two groups was not as large as on the phonological task, the difference was still statistically significant.

Christopher and MacDonald also administered four tests that assessed the central executive. The two groups of participants performed similarly on two of these tasks, the Brown/Peterson & Peterson task (see pp. 97–98) and a verbal reasoning task.

However, differences emerged on two other tests of central-executive functioning. Specifically, one task required participants to listen to a series of letters and then report them in the reverse order. The individuals with depression had an average span of 2.8, in contrast to an average span of 4.9 for individuals without depression. A final central-executive task required participants to recall the last four letters of a string of letters that varied in length from four to eight letters. The individuals with depression had an average span of 3.2, in contrast to an average span of 7.4 for individuals without depression.

At this point, it's not clear why people with major depression have difficulty with some working-memory tasks, but not others. Still, the general results are consistent with clinical reports: People with depression often comment that they have trouble concentrating. Many report that they are especially distracted by automatic negative thoughts, a topic we considered in Chapter 3. As Christopher and MacDonald (2005) conclude, "These findings emphasize the profound impact that depression has on the day-to-day cognitive activity of people suffering from depression" (p. 397). Poor performance on these daily activities probably increases the level of depression even further. Clearly, clinical psychologists and other mental-health professionals need to know about these important deficits in working memory.

⚙ Section Summary: *The Working-Memory Approach*

1. Alan Baddeley and his coauthors proposed a working-memory approach in which immediate memory is not a passive storehouse; instead, it resembles a workbench where material is continuously being combined and transformed.

2. In a classic study, Baddeley and Hitch (1974) demonstrated that people could perform a verbal task and a spatial task simultaneously, with minimal reduction in speed and accuracy.

3. In the working-memory approach, the phonological loop briefly stores a limited number of sounds, as demonstrated by the pronunciation-time research; additional research shows that items stored in the loop can be confused with other similar-sounding items.

4. The phonological loop is also used for tasks such as reading, learning vocabulary, problem solving, and remembering information.

5. Neuroscience research reveals that phonological tasks typically activate the left hemisphere, including the frontal lobe, the temporal lobe, and the parietal lobe.

6. A second component of the working-memory approach is the visuospatial sketchpad, which stores visual and spatial information. The capacity of this feature is also limited; two visuospatial tasks will interfere with each other if they are performed simultaneously.

7. Activation of the visuospatial sketchpad is typically associated with the right hemisphere, especially the occipital region (for visual tasks), the frontal region, and the parietal region.

8. The central executive integrates information from the phonological loop, the visuospatial sketchpad, and the episodic buffer—as well as from long-term memory. The central executive is important in such tasks as focusing attention, selecting strategies, and suppressing irrelevant information. However, it does not store information.

9. The central executive cannot perform two challenging tasks simultaneously; for example, daydreaming interferes with generating a random-number sequence.

10. According to neuroscience research, the central executive primarily activates various regions within the frontal lobe.

11. A relatively new component to Baddeley's working-memory approach is called the "episodic buffer"; this component temporarily stores material from the phonological loop, the visuospatial sketchpad, and long-term memory.

12. Many psychologists are investigating individual differences in working memory that are related to components of working memory. This research shows that high scores on working-memory tasks are correlated with intelligence, grades in school, verbal fluency, and reading comprehension. Also, children with ADHD have difficulty on many central-executive tasks.

13. Adults who experience major depression have difficulty with a variety of tasks involving the phonological loop, the visuospatial sketchpad, and the central executive.

CHAPTER REVIEW QUESTIONS

1. Describe Miller's classic concept about the magical number 7 ± 2. Why are chunks relevant to this concept? How did the Atkinson-Shiffrin model incorporate the idea of limited memory?

2. What is the serial position effect? Why is this effect related to short-term memory? Also discuss another classic method of measuring short-term memory.

3. What does the research on pronunciation time tell us about the limits of working memory? What specific aspect of Baddeley's model is most likely to be related to pronunciation time?

4. Suppose that you have just been introduced to five students from another college. Using the information on pronunciation time and semantic similarity, why would you find it difficult to remember their names immediately after they have been introduced? How could you increase the likelihood of your remembering their names?

5. According to the discussion of Baddeley's approach, working memory is not just a passive storehouse. Instead, it is like a workbench where material is continually being handled, combined, and transformed. Why is the workbench metaphor more relevant for Baddeley's model than for the Atkinson-Shiffrin model?

6. This chapter describes Baddeley and Hitch's (1974) research on remembering numbers while performing a spatial reasoning task. Why does this research suggest that a model of working memory must have at least two separate stores?

7. Name some tasks that you have performed today that required the use of your phonological loop, the visuospatial sketchpad, the central executive, and the episodic buffer. Can you think of a specific task that uses all four of these working-memory components, as well as long-term memory?

8. What does the central executive do? Why is the metaphor of a business executive relevant when discussing its role in working memory?

9. Turn to Figure 2.1 on page 35. Using the descriptions that you have read in the current chapter, point out which parts of the brain are active for tasks that require (a) the phonological loop, (b) the visuospatial sketchpad, and (c) the central executive.

10. For many decades, researchers in the area of human memory primarily studied college students who are enrolled in introductory psychology courses. Why would the research on working memory not be applicable for someone who is currently experiencing major depression?

KEYWORDS

working memory	chunk	recency effect
short-term memory	rehearsal	primacy effect
long-term memory	serial position effect	control processes

KEYWORDS (continued)

semantics
proactive interference (PI)
release from proactive
   interference
working-memory approach

phonological loop
subvocalization
acoustic confusions
visuospatial sketchpad
central executive

episodic buffer
attention-deficit/hyperactivity
   disorder (ADHD)
major depression

RECOMMENDED READINGS

Conway, A. R. A., et al. (Eds.). (2007). *Variation in working memory*. New York: Oxford University Press. Here is an upper-level book with eleven chapters that focus on individual differences in both normal and atypical individuals. Each chapter concludes with a discussion about a standard set of four theoretical issues, a feature that increases the readability of this book.

Cowan, N. (2005). *Working memory capacity*. New York: Psychology Press. Here's a book for any student who is considering graduate work in cognitive psychology. Cowan discusses theories and research about limits in memory capacity, but he also asks *why* human memory should have limitations.

Logie, R. H. (2003). Spatial and visual working memory: A mental workspace. *The Psychology of Learning and Motivation*, *42*, 37–78. This article is an unusually clear description of the research about the visuospatial sketchpad. The examples are especially well chosen.

Miyake, A. (Ed.). (2001b). Individual differences in working memory [Special issue]. *Journal of Experimental Psychology: General*, *130*, 163–168. The June 2001 issue of this journal presents six articles about individual differences in working memory. The topics include children's working-memory capacity, working memory and math anxiety, and working memory and the Scholastic Assessment Test.

Pickering, S. J. (Ed.) (2006c). *Working memory and education*. Burlington, MA: Elsevier. I strongly recommend this book for undergraduate libraries, because the chapters emphasize applications of working memory to education, rather than focusing on theoretical approaches. A clearly written chapter by Alan Baddeley provides a current discussion of his approach to working memory.

CHAPTER 5

Using Long-Term Memory

PREVIEW

Chapter 5 focuses on long-term memory, in other words, the memories that you've gathered throughout your lifetime. This chapter first examines factors that are relevant when you acquire new information. For example, the research on depth of processing shows that memory is typically more accurate if you process information in terms of its meaning, rather than more superficial characteristics. If you have ever returned to a once-familiar location and experienced a flood of long-lost memories, you know the importance of another factor, called encoding specificity. In addition, emotional factors influence your memory in several ways. For example, if you have been watching a violent show on television, your memory will be relatively poor for the advertisements appearing during that show. We'll also discuss how personality characteristics can influence the way you recall the components of a story.

The next section of the chapter, on the retrieval of memories, demonstrates that memory accuracy can also be influenced by the way memory retrieval is measured. For instance, individuals with amnesia earn low scores on traditional recall tests, but they perform quite well on some nontraditional memory tests. This section also looks at the memory abilities of individuals with expertise in a particular subject area.

Autobiographical memory, the topic of the last section in this chapter, refers to your memory for the everyday events in your life. Your memory is influenced by your general knowledge about objects and events; this general knowledge is usually helpful, but it may create memory errors. This section also examines source monitoring, a process you use when you try to determine whether you really performed an action or merely imagined it. This discussion points out that so-called flashbulb memories are typically not very accurate. Finally, the chapter looks at eyewitness testimony, which shows that misleading information can sometimes alter your memory.

INTRODUCTION

Take a minute to think about the contents of your own long-term memory. For example, can you remember some of the details about the first day that you attended the class for which you are using this textbook? Now try to recall the names of your high school science teachers. Can you remember some of the characteristics of your closest friends during fifth grade? Memory is one of our most important cognitive activities. Consistent with Theme 4 of this book, it is closely connected with numerous other cognitive processes (Einstein & McDaniel, 2004).

Chapter 4 emphasized the fragility of working memory. As that chapter illustrated, information that we want to retain can disappear from memory after less than a minute. In contrast, Chapter 5 demonstrates that your long-term memory can retain material for many decades.

Before we examine long-term memory, let's review some familiar terminology and introduce some important new distinctions. As we noted in earlier chapters, psychologists often divide memory into two basic categories called **working memory** (the brief, immediate memory for material we are currently processing) and long-term memory. **Long-term memory** has a large capacity; it contains our memory for experiences and information that we have accumulated over a lifetime.

Like many psychologists, I'm not firmly convinced that working memory and long-term memory are two distinctly different kinds of memory. However, I *do* believe that the division is a convenient way to partition the enormous amount of research about our memory processes.

Psychologists often subdivide long-term memory into more specific categories. Once again, this subdivision reflects convenience, rather than a conviction that the subdivisions represent distinctly different kinds of memory. One popular system subdivides long-term memory into episodic memory, semantic memory, and procedural memory (Herrmann, Yoder, Gruneberg, & Payne, 2006; Hoerl, 2001; Tulving, 2002).

Episodic memory focuses on your memories for events that happened to you; it allows you to travel backward in subjective time to reminisce about earlier *episodes* in your life. Episodic memory includes your memory for an event that occurred ten years ago, as well as a conversation you had 10 minutes ago. Episodic memory is the major focus of this chapter.

In contrast, **semantic memory** describes your organized knowledge about the world, including your knowledge about words and other factual information. For example, you know that the word *semantic* is related to the word *meaning*, and you know that Ottawa is the capital of Canada. Chapter 8 of this textbook focuses on semantic memory and our general knowledge about the world.

Finally, **procedural memory** refers to your knowledge about how to do something. For instance, you know how to ride a bicycle, and you know how to send an e-mail message to a friend. We will mention some aspects of procedural memory in this chapter, in connection with implicit memory (pp. 136–140), and also in Chapter 6, in connection with prospective memory (pp. 177–180).

In the current chapter, we'll look at three aspects of long-term memory. We'll begin with **encoding,** which refers to your initial acquisition of information; during encoding, information is embedded in your memory (Einstein & McDaniel, 2004). Then we'll explore **retrieval,** which refers to locating information in storage and accessing that information. Our final section examines autobiographical memory. **Autobiographical memory** * refers to memory for events and topics related to your own everyday life. Incidentally, we'll continue to examine long-term memory in Chapter 6, which emphasizes memory-improvement strategies.

---

*Many psychologists consider episodic memory and autobiographical memory to be highly similar. However, others argue that the research on episodic memory emphasizes accuracy, whereas the research on autobiographical memory emphasizes the qualitative "match" between the event and the memory for the event (Koriat et al., 2000). Some psychologists also argue that autobiographical memory may include some semantic information. For example, you know the date on which you were born, even if you have no recall for that life event (Roediger & Marsh, 2003).

ENCODING IN LONG-TERM MEMORY

In this section, we'll look at four important questions about encoding in long-term memory:

1. Are we more likely to remember items that we processed in a deep, meaningful fashion, rather than items processed in a shallow, superficial fashion?

⦿ Demonstration 5.1

Levels of Processing

Read each of the following questions and answer "yes" or "no" with respect to the word that follows.

1.	Is the word in capital letters?	BOOK
2.	Would the word fit this sentence:	
	"I saw a _____ in a pond"?	duck
3.	Does the word rhyme with BLUE?	safe
4.	Would the word fit this sentence:	
	"The girl walked down the _____"?	house
5.	Does the word rhyme with FREIGHT?	WEIGHT
6.	Is the word in small letters?	snow
7.	Would the word fit this sentence:	
	"The _____ was reading a book"?	STUDENT
8.	Does the word rhyme with TYPE?	color
9.	Is the word in capital letters?	flower
10.	Would the word fit this sentence:	
	"Last spring we saw a _____"?	robin
11.	Does the word rhyme with BALL?	HALL
12.	Is the word in small letters?	TREE
13.	Would the word fit this sentence:	
	"My _____ is 6 feet tall"?	TEXTBOOK
14.	Does the word rhyme with SAY?	Day
15.	Is the word in capital letters?	FOX

Now, without looking back over the words, try to remember as many of them as you can. Calculate the percentage of items you recalled correctly for each of the three kinds of tasks: physical appearance, rhyming, and meaning.

---

2. Are we more likely to remember items if the context at the time of encoding matches the context at the time of retrieval?

3. How do emotional factors influence memory accuracy?

4. How do people's goals about social relationships influence memory accuracy?

Before you read further, though, be sure to try Demonstration 5.1 on page 122.

Levels of Processing

In 1972, Fergus Craik and Robert Lockhart wrote an article about the depth-of-processing approach. This article became one of the most influential publications in the history of research on memory (Roediger, Gallo, & Geraci, 2002). The **levels-of-processing approach** argues that deep, meaningful kinds of information processing lead to more permanent retention than shallow, sensory kinds of processing. (This theory is also called the **depth-of-processing approach.**)

The levels-of-processing approach predicts that your recall will be relatively accurate when you use a deep level of processing. In Demonstration 5.1, for instance, you used deep processing when you considered a word's meaning (e.g., whether it would fit in a sentence). The levels-of-processing approach predicts that your recall will be relatively poor when you use a shallow level of processing. For example, you will be less likely to recall a word when you considered its physical appearance (e.g., whether it is typed in capital letters) or its sound (e.g., whether it rhymes with another word).

In general, then, people achieve a deeper level of processing when they extract more meaning from a stimulus. When you analyze for meaning, you may think of other associations, images, and past experiences related to the stimulus. You are especially likely to remember a stimulus that you analyzed at a very deep level (Roediger, Gallo, & Geraci, 2002). As we'll see in Chapter 6, most memory-improvement strategies emphasize deep, meaningful processing.

Let's examine some of the research on the levels-of-processing approach. We'll first consider general material, and then we'll consider an especially deep level of processing called *self-reference*.

Levels of Processing and Memory for General Material. The major hypothesis emerging from Craik and Lockhart's (1972) paper was that deeper levels of processing should produce better recall. For example, in an experiment similar to Demonstration 5.1, Craik and Tulving (1975) found that people were about three times as likely to recall a word if they had originally answered questions about its meaning rather than if they had originally answered questions about the word's physical appearance. Numerous reviews of the research conclude that deep processing of verbal material generally produces better recall than shallow processing (Craik, 1999, 2006; Lockhart, 2001; Roediger & Gallo, 2001).

Deep levels of processing encourage recall because of two factors: distinctiveness and elaboration. **Distinctiveness** means that a stimulus is different from other memory traces. Suppose that you are interviewing for a job. You've just learned that one man is especially important in deciding whether you will be hired, and you want to be sure to remember his name. You'll need to use deep processing and spend extra time processing his name. You'll try to figure out something unusual about his name that makes it different from other names you've heard in this interview context (Hunt, 2006). Furthermore, when you provide a distinctive encoding for a person's name, it will be less vulnerable to interference from other names (Craik, 2006; Schacter & Wiseman, 2006; Tulving & Rosenbaum, 2006).

The second factor that operates with deep levels of processing is **elaboration,** which requires rich processing in terms of meaning and interconnected concepts (Craik, 1999, 2006; Smith, 2006). For example, if you want to understand the term *levels of processing*, you'll need to appreciate how this concept is related to both distinctiveness and elaboration. Think about the way you processed the word *duck* in Demonstration 5.1, for example. Perhaps you thought about the fact that you had indeed seen ducks on ponds and that a restaurant menu had listed duck with an orange sauce. This kind of semantic encoding encouraged rich processing. In contrast, if the instructions for that item had asked whether the word *duck* was printed in capital letters, you would simply have answered "yes" or "no." You would not need to spend time on extensive elaboration.

Let's consider research on the importance of elaboration. Craik and Tulving (1975) asked participants to read sentences and decide whether the words that followed were appropriate to the sentences. Some of the sentence frames were simple, such as "She cooked the _____." Other sentence frames were elaborate, such as "The great bird swooped down and carried off the struggling _____." The word that followed these sentences was either appropriate (for example, *rabbit*) or inappropriate (for example, *rock*). You'll notice that both kinds of sentences required deep or semantic processing. However, the more elaborate, more detailed sentence frame produced far more accurate recall.

Other research demonstrates that deep processing also enhances our memory for faces. For instance, people recognize more photos of faces if they had previously judged whether the person looked honest, rather than judging a more superficial characteristic, such as the width of the person's nose (Bloom & Mudd, 1991; Sporer, 1991). People also recall faces better if they have been instructed to pay attention to the distinctions between faces (Mäntylä, 1997).

Levels of Processing and the Self-Reference Effect. According to the **self-reference effect,** you will remember more information if you try to relate that information to yourself (Burns, 2006; Gillihan & Farah, 2005; Rogers et al., 1977; Schmidt, 2006). Self-reference tasks tend to encourage especially deep processing. Let's look at some representative research on the self-reference effect and then consider a problem with participants who do not follow instructions. Then we'll discuss several factors that help to explain the self-reference effect.

1. *Representative research.* In the classic demonstration of the self-reference effect, T. B. Rogers and his coauthors (1977) asked participants to process lists of words according to three kinds of instructions usually studied in levels-of-processing research. These three instructions included: (1) the words' visual characteristics, (2) their acoustic (sound)

characteristics, or (3) their semantic (meaning) characteristics. Another group processed the words in terms of self-reference: (4) the participants were told to decide whether a particular word could be applied to themselves.

The results showed that recall was poor for the two tasks that used shallow processing—that is, processing in terms of visual characteristics or acoustic characteristics. The recall was much better when people had processed in terms of semantic characteristics. However, the self-reference task produced much better recall than all other tasks.

Apparently, when we think about a word in connection with ourselves, we develop a particularly memorable coding for that word. For example, suppose that you are trying to decide whether the word *generous* applies to yourself. You might remember how you loaned your notes to a friend who had missed class, and you shared a box of candy with your friends—yes, *generous* does apply. The self-reference task requires organization and elaboration. These mental processes increase the probability of recalling an item.

The research on the self-reference effect also demonstrates one of the themes of this book. As Theme 3 proposes, our cognitive system handles positive instances more effectively than negative instances. In the self-reference studies, people are more likely to recall a word that *does* apply to themselves rather than a word that *does not* apply (Bellezza, 1992; Ganellen & Carver, 1985; Roediger & Gallo, 2001). For example, the participants in Bellezza's (1992) study recalled 46% of the adjectives that applied to themselves, compared with 34% of the adjectives that did not apply.

Research shows that the self-reference effect improves recall for participants from different age groups, using a variety of instructions and stimuli (e.g., Thompson et al., 1996). Furthermore, Symons and Johnson (1997) gathered the results of 129 different studies that had been conducted on the self-reference effect, and they performed a meta-analysis. The **meta-analysis technique** is a statistical method for synthesizing numerous studies on a single topic. A meta-analysis computes a statistical index that tells us whether a variable has a statistically significant effect. Symons and Johnson's meta-analysis confirmed the pattern we have described: People recall significantly more items when they use the self-reference technique, rather than semantic processing or any other processing method.

2. Participants' failure to follow instructions. The self-reference effect is definitely robust. However, Mary Ann Foley and her coauthors (1999) have demonstrated that the research may actually *underestimate* the power of self-reference. Specifically, these investigators speculated that research participants might sometimes "cheat" when they have been instructed to use relatively shallow processing for stimuli. In fact, the participants might actually use the self-reference technique instead.

In one of their studies, Foley and her coauthors (1999) instructed students to listen to a list of familiar, concrete nouns. However, before hearing each word, they were told about the kind of mental image they should form. Let's consider two of the conditions, in which the students were instructed (1) to "visualize the object," or (2) to "imagine yourself using the object."

For the first analysis of the data, Foley and her colleagues classified the results according to the instructions supplied by the experimenter, prior to each word. Notice in Table 5.1 that this first analysis produced identical recall for the two conditions.

TABLE 5.1

Percentage of Items Recalled, as a Function of Imagery Condition and Analysis Condition

	Visualize the Object	Imagine Yourself Using the Object
First analysis of data	42%	42%
Second analysis of data	23%	75%

Source: Based on Foley et al., 1999.

That is, students recalled 42% of the words, whether they had been instructed to use relatively shallow processing or deep, self-reference processing.

Fortunately, however, Foley and her colleagues had also asked the students to describe their visual image for each word during the learning task. As the researchers had suspected, people in the "visualize the object" condition often inserted themselves into the mental image, so that they had actually used self-reference processing. In a second analysis, the researchers sorted the words according to the processing methods that the students had actually used, rather than the instructions they had received. As you can see, the second analysis revealed that the recall was more than three times as high for the self-reference condition as for the visualized-object condition.

The research by Foley and her colleagues (1999) has important implications beyond this particular study. The research shows that our cognitive processes are active (Theme 1). People do not just passively follow instructions and do what they are told. Researchers need to keep in mind that participants are likely to transform the instructions, and this transformation can influence the results of the study.

3. *Factors responsible for the self-reference effect.* Let's now turn our attention to another issue: Why should we recall information especially well when we apply it to ourselves? As Tulving and Rosenbaum (2006) emphasize, a cognitive phenomenon typically requires more than just one explanation. Let's consider three factors that contribute to the self-reference effect.

One factor is that the self produces an especially rich set of cues. You can easily link these cues with new information that you are trying to learn. These cues are also distinctive; they seem very different from one another. For example, your trait of honesty seems different from your trait of intelligence (Bellezza, 1984; Bellezza & Hoyt, 1992).

A second factor is that self-reference instructions encourage people to consider how their personal traits are related to one another. As a result, retrieval will be easier and more effective (Burns, 2006; Klein & Kihlstrom, 1986; Thompson et al., 1996).

A third factor is that you rehearse material more frequently if it is associated with yourself. You're also more likely to use rich, complex rehearsal when you associate material with yourself (Thompson et al., 1996). These rehearsal strategies facilitate later recall.

In short, several major factors work together to help you recall material related to yourself. Several years ago, some research also suggested neurological correlates for the self-reference effect (e.g., Craik et al., 1999; Kircher et al., 2000; Macrae et al., 2004).

Unfortunately, however, a careful analysis of the research uncovered inconsistencies in the findings (Gillihan & Farah, 2005). Specifically, when people think about themselves, the instructions do not automatically activate one specific region of the brain. The self-reference effect is well established. Unfortunately, the biological explanation for this effect remains elusive.

The Effects of Context: Encoding Specificity

Does this scenario sound familiar? You are in the bedroom and realize that you need something from the kitchen. Once you arrive in the kitchen, however, you have no idea why you made the trip. Without the context in which you encoded the item you wanted, you cannot retrieve this memory. You return to the bedroom, which is rich with contextual cues, and you immediately remember what you wanted. Similarly, an isolated question on an exam may look completely unfamiliar, although you could probably remember the answer in the appropriate context.

These examples illustrate the **encoding specificity principle,** which states that recall is better if the retrieval context is similar to the encoding context (Brown & Craik, 2000; Nairne, 2005; Tulving & Rosenbaum, 2006). In contrast, forgetting often occurs when the two contexts do not match. Three other, similar terms for the encoding specificity principle are context-dependent memory, transfer-appropriate processing, and reinstatement of context (Craik, 2006; Roediger & Guynn, 1996). Let's now consider this topic of encoding specificity in more detail. We'll begin with some representative research, and then we'll see how the research forces us to modify our earlier conclusions about levels of processing.

Research on Encoding Specificity. In a representative study, Viorica Marian and Caitlin Fausey (2006) tested people living in Chile who were fluent in both English and Spanish. The participants listened to four stories about topics such as chemistry and history. They heard two stories in English and two in Spanish.

After a short delay, the participants listened to questions about each story. Half of the questions were asked in the language that matched the language of the original story (e.g., Spanish-Spanish), and half had a mismatch between the language of the story and the language of the questions (e.g., Spanish-English). The participants were instructed to answer in the same language that was used for the questions.

As you can see on page 128, Figure 5.1 illustrates encoding specificity. For example, people were relatively accurate if they had heard the story in Spanish, and they also answered the questions in Spanish. They were less accurate if they heard the story in Spanish and answered the questions in English. (Incidentally, we will examine bilingualism in more detail in Chapter 10.)

In an earlier, conceptually similar study, participants were relatively accurate when the gender of the voice during encoding matched the gender of the voice during retrieval (Geiselman & Glenny, 1977). They were less accurate when the gender of the voices did not match.

Everyone reading this book can readily recall real-life examples of the encoding specificity principle. Psychologists have also explained why context effects help us to

FIGURE 5.1

Percentage of Items Correctly Recalled, as a Function of Language used during Encoding and Language used during Retrieval.

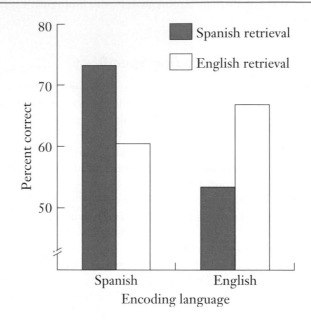

Source: Based on Marian & Fausey, 2006.

function competently in our daily lives. Basically, we often forget material associated with contexts other than our present context. After all, we don't need to remember numerous details that might have been important in a previous setting but are no longer relevant at the present time (Bjork & Bjork, 1988). For instance, you don't want your memory to be cluttered with details about the math textbook you used in fifth grade or the senior trip you took in high school.

Context effects are easy to demonstrate in real life. However, context effects are often inconsistent in the laboratory (e.g., Baddeley, 2004; Nairne, 2005; Roediger & Guynn, 1996). For example, why should context effects be important in one experiment (e.g., Smith et al., 1978), and yet have absolutely no influence in a highly similar replication experiment (e.g., Bjork & Richardson-Klavehn, 1987)? Let's consider two potential explanations.

1. *Different kinds of memory tasks.* One explanation for the discrepancy between real life and the laboratory is that the two situations typically test different kinds of memory (Roediger & Guynn, 1996). To explore this point, we need to introduce two important terms: *recall* and *recognition*. When memory researchers test **recall,** the participants must reproduce the items they learned earlier. (For example, can you recall the definition for *elaboration?*) In contrast, when memory researchers test **recognition,** the participants

must identify whether they saw a particular item at an earlier time. (For example, did the word *morphology* appear earlier in this chapter?)

Let's return to encoding specificity. Our real-life examples often describe a situation in which we *recall* an earlier experience, and that experience occurred many years earlier (Roediger & Guynn, 1996). Encoding specificity is typically strong in these real-life, long-delay situations. For example, when I smell a particular flower called verbena, I am instantly transported back to a childhood scene in my grandmother's garden. I specifically recall walking through the garden with my cousins, an experience that happened decades ago. In contrast, the laboratory research focuses on *recognition,* rather than *recall:* "Did this word appear on the list you saw earlier?" Furthermore, that list was typically presented less than an hour earlier. Encoding specificity is typically weak in these laboratory, short-delay situations.

In summary, then, the encoding-specificity effect is most likely to occur in memory tasks that (a) assess your recall, (b) use real-life incidents, and (c) examine events that happened long ago.

2. *Physical versus mental context.* In their studies on encoding specificity, researchers often manipulate the *physical* context in which material is encoded and retrieved. However, physical context may not be as important as *mental* context. It is possible that physical details—such as the characteristics of the room—are relatively trivial in determining whether the encoding context matches the retrieval context. Instead, as Eich (1995) points out, "How well information transfers from one environment to another depends on how similar the environments feel, rather than on how similar they look" (p. 293).

Eich's comment should remind you of the study by Foley and her colleagues (1999), in which participants' mental activities often did not match the researchers' specific instructions. (See pp. 125 to 126, earlier in this chapter.) Researchers need to look beyond the variables that they believe they are manipulating and pay attention to the processes going on inside the participants' heads. This importance of mental activities is also crucial to the next topic, which brings us back to the level-of-processing issue.

Levels of Processing and Encoding Specificity. Craik and Lockhart's (1972) original description of the levels-of-processing approach emphasized *encoding,* or how items are placed into memory. It did not mention details about *retrieval,* or how items are recovered from memory. However, people recall more material if the retrieval conditions match the encoding conditions (Moscovitch & Craik, 1976). Thus, encoding specificity can override level of processing. In fact, shallow processing can be more effective than deep processing when the retrieval task emphasizes superficial information. Notice that this point is *not* consistent with the original formulation of the levels-of-processing approach.

Let's consider a study that demonstrates the importance of the similarity between encoding and retrieval conditions (Bransford et al., 1979). Suppose that you performed the various encoding tasks in Demonstration 5.1 on page 122. Imagine, however, that you were then tested in terms of rhyming patterns, rather than in terms of recalling the words on that list. For example, you might be asked, "Was there a word on the list that rhymed with *toy?*" People usually perform better on this rhyming test if they had originally performed the shallow-encoding task (rhyming), rather than the deep-encoding task (meaning). This area of research demonstrates that deep, semantic processing is effective only if the retrieval conditions also emphasize these deeper, more meaningful features (Roediger & Guynn, 1996).

Theme 4 of this textbook points out that our cognitive processes are often interrelated. The research on encoding specificity emphasizes that memory often requires problem solving: To determine how to store some information, you'll need to figure out the characteristics of the retrieval task (Phillips, 1995). For example, how would you study the material in this chapter if you knew you would be tested on your *recall* (e.g., by answering essay questions like those at the end of each chapter)? Would your study techniques be different if you were tested on your *recognition* (e.g., by having to answer multiple-choice questions)?

In summary, then, memory is sometimes—but not always—enhanced when the retrieval context resembles the encoding context (Nairne, 2005). However, the benefits of encoding specificity are more likely when items are tested by recall (rather than recognition), when the stimuli are real-life events, and when the items have been in memory for a long time. In addition, encoding specificity depends on mental context more than physical context. Furthermore, we've seen that encoding specificity can modify the level-of-processing effect; in some cases, the match between encoding and retrieval is even more important than deep processing. As you'll see next, context is also relevant when we examine how emotions and mood can influence memory.

Emotions, Mood, and Memory

During the last decade, the amount of psychological research on emotions, mood, and memory has increased dramatically (Uttl, Siegenthaler, & Ohta, 2006). In everyday speech, we often use the terms *emotion* and *mood* interchangeably, and the terms are somewhat similar. However, psychologists define **emotion** as a reaction to a specific stimulus. In contrast, **mood** refers to a more general, long-lasting experience (Bower & Forgas, 2000). For example, you may have a negative emotional reaction to the unpleasant fragrance you just smelled in a locker room, whereas you may be in a relatively positive mood today. Before you read further, try Demonstration 5.2.

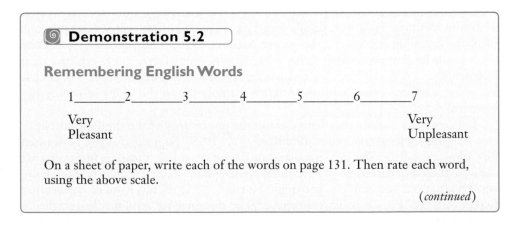

⑨ Demonstration 5.2

Remembering English Words

1_____2_____3_____4_____5_____6_____7

Very   Very
Pleasant   Unpleasant

On a sheet of paper, write each of the words on page 131. Then rate each word, using the above scale.

(*continued*)

1. Hope	9. Loss	17. Insult
2. Fool	10. Trust	18. Praise
3. Style	11. Theft	19. Panic
4. Interest	12. Liberty	20. Grudge
5. Quarrel	13. Decay	21. Travel
6. Hunger	14. Comfort	22. Fraud
7. Cure	15. Benefit	23. Wisdom
8. Beauty	16. Trouble	24. Rumble

Now cover up this list for the remainder of the demonstration. Take a break for a few minutes. Then write down as many words as you can recall. Count how many of the following words you remembered correctly: Hope, Style, Interest, Cure, Beauty, Trust, Liberty, Comfort, Benefit, Praise, Travel, Wisdom.

Then count how many of the following words you remembered correctly: Fool, Quarrel, Hunger, Loss, Theft, Decay, Trouble, Insult, Panic, Grudge, Fraud, Rumble.

Did you recall more from the first category or the second category?

Source: Balch, 2006b.

Cognitive psychologists acknowledge that emotion and mood can influence our cognitive processes. Let's consider two ways in which emotion and mood can affect our memory:

1. We typically remember pleasant stimuli more accurately than other stimuli;
2. We typically recall material more accurately if our mood matches the emotional nature of the material, an effect called *mood congruence.*

Memory for Items Differing in Emotion. In 1978, my coauthor and I proposed that the people's enhanced recall of pleasant items is part of a more general *Pollyanna Principle* (Matlin & Stang, 1978). The **Pollyanna Principle** states that pleasant items are usually processed more efficiently and more accurately than less pleasant items. The principle holds true for a wide variety of phenomena in perception, language, and decision making (Matlin, 2004). However, our focus in this chapter is on long-term memory. Let's consider several ways in which the emotional nature of the stimuli can influence memory.

1. *More accurate recall for pleasant items.* For nearly a century, psychologists have been interested in the way that emotional tone can influence memory (e.g., Balch, 2006b; Hollingworth, 1910; Thompson et al., 1996). In a typical study, people learn lists of words that are pleasant, neutral, or unpleasant. Then their recall is tested after a delay of several minutes to several months. In a review of the literature, we found that

pleasant items are often recalled better than negative items, particularly if the delay is long (Matlin, 2004; Matlin & Stang, 1978). For example, in 39 of the 52 studies that we located on long-term memory, pleasant items were recalled significantly more accurately than unpleasant items. Incidentally, neutral items are usually recalled *least* accurately of all, suggesting that the intensity of an item's emotional tone is also important (Bohanek et al., 2005; Talarico et al., 2004).

Demonstration 5.2 is a simplified version of a study conducted by William Balch (2006b). Check back to page 131 and count how many pleasant words you recalled from this list: 1, 3, 4, 7, 8, 10, 12, 14, 15, 18, 21, 23. Then count how many words you recalled from this list of unpleasant words: 2, 5, 6, 9, 11, 13, 16, 17, 19, 20, 22, 23. Was your recall more accurate for the pleasant words than for the unpleasant words? When Balch tested introductory psychology students, he found that they recalled significantly more of the positive words.

Furthermore, people generally recall pleasant events more accurately than unpleasant events (Mather, 2006; Walker et al., 1997). One potential explanation is that people's memory for pleasant events is more vivid and clear than for unpleasant events (D'Argembeau et al., 2003; Levine & Bluck, 2004). A related finding is that drivers quickly forget their near-accidents; in fact, they remember only 20% of these accidents just two weeks later (Chapman & Underwood, 2000).

2. *More accurate recall for neutral stimuli associated with pleasant stimuli.* Media violence is an important issue in North American culture. Surveys suggest that about 60% of television programs depict violence. Furthermore, numerous studies have concluded that media violence has an impact on children's aggression (Bushman, 2003; Bushman & Huesmann, 2001; Kirsh, 2006).

However, we'll consider a different component of media violence: Do people remember commercials less accurately when they are associated with violent material? To answer this question, Bushman (1998) recorded 15-minute segments of two videos. One video, *Karate Kid III*, showed violent fighting and destruction of property. The other video, *Gorillas in the Mist*, was judged equally exciting by undergraduate students, but it contained no violence. Bushman then inserted two 30-second advertisements for neutral items into each of the two video clips.

College students watched either the violent or the nonviolent film clip. Then they were asked to recall the two brand names that had been featured in the commercials and to list everything they could recall about the commercials. The results showed significantly better recall—on both measures—for commercials that had appeared in the nonviolent film. Additional research demonstrates that anger and violence typically reduce memory accuracy (Bushman, 1998, 2003, 2005; Gunter et al., 2005; Levine & Burgess, 1997).

Individuals who are concerned about societal violence should be interested in Bushman's research, because they can use this research in persuading advertisers to place their ads during nonviolent programs. Advertisers obviously want viewers to remember their product's name, as well as information about the product. In light of this research, advertisers should be hesitant to sponsor violent programs.

3. *Over time, unpleasant memories fade faster.* Richard Walker and his coauthors (1997) asked undergraduate students to record one personal event each day for about fourteen

weeks and to rate both the pleasantness and the intensity of the event. Three months later, the participants returned, one at a time, for a second session. A researcher read off each event from the previous list, and the student was instructed to rate the current pleasantness of that event. In the analysis of the results, the rating did not change for those events that were originally considered to be neutral. However, the events originally considered to be pleasant were now considered to be slightly less pleasant. In contrast, the events originally considered to be unpleasant were now considered to be much more pleasant. Consistent with the Pollyanna Principle, people tend to rate past events more positively with the passage of time, a phenomenon called the **positivity effect**.

Additional research shows that elderly people are especially likely to show this positivity effect (Kennedy et al., 2004; Mather, 2006). Furthermore, Walker and his colleagues (2003) studied two groups of students; one group consisted of students who did not have tendencies toward depression, and one group had depressive tendencies. Those who did not have depressive tendencies showed the usual positivity effect. In contrast, the students with depressive tendencies showed equal fading for unpleasant and pleasant events. In other words, when people at risk for depression look back on their lives, the unpleasant events still remain unpleasant! As you can imagine, this research has important implications for clinical psychologists. Therapists must address a depressed client's interpretation of past events, as well as the current situation.

So far, we have considered how the pleasantness of the stimuli influences memory. As we've seen, pleasant stimuli usually fare better than less pleasant ones: (1) We often remember them more accurately; (2) we tend to forget information when it is associated with violent, unpleasant stimuli; and (3) over time, pleasant memories fade less than unpleasant memories. Let's now see how memory is influenced by the match between your mood and the emotional tone of the stimuli.

Mood Congruence. A second major category of studies about mood and memory is called *mood congruence*. **Mood congruence** means that you recall material more accurately if it is congruent with your current mood (Fiedler et al., 2003; Joorman & Siemer, 2004; Schwarz, 2001). For example, a person who is in a pleasant mood should remember pleasant material better than unpleasant material, whereas a person in an unpleasant mood should remember unpleasant material better.*

Consider a study by Laura Murray and her colleagues (1999). Like Walker and his colleagues (2003), these researchers tested one group of students who did not have tendencies toward depression, and one group with depressive tendencies. The participants were instructed to look at a series of 20 positive- and 20 negative-trait words. Later, the participants recalled as many words as possible from the original list.

Murray and her colleagues found results that were consistent with earlier research, as well as the research on depression and working memory we considered

---

*A similar-sounding phenomenon is called *mood-dependent memory* in which you may remember more material if your mood at the time of retrieval matches your mood at the time of encoding. Mood-dependent memory is one example of the encoding specificity principle, and the research shows that this effect is often weak or nonexistent (Forgas, 2001; Ryan & Eich, 2000).

TABLE 5.2

Percentage of Items Recalled, as a Function of Mood and the Nature of the Stimulus.

	Type of Stimulus	
Mood category	Positive	Negative
No depressive tendencies	49%	38%
Depressive tendencies	35%	39%

Source: Murray et al., 1999.

in Chapter 4. Specifically, the nondepressed individuals recalled a greater overall percentage of the words than did the depression-prone individuals. In addition, as you can see from Table 5.2, the nondepressed students recalled a significantly greater percentage of positive words than negative words. In contrast, the depression-prone students recalled a slightly greater percentage of negative words than positive words.

In these studies about mood congruence, nondepressed people typically recall more positive than negative material. In contrast, depression-prone people tend to recall more negative material (Fiedler et al., 2003; Mather, 2006; Parrott & Spackman, 2000; Schwarz, 2001). Like the results of the research by Walker and his colleagues (2003), these findings are important for clinical psychologists. If depressed people tend to forget the positive experiences they have had, their depression could increase still further (Schacter, 1999).

Individual Differences: Social Goals and Memory

So far, the Individual Differences features in this book have focused on psychological disorders. In Chapter 2, you saw that people with schizophrenia have difficulty perceiving human faces. Chapter 3 showed that individuals with obsessive-compulsive disorder have more trouble than other people when they try to push a specific thought out of their consciousness. Chapter 4 pointed out that people with major depression typically have deficits in several components of working memory.

In this chapter—and many others in this textbook—our Individual Differences feature will not focus on a psychological problem that might interest clinical psychologists. In this chapter, for example, we will explore a personality characteristic that varies in the general population. In connection with long-term memory, let's consider a dimension called social goals (Strachman & Gable, 2006). **Social goals** refers to your style of interacting with other people, in terms of friendships and other interpersonal relationships.

If you have a high score in **approach social goals,** you tend to emphasize close relationships with other people. On a standardized questionnaire assessing social goals, you would supply a high rating to questions such as "I will be trying to deepen my relationships with my friends this quarter" and "I will be trying to enhance the bonding and intimacy in my close relationships" (Strachman & Gable, 2006, p. 1449). If you have a high score in **avoidance social goals**—as the name suggests—you tend to avoid close relationships with other people. On a questionnaire, you would supply a high rating to questions such as "I will be trying to avoid getting embarrassed, betrayed, or hurt by my friends" and "I will be trying to make sure that nothing bad happens to my close relationships" (p. 1449).

Amy Strachman and Shelly Gable (2006) asked college students to read a story that focused on interpersonal relationships. This story included a variety of statements from all three emotional categories, positive, neutral, and negative. After completing the story, the students were instructed to recall the essay as accurately as possible.

The results of this study showed that social goals were not related to the actual number of items that students recalled correctly. However, the students who were high in approach social goals tended to recall the neutral statements as being more positive than they actually were in the story. In contrast, students who were high in avoidance social goals tended to recall the neutral and positive statements as being more negative than they actually were in the story. This group also remembered more of the negative statements and fewer of the positive statements, compared to those who were high in approach social goals. The research also showed that the differences in recall could not be explained by the participants' mood—the topic we discussed on pages 133 to 134.

In summary, people's personal characteristics help to explain their memory patterns. Specifically, their social goals influence which items they will remember. These social goals also influence whether they remember items as being more positive or more negative than they actually were.

Section Summary: *Encoding in Long-Term Memory*

1. Long-term memory can be subdivided into three categories: episodic memory, semantic memory, and procedural memory; episodic memory is most relevant for the current chapter.

2. The research on levels of processing shows that stimuli are remembered better with deep, meaningful processing, rather than with shallow, sensory processing.

3. Deep processing encourages recall because of distinctiveness and elaboration.

4. Research on the self-reference effect demonstrates that memory is greatly improved by relating stimuli to your own personal experience; to obtain a valid assessment of the self-reference effect, the stimuli must be classified in terms of the participant's actual mental activities, rather than in terms of the experimenter's instructions.

5. The self-reference effect works because the self is a rich source of memory ideas, and because self-reference instructions encourage people to think about how their own characteristics are interrelated. Furthermore, self-reference increases elaborative rehearsal.

6. The encoding-specificity effect is most likely to operate when memory is tested by recall, when real-life events are studied, when the original event happened long ago, and when mental context is emphasized. In addition, encoding specificity can modify the depth-of-processing effect.

7. Research on the influence of emotions and mood on memory shows that (a) people generally recall pleasant stimuli more accurately than unpleasant stimuli; (b) people recall less information if they see the material during a violent television program; (c) unpleasant memories grow more neutral over time, compared to pleasant memories.

8. Memory is more accurate when the material to be learned is congruent with a person's current mood (mood congruence).

9. Students with high scores in "approach social goals" tend to recall stories with neutral statements as being relatively positive. In contrast, students with high scores on "avoidance social goals" tend to recall neutral and positive statements as being relatively negative.

RETRIEVAL IN LONG-TERM MEMORY

So far in this chapter, we have emphasized encoding processes. We examined how your long-term memory could be influenced by the level of processing that you used in encoding the material, by the context at the time of encoding, by emotional and mood-related factors during encoding, and by your social goals.

Naturally, we cannot discuss encoding without also mentioning retrieval. After all, psychologists need to test how accurately you can *retrieve* information in order to examine how effectively you *encoded* the information. Furthermore, many memory errors can be traced to inadequate retrieval strategies (Einstein & McDaniel, 2004).

However, retrieval was relatively unimportant in the preceding section of this chapter. Now we'll move retrieval to the center stage. Let's first consider the distinction between two types of retrieval tasks, called explicit and implicit memory tasks. Then we'll focus on the two extremes of memory ability by exploring the topics of amnesia and memory expertise.

Throughout this section, keep Theme 1 in mind: Our cognitive processes are active, rather than passive. Yes, sometimes we retrieve material from memory in an effortless fashion; you see a friend, and her name seems to spontaneously appear in your memory. Other times, retrieval requires hard work! For example, you might try to recover someone's name by strategically re-creating the context in which you met this person (Koriat, 2000; Roediger, 2000). Who else was present, how long ago was it, and where did this event take place?

Explicit Versus Implicit Memory Tasks

Imagine this scene: A young woman is walking aimlessly down the street, and she is eventually picked up by the police. She seems to be suffering from an extreme form of amnesia, because she has lost all memory of who she is. Unfortunately, she is carrying no identification. Then the police have a breakthrough idea: They ask her to begin dialing phone numbers. As it turns out, she dials her mother's number, even though she is not aware whose number she is dialing.

Daniel Schacter tells this story to illustrate the difference between explicit and implicit measures of memory (as cited in Adler, 1991). This difference can be demonstrated for people with normal memory as well as for those who have amnesia. Let us clarify the basic concepts of this distinction and then look at some research.

---

⑨ Demonstration 5.3

Explicit and Implicit Memory Tasks

Take out a piece of paper. Then read the following list of words:

> picture   commerce   motion   village   vessel
> window   number   horse   custom   amount
> fellow   advice   dozen   flower   kitchen   bookstore

Now cover up that list for the remainder of the demonstration. Take a break for a few minutes and then try the following tasks:

A. *Explicit Memory Tasks*

1. *Recall:* On the piece of paper, write down as many of those words as you can recall.
2. *Recognition:* From the list below, circle the words that appeared on the original list:

> woodpile   fellow   leaflet   fitness   number   butter
> motion   table   people   dozen   napkin
> picture   kitchen   bookstore   horse   advice

B. *Implicit Memory Tasks*

1. *Word completion:* From the word fragments below, provide an appropriate, complete word. You may choose any word you wish.

> v_s_e_   l_t_e_   v_l_a_e   p_a_t_c   m_t_o_   m_n_a_
> n_t_b_o_   c_m_e_c   a_v_c_   t_b_e_   f_o_e_   c_r_o_
> h_m_w_r_   b_o_s_o_e

2. *Repetition priming:* Perform the following tasks:

- Name three rooms in a typical house.
- Name three different kinds of animals.
- Name three different kinds of stores.

Definitions and Examples. Demonstration 5.3 provides two examples of explicit memory tasks and two examples of implicit memory tasks. Try these examples before you read further.

So far, we have focused on explicit memory tasks. On an **explicit memory task,** the researcher directly instructs participants to remember information; the participants are conscious that their memory is being tested, and the test requires them to intentionally retrieve some information they previously learned (Roediger & Amir, 2005).

Almost all the research we have discussed in Chapters 4 and 5 has used explicit memory tests. The most common explicit memory test is *recall*. As we discussed in the preceding section, a recall test requires the participant to reproduce items that were learned earlier. Another explicit memory test is *recognition*, in which the participant must identify which items on a list had been presented at an earlier time.

In contrast, an implicit memory task assesses memory indirectly. On an **implicit memory task,** people see the material (usually a series of words or pictures); later, during the test phase, people are instructed to complete a cognitive task that does not directly ask for either recall or recognition (Lockhart, 2000; Roediger & Amir, 2005). For example, in Part B1 of Demonstration 5.3, you filled in the blanks in several words. Previous experience with the material—in this case, the words at the beginning of the demonstration—facilitated your performance on the task (Roediger & Amir, 2005).

On an implicit memory task, the researchers avoid using words such as *remember* or *recall*. For example, in Schacter's anecdote about the woman with amnesia, dialing a phone number was a test of implicit memory. Implicit memory shows the effects of previous experience that creep out in our ongoing behavior, when we are not making a conscious effort to remember the past (Kihlstrom et al., 2007; Roediger & Amir, 2005).

Researchers have devised numerous measures of implicit memory (Amir & Selvig, 2005; Roediger & Amir, 2005; Wiers & Stacy, 2006). You tried two of these in Demonstration 5.3 . For example, in Task B1, if you stored the words in the original list in your memory, you would be able to complete those words (for example, *commerce* and *village*) faster than the words in Task B1 that had not been on the list (for example, *letter* and *plastic*).

Task B2 illustrates a second measure of implicit memory, called a repetition priming task. In a **repetition priming task,** recent exposure to a word increases the likelihood that you'll think of this particular word, when you are given a cue that could evoke many different words. For example, on Task B2, you were likely to supply the words *kitchen, horse,* and *bookstore*—words you had seen at the beginning of the demonstration. In contrast, you were less likely to supply words you had not seen, such as *dining room, cow,* and *drugstore*.

During the last twenty five years, implicit memory has become a popular topic in research on memory (Roediger & Amir, 2005). For example, we'll see in Chapter 8 that researchers can use implicit memory tasks to assess people's unconscious attitudes about gender, ethnicity, and other social categories (Nosek et al., 2007).

Research with Normal Adults. A variety of studies demonstrate that normal adults often cannot remember stimuli when they are tested on an explicit memory task. However, they do remember the stimuli when tested on an implicit memory task.

One intriguing finding focuses on normal adults who have received anesthesia during surgery. These people often show no evidence of memory for information transmitted under anesthesia (for example, a conversation between the surgeon and the anesthesiologist) when memory is assessed with explicit memory tests. However, in most of the research studies, these people do remember a substantial amount of information when memory is assessed with implicit memory tests (Kihlstrom & Cork, 2007).

Some of the studies on explicit and implicit memory illustrate a pattern that researchers call a dissociation. A **dissociation** occurs when a variable has large effects on Test A, but little or no effects on Test B; a dissociation also occurs when a variable has one kind of effect if measured by Test A, and exactly the opposite effect if measured by Test B. The term *dissociation* is similar to the concept of a statistical interaction, a term that might sound familiar if you've taken a course in statistics.

Let's consider an illustration of a dissociation based on the research on the level-of-processing effect. As you know from the first section of this chapter, people typically recall more words if they have used deep levels of processing to encode them. For example, participants recall more items on an explicit memory test if they had originally used semantic encoding rather than encoding physical appearance. However, on an *implicit* memory test, semantic and perceptual encoding may produce similar memory scores, or people may even score lower if they had used semantic encoding (e.g., Jones, 1999; Richardson-Klavehn & Gardiner, 1998). Notice that these results fit the definition of a dissociation because depth of processing has a large positive effect on memory scores on Test A (an explicit memory task), but depth of processing has no effect or even a negative effect on memory scores on Test B (an implicit memory task).

We need to emphasize, however, that some variables have the same effect on both explicit and implicit memory. For example, in Chapter 4 we discussed proactive interference. **Proactive interference** means that people have trouble learning new material because previously learned material keeps interfering with new learning. According to the research, proactive interference operates on both explicit and implicit memory tasks (Lustig & Hasher, 2001a, 2001b). In both cases, memory for new material is less accurate because the earlier material keeps interfering.

The research on implicit memory illustrates that people often know more than they can reveal in actual recall. As a result, this research has potential implications for applied areas such as education, clinical psychology, and advertising (Jones, 1999).

Individuals with Amnesia

In this section and the next, we'll consider individuals who have unusual memory abilities. We'll first discuss people with **amnesia,** who have severe deficits in their episodic memory (Kalat, 2007). Then we'll examine the impressive performance of memory experts.

One form of amnesia is **retrograde amnesia,** or loss of memory for events that occurred *prior* to brain damage; the deficit is especially severe for events that occurred during the years just before the damage (Brown, 2002; Meeter et al., 2006; Meeter & Murre, 2004). For example, one woman known by the initials L.T. cannot recall events in her life that happened prior to an accident that injured her brain. However, her memory is normal for events after the injury (Conway & Fthenaki, 2000; Riccio et al., 2003).

The other form of amnesia is **anterograde amnesia,** or loss of memory for events that have occurred *after* brain damage (Kalat, 2007). For several decades, researchers have studied a man with anterograde amnesia who is known only by his initials, H.M. (James & MacKay, 2001; Milner, 1966). H.M. had such serious epilepsy that neurosurgeons operated on his brain in 1953. Specifically, they removed a portion of his temporal lobe region, as well as his **hippocampus,** a structure underneath the cortex that is important in many learning and memory tasks (Thompson, 2005).

The operation successfully cured H.M.'s epilepsy, but it left him with a severe kind of memory loss. H.M. has normal semantic memory, and he can accurately recall events that occurred before his surgery. However, he cannot learn or retain new information. For example, in 1980, he moved to a nursing home. Four years later, he still could not describe where he lived. For many years after the operation, he persisted in reporting that the year was 1953 (Corkin, 1984).

The research demonstrates that people with anterograde amnesia often recall almost nothing on tests of explicit memory such as recall or recognition. That is, they do poorly when asked to *consciously* remember an event that happened after they developed amnesia. Interestingly, however, they perform fairly accurately on tests of implicit memory (Schacter & Badgaiyan, 2001; Weiskrantz, 2000).

Let's consider the pioneering work conducted by Elizabeth Warrington and Lawrence Weiskrantz (1970). These researchers presented some English words to individuals with anterograde amnesia. Then the researchers administered several recall and recognition tasks. Compared to normal control-group participants, the individuals with amnesia performed much more poorly on both kinds of explicit memory tasks. So far, then, the results are not surprising.

However, Warrington and Weiskrantz (1970) also administered implicit memory tasks. The tasks were presented as word-guessing games, though they actually assessed memory for the words shown earlier. For example, they showed the previously presented English words in a mutilated form that was difficult to read. The participants were told to guess which word was represented. Amazingly, the implicit memory scores of the participants with amnesia and the control-group participants were virtually identical. Both groups correctly supplied the words from the previous list for about 45% of the mutilated stimuli. These results have been replicated many times since the original research, using both visual and auditory tasks (e.g., Bower, 1998; Roediger & Amir, 2005; Schacter et al., 1994).

Notice that the research by Warrington and Weiskrantz (1970) is an excellent example of a dissociation. As we noted, a dissociation occurs when a variable has a large effect on one kind of test, but little or no effect on another kind of test. In this case, the dissociation was evident because the variable of memory status (amnesic versus control) had a major effect when measured by explicit memory tests, but this same variable had no effect when measured by implicit memory tests.

The research on individuals with amnesia reminds us that memory is an extremely complex cognitive process. Specifically, people who apparently remember nothing when their memory is tested on a recall task can actually perform quite well when memory is measured in a different fashion.

Expertise

Whereas people with amnesia experience severe memory deficits, people with expertise demonstrate impressive memory abilities. A person with **expertise** shows consistently exceptional performance on representative tasks in a particular area (Ericsson, 2003a, 2003b, 2006). K. Anders Ericsson is the psychologist who currently has the greatest "expertise" in the area of expertise. As Ericsson emphasizes (cited in Schraw, 2005), practice is more important than inborn skill. In fact, expertise in a particular domain requires intensive, practice on a daily basis (Ericsson, 2003a; Ericsson et al., 2004).

Our first topic in this discussion illustrates that people's expertise is context specific. Next, we'll examine some of the ways in which memory experts and novices differ. Our final topic—indirectly related to expertise—explores how people can identify individuals from their own ethnic background more accurately than individuals from another ethnic group.

The Context-Specific Nature of Expertise. Researchers have studied memory experts in numerous areas, such as chess, sports, ballet, maps, musical notation, and memorizing extremely long sequences of numbers. In general, researchers have found a strong positive correlation between knowledge about an area and memory performance in that area (Schraw, 2005; Vicente & Wang, 1998). Experts remember material significantly more accurately than nonexperts, in terms of both recognition and recall (Brandt et al., 2005). Furthermore, experts' memory is more accurate immediately after the material is presented, and also after a long delay (Noice & Noice, 2002).

Interestingly, however, people who are expert in one area seldom display outstanding *general* memory skills (Kimball & Holyoak, 2000; Wilding & Valentine, 1997). For instance, chess masters are outstanding in their memory for chess positions, but they do not differ from nonexperts in their basic cognitive and perceptual abilities (Cranberg & Albert, 1988).

Furthermore, memory experts typically do not receive exceptional scores on tests of intelligence (Wilding & Valentine, 1997). For example, men who are experts in remembering information at the horse races do not score especially high on standard IQ tests. In fact, one horse race expert had an eighth-grade education and an IQ of 92 (Ceci & Liker, 1986). Incidentally, in Chapter 11, we'll see that memory expertise for specific areas of knowledge also helps people solve problems in these areas.

How Do Experts and Novices Differ? From the information we've discussed—as well as from other resources—we know that memory experts have several advantages over nonexperts (Ericsson & Kintsch, 1995; Ericsson & Lehmann, 1996; Herrmann, Gruneberg, et al., 2006; Herrmann, Yoder, et al., 2006; Kimball & Holyoak, 2000; McCormick, 2003; Noice & Noice, 1997; Roediger, Marsh, & Lee, 2002; Schraw, 2005; Simon & Gobet, 2000; Van Overschelde et al., 2005; Wilding & Valentine, 1997). Let's consider these advantages:

1. Experts possess a well-organized, carefully learned knowledge structure, which assists them during both encoding and retrieval. For instance, chess players store a number of common patterns that they can quickly access.

2. Experts are more likely to reorganize the new material they must recall, forming meaningful chunks in which related material is grouped together.

3. Experts typically have more vivid visual images for the items they must recall.

4. Experts work hard to emphasize the distinctiveness of each stimulus during encoding. As we saw on pages 123 to 124, distinctiveness is essential for accurate memory.

5. Experts rehearse in a different fashion. For example, an actor may rehearse his or her lines by focusing on words that are likely to trigger recall.

6. Experts are better at reconstructing missing portions of information from material that they partially remember.

7. Experts are more skilled at predicting the difficulty of a task and at monitoring their progress on this task.

Throughout this book, we have emphasized that our cognitive processes are active, efficient, and accurate (Themes 1 and 2). These cognitive processes also employ both top-down and bottom-up strategies (Theme 5). As we can see from the previous list, these characteristics are especially well developed for someone with memory expertise in a given area.

Own-Race Bias.   The information on expertise has interesting implications for face recognition. Specifically, people are generally more accurate in identifying members of their own ethnic group than members of another ethnic group, a phenomenon called **own-race bias** (Brigham et al., 2007; Meissner et al., 2005; Walker & Hewstone, 2006). This effect is also known as the *other-race effect* or the *cross-race effect*.

Research in the United States typically shows that both Black and European American individuals are more accurate in recognizing faces of people from their own ethnic group (MacLin & Malpass, 2001; Meissner et al., 2005; Wright et al., 2003). Similar findings are reported for face recognition with European American and Asian individuals (Brigham et al., 2007; Ng & Lindsay, 1994).

One explanation for the own-race bias is that people develop expertise for the facial features of the ethnic group with whom they frequently interact. As a result, faces representing their own ethnic group acquire distinctiveness. As you know from previous discussions in this chapter, memory is most accurate when the stimuli are distinctive. Consistent with this research, Van Wallendael and Kuhn (1997) found that Black students rated Black faces as more distinctive than European American faces. In contrast, European American students rated European American faces as more distinctive than Black faces.

In the United States, Blacks represent about 13% of the population, and Latinas/os represent about 14% of the population (U.S. Census Bureau, 2006). In contrast, the largest non-White population in Great Britain is South Asian, a group with origins in countries such as India, Pakistan, and Bangladesh. South Asians represent only about 4% of the British population (Walker & Hewstone, 2006). As a result, White people would have relatively little experience in interacting with South Asian people. In contrast, South Asian people would have relatively extensive experience interacting with White people.

Pamela Walker and Miles Hewstone (2006) studied facial recognition in British high school students who were either White or South Asian. Each student looked at photographs of faces that had been altered. Within each gender category, the faces differed along a continuum. On one end of the continuum, the faces looked clearly South Asian; at the other end, the faces looked clearly White. Other faces represented intermediate combinations of the two sets of facial features. In each case, the student saw photos of two faces—one after the other—and then judged whether the faces were the same or different.

As you can see in Figure 5.2, the British White students made more accurate judgments for White faces than for South Asian faces. In contrast, the British South Asian students were equally accurate for both kinds of faces. It would be interesting to see whether British White students also demonstrate more of the own-race bias in long-term memory for faces, compared to South Asian students.

We would expect to find that own-race bias decreases when people have greater contact with members of other ethnic groups. (In fact, the research by Walker and Hewstone suggests this outcome.) The research generally shows some support for the contact hypothesis, although the evidence is not strong (Brigham et al., 2007; Meissner & Brigham, 2001; Wright et al., 2003).

FIGURE 5.2

Percentage of Accurate Responses in a Discrimination Task, as a Function of the Ethnic Group of the Student and the Ethnic Group of the Faces.

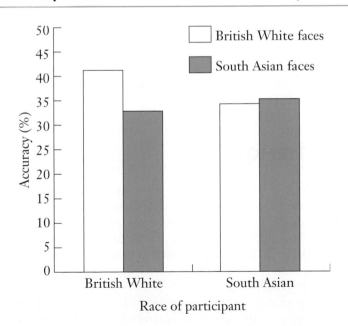

Source: Based on Walker and Hewstone (2006).

Some researchers have explored expertise in social categories other than ethnicity. For example, Anastasi and Rhodes (2003) studied younger-adult and older-adult participants. They found that participants from these two age groups were most accurate in identifying people in their own group. In the next section, we will explore several additional factors that influence accuracy in identifying faces.

Section Summary: *Retrieval in Long-Term Memory*

1. Explicit memory tasks instruct participants to recall or recognize information. In contrast, implicit memory tasks require participants to perform a cognitive task, such as completing a word that has missing letters.

2. When people hear information while they are anesthetized, they may recall much more of that information on an implicit task than on an explicit task. Research also indicates that depth of processing has no impact on an implicit memory task, even though it has a major effect on an explicit memory task.

3. Individuals with retrograde amnesia have difficulty recalling events that occurred prior to brain damage.

4. Individuals with anterograde amnesia have difficulty recalling events that occurred after brain damage. They may recall almost nothing on tests of explicit memory; however, on tests of implicit memory, they can perform as accurately as people without brain damage.

5. Expertise has an important effect on long-term memory, although expertise is context-specific. Compared to novices, experts have cognitive advantages such as well-organized knowledge structures and vivid visual images.

6. According to the research on own-race bias, people have more expertise in recognizing faces from their own ethnic group, in part because their expertise makes these faces more distinctive.

AUTOBIOGRAPHICAL MEMORY

As we noted at the beginning of the chapter, autobiographical memory is memory for events and issues related to yourself. Autobiographical memory usually includes a verbal narrative; it may also include imagery about the events, emotional reactions, and procedural information (Roediger, Marsh, & Lee, 2002). In general, the research in this area examines recall for naturally occurring events that happen outside the laboratory. Your autobiographical memory is a vital part of your identity, shaping your personal history and your self-concept (Lampinen et al., 2004; Lieberman, 2007; McAdams, 2004).

The previous two sections in this chapter focused on encoding and retrieval in long-term memory, and they primarily examined laboratory research. In general, the dependent variable in these studies is the number of items correctly recalled—a *quantity*-oriented approach to memory (Koriat et al., 2000). In contrast, in autobiographical memory, the dependent variable is memory *accuracy;* does your recall match the actual events that happened, or does it distort the events? Therefore, autobiographical memory usually focuses on the correspondence between an actual event and an individual's memory for that event.

The studies of autobiographical memory are typically high in ecological validity (Bahrick, 2005; Esgate & Groome, 2005; Lampinen et al., 2004). As we noted in Chapter 1, a study has **ecological validity** if the conditions in which the research is conducted are similar to the natural setting to which the results will be applied.

Interest in autobiographical memory has grown rapidly during the last thirty years. Here are some representative topics:

1. Immigrant Latinas/os recalling their life stories in both English and Spanish (Schrauf & Rubin, 2001).

2. Older adults describing themes in their life stories (Bluck & Habermas, 2001; Pasupathi, 2001).

3. Memory failures that people experience in their everyday life (Gennaro et al., 2005; Herrmann & Gruneberg, 2006).

4. "Earwitness testimony," or accuracy in identifying someone's voice (Kerstholt et al., 2006; Yarmey, 2007).

5. Brain-imaging studies of autobiographical memory (Conway, 2001; Lieberman, 2007).

This discussion of autobiographical memory first looks at schemas. Schemas can shape your memory for previous event, so that this memory becomes more consistent with your current viewpoint. Next, we'll examine source monitoring, which shows that you can make mistakes when you try to remember where and when you learned certain information. Then an in-depth section on the so-called "flashbulb memory" examines some especially vivid memories. Our final topic is eyewitness testimony, an area of research that has obvious applications in the courtroom.

This discussion of autobiographical memory illustrates several important characteristics of our memory for life events:

1. Although we sometimes make errors, our memory is often accurate for a variety of information (Theme 2). For example, adults can recall the names of streets near their childhood home and material from their elementary school textbooks (Read & Connolly, 2007).

2. When people do make mistakes, they generally concern peripheral details and specific information about commonplace events, rather than central information about important events (Goldsmith et al., 2005; Sutherland & Hayne, 2001; Tuckey & Brewer, 2003). In fact, it's usually helpful *not* to remember numerous small details that would interfere with memory for more important information (Bjork et al., 2005).

3. Our memories often blend together information; we actively construct a memory at the time of retrieval (Davis & Loftus, 2007; Kelley & Jacoby, 2000; Koriat, 2000). Notice that this constructive process is consistent with Theme 1: Our cognitive processes are typically active, rather than passive.

Schemas and Autobiographical Memory

This discussion of schemas emphasizes how you remember common, ordinary events. A **schema** consists of your general knowledge or expectation, which is distilled from your past experiences with an event or a person (Davis & Loftus, 2007; Koriat et al., 2000). For example, you have probably developed a schema for "eating lunch." You tend to sit in a particular area with the same group of people. Your conversation topics may also be reasonably standardized. You have also developed a schema for the events that occur during the first day of a class and for purchasing items in a grocery store. You have even developed a schema for yourself.

We use schemas to guide our recall. As time passes, we still remember the gist of an event, although we may forget the schema-irrelevant information (Davis & Loftus, 2007; Goldsmith et al., 2005; Tuckey & Brewer, 2003). Chapter 8 explores in more detail how schemas influence a variety of cognitive processes. However, in the present chapter, we'll examine a topic that is especially relevant to autobiographical memory, called the consistency bias.

During recall, we often reveal a **consistency bias;** that is, we tend to exaggerate the consistency between our past feelings and beliefs and our current viewpoint (Davis & Loftus, 2007; Schacter, 1999, 2001). As a consequence, our memory of the past may be distorted. For example, suppose that a researcher asks you today to recall how you felt about feminism when you were a high school student. You would tend to construct your previous emotions so that they would be consistent with your current emotions. We generally see ourselves as being consistent and stable (Greenwald et al., 2002). As a result, we underestimate how we have changed throughout our lives. For example, we recall that our previous political views and activities are highly similar to our current perspective. As Schacter (2001) summarizes the consistency bias, "The way we were depends on the way we are" (p. 139).

The consistency bias suggests that we tell our life stories so that they are consistent with our current schemas about ourselves (Ceballo, 1999). For example, Honig (1997), a historian, interviewed Chicana garment workers who had participated in a strike at a garment manufacturing company in El Paso, Texas. Shortly after the strike, these women viewed the strike as a life-transforming experience that had changed them from timid factory workers into fearless, self-confident activists.

When Honig returned to interview these same women several years later, they recalled that they had *always* been assertive and nonconforming—even prior to the strike. It's possible that they selectively recalled assertive episodes from their pre-strike lives—episodes consistent with their current self-schemas. As Honig argues, these Chicana garment workers are "not inventing nonexistent past experiences, but they are retelling them with the language, perceptions, and mandates of their present" (1997, p. 154). Notice the interdisciplinary nature of research on the consistency bias: It explores the interface of cognitive psychology, personality/social psychology, and history.

We have seen that schemas can influence our memories of the past, so that they seem more similar to our present feelings, beliefs, and actions. Now let's move away from schemas to consider another component of autobiographical memory, called source monitoring.

Source Monitoring

Something like this has certainly happened to you: You borrowed a book from a friend, and you distinctly remember returning it. However, the next day, you find that the book is still on your desk. Apparently, you simply *imagined* returning the book. Or perhaps you are trying to recall where you learned some background information about a movie you saw. Did a friend tell you this information, or did you learn it from a review of the movie? This process of trying to identify the origin of memories and beliefs is called **source monitoring** (Johnson, 1997, 2002; Pansky et al., 2005).

According to Marcia Johnson and Carol Raye (2000), we often try to sort out the source of information in our memory. We include cues such as our schemas and expectations, as well as the nature of the details. Unfortunately, our source monitoring sometimes produces mistakes.

For example, suppose that you are working on a project with a classmate, and you are trying to anticipate what suggestions your classmate will supply. Later on, you are likely to remember that your friend actually *did* provide these suggestions (Foley et al., 2006).

In a related study, Marsh and his colleagues (1997) asked two groups of college students to discuss an open-ended question on a topic such as methods for improving their university. One week later, the participants in both groups returned for a second session. One group took a recognition test. Specifically, the participants identified whether each item on a list had been their own idea or someone else's idea. The participants in this group seldom made source-monitoring mistakes; that is, they seldom claimed that an idea generated by another person had really been their own idea.

When the other group returned for the second session, they were given the original open-ended topic. The experimenter asked them to write down new answers to the question—answers that no one had supplied before. Interestingly, this group of individuals frequently committed source-monitoring errors. That is, they frequently wrote down answers that another person had supplied one week earlier. Apparently, a recognition test forces us to adopt stricter criteria with respect to source monitoring. In contrast, our criteria are more relaxed when we generate ideas.

Source-monitoring errors are puzzling. Can't we even remember what we ourselves said, as opposed to what another person said? According to Defeldre (2005), people may also plagiarize inadvertently. For example, one student believed that he had composed a truly new song. However, in reality, the melody of the song was based on a melody composed by another songwriter.

Earlier in the chapter, we saw that our memory has a positive bias; we tend to remember pleasant events, and negative events become more positive as time passes. Similarly, we seem to have a "wishful thinking bias," which leads us to make errors in source monitoring. For example, suppose you consulted a number of sources before you bought a new PDA made by the Handy Dandy company. A friend asks you what information you consulted before making the decision. You'll tend to recall that the extremely positive review for the Handy Dandy model came from a trustworthy source, such as *Consumer Reports*, rather than a less reliable source, such as an e-mail from a friend (Gordon et al., 2005).

In some cases, the mistakes in source monitoring can have much more serious consequences. For many years, Marcia Johnson (1996, 1998, 2002) has emphasized that source-monitoring errors occur at a societal level, not just at the individual level. Our government, the media, and corporations must engage in vigorous source monitoring in order to determine which events really happened and which are fictional. Unfortunately, individuals are seldom aware of source monitoring until they make a source-monitoring error. Similarly, society is seldom aware of source monitoring until we discover that this monitoring has failed.

A representative source-monitoring failure occurred in 2003, when President George W. Bush was trying to provide justifications for starting the Iraq War. In his State of the Union address in early 2003, Bush discussed one important reason to justify invading Iraq. Specifically, he announced that Iraq was negotiating with an African country to buy uranium (an ingredient used in making nuclear weapons).

Six months later, the public learned that this claim was based on clearly falsified documents from Niger, a country in west-central Africa. Also, the Central Intelligence Agency claimed that their agents had tried to warn the President that the information from Niger was false. Furthermore, the President maintained that his State of the Union address had been cleared by the CIA (Isikoff & Lipper, 2003). Unfortunately, several different errors in source monitoring on "the uranium question" probably helped to push the United States into an expensive, destructive war.

Marcia Johnson (2002) emphasizes that government agencies, the media, and corporation executives need to be meticulous about checking the accuracy of their information. Their goal should be to limit both the frequency and the size of source-monitoring errors.

So far, our discussion of autobiographical memory has explored memory schemas and source monitoring. Now let's consider the related topic of "flashbulb memories," which are memories that seem especially vivid. As you'll see, people commit errors when they try to recall the circumstances in which they learned about an important event—just as they commit errors in recalling the circumstances during source monitoring.

IN DEPTH

Flashbulb Memories

At some point in the near future, try Demonstration 5.4. This demonstration illustrates the so-called flashbulb-memory effect. **Flashbulb memory** refers to your memory for the circumstances in which you first learned about a very surprising and emotionally arousing event. Many people believe that they can accurately recall trivial details about what they were doing at the time of this event (Brown & Kulik, 1977; Esgate & Groome, 2005).

One of my clearest flashbulb memories, like many of my generation, is of learning that President John Kennedy had been shot. I was a sophomore at Stanford University, just ready for a midday class in German. As I recall, I had entered the classroom from

> ### ⑨ Demonstration 5.4
>
> #### Flashbulb Memory
>
> Ask several acquaintances whether they can identify any memories of a very surprising event. Tell them, for example, that many people believe that they can recall—in vivid detail—the circumstances in which they learned about the death of President Kennedy, or the September 11, 2001, terrorist attacks.
>
> Also tell them that other vivid memories focus on more personal important events. Ask them to tell you about one or more memories, particularly noting any small details that they recall.

the right, and I was just about to sit down at a long table on the right-hand side of the room. The sun was streaming in from the left. Only one other person was seated in the classroom, a blond fellow named Dewey. He turned around and said, "Did you hear that President Kennedy has been shot?" I also recall my reaction and the reactions of others as they entered the room.

President Kennedy was shot more than forty years ago, yet trivial details of that news still seem stunningly clear to many people (Neisser & Libby, 2000). You can probably think of personal events in your own life that triggered flashbulb memories, such as the death of a relative, a political tragedy, or an amazing surprise.

People also report extremely vivid memories for highly positive events, as well as tragedies. For example, an Indian friend of mine recalls in detail the circumstances in which he heard Mohandas Gandhi—the nonviolent political leader—speaking to a crowd of people in Gauhati, India. My friend was only 5 years old at the time, yet he vividly recalls that Gandhi was wearing a white outfit, and he was accompanied by two women. He can recall that his aunt, who was with him, was wearing a white sari with a gold and red border. He can also distinctly remember how the heat of the day had made him very thirsty.

Let's first consider the classic study by Brown and Kulik (1977) which introduced the term "flashbulb memory." Then we'll discuss the research that focuses on memory for the events of September 11, 2001.

The Classic Study. Roger Brown and James Kulik (1977) were the first researchers to study whether various important political events triggered contextually rich memories. They found that people tended to describe details such as their location when they heard the news and the person who gave them the news. Notice whether your friends included this information in their responses to Demonstration 5.4.

Brown and Kulik (1977) suggested that people's flashbulb memories are more accurate than memories of less surprising events. However, many later studies suggested that people made numerous errors in recalling details of national events, even though they claimed that their memories for these events were very vivid (Roediger, Marsh, & Lee, 2002; Schooler & Eich, 2000).

Memories about September 11, 2001. Several researchers have studied recall of a tragedy that is especially vivid for most U.S. students—the terrorist attacks of September 11, 2001. Let's look at an especially thorough study by Jennifer Talarico and David Rubin (2003), and then we'll discuss additional observations about people's memory for that event.

On September 12, the day after the attacks, Talarico and Rubin asked students at a North Carolina university to report specific details about how they had learned about the attacks. The students also provided similar information for an ordinary event that had occurred at about the same time. This ordinary event served as a control condition that could be contrasted with the "flashbulb memory" of the attack.

After the initial session, the students were randomly assigned to one of three recall-testing sessions. Some returned to be tested one week later, others returned six weeks later, and still others returned thirty-two weeks later. At these recall-testing sessions, Talarico and Rubin asked the students a variety of questions, including the details of their memory for the attack and for the everyday event. These details were checked against the details that had been supplied on September 12, and the researchers counted the number of consistent and inconsistent details.

Figure 5.3 shows the results. The number of details provided on September 12 provides the baseline for the number of consistent details. As you can see, the consistency

FIGURE 5.3

Average Number of Consistent and Inconsistent Details Reported for a Flashbulb Event (September 11, 2001, Attacks) and an Ordinary Event, as a Function of the Passage of Time.

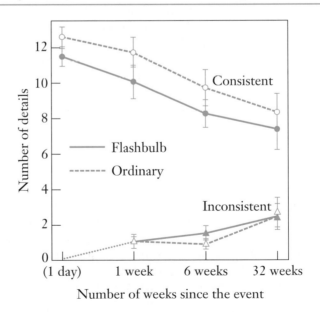

Source: Talarico & Rubin, 2003.

drops over time for each of the three testing sessions. However, the drop was similar for the terrorist-attack memory and for the everyday memory. The number of inconsistent details could not be assessed until the one-week recall-testing session. As the figure shows, the number of inconsistent details increases slightly over time for both kinds of memories. Interestingly, however, the students in all conditions reported that they were highly confident that their recall of the terrorist attacks had been accurate.

A related study by Kathy Pezdek (2003b) examined whether students' proximity to New York City influenced their memories about September 11, 2001. She found that students at a college in New York City recalled significantly more factual details about the tragedy than students at colleges in California and Hawaii. This finding makes sense because the New York City students were an average of only 27 blocks from the World Trade Center at the time they learned about the attack. Also, they were much more likely than the other students to have family members and friends whose lives were impacted by the event. In contrast, the New York City students were less likely than others to provide details about how they learned about the event.

Pezdek suggests that the New York students focused on rehearsing and remembering the detailed events of the tragedy, because these objective details could impact the lives of people they knew. In contrast, most of the students from California and Hawaii did not need to know these details, so they could focus on their own personal memories that focused on how they first learned about the tragedy.

So, what can we conclude from all this information about flashbulb memories? It's likely that we do not need to invent any special mechanism to explain them. Yes, these memories can sometimes be more accurate than our memories for ordinary events. However, these enhanced memories can usually be explained by standard mechanisms such as rehearsal frequency, distinctiveness, and elaboration (Koriat et al., 2000; Neisser, 2003; Read & Connolly, 2007). Furthermore, both flashbulb memories and "ordinary memories" grow less accurate with the passage of time (Kvavilashvili et al., 2003; Read & Connolly, 2007; Schmolck et al., 2000).

Eyewitness Testimony

So far, our discussion of autobiographical memory has explored memory schemas, source monitoring, and flashbulb memories. Now let's consider eyewitness testimony, the most extensively researched topic within the domain of autobiographical memory. Memory schemas can alter a witness's testimony. You'll also see that some of the errors in eyewitness testimony can be traced to faulty source monitoring. People believe they really witnessed something that had actually been suggested to them in a different situation (Mitchell & Johnson, 2000).

We have seen throughout this chapter that people's long-term memory is reasonably accurate, especially if we consider memory for the gist of a message. However, eyewitness testimony requires people to remember specific details about people and events. In these cases, mistakes are more likely (Castelli et al., 2006; Wells & Olson, 2003). When eyewitness testimony is inaccurate, the wrong person may go to jail or—in the worst cases—be put to death.

Consider the case of Gary Graham, who was a suspect in the murder of Bobby Lambert. In truth, there was no convincing evidence for Graham's guilt—nothing like

DNA or fingerprint evidence. When Graham came to trial, jury members were informed that Graham had a pistol *similar* to one that had shot Lambert. They were not told that the Houston police had concluded that it was not the *same* pistol.

Furthermore, eight eyewitnesses had seen the killer near the store, but seven of them were unable to identify Graham as the killer. His fate—the death penalty—was sealed by one woman's eyewitness testimony, even though she testified that she had seen his face at night for about 3 seconds, from a distance of about 30 feet. In addition, the court never heard the testimony of two eyewitnesses whose information contradicted the testimony of that one woman. Graham's case was never reviewed. Was Gary Graham genuinely guilty? We'll never know, because he was executed on June 22, 2000 (Alter, 2000).

Reports like this one have led psychologists to question the validity of eyewitness testimony. In many criminal cases, the only evidence available for identifying the culprit is the eyewitness testimony provided by people who were present at the crime scene.

Fortunately, DNA testing became more common during the late 1990s, and it was used for some individuals who had been convicted before the tests were available (Herrmann, Gruneberg, et al., 2006). Researchers analyzed samples of imprisoned people whose DNA did not match the biological sample from the scene of the crime. More than 75% of these people had been pronounced guilty because of erroneous eyewitness testimony (Castelli et al., 2006; Wells & Olson, 2003).

In our discussion of eyewitness testimony, let's first consider how inaccuracies can arise when people are given misleading information after the event that they had witnessed. Next, we'll summarize several factors that can influence the accuracy of eyewitness testimony. Then we'll see whether witnesses who are *confident* about their eyewitness testimony are also more *accurate* about their judgments. Our final topic in this discussion is the recovered memory/false memory debate.

The Post-Event Misinformation Effect.   Errors in eyewitness testimony can often be traced to incorrect information. In the **post-event misinformation effect,** people first view an event, and then afterward they are given misleading information about the event; later on, they mistakenly recall the misleading information, rather than the event they actually saw (Davis & Loftus, 2007; Pansky et al., 2005; Pickrell et al., 2004).

Earlier in the chapter, on page 139, we discussed proactive interference, which means that people have trouble recalling new material because previously learned, old material keeps interfering with new memories. The misinformation effect resembles another kind of interference called retroactive interference. In **retroactive interference,** people have trouble recalling old material because some recently learned, new material keeps interfering with old memories. For example, suppose that an eyewitness saw a crime, and then a lawyer supplied some misinformation while asking a question. Later on, the eyewitness may have trouble remembering the events that actually occurred at the scene of the crime, because the new misinformation is interfering.

In the classic experiment on the misinformation effect, Elizabeth Loftus and her coauthors (1978) showed participants a series of slides. In this sequence, a sports car stopped at an intersection, and then it turned and hit a pedestrian. Half the participants saw a slide with a yield sign at the intersection; the other half saw a stop sign.

Twenty minutes to a week after the participants saw the slides, they answered a questionnaire about the details of the accident. A critical question contained information that was either consistent with a detail in the original slide series, inconsistent with that detail, or neutral (i.e., did not mention the detail). For example, some people who had seen the yield sign were asked, "Did another car pass the red Datsun while it was stopped at the yield sign?" (consistent). Other people were asked, "Did another car pass the red Datsun while it was stopped at the stop sign?" (inconsistent). For still other people, the question did not mention the sign (neutral). To answer this question, all participants saw two slides, one with a stop sign and one with a yield sign. They were asked to select which slide they had previously seen.

As Figure 5.4 shows, people who saw the inconsistent information were much less accurate than people in the other two conditions. They selected a sign, based on the

FIGURE 5.4

The Effect of Type of Information and Delay on Proportion of Correct Answers.

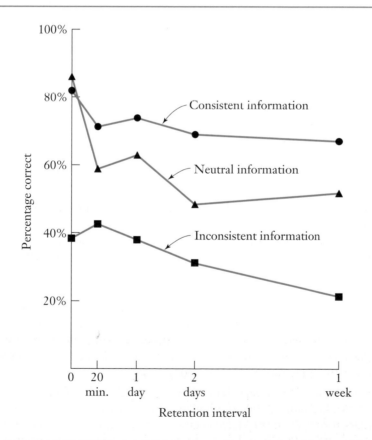

Source: Loftus et al., 1978.

information in the questionnaire, rather than the original slide. Many studies have replicated the detrimental effects of misleading post-event information (e.g., Pickrell et al., 2004; Roediger & McDermott, 2000; Schacter, 2001; Wade et al., 2002).

The misinformation effect can be at least partly traced to faulty source monitoring (Davis & Loftus, 2007; Schacter et al., 1998). For example, in the study by Loftus and her colleagues (1978), the post-event information in the inconsistent-information condition encouraged people to create a mental image of a stop sign. During testing, they had trouble deciding which of the two images—the stop sign or the yield sign—they had actually seen in the original slide series.

The research on the misinformation effect emphasizes the active, constructive nature of memory. As Theme 1 points out, cognitive processes are active, rather than passive. The **constructivist approach** to memory argues that we construct knowledge by integrating what we know, so that our understanding of an event or a topic is coherent, and it makes sense (Davis & Loftus, 2007; Mayer, 2003; Pansky et al., 2005). In the case of the study by Loftus and her colleagues (1978), the people in the inconsistent condition made sense of the event by concluding that the car had paused at the stop sign.

Notice, then, that the consistency bias—discussed on page 146—is one component of the constructivist approach. In short, memory does not consist of a list of facts, all stored in intact form and ready to be replayed like a videotape. Instead, we construct a memory by blending information from a variety of sources (Davis & Loftus, 2007; Hyman & Kleinknecht, 1999).

Factors Affecting the Accuracy of Eyewitness Testimony. As you can imagine, a variety of factors influence whether eyewitness testimony is accurate. We have already mentioned three potential problems in eyewitness testimony: (1) People may create memories that are consistent with their schemas; (2) people may make errors in source monitoring; and (3) post-event misinformation may distort people's recall. Here are several other important variables:

1. *Errors are more likely when there is a long delay between the original event and the time of the testimony.* As time passes, recall accuracy decreases for most of our ordinary memories. A long delay in eyewitness testimony also allows more opportunities for "contamination" from post-event misinformation (Dysart & Lindsay, 2007; Esgate & Groome, 2005; Read & Connolly, 2007).

2. *Errors are more likely if the misinformation is plausible.* For instance, in the classic study by Loftus and her colleagues (1978), a stop sign is just as plausible as a yield sign, so participants in that study often made errors. People are also likely to say that an event occurred in their own life (when it really did not) if the event seems consistent with other similar experiences (Castelli et al., 2006; Davis & Loftus, 2007; Hyman & Loftus, 2002).

3. *Errors are more likely if there is social pressure* (Roebers & Schneider, 2000; Roediger & McDermott, 2000; Smith et al., 2003). People make many errors in eyewitness testimony if they have been pressured to provide a specific answer (for example, "Exactly when did you first see the suspect?"). In contrast, the testimony is more accurate when people are allowed to report in their own words,

when they are given sufficient time, and when they are allowed to say, "I don't know" (Koriat et al., 2000; Wells et al., 2000).

4. *Errors are more likely if eyewitnesses have been given positive feedback.* Eyewitnesses are much more certain about the accuracy of their decision if they had previously been given positive feedback—even a simple "Okay" (Douglass & Steblay, 2006; Semmler & Brewer, 2006; Wells & Bradfield, 1999). Unfortunately, in real-life lineups, the eyewitnesses often hear this kind of encouragement (Wells & Olson, 2003). Now try Demonstration 5.5, below.

The Relationship Between Memory Confidence and Memory Accuracy. In some studies, researchers ask participants to judge how confident they are about the accuracy of their eyewitness testimony. Interestingly, in many situations, participants are almost as confident about their misinformation-based memories as they are about their genuinely correct memories (Koriat et al., 2000; Penrod & Cutler, 1999; Perfect, 2004;

---

⑥ Demonstration 5.5

Remembering Lists of Words

For this demonstration, you must learn and recall two lists of words. Before beginning, take out two pieces of paper. Next, read List 1, then close the book and try to write down as many of the words as possible. Then do the same for List 2. After you have recalled both sets of words, check your accuracy. How many items did you correctly recall?

List 1	List 2
bed	water
rest	stream
awake	lake
tired	Mississippi
dream	boat
wake	tide
snooze	swim
blanket	flow
doze	run
slumber	barge
snore	creek
nap	brook
peace	fish
yawn	bridge
drowsy	winding

Wells & Olson, 2003). In other words, people's confidence about their eyewitness testimony is not strongly correlated with the accuracy of their testimony. In fact, the correlations are typically between +.30 and +.50* (Leippe & Eisenstadt, 2007).

This research has a practical application for the legal system. Jury members are much more likely to believe a confident eyewitness than an uncertain one (Brewer et al., 2005; Koriat et al., 2000; Penrod & Cutler, 1999). Unfortunately, however, the research shows that a *confident* eyewitness is not necessarily an *accurate* eyewitness.

The Recovered Memory/False Memory Controversy. If you scan popular magazines such as *Newsweek* or *People*, you seldom come across articles on working memory, the encoding-specificity principle, or source monitoring. However, between about 1995 and 2005, one topic from cognitive psychology attracted media attention: the controversy about recovered memory versus false memory (e.g., Eisen et al., 2002; Freyd & DePrince, 2001; Gallo, 2006; Goodman et al., 2007; Lynn & McConkey, 1998; Williams & Banyard, 1999). During this period, cognitive psychologists, therapists, and lawyers published more than 800 books and articles about this topic (Smith & Gleaves, 2007).

A complete discussion of this controversy is beyond the scope of a cognitive psychology textbook. Furthermore, the so-called "memory wars" have not been resolved, though most professionals now seem to favor a compromise position. We will summarize five important components of this issue. Before you read further, however, be sure that you have tried Demonstration 5.5 on page 155.

1. *The two contrasting positions in the controversy.* Most of the discussion about false memory focuses on childhood sexual abuse. One group of researchers argues that memories can be forgotten and then recovered. According to this **recovered-memory perspective,** some individuals who experienced sexual abuse during childhood managed to forget that memory for many years. At a later time, often prompted by a specific event or by encouragement from a therapist, this presumably forgotten memory comes flooding back into consciousness (Smith & Gleaves, 2007; Schacter, 2001).

A second group of researchers interprets phenomena like this in a different light. We must emphasize that this second group agrees that childhood sexual abuse is a genuine problem that needs to be addressed. However, these people deny the accuracy of many reports about the sudden recovery of early memories. Specifically, the **false-memory perspective** proposes that many of these recovered memories are actually incorrect memories; that is, they are constructed stories about events that never occurred (Davis & Loftus, 2007; Gerrie et al., 2005; Hyman & Loftus, 2002; Loftus & Guyer, 2002a, 2002b; Reyna et al., 2007).

2. *The potential for memory errors.* Our discussion throughout this section on autobiographical memory should convince you that memory is less than perfect. For example, people are often guided by schemas, rather than their actual recall of an event. Also, the research on source monitoring shows that people cannot recall with absolute

---

*A correlation is a statistical measure of the relationship between two variables, in which .00 represents no relationship and +1.00 represents a strong positive relationship.

accuracy whether they performed an action or merely imagined performing it. We also saw that eyewitness testimony can be flawed, especially when witnesses receive misinformation (Hyman & Loftus, 2002).

Similar problems arise in recalling memories from childhood. For instance, some psychotherapists suggest to clients that they had been sexually abused during childhood. This suggestion could easily be blended with reality to create a false memory (Kihlstrom, 1998). These statements encourage clients to invent a false memory, especially because we noted earlier that people make more errors when they have experienced social pressure (Smith et al., 2003).

We cannot easily determine whether a memory of childhood abuse is correct. After all, the situation is far from controlled, and other, independent witnesses are rarely available (Berliner & Briere, 1999; Koriat et al., 2000). Furthermore, PET scans and other techniques cannot reliably distinguish between correct and incorrect recall of abuse (McNally, 2003; Schacter, 2001).

However, psychologists have conducted research and created theories that are designed to address the recovered memory/false memory issue. Let's first consider laboratory research that demonstrates false memory. Then we'll discuss why the situation of sexual abuse during childhood may sometimes require a different kind of explanation, rather than one that can explain false memory for emotionally neutral material.

3. *Laboratory evidence of false memory.* Research in the psychology laboratory clearly demonstrates that people often "recall" seeing a word that was never actually presented. In contrast to the real-life recall of sexual abuse, the laboratory research is very straightforward and unemotional. Researchers simply ask participants to remember a list of words they had seen earlier, and their accuracy can be objectively measured. For example, Demonstration 5.5 asked you to memorize and recall two lists of words, and then you checked your accuracy. Take a moment now to check something else. On List 1, did you write down the word *sleep?* Did you write *river* on List 2?

If you check the original lists on page 155, you'll discover that neither *sleep* nor *river* was listed. In research with lists of words like these, Roediger and McDermott (1995) found a false-recall rate of 55%. People made intrusion errors by listing words that did not appear on the lists. Intrusions are common on this task because each word that *does* appear on a list is commonly associated with a missing word, in this case either *sleep* or *river.* This experiment has been replicated numerous times, using different stimuli and different testing conditions (e.g., Foley et al., 2006; Neuschatz et al., 2007; Roediger & Gallo, 2004). These researchers argue that similar intrusions could occur with respect to childhood memories. People may "recall" events that are related to their actual experiences, but these events never actually occurred.

Other studies have demonstrated that laboratory-research participants can construct false memories for events during childhood that never actually happened. These false memories include being attacked by a small dog, being lost in a shopping mall, seeing someone possessed by demons, and becoming ill after eating hard-boiled eggs (e.g., Bernstein et al., 2005; Gerrie et al., 2005; Hyman & Kleinknecht, 1999; Pickrell et al., 2004).

However, we need to emphasize that only a fraction of participants actually claim to remember an event that did not occur. For example, researchers tried to implant a false memory that the research participant had attended a wedding at the age of 6. According to this fake story, the 6-year-old had accidentally bumped into a table containing a punch bowl, spilling punch on a parent of the bride. Interestingly, 25% of the participants eventually recalled this false memory—an entire event that did not actually occur (Hyman et al., 1995; Hyman & Loftus, 2002). Notice, however, that 75% of the students refused to "remember" the specific event.

4. *Arguments for recovered memory.* One problem is that these laboratory studies have little ecological validity with respect to memory for childhood sexual abuse (Freyd & Quina, 2000). Consider the studies on recalling word lists. There's not much similarity between "remembering" a word that never appeared on a list and a false memory of childhood sexual abuse. In addition, the events—such as spilling the contents of a punch bowl—are somewhat embarrassing. However, these events have no sexual content, and they could be discussed in public. In contrast, students cannot be convinced to create false memories for more embarrassing events, such as having had an enema as a child (Pezdek et al., 1997).

Many people who have been sexually abused as children have continually remembered the incidents, even decades later. However, some people may genuinely not recall the abuse. For example, researchers have studied individuals who had been treated in hospital emergency rooms for childhood sexual abuse, or individuals whose sexual abuse had been documented by the legal system. Still, some of them fail to recall the episode when interviewed as adults (Goodman et al., 2003; Pezdek & Taylor, 2002; Schooler, 2001). Indeed, some people can forget about the incident for many years, but they suddenly recall it decades later.

Jennifer Freyd and Anne DePrince propose an explanation for these cases of recovered memory (DePrince & Freyd, 2004; Freyd, 1996, 1998). They emphasize that childhood sexual abuse is genuinely different from relatively innocent episodes such as spilled wedding punch. In particular, they propose the term **betrayal trauma** to describe how a child may respond adaptively when a trusted parent or caretaker betrays him or her by sexual abuse. The child depends on this adult and must actively inhibit memories of abuse in order to maintain an attachment to the adult (Anderson, 2001).

5. *Both perspectives are partially correct.* In reality, we must conclude that both the recovered-memory perspective and the false-memory perspective are at least partially correct (Castelli et al., 2006; Herrmann et al., 2006). Indeed, some people have truly experienced childhood sexual abuse, and they may forget about the abuse for many decades until a critical event triggers their recall. Furthermore, other people may never have experienced childhood sexual abuse, but a suggestion about abuse creates a false memory of childhood experiences that never really occurred. In still other cases, people can provide accurate testimony about how they have been abused, even years afterwards (Brainerd & Reyna, 2005; Castelli et al., 2006; Goodman & Paz-Alonso, 2006).

We have seen throughout this chapter that human memory is both flexible and complex. This memory process can account for temporarily forgetting events, it can account for the construction of events that never actually happened, and it can also account for accurate memory—even when the events are horrifying.

◉ Section Summary: *Autobiographical Memory*

1. Research on autobiographical memory typically has high ecological validity; this research shows that our memories are usually accurate, although we may make errors on some details, and we may blend together information from different events.

2. Memory schemas encourage us to make errors in recalling events; in addition, we may reveal a consistency bias by exaggerating the similarity between our current self-schema and our previous characteristics.

3. The research on source monitoring shows that we may have difficulty deciding whether something really happened, instead of imagining it, and we may have difficulty deciding where we learned some information.

4. Flashbulb memories are rich with information, and we are often confident that they are accurate; however, even memories for tragedies—such as the September 11, 2001 tragedy—are typically no more accurate than memories for important personal events.

5. In eyewitness testimony, the post-event misinformation effect can occur if misleading information is introduced after a witness has seen an event. The research is consistent with the constructivist approach to memory.

6. Errors in eyewitness memory are more likely if the witness observed an event long ago, if the misinformation is plausible, if social pressure was applied, or if positive feedback was supplied.

7. An eyewitness's self-confidence is not strongly correlated with his or her memory accuracy.

8. Both sides of the recovered memory/false memory controversy are at least partially correct. Some people may indeed forget about a painful childhood memory, recalling it years later. Other people apparently construct a memory of abuse that never really occurred, and still other people continue to have accurate memory for abuse, long afterwards.

CHAPTER REVIEW QUESTIONS

1. Suppose that you are in charge of creating a public service announcement for television. Choose an issue that is important to you, and describe at least five tips from this chapter that would help you make an especially memorable advertisement. Be sure to include depth of processing as one of the tips.

2. What is encoding specificity? Think of a recent example where encoding specificity explained why you temporarily forgot something. How strong are the effects of encoding specificity?

3. Give several examples of explicit and implicit memory tasks you have performed in the past few days. What is dissociation, and how is it relevant in the research that has been conducted with both normal adults and people with amnesia?

4. According to one saying, "The more you know, the easier it is to learn." What evidence do we have for this statement, based on the material discussed in this chapter? Be sure to include information on expertise and schemas as part of your answer.

5. Although this textbook focuses on cognitive psychology, several topics discussed in this chapter are relevant to other areas, such as social psychology, personality psychology, and abnormal psychology. Summarize this research, discussing topics such as the self-reference effect, emotions and memory, and the consistency bias.

6. Define the term "autobiographical memory," and mention several topics that have been studied in this area. How does research in this area differ from more traditional laboratory research? List the advantages and disadvantages of each approach. Point out how Roediger and McDermott's (1995) study on false memory for English words highlights both the advantages and disadvantages of the laboratory approach.

7. Describe how schemas could lead to a distortion in the recall of a flashbulb memory. How might misleading post-event information also influence this recall? In answering the two parts of this question, use the terms *proactive inhibition* and *retroactive inhibition*.

8. The constructivist approach to memory emphasizes that we actively revise our memories in the light of new concerns and new information. How would this approach be relevant if a woman were to develop a false memory about her childhood, and she also shows a strong consistency bias? How would this approach be relevant for other topics in the section about autobiographical memory?

9. Chapter 6 emphasizes methods for improving your memory. However, the present chapter also contains some relevant information and hints about memory improvement. Review Chapter 5, and make a list of suggestions about memory improvement that you could use when you study for the next examination in cognitive psychology.

10. Researcher Daniel Schacter (2001) wrote a book describing several kinds of memory errors. He argues, however, that these errors are actually byproducts of a memory system that usually functions quite well. What textbook theme is related to his argument? Review this chapter and list some of the memory errors people may commit. Explain why each error is a byproduct of a memory system that works well in most everyday experiences.

KEYWORDS

working memory
long-term memory
episodic memory
semantic memory
procedural memory
encoding
retrieval
autobiographical memory
levels-of-processing approach
depth-of-processing
  approach
distinctiveness
elaboration
self-reference effect
meta-analysis technique
encoding specificity principle
recall

recognition
emotion
mood
Pollyanna Principle
positivity effect
mood congruence
social goals
approach social goals
avoidance social goals
explicit memory task
implicit memory task
repetition priming task
dissociation
proactive interference
amnesia
retrograde amnesia
anterograde amnesia

hippocampus
expertise
own-race bias
ecological validity
schema
consistency bias
source monitoring
flashbulb memory
post-event misinformation
  effect
retroactive interference
constructivist approach
recovered-memory
  perspective
false-memory perspective
betrayal trauma

RECOMMENDED READINGS

Handbook of eyewitness psychology. Memory for people (Vol. 1, Toglia, M. P., et al., Eds.), *Memory for events* (Vol. 2, Lindsay, R. C. L., et al., Eds.) (2007). Mahwah, NJ: Erlbaum. I strongly recommend this two-volume handbook for college libraries, as well as anyone interested in the psychological or legal components of eyewitness testimony. The chapters are clearly written, with references to recent psychological research and legal cases.

Hunt, R. R., & Worthen, J. B. (Eds.). (2006). *Distinctiveness and memory.* New York: Oxford University Press. This book features nineteen chapters that explore the nature of distinctiveness, as well as methods to enhance distinctiveness.

Pezdek, K. (Ed.). (2003b). Memory and cognition for the events of September 11, 2001 [Special issue]. *Applied Cognitive Psychology, 17* (9). Most of the articles in this special issue focus on some component of flashbulb memory, but others look at other cognitive reactions to the terrorist attack, such as decision making and categorizing the faces of Arab individuals.

Uttl, B., Ohta, N., & Siegenthaler, A. L. (Eds.). (2006). *Memory and emotion: Interdisciplinary perspectives.* Malden, MA: Blackwell. The twelve chapters in this book are relevant to many topics in the current chapter, including autobiographical memory and the influence of mood and emotions on memory.

CHAPTER 6

Using Memory Strategies and Metacognition

Introduction

Memory Strategies

Suggestions from Previous Chapters: A Review
   Practice
Mnemonics Using Imagery
Mnemonics Using Organization
A Comprehensive Approach to Memory Improvement
Improving Prospective Memory

Metacognition

Metamemory and the Prediction of Memory Performance
Individual Differences: Metamemory and Adults with
   Attention-Deficit/Hyperactivity Disorder
Metamemory About Factors Affecting Memory
In Depth: Metamemory and the Regulation of Study Strategies
The Tip-of-the-Tongue Phenomenon
Metacomprehension

PREVIEW

Chapter 4 focused on working memory, which is the brief, immediate memory for material you are currently processing. Chapter 5 explored long-term memory, or memory for events that occurred minutes, days, or even years earlier. Both of those chapters emphasized the research and theory about memory. In contrast, Chapter 6 explores more practical issues concerned with memory strategies and metacognition (knowledge and control of your cognitive processes). The information in this chapter should help you develop more effective memory strategies; it should also help you learn how to monitor both your memory and your reading techniques.

The section on memory strategies begins by reviewing some memory suggestions derived from Chapters 3 and 5. Next, we'll consider several ways in which different aspects of practice can enhance your memory. We'll then look at memory techniques that emphasize imagery and organization. However, we'll see that genuine memory improvement requires a comprehensive approach, which includes factors such as mental and physical health. Our final topic in this section explores ways to improve prospective memory, or remembering to do something in the future.

The second section examines metacognition. The research on metamemory suggests that college students are often overconfident when estimating their total score on a memory test. However, they can accurately predict which items they will remember on a memory test. College students with Attention-Deficit/Hyperactivity Disorder are similarly accurate in predicting which specific test items they will recall. In general, the research on college students shows that they often spend too long studying material they already know.

The tip-of-the-tongue phenomenon represents another dimension of metacognition: People are fairly knowledgeable about characteristics of the target word, such as the first letter of this word. Unfortunately, however, the research suggests that students are often overconfident in judging whether they have understood a passage they have recently read. Throughout the discussion of metacognition, we'll point out techniques to help you learn course material more effectively.

INTRODUCTION

Take a moment to consider the thousands of hours that you spent during high school listening to lectures, engaging in class discussions, taking notes, reading textbooks, and then studying for examinations. Now think about the amount of time your high school teachers spent in teaching you how to improve your memory. Perhaps a history teacher urged the class to begin studying early for an upcoming exam, rather than trying to master everything the night before the exam. Maybe a math teacher taught you how to remember the abbreviations for the three basic trigonometry formulas. Possibly a French-language teacher mentioned that you could learn vocabulary terms by using mental imagery. Try to estimate the total amount of time your teachers spent helping you learn how to improve your memory.

When my cognitive psychology class begins the chapter on memory strategies and metacognition, we try the exercise I've just described. In contrast to the thousands of hours my students have spent learning and remembering, most of them estimate that all of their high school teachers—combined—spent a grand total of about 1 hour discussing memory improvement.

Furthermore, some students report that their teachers recommended some study strategies that contradict the information they have learned about human memory. For instance, one student told our class about her history teacher's recommendations: Repeat a sentence out loud three times, and then write it three times, and you'll have it memorized. Pause for a moment, right now. Why should students avoid this particular recommendation?

We'll start this chapter by reviewing some strategy tips that you learned about memory improvement, based on the chapters you've already read. Then we'll look at several other useful memory strategies that psychology researchers have discovered. Furthermore, your choice of memory strategies will be guided by your **metacognition,** which is your knowledge about your cognitive processes, as well as your control of these cognitive processes. The second half of this chapter will encourage you to explore how metacognition can help you use your cognitive processes more effectively.

MEMORY STRATEGIES

When you use a **memory strategy,** you perform mental activities that can help you improve your encoding and retrieval (Bransford et al., 2000; Herrmann et al., 2002). Most memory strategies help you remember something that you learned in the past. For example, when you take a test in Art History, your professor may ask you to write an essay about the stylistic differences between Renaissance and Baroque paintings. To answer this question, you'll need to remember information from the professor's lecture last week and from the textbook chapter you finished reading last night. Most of this part of Chapter 6 explores strategies for remembering something you learned in the past. Our last topic in this section is different, however, because it focuses on improving your memory for the tasks that you must remember to do in the future.

Suggestions from Previous Chapters: A Review

Let's begin the advice about memory from previous chapters with some information that you learned in Chapter 3 about divided attention. Then we'll review some important concepts from Chapter 5: levels of processing, distinctiveness, the encoding-specificity principle, and the overconfidence problem.

Divided Attention. The material in Chapter 3 provides an important caution. You'll recall that people usually cannot pay complete, full attention to two simultaneous tasks. Suppose that you are trying to pay attention to your biology professor's lecture at the same time you are thinking about your plans for next weekend. You will discover that some of the biology material failed to make its way into your working memory, and it had no hope of reaching long-term memory! Research confirms that memory performance is substantially reduced if people had used divided attention during the encoding phase (deWinstanley & Bjork, 2002; Naveh-Benjamin et al., 1998; Payne et al., 1999).

Let's consider some additional research on the topic of divided attention and memory. My students often ask whether their memory will be helped or hindered by listening to background music while they study. The answer—like many answers in psychology—is, "It depends." Outgoing people who are extraverts typically remember about the same amount, whether they are listening simultaneously to quiet background music or listening to no music at all (Furnham & Bradley, 1997).

In contrast, people who are introverts—that is, shy and withdrawn—typically remember less if they listen to background music during a memory task. During divided-attention tasks like this, introverted individuals are apparently more distracted by the music, and they cannot focus their attention sufficiently on the memory task (Furnham & Bradley, 1997).

Levels of Processing.   One of the most useful general principles for memory improvement comes from the discussion about levels of processing in Chapter 5. Specifically, the research on **levels of processing** shows that you will recall information more accurately if you process it at a deep level, rather than a shallow level (Esgate & Groome, 2005).

We noted that deep levels of processing facilitate learning because of two factors, elaboration and distinctiveness. Suppose that you need to learn some material in a chapter for a course in U.S. History. If you want to emphasize elaboration, be sure to concentrate on the meaning, and relate it to your prior knowledge about U.S. History. Try to develop rich, elaborate encoding (deWinstanley & Bjork, 2002; Esgate & Groom, 2005; Herrmann et al., 2002). In contrast, simple **rehearsal,** or repeating the information you want to learn, is basically a waste of time!

Here's a specific application of the elaboration factor, which you can use when you need to master a complex topic. Giles Einstein and Mark McDaniel (2004) propose that you can learn and remember complex material more easily if you create and answer "why questions." To answer these questions, you must use deep processing to think about the meaning of the material and interconnect this new material with information you already know.

For example, suppose that your American History professor requires you to learn the Ten Amendments in the U.S. Bill of Rights. I recall having trouble remembering the Third Amendment. According to this Amendment, when citizens are asked to provide housing and food for soldiers, these citizens must be paid appropriately. This Amendment is difficult to remember because it is meaningless to most U.S. residents in the current era. Einstein and McDaniel propose that we ask why this issue was important enough in American history to deserve an amendment. They suggest that we think about the citizens of that era. They had little money, and yet they had been forced to house and feed soldiers during the Revolutionary War. Now we can understand why this amendment was so necessary! (Similarly, why did I ask you the "why question" about memory strategies in paragraph 2 on page 165?)

Research also shows that deep processing helps students remember more information in their psychology courses. For instance, students earned higher grades in a developmental psychology course if they tried to analyze newspaper-advice columns from a developmental perspective (Cabe et al., 1999). Also, students learned more in a psychology course on personality theories if they had maintained a journal in which they applied various theories to personal friends, political figures, and characters from television programs (Connor-Greene, 2000). In both these cases, students elaborated on the material and analyzed it in a complex, meaningful fashion, rather than simply rehearsing the material.

In Chapter 5, we emphasized that deep levels of processing enhance your memory for two reasons, elaboration and distinctiveness. We've already considered elaboration, so let's discuss distinctiveness. People tend to forget information if it is not distinctly different from the other memory traces in their long-term memory.

Distinctiveness is an especially important factor when we try to learn names. For example, I often need to recall someone's name. Let's say that I have just met a young woman named Kate. I've often made the mistake of telling myself, "That's easy. I'll just remember that she looks like the student in my Cognitive Psychology class named Kate." Later on, I'll realize that I have two or three students in that class named Kate. My encoding had not been sufficiently distinctive. As a result, the face I was trying to recall was extremely vulnerable to interference from other students' faces. With interference from other names, we easily forget the target name (Craik, 2006; Schacter & Wiseman, 2006; Tulving & Rosenbaum, 2006).

As we emphasized in Chapter 5, one especially deep level of processing takes advantage of the **self-reference effect,** in which you enhance long-term memory by relating the material to your own experiences. For example, one of the reasons that I include demonstrations in this textbook is to provide you with personal experiences focusing on some of the important principles of cognitive psychology.

If you read your textbook in a reflective fashion, you'll try to think how to apply major concepts to your own life. I'm hopeful, for instance, that this chapter will encourage you to see how memory strategies and metacognitive principles can be applied to the way you learn in all of your college courses.

Encoding Specificity.   Chapter 5 also discussed the **encoding-specificity principle,** which states that recall is often better if the context at the time of encoding matches the context at the time when your retrieval will be tested. As we noted in Chapter 5, context effects are often inconsistent (e.g., Baddeley, 2004; Nairne, 2005). For example, you probably will not improve your grade if you decide to study for an upcoming exam by reviewing the material in the classroom where you'll be taking this exam.

However, the research on encoding specificity does provide some other strategies. For instance, when you are trying to devise study strategies, one specific suggestion is that you should consider how you will be tested on your next examination (Herrmann et al., 2006; Koriat, 2000; Payne et al., 1999). For example, suppose that your exam will contain essays. This format requires you to *recall* information—not simply to *recognize* it. As you are learning the material, make an effort to quiz yourself periodically by closing your notebook and trying to recall the material on the pages you've just read. During studying, you can also try to create some essay questions and then answer them, a strategy that would also increase your deep processing of the material.

Overconfidence. Our examination of autobiographical memory in Chapter 5 provides a general caution, rather than a specific memory strategy. In that section, we saw that people often believe that their memories about their life experiences are highly accurate. However, even their so-called flashbulb memories may contain some errors. This area of research suggests that we are sometimes overconfident about our memory skills. If we can make mistakes in remembering important life events, then we can certainly make mistakes in remembering material from a course! The issue of overconfidence is also an important topic in the second half of the chapter. Now, before you read further, be sure to try Demonstration 6.1.

---

⑨ Demonstration 6.1

Instructions and Memory

Learn the following list of pairs by repeating the members of each pair several times. For example, if the pair were CAT–WINDOW, you would say over and over to yourself, "CAT–WINDOW, CAT–WINDOW, CAT–WINDOW." Just repeat the words, and do not use any other study method. Allow yourself 1 minute to learn this list.

CUSTARD–LUMBER	IVY–MOTHER
JAIL–CLOWN	LIZARD–PAPER
ENVELOPE–SLIPPER	SCISSORS–BEAR
SHEEPSKIN–CANDLE	CANDY–MOUNTAIN
FRECKLES–APPLE	BOOK–PAINT
HAMMER–STAR	TREE–OCEAN

Now, cover up the pairs above. Try to recall as many responses as possible:

ENVELOPE	_____	JAIL	_____
FRECKLES	_____	IVY	_____
TREE	_____	SHEEPSKIN	_____
CANDY	_____	BOOK	_____
SCISSORS	_____	LIZARD	_____
CUSTARD	_____	HAMMER	_____

Next, learn the list of pairs at the top of page 169 by visualizing a mental picture in which the two objects in each pair are in some kind of vivid interaction. For example, if the pair were CAT–WINDOW, you might make up a picture of a cat jumping through a closed window, with the glass shattering all around. Just make up a mental image and do not use any other study method. Allow yourself 1 minute to learn this list.

(continued)

SOAP–MERMAID   MIRROR–RABBIT
FOOTBALL–LAKE   HOUSE–DIAMOND
PENCIL–LETTUCE   LAMB–MOON
CAR–HONEY   BREAD–GLASS
CANDLE–DANCER   LIPS–MONKEY
DANDELION–FLEA   DOLLAR–ELEPHANT

Now, cover up the pairs above. Try to recall as many responses as possible:

CANDLE   _____   DOLLAR   _____
DANDELION   _____   CAR   _____
BREAD   _____   LIPS   _____
MIRROR   _____   PENCIL   _____
LAMB   _____   SOAP   _____
FOOTBALL   _____   HOUSE   _____

Now, count the number of correct responses on each list. Did you recall a greater number of words with the imagery instructions? Incidentally, you may have found it very difficult to avoid using imagery on the first list, because you are reading a section about memory improvement. In that case, your recall scores were probably similar for the two lists. You may wish to test a friend instead. We will discuss imagery on pages 171 to 173.

Practice

So far, we've considered several memory-improvement suggestions based on concepts discussed in earlier chapters. Let us now turn to some new suggestions about memory strategies.

The Total-Time Hypothesis. The first of these memory-improvement strategies sounds almost too obvious to mention. According to the **total-time hypothesis,** the amount you learn depends on the total time you devote to learning (Baddeley, 1997).

However, if you simply reread the material over and over, this additional practice will not be helpful. For instance, researchers have found that the variable "number of hours spent studying" is not a good way of predicting a student's grade-point average. Instead, study time predicted grade-point average only when the researchers also assessed the quality of study strategies (Plant et al., 2005). For instance, 1 hour spent actively learning the material— using deep levels of processing—will usually be more helpful than 2 hours in which your eyes simply drift across the pages.

To prepare for an examination, you need to read your lecture notes and textbooks at least twice. Each time, you should also practice retrieving the information. (For example, what are the memory-improvement techniques we have discussed so far in this chapter?) The research shows that retrieval practice improves test performance (Bjork, 1999; deWinstanley & Bjork, 2002; Herrmann et al., 2002).

The Distributed-Practice Effect. According to the **distributed-practice effect** (also called the **spacing effect**), you will remember more material if you spread your learning trials over time **(spaced learning).** You'll remember less if you learn the material all at once **(massed learning).** The studies generally support this effect for both recall tasks and recognition tasks (Bahrick & Hall, 2005; Balch, 2006a; Cepeda et al., 2006; Koriat & Helstrup, 2007). Research also confirms the spacing effect with real-life material, such as math knowledge, Spanish vocabulary, and people's names (Bahrick et al., 1993; Carpenter & DeLosh, 2005; P.E. Morris et al., 2005; Pashler et al., 2007; Payne & Wenger, 1992; Rohrer & Taylor, 2006).

One reason that distributed practice is helpful for long-term recall is that it introduces **desirable difficulties,** in other words, a learning situation that is somewhat challenging, but not too difficult (Bjork, 1999; Koriat & Helstrup, 2007; McDaniel & Einstein, 2005). Suppose that you need to learn some key concepts for a biology class. If you test yourself on one concept several times in a row, the concept will seem easy by your third or fourth repetition.

However, if you allow several minutes to pass before the second repetition, you'll pay more attention to the concept. In addition, the task will be slightly more difficult because you will have begun to forget the concept (Bjork, 1999; deWinstanley & Bjork, 2002; Einstein & McDaniel, 2004). As a result, you'll make some mistakes, and you will not be overconfident that you have mastered the concepts. According to the current research, a delay of at least one day between practice sessions is even more effective in boosting long-term retention (Bahrick & Hall, 2005; Cepeda et al., 2006).

I have tried to apply the distribution of practice effect to some extent in this textbook. For instance, this chapter began with a review of some concepts you learned in Chapter 5. Furthermore, you'll have another opportunity to review many memory concepts in Chapter 13, when we examine memory processes in children and elderly adults.

The Testing Effect. Professors administer tests in an academic course so that they can assess how much you have learned. However, the research demonstrates a second function of tests, called the **testing effect**—taking a test is actually an excellent way to boost your long-term recall for academic material.

Henry Roediger and Jeffrey Karpicke (2006b) asked students to read short essays on a science-related topic. Then half of the students studied the same essays again. The other half took a test on the contents of the essay. They received a blank sheet of paper and wrote down as much as they could recall from the essay. They did not receive feedback about the accuracy of their recall.

During the last step of the study, everyone received a final test in which they wrote down their recall from the essay. Some completed this final test just 5 minutes after the last activity (either studying or taking the first test). Others were tested after a delay of either 2 days or 1 week.

Figure 6.1 shows the results. As you can see, when students took the test only 5 minutes after the last activity, those who had restudied the material performed somewhat better than those who had completed a test on the material. However, after a delay of 2 days or 1 week, students earned much higher scores if their last activity had been taking a test—even though they had received no feedback about their accuracy on that test.

FIGURE 6.1

The Effects of Learning Condition (Repeated Study Versus Testing) and Retention Interval on Percentage of Idea Units Correctly Recalled.

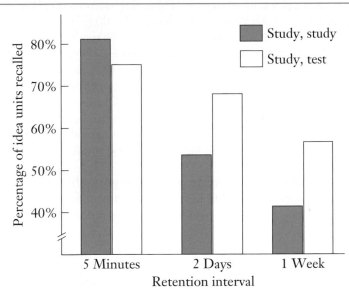

Source: Roediger & Karpicke (2006b).

Apparently, when you take a test, this testing provides practice in retrieving the relevant material. Furthermore, that test produces desirable difficulties. When you try to recall the content of the essay, you'll see that the task is somewhat challenging, and you will not be overconfident (Pashler et al., 2007; Roediger & Karpicke, 2006a, 2006b). I'm hopeful that Figure 6.1 will encourage you to test yourself on the new terms and the review questions at the end of each chapter in this textbook.

Mnemonics Using Imagery

The preceding discussion demonstrated the usefulness of strategies related to practice. This section, as well as the next one on organization, emphasizes the use of mnemonics (pronounced "ni-*mon*-icks," with a silent initial *m*). **Mnemonics** are mental strategies designed to improve your memory (Hunter, 2004b). When we use mnemonics that emphasize **imagery,** we mentally represent objects or actions that are not physically present. Chapter 7 examines the nature of these mental images; in the present chapter, however, we'll focus on how imagery can enhance memory.

Now check your results for Demonstration 6.1. This demonstration is a simplified version of a study by Bower and Winzenz (1970), who asked one group of participants to simply repeat pairs of words silently to themselves. Other participants tried to construct a mental image of the two words in vivid interaction with each other. Later, the participants saw the first word of each pair, and they were asked to supply the second word. The results showed that people in the imagery condition recalled more than twice as many items as did the people in the repetition condition.

Visual imagery is a powerful strategy for enhancing memory (De Beni & Moe, 2003; deWinstanley & Bjork, 2002; Einstein & McDaniel, 2004). The research shows that imagery is especially effective when the items that must be recalled are shown interacting with each other (Esgate & Groome, 2005; McKelvie et al., 1994; West, 1995). For example, if you want to remember the pair *piano-toast*, try to visualize a piano chewing a large piece of toast, rather than these two items separated from each other. In general, an interacting image is especially helpful if the image is bizarre (Davidson, 2006; Worthen, 2006).

One reason that visualization mnemonics are effective is that they are motivating and interesting (Herrmann et al., 2002; Higbee, 1999). Let's now consider two specific mnemonic devices that employ mental imagery: the keyword method and the method of loci.

The Keyword Method. If you need to remember unfamiliar vocabulary items, the keyword method is especially helpful. In the **keyword method,** you identify an English word (the keyword) that sounds similar to the new word you want to learn; then

FIGURE 6.2

The Keyword Representation for the Pair of Words Turkey-*Chompipe*.

⟲ Demonstration 6.2

Remembering Lists of Letters

Read this list of letters and then cover up the list. Try to recall them as accurately as possible.

   YMC AJF KFB INB CLS DTV

Now read this list of letters and then cover them up. Try to recall them as accurately as possible.

   AMA PHD GPS VCR CIA CBS

---

you create an image that links the keyword with the meaning of the new word (Bellezza, 1996; Iannuzzi et al., 1998). For example, one Thanksgiving, our Spanish-speaking guests were from Nicaragua, where the word for turkey is *chompipe* (pronounced, "chom-*pea*-pay." I had trouble remembering this word until I created an image of a turkey chomping down on an enormous pipe, as in Figure 6.2.

The research on the keyword method shows that it seems to help students who are trying to learn new English vocabulary words, vocabulary in another language, or people's names (Esgate & Groome, 2005; Groninger, 2000; Herrmann et al., 2002).

In a representative study, Carney and Levin (2001) showed sketches of unfamiliar animals, each paired with the animal's name. For the students in the experimental group, the instructions said that they should imagine an animal called a *capybara* with a *cap* pulled down over its eyes. Students in the control group were told to use their customary memorization method. According to the results, the imagery-group students were significantly more accurate than the control-group students in identifying the names of animal in video clips, as well as in sketches.

The Method of Loci. If you want to use the **method of loci,** you must associate the items to be learned with a series of visual images of physical locations. The method of loci (pronounced "*low*-sigh") is especially useful when you want to learn a list of items in a specific order (Einstein & McDaniel, 2004; Herrmann et al., 2002; Hunter, 2004b).

For example, you might use the method of loci for a familiar sequence of loci associated with a home, such as the driveway, the garage, and the front door. Suppose that you need to remember a grocery-shopping list, which begins with hot dogs, cat food, and tomatoes. You could make up a vivid image for each item and then imagine each item in its appropriate place. You could imagine giant *hot dogs* rolling down the *driveway*, a monstrous *cat eating food* in the *garage*, and ripe *tomatoes* splattering all over the *front door*. When you enter the supermarket, you can mentally walk the route from your driveway to the kitchen sink, recalling the items in order. In a classic experiment, participants in the method of loci condition recalled about twice as many words as participants in the control condition, when recall was measured five weeks after the original learning session (Groninger, 1971).

Mnemonics Using Organization

Organization is the attempt to bring systematic order to the material we learn. This category of mnemonics makes sense, because you need to use deep processing to sort items into categories (Esgate & Groome, 2005). Furthermore, retrieval is easier when you have constructed a well-organized framework (Bellezza, 1996; Wolfe, 2005). Let's consider four mnemonics that emphasize organization.

Chunking. Chapter 4 discussed an organizational strategy called **chunking,** in which we combine several small units into larger units. For instance, Demonstration 6.2 on page 173 is a modification of a study by Bower and Springston (1970). These researchers found that people recalled much more material when a string of letters was grouped according to meaningful, familiar units, rather than in arbitrary groups of three. In Demonstration 6.2, did you recall a larger number of items on the second list, which was organized according to familiar chunks?

Hierarchy Technique. A second effective way to organize material is to construct a hierarchy. A **hierarchy** is a system in which items are arranged in a series of classes, from the most general classes to the most specific. For example, Figure 6.3 presents part of a hierarchy for animals.

Gordon Bower and his colleagues (1969) asked people to learn words that belonged to four hierarchies similar to the one in Figure 6.3. Some people learned the words in an organized fashion, in the format of the upside-down trees you see in Figure 6.3. Other people saw the same words, but the words were randomly scattered throughout the different positions in each tree. The group who had learned the organized

FIGURE 6.3

An Example of a Hierarchy.

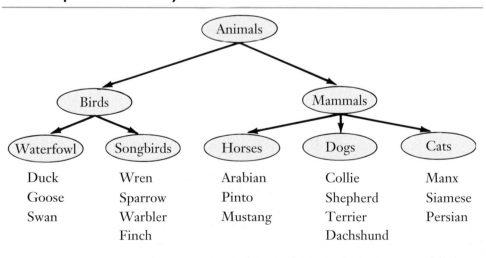

structure recalled more than three times as many words as the group who learned the random structure. Structure and organization clearly enhance recall (Baddeley, 1999; Herrmann et al., 2002).

An outline is a form of a hierarchy, because an outline is divided into general categories, and each general category is further subdivided. An outline is valuable because it provides organization and structure for concepts that you learn in a particular discipline. For example, this chapter is divided into two general categories: memory strategies and metacognition. When you have finished reading this chapter, see if you can construct—from memory—a hierarchy similar to Figure 6.3. Begin with the two general categories, and then subdivide these categories into more specific topics. Then check the chapter outline on page 163 to see whether you omitted anything. If you study the outline of each chapter, you will have an organized structure that can enhance your recall on an examination.

Unfortunately, students in introductory psychology classes report that they seldom use chapter outlines when studying for exams (Gurung, 2003). However, it's possible that students in more advanced courses (such as cognitive psychology!) know that they can learn more effectively if they understand how a topic is organized.

First-Letter Technique. Another popular mnemonic that makes use of organization is the **first-letter technique;** you take the first letter of each word you want to remember and compose a word or a sentence from those letters. Maybe you learned the order of the colors of the rainbow by using the letters ROY G. BIV to recall Red, Orange, Yellow, Green, Blue, Indigo, and Violet. As you may have learned in a statistics class, the nominal, ordinal, interval, and ratio scales conveniently spell *noir*, the French word for "black."

Students frequently use first-letter mnemonics. Unfortunately, however, the effectiveness of this technique has not been consistently demonstrated in laboratory research (Herrmann et al., 2002). In cases where it *does* work, its effectiveness can probably be traced to the fact that these first letters frequently enhance retrieval. For instance, suppose that you are experiencing a memory block for a certain term. If you know the first letter of that term, you'll be more likely to retrieve the item (Herrmann et al., 2002).

Narrative Technique. So far, we have looked at three mnemonic strategies that focus on organization: chunking, hierarchies, and the first-letter technique. A fourth organizational method, called the **narrative technique,** instructs people to make up stories that link a series of words together.

In a classic study, Bower and Clark (1969) told a group of people to make up narrative stories that incorporated a set of English words. People in a control group received no special instructions. In all, each group learned twelve lists of words. The results showed that the people in the narrative-technique group recalled about six times as many words as those in the control group.

The narrative technique is clearly an effective strategy for enhancing memory, and it has also been used successfully with memory-impaired individuals (Wilson, 1995). However, techniques such as this are effective only if you can generate the narrative easily and reliably during both learning and recall.

A Comprehensive Approach to Memory Improvement

Some psychologists complain that the traditional approach to memory improvement has been too simplistic (e.g., Baddeley et al., 1995; Herrmann et al., 2002; Searleman & Herrmann, 1994). That approach implies that we can find a single solution to help all people with their memory problems, which can be solved with just a few days' effort.

Psychologists propose that we need a more comprehensive approach to solving memory problems. For example, Douglas Herrmann's **multimodal approach** emphasizes that people who seriously want to enhance their memory must adopt a comprehensive approach to memory improvement; this approach focuses on many different *modes* or factors (Herrmann, 1991; Herrmann et al., 2002). Specifically, a comprehensive approach requires you to pay attention to your physical condition, for example, by getting sufficient sleep and attending to health problems (Winerman, 2006).

As you might expect, students who have a strong motivation to achieve success are also likely to have high grade-point averages (Robbins et al., 2004). Psychological well-being is also important. As you saw in Chapter 4, depressed individuals are more likely than others to experience working-memory problems. Depressed individuals are also more likely to experience memory problems on tests of both explicit and implicit memory (Gilbert, 2002; Jenkins & McDowall, 2001; Kizilbash et al., 2002).

People who want to improve their memories should develop a repertoire of several memory-improvement techniques. According to the research, students who earn high grades in a college course typically report using a large number of different memory strategies, compared to students who earn average grades (Herrmann et al., 2002). Furthermore, students who had completed a course in study strategies showed greater improvements in their grade-point averages, compared to students in a control group (Tuckman, 2003).

Ellen Langer has developed a perspective called mindfulness that provides another dimension to comprehensive memory improvement (Carson & Langer, 2006; Langer, 2000). According to Langer, **mindfulness** requires a flexible approach to the world, with a particular sensitivity to new things and an appreciation for new ways of approaching a problem. In contrast, we demonstrate mindlessness when we approach everything in the same, routine fashion we've used in the past.

I recall a student in my introductory psychology course several years ago who provided an unfortunate example of mindlessness. Dave had earned a low D grade on the first exam in the course, so I wrote a note asking him to come to my office to discuss study strategies. Together we discussed several of concepts mentioned in this chapter, including a heavy emphasis on metacognition (the topic we'll address in the second half of this chapter). Eagerly, I inspected Dave's second exam. Another low D. Later, I asked Dave whether he had tried any of the ideas we had discussed. He replied, "No, they would have been too much work, so I studied the way I always study."

The current research suggests that Dave's mindless perspective is fairly common. Students often resist using resources that could help them. For instance, students enrolled in a Web-based introductory psychology course seldom used any of the online study material until just two days before their exam (Maki & Maki, 2000). Furthermore, students enrolled in traditional introductory psychology courses sometimes make use of the boldface terms in their textbook. However, they seldom use other helpful features, such as outlines (as we noted earlier), chapter summaries, or practice-test questions (Gurung, 2003, 2004).

Let's take a moment to review the strategies we've examined for improving your memory for information you've acquired in the past. As we noted, Chapter 4 had emphasized the problem of divided attention. We also discussed several suggestions from Chapter 5, including the value of deep processing, for example, by using elaborate encodings, distinctiveness, and the self-reference approach. Chapter 5 also provided advice about the usefulness of encoding specificity, as well as the importance of not being overconfident.

The current chapter pointed out the helpfulness of three components of practice (the total-time hypothesis, the distributed practice effect, and the testing effect). This chapter also explored mnemonics using imagery (visualizing the objects in vivid interaction, the keyword method, and the method of loci) and mnemonics using organization (chunking, the hierarchy technique, the first-letter technique, and the narrative technique). Finally, we emphasized the value of a comprehensive orientation to memory, which includes Herrmann's multimodal approach and Langer's concept of mindfulness.

Improving Prospective Memory

Let's move away from memory for information that you acquired in the past. Instead, we'll focus on **prospective memory,** or remembering that you need to do something in the future. A prospective-memory task has two components. First, you must establish that you intend to accomplish a particular task at some future time. Second, at that future time, you must fulfill your intention (Einstein & McDaniel, 2004; Marsh et al., 1998; McDaniel & Einstein, 2000, 2007).

Some typical prospective-memory tasks might include remembering to pick up a friend at work this afternoon, to let the dog out before you leave the house, and to keep your office-hour appointment with a professor. According to surveys, people say that they are more likely to forget a prospective memory task than any other memory task (Einstein & McDaniel, 2004).

Occasionally, the primary challenge is to remember the *content* of the action (Schaefer & Laing, 2000). You've probably experienced the feeling that you know you are supposed to do something, but you cannot remember what it is. However, most of the time, the primary challenge is simply to remember to perform an action in the future (McDaniel & Einstein, 2007).

Before we can examine the methods for improving prospective memory, we need to understand how this aspect of memory operates. Let's first compare prospective memory with more standard memory tasks, and then we'll consider some of the research on prospective memory. Next, we'll explore the related topic of absentmindedness. With this background in mind, we'll consider several specific suggestions about how to improve prospective memory.

Comparing Prospective and Retrospective Memory. This textbook's discussions of memory have focused on **retrospective memory,** or recalling information that you have previously learned. Researchers study retrospective memory much more often than prospective memory. However, most people rank prospective memory errors among the most common memory lapses and also among the most embarrassing (Cook et al., 2005; Einstein & McDaniel, 2004; McDaniel & Einstein, 2007).

In contrast to retrospective memory, prospective memory requires you to plan something you must do in the future. In this respect, prospective memory resembles problem solving, a topic we'll explore in Chapter 11, and it also focuses on action (Einstein & McDaniel, 1996, 2004). Retrospective memory is more likely to focus on remembering information and ideas.

Despite their differences, prospective memory and retrospective memory are governed by some of the same variables. For example, your memory is more accurate for both kinds of memory tasks if you use both distinctive encoding and effective retrieval cues. Furthermore, both kinds of memory are less accurate when you have a long delay, filled with irrelevant activities, prior to retrieval (Einstein & McDaniel, 2004; Roediger, 1996). Finally, prospective memory relies on regions of the frontal lobe that also play a role in retrospective memory (Einstein & McDaniel, 2004; West et al., 2000).

Research on Prospective Memory.   Most of the research on prospective memory is reasonably high in ecological validity. The researchers try to design tasks that resemble the prospective memory tasks we face in our daily lives. Here is a small sample of the results of some of this research:

1. Suppose that you are working on a task that is very demanding, such as a project that requires divided attention. In this situation, you will be very likely to forget to complete an unrelated prospective-memory task (Einstein et al., 2003; McDaniel et al., 2004).

2. Suppose that you are working on Task 1, and you are supposed to complete a prospective-memory task later on. If you suddenly need to switch to working on Task 2, you will be less like to complete the prospective-memory task (Finstad et al., 2006).

3. You know that the encoding-specificity principle sometimes enhances memory. If you need to do a prospective-memory task tonight, would it help to associate that task with a mental image of the place where you will be tonight? The answer is "Yes," if you actually end up in that place, but the answer is "No," if you end up in a different setting (Cook et al., 2005).

Absentmindedness.   One intriguing component of prospective memory is absentmindedness. Most people do not publicly reveal their absentminded mistakes. You may therefore think that you are the only person who forgets to pick up a quart of milk on your way home from school, who dials Chris's phone number when you want to speak to Alex, or who fails to include an important attachment when sending an e-mail.

One problem is that the typical prospective-memory task represents a divided-attention situation. You must focus on your ongoing activity, as well as on the task you need to remember in the future (Marsh et al., 2000; McDaniel & Einstein, 2000). Absentminded behavior is especially likely when the intended action causes you to disrupt a customary schema. That is, you have a customary schema or habit that you usually perform, which is Action A (for example, driving from your college to your home). You also have a prospective-memory task that you must perform on this specific occasion, which is Action B (for example, stopping at the grocery store). In cases like this, your long-standing habit dominates the more fragile prospective memory, and you fall victim to absentminded behavior (Hay & Jacoby, 1996).

Prospective-memory errors are more likely in highly familiar surroundings when you are performing tasks automatically (Schacter, 2001). Errors are also more likely if you are preoccupied or distracted, or if you are feeling time pressure. In most cases, absentmindedness is simply irritating. However, sometimes these slips can produce airplane collisions, industrial accidents, and other disasters that influence the lives of hundreds of individuals (Finstad et al., 2006).

Suggestions for Improving Prospective Memory. Earlier in the chapter, we discussed numerous suggestions that you could use to aid your retrospective memory. Some of these internal strategies could presumably be used to aid your prospective memory as well. For example, a vivid, interactive mental image of a quart of milk might help you avoid driving past the grocery store in an absentminded fashion (Einstein & McDaniel, 2004).

However, the reminders that you choose must be distinctive if you want to perform a prospective-memory task (Engelkamp, 1998; Guynn et al., 1998). For example, suppose you want to remember to give Tonya a message tomorrow. It won't be helpful just to rehearse her name or just to remind yourself that you have to convey a message. Instead, you must form a strong connection between these two components, linking both Tonya's name and the fact that you must give her a message.

Another problem is that people are often overconfident that they will remember to perform specific prospective memory task. After all, the actual task of buying a quart of milk is extremely simple . . . but remembering to actually *do* this task is challenging.

External memory aids are especially helpful on prospective-memory tasks (McDaniel & Einstein, 2007). An **external memory aid** is defined as any device, external to yourself, that facilitates your memory in some way (Herrmann et al., 2002). Some examples of external memory aids include a shopping list, a rubber band around your wrist, asking someone else to remind you to do something, and the ring of an alarm clock, to remind you to make an important phone call.

The placement of your external memory aid is especially important. For example, my nephew sometimes drives to his mother's home for dinner, and she typically tells him about some items in the refrigerator that he must remember to take home when he leaves. After several prospective-memory lapses, he thought of an ideal external memory aid: When he arrives for dinner, he places his car keys in the refrigerator (White, 2003). Notice his mindfulness in designing the placement of this memory aid; he is highly unlikely to drive home without the refrigerated items.

My students report that they often use informal external mnemonics to aid their prospective memory. When they want to remember to bring a book to class, they place it in a location where they will have to confront the book on the way to class. They also place letters to be mailed in a conspicuous position on the dashboard of their car. Other students describe the sea of colored sticky notes that decorate their dormitory rooms.

Many commercial memory aids are also available to assist your prospective memory (Herrmann et al., 2002; Herrmann et al., 2006). For example, many people now carry PDAs, which can be programmed to provide reminders about prospective-memory tasks. However, these external memory aids are helpful only if you can use them easily and if they successfully remind you of what you are supposed to remember. Now that you are familiar with the challenges of prospective memory, try Demonstration 6.3. Also, review the memory-improvement techniques listed in Table 6.1.

Demonstration 6.3

Prospective Memory

Make a list of five prospective-memory tasks that you need to accomplish within the next day or two. These should be tasks that you must remember to complete on your own, without anyone else providing a reminder.

For each item, first describe the method you would customarily use to remember to do the task. Also note whether this method is typically successful. Then, for each task where you typically make a prospective-memory error, try to figure out a more effective reminder. (Incidentally, one prospective-memory task that you may forget to do is to complete this demonstration!)

TABLE 6.1

Memory-Improvement Strategies.

1. Suggestions from previous chapters

   a. Do not divide your attention between several simultaneous tasks.

   b. Process information in terms of its meaning, rather than at a shallow level, by emphasizing elaborative encodings, distinctiveness, and self-reference.

   c. Try to learn material in the same context as the one in which you will be tested.

   d. Don't be overconfident about the accuracy of your memory for life events.

2. Techniques related to practice

   a. The amount you learn depends on the total time you spend practicing.

   b. You'll learn more if you spread your learning trials over time (the distributed-practice effect).

   c. You'll also enhance your memory just by taking tests on the material.

3. Mnemonics using imagery

   a. Use imagery, especially imagery that shows an interaction between the items that need to be recalled.

   b. Use the keyword method; for example, if you are learning vocabulary in another language, identify an English word that sounds like the target word, and link the English word with the meaning of that target word.

   c. Use the method of loci when learning a series of items by associating each item with a physical location.

4. Mnemonics using organization

a. Use chunking by combining isolated items into meaningful units.

b. Construct a hierarchy by arranging items in a series of classes (e.g., Figure 6.3 on p. 174).

c. Take the first letter of each item you want to remember, and compose a word or sentence from these letters (first-letter technique).

d. Create a narrative, or a story that links a series of words together.

5. The multimodal approach

Memory improvement must be comprehensive, with attention to physical and mental health, social factors, and the flexible use of memory strategies; it must also be mindful.

6. Improving prospective memory

a. Create a vivid, interactive mental image to prompt future recall.

b. Create a specific reminder or an external memory aid.

◎ Section Summary: *Memory Strategies*

1. Previous chapters presented several strategies for memory improvement, specifically, avoiding divided attention, using deep levels of processing (including elaborate encodings, distinctiveness, and the self-reference method), using encoding specificity, and avoiding the dangers of overconfidence.

2. Three general memory-improvement strategies focus on aspects of practice: the total-time hypothesis, the distributed-practice effect, and the testing effect.

3. Some useful mnemonics focus on imagery; these include visualizing the items in vivid interaction, the keyword method, and the method of loci.

4. Other useful mnemonics focus on organization; these include chunking, the hierarchy technique, the first-letter technique, and the narrative technique.

5. A comprehensive approach to memory improvement proposes that memory problems require multifactor solutions that focus on physical, mental, and social factors, as well as training in the flexible use of a variety of memory strategies. The comprehensive approach also emphasizes a mindful approach to memory.

6. Whereas most of the research focuses on retrospective memory, the area of prospective memory examines how people remember to do something in the future. Although the two kinds of memory have somewhat different focuses, they share some important similarities.

7. People make more errors on prospective-memory tasks if the ongoing activity is demanding, if they switch projects, and if the location for the prospective-memory task is switched.

8. Prospective memory may create a divided-attention situation, which can lead to absentmindedness.

9. In general, prospective memory is more accurate if people use the same memory strategies they use in retrospective-memory tasks and if they use external memory aids.

METACOGNITION

The first half of this chapter focused on memory strategies, or methods of improving our memory. This second half focuses on the related topic of metacognition. We noted earlier that *metacognition* refers to your knowledge and control of your cognitive processes. One important function of metacognition is to supervise the way you select and use your memory strategies. Consistent with Theme 1, metacognition is an extremely active process (Koriat & Helstrup, 2007; McCormick, 2003).

Think about the variety of metacognitive knowledge you possess. For example, you know what kind of factors influence your own memory—factors such as the time of day, your motivation, the type of material, and social circumstances. If you have studied the information in this textbook and in your cognitive psychology class, you already know more than most people about the general factors that influence your memory (Magnussen et al., 2006).

In addition, you know how to control or regulate your study strategies. If something looks difficult to remember, you'll spend more time trying to commit it to memory. You also have metacognitive knowledge about whether information is currently on the "tip of your tongue." Try to recall, for instance, the name of the psychologist who is primarily responsible for developing the theory of working memory, which we discussed in Chapter 4. Is his name on the tip of your tongue? Still another kind of metacognitive knowledge focuses on your understanding of material that you've read. For example, do you understand the definition of *metacognition*? All these examples apply to your knowledge and awareness of your cognitive processes.

Metacognition is an intriguing topic because we use our cognitive processes to think about our cognitive processes. It is important because our knowledge about our cognitive processes can guide us in selecting strategies to improve our future cognitive performance. Metacognition is also important because a general goal in college should be to learn how to think and how to become a reflective person. As a reflective person, you can consider what you have done and what you plan to do in the future (Dominowski, 2002).

Let's review topics related to metacognition that were described in previous chapters of this book. For instance, in Chapter 3, we saw that people often have limited consciousness about their higher mental processes. As a result, they may not be able to identify which factors helped them solve a problem. In addition, Chapter 4 explored Alan Baddeley's (2001) theory of working memory. That theory proposes that the central executive plays an important role in planning behavior. One example is the metacognitive task of planning which topics you'll spend the most time studying in preparation for an exam.

Chapter 5 discussed how people may have difficulty on source-monitoring tasks. For instance, you may not be able to recall whether you actually gave a book to a friend—or whether you merely imagined you had done so. We also noted that people are sometimes unaware of the errors they make in flashbulb memory or courtroom testimony.

In this section of the current chapter, we will examine three important kinds of metacognition. Our first topic is **metamemory,** a topic that refers to people's knowledge and control of their memory. Metamemory plays a major part in memory improvement.

We will therefore explore several components of metamemory. Two related kinds of metacognition are metacomprehension and the tip-of-the-tongue phenomenon.

We'll also examine related components of metacognition in later chapters. For example, in Chapter 11 we will discuss whether people can accurately judge how close they are to solving a cognitive problem. Also, Chapter 13 addresses the development of metamemory across the lifespan. Let's begin by focusing on three different aspects of metamemory: (1) People's accuracy in predicting memory performance; (2) people's knowledge about memory strategies; and (3) people's knowledge about how to regulate their study strategies. This third topic will be the focus of this chapter's In Depth feature.

Metamemory and the Prediction of Memory Performance

Have you ever been in this situation? You thought that you knew the material for a midterm, and—in fact—you expected to receive a fairly high grade. However, when the midterms were handed back, you received a C. If this sounds familiar, you realize that your metamemory isn't always accurate in predicting memory performance.

In what circumstances does metamemory accurately predict memory performance? In other words, if you are confident about your performance on some memory task, is your memory indeed accurate? The answer to this question depends on which aspect of metamemory we are examining:

1. When people estimate their *total score* on a memory test, they are generally overconfident, rather than accurate.

2. When people have a number of items to remember, they can accurately predict which *individual items* they'll remember and which ones they'll forget.

Metamemory on a Total-Score Basis. In some of the metamemory studies, students begin by studying a list of paired associates, such as *coat-sandwich*. In other words, when they see the word *coat*, they know that they must respond *sandwich*. Then they are asked to predict the total number of correct responses they will supply on a later test (Koriat, 2007; Koriat & Bjork, 2005, 2006a, 2006b). In this situation, they are likely to commit the **foresight bias;** they overestimate the number of answers they will correctly supply on a future test.

The problem here is that they are studying those word pairs while the correct responses are visible, so their prediction probably won't be realistic. Keep this issue in mind if you are learning terminology or vocabulary in another language. You would be more likely to provide an accurate estimate if you used flashcards, let's say, with the English word on one side and the French word on the other side. Similarly, if you have a psychology exam, based on a textbook, read the material on a page, close the book and summarize the information on that page. You may have a general idea about the material, but you might not provide specific information when the book is closed!

In other studies, students estimate their total scores *after* finishing an exam. For example, Dunning and his coauthors (2003) asked students in a sophomore-level psychology course to estimate the total score they thought they had earned on an examination they had just completed. Then these researchers graded the test and divided the students into four groups, based on their actual test score.

FIGURE 6.4

Estimated Total Score vs. Actual Total Score, as a Function of Actual Test Performance.

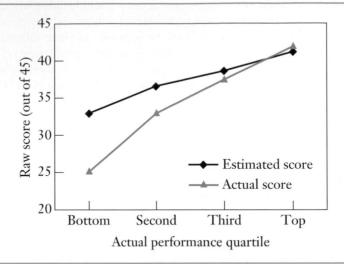

Source: Dunning et al., 2003.

Figure 6.4 shows the performance for the four groups, the bottom quartile, second quartile, third quartile, and top quartile. Notice that the students in the top quartile estimated their total actual scores very accurately and that students in the third quartile were almost as accurate. However, the less competent students clearly overestimated their performance. For instance, the students in the bottom quarter of the class overestimated their performance by about 30%. Ironically, this group of students is unaware of their limitations; they do not know that they do not know the material!

In other research, Dunning (2005) tested college students on a variety of other cognitive skills (e.g., English grammar). Again, the students with the weakest cognitive skills were especially likely to overestimate their total scores on these tests.

Metamemory on an Item-by-Item Basis. We've seen that people tend to be overconfident when they estimate the total number of correct items. The situation is more hopeful when we measure metamemory in a different fashion. Specifically, people's metamemory can be highly accurate when we consider their predictions about which individual items they'll remember and which ones they'll forget.

In a classic study, Eugene Lovelace (1984) presented pairs of unrelated English words, such as *disease–railroad*. The participants were told that they would be tested for paired-associate learning; that is, they would later see the first word in each pair and be asked to supply the second word. Let's consider the predictions of students who saw each pair for 8 seconds. After the final exposure of each pair, the participants rated the likelihood of their answering the item correctly on a later test. After these ratings, the participants saw the first word of each pair, and they were told to supply the appropriate second word.

FIGURE 6.5

Probability of Recalling an Item, as a Function of Rated Likelihood of Answering the Question.

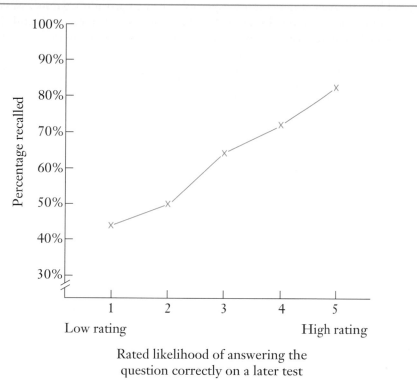

Source: Lovelace, 1984.

As you can see from Figure 6.5, people *can* accurately predict their likelihood of recalling an item. When they give an item a rating of 1, they recall it only about 45% of the time when they are tested later. In contrast, when they give a rating of 5, they recall the item about 80% of the time.

You can apply these findings to your classroom performance. Suppose that you know you'll be tested on a specific list of items, such as Spanish vocabulary or definitions for specific psychology terms. In this situation, you are likely to be reasonably accurate in identifying which items you'll recall and which you'll forget.

In general, the research shows that college students are fairly accurate in predicting which items they'll remember when they are learning straightforward material like pairs of words (Izaute et al., 2002; Koriat & Helstrup, 2007; McCormick, 2003). One factor that students use in making these predictions is whether they could easily generate an image linking the two words together (Hertzog et al., 2003). However, metamemory is less accurate when the task is less clear-cut than in paired associate learning (Nelson, 1999).

Researchers have discovered that people are even more accurate in predicting which item they will recall if they delay their judgments, rather than making them immediately after learning (Dunlosky et al., 2002; Koriat & Helstrup, 2007; Son & Schwartz, 2002). These delayed judgments are especially likely to provide accurate assessments of your memory performance because they assess long-term memory—and the actual memory task requires long-term memory.* In contrast, immediate judgments assess working memory, which is less relevant to this memory task.

These particular findings suggest an important practical application. Suppose that you are studying your notes for an exam, and you are trying to determine which topics need more work. Be sure to wait a few minutes before assessing your memory. Your metamemory is more likely to be accurate if you wait than if you make an immediate judgment.

Individual Differences: Metamemory and Adults with Attention-Deficit/Hyperactivity Disorder.

A primary cognitive characteristic of people with **Attention-Deficit/Hyperactivity Disorder (ADHD)** is that they have difficulty paying close attention at school, at work, and in other activities (American Psychiatric Association, 2000). According to estimates, about 4 to 5% of the adult population have ADHD. In general, people with ADHD are even more likely than other people to overestimate their total score on memory tasks (Knouse et al., 2006). For example, college students with ADHD might overestimate their scores on a specific memory task by 30%, whereas college students without ADHD may overestimate these scores by 20%.

Laura Knouse and her coauthors (2006) wanted to discover how people with ADHD performed on a task where metamemory was measured on an item-by-item basis. They located a sample of 28 people from a university and the surrounding community who met the criteria for ADHD. All participants were between the ages of 18 and 60. Then they located 28 people without ADHD, who matched the first group in age, gender, and university versus community status. On the day of the metamemory study, the individuals with ADHD received no medication.

Using a method somewhat similar to Lovelace's (1984) setup, Knouse and her coauthors showed each item pair (e.g., DISEASE-RAILROAD) on a computer screen for 8 seconds. Then the participants were asked to estimate, on a scale from 0 to 100%, the likelihood that they would recall the second word, when given the first word. For 30 pairs, everyone provided metamemory estimates immediately after the initial exposure. For 30 additional pairs, everyone provided delayed metamemory estimates, after a random number of intervening items.

Figure 6.6a and 6.6b show the results for the immediate judgments and the delayed judgment, respectively. Notice the diagonal line in solid black. This line represents the performance of people who have "perfect calibration." For example, if these people

---

*In fact, it could be argued that this measure is actually a long-term memory test, rather than a true test of metamemory (Lovelace, 1996).

FIGURE 6.6

Accuracy of Predicting Which Items Will Be Correctly Recalled, when Making Judgments of Learning Immediately After Seeing a Pair (Figure 6.6a) and When Making Delayed Judgments (Figure 6.6b).

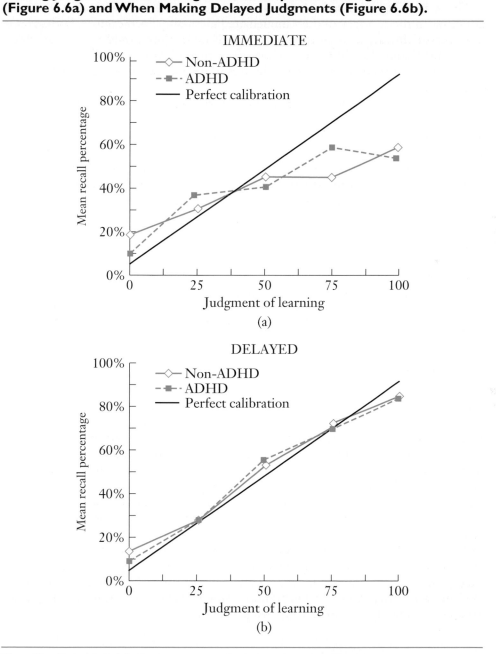

(a)

(b)

Note: The diagonal straight line represents perfectly accurate predictions.

Source: Based on Knouse et al., 2006.

estimated that they would have a 50% chance of correctly recalling these items, then they indeed did correctly recall them 50% of the time. Their predictions were equally accurate for all levels of item difficulty.

Now look at Figure 6.6a. As you can see, people with and without ADHD did not differ in the accuracy of their immediate judgments. Furthermore, both groups were reasonably accurate in predicting which items they would recall and which they would miss. As Figure 6.6b shows, the two groups again did not differ in the accuracy of their delayed judgments. Both groups were also extremely "well calibrated."

In other words, people with ADHD may overestimate their total scores on a memory test. However, they are highly accurate in estimating their performance on an item-by-item basis, especially when there is a delay prior to estimation. As Knouse and her colleagues point out, their sample of people with ADHD was unusual. People with ADHD who are university students—or who live near a university—are likely to function better than people with ADHD in the general population. Still, this study demonstrates that, in these circumstances, people with ADHD can make highly accurate judgments about an important component of memory.

Metamemory About Factors Affecting Memory

According to the research, many college students are not sufficiently aware of the importance of strategic factors that may affect their memory performance (Cornoldi, 1998; Gurung, 2003, 2004). In fact, students who earn low scores on exams are likely to use no specific memory strategies in learning material for an exam (McDougall & Gruneberg, 2002).

Furthermore, metamemory should also help students identify which memory strategies work best for them and which ones are ineffective. However, Suzuki-Slakter (1988) found that students weren't aware that "all memory strategies are not created equal." For example, she instructed one group of students to memorize material by simply repeating it—a strategy that you know is relatively ineffective. These students severely overestimated their performance. Another group was told to make up stories and images about the items—a strategy you know to be effective. These students actually *underestimated* their performance.

Other studies have found that people are not aware that the keyword method (illustrated in Figure 6.2 on p. 172) is more effective than mere repetition (Pressley et al., 1984, 1988). However, when people practiced both methods and saw their superior performance with the keyword method, they were much more likely to use this method in the future. This research highlights an important point: Try using various study strategies. Then on your next test, see how you do. Identify which method or methods were most effective. You'll be much more likely to revise your strategies if you can demonstrate that they improve your own performance.

IN DEPTH

Metamemory and the Regulation of Study Strategies

You may have developed your metamemory to the point that you know exactly which study strategies work best in which circumstances. However, your exam performance may still be poor unless you effectively regulate your study strategies by spending more time studying the difficult topics. The research on the regulation of study strategies emphasizes that memory tasks require a substantial amount of *decision making* as you plan how to master the material (Koriat & Helstrup, 2007; Metcalfe, 2000). Consistent with Theme 4, you must often coordinate at least two cognitive processes—in this case, memory and decision making.

This In Depth feature examines the way students make decisions about how they will allocate their study time, in preparing for a memory test. As you'll see, in some circumstances, students will spend more time on the difficult items than on the easy items. However, when the material is more challenging and the time is limited, students will spend the most time learning the items that are just within their grasp (Kornell & Metcalfe, 2006).

Allocating Time When the Task is Easy.   In a classic study, Thomas Nelson and R. Jacob Leonesio (1988) examined how students distribute their study time when they can study at their own pace. In this study, students were allowed a reasonable amount of time to study the material.

Nelson and Leonesio found that students allocated more study time for the items that they believed would be difficult to master. The correlations here averaged about +.30 (where .00 would indicate no relationship and +1.00 would be a perfect correlation between each item's judged difficulty and its study time). In other words, the students did not passively review all the material equally. The research on metamemory reveals that people take an active, strategic approach to this cognitive task, a finding that is consistent with Theme 1 about active processing.

One of my professors in graduate school suggested an interesting strategy for examining research data (Martin, 1967). As he pointed out, whenever you see a number, you should ask yourself, "Why is it so high, and why is it so low?" In this case, the correlation is as *high* as +.30 because students do realize the difficult items require more time. This general relationship has been replicated in later research (Koriat, 1997; Nelson et al., 1994; Son & Schwartz, 2002). But why is this crucial correlation as *low* as +.30? Unfortunately, students are less than ideal in regulating their study strategies. They spend longer than necessary studying items they already know, and not enough time studying the items they have not yet mastered.

Lisa Son and Janet Metcalfe (2000) reviewed the research on students' allocation of study time. They discovered that 35 out of the 46 published studies demonstrated that these students spend more time on the difficult items. However, they found that all these studies examined relatively easy material, such as learning pairs of words. In addition, these students typically had enough time to study all of the items. Son and Metcalfe speculated that students might choose a different strategy in other circumstances.

Allocating Time When the Task is Difficult. Think about the exams you've taken so far this term. In psychology courses, for instance, your exams require you to remember conceptual information about psychology, rather than a list of paired words. In addition, students in real-life settings have only a limited time to study for their exams (Kornell & Metcalfe, 2006). Son and Metcalfe (2000) decided to design a situation that more closely resembles the challenging learning situation that college students often face.

Let's consider the details of one of Son and Metcalfe's (2000) three studies. The test material was a series of eight encyclopedia-style biographies; a good reader would need about 60 minutes to read them all completely. The researchers increased the time pressure for this task by allowing the students only 30 minutes to read all the material. The students began by reading a single paragraph from each biography; they ranked the biographies in terms of their perceived difficulty. Then the researchers informed them that they had 30 minutes to read the material, and they could choose how to spend their time.

The results of this study showed that students spent the majority of their study time on the biographies they considered easy, rather than those they considered difficult. Notice that this strategy is wise, because they can master more material within the limited time frame.

Additional studies showed that—when students are facing time pressure—they choose to study material that seems relatively easy to master (Kornell & Metcalfe, 2006; Metcalfe, 2002). Furthermore, Metcalfe (2002) tested students who had expertise in a given area. These students chose to concentrate their time on more challenging material, compared to the novices.

Conclusions About the Regulation of Study Strategies. As you can see from this In Depth feature, students can regulate their study strategies in a sophisticated fashion. When they have time to master a relatively easy task, they allocate the most time to the difficult items. On a more challenging task, with time pressure, they realistically adjust their study strategies so that they focus on the items they are likely to master in the limited time frame (Kornell & Metcalfe, 2006).

We have seen that students regulate their study strategies. Furthermore, they also regulate the *regulation* of their study strategies! That is, they choose one style for easy tasks and a different style for difficult tasks. As Metcalfe (2000) concludes, "Rather than simply being passive repositories for knowledge and memories, humans can use their knowledge of what they know to exert control over what they know [and] what they will know" (p. 207).

Let's review the information about metamemory. We have explored how attention to your metamemory can improve your performance. Naturally, you need to know memory strategies, such as those described in the first part of this chapter. You also need to have the time and motivation to devise an appropriate plan for mastering the material (Langer, 2000; Robbins et al., 2004). Finally, you need to know how to use memory strategies effectively by selecting those strategies that work well for you and by distributing your study time appropriately.

The Tip-of-the-Tongue Phenomenon

Try Demonstration 6.4 to see whether any of the definitions encourages a tip-of-the-tongue experience. The **tip-of-the-tongue phenomenon** refers to the subjective feeling you have when you are confident that you know the target word for which you are searching, yet you cannot recall it (Schwartz, 1999, 2002). In our discussion of this topic, let's first consider the classic study by Brown and McNeill (1966). Then we'll examine some of the later research, as well as the related topic of the feeling of knowing.

⊚   Demonstration 6.4

The Tip-of-the-Tongue Phenomenon

Look at each of the definitions below. For each definition, supply the appropriate word if you know it. Indicate "don't know" for those that you are certain you don't know. Mark "TOT" next to those for which you are reasonably certain you know the word, though you can't recall it now. For these TOT words, supply at least one word that sounds similar to the target word. The answers appear at the end of the chapter. Check to see whether your similar-sounding words actually do resemble the target words.

1. An absolute ruler, a tyrant.
2. A stone having a cavity lined with crystals.
3. A great circle of the earth passing through the geographic poles and any given point on the earth's surface.
4. Worthy of respect or reverence by reason of age and dignity.
5. Shedding leaves each year, as opposed to evergreen.
6. A person appointed to act as a substitute for another.
7. Five offspring born at a single birth.
8. A special quality of leadership that captures the popular imagination and inspires unswerving allegiance.
9. The red coloring matter of the red blood corpuscles.
10. A flying reptile that was extinct at the end of the Mesozoic Era.
11. A spring from which hot water, steam, or mud gushes out at intervals, found in Yellowstone National Park.
12. The second stomach of a bird, which has thick, muscular walls.

Brown and McNeill's Classic Research. Roger Brown and David McNeill (1966) conducted the first formal investigation in this area. Their description of a man "seized" by a tip-of-the-tongue state may capture the torment you sometimes feel when you fail to snatch a word from the tip of your tongue:

> The signs of it were unmistakable; he would appear to be in mild torment, something like the brink of a sneeze, and if he found the word his relief was considerable. (p. 326)

In their research, Brown and McNeill produced the tip-of-the-tongue state by giving people the definition for an uncommon English word—such as *sampan*, *ambergris*, or *nepotism*—and asking them to identify the word. Sometimes people supplied the appropriate word immediately, and other times they were confident that they did not know the word. However, in still other cases, the definition produced a tip-of-the-tongue state. In these cases, the researchers asked people to provide words that resembled the target word in terms of sound, but not meaning. For example, when the target word was *sampan*, people provided these similar-sounding words: *Saipan, Siam, Cheyenne, sarong, sanching,* and *symphoon.*

When Brown and McNeill analyzed the results, they found that the similar-sounding words did indeed resemble the target words. Specifically, the similar-sounding words matched the target's first letter 49% of the time, and they matched the target's number of syllables 48% of the time.

Think about why the tip-of-the-tongue phenomenon is one kind of metacognition. People know enough about their memory for the target word to be able to say, "This word is on the tip of my tongue." Their knowledge is indeed fairly accurate, because they are likely to be able to identify the first letter and other attributes of the target word. They are also likely to provide similar-sounding words that really do resemble the target word.

In addition to metacognition, the tip-of-the-tongue phenomenon is related to several other topics in cognitive psychology, including consciousness (discussed in Chapter 3), semantic memory (discussed in Chapter 8), and language production (discussed in Chapter 10). As we have seen repeatedly, cognitive processes are interrelated.

Later Research on the Tip-of-the-Tongue Phenomenon. Researchers conclude that people report having approximately one tip-of-the-tongue experience each week in their daily lives (James & Burke, 2000; Schwartz, 2002). However, bilingual individuals experience the tip-of-the-tongue effect more frequently than monolinguals. One reason for this difference is that bilinguals have a greater total number of separate words in their semantic memory, compared to monolinguals (Gollan & Acenas, 2004; Gollan et al., 2005).

People successfully retrieve the word they are seeking about half the time, often within the first 2 minutes of the tip-of-the-tongue feeling. As you might expect, words that produce a strong tip-of-the-tongue sensation are especially likely to be correctly recognized at a later time (Schwartz, 2002; Schwartz et al., 2000).

When people are experiencing a tip-of-the-tongue state, they correctly guess the first letter of the target word between 50 and 70% of the time. They are also highly accurate in identifying the appropriate number of syllables, with accuracy rates between 45 and 85% (Brown, 1991; Schwartz, 2002). Furthermore, they can usually identify semantic characteristics of the target, for example, whether this target is pleasant, neutral, or unpleasant (Koriat et al., 2003).

Researchers have also documented the tip-of-the-tongue phenomenon in non-English languages such as Polish, Japanese, and Italian (Schwartz, 1999, 2002,). Research in these other languages demonstrates that people can retrieve other characteristics of the target word, in addition to its first letter and number of syllables. For example, Italian speakers can often retrieve the grammatical gender of the target word that they are seeking (Caramazza & Miozzo, 1997; Miozzo & Caramazza, 1997).

Feeling of Knowing. Another topic related to the tip-of-the-tongue phenomenon is called the **feeling of knowing,** or the prediction about whether you could correctly recognize the correct answer to a question (Schwartz & Perfect, 2002). The tip-of-the-tongue phenomenon is generally an involuntary effect. In contrast, the feeling of knowing is more conscious; you thoughtfully assess whether you could recognize the answer if you were given several options (Koriat & Helstrup, 2007).

You may also have a feeling of knowing if someone asks you to list as many members of a specific category as possible—say a list of vegetables or a list of students from your high school. You know whether you can supply dozens of additional items and when that category is nearly empty (Young, 2004).

People are likely to have a strong feeling of knowing if they can retrieve a large amount of partial information (Koriat & Helstrup, 2007; Schwartz et al., 1997; Schwartz & Smith, 1997). For example, I recently compiled an informal list of novels that focused on individuals in non-Western cultures. I wanted to include a book called *The Kite Runner*, about a boy growing up in Afghanistan. The author's last name was "Husseini," but what was his first name? A strong feeling of knowing enveloped me. The available mental clues were that this first name had two syllables and that it had a combination of consonants that would not occur in English. In this case, however, the first name wasn't really on the tip of my tongue, and I wasn't able to recall the answer. However, I knew I could select the correct answer from a set of options. A quick check of some resources revealed that the author's first name was "Khaled." Presumably this feeling of knowing would have been weaker if fewer mental clues had been available.

Metacomprehension

Did you understand the material on the tip-of-the-tongue phenomenon? Are you aware that you've started reading a new subtopic, in this current section on metacognition? How much longer can you read today before you feel that you can't absorb any more? As you think about these issues, you are engaging in metacomprehension. **Metacomprehension** refers to our thoughts about comprehension. Most research on metacomprehension focuses on reading comprehension, rather than on the comprehension of spoken speech (Maki & McGuire, 2002). Remember that the general term, *metacognition*, includes both metamemory (pp. 182 to 193) and metacomprehension (pp. 193 to 196).

Let's consider two topics in connection with metacomprehension. First, how accurate is the typical college student's metacomprehension? Second, how can you improve your metacomprehension skills?

Metacomprehension Accuracy.   In general, college students are not very accurate in their metacomprehension skills. For example, they may not notice inconsistencies or missing information in a written passage. Instead, they think they understand it (Maki, 1998; Mayer, 2004; McNamara & Shapiro, 2005).

Furthermore, students often believe that they have understood something they have read because they are familiar with its general topic. However, they often fail to retain specific information, and they may overestimate how they will perform when they are tested on the material (Chi, 2000; Maki, 1998; Maki & McGuire, 2002).

Let's consider a representative study on metacomprehension. Pressley and Ghatala (1988) tested introductory psychology students to assess their metacomprehension as well as their performance on tests of reading ability. Specifically, these researchers selected reading comprehension tests from the Scholastic Aptitude Test, an earlier form of the current SAT. If you took the SAT, you'll recall that the items on this portion of the test typically contain between one and three paragraphs, in essay form. The essay remains visible while you answer several multiple-choice questions. Each question has five possible answers. Therefore, a person who simply guessed on an answer would be correct 20% of the time.

The students in Pressley and Ghatala's study answered the multiple-choice questions, and then they rated how certain they were that they had answered each question correctly. If they were absolutely certain that their answer had been correct, they were told to answer 100%. If they were just guessing, they were told to report 20%. This certainty rating served as the measure of metacomprehension. (Notice, incidentally, that this task would have assessed metamemory—rather than metacomprehension—if there had been a delay between the reading task and the presentation of the multiple-choice questions.)

Let's consider the results. When a student had answered a reading comprehension question *correctly*, he or she supplied an average certainty rating of 73%. In other words, the students were fairly confident about these items, which is appropriate. However, when a student answered a question *incorrectly*, he or she supplied an average certainty rating of about 64%. Unfortunately, this is about the same level of confidence they showed for the items they answered correctly! Furthermore, these data suggest that students are highly overconfident in many cases. About two-thirds of these students believed that they understood the material they had just finished reading, even when they answered the questions incorrectly.

People with excellent metacomprehension often receive higher scores on tests of reading comprehension (Maki & Berry, 1984; Maki & McGuire, 2002; Schraw, 1994). For example, Maki and her coauthors (1994) reported that readers who were good at assessing which sections of a text they had understood were also likely to receive higher scores on a reading-comprehension test. In fact, metacomprehension accuracy and reading comprehension scores were significantly correlated (r = +.43).

In general, college students with low reading ability are overconfident when they estimate their scores on a difficult reading test. In contrast, high-ability students tend to be underconfident (Maki et al., 2005).

Students also become somewhat more accurate in assessing their performance as they gain experience in reading the text and as they receive feedback (Maki & Berry, 1984; Maki & Serra, 1992; Schooler et al., 2004). However, the improvement is not dramatic. College students clearly need some hints on how to increase their metacomprehension abilities and how to take advantage of their reading experiences.

Improving Metacomprehension. Ideally, students should be accurate in assessing whether they understand what they have read. In other words, their subjective assessments should match their performance on an objective test. One effective way to improve metacomprehension is to take a pretest—which can supply feedback about comprehension—before taking the actual examination (Glenberg et al., 1987; Maki, 1998).

Another effective method for improving metacomprehension is to read a passage, wait a few minutes, and then try to summarize the passage. This procedure not only improves your judgment about how well you know the passage, but it should also increase your score on a test about this material (Baker & Dunlosky, 2006; Dunlosky et al., 2005; Thiede et al., 2005). Furthermore, when you use this kind of active reading, you are less likely to "zone out" and fail to notice that you are no longer paying attention to your reading (Schooler et al., 2004).

As we have seen, one component of metacomprehension requires you to accurately assess whether you understand a written passage. However, metacomprehension also requires you to *regulate* your reading, so that you know how to read more effectively. For example, good and poor readers differ in their awareness that certain reading strategies are useful. Good readers are more likely to report that they try to make connections among the ideas they have read. They also try to create visual images, based on descriptions in the text (Kaufman et al., 1985; Pressley, 1996). In addition, good readers outline and summarize material in their own words when they are reading textbooks (McDaniel et al., 1996).

Demonstration 6.5 will help you consider your own metacomprehension skills and think about some strategies for self-management. As researchers emphasize, metacomprehension and strategy use are essential components of skilled reading (McCormick, 2003; Schooler et al., 2004).

◉ Demonstration 6.5

Assessing Your Metacomprehension Skills

Answer each of the following questions about your own metacomprehension. If you answer "no" to any question, devise a plan for improving metacomprehension that you can apply as you read the next assigned chapter in this textbook.

1. Before beginning to read an assignment, do you try to assess how carefully you should read the material?
2. In general, are you accurate in predicting your performance on the exam questions that focus on the reading assignments?

(continued)

> ⊚ **Demonstration 6.5**
>
> **Assessing Your Metacomprehension Skills**   (*continued*)
>
> 3. After you read a short section (roughly a page in length), do you make yourself summarize what you have just read—using your own words?
>
> 4. After reading a chapter in this textbook, do you test yourself on the list of new terms and on the review questions?
>
> 5. Do you reread a portion when it doesn't make sense or when you realize that you haven't been paying attention?
>
> 6. Do you try to draw connections among the ideas in your textbook?
>
> 7. Do you try to draw connections between the ideas in your textbook and the information you have learned in class?
>
> 8. When you read a term you do not know, do you try to determine its meaning by looking it up in a dictionary or in the glossary of this textbook?
>
> 9. When you review material prior to a test, do you spend more time reviewing the reading that you consider difficult than the concepts that you have already mastered?
>
> 10. When reading through several journal articles to see whether they might be relevant for a paper you are writing, do you first try to assess—without reading every word—the general scope or findings of each article?

⊚ Section Summary: *Metacognition*

1. Metacognition is your knowledge and control of your cognitive processes; three important components of metacognition are metamemory, the tip-of-the-tongue phenomenon, and metacomprehension.

2. People are often overconfident when they are judging their overall performance on a memory task. However, metamemory skills are quite accurate when people are judging which specific items they will remember best.

3. In a study by Knouse and her coauthors (2006), adults with ADHD were similar to adults without ADHD in judging which specific items they would remember best.

4. In general, students are not sufficiently aware that some memory strategies are more effective than others.

5. When the task is easy, students spend somewhat more time studying difficult material, rather than easy material. When the task is difficult, and time is limited, they study material that they are likely to master.

6. The research on the tip-of-the-tongue phenomenon shows that—even when people cannot remember the word for which they are searching—they often can identify important attributes such as the first letter, the number of syllables, similar-sounding words, and semantic characteristics of the target.

7. The phrase "feeling of knowing" refers to situations in which you think you could identify a correct answer from several choices, even though the target isn't actually on the tip of your tongue.

8. Studies on metacomprehension suggest that students are often overconfident in judging whether they understand the material they have read, especially if they have low reading ability.

9. Students' metacomprehension can be improved if they take a pretest, and if they wait a few minutes and then summarize the material. Good readers also use a variety of strategies to regulate their reading.

CHAPTER REVIEW QUESTIONS

1. One trend throughout this chapter is that memory is enhanced by deep levels of processing. Review the material in the section on memory strategies, identifying how almost every strategy makes use of some form of deep processing. Also explain why deep processing would be important in metacognition.

2. Discuss as many of the memory-improvement techniques from this chapter as you can remember. Which techniques focus on strategies, and which focus on metacognition? In each case, tell how you can use each one to remember some information from this chapter for your next examination in cognitive psychology.

3. Why are some current memory researchers critical of the traditional approaches to memory improvement? Describe how the multimodal approach emphasizes a more comprehensive and complex view of memory improvement.

4. Describe Langer's concepts of mindlessness and mindfulness. Then turn to the chapter outline on page 163. Using these topics as a guide, point out how you can be more mindful in reading and studying for your next exam in cognitive psychology.

5. Why is prospective memory different from retrospective memory? How is it different? Think of a specific elderly person you know who complains about his or her memory. What hints can you provide to this person to encourage better prospective-memory performance?

6. In general, how accurate is our metacognition? Provide examples from various metamemory studies, the tip-of-the-tongue phenomenon, and metacomprehension. When you describe the research on metamemory, be sure to describe situations in which people are relatively accurate and the situations in which they are less accurate. Finally, how do people with ADHD perform on these metamemory tasks?

7. Several parts of this chapter emphasized that people tend to be overconfident about their ability to remember material and to understand written material. Summarize this information, mentioning a group of people who are *underconfident*. Then describe how you can apply this information when you are reading and studying for your next exam in your course on cognitive psychology.

8. Some parts of the section on metacognition emphasized the control of study strategies and reading strategies, rather than simply knowledge about cognitive processes. Describe the research on strategy regulation and point out how your own strategy regulation has improved since you began college.

9. What evidence suggests that people are reasonably accurate when they report that a word is on the tip of their tongue? Why is this topic related to metacognition? What other components of the tip-of-the-tongue phenomenon would be interesting topics for future research?

10. What kind of metacomprehension tasks are relevant when you are reading this textbook? List as many tasks as possible. Why do you suppose that metacomprehension for reading passages of text would be less accurate than metamemory for learning pairs of words (for example, refer to the 1984 study by Lovelace, described on pp. 184 to 185)?

KEYWORDS

metacognition
memory strategy
levels of processing
rehearsal
self-reference effect
encoding-specificity principle
total-time hypothesis
distributed-practice effect
spacing effect
spaced learning
massed learning
desirable difficulties
testing effect

mnemonics
imagery
keyword method
method of loci
organization
chunking
hierarchy
first-letter technique
narrative technique
multimodal approach
mindfulness
prospective memory
retrospective memory

external memory aid
metamemory
foresight bias
Attention-
   Deficit/Hyperactivity
   Disorder
ADHD
tip-of-the-tongue
   phenomenon
feeling of knowing
metacomprehension

RECOMMENDED READINGS

Einstein, G. O., & McDaniel, M. A. (2004). *Memory fitness: A guide for successful aging.* New Haven: Yale University Press. Don't be misled by the title of this book, because it would actually be useful for adolescents and adults. It also provides an ideal blend of research summaries and practical suggestions.

Herrmann, D., Raybeck, D., & Gruneberg, M. (2002). *Improving memory and study skills.* Kirkland, WA: Hogrefe & Huber. Many books on memory improvement are based on the author's whims. In contrast, the authors of this book are well-respected researchers in the area, and they approach the topic from a comprehensive perspective.

McDaniel, M. A., & Einstein, G. O. (2007). *Prospective memory: An overview and synthesis of an emerging field.* Thousand Oaks, CA: Sage. Two of the leading researchers in the area of prospective memory have written a book that is both research based and student oriented.

Perfect, T. J., & Schwartz, B. L. (Eds.). (2002). *Applied metacognition.* Cambridge, UK: Cambridge University Press. I highly recommend this book if you want additional information about metacognition! It includes chapters on topics such as metamemory monitoring, metacomprehension, overconfidence, and the development of metacognition.

ANSWERS TO DEMONSTRATION 6.4

1. despot
2. geode
3. meridian
4. venerable
5. deciduous
6. surrogate

7. quintuplets
8. charisma
9. hemoglobin
10. pterodactyl
11. geyser
12. gizzard

CHAPTER 7

Using Mental Imagery and Cognitive Maps

PREVIEW

Chapters 4, 5, and 6 have emphasized how we remember verbal material. Now we shift our focus to more pictorial material as we investigate three components of mental imagery: the characteristics of mental images, neuroscience research on mental images, and cognitive maps.

Psychologists have devised some creative research techniques to examine the characteristics of mental images. In many ways, mental imagery and the perception of real objects are similar. For example, if you were asked to imagine the sound of a flute, you would have trouble perceiving the sound of a harmonica—just as the real sound of a flute would interfere with perceiving that harmonica's sound. The first section of this chapter also examines a controversy about how we store mental images in memory: Are images stored in a picture-like code or in a more abstract, language-like description? A final topic in this first section is the complex pattern of gender comparisons in spatial ability.

The second section explores the recent evidence from cognitive neuroscience research. This research suggests that visual images activate some of the same brain structures that are activated during vision. This section also examines neuroscience correlates of mental rotation tasks.

A cognitive map is a representation of your external environment. For instance, you have developed a cognitive map of the town or city in which your college is located. Our cognitive maps show certain systematic distortions. For example, you may remember that two streets intersect at right angles, even when the angles are far from 90 degrees. Because of these distortions, our mental maps are a more organized and more standardized version of reality. The In Depth feature in this chapter considers how people can create cognitive maps of their environment, based on verbal descriptions.

INTRODUCTION

Take a moment to create a clear mental image of the cover of this textbook. Be sure to include details such as its size, shape, and color, as well as the photo of the nautilus shell. Next, create a "mental map" of the most direct route between your current location and the nearest grocery store. These tasks require **imagery,** which is the mental representation of stimuli when those stimuli are not physically present (Kosslyn et al., 2002).

Imagery relies exclusively on top-down processing, because your sensory receptors do not receive any input when you create a mental image (Kosslyn & Thompson, 2000). We discussed perceptual processes in Chapters 2 and 3 of this book. In contrast to imagery, perception requires you to register information through the receptors in your sensory organs, such as your eyes and ears (Kosslyn, Ganis, & Thompson, 2001). As we emphasized earlier, perception requires both bottom-up and top-down processing.

| 🌀 **Demonstration 7.1** |

The Relevance of Mental Imagery in Earlier Chapters of this Book

Look back at the Table of Contents (just before Chapter 1) to review the outlines for Chapters 2–6. How would visual imagery or auditory imagery be relevant in each of these chapters? For some representative answers, look on page 237, at the end of this chapter.

We use imagery for a wide variety of familiar cognitive activities (Denis et al., 2004; Tversky, 2005a). Try Demonstration 7.1 to illustrate how imagery was relevant in the earlier chapters of this book. Imagery is also relevant in the cognitive processes we'll discuss later in this textbook. For example, you'll see in Chapter 11 that mental imagery is immensely helpful when you want to solve a spatial problem or work on a task that requires creativity.

In addition, some professions emphasize mental imagery. Would you want to fly on an airplane if your pilot had weak spatial imagery? Imagery is also useful in clinical psychology. For example, therapists often treat problems such as phobias and obsessive-compulsive disorders by encouraging clients to use mental imagery (Singer, 2006).

What kind of imagery do we use most often? Stephen Kosslyn and his coauthors (1990) asked students to keep diaries about their mental imagery. They reported that about two-thirds of their images were visual. Images for hearing, touch, taste, and smell were much less common. Psychologists show a similar lopsidedness in their research preferences. Researchers occasionally study topics such as auditory imagery or smell imagery. However, most of the studies examine visual imagery (Djordjevic et al., 2004; Olivetti Belardinelli, 2004; Reisberg & Heuer, 2005).

Wilhelm Wundt and other early psychologists considered imagery to be an important part of the discipline (Palmer, 1999). In contrast, behaviorists such as John Watson strongly opposed research on mental imagery because it could not be connected to observable behavior. As a consequence, North American psychologists seldom studied imagery during the period between 1920 and 1960 (Kosslyn et al., 2006; Tversky, 2000b). As cognitive psychology gained popularity, researchers rediscovered imagery. The topic continues to be important in contemporary cognitive psychology (Allen, 2004; Kosslyn et al., 2006).

This chapter explores three aspects of imagery that have intrigued contemporary researchers. First, we examine the nature of mental images, with an emphasis on the way we transform these images. Then we'll explore some cognitive neuroscience research on different types of mental imagery. Our final topic is cognitive maps, or the mental representation of geographic information.

THE CHARACTERISTICS OF MENTAL IMAGES

As you might expect, research on mental imagery is difficult to conduct, especially because researchers cannot directly observe mental images and because they fade so quickly (Kosslyn et al., 2003; Kosslyn et al., 2006; Richardson, 1999). However, psychologists

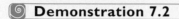 **Demonstration 7.2**

Mental Rotation

Which of these pairs of objects are the same, and which are different?

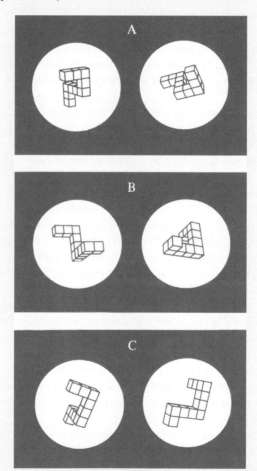

Source: Reprinted with permission from Shepard, R. N., & Metzler, J. (1971). Mental rotation of three-dimensional objects. *Science*, *171*, 701–703. Copyright 1971 American Association for the Advancement of Science.

have modified some research techniques developed for studying visual perception. These techniques can now be applied to mental images (Allen, 2004). As a result, the investigation of imagery has made impressive advances. Try Demonstration 7.2 on page 204, which illustrates an important research technique that we'll examine shortly.

Steven Kosslyn and his colleagues (2006) use the term the **imagery debate** to refer to an important controversy: Do our mental images resemble perception (using an analog code), or do they resemble language (using a propositional code)? We'll introduce that controversy now and return to discuss it in more detail once we've examined the evidence.

The majority of theorists argue that information about a mental image is stored in an analog code (Howes, 2007; Kosslyn et al., 2002; Kosslyn et al., 2006; Reisberg et al., 2003). An **analog code** (also called a **depictive representation** or a **pictorial representation**) is a representation that closely resembles the physical object. Notice that the word *analog* suggests the word *analogy*, such as the analogy between the real object and the mental image.

According to the analog-code approach, mental imagery is a close relative of perception (Tversky, 2005a). When you look at a photograph of a triangle, the physical features of that triangle are registered in your brain in a form that preserves the physical relationship among the three lines. Those who support analog coding argue that your mental image of a triangle is registered in a similar fashion, preserving the same relationship among the lines.

However, supporters of the analog approach do not argue that people literally have a picture in their head (Kosslyn et al., 2006). Furthermore, they point out that people often fail to notice precise details when they look at an object. Similarly, these details will also be missing from their mental image of this object (Howes, 2007; Kosslyn et al., 2006).

In contrast to the analog-code position, other theorists argue that we store images in terms of a propositional code (Pylyshyn, 1984, 2003, 2006). A **propositional code** (also called a **descriptive representation**) is an abstract, language-like representation; storage is neither visual nor spatial, and it does not physically resemble the original stimulus.

According to the propositional-code approach, mental imagery is a close relative of language, not perception. For example, if you try to create a mental image of a triangle, your brain will register a language-like description of the lines and angles. Theorists have not specified the precise nature of the verbal description. However, it is abstract, and it does not resemble any natural language, such as English (Kosslyn et al., 2006).

The controversy about analog versus propositional coding has not been resolved. The majority of people who conduct research on visual imagery support the analog position, perhaps partly because they personally experience vivid, picture-like images (Reisberg et al., 2003). Like most controversies in psychology, both the analog and the propositional approaches are probably at least partially correct. As you read the following pages, keep a list of the studies that support each viewpoint. This list will help you appreciate the summary toward the end of this section, on pages 219–220.

We noted earlier that mental imagery is a challenging topic to study. Compared with topics such as verbal memory, mental imagery is elusive and inaccessible. Researchers have attacked this problem by using the following logic: If a mental image really does resemble a physical object, then people must make judgments about a mental image in the same way that they make judgments about the corresponding physical object.

For example, we should be able to rotate a mental image in the same way we can rotate a physical object. Judgments about distance and shape should also be similar. In addition, a mental image should interfere with the perception of a physical object. Furthermore, we should be able to discover two interpretations of a mental image of an ambiguous figure, and we should be able to produce other vision-like effects when we construct a mental image. Let's now consider these potential parallels between imagery and perception.

Imagery and Rotation

Suppose that you are a researcher who wants to study whether people rotate a mental image in the same way they rotate a physical object. It's tempting to think that you could simply ask people to analyze their mental images and use these reports as a basis for describing mental imagery. However, these introspective reports can be inaccurate and biased, because people may not have conscious access to the processes associated with our mental imagery (Anderson, 1998; Pinker, 1985; Pylyshyn, 2006). You may recall that the discussion of consciousness in Chapter 3 explored this issue.

More research has been conducted on mental imagery and rotation than on any other imagery-related topic. Let's first consider the original study by Shepard and Metzler (1971), and then we'll examine the more recent research.

Shepard and Metzler's Research.   Demonstration 7.2 illustrates a classic experiment by Roger Shepard and his coauthor Jacqueline Metzler (1971). Notice that in the top pair of designs (Part A), the left-hand figure can be changed into the right-hand figure by keeping it flat on the page and rotating it clockwise. Suddenly, the two figures match up, and you conclude "same." You can match these two figures by using a two-dimensional rotation. In contrast, the middle pair (Part B) requires a rotation in a third dimension. You may, for example, take the two-block "arm" that is jutting out toward you and push it over to the left and away from you. Suddenly, the figures match up, and you conclude "same." In the case of the bottom pair (Part C), you cannot rotate the figure on the left so that it matches the figure on the right. Therefore, you conclude "different."

Shepard and Metzler (1971) asked eight participants to judge 1,600 pairs of line drawings like these. They were instructed to pull a lever with their right hand if they judged the figures to be the same, and to pull a different lever with their left hand if they judged the figures to be different. In each case, the experimenters measured the amount of time required for a decision. Notice, then, that the dependent variable is *reaction time*, in contrast to the dependent variable of *accuracy* in most of the research we have examined in previous chapters.

Part A of Figure 7.1 shows the results for figures like Pair A in Demonstration 7.1. These figures require only a two-dimensional rotation, similar to rotating a flat picture. In contrast, Part B of Figure 7.1 shows the results for figures like Pair B in Demonstration 7.1. These figures require a three-dimensional rotation, similar to

FIGURE 7.1

Reaction Time for Deciding That Pairs of Figures Are the Same, as a Function of the Angle of Rotation and the Nature of Rotation. Note: The centers of the circles indicate the means, and the bars on either side provide an index of the variability of those means.

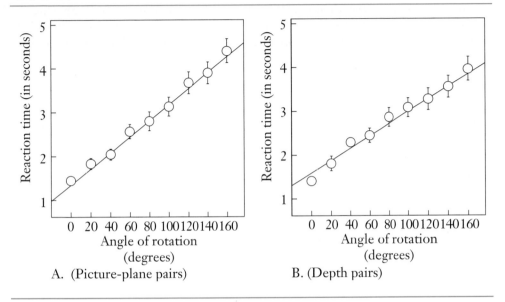

A. (Picture-plane pairs)   B. (Depth pairs)

Source: Shepard & Metzler, 1971.

rotating an object in depth. As both graphs show, people's decision time was strongly influenced by the amount of rotation required to match a figure with its mate. For example, rotating a figure 160 degrees requires much more time than rotating it a mere 20 degrees. Furthermore, notice the similarity between Figures 7.1A and 7.1B. In other words, the participants in this study performed a three-dimensional rotation just as quickly as a two-dimensional rotation.

As you can see, both figures show that the relationship between rotation and reaction time is a straight line. This research supports the analog code, because you would take much longer to rotate an actual physical object 160 degrees than to rotate it a mere 20 degrees. In contrast, a propositional code would predict similar reaction times for these two conditions; the language-like description of the figure would not vary with the amount of rotation (Howes, 2007).

Recent Research on Mental Rotation. The basic findings about mental rotation have been replicated many times. Using a variety of other stimuli, such as letters of the alphabet, researchers have found a clear relationship between angle of rotation and reaction time (e.g., Bauer & Jolicoeur, 1996; Cooper & Lang, 1996; Kosslyn et al., 2006; Newcombe, 2002).

We also know that elderly people perform more slowly than younger people on a mental-rotation task. In contrast, age is not consistently correlated with other imagery skills, such as sense of direction or the ability to scan mental images (Beni et al., 2006; Dror & Kosslyn, 1994).

Surprisingly, however, practice on one mental-rotation task may not improve your performance on a different mental-rotation task (Sims & Mayer, 2002). Specifically, after students had spent 12 hours practicing the video game Tetris, they performed better than control-group students on mental-rotation tasks in which the stimuli resembled Tetris-game figures. In contrast, when the mental-rotation task used visually different stimuli, all those hours of practice had no effect.

Other research shows that deaf individuals who are fluent in American Sign Language (ASL) are especially skilled in looking at an arrangement of objects in a scene and mentally rotating that scene by 180 degrees (Emmorey et al., 1998). After all, individuals who use sign language have had extensive experience in watching a narrator produce a sign, and then they must rotate this sign 180 degree. They need to perform this rotation frequently so that they can match the perspective that they would use when producing this sign. (If you are not fluent in ASL, stand in front of a mirror and notice how you and a viewer would have very different perspectives on your hand movements.)

In general, the research on rotating geometric figures provides some of the strongest support for the analog-coding approach. We seem to treat mental images the same way we treat physical objects when we rotate them through space. In both cases, it takes longer to perform a large mental rotation than a small one.

As we noted earlier, the topic of mental rotation has inspired more research than any other component of mental imagery. Furthermore, several neuroscience studies specifically focus on mental rotation. Therefore, we'll return to this task in the section about neuroscience research on mental imagery.

Imagery and Distance

As we have seen, the first systematic research on imagery demonstrated the similarity between rotating mental images and rotating physical objects. Researchers soon began to examine other attributes of mental images, such as the distance between two points and the shape of the mental image

Stephen Kosslyn is one of the most important researchers in the field of mental imagery. Some of his early research focused on the relationship between the distance between two points in a mental image and the participants' response time. For example, Kosslyn and his colleagues (1978) showed that people required a long time to scan the distance between two widely separated points on a mental map that they had created. In contrast, they scanned the distance between two nearby points very rapidly. Later research confirms that there is a linear relationship between the distance to be scanned in a mental image and the amount of time required to scan this distance (Denis & Kosslyn, 1999b; Kosslyn et al., 2006).

Researchers have also designed additional studies on imagery and distance so that they could examine an important issue concerning research methods. Could the results of Kosslyn and his colleagues (1978) be explained by experimenter expectancy, rather than a genuine influence from the distance between the two points in the mental image? In **experimenter expectancy**, the researchers' biases and expectations influence the outcomes of the experiment. For example, the psychology researchers who conduct research about mental imagery know that longer distances should require longer search times. Perhaps these researchers could somehow transmit their expectations to the participants in the study. These participants might—either consciously or unconsciously—adjust their search speeds according to the expectations (Denis & Kosslyn, 1999a; Intons-Peterson, 1983).

To answer this criticism, Jolicoeur and Kosslyn (1985a, 1985b) repeated the mental-map experiment designed by Kosslyn and his coauthors (1978). However, they made certain that the two research assistants who actually administered the new study were not familiar with the research on mental imagery. Specifically, they did not know about the typical linear relationship found in the previous research. Instead, the assistants were given an elaborate and convincing (but incorrect) explanation about why their results should show a U-shaped relationship between distance and scanning time.

Interestingly, the research assistants did not obtain the U-shaped curve that they were told they would find. Instead, their results demonstrated—once again—the standard linear relationship, in which participants took longer when they scanned a large mental distance. Experimenter expectancy therefore cannot account for the obtained results (Denis & Kosslyn, 1999b; Kosslyn et al., 2006).

Up to this point, we have considered only visual images, asking questions about the distances on imagined maps. Other research has examined auditory imagery. This research shows that people can quickly "travel" the distance between two musical notes that are similar in pitch. In contrast, people require more travel time if the two notes are widely separated on the musical scale (Intons-Peterson et al., 1992).

Imagery and Shape

So far, we've seen that our mental images resemble real, physical images in the research on rotation and in the research on distance. The research on shape shows the same relationship.

Consider, for example, another classic study on visual imagery. Allan Paivio (1978) asked participants to make judgments about the angle formed by the two hands on an imaginary clock. For example, try to visualize the two hands on a standard, nondigital clock. Next, create a mental image of the angle formed by the two hands if the time were 3:20. Now create a mental image of the angle between the two hands if the time were 7:25. Which of these two "mental clocks" has the smaller angle between the two hands?

Paivio also gave the participants several standardized tests to assess their mental-imagery ability. As you can see in Figure 7.2, the high-imagery participants made decisions much more quickly than the low-imagery participants. As Figure 7.2 also shows, participants in both groups made decisions very slowly when they compared the angle formed by the hands at 3:20 with the angle of the hands at 7:25. After all, these two angles are quite similar. In contrast, their decisions were relatively fast if the two angles were very different in size, perhaps 3:20 and 7:05.

FIGURE 7.2

The Influence of Angle Difference on Reaction Time for High-Imagery and Low-Imagery People.

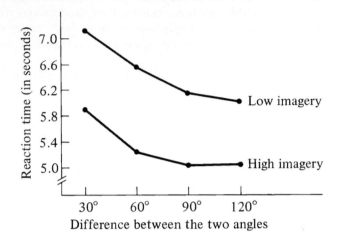

Source: Paivio, 1978.

With real objects, people take a long time to make decisions when the objects are similar to each other. When the objects are different, people respond quickly. People show the same pattern with their mental images of objects. According to Paivio (1978), this study demonstrates strong support for the proposal that people use analog codes, rather than propositional codes.

Additional support for analog codes comes from research with mental images that represent more complex shapes. Shepard and Chipman (1970) asked participants to construct mental images of the shapes of various U.S. states, such as Colorado and Oregon. Then they judged the similarity between the two mental images, with respect to their shapes. For example—without looking at a map—how similar in shape do Colorado and Oregon seem to you? How about Colorado and West Virginia?

The same participants also made shape-similarity judgments about pairs of states while they looked at an actual physical sketch of each state (rather than only its name). The participants' judgments were highly similar in the two conditions. Once again, people's judgments about the shape of mental images are similar to their judgments about the shape of physical stimuli.

Let's review our conclusions about the characteristics of mental images, based on the research we have discussed so far:

1. When people *rotate* a mental image, a large rotation takes them longer, just as they take longer when making a large rotation with a physical stimulus.

2. People make *distance* judgments in a similar fashion for mental images and physical stimuli; this conclusion holds true for both visual and auditory images.

3. People make decisions about *shape* in a similar fashion for mental images and physical stimuli; this conclusion holds true for both simple shapes (angles formed by hands on a clock) and complex shapes (geographic regions, like Colorado or West Virginia).

Now, let's consider a fourth topic that demonstrates some similarity between mental images and physical stimuli. As you'll see, the research shows how mental images and physical stimuli can interfere with each other.

Imagery and Interference

A number of studies show that mental images and physical images can interfere with one another (e.g., Baddeley & Andrade, 1998; Brooks, 1968; Craver-Lemley & Reeves, 1987, 1992; Kosslyn et al., 2006; Richardson, 1999). Let's examine research related to interference, specifically focusing on (1) visual and auditory imagery and (2) motor imagery.

Visual and Auditory Imagery. Try to create a mental image of a close friend's face, and simultaneously let your eyes wander over this page. You will probably find the task to be difficult, because you are trying to look at your friend (in a visual image) at the same time that you are trying to look at the words on the page (a physical stimulus). In other words, you experience interference. Research has confirmed that visual imagery can interfere with visual perception. Furthermore, auditory imagery can interfere with auditory perception.

Consider the research of Segal and Fusella (1970), who asked participants to create either a visual image (for example, an image of a tree) or an auditory image (for example, the sound of an oboe). As soon as each person had formed the requested image, the experimenters presented a real physical stimulus—either a sound on a harmonica (auditory stimulus) or a small blue arrow (visual stimulus). In each case, the researchers measured the participants' ability to detect the physical stimulus.

Segal and Fusella's (1970) results showed that people had more problems detecting the physical stimulus when the image and the signal were in the same sensory mode. For example, participants often failed to report the arrow when they had been imagining the shape of a tree (that is, the same sensory modes). The visual image interfered with the real visual stimulus. In contrast, when they had been imagining the sound of an oboe, they had no trouble reporting that they saw the arrow (two different sensory modes). Similarly, participants had more trouble hearing a harmonica when they had been imagining the sound of an oboe (same sensory modes) than when they had been imagining the shape of a tree (different sensory modes).

In another study on visual interference, Mast and his colleagues (1999) told participants to create a visual image of a set of narrow parallel lines. Next, they were instructed to rotate their mental image of this set of lines, so that the lines were in a diagonal orientation. Meanwhile, the researchers presented a physical stimulus, a short line segment. The participants were told to judge whether this line segment had an exactly vertical orientation. The results showed that the imagined and the real set of lines produced similar distortions in participants' judgments about the orientation of the line segment.

Motor Imagery. So far, the research we've discussed has emphasized visual images and auditory images. However, in our daily lives we also create images of motor movements. For example, if you are taking a tennis class, you might imagine yourself serving the ball. Interestingly, if you are performing an actual motor movement at the same time (perhaps rotating the steering wheel while driving), you may have more difficulty creating an appropriate motor image.

Wexler and his colleagues (1998) conducted research on motor imagery, using a modification of the mental-rotation task. These researchers selected a motor-movement task that required participants to rotate a motor-controlled joystick at a steady rate, in either a clockwise or a counterclockwise direction. The joystick was positioned so that the participants could not see their hand movements. As a result, this task required motor movement but no visual perception.

At the same time as this motor task, participants were instructed to look at a geometric figure. Each figure was a simplified, two-dimensional version of the figures in Demonstration 7.2. In that demonstration, you saw both members of each geometric pair at the same time. However, in the study by Wexler and his colleagues (1998), the participants first saw one member of the pair. Then they saw an arrow indicating whether they should rotate this figure clockwise or counterclockwise. Finally, they saw the second member of the pair, and they judged whether the two members matched.

As you can see from Figure 7.3, the participants made the judgments about their mental images relatively quickly when their hand was moving in the same direction

FIGURE 7.3

Reaction Time, as a Function of the Amount of Mental Rotation and Whether the Mental Rotation Was in the Same Direction as the Hand Movement or in the Opposite Direction.

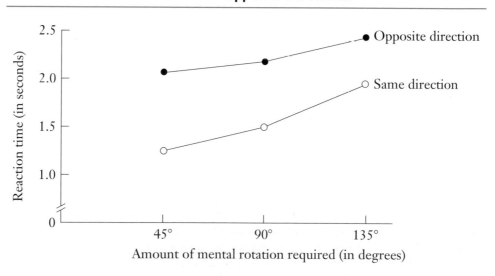

Source: Based on Wexler et al., 1998.

⊚ Demonstration 7.3

Imagery and an Ambiguous Figure

Look at the figure below, and form a clear mental image of the figure. Then turn to the paragraph labeled "Further instructions for Demonstration 7.3" at the bottom of Demonstration 7.4, on page 215.

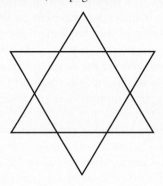

that their mental image was moving. In contrast, their judgments were slower when the two movements were in opposite directions (for example, with the hand moving clockwise and the mental image moving counterclockwise).

The research by Wexler and his colleagues (1998) showed that an actual motor movement can interfere with a mental image of movement. Related research by Wohlschläger (2001) demonstrated that simply *planning* a motor movement can interfere with trying to rotate a mental image. Specifically, participants were instructed to get ready to rotate their hand in a particular direction, and then they performed a mental-rotation task similar to the Shepard and Metzler (1971) task you tried in Demonstration 7.2. Participants performed the mental-rotation task much more slowly if they had been planning to rotate their hand in the opposite direction, rather than the same direction. Clearly, then, interference effects can be found for motor imagery as well as for visual imagery and auditory imagery.

Imagery and Ambiguous Figures

Before you read further, try Demonstration 7.3 and note whether you were able to reinterpret the figure. Most people have difficulty with tasks like this. The research suggests that people sometimes use analog codes and sometimes use propositional codes, when they create a mental image of an ambiguous figure.

Stephen Reed (1974) was interested in people's ability to decide whether a pattern was a portion of a design they had seen earlier. He therefore presented a series of paired figures: first a pattern like the Star of David in Demonstration 7.3, and then—after a brief delay—a second pattern (for example, a parallelogram). In half of the cases, the second pattern was truly part of the first one. In the other half, it was not (for example, a rectangle).

If people store mental images in their heads that correspond to the physical objects they have seen, then they should be able to create a mental image of the star and quickly discover the parallelogram shape hidden within it. However, the participants in Reed's (1974) study were correct only 14% of the time on the star/parallelogram example. Across all stimuli, they were correct only 55% of the time, hardly better than chance.

According to Reed (1974), this poor performance suggests that people could not have stored mental pictures. Instead, Reed proposed that people store pictures as descriptions, in propositional codes. You may have stored the description in Demonstration 7.3 as "two triangles, one pointing up and the other pointing down, placed on top of each other." When asked whether the figure contained a parallelogram, you may have searched through that verbal description and found only triangles, not parallelograms. Notice that Reed's research supports the propositional-code approach, rather than the analog-code approach.

Similar research has examined whether people can provide reinterpretations for a mental image of an ambiguous figure. For example, you can interpret the ambiguous stimulus in Figure 7.4 in two ways: a rabbit facing to the right or a duck facing to the left. Chambers and Reisberg (1985) asked participants to create a clear mental image of this figure, and then they removed the figure. Participants were then asked to give a second, different interpretation of the figure. None of the fifteen people could do so.

Next, the participants were asked to draw the figure from memory. Could they reinterpret this physical stimulus? All fifteen looked at the figure they had drawn and supplied a second interpretation. Chambers and Reisberg's research suggests that a strong verbal propositional code can dominate over an analog code. Other similar research has also replicated these findings: It's easy to reverse an image while you are looking at an ambiguous physical picture. In contrast, reversing a mental image is difficult (Reisberg & Heuer, 2005). Now try Demonstration 7.4. before you read further.

FIGURE 7.4

An Example of an Ambiguous Figure from Chambers and Reisberg's Study.

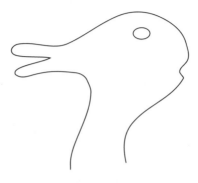

@ **Demonstration 7.4**

Reinterpreting Ambiguous Stimuli

Imagine the capital letter **H.** Now imagine the capital letter **X** superimposed directly on top of the **H,** so that the four corners of each letter match up exactly. From this mental image, what new shapes and objects do you see in your mind's eye?

(Further instructions for Demonstration 7.3: Without glancing back at the figure in Demonstration 7.3, consult your mental image. Does that mental image contain a parallelogram?)

The research that supports the analog code often uses fairly simple figures (like the two hands of a clock). In contrast, people may use a propositional code when the figures are more complex, as in the case of the research by Reed (1974) and Chambers and Reisberg (1985). As Kosslyn and his coauthors (2006) point out, our memory has a limited capacity for imagery. We may therefore have difficulty storing complex visual information in an analog code and then making accurate judgments about these mental images.

Verbal labels (and a propositional code) may be especially helpful when a visual stimulus is complex. For example, when I work on a jigsaw puzzle, I often find that I've attached a verbal label—such as "angel with outstretched wings"—to aid my search for a missing piece. In the case of these complex shapes, storage may be predominantly propositional.

In other research, Finke and his colleagues (1989) asked people to combine two mental images, as in Demonstration 7.4. The participants in this study were indeed able to come up with new interpretations for these ambiguous stimuli. In addition to a combined **X** and **H** figure, they reported some new geometric shapes (such as a right triangle), some new letters (such as **M**), and some objects (such as a bow tie). Other research confirms that observers can locate similar, unanticipated shapes in their mental images (Brandimonte & Gerbino, 1996; Cooper & Lang, 1996; Kosslyn et al., 2006; Rouw et al., 1997).

In summary, the research on ambiguous figures shows that people create mental images using both propositional and analog codes. That is, we often use analog codes to provide picture-like representations to capture our mental images. However, when the stimuli and situations make it difficult to use analog codes, we may use a propositional code to create a language-like representation.

Imagery and Other Vision-Like Processes

So far, we have examined a variety of characteristics related to visual imagery. These include rotation, distance, shape, interference, and ambiguous figures. Let's briefly consider other less obvious characteristics of visual perception. We'll see that each visual characteristic has a mental-imagery counterpart.

For example, research by Ishai and Sagi (1995) shows that people can see a visual target more accurately if the target is presented with masking stimuli on each side of this target. They also showed that mental imagery produces the same masking effect. That is, people can see a visual target more accurately if they create mental images of masks on each side of the target.

This study on the masking effect is especially important because of a research-methods issue called "demand characteristics." **Demand characteristics** are all the cues that might convey the experimenter's hypothesis to the participant.

You already learned about a research-methods concept called "experimenter expectancy." As we noted, researchers may transmit their expectations to participants in an experiment (see pp. 208 to 209). As it happens, experimenter expectancy is one kind of demand characteristic.

However, experiments provide numerous other demand characteristics. Some critics of the analog approach have proposed that the experimental results in imagery experiments might be traceable to one or more of these demand characteristics (Pylyshyn, 2003, 2006). For example, participants may be able to guess the results that the experimenter wants. Perhaps they might guess that an auditory image is supposed to interfere with an auditory perception.

However, the masking effect is virtually unknown to people without a background in the field of perception. The participants in the study by Ishai and Sagi (1995) would never have guessed that visual targets are especially easy to see if they are surrounded by masking stimuli. Therefore, demand characteristics cannot account for the masking effect with mental images. As a result, we can be more confident that visual imagery really can produce the masking effect, just as visual stimuli can produce the masking effect.

Researchers have also examined whether mental images resemble visual perception in other respects. For example, people have especially good acuity for mental images that are visualized in the center of the retina, rather than in the periphery; visual perception operates the same way (Kosslyn, 1983). People can even create illusory conjunctions—like the ones we discussed in Chapter 3 by combining features of visual images and mental images (Craver-Lemley et al., 1999). Other studies demonstrate additional parallels between mental images and visual perception (Kosslyn, 2001; Kosslyn & Thompson, 2000; Kosslyn et al., 2006).

Revisiting the Imagery Controversy

The imagery controversy has been an important and long-lasting debate in cognitive psychology (Kosslyn et al., 2004; Kosslyn et al., 2006; Pylyshyn, 2004, 2006). At the beginning of this chapter, we introduced the analog and propositional perspectives on imagery. Now that you are familiar with the research, let's examine the two perspectives in more detail. The two viewpoints definitely differ in their emphasis on the similarity between mental images and physical stimuli. However, the two positions are not *completely* different from each other, and they may apply to different kinds of tasks.

The Analog Viewpoint. According to the analog perspective, we create a mental image of an object that closely resembles the actual, physical object (Kosslyn et al.,

2003, 2004; Kosslyn et al., 2006). Take a minute to review pages 205 to 216, and you'll see that our responses to mental images are frequently similar to our responses to physical objects. Indeed, the majority of the research supports this position. Of course, no one argues that vision and mental imagery are identical (Kosslyn et al., 2006). After all, you can easily differentiate between your *mental image* of your textbook's cover and your *perception* of that cover. However—as you'll see in the next section of this chapter—the neuropsychology research provides especially strong evidence for the analog viewpoint, because visual imagery and visual perception activate many similar structures in the cortex (Kosslyn et al., 2006).

Kosslyn and his coauthors have developed the analog approach to visual imagery still further by designing a model with several different subsystems. Both visual imagery and visual perception share these subsystems (Kosslyn et al., 2004; Kosslyn & Thompson, 2000; Kosslyn et al., 2006).

A representative subsystem in this model is the shifting of attention, a cognitive process we explored in Chapter 3. Humans can also shift their attention in mental imagery. For example, try forming a mental image of a cat. Now answer this question: Does the cat have curved claws on its front paws? Most people say that the original mental image did not include the claws. However, their attention then shifts to the front end of the cat and zooms in, once they must answer a question about the cat's claws (Kosslyn, 2001).

In summary, the analog viewpoint proposes that imagery resembles perception in many respects. The two processes even activate similar structures within the cerebral cortex, as we'll emphasize in the next section. In addition, several different subsystems can manipulate our mental images. As a result, our mental imagery can be extremely flexible and useful for a wide variety of cognitive tasks.

The Propositional Viewpoint. According to the propositional perspective, mental images are stored in an abstract, language-like form that does not physically resemble the original stimulus. Zenon Pylyshyn (1984, 2003, 2004, 2006) has been the strongest opponent of the analog hypothesis. Pylyshyn agrees that people do experience mental images; it would be foolish to argue otherwise. However, Pylyshyn says that these images are not a necessary, central component of imagery.

Pylyshyn argues that it would be awkward—and perhaps even unworkable—to store information in terms of mental images. For instance, people would need a huge space to store all the images that they claim to have.

Pylyshyn (2004, 2006) also emphasizes the differences between perceptual experiences and mental images. For example, you can re-examine and reinterpret a real photograph. However, Chambers and Reisberg's (1985) study illustrated that people usually cannot reinterpret an ambiguous mental image—such as a rabbit—even though they can easily reinterpret a visual stimulus.

In reality, we may not be able to resolve the imagery controversy. At present, the majority of imagery researchers favor an analog code to explain most stimuli and most tasks (Farah, 2000a; Kosslyn et al., 2006; Reisberg et al., 2003). However, for some kinds of stimuli and several specific tasks, people may use a propositional code. A later section of this chapter explores cognitive neuroscience research. As you'll see, our mental images and our perceptual experiences employ many of the same brain structures.

Individual Differences: Gender Comparisons in Spatial Ability

When psychologists conduct research on individual differences in cognition, one of the most popular topics is gender comparisons. Talk-show hosts, politicians—and even university presidents—feel free to speculate about gender differences. Unfortunately, they rarely consult the psychology research. As a result, they rarely learn that most gender differences in cognitive abilities are small (Hyde, 2005; Matlin, 2008; Yoder, 2007). In Chapters 2 through 6, our Individual Differences feature all focused on one single study. However, researchers have conducted literally hundreds of studies on gender comparisons in cognitive abilities. If we want to understand gender comparisons in spatial imagery, we cannot focus on just one study.

When the research on a topic is abundant, psychologists often use a statistical technique called "meta-analysis." **Meta-analysis** provides a statistical method for combining numerous studies on a single topic. Researchers begin by locating all appropriate studies on a topic, for example, gender comparisons in verbal ability. Then they perform a meta-analysis that combines the results of all these studies.

A meta-analysis yields a number called effect size, or *d*. For example, suppose that researchers conduct a meta-analysis of 18 studies about gender comparisons in reading comprehension scores. Furthermore, suppose that—averaging across all 18 studies—females and males receive very similar scores on reading comprehension tests. In this case, the *d* would be close to zero. For the sake of comparison, consider the gender differences in height, where *d* is 2.0.

Psychologists have conducted numerous meta-analyses on cognitive gender comparisons. Janet Hyde (2005) wrote an important article that summarized these previous meta-analyses. Table 7.1 shows a tally of the effect sizes for the meta-analyses that have been conducted in three areas of cognitive ability.

According to Table 7.1, four meta-analyses on verbal ability showed extremely small gender differences, with *d* values close to zero. One additional meta-analysis produced a *d* value considered to be "small," and no meta-analyses yielded a *d* value considered to be either moderate or large. You can also see that all four meta-analyses on

TABLE 7.1

The Distribution of Effect Sizes (*d*) Reported in Meta-Analyses of Cognitive Skills

Skill	Magnitude of *d*			
	Close to Zero ($d \leq 0.10$)	Small ($d = 0.11$ to 0.35)	Moderate ($d = 0.36$ to 0.65)	Large ($d = 0.66$ to 1.00)
Verbal Ability	4	1	0	0
Mathematics Ability	4	0	0	0
Spatial Ability	0	4	3	1

Source: Based on Hyde (2005).

mathematics ability produced *d* values that are close to zero. These gender similarities in math ability are extremely important, especially because the headlines in the media usually claim that males are much better than females in their math skills (Barnett & Rivers, 2004; Hyde, 2005).

The gender differences are more substantial in spatial ability, the topic related to our current chapter. Notice, however, that only one meta-analysis yielded a *d* value in the "large" category.

An important point is that spatial ability represents several different skills; it is not unitary (Caplan & Caplan, 1999; Chipman, 2004; Tversky, 2005b). One skill is spatial visualization. A typical task would be looking at a sketch of a busy street to find drawings of human faces. Gender differences in spatial visualization are small, according to Hyde's (2005) summary of meta-analyses.

The second component of spatial ability is spatial perception. A typical task would be sitting in a dark room and adjusting an illuminated rod so that it is in an exactly vertical position. The two meta-analyses that specifically focused on spatial perception both produced *d* values of 0.44, a moderate gender difference (Hyde, 2005).

The third component of spatial ability is mental rotation. As the name suggests, a typical task would be looking at two figures and determining whether they would be identical if you rotated one of the figures. You already tried this task in Demonstration 7.2. The two meta-analyses that specifically focused on mental rotation produced *d* values of 0.56 and 0.73 (Hyde, 2005).

In other words, mental rotation is the one cognitive skill where a group of males is most likely to earn higher scores than a group of females. It is possible that biological factors might partially explain these gender differences (Halpern & Collaer, 2005). However, we must emphasize that some studies report no gender differences in mental rotation. Furthermore, some studies report that the gender differences disappear when the task instructions are changed and when people receive training on spatial skills (Matlin, 2008; Newcombe, 2006; Sharps et al., 1994). Furthermore, a large portion of the gender differences in spatial rotation can be traced to experience with toys and sports that emphasize spatial skills (Voyer et al., 2000). In other words, even this one area of cognitive gender differences is not inevitable; it can be modified by providing experience in spatial activities.

Section Summary: *The Characteristics of Mental Images*

1. A major controversy in cognitive psychology focuses on mental imagery, specifically, whether information is stored in picture-like analog codes or language-like propositional codes. Research on the characteristics of mental images addresses this issue.

2. The amount of time that people take to rotate a mental image depends on the extent of the rotation, just as when we rotate a real, physical object.

3. People take longer to "travel" a long mental distance, whether that distance is visual or auditory.

4. When judging the shapes of mental images or visual images, people take longer to make decisions when the two stimuli have very different shapes; this conclusion applies to simple shapes (e.g., the hands on a clock) and complex shapes (e.g., the shapes of U.S. states).

5. Visual images can interfere with visual perception; auditory images can interfere with auditory perception; and motor movement can interfere with motor images.

6. People have difficulty identifying that a part belongs to a whole if they did not include the part in their original verbal description of the whole. Also, some ambiguous figures are difficult to reinterpret in a mental image; others can be reinterpreted fairly easily.

7. Other vision-like properties of mental images include enhanced acuity when a target is flanked by imaginary masks, enhanced acuity for stimuli seen in the center portion of the retina, and illusory conjunctions. This area of research is important because demand characteristics are minimal in these studies.

8. The majority of research supports the analog viewpoint, as described by Kosslyn and his colleagues; this model now includes several specific operations that can be performed on both mental images and real objects.

9. In contrast, Pylyshyn's propositional viewpoint argues that analog images are not a necessary component of mental imagery, because people can perform perceptual tasks that they cannot perform with mental images.

10. Meta-analyses on spatial ability reveal small to moderate gender differences in spatial visualization and spatial perception; gender differences are somewhat larger in mental rotation, but these differences can be reduced by experience in spatial activities.

COGNITIVE NEUROSCIENCE RESEARCH ON MENTAL IMAGERY

In Chapter 1, we discussed a variety of neuroscience research techniques that can help us understand how cognitive processes operate. These techniques are especially useful when we consider mental imagery. We'll first examine a general issue: Do visual imagery and perception activate similar parts of the brain? Then we'll explore cognitive neuroscience research on one specific topic, mental rotation, which is the most popular of the visual imagery tasks.

Neuroscience Research Comparing Visual Imagery and Visual Perception

We have considered many studies that illustrate how people seem to treat visual images and visual stimuli in a similar fashion. In general, imagery and perception seem to demonstrate similar psychological processes. But how similar are imagery and perception at the biological level? Obviously, the two processes are not identical (Kosslyn & Thompson,

2000; Kosslyn et al., 2006). After all, mental imagery relies on top-down processing. In contrast, visual perception activates the rods and cones in the retina. When you create a mental image of an elephant, no one would suggest that the rods and cones in the back of your retina are registering an elephant-shaped pattern of stimulation.

However, numerous neuroscience studies demonstrate that brain structures at more advanced levels of visual processing—beyond the retina—do seem to be activated when we construct mental images (Kosslyn et al., 2006; Reisberg & Heuer, 2005; Thompson & Kosslyn, 2000). Surveying a large number of studies, Kosslyn (2004) concludes that visual imagery activates about two-thirds of the same brain regions that are activated during visual perception.

Researchers have studied individuals with lesions (damage) in the visual cortex and other areas of the cortex that process visual stimuli. Many of these people cannot register perceptual images, and they also cannot produce mental images. Still, their other cognitive abilities are normal. In general, individuals with these lesions show mental-imagery impairments that resemble their perceptual impairments. (Farah, 2000a, 2000b; Kosslyn, Ganis, & Thompson, 2001; Kosslyn et al., 2006).

Many other studies have used PET scans, fMRIs, and other brain-imaging techniques to assess which areas of the brain show increased blood flow when people work on a variety of tasks that require visual imagery. For example, Stephen Kosslyn and his coauthors (1996) asked people to create visual images for various letters of the alphabet. Then the participants were asked a question about each letter's shape (for example, whether the letter had any curved lines). Meanwhile, a PET scan recorded the blood flow to the cortex. The researchers found that this task activated the primary visual cortex, located at the back of the brain. (See Figure 2.1 on p. 35.) This part of the cortex is the same region that is active when we perceive the shape of actual visual stimuli.

Two studies using fMRI (functional magnetic resonance imaging) asked participants either to look at or to create a visual image of a simple object, such as a bow tie or a tree (Ganis et al., 2004; Klein et al., 2004). Visual perception and visual imagery produced closely matching patterns of stimulation.

Other neuroscience research on imagery demonstrates that different tasks activate different areas of the brain. For instance, the research confirms that the primary visual cortex is especially active when people need to carefully inspect a mental image of a visual image, for example, examining features contained in letters of the alphabet (Kosslyn et al., 2006; Sparing et al., 2002). Notice that these results support the analog perspective on imagery, because the primary visual cortex is active when we look at shapes; it does not process language-like material (Kosslyn et al., 2006).

Different regions of the brain specialize in different methods of processing visual imagery. For example, part of the parietal lobe—as shown in Figure 2.1 on page 35— is especially active when people need to make changes in the structure of their visual images (Newcombe, 2002).

This neuroscience evidence is particularly compelling because it avoids the problem of demand characteristics that we discussed on page 216. As Farah (2000a) points out, people are not likely to know which parts of their brain are typically active during vision. When you create a mental image of a bow tie, you cannot voluntarily activate the relevant cells in your primary visual cortex! These similarities between perception and imagery are especially persuasive because they cannot be explained by social expectations.

Neuroscience Research on Mental Rotation Tasks

In this section on neuroscience, we have seen that the brain typically processes visual imagery and visual perceptual in a similar fashion. Let's shift our focus and re-examine the mental rotation task (pages 206 to 208), this time within the framework of neuroscience research.

In one of the early studies on this topic, Kosslyn, Thompson, and their coauthors (2001) examined whether people use the motor cortex when they imagine themselves rotating one of the geometric figures in Demonstration 7.2. These researchers instructed some participants to rotate—with their own hands—one of the geometric figures that had been used in Shepard and Metzler's (1971) study. They instructed other participants to simply watch as an electric motor rotated this same figure.

Next, the people in both groups performed the matching task you tried in Demonstration 7.2 (page 204), by rotating the figures mentally. Meanwhile, the researchers conducted PET scans to see which areas of the brain the participants used during the mental-rotation task. The PET-scan results were clear-cut. Those participants who had rotated the original geometric figure with their hands now showed activity in the primary motor cortex—the same part of the brain that was active during the manual rotation task. In contrast, consider the participants who had simply watched the electric motor as it rotated the figure. These people showed no activity in the primary motor cortex.

Researchers have also found that the nature of the instructions can influence whether a mental-rotation task activates certain regions of the cortex. Specifically, the standard "rotate this figure" instructions activate the primary motor cortex and the right parietal cortex (Wraga et al., 2005; Zacks et al., 2003).

Does the pattern of activation change when researchers modify the instructions? Now, the participants are instructed to imagine rotating *themselves* so that they can "see" the figure from a different perspective. These instructions produced increased activity in the left temporal lobe, as well as a different part of the motor cortex. However, the instructions did *not* activate the primary motor cortex (Wraga et al., 2005; Zacks et al., 2003). Apparently, when we imagine ourselves rotating around a figure, we do not imagine ourselves walking or our muscles moving.

⊙ Section Summary: *Cognitive Neuroscience Research on Mental Imagery*

1. Neuroscience research, using case studies, has demonstrated that people with lesions in the visual cortex have the same difficulties with visual imagery that they have with visual perception.
2. Other neuroscience research has used PET scans, fMRIs, and other brain-imaging techniques to show that visual imagery activates specific visual-processing

areas of the cerebral cortex, such as the primary visual cortex and the parietal region of the cortex.

3. Neuroscience research on mental rotation shows that the primary motor cortex is activated when people have recently rotated geometric figures with their hands. However, the primary motor cortex is not activated when people imagine themselves rotating—while a geometric figure remains in the same position.

COGNITIVE MAPS

You have probably had an experience like this: You've just arrived in a new environment, perhaps for your first year of college. You ask for directions, let's say, to the library. You hear the reply, "OK, it's simple. You go up the hill, staying to the right of the Blake Building. Then you take a left, and Newton Hall will be on your right. The library will be over on your left." You struggle to recall some landmarks from the orientation tour. Was Newton Hall next to the College Union, or was it over near the Administration Building? Valiantly, you try to incorporate this new information into your discouragingly hazy mental map.

So far, this chapter has examined the general characteristics of mental images. This discussion primarily focused on a theoretical issue that has intrigued cognitive psychologists—how mental images are stored in memory—and the neuroscience of mental imagery.

Now we consider cognitive maps, a topic that clearly relies on mental images. However, the research on cognitive maps focuses on the way we represent geographic space. More specifically, a **cognitive map** is a mental representation of the environment that surrounds us (Tversky, 2000a; Wagner, 2006). Notice, then, that the first two sections of this chapter emphasize our mental images of objects. In contrast, this third section emphasizes our mental images of the *relationships* among objects, such as buildings on a college campus.

Let's discuss some background information about cognitive maps, and then we'll see how distance, shape, and relative position are represented in these cognitive maps. We'll conclude this chapter with an In Depth feature that explores the way we create mental maps from verbal descriptions.

Background Information About Cognitive Maps

Our cognitive maps typically represent neighborhoods, cities, and countries. In general, our cognitive maps represent areas that are too large to see in a single glance (Wagner, 2006). As a result, we create a cognitive map by integrating information we have acquired from many successive views (Shelton, 2004). In general, the research on cognitive maps emphasizes real-world settings and ecological validity.

The study of cognitive maps is part of a larger topic called spatial cognition. **Spatial cognition** refers to our thoughts about spatial issues; this broad area includes not only cognitive maps, but also how we remember the world we navigate and how we keep track of objects in a spatial array (Newcombe, 2002; Shelton, 2004). Within

---

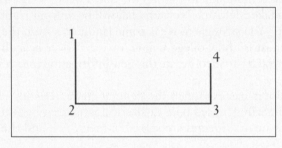

🌀 **Demonstration 7.5**

Learning from a Map

Study the diagram at the bottom of this demonstration for about 30 seconds, and then cover it completely. Now answer the following questions:

1. Imagine that you are standing at Position 3, facing Position 4. Point to Position 1.

2. Now, glance quickly at the diagram and then cover it completely. Imagine that you are now standing at Position 1, facing Position 2. Point to Position 4.

---

psychology, spatial cognition is often discussed in courses on environmental psychology (García-Mira & Real, 2005; Wagner, 2006).

Furthermore, spatial cognition is interdisciplinary in its scope. For example, computer scientists try to create models of spatial knowledge. Linguists analyze how people talk about spatial arrangements. Anthropologists study how different cultures use different frameworks to describe locations. Geographers examine all of these dimensions, with the goal of creating efficient maps and other sources of information (Tversky, 1999). The topic is also relevant when architects design buildings and when urban planners construct new communities (Devlin, 2001; Tversky, 2000b).

We are often unaware just how much information we know about spatial cognition. Research in artificial intelligence has demonstrated the complexity of our knowledge base (Montello, 2005). As Laszlo and his colleagues (1996) point out:

> It was discovered, much to the consternation of the programmers, that without exquisitely elaborate programs, computers made unbelievably stupid errors. A simulation of a restaurant scene, for instance, might find the patrons entering by walking directly through the walls, whereupon they might seat themselves on the floor (exactly where the computer probably has the waiter serve the food) and eventually tip the cook before leaving. To get this scene right, the programmer must supply the computer with an enormous amount of commonsense information of the kind that makes up the basic cognitive maps that guide human behavior. (p. 9)

As you might expect, individual differences in spatial-cognition skills are quite large (Shelton & McNamara, 2004; Tversky, 2005b; Wagner, 2006). However, people tend to be accurate in judging their ability to find their way to unfamiliar locations (Kitchin & Blades, 2002; Taylor et al., 1999). In other words, their metacognitions about spatial ability are reasonably correct. Furthermore, these individual differences in spatial cognition are correlated with performance on the spatial tasks that we discussed in the first section of this chapter (Newcombe, 2002; Sholl et al., 2006). For example, people who are good at mental rotation pages 206 to 208 are more skilled than others in using a map to find a particular location (Fields & Shelton, 2006; Shelton & Gabrieli, 2004)

Also, suppose that you are visiting an unfamiliar college campus. You park your car, and you set out to find a specific building. You'll increase your chances of finding your way back to your car if you periodically turn around and study the scene you'll see on your return trip (Heth et al., 2002; Montello, 2005).

Try Demonstration 7.5 before you read further. This demonstration is based on research by Roskos-Ewoldsen and her colleagues (1998), which we will discuss shortly.

In general, researchers have not discussed the way in which cognitive maps are encoded—that is, whether the code for these maps is analog or propositional. However, most researchers who have raised this issue conclude that cognitive maps must be both analog and propositional in nature (e.g., Kitchin & Blades, 2002; Montello et al., 2004; Taylor et al., 1999). Your mental map for a particular city may therefore include a series of picture-like images of the relationship among several streets and buildings. This mental map will also include propositions, such as "The Ethiopian restaurant is in downtown Toronto, northwest of the CN Tower." Information on your mental map may also include landmark knowledge and procedural knowledge (for example, "To get to the Ethiopian restaurant, go north from the hotel parking lot and turn left on Bloor").

Your mental map may also include survey knowledge, which is the relationship among locations that you directly acquire by learning a map or by repeatedly exploring an environment. Now look back at Demonstration 7.5; which of the two tasks was easier? As you might imagine, your mental map will be easier to judge and more accurate if you acquire spatial information from a physical map that is oriented in the same direction that you are facing in your mental map.

In Question 1 of this demonstration, your mental map and the physical map have the same orientation, so that task is relatively easy. In contrast, you need to perform a mental rotation in order to answer Question 2, so that task is more difficult. Research confirms that judgments are easier when your mental map and the physical map have matching orientations (Devlin, 2001; Montello, 2005; Montello et al., 2004; Roskos-Ewoldsen et al., 1998).

The next three topics will consider how our cognitive maps represent three geographic attributes: distance, shape, and relative position. Theme 2 of this book states that our cognitive processes are generally accurate. This generalization also applies to cognitive maps. In fact, our mental representations of the environment usually reflect reality with reasonable accuracy, whether these cognitive maps depict college campuses or larger geographic regions.

According to Chapter 1's discussion of Theme 2, however, when people do make errors in their cognitive processes, those errors can often be traced to a rational strategy.

The mistakes that people display in their cognitive maps usually "make sense" because they are systematic distortions of reality (Devlin, 2001; Koriat et al., 2000; Tversky, 2000b). The mistakes reflect a tendency to base our judgments on variables that are typically relevant. They also reflect a tendency to judge our environment as being more well-organized and orderly than it really is. We will see that people tend to show systematic distortions in distance, shape, and relative position.

Cognitive Maps and Distance

How far is it from your college library to the classroom in which your cognitive psychology course is taught? How many miles separate the city in which you were born from the city where your home is currently located? When people make distance estimates like these, their estimates are often distorted by factors such as the number of intervening cities, semantic categories, and whether their destination is a landmark.

Number of Intervening Cities.   In one of the first systematic studies about distance in cognitive maps, Thorndyke (1981) constructed a map of a hypothetical region with cities distributed throughout the map. Between any two cities on the map, there were 0, 1, 2, or 3 other cities along the route. Participants studied the map until they could accurately reconstruct it. Then they estimated the distance between specified pairs of cities.

The number of intervening cities had a clear-cut influence on their estimates. For example, when the cities were really 300 miles apart on the map, people estimated that they were only 280 miles apart when there were no intervening cities. In contrast, these target cities were estimated to be 350 miles apart with three intervening cities. Notice that this error is a sensible one. If cities are randomly distributed throughout a region, two cities are usually closer together when there are no intervening cities between them. In contrast, two target cities with three intervening cities are likely to be further apart.

Variations of this study confirm that the distance seems longer when the route is "cluttered" with objects along the way (Koriat et al., 2000; Tversky, 2000a; Wagner, 2006). Furthermore, the distance seems longer when the road features a number of complex turns, rather than a straight route (Tversky et al., 2004).

Semantic Categories.   The Fine Arts Building on my college campus seems closer to the College Union than it is to Buzzo's Music Store. The music store is actually closer. However, my distance estimate is distorted because the Fine Arts Building and the College Union are clustered together in my semantic memory under the category "college buildings." The music store does not belong within this semantic cluster, even though there is no physical boundary between the campus buildings and the stores located outside our campus.

Research shows that semantic factors influence distance estimates for specific locations within a town. For example, Hirtle and Mascolo (1986) showed participants a hypothetical map of a town, and they learned the locations on the map. Then the map was removed, and people estimated the distance between pairs of locations. The results showed that people tended to shift each location closer to other sites that belonged to the same semantic cluster. For example, the courthouse might be remembered as being close to the police station and other government buildings. These shifts did not occur for members of different semantic clusters. For instance, people did not move the courthouse closer to the golf course.

The same clustering bias appeared when University of Michigan students estimated distances between pairs of locations on campus and outside the campus in Ann Arbor (Hirtle & Jonides, 1985). That is, members of the same category were judged to be closer to each other than to members of different categories.

In summary, these studies confirm an additional distortion in distance estimates: When two places belong to the same category, we believe that they are also geographically close (Tversky, 2000b; Wagner, 2006). Once again, however, this error makes sense. In general, our real-life experience tells us that locations with similar functions are likely to be close to each other.

People show a similar distortion when they estimate large-scale distances. For instance, Friedman and her colleagues asked college students to estimate the distance between various North American cities (Friedman et al., 2005; Friedman & Montello, 2006). Students from Canada, the United States, and Mexico judged that distances were greater when they were separated by an international border. Specifically, they judged two cities to be an average of 1,225 miles from each other if the cities were located in the same country. In contrast, they judged two cities to be an average of 1,579 miles from each other if they were located in different countries. In other words, the difference was 354 miles when the cities were separated by an international border; in reality, the actual difference was only 63 miles (Friedman & Montello, 2006).

Landmarks Versus Nonlandmarks as Destinations. We have some friends who live in Rochester, the major city in our region of upstate New York. We sometimes invite them to come down for a meeting in Geneseo, about 45 minutes away. "But it's so far away," they complain. "Why don't you come up here instead?" They are faintly embarrassed when we point out that the distance from Geneseo to Rochester is exactly the same as the distance from Rochester to Geneseo!

The research confirms the **landmark effect**, which is the general tendency to provide shorter estimates when traveling to a landmark, rather than a nonlandmark (Devlin, 2001; Tversky, 2005b; Wagner, 2006). For example, McNamara and Diwadkar (1997) asked students to memorize a map that displayed various pictures of objects. The map included some objects that were described as landmarks, and some objects that were not landmarks. After learning the locations, the students estimated the distance on the map (in inches) between various pairs of objects.

Consistent with the landmark effect, the students showed an asymmetry in their distance estimates. In one study, for instance, they estimated that the distance was an average of 1.7 inches when traveling from the landmark to the nonlandmark. However, the estimated distance was an average of only 1.4 inches when traveling from the nonlandmark to the landmark. Prominent destinations apparently seem closer than less important destinations. This research also demonstrates the importance of context when we make decisions about distances and other features of our cognitive maps.

Cognitive Maps and Shape

Our cognitive maps represent not only distances, but shapes. These shapes are evident in map features such as the angles formed by intersecting streets and the curves illustrating the bends in rivers. Once again, the research shows a systematic distortion: We tend to construct cognitive maps in which the shapes are more regular than they are in reality.

Angles. Consider the classic research by Moar and Bower (1983), who studied people's cognitive maps of Cambridge, England. All the participants in the study had lived in Cambridge for at least five years. Moar and Bower wanted to determine people's estimates for the angles formed by the intersection of two streets. The participants showed a clear tendency to "regularize" the angles so that they were more like 90 degree angles. For example, three intersections in Cambridge had "real" angles of 67, 63, and 50 degrees. However, people estimated these same angles to be 84, 78, and 88 degrees. In fact, this study showed that seven of the nine angles were significantly biased in the direction of a 90 degree angle.

What explains this systematic distortion? Moar and Bower (1983) suggest that we employ a heuristic. A **heuristic** (pronounced "hyoo-*riss*-tick") is a general problem-solving strategy that usually produces a correct solution. When two roads meet in most urban areas, they generally form a 90 degree angle. When people use the **90 degree-angle heuristic**, they represent angles in a mental map as being closer to 90 degrees than they really are. Similarly—as you may recall from Chapter 5's discussion of memory schemas on pages 146–147—it is easier to store a schematic version of an event, rather than a precise version of the event that accurately represents all the little details. This 90 degree-angle heuristic has also been replicated in other settings (Montello et al., 2004; Tversky, 2005b; Tversky & Lee, 1998; Wagner, 2006).

Curves. The New York State Thruway runs in an east-west direction across the state, although it curves somewhat in certain areas. To me, the upward curve south of Rochester seems symmetrical, equally arched on each side of the city. However, when I checked the map, the curve is much steeper on the eastern side.

Research confirms that people tend to use a **symmetry heuristic;** we remember figures as being more symmetrical and regular than they truly are (Montello et al., 2004; Tversky, 2000a; Tversky & Schiano, 1989). Again, these results follow the general pattern: The small inconsistencies of geographic reality are smoothed over, creating cognitive maps that are idealized and standardized.

Cognitive Maps and Relative Position

Which city is farther west—San Diego, California, or Reno, Nevada? If you are like most people—and the participants in a classic study by Stevens and Coupe (1978)—the question seems ludicrously easy. Of course, San Diego would be farther west, because California is west of Nevada. However, if you consult a map, you'll discover that Reno is in fact west of San Diego. Which city is farther north—Detroit or its "twin city" across the river, Windsor, in Ontario, Canada? Again, the answer seems obvious; any Canadian city must be north of a U.S. city!

Barbara Tversky (1981, 1998) points out that we use heuristics when we represent relative positions in our mental maps—just as we use heuristics to represent the angles of intersecting streets as being close to 90 degree angles, and just as we represent curves as being symmetrical. In particular, Tversky argues: (1) We remember a tilted geographic structure as being either more vertical or more horizontal than it really is (the rotation heuristic); and (2) We remember geographic structures as being arranged in a straighter line than they really are (the alignment heuristic).

The Rotation Heuristic. According to the **rotation heuristic,** a figure that is slightly tilted will be remembered as being either more vertical or more horizontal than it really is (Taylor, 2005; Tversky, 1981, 1997, 2000b; Wagner, 2006). For example, Figure 7.5 shows that the coastline of California is slanted at a significant angle. When we use the rotation heuristic for our cognitive map of California, we make the orientation more vertical by rotating the coastline in a clockwise fashion. If your cognitive map suffers from the distorting effects of the rotation heuristic, you will conclude (erroneously) that San Diego is west of Reno. Similarly, the rotation heuristic encourages you to create a horizontal border between the United States and Canada. Therefore, you'll make the wrong decision about Detroit and Windsor. In reality, Windsor, in Canada, is south of Detroit.

Let us look at some research on the rotation heuristic. Tversky (1981) studied people's mental maps for the geographic region of the San Francisco Bay Area. She found that 69% of the students at a Bay Area university showed evidence of the rotation heuristic. When constructing their mental maps, they rotated the California coastline in a more north-south direction than is true on a geographically correct map. Keep in mind, though, that some students—in fact, 31% of them—were not influenced by this heuristic.

FIGURE 7.5

The Correct Locations of San Diego and Reno. This figure shows that Reno is farther west than San Diego. According to the rotation heuristic, however, we tend to rotate the coastline of California into a more nearly vertical orientation. As a result, we incorrectly conclude that San Diego is farther west than Reno.

We also have cross-cultural evidence for the rotation heuristic. People living in Israel, Japan, and Italy also tend to rotate geographic structures. As a result, these structures appear to have a more vertical or horizontal orientation in a mental map than in reality (Glicksohn, 1994; Tversky et al., 1999).

The Alignment Heuristic. According to the **alignment heuristic,** a series of geographic structures will be remembered as being more lined up than they really are (Taylor, 2005; Tversky, 1981, 2000b). To test the alignment heuristic, Tversky (1981) presented pairs of cities to students, who were asked to select which member of each pair was north (or, in some cases, east). For example, one pair was Rome and Philadelphia. As Figure 7.6 shows, Rome is actually north of Philadelphia. However, because of the alignment heuristic, people tend to line up the United States and Europe so that they are in the same latitude. We know that Rome is in the southern part of Europe and that Philadelphia is in the northern part of the United States. Therefore, we conclude—incorrectly—that Philadelphia is north of Rome.

Tversky's results indicated that many students showed a consistent tendency to use the alignment heuristic. For example, 78% judged Philadelphia to be north of Rome, and 12% judged that they were at the same latitude. Only 10% correctly answered that Rome is north of Philadelphia. On all eight pairs of items tested by Tversky, an average of 66% of participants supplied the incorrect answer. According to additional research, people's cognitive maps are most likely to be biased when northern cities in North America are compared with southern cities in Europe (Friedman et al., 2002).

The rotation heuristic and the alignment heuristic may initially sound similar. However, the rotation heuristic requires rotating a *single* coastline, country, building,

FIGURE 7.6

The Correct Locations of Philadelphia and Rome. This figure shows that Philadelphia is farther south than Rome. According to the alignment heuristic, however, we tend to line up Europe and the United States. As a result, we incorrectly conclude that Philadelphia is north of Rome.

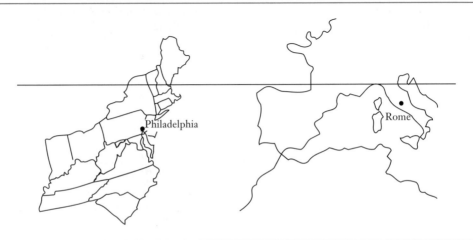

or other figure in a clockwise or counterclockwise fashion so that its border is oriented in a nearly vertical or horizontal direction. In contrast, the alignment heuristic requires lining up *several separate* countries, buildings, or other figures in a straight row. Both heuristics are similar, however, because they encourage us to construct cognitive maps that are more orderly and schematic than geographic reality.

The heuristics we have examined in this chapter make sense. For example, our city streets tend to have right-angle intersections. Furthermore, a picture is generally hung on a wall in a vertical orientation, rather than at a slant, and a series of houses is typically lined up so that they are equally far from the street.

However, when our mental maps rely too strongly on these heuristics, we miss the important details that make each stimulus unique. When our top-down cognitive processes are too active, we fail to pay sufficient attention to bottom-up information. In fact, the angle at that intersection may really be 70 degrees, that coastline may not run exactly north-south, and those two continents are not really arranged in a neat horizontal line.

At this point, you may be reasonably skeptical about the validity of Theme 2; perhaps our cognitive processes are *not* impressively accurate. However, Mary Smyth and her coauthors (1994) place these errors in perspective:

> The errors people make when they straighten edges, make junctions more like right angles, put things closer to landmarks, and remember average rather than specific positions, are indications of the way in which knowledge of spatial information is dealt with. Like the formation of concepts, the regularizing of spatial information reduces the need to maintain all the features of an environment which might possibly be relevant and allows approximate solutions to problems for which precise location is unnecessary. (p. 326)

IN DEPTH

Creating Cognitive Maps

In everyday life, we often hear or read descriptions of a particular environment. For instance, a friend calls to give you directions to her house. You have never traveled there before, yet you create a cognitive map as you hear her describing the route. Similarly, a neighbor describes the setting in which his car was hit by a truck, or you read a mystery novel explaining where the dead body was found in relation to the broken vase and the butler's fingerprints. In each case, you typically create a cognitive map. These cognitive maps help us represent the spatial aspects of our external environment.

When we hear a description, we do not simply store these isolated statements in a passive fashion. Instead—consistent with Theme 1—we actively create a cognitive map that represents the relevant features of a scene (Tversky, 2005a, 2005b). In fact, the mental maps that people create from a description are similar to the mental maps they create from looking at a scene (Bryant, 1998; Carr & Roskos-Ewoldsen, 1999; Tversky, 2000b, 2005a, 2005b). Furthermore, people integrate information from separate statements and combine them to form an integrated cognitive map (Newcombe & Huttenlocher, 2000).

In this In Depth feature, we will examine how people create these cognitive maps, typically based on verbal description. Let us begin by considering the classic research on this topic. Then we will examine the spatial framework model, as well as other information about the characteristics of cognitive maps.

⊚ Demonstration 7.6

Creating a Cognitive Map

Take a piece of paper and cover the portion of this demonstration labeled "Further Instructions." Now read the story. When you have finished reading it, cover up the story and follow the Further Instructions.

The Story

You are at the Jefferson Plaza Hotel, where you have just taken the escalator from the first to the second floor. You will be meeting someone for dinner in a few minutes. You now stand next to the top of the escalator, where you have a view of the first floor as well as the second floor. You first look directly to your left, where you see a shimmering indoor fountain about 10 yards beyond a carpeted walkway. Although you cannot see beyond the low stone wall that surrounds it, you suppose that its bottom is littered with nickels and pennies that hotel guests have tossed in. The view down onto the first floor allows you to see that directly below you is a darkened, candle-lit tavern. It looks very plush, and every table you see seems to be filled with well-dressed patrons.

Looking directly behind you, you see through the window of the hotel's barbershop. You can see an older gentleman, whose chest is covered by a white sheet, being shaved by a much younger man. You next look straight ahead of you, where you see a quaint little gift shop just on the other side of the escalator. You're a sucker for little ceramic statues, and you squint your eyes to try to read the hours of operation posted on the store's entrance. Hanging from the high ceiling directly above you, you see a giant banner welcoming the Elks convention to the hotel. It is made from white lettering sewn onto a blue background, and it looks to you to be about 25 feet long.

Further Instructions

Now imagine that you have turned to face the barbershop. Cover up the story above and answer the following questions:

1. What is above your head?
2. What is below your feet?
3. What is ahead of you?
4. What is behind you?
5. What is to your right?

Source: Based on Tversky, 1991, p. 133.

Franklin and Tversky's Research. Before you read further, try Demonstration 7.6, which is based on a story used in a series of studies conducted by Nancy Franklin and Barbara Tversky (1990). Franklin and Tversky presented verbal descriptions of ten different scenes, such as a hotel lobby, an opera theater, a barn, and so forth. Each description mentioned five objects located in a plausible position in relation to the observer (either above, below, in front, in back, or to either the left or the right side). Only five objects were mentioned, so that the memory load would not be overwhelming. After the participants had read each description, they were instructed to imagine that they were turning around to face a different object. They were then asked to specify which object was located in each of several directions (for example, "above your head"). In all cases, the researchers measured how long the participant took to respond to the question.

Franklin and Tversky (1990) were especially interested in discovering whether response time depended upon the location of the object that was being tested. Do we make all those decisions equally quickly? Alternatively, did your experience with Demonstration 7.6 suggest that some decisions are easier than others?

Franklin and Tversky (1990) found that people could rapidly answer which objects were above and below; reaction times were short for these judgments. People required somewhat longer to decide which objects were ahead or behind. Furthermore, they took even longer to decide which objects were to the right or to the left. This research has been replicated in additional research (Bryant & Tversky, 1999; Franklin & Tversky, 1990). In all these studies, people judged the vertical dimension more quickly.

Franklin and Tversky (1990) also asked participants to describe how they thought they had performed the task. All participants reported that they had constructed images of the environment as they were reading. Most also reported that they had constructed imagery that represented their own point of view as an observer of the scene. Do these reports match your own experience with Demonstration 7.6?

The Spatial Framework Model. To explain their results, Franklin and Tversky proposed the spatial framework model (Franklin & Tversky, 1990; Tversky, 1991, 1997, 2005a, 2005b). The **spatial framework model** emphasizes that the above-below spatial dimension is especially important in our thinking, the front-back dimension is moderately important, and the right-left dimension is least important.

When we are in a typical upright position, the vertical or above-below dimension is especially important for two reasons:

1. The vertical dimension is correlated with gravity, an advantage that neither of the other two dimensions share. Gravity has an important asymmetric effect on the world we perceive; objects fall downward, not upward. Because of its association with gravity, the above-below dimension should be particularly important and thus particularly accessible.

2. The vertical dimension on an upright human's body is physically asymmetric. That is, the top (head) and the bottom (feet) are very easy to tell apart, and so we do not confuse them with each other.

These two factors combine to help us make judgments on the above-below dimension very rapidly.

The next most prominent dimension is the front-back dimension. When we are upright, the front-back dimension is not correlated with gravity. However, we usually interact with objects in front of us more easily than with objects in back of us, introducing an asymmetry. Also, the human's front half is not symmetric with the back half, again making it easy to distinguish between front and back. These two characteristics lead to judgment times for the front-back dimension that are fairly fast, although not as fast as for the above-below dimension.

The least prominent dimension is right-left. This dimension is not correlated with gravity, and we can perceive objects equally well whether they are on the right or the left. Furthermore—except for the minor preferences most of us show with our right or left hand when we manipulate objects—this dimension does not have the degree of asymmetry we find for the front-back dimension. Finally, a human's right half is roughly symmetrical with the left half. You can probably remember occasions when you confused your right hand with your left hand, or when you told someone to turn left when you meant right. Apparently, we need additional processing time to ensure that we do not make this error. Therefore, right-left decisions take longer than either above-below or front-back decisions.

In related studies, researchers have examined how people process directions on a physical map. The results demonstrate that people can make north-south decisions significantly faster than east-west decisions (Newcombe, 2002; Wagner, 2006). On a typical map in our culture, north-south corresponds to above-below, whereas right-left corresponds to east-west. In other words, these results provide further support for the spatial framework model.

In summary, then, Franklin and Tversky's spatial framework model proposes that the vertical or above-below dimension is most prominent for the upright observer (Franklin & Tversky, 1990; Tversky, 2005a, 2005b). The front-back dimension is next most prominent, and the right-left dimension is least prominent. Our cognitive maps therefore reveal certain biases. These biases are based on our long-term interactions with our bodies and with the physical properties of the external world (Tversky, 2005a, 2005b).

Further Research on Creating Cognitive Maps.   So far, all the research we have discussed has used scenarios written in the second person. (Notice the number of "you" sentences in Demonstration 7.6, for example.) Perhaps people can construct cognitive maps from verbal descriptions when the text suggests that the reader is observing a scene. However, do people still construct these models when the text describes the experience of another person? Suppose that you are reading a mystery novel, which describes what Detective Brown sees when she arrives at the scene of the crime. Do you jump into the scene and adopt Detective Brown's perspective? Bryant, Tversky, and Franklin (1992) found that readers typically prefer to adopt the perspective of the observer. They were less likely to remain outside the scene, like a viewer watching a movie.

We have seen that the cognitive maps we derive from verbal descriptions represent both orientation and point of view. We also tend to establish important landmarks when we hear or read a story (Ferguson & Hegarty, 1994). Then we use those landmarks as reference points for adding other locations to our cognitive maps. Notice that this information about landmarks is consistent with the research about cognitive maps and distance, discussed on page 227. Landmarks apparently have special, privileged status, whether we are constructing cognitive maps based on a physical diagram or based on a verbal narrative.

Our cognitive maps also represent distance, even if distance is not explicitly mentioned. For example, when people read that Joe has been walking for a long time, they make an inference about distance. Consequently, their cognitive maps show a great distance between Joe's starting point and his final destination (Rapp & Taylor, 2004; Rinck, 2005).

All the research on cognitive maps provides strong testimony for the active nature of human cognitive processes. We take in information, synthesize it, and go beyond the information we have received; we create a model to represent our knowledge (Tversky, 2000b, 2005b). As you will see throughout the rest of this textbook, an important general characteristic of our cognitive processes is our tendency to make inferences, so that we go beyond the given information.

Section Summary: *Cognitive Maps*

1. A cognitive map is a mental representation of the external environment; the research on this topic often emphasizes real-world settings, and it is interdisciplinary in scope.

2. Cognitive maps often represent complex knowledge. Individual differences in spatial cognition are large, and they are correlated with mental-rotation ability.

3. We can make judgments about spatial cognition more easily if our cognitive map matches the orientation of a physical map.

4. Cognitive maps usually represent reality with reasonable accuracy. However, systematic errors in these maps usually reflect the tendency to base our judgments on heuristics. We judge according to variables that are typically relevant, and we represent our environment as being more regular than it really is.

5. Estimates of distance on cognitive maps can be distorted by the number of intervening cities and by the semantic categories of the buildings on the cognitive maps. In addition, we estimate that landmarks are closer than nonlandmarks.

6. Shapes on cognitive maps can be distorted so that angles of intersecting streets are closer to 90 degrees than they are in reality, and so that curves are more nearly symmetrical than they are in reality.

7. The relative positions of geographic structures on cognitive maps can be distorted so that a slightly tilted structure will be remembered as being more vertical or more horizontal than it really is (rotation heuristic). Furthermore, a series of geographic structures will be remembered as being more lined up than they really are (alignment heuristic).

8. We often create cognitive maps of an environment on the basis of a verbal description. In these maps, the up-down dimension has special prominence, followed by the front-back dimension. The right-left dimension is most difficult. Franklin and Tversky (1990) explain these data in terms of the spatial framework model. We also make inferences to fill in other details in a cognitive map.

CHAPTER REVIEW QUESTIONS

1. Summarize the two theories of the characteristics of mental images: the analog code and the propositional code. Describe the findings about mental rotation, size, shape, reinterpreting ambiguous figures, and any other topics you recall. In each case, note which theory the results support.

2. Almost all of this chapter dealt with visual imagery, because little information is available about imagery in the other senses. How might you design a study on taste imagery that would be conceptually similar to one of the studies mentioned in the section on mental imagery? See whether you can also design studies to examine smell, hearing, and touch, basing these studies on the research techniques discussed in the first section of this chapter.

3. How do the studies on imagery and interference support the viewpoint that mental images operate like actual perceptions? Answer this question with respect to research on visual, auditory, and motor images. Describe how the research on interference provides strong support for the analog storage of information about objects.

4. Suppose that you see a newspaper headline, "Males Have Better Spatial Ability, Study Shows." When reading this article, what cautions should you keep in mind, based on the discussion of gender comparisons in spatial ability?

5. According to the research from cognitive neuroscience, what evidence do we have that visual imagery resemble perception? Why does this research avoid the problem of demand characteristics, which might be relevant in other imagery research?

6. Cognitive maps sometimes correspond to reality, but sometimes they show systematic deviations. Discuss the factors that seem to produce systematic distortions when people estimate distance on mental maps.

7. What heuristics cause systematic distortions in geographic shape and in relative position represented on cognitive maps? How are these related to two concepts we discussed in earlier chapters—namely, top-down processing (Chapter 2) and schemas (Chapter 5)?

8. According to Franklin and Tversky's spatial framework model, the three dimensions represented in our cognitive maps are not equally important. Which dimension has special prominence? How does the spatial framework model explain these differences?

9. The research we discussed in the first portion of this chapter emphasized that mental imagery often resembles perception. However, the material in the second portion emphasized that cognitive maps may be influenced by our concepts, as well as by our perceptions. Discuss these points, including some information about cognitive maps.

10. Cognitive psychologists often tend to ignore individual differences. However, this chapter examined several ways in which individuals differ with respect to mental imagery and spatial cognition. Describe this information, and speculate about other areas in which researchers could examine individual differences.

KEYWORDS

imagery	experimenter expectancy	90 degree-angle heuristic
imagery debate	demand characteristics	symmetry heuristic
analog code	meta-analysis	rotation heuristic
depictive representation	cognitive map	alignment heuristic
pictorial representation	spatial cognition	spatial framework model
propositional code	landmark effect	
descriptive representation	heuristic	

RECOMMENDED READINGS

Kosslyn, S. M., Thompson, W. L., & Ganis, G. (2006). *The case for mental imagery*. New York: Oxford University Press. As the title suggests, Steven Kosslyn and his colleagues focus their discussion on the analog approach to mental imagery; the book also emphasizes neuroscience support for this approach.

Shah, P., & Miyake, A. (Eds.). (2005). *The Cambridge handbook of visuospatial thinking*. New York: Cambridge University Press. This excellent reference book includes information on cognitive maps, gender comparisons, and applications of the imagery research; a chapter by Reisberg and Heuer also provides useful perspectives on the imagery debate.

Tversky, B. (2005b). Visuospatial reasoning. In K. J. Holyoak & R. G. Morrison (Eds.), *The Cambridge handbook of thinking and reasoning* (pp. 209–240). New York: Cambridge University Press. This chapter provides a good review of topics such as mental imagery and cognitive maps, and it also discusses the importance of inferences in cognitive psychology.

Wagner, M. (2006). *The geometries of visual space*. Mahwah, NJ: Erlbaum. In Mark Wagner's book, Chapter 8 is especially relevant to our discussion of cognitive maps. The remainder of the book focuses on philosophical and mathematical explorations of space perception.

ANSWERS TO DEMONSTRATION 7.1

In Chapter 2, people need to consult some sort of mental image to identify a shape (e.g., a letter of the alphabet) or to identify a sound (e.g., a speech sound). In Chapter 3, when people conduct a search for a target—perhaps for a blue X, as in Demonstration 3.2—they must keep a mental image in mind as they inspect the potential targets. In Chapter 4, the entire discussion of the visuospatial sketchpad is based on visual imagery. In Chapter 5, visual imagery is relevant to the material on face recognition in long-term memory. Chapter 6 discussed visual imagery as a helpful class of mnemonic devices for retrospective memory. In addition, you may use visual imagery or motor imagery in order to prompt your prospective memory for some action you must perform in the future.

CHAPTER 8
Using General Knowledge

PREVIEW

This chapter examines our background knowledge—the knowledge that informs and influences cognitive processes such as memory and spatial cognition. We will explore two major topics: semantic memory and schemas.

Semantic memory refers to our organized knowledge about the world. We will look at four categories of theories that attempt to explain how all this information could be stored. These theories are partly compatible with one another, but they emphasize different aspects of semantic memory. Suppose that you are trying to decide whether an object in the grocery store is an apple. (1) The feature comparison model proposes that you examine a list of necessary features—such as color, size, and shape—to decide if it is an apple. (2) The prototype approach argues that you decide whether this object is an apple by comparing it with an apple that is most typical of the category; however, people who are experts don't use this particular approach. (3) The exemplar approach emphasizes that you decide whether it is an apple by comparing it with some specific examples of apples with which you are familiar (perhaps a McIntosh, an Ida Red, and a Fuji apple).

These first three theories—feature comparison, prototype, and exemplar—are primarily concerned about category membership. (4) The network models, in contrast, emphasize the interconnections among related items; for example, an apple may be related to other items such as *red*, *seed-bearing*, and *pear*. (Incidentally, Chapter 1 introduced you to the most prominent network model, the parallel distributed processing approach.)

Schemas and scripts apply to larger clusters of knowledge. A schema is a generalized kind of knowledge about situations and events. One kind of schema is called a script; scripts describe an expected sequence of events. For example, most people have a well-defined "restaurant script," which specifies all the events that are likely to occur when you dine in a restaurant. Schemas influence our memories in several ways: (1) selecting the material we want to remember, (2) extending the boundaries for visual scenes, (3) storing the general meaning of a verbal passage, (4) interpreting the material by making inferences, and (5) forming a single, integrated representation in memory. Schemas can cause inaccuracies during these stages, but we are often more accurate than schema theory proposes.

INTRODUCTION

Consider the following sentence:

When Lisa was on her way back from the store with the balloon, she fell and the balloon floated away.

Think about all the information that you assume and all the reasonable inferences that you make while reading this brief sentence. For instance, consider just the word *balloon*. You know that balloons can be made of several lightweight substances, that they can be filled with air or a lightweight gas, and that their shape can resemble an animal or a cartoon character. However, a balloon is unlikely to be created from a sock, it is unlikely to be filled with raspberry yogurt, and it is unlikely to be shaped like a spear of broccoli.

Now reread that entire sentence about the balloon, and think about the inferences you are likely to make. For instance, Lisa is probably a child, not a 40-year-old woman. Also, she probably bought the balloon in the store. You might also guess that the balloon was attached to a string, but the other end of the string was not firmly attached to Lisa. When she fell, she probably let go of the string. She may have scraped her knee, and it may have bled. A sentence that initially seemed simple is immediately enriched by an astonishing amount of general knowledge about objects and events in our world.

To provide a context for Chapter 8, let's briefly review the topics we've considered so far in this textbook. In Chapter 2, on visual and auditory recognition, we examined how the senses gather stimuli from the outside world, and how these stimuli are then interpreted by our previous knowledge. Chapter 3 emphasized that we have difficulty paying attention to more than one message at a time; our knowledge may influence which message we choose to process and which we choose to ignore.

In Chapters 4 through 7, we discussed how these stimuli from the outside world are stored in memory. In many cases, we saw that our previous knowledge can influence memory. For example, it can help us chunk items together to aid working memory (Chapter 4). Furthermore, our knowledge provides the kind of expertise that enhances long-term memory, and it can influence our memory for the events in our lives (Chapter 5). In addition, our knowledge can help us organize information in order to recall it more accurately (Chapter 6). Finally, when we apply general principles such as the rotation heuristic and the alignment heuristic, our previous knowledge can distort our memories of spatial relationships, making them more regular than they actually are (Chapter 7). All these cognitive processes rely on general knowledge, demonstrating again that our cognitive processes are interrelated (Theme 4).

During the first half of the book, then, we've emphasized how information from the outside world is taken into your cognitive system and is somehow influenced by your general knowledge. This knowledge allows you to go beyond the information in the stimulus in a useful, productive fashion (Billman, 1996; Landauer & Dumais, 1997).

Now we need to focus specifically on the nature of this general knowledge by examining two components:

1. First, we'll consider semantic memory. If you are a typical English-speaking adult, you know the meaning of at least 20,000 to 40,000 words (Baddeley, 1990; Saffran & Schwartz, 2003). You also know a tremendous amount of information about each of these words. For example, you know that a cat has fur and that an apple has seeds. You also know that a car is a good example of a vehicle . . . but an elevator is a bad example.

2. We will also consider the nature of schemas, or general knowledge about an object or event. Schemas allow us to know much more than the simple combination of words within a sentence.

This chapter emphasizes our impressive cognitive abilities (Theme 2). We have an enormous amount of information at our disposal, and we use this information efficiently and accurately. This chapter also confirms the active nature of our cognitive processes (Theme 1). In the last part of Chapter 7, for example, we saw that people can use the information in a verbal description to actively construct a mental model of an environment. As we'll see in the current chapter, people who are given one bit of information can go beyond that specific information to actively retrieve additional stored knowledge about word relationships and other likely inferences. Let us explore the nature of general knowledge as we see how people go beyond the given information in semantic memory and in schemas.

THE STRUCTURE OF SEMANTIC MEMORY

As we discussed in earlier chapters, **semantic memory** is our organized knowledge about the world (Wheeler, 2000). We contrasted semantic memory with **episodic memory,** which contains information about events that happen to us. Chapters 4, 5, and 6 emphasized different aspects of episodic memory.

The distinction between semantic and episodic memory is not clear-cut (McNamara & Holbrook, 2003). In general, though, semantic memory refers to knowledge or information; it does not mention how we acquired that information. An example of semantic memory would be: "Managua is the capital of Nicaragua." In contrast, episodic memory always implies a personal experience, because episodic memory emphasizes when, where, or how this event happened to you (McNamara & Holbrook, 2003). An example of episodic memory would be: "This morning in my Political Science course, I learned that Managua is the capital of Nicaragua." Let's discuss some background information about semantic memory before we examine several theoretical models of how it operates.

Background on Semantic Memory

Psychologists use the term *semantic memory* in a broad sense—much broader than the word *semantic* implies in normal conversation (McNamara & Holbrook, 2003). For example, semantic memory includes encyclopedic knowledge (e.g., "Martin Luther King, Jr., was born in Atlanta, Georgia"). It also includes lexical or language knowledge (e.g., "The word *justice* is related to the word *equality*"). In addition, semantic memory includes conceptual knowledge (e.g., "A square has four sides"). Semantic memory influences most of our cognitive activities. For instance, we need this form of memory so that we can determine locations, read sentences, solve problems, and make decisions.

Categories and concepts are essential components of semantic memory. In fact, we need to divide up the world into categories in order to make sense of our knowledge

(Goldstone & Kersten, 2003; Schwarz, 1995). A **category** is a set of objects that belong together. For example, the category called "fruit" represents a certain category of food items; your cognitive system treats these objects as being equivalent (Markman & Ross, 2003).

Psychologists use the term **concept** to refer to our mental representations of a category (Wisniewski, 2002). For instance, you have a concept of "fruit," which refers to your mental representation of the objects in that category. (Incidentally, in this chapter I'll follow the tradition in cognitive psychology of using italics for the actual word names, and quotation marks for categories and concepts.)

Every academic course in which you are enrolled requires you to form concepts (Goldstone & Kersten, 2003). In an art history course, you may need to create a concept called "15th-century Flemish painting," and in a Spanish course you learn a concept called "people with whom you use the 'usted' form of verbs."

Your semantic memory allows you to code the objects you encounter. Even though the objects are not identical, you can combine together a wide variety of similar objects by using a single, one-word concept (Milton & Wills, 2004; Wisniewski, 2002; Yamauchi, 2005). This coding process greatly reduces the storage space, because many objects can all be stored with the same label (Sternberg & Ben-Zeev, 2001).

Your concepts also allow you to make numerous inferences when you encounter new examples from a category (Keil, 2003; Yamauchi, 2005). For example, even a young child knows that a member of the category "fruit" has the attribute "you can eat it." When she encounters a new kind of fruit, she makes the inference (usually correctly) that you can eat it. As we noted earlier, these inferences allow us to go beyond the given information, greatly expanding our knowledge. Otherwise—if you had no concepts— you would need to examine each new chair you encountered, in order to figure out how to use it (Murphy, 2002).

We noted that semantic memory allows us to combine similar objects into a single concept. But how do we decide which objects are similar? As you'll soon see, each of four approaches to semantic memory has a slightly different perspective on the nature of similarity (Markman & Gentner, 2001). Let's now consider these four major approaches. They include the feature comparison model, the prototype approach, the exemplar approach, and network models.

Most theorists in the area of semantic memory believe that each model may be at least partly correct. Furthermore, each model can account for some aspect of semantic memory (Markman, 2002). In fact, it's unlikely that the wide variety of concepts would all be represented in the same way in our semantic memory (Haberlandt, 1999; Hampton, 1997a). Therefore, as you read about these four approaches, you do not need to choose which single approach is correct and which three must consequently be wrong.

The Feature Comparison Model

One logical way to organize semantic memory would be in terms of lists of features. According to an early theory, called the **feature comparison model,** concepts are stored in memory according to a list of necessary features or characteristics. People use

---

Demonstration 8.1

The Sentence Verification Technique

For each of the items below, answer as quickly as possible either "True" or "False."

1. A poodle is a dog.
2. A squirrel is an animal.
3. A flower is a rock.
4. A carrot is a vegetable.
5. A mango is a fruit.
6. A petunia is a tree.
7. A robin is a bird.
8. A rutabaga is a vegetable.

---

a decision process to make judgments about these concepts (Smith et al., 1974). Before you read further, try Demonstration 8.1.

Description of the Feature Comparison Model. Consider the concept "cat" for a moment. We could make up a list of features that are often relevant to cats:

> has fur
>
> has four legs
>
> meows
>
> has a tail
>
> chases mice

Smith and his coauthors (1974) propose that the features used in this model are either defining features or characteristic features. **Defining features** are those attributes that are necessary to the meaning of the item. For example, the defining features of a robin include that it is living and has feathers and a red breast. **Characteristic features** are those attributes that are merely descriptive but are not essential. For example, the characteristic features of a robin include that it flies, perches in trees, is not domesticated, and is small in size. If the distinction between defining features and characteristic features seems somewhat arbitrary, you'll be pleased to know that the research confirms this impression!

Research on the Feature Comparison Model. The sentence verification technique is one of the major tools used to explore the feature comparison model. In the **sentence verification technique,** people see simple sentences, and they must consult their stored semantic knowledge to determine whether the sentences are true or false. Demonstration 8.1 shows the kinds of items presented in the sentence verification technique. In general, people are highly accurate on this task, so it's not useful to compare the error rates across experimental conditions. Instead, researchers measure reaction times.

One common finding in research using the sentence verification technique is the typicality effect. In the **typicality effect,** people reach decisions faster when an item is a typical member of a category, rather than an unusual member (McNamara & Holbrook, 2003; Olson et al., 2004). For example, in Demonstration 8.1, you probably decided quickly that a carrot is a vegetable, but you may have paused before deciding that a rutabaga is a vegetable.

The feature comparison model can explain the typicality effect (Smith, 1978). For example, a carrot is a typical member of its category, so the features of carrots and the features of vegetables are highly similar. Therefore, people quickly answer the question, "Is a carrot a vegetable?" However, a rutabaga is an example of an atypical vegetable. People require much longer to answer the question, "Is a rutabaga a vegetable?" According to the model, when people encounter an atypical item, they need to compare the defining features for the item and its category (Smith, 1978). This extra step requires more time.

Research on another aspect of the feature comparison model clearly contradicts this approach. Specifically, a major problem with the feature comparison model is that very few of the concepts we use in everyday life can be captured by a specific list of necessary, defining features (Burgess & Lund, 2000; Hahn & Chater, 1997; Wisniewski, 2002). For example, Sloman and his colleagues (1998) asked college students to judge whether they could imagine an example of a concept that lacked a given characteristic. When judging a robin, for example, they could imagine a robin that didn't fly, didn't eat, didn't have feathers, and didn't have a red breast! Notice, then, that the participants did not believe that any specific feature is absolutely necessary in order to qualify for the category of "robin."

Conclusions About the Feature Comparison Model. We have seen that the feature comparison model can account for the typicality effect. However, the research does not support the idea that category membership is based on a list of necessary features.

Another problem with the feature comparison model is its assumption that the individual features are independent of one another. However, many features are correlated for the concepts we encounter in nature. For example, objects that have leaves are not likely to have legs or fur. In contrast, objects that have fur are highly likely to have legs (Goldstone & Kersten, 2003; Markman, 2002; Rogers & McClelland, 2004). Finally, the feature comparison model does not explain how the members of categories are related to one another (Barsalou, 1992).

Our next topic is the prototype approach to concepts. Like the feature comparison model, the prototype approach emphasizes that we ignore many details that make each item in a category unique (Heit & Barsalou, 1996). Also, like the feature comparison model, the prototype approach does not explain how the members of categories are related to one another. However, the feature comparison model is based on the similarity between an item and a list of features that are necessary for category membership.

In contrast, the prototype model is based on the similarity between an item and an idealized object that represents the category (Sternberg & Ben-Zeev, 2001).

The Prototype Approach

According to a theory proposed by Eleanor Rosch, we organize each category on the basis of a **prototype,** which is the item that is most typical and representative of the category (Murphy, 2002; Rosch, 1973). According to this **prototype approach,** you decide whether an item belongs to a category by comparing that item with a prototype. If the item is similar to the prototype, you include that item in the category (Sternberg & Ben-Zeev, 2001; Wisniewski, 2002). For example, you conclude that a robin is a bird because it matches your ideal prototype for a bird. Suppose, however, that the item you are judging is sufficiently different from the prototype, for example, a bee. In this case, you place the item in another category (the category "insect") where it more closely resembles that category's prototype.

In some cases, the prototype of a category may not even exist (Markman, 1999; Murphy, 2002). For example, suppose that I asked you to describe a prototypical animal. You might tell me about a four-legged creature with fur, a tail, and a size somewhere between a large dog and a cow—something that does not precisely resemble any creature on earth. Thus, a prototype is an abstract, idealized example.

Rosch (1973) also emphasizes that members of a category differ in their **prototypicality,** or degree to which they are prototypical. A robin and a sparrow are very prototypical birds, whereas ostriches and penguins are nonprototypes. Think of a prototype, or most typical member, for a particular group of students on your campus, perhaps students with a particular academic major. Also think of a nonprototype ("You mean he's an art major? He doesn't seem at all like one!"). Now think of a prototype for a professor, a fruit, and a vehicle; then think of a nonprototype for each category. For example, a tomato is a nonprototypical fruit, and an elevator is a nonprototypical vehicle.

The prototype approach represents a different perspective from the feature comparison model that we just examined. According to the feature comparison model, an item belongs to a category as long as it possesses the necessary and sufficient features (Markman, 1999). The feature comparison perspective therefore argues that category membership is very clear-cut. For example, for the category "bachelor," the defining features are *male* and *unmarried.*

However, don't you think that your 32-year-old unmarried male cousin represents a better example of a bachelor than does your 2-year-old nephew or an elderly Catholic priest? All three individuals are indeed male and unmarried, so the feature comparison model would conclude that all three deserve to be categorized as "bachelors." In contrast, the prototype approach would argue that not all members of the category "bachelor" are created equal. Instead, your cousin is a more prototypical bachelor than your nephew or the priest (Lakoff, 1987). The prototype approach to semantic memory is especially useful when we consider social relationships such as "bachelor" and "love" (Fehr, 2005).

Eleanor Rosch and her coauthors, as well as other researchers, have conducted numerous studies on the characteristics of prototypes. Their research demonstrates that all members of categories are *not* created equal (Medin & Rips, 2005; Murphy, 2002;

Rogers & McClelland, 2004). Instead, a category tends to have a **graded structure,** beginning with the most representative or prototypical members and continuing on through the category's nonprototypical members. Let us examine several important characteristics of prototypes. Then we will discuss another important component of the prototype approach, which focuses on several different levels of categorization.

Characteristics of Prototypes. Prototypes differ from the nonprototypical members of categories in several respects. As you will see, prototypes have a special, privileged status within a category.

1. *Prototypes are supplied as examples of a category.* Several studies have shown that people judge some items to be better examples of a concept than other items. In one study, for example, Mervis and her colleagues (1976) examined some norms in which people had provided examples of categories, such as "birds," "fruit," and "sports." Mervis and her coauthors asked a different group of people to supply prototype ratings for each of these examples.

A statistical analysis showed that the items that were rated most prototypical were the same items that people had supplied most often in the category norms. For instance, for the category "bird," people judged a robin to be very prototypical, and *robin* was very frequently listed as an example of the category "bird." In contrast, people rated *penguin* as low on the prototype scale, and penguin was only rarely listed as an example of the category "bird." In other words, if someone asks you to name a member of a category, you will probably name a prototype.

Our earlier explanation of the feature comparison model discussed the typicality effect. As it happens, the prototype approach accounts well for the typicality effect (Murphy, 2002; Rogers & McClelland, 2004). That is, when people are asked to judge whether an item belongs to a particular category, they judge typical items (prototypes) faster than atypical items (nonprototypes). For instance, when judging whether items belong to the category "bird," people judge *robin* more quickly than *penguin.* This rapid judging holds true for both pictures of objects and names of objects (Hampton, 1997b; Heit & Barsalou, 1996). To summarize this first characteristic of prototypes, we can conclude that people supply prototypes more often as examples, and people also make quicker judgments about category membership when assessing prototypes.

2. *Prototypes are judged more quickly after semantic priming.* The **semantic priming effect** means that people respond faster to an item if it was preceded by an item with similar meaning. For example, you would make judgments about apples more quickly if you had just seen the word *fruit* than if you had just seen the word *giraffe.* The semantic priming effect helps cognitive psychologists understand important information about how we retrieve information from memory (McNamara, 2005; McNamara & Holbrook, 2003).

The research shows that priming facilitates the responses to prototypes more than it facilitates the responses to nonprototypes. Imagine, for example, that you are participating in a study on priming. Your task is to judge pairs of similar colors and to answer whether they are the same. On some occasions, you see the name of the color before you must judge the pair of colors; these are the primed trials. On other occasions, you do not see a color name as a "warning"; these are the unprimed trials. Rosch (1975) tried this priming setup for both prototype colors (for example, a good, bright red) and nonprototype colors (for example, a muddy red).

Rosch's results showed that priming was very helpful when people made judgments about prototypical colors; they responded more quickly after primed trials than after nonprimed trials. However, priming actually *inhibited* the judgments for nonprototypical colors. In other words, if you see the word *red*, you expect to see a true, fire-engine red color. However, if you see a dark, muddy red color, the priming offers no advantage. Instead, you actually need extra time in order to reconcile your image of a bright, vivid color with the muddy color you actually see before you.

3. *Prototypes share attributes in a family resemblance category.* Before we examine this issue, let's introduce a new term, family resemblance. **Family resemblance** means that no single attribute is shared by all examples of a concept; however, each example has at least one attribute in common with some other example of the concept (Milton & Wills, 2004; Rosch & Mervis,1975).

Rosch and Mervis (1975) examined the role of prototypes in family resemblance categories. They asked a group of students to make prototypicality judgments about members of several categories. As you can see in Table 8.1, for example, the students rated a car as being the most prototypical vehicle and a wheelchair as being the least prototypical vehicle on this list.

TABLE 8.1

Prototype Ratings for Words in Three Categories.

Item	Vehicle	Vegetable	Clothing
1	Car	Peas	Pants
2	Truck	Carrots	Shirt
3	Bus	String beans	Dress
4	Motorcycle	Spinach	Skirt
5	Train	Broccoli	Jacket
6	Trolley car	Asparagus	Coat
7	Bicycle	Corn	Sweater
8	Airplane	Cauliflower	Underwear
9	Boat	Brussels sprouts	Socks
10	Tractor	Lettuce	Pajamas
11	Cart	Beets	Bathing suit
12	Wheelchair	Tomato	Shoes

Source: Rosch & Mervis, 1975.

Then, Rosch and Mervis asked a different group of people to list the attributes possessed by each item. They found that the most prototypical item also had the largest number of attributes in common with the other items in the category. For example, a car (the most prototypical vehicle) has wheels, moves horizontally, and uses fuel. In contrast, a wheelchair has relatively few attributes in common with other items. Check the categories "vegetable" and "clothing" in Table 8.1. Do the most prototypical items share more attributes with other items, compared to the nonprototypical items?

Most researchers in semantic memory agree that categories tend to have a structure based on family resemblance (Murphy, 2002; Pinker & Prince, 1999). That is, members of a category share attributes with other members of that category. However, no single attribute serves as the necessary and sufficient criterion for membership in that category.

Levels of Categorization. We have just examined three characteristics of proto-types that differentiate them from nonprototypes. The second major portion of Eleanor Rosch's prototype theory examines the way that our semantic categories are structured in terms of different levels.

Consider these examples: Suppose that you are sitting on a wooden structure that faces your desk. You can call that structure by several different names: *furniture, chair,* or *desk chair.* You can also refer to your pet as a *dog,* a *spaniel,* or a *cocker spaniel.* You can tighten the mirror on your car with a *tool,* a *screwdriver,* or a *Phillips screwdriver.*

An object can be categorized at several different levels. Some category levels are called **superordinate-level categories**, which means they are higher-level or more general categories. "Furniture," "animal," and "tool" are all examples of superordinate-level categories. **Basic-level categories** are moderately specific. "Chair," "dog," and "screwdriver" are examples of basic-level categories. Finally, **subordinate-level categories** refer to lower-level or more specific categories. "Desk chair," "collie," and "Phillips screwdriver" are examples of subordinate categories.

As you continue to read the rest of this description of prototype theory, keep in mind that a prototype is *not* the same as a basic-level category. A prototype is the best example of a category. In contrast, a basic-level category refers to a category that is neither too general nor too specific.

Basic-level categories seem to have special status (Rogers & McClelland, 2004; Rosch et al., 1976; Wisniewski, 2002). In general, they are more useful than either superordinate-level categories or subordinate-level categories. Let's examine how these basic-level categories seem to have special privileges, in contrast to the other two category levels.

1. *Basic-level names are used to identify objects.* Try naming some of the objects that you can see from where you are sitting. You are likely to use basic-level names for these objects. You will mention *pen,* for example, rather than the superordinate *writing instrument* or the subordinate *Bic fine-point pen.*

Eleanor Rosch and her colleagues (1976) asked people to look at pictures and identify the objects. They found that people preferred to use basic-level names. Apparently, the basic-level name gives enough information without being overly detailed (Medin et al., 2000; Rogers & McClelland, 2004; Wisniewski, 2002). In addition, people produce basic-level names faster than superordinate or subordinate names (Kosslyn et al., 1995; Rogers & McClelland, 2004). Furthermore, when people see superordinate or subordinate terms, they frequently remember the basic-level version of these terms when they are later tested for recall (Pansky & Koriat, 2004). In other words, the basic level does have special, privileged status.

2. *Basic-level names are more likely to produce the semantic priming effect.* Eleanor Rosch and her colleagues (1976) used a variant of the semantic priming task. In this version, the researchers present the name of an object, followed by two pictures. The participant must decide whether these two pictures are the same as one another. For example, you might hear the word *apple* and see pictures of two identical apples. The priming is effective because the presentation of the word allows you to create a mental representation of this word, which helps when you make the decision more quickly.

Rosch and her coworkers showed that priming with basic-level names was indeed helpful. The participants made faster judgments if they saw a basic-level term like *apple* before judging the apples. However, priming with superordinate names (such as *fruit*) was not helpful. Apparently, when you hear the word *fruit*, you create a general representation of fruit, rather than a representation that is specific enough to prepare you for judging apples.

3. *Different levels of categorization activate different regions of the brain.* Neuroscience research using PET scans has examined whether different regions of the brain tend to process different category levels (Kosslyn et al., 1995). On a typical trial, a participant might be asked to judge whether a word (e.g., *toy, doll,* or *rag doll*) matched a particular picture. This research showed that superordinate terms (e.g., *toy*) are more likely than basic-level terms (e.g., *doll*) to activate part of the prefrontal cortex. This finding makes sense, because this part of the cortex processes language and associative memory. To answer whether the picture of the doll qualifies as a toy, you must consult your memory about category membership.

In contrast, the research showed that subordinate terms (e.g., *rag doll*) are more likely than basic-level terms (e.g., *doll*) to activate part of the parietal region of the brain. As Chapter 3 noted, the parietal lobe is active when we shift visual attention. Again, this finding makes sense. To answer this question, you must shift your attention from the general shape of the object to determine if the fabric and style of the doll indeed permit it to be categorized as a "rag doll."

Conclusions About the Prototype Approach. One advantage of the prototype approach is that it can account for our ability to form concepts for groups that are loosely structured. For example, we can create a concept for stimuli that merely share a family resemblance, when the members of a category have no single characteristic in common. Another advantage of the prototype approach is that it can be applied to social relationships, as well as inanimate objects and nonsocial categories (Fehr, 2005).

However, an ideal model of semantic memory must also acknowledge that concepts can be unstable and variable. For example, our notions about the ideal prototype can shift as the context changes (Barsalou, 1993). Novick (2003) found that U.S. college students rated *airplane* as being a prototypical vehicle during the period immediately following the terrorist attack of September 11, 2001. In contrast, *airplane* was considered a non-prototypical vehicle in studies that had gathered norms on vehicles during the five years prior to this date. Furthermore, as the media coverage decreased after the attack, *airplane* decreased in prototypicality. In fact, $4\frac{1}{2}$ months after the attack, *airplane* was no longer a prototypical vehicle.

Another problem with the prototype approach is that we often *do* store specific information about individual examples of a category. An ideal model of semantic memory would therefore need to include a mechanism for storing this specific information, as well as abstract prototypes (Barsalou, 1990, 1992).

The prototype theory clearly accounts for a number of phenomena. Unfortunately, however, research on prototype theory has decreased since the 1980s, and it has not been developed to account for some complexities of the categories that people use in their daily lives. An additional problem is that the prototype approach may operate well when we consider the general population, but not when we examine experts in a particular discipline.

Individual Differences: Expertise and Prototypes

An individual with **expertise** shows consistently exceptional performance on representative tasks in a particular area (Ericsson, 2003a, 2003b, 2006). People who are experts deliberately challenge themselves and practice tasks in their specific area (Ericsson, 2004; Zimmerman, 2006). Researchers frequently specify that an individual must have practiced for at least ten years in his or her area in order to qualify as an expert (Ericsson, 2003b; Kellogg, 2006).

The earlier description of prototypes on pages 246–249 emphasized that a prototype is the item that is most typical and representative of the category. In other words, a prototype is most similar to other members of its category; therefore, a prototype represents a central tendency (Lynch et al., 2000). Research suggests, however, that experts construct prototypes in a different fashion (Rogers & McClelland, 2004).

Elizabeth Lynch, John Coley, and Douglas Medin (2000) examined whether people with expertise in an area would select the same prototype as novices (nonexperts). Specifically, they tested twenty-four tree experts from the Chicago area. The experts included people from three categories: landscapers who choose trees to be planted in appropriate settings, academic researchers who study the names of trees, and parks maintenance workers who plant trees and take care of them. The novices were twenty undergraduate students. In each case, the participants were instructed to use a 7-point rating scale to indicate whether each of forty-eight tree species was a very good example of the category "tree," a very bad example, or somewhere in between.

If the prototype approach applies to the experts' decisions, then the best example of a tree should be one with an average height. However, the experts did not choose a tree of average height; instead, they gave the highest ratings to the taller trees and the lowest ratings to the shorter trees. The experts' ratings also showed that the best examples of trees could not be "weedlike." That is, the best trees could not have weak wood, they couldn't create a mess (for instance, by staining sidewalks), and they could not spring up in inappropriate locations. In other words, the experts' best examples were very tall, well-behaved trees . . . rather than typical, average trees.

As it happened, the novice undergraduate students also failed to give the highest rating to typical trees. Instead, they rated the trees almost entirely on the basis of their familiarity with the tree names. Their "best trees" were ones that included familiar names such as *maple* and *oak*; their "worst trees" included unfamiliar names such as *catalpa* and *ginko*.

We discussed different levels of categorization on pages 249–251. Research on this topic shows that experts and novices also prefer different levels of categorization (Medin & Atran, 2004; Rogers & McClelland, 2004). For example, Johnson and Mervis (1997) found that bird-watching experts provided very specific names for birds, such as *yellow-throated warbler*, whereas the novices uniformly supplied the basic-level term *bird*.

In short, the best example of a tree is not a typical tree—for either experts or novices. Furthermore, novices may prefer basic-level terms, but experts prefer terms that are even more specific than the subordinate terms. Let's now consider the exemplar approach to semantic memory, in which a category is represented in terms of all its members, not just the most typical member.

The Exemplar Approach

The **exemplar approach** argues that we first learn some specific examples of a concept; then we classify each new stimulus by deciding how closely it resembles those specific examples (Medin & Rips, 2005; Wisniewski, 2002). Each of those examples stored in memory is called an **exemplar.** The exemplar approach emphasizes that your concept of "dog" would be represented by numerous examples of dogs you have known (Murphy, 2002). In contrast, the prototype approach would argue that your *prototype* of a dog would be an idealized representation of a dog, with average size for a dog and average other features—but not necessarily like any particular dog you've ever seen.

Consider another example. Suppose that you are taking a course in abnormal psychology. Suppose also that you have just read four case studies in your textbook, and each case study described a depressed individual. You then read an article that describes a woman's psychological problems, but the article does not specify her disorder. You decide that she fits into the category "depressed person" because this description closely resembles the characteristics of some earlier exemplars. Furthermore, this individual does not resemble any exemplars in a set of case studies you read last week when you were learning about anxiety disorder.

A Representative Study on the Exemplar Approach. The exemplar approach predicts performance on artificial categories, such as cartoon faces that can be shown with or without glasses, smiling or frowning, and so on (Medin & Rips, 2005; Rehder & Hoffman, 2005). How does this approach work with categories we use in our everyday lives? Before you read further, try Demonstration 8.2, which is based on a study by Evan Heit and Lawrence Barsalou (1996).

Demonstration 8.2

Exemplars and Typicality

A. For the first part of this demonstration, take out a sheet of paper and write the numbers 1 through 7 in a column. Then, next to the appropriate number, write the first example that comes to mind for each of the following categories:

    1. amphibian

    2. bird

    3. fish

    4. insect

    5. mammal

    6. microorganism

    7. reptile

B. For the second part of the demonstration, look at each of the items you wrote on the sheet of paper. Rate how typical each item is for the category "animal." Use a scale where 1 = not at all typical, and 10 = very typical. For example, if you wrote *barracuda* on the list, supply a number between 1 and 10 to indicate the extent to which *barracuda* is typical of an animal.

C. For the final part of this demonstration, rate each of the seven categories in Part A in terms of how typical each category is for the superordinate category "animal." Use the same rating scale as in Part B.

Source: Partly based on a study by Heit & Barsalou, 1996.

Heit and Barsalou (1996) wanted to determine whether the exemplar approach could explain the structure of several superordinate categories, such as "animal." When people make judgments about animals, do they base these judgments on specific exemplars or general prototypes?

Heit and Barsalou (1996) asked a group of undergraduates to supply the first example that came to mind for each of the seven basic-level categories in Part A of Demonstration 8.2. Then a second group of undergraduates rated the typicality of each of those examples, with respect to the superordinate category "animal." For instance, this second group would rate each example—such as *frog* or *salamander*—in terms of whether it was typical of the concept "animal." That second group also rated the seven basic-level categories. (To make the demonstration simpler—though not as well controlled—you performed all three tasks.)

Heit and Barsalou (1996) then assembled all the data. They wanted to see whether they could create an equation that would accurately predict—for the category "animal"—the typicality of the rating of the seven categories ("amphibian," "bird," "fish," and so on), based on the exemplars generated in a task like Task A of Demonstration 8.2 . Specifically, they took into account the frequency of each of those exemplars. For example, the basic-level category "insect" frequently produced the exemplar *bee* but rarely produced the exemplar *Japanese beetle*. They also took into account the typicality ratings, similar to those you provided in Task B of the demonstration.

The information about exemplar frequency and exemplar typicality did accurately predict which of the seven categories were most typical for the superordinate category "animal" (Task C). In fact, the correlation between the predicted typicality and the actual typicality was r = +.92, indicating an extremely strong relationship. For example, mammals were considered the most typical animals, and microorganisms were the least typical.

The prototype approach suggests that our categories consider only the most typical items (Wisniewski, 2002). If this proposal is correct, then we can forget about the less typical items, and our categories would not be substantially changed. In another part of their study, Heit and Barsalou (1996) tried eliminating the less typical exemplars from the equation. The correlation between predicted typicality and actual typicality decreased significantly.

Notice the implications of this study: Suppose that you are asked a question such as, "How typical is an insect, with respect to the category 'animal'?" To make that judgment, you don't just take into account a very prototypical insect—perhaps a combination of a bee and a fly. Instead, you also include some information about a caterpillar, a grasshopper, and maybe even a Japanese beetle.

Comparing the Exemplar Approach with Other Approaches. On pages 243 to 245, we discussed the feature comparison approach. That approach has an important disadvantage: People usually cannot create a list of necessary and sufficient features for a category (Hahn & Chater, 1997). In contrast, the exemplar approach proposes that we do not need any list of features, because all the necessary information is stored in the specific exemplars.

How does the exemplar approach compare with the prototype approach? Both approaches say that we make decisions about category membership by comparing a new item against some stored representation of the category (Markman, 1999; Murphy, 2002). If the similarity is strong enough, we conclude that this new item does indeed belong to the category. However, the prototype approach says that this stored representation is a typical member of the category. In contrast, the exemplar approach says that the stored representation is a collection of numerous specific members of the category (Medin & Rips, 2005; J. D. Smith, 2002; Yang & Lewandowsky, 2004).

Furthermore, the exemplar approach says that people do not need to perform any kind of abstraction process (Barsalou, 2003; Heit & Barsalou, 1996; Knowlton, 1997). For example, suppose that you had read four case studies about depressed people. In this case, you would not need to figure out a list of necessary and sufficient features that the individuals had in common, as the feature comparison model would suggest. You also would not need to devise a prototype—an ideal, typical person with depression. The exemplar approach argues that creating a list of characteristics or creating a prototypical person would force you to discard useful, specific data about individual cases.

One problem with the exemplar approach, however, is that our semantic memory would quickly become overpopulated with numerous exemplars for numerous categories (Nosofsky & Palmieri, 1998; Sternberg & Ben-Zeev, 2001). The exemplar approach may therefore be more suitable when considering a category that has relatively few members (Knowlton, 1997). For instance, the exemplar approach might operate for the category "tropical fruit," unless you happen to live in a tropical region of the world.

In contrast, the prototype approach may be more suitable when considering a category that has numerous members. For example, a prototype may be the most efficient approach for a large category such as "fruit" or "animal." Despite the encouraging results from Heit and Barsalou's (1996) study, the exemplar approach may be simply too bulky for some purposes. In many situations, it is not effective to use a classification strategy based purely on exemplars (Erickson & Kruschke, 1998, 2002).

Individual differences may be substantial in the way people represent categories. Perhaps some people store information about specific exemplars, especially for categories in which they have expertise. Other people may construct categories that do not include information about specific exemplars (Thomas, 1998). These individuals may construct categories based on more generic prototypes.

In reality, the prototype approach and the exemplar approach may coexist, so that a concept includes information about both prototypes and specific exemplars (Murphy, 2002; Ross & Makin, 1999; Wisniewski, 2002). In fact, one possibility is that the brain uses both prototype processing and exemplar processing, but each is handled by a different hemisphere. Specifically, the left hemisphere may store prototypes and the right hemisphere may store exemplars (Bruno et al., 2003; Gazzaniga et al., 2002; Laeng et al., 2003). Furthermore, different kinds of categories may require different strategies for category formation (E. E. Smith et al., 1998; J. D. Smith, 2002). People may in fact use a combination of prototype strategies and exemplar strategies when they form categories in everyday life.

Network Models

The feature comparison model, the prototype approach, and the exemplar approach all emphasize whether an item belongs to a category. In contrast, network theories are more concerned about the interconnections among related items.

Think for a moment about the large number of associations you have to the word *apple*. How can we find an effective way to represent the different aspects of meaning for *apple* that are stored in memory? A number of theorists favor network models. The **network models** of semantic memory propose a netlike organization of concepts in memory, with many interconnections. The meaning of a particular concept, such as "apple," depends on the concepts to which it is connected.

Here, we will briefly consider the network model developed by Collins and Loftus (1975), as well as Anderson's (1983, 2000) ACT theory. We'll conclude our section on the structure of semantic memory with a third network theory, the parallel distributed processing (PDP) approach. The PDP approach, which we introduced in Chapter 1, argues that cognitive processes can be understood in terms of networks that link together neuron-like units.

The Collins and Loftus Network Model. According to the **Collins and Loftus network model,** semantic memory is organized in terms of netlike structures, with numerous interconnections. When we retrieve information, activation spreads to related concepts.

In this model, each concept can be represented as a **node,** or location in the network. Each **link** connects a particular node with another concept node. The collection of nodes and links forms a network. Figure 8.1 shows a small portion of the network that might surround the concept "apple."

How does this network model work? When the name of a concept is mentioned, the node representing that concept is activated. The activation expands or spreads from that node to other nodes with which it is connected, a process called **spreading activation.** The activation requires longer to spread to the more remote nodes in the network (Markman, 2002).

Let's consider how the Collins and Loftus (1975) model would explain what happens in a sentence verification task, such as the one you tried in Demonstration 8.1, on page 244. Suppose you hear the sentence, "A McIntosh is a fruit." This model proposes that activation will spread from "McIntosh" and "fruit" to the node "apple." A search of memory notes the intersection of these two activation patterns. As a consequence, the sentence, "A McIntosh is a fruit" deserves a "yes" answer.

In contrast, suppose you hear the sentence, "An apple is a mammal." Activation spreads outward from both "apple" and "mammal." but the memory search does not locate an intersection. This sentence deserves a "no" answer.

Collins and Loftus (1975) also propose that frequently used links have greater strengths. As a result, activation travels faster between the nodes. Therefore, it is easy to explain the typicality effect, in which people reach decisions faster when an item is

FIGURE 8.1

An Example of a Network Structure for the Concept "Apple," as in the Collins and Loftus Network Model.

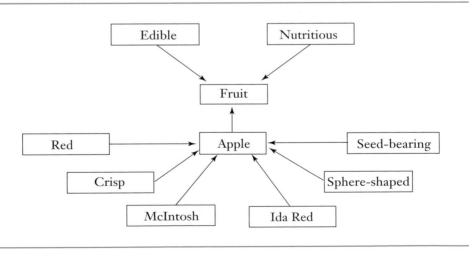

a typical member of a category (such as a carrot), rather than an unusual one (such as a rutabaga). The model also provides a useful explanation of semantic priming (McNamara & Holbrook, 2003).

The concept of spreading activation is an appealing one. However, Collins and Loftus's (1975) model has been superseded by more complex theories that attempt to explain broader aspects of general knowledge (Rogers & McClelland, 2004). Two theories that have superseded the Collins and Loftus model are Anderson's ACT theories and the parallel distributed processing approach.

Anderson's ACT Theories. John Anderson of Carnegie Mellon University and his colleagues have constructed a series of network models, which they now call ACT-R (Anderson, 1983, 2000; Anderson & Schooler, 2000; Anderson & Schunn, 2000; Anderson et al., 2004). **ACT-R** is an acronym for "Automatic Components of Thought-Rational"; it attempts to account for all of cognition (Anderson et al., 2005). The models we've considered so far have a limited goal: to explain how we organize our cognitive concepts. In contrast, Anderson created ACT-R and its variants to explain all of this textbook's topics, including memory, learning, spatial cognition, language, reasoning, and decision making (Anderson et al., 2004).

Obviously, a theory that attempts to explain all of cognition is extremely complex. However, we will focus on the model's more specific view of **declarative knowledge,** or knowledge about facts and things—the essence of this current chapter. As you have just seen, the network model devised by Collins and Loftus (1975) focuses on networks for individual words. Anderson, in contrast, designed a model based on larger units of meaning. According to Anderson (1990), the meaning of a sentence can be represented by a *propositional network*, or pattern of interconnected propositions.

Anderson and his coauthors define a **proposition** as the smallest unit of knowledge that can be judged either true or false. For instance, the phrase *white cat* does not qualify as a proposition because we cannot determine whether it is true or false. According to the model, each of the following three statements is a proposition:

1. Susan gave a cat to Maria.
2. The cat was white.
3. Maria is the president of the club.

These three propositions can appear by themselves, but they can also be combined into a sentence, such as the following:

Susan gave a white cat to Maria, who is the president of the club.

Figure 8.2 shows how this sentence could be represented by a propositional network. As you can see, each of the three propositions in the sentence is represented by a node, and the links are represented by arrows. Notice, too, that the network represents the important relations in the three propositions, but not the exact wording. Propositions are abstract; they do not represent a specific set of words.

FIGURE 8.2

A Propositional Network Representing the Sentence "Susan gave a white cat to Maria, who is the president of the club."

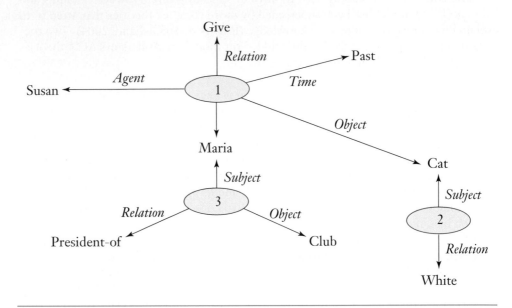

Furthermore, Anderson suggests that each of the concepts in a proposition can be represented by its own individual network. Figure 8.3 illustrates just a small part of the representation of the word *cat* in memory. Imagine what the propositional network in Figure 8.2 would look like if we could replace each of the concepts in that network with an expanded network representing the richness of meanings you have acquired. These networks need to be complicated in order to accurately represent the dozens of associations we have for each item in semantic memory.

Anderson's model of semantic memory makes some additional proposals. For example, similar to Collins and Loftus's (1975) model, the links between nodes become stronger as they are used more often (Anderson, 2000; Anderson & Schunn, 2000; Sternberg & Ben-Zeev, 2001). Practice is vitally important in developing more extensive semantic memory (Anderson & Schooler, 2000).

Also, the model assumes that, at any given moment, as many as ten nodes are represented in your working memory. In addition, the model proposes that activation can spread. However, Anderson argues that the limited capacity of working memory can restrict the spreading. Also, if many links are activated simultaneously, each link receives relatively little activation (Anderson, Reder, & Lebiere, 1996; Markman, 2002; Schooler & Hertwig, 2005). As a consequence, this knowledge will be retrieved relatively slowly (Anderson, 2000).

Anderson's model has been highly praised for its skill in integrating cognitive processes and for its scholarship. Anderson and his colleagues are currently conducting

FIGURE 8.3

A Partial Representation of the Word *Cat* in Memory.

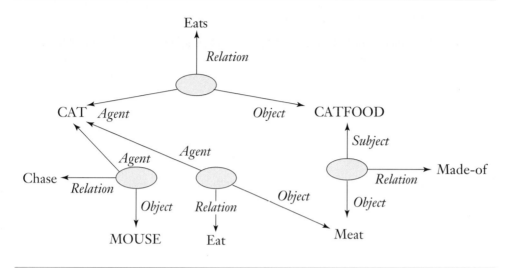

research, using functional magnetic resonance imaging to examine how changes in learning are reflected in selected regions of the cortex and the subcortex (Anderson et al., 2005; Anderson et al., 2004).

The parallel distributed processing approach—which we discuss next—incorporated neuroscience from the beginning. In fact, the creators specifically designed this approach in terms of the neural networks found in the cerebral cortex.

The Parallel Distributed Processing Approach. The **parallel distributed processing (PDP) approach** argues that cognitive processes can be represented by a model in which activation flows through networks that link together a large number of simple, neuron-like units (Markman, 1999; McClelland & Rogers, 2003; Rogers & McClelland, 2004).

Two other names—**connectionism** and **neural networks**—are often used interchangeably with *PDP approach*. The researchers who designed this approach tried to construct their model by taking into account the physiological and structural properties of human neurons (McClelland & Rogers, 2003). We briefly introduced the PDP approach in Chapter 1; now let's consider it in more detail.

The designers of the PDP approach also emphasize that the earlier models based on categorization are too restrictive. As a result, they fail to account for the subtlety of our knowledge about the world. Here are three central characteristics of the PDP approach:

1. As suggested by the name "parallel distributed processing," cognitive processes are based on parallel operations, rather than serial operations. Therefore, many patterns of activation may be proceeding simultaneously.

2. A network contains basic neuron-like units or nodes, which are connected together so that a specific node has many links to other nodes (hence the alternate name

---

⑨ Demonstration 8.3

Parallel Distributed Processing

For each of the two tasks below, read the set of clues and then guess as quickly as possible what thing is being described.

Task A

1. It is orange.
2. It grows below the ground.
3. It is a vegetable.
4. Rabbits characteristically like this item.

Task B

1. Its name starts with the letter *p*.
2. It inhabits barnyards.
3. It is typically yellow in color.
4. It says, "Oink."

---

for the theory: *connectionism*). PDP theorists argue that most cognitive processes can be explained by the activation of these networks (McNamara & Holbrook, 2003; Rogers & McClelland, 2004).

3. As the name "parallel distributed processing" also suggests, a concept is represented by the pattern of activity distributed throughout a set of nodes (McClelland, 2000; Rogers & McClelland, 2004; Shanks, 1997). Notice that this view is very different from the commonsense idea that all the information you know about a particular person or object is stored in one specific location in the brain.

Before you read further, try Demonstration 8.3, which illustrates some features of the PDP approach.

Each of the clues in Task A of Demonstration 8.3 probably reminded you of several possible candidates. Perhaps you thought of the correct answer after just a few clues, even though the description was not complete. Notice, however, that you did not use a **serial search,** conducting a complete search of all orange objects before beginning a second search of all below-ground objects, then all vegetables, then all rabbit-endorsed items. As we just noted, you used a **parallel search,** in which you considered all attributes simultaneously (Protopapas, 1999; Rogers & McClelland, 2004; Sternberg & Ben-Zeev, 2001).

Furthermore, notice that your memory can cope quite well, even if one of the clues is incorrect (Shanks, 1997). For instance, in Task B you searched for a barnyard-dwelling, oink-producing creature whose name starts with *p*. The word *pig* emerged, despite the misleading clue about the yellow color. Similarly, if someone describes a classmate from Saratoga Springs who is a tall male in your child development course, you can identify the appropriate student, even if he is from Poughkeepsie.

According to James McClelland, our knowledge about a group of individuals might be stored by connections that link these people with their personal characteristics. His original example portrayed members of two gangs of small-time criminals, the Jets and the Sharks (McClelland, 1981). We'll use a simpler and presumably more familiar example that features five college students. Table 8.2 lists these students, together with their college majors, years in school, and political orientations.

Figure 8.4 shows how this information could be represented in network form. Notice that this figure represents only a fraction of the number of people a college student is likely to know and also just a fraction of the characteristics associated with each person. Take a minute to imagine how large a piece of paper you would need in order to represent all the people you know, together with all the characteristics you consider relevant.

According to the PDP approach, each individual's characteristics are connected in a mutually stimulating network. If the connections among the characteristics are well established through extensive practice, then an appropriate clue allows you to locate the characteristics of a specified individual (McClelland, 1995; McClelland et al., 1986; Rumelhart et al., 1986).

One advantage of the PDP model is that it allows us to explain how human memory can help us when some information is missing. Specifically, people can make a **spontaneous generalization** by using individual cases to draw inferences about general information (Protopapas, 1999; Rogers & McClelland, 2004).

For example, suppose that your memory stores the information in Figure 8.4 and similar information on other college students. Suppose, also, that someone were to ask you whether engineering students tend to be politically conservative. PDP theory suggests that the clue *engineering student* would activate information about all the engineering students you know, including information about their political orientation. You

TABLE 8.2

Attributes of Representative Individuals Whom a College Student Might Know.

Name	Major	Year	Political Orientation
1. Joe	Art	Junior	Liberal
2. Marti	Psychology	Sophomore	Liberal
3. Sam	Engineering	Senior	Conservative
4. Liz	Engineering	Sophomore	Conservative
5. Roberto	Psychology	Senior	Liberal

FIGURE 8.4

A Sample of the Units and Connections That Represent the Individuals in Table 8.2.

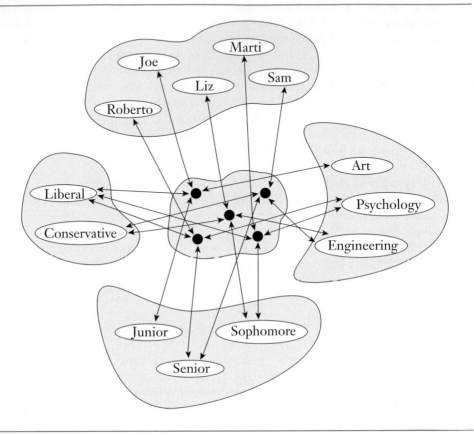

would reply that they do tend to be politically conservative, even though you did not directly store this statement in your memory. (Our ability to make inferences will be discussed in more detail later in this chapter, and also in Chapters 9 and 12.)

Spontaneous generalization accounts for some of the memory errors and distortions we discussed in Chapter 5, on long-term memory. Spontaneous generalization can also help to explain stereotyping (Bodenhausen et al., 2003), a complex cognitive process discussed later in this chapter and also in Chapter 12, on decision making. The PDP model argues that we do not simply retrieve a memory in the same fashion that we might retrieve a book from a library. Instead, we reconstruct a memory, and that memory sometimes includes inappropriate information (McClelland, 1999).

PDP models also allow us to fill in missing information about a particular person or a particular object by making a best guess; we can make a **default assignment** based on information from other similar people or objects (Rogers & McClelland, 2004). Suppose, for example, that you meet Christina, who happens to be an engineering student. Someone asks you about Christina's political preferences, but you have never discussed politics with her. This question will activate information in the network about the political leanings of other engineers. Based on a default assignment, you will reply that she is probably conservative.

Incidentally, students sometimes confuse the terms *spontaneous generalization* and *default assignment*. Remember that spontaneous generalization means that we draw a conclusion about a general category (for example, "engineering students"), whereas default assignment means that we draw a conclusion about a specific member of a category (for example, a particular engineering student).

Notice, however, that both spontaneous generalization and default assignment can produce errors. For example, Christina may really be the president of your university's Anti-War Coalition.

So far, our discussion of parallel distributed processing has been concrete and straightforward. In reality, the theory is extremely complex, sophisticated, and abstract (e.g., Gluck & Myers, 2001; Protopapas, 1999; Rogers & McClelland, 2004). Some other important characteristics of the PDP approach include the following:

1. The connections between these neuron-like units are weighted, and the **connection weights** determine how much activation one unit can pass on to another unit (McClelland, 1999).

2. When a unit reaches a critical level of activation, it may affect another unit, either by exciting it (if the connection weight is positive) or by inhibiting it (if the connection weight is negative). Notice that this design resembles the excitation and inhibition of neurons in the human brain (Gluck & Myers, 2001; Markman, 1999). Incidentally, Figure 8.4 shows only excitatory connections, but you can imagine additional, inhibitory connections. For example, the characteristic *polite* might have a negative connection weight associated with some of the less civilized students in this figure.

3. Every new piece of information you learn will change the strength of connections among relevant units by adjusting the connection weights (Barsalou, 2003; McNamara & Holbrook, 2003; Rogers & McClelland, 2004). For example, while you have been reading about the PDP approach, you have been changing the strength of connections between the name *PDP approach* and such terms as *network* and *spontaneous generalization*. The next time you encounter the term *PDP approach*, all these related terms are likely to be activated.

4. Sometimes we have only partial memory for some information, rather than complete, perfect memory. The brain's ability to provide partial memory is called **graceful degradation.** For example, Chapter 6 discussed the **tip-of-the-tongue phenomenon,** which occurs when you know which target you are seeking; however, you cannot retrieve the actual target. Consistent with graceful degradation, you may know the target's first letter and the number of syllables—even though the word itself refuses to leap into memory. Graceful degradation also explains why the brain continues to work somewhat accurately, even when an accident, stroke, or dementia has destroyed portions of the cortex (McNamara & Holbrook, 2003; Rogers & McClelland, 2004).

We've examined some of the most important characteristics of the PDP approach. Let's now briefly discuss the current status of this theory. Clearly, the PDP perspective is one of the most important shifts in cognitive psychology in recent decades (Levine, 2002; McNamara & Holbrook, 2003). However, the approach is relatively new, and researchers have not yet developed PDP models for numerous cognitive tasks.

Some supporters are enthusiastic that the PDP approach seems generally consistent with the neurological design of neurons and the brain (Bressler, 2002; Gluck & Myers, 2001; Rogers & McClelland, 2004). Many are therefore hopeful that PDP research may provide important links between psychology and neuroscience.

Theorists argue that the PDP approach works better for tasks in which several processes typically operate simultaneously, as in pattern recognition, categorization, and memory search. However, many other cognitive tasks demand primarily serial processing. Later in this textbook, we will consider language use, problem solving, and reasoning. Many components of these cognitive skills require serial processing, rather than parallel operations. For these "higher" mental processes, artificial intelligence approaches and other models may be more effective (Baddeley, 1997; Pinker, 1997).

So, what are some of the cognitive tasks that can be explained by the PDP approach? These include the word superiority effect (Markman, 2002), retroactive interference (McClelland, 2000), category formation (Levine, 2002; McClelland, 2000), and complex decision making (Levine, 2002; Lord et al., 2003). Researchers have also applied the PDP approach to areas such as social psychology (Van Overwalle & Labiouse, 2004; Van Rooy et al., 2003) and to developmental psychology (Munakata & McClelland, 2003; Quinlan, 2003a).

The PDP approach has also been used to explain cognitive disorders, such as the reading problems experienced by people with dyslexia (Levine, 2002; O'Reilly & Munakata, 2000). It can also account for the cognitive difficulties found in people with schizophrenia (Chen & Berrios, 1998) and semantic-memory deficits (Leek, 2005; McClelland & Rogers, 2003; Tippett et al., 1995).

In general, the current PDP models can explain situations where learning accumulates gradually across trials (McClelland & Rogers, 2003). However, some critics say that the PDP model is not currently structured enough to handle the subtleties and complexities of semantic memory (McClelland & Rogers, 2003). The PDP approach also has trouble explaining why we sometimes quickly forget extremely well-learned information that occurs when we learn additional information (Ratcliff, 1990). On the other hand, the model cannot explain why we sometimes can recall earlier material when it has been replaced by more current material (Lewandowsky & Li, 1995).

Earlier in the chapter, we discussed the feature comparison model, the prototype approach, the exemplar approach, and two other network theories. All of those theoretical approaches also generated enthusiasm when they were first proposed. However, the PDP approach is broader than most of these theories because it addresses perception, language, and decision making, as well as numerous aspects of memory. Will the enthusiasm for this approach eventually fade as it did for some of the earlier explanations? At present, many of the features of connectionism are speculative. It is possible, however, that the PDP approach will eventually become the standard framework for analyzing human knowledge.

⑨ Section Summary: *The Structure of Semantic Memory*

1. One early theory of semantic memory, the feature comparison model, proposes that concepts are stored in terms of a list of necessary features.

2. According to prototype theory, people compare new stimuli with an idealized prototype in order to categorize them. People frequently supply prototypes as examples of a category, and they judge prototypes more quickly after semantic priming. Prototypes also share a large number of attributes with other items in the same family-resemblance category.

3. Prototype theory also proposes that people use basic-level categories more often than subordinate- or superordinate-level categories when identifying objects. Basic-level names are more likely to produce the priming effect, and different levels of categorization activate different regions of the brain.

4. Experts and novices may choose different prototypes, for example, as the "best example" of a tree. Experts are also more likely than other people to use subordinate terms and even more specific terms, rather than basic-level terms.

5. The exemplar approach proposes that we classify a new stimulus by deciding how closely it resembles specific examples (or exemplars) that we have already learned; research suggests that our concepts may indeed include information about less typical exemplars. It's possible that people may use both prototypes and exemplars to represent concepts.

6. Collins and Loftus (1975) proposed an early network model, in which concepts are interconnected in semantic memory and activation spreads to related concepts.

7. Anderson's series of ACT models attempt to explain a wide variety of cognitive processes. His model of declarative memory represents both sentences and concepts with a network structure.

8. The third network model, the parallel distributed processing (PDP) approach, proposes that (a) cognitive processes are based on parallel operations, (b) networks link numerous neuron-like nodes, and (3) a concept is represented by a pattern of activity throughout that set of nodes.

9. The PDP approach also proposes features to explain cognitive phenomena such as spontaneous generalization, default assignment, and graceful degradation. It also attempts to explain a variety of cognitive tasks, as well as the cognitive difficulties faced by people with psychological disorders.

SCHEMAS AND SCRIPTS

So far, our discussion of general knowledge has focused on words, concepts, and—occasionally—sentences. However, our cognitive processes also handle knowledge units that are much larger and more complex. For example, our knowledge includes information about familiar situations, behavior, and other "packages" of things we know. This generalized knowledge about a situation, an event, or a person is called a **schema;** this

---

⑨ Demonstration 8.4

The Nature of Scripts

Read the following paragraph, which is based on a description from Trafimow and Wyer (1993, p. 368):

> After doing this, he found the article. He then walked through the doorway and took a piece of candy out of his pocket. Next, he got some change and saw a person he knew. Subsequently, Joe found a machine. He realized he had developed a slight headache. After he aligned the original, Joe put in the coin and pushed the button. Thus, Joe had copied the piece of paper.

Now turn to the list of new terms for Chapter 8, on page 284. Look at the first two columns of terms and write out the definition for as many of these terms as you know. Take about 5 minutes on the task. Then look at the paragraph labeled "Further instructions for Demonstration 8.4," which appears at the bottom of Demonstration 8.5, on page 269.

---

schema influences the way we understand a situation or an event. Incidentally, the plural form for *schema* is either *schemas* or *schemata;* we will use *schemas.*

Consider, for example, the schema you have for the interior of a hardware store. It should have wrenches, cans of paint, garden hoses, and light bulbs. The store certainly should not have psychology textbooks, DVDs of Verdi operas, or birthday cakes.

Schema theories are especially helpful when psychologists try to explain how people process complex situations and events (Davis & Loftus, 2007; Markman, 1999). In this section of the chapter, we'll consider some background information on schemas and a subcategory called *scripts.* Then we'll discuss how schemas can influence various phases of memory. First, however, try Demonstration 8.4.

Background on Schemas and Scripts

Schema theories propose that people encode, in their memory, "generic" information about a situation (Bodenhausen et al., 2003; Chi & Ohlsson, 2005). Then they use this information to understand and remember new examples of the schema. Specifically, schemas guide your recognition and understanding of new examples because you say to yourself, "This is just like what happened when . . ." (Endsley, 2006).

Clearly, schemas emphasize how top-down processing and bottom-up processing work together, a principle of cognitive processes highlighted in Theme 5. Schemas allow us to predict what will happen in a new situation. These predictions will usually be correct. Schemas are **heuristics,** or general rules that are typically accurate.

Schemas also emphasize the active nature of our cognitive processes (Theme 1). An event happens, and we immediately try to think how the event is related to an established schema. If the event is not consistent with a schema, we usually feel obligated to reconcile the inconsistency.

However, schemas can sometimes lead us astray, and we make errors (Davis & Loftus, 2007). Still, these errors usually make sense within the framework of that schema. Consistent with Theme 2, our cognitive processes are generally accurate, and our mistakes are typically rational.

The concept of schemas has had a long history in psychology. For example, Piaget's work in the 1920s investigated schemas in infants, and Bartlett (1932) tested adults' memory for schemas. Schemas were not popular during the behaviorist era, because they emphasize unseen cognitive processes. In recent decades, however, cognitive psychologists have conducted numerous studies on this topic, so that *schema* is a standard term in contemporary cognitive psychology.

Schemas are also important in areas other than cognitive psychology, such as social psychology (Bodenhausen et al., 2003). For instance, Baldwin and Dandeneau (2005) examined how we have schema-based expectations about what will happen in a social interaction with a specific individual. Furthermore, Hong and her coauthors (2000) examined how bicultural individuals develop a different set of schemas for each of their two cultures. A young boy may see the world through U.S.-based schemas while at school, but he uses Mexican-based schemas when he returns to his home.

An interesting approach in clinical psychology is called schema therapy (Young et al., 2003). In **schema therapy,** the clinician works together with the client in order to create appropriate new schemas that can replace the maladaptive schemas developed early in life, such as the "mistrust schema" or a "self-sacrifice schema."

One common kind of schema is called a script. A **script** is a simple, well-structured sequence of events—in a specified order—that are associated with a highly familiar activity (Markman, 2002). A script is an abstraction, a prototype of a series of events that share an underlying similarity. The terms *schema* and *script* are often used interchangeably. However, *script* is actually a narrower term, referring to a sequence of events that unfold in a specified order (Woll, 2002; Zacks et al., 2001).

Consider a typical script, describing the standard sequence of events that a customer might expect in a restaurant (Abelson, 1981; Schank & Abelson, 1977). The "restaurant script" includes events such as sitting down, looking at the menu, eating the food, and paying the bill. We could also have scripts for visiting a dentist's office, for a trip to the grocery store, and for the first day of class in a college course. In fact, much of our education consists of learning the scripts that we are expected to follow in our culture (Schank & Abelson, 1995).

A violation of a familiar script can be both surprising and unsettling. For example, some years ago, several friends and I were watching a Russian movie at another college campus. At the beginning, a young boy rescues a wolf pup. The two grow up together, sharing many adventures. If you have been raised on a diet of Hollywood films about children, you know exactly what happens next: The boy is in great danger, and the wolf rescues him. However, in this particular movie, the wolf kills the boy. At this point, the audience gasped collectively—the script violation was simply too devastating!

In general, the research demonstrates that people recall a script significantly more accurately if the script has been clearly identified in advance. For example, Trafimow and Wyer (1993) developed four different scripts, each describing a familiar sequence of actions: photocopying a piece of paper, cashing a check, making tea, and taking the subway. Some details irrelevant to the script (such as taking a piece of candy out of a pocket) were also added. In some cases, the script-identifying event was presented first. In other cases, the script-identifying event was presented last. For instance, in Demonstration 8.4, you saw the information about copying the piece of paper after you had read the script.

Five minutes after reading all four descriptions, the participants were asked to recall the events from the four original descriptions. When the script-identifying event had been presented first, participants recalled 23% of those events. In contrast, they recalled only 10% when the script-identifying event had been presented last. As you might expect, the events in a sequence are much more memorable if you understand—from the very beginning—that these events are all part of a standard script (Davis & Friedman, 2007).

For the remainder of the chapter, let's examine five ways in which schemas and scripts can operate during cognitive processing:

1. During the selection of material to be remembered.
2. In boundary extension (when you store a scene in memory).
3. During abstraction (when you store the meaning, but not the specific details of the material).
4. During interpretation (when you make inferences about the material).
5. During integration (when you form a single memory representation of the material).

Schemas and Memory Selection

The research on schemas and memory selection has produced contradictory findings. Sometimes people remember material best when it is *consistent* with a schema; other times they remember material best when it is *inconsistent* with the schema (Hirt et al., 1998). Let's first consider two studies that favor schema-consistent memory.

Enhanced Memory for Schema-Consistent Material. Try Demonstration 8.5 when you have the opportunity. This demonstration is based on a study by Brewer and Treyens (1981). These authors asked participants in their study to wait, one at a time, in the room pictured in the demonstration. Each time, the experimenter explained that this was his office, and he needed to check the laboratory to see if the previous participant had completed the experiment. After 35 seconds, the experimenter asked the participant to move to a nearby room. Here, the experimenter asked the participants to remember everything in the room in which they had waited.

The results showed that people were highly likely to recall objects consistent with the "office schema." Nearly everyone remembered the desk, the chair next to the desk, and the wall. However, few recalled the wine bottle, the coffee pot, and the picnic basket. These items were not consistent with the office schema.

In addition, some people in Brewer and Treyens's (1981) study "remembered" items that were not in the room. For example, nine said they remembered books, though none

◎ Demonstration 8.5

Schemas and Memory

After reading these instructions, cover them and the rest of the text in this demonstration so that only the picture shows. Present the picture to a friend, with the instructions, "Look at this picture of a psychology professor's office for a brief time." Half a minute later, close the book and ask your friend to list everything that was in the room.

(Further instructions for Demonstration 8.4: Now without looking back at Demonstration 8.4, write down the story from that demonstration, being as accurate as possible.)

Source: Based on Brewer & Treyens, 1981.

had been visible. Other research shows that the number of schema-consistent errors is even greater two days later (Lampinen et al., 2001). This tendency to supply schema-consistent items represents an interesting reconstruction error (Neuschatz et al., 2007).

Similarly, Neuschatz and his coauthors (2002) instructed students to watch a video of a man giving a lecture. The students were likely to falsely remember events that were consistent with the "lecture schema," such as referring to a concept from the previous lecture. They were not likely to falsely remember events inconsistent with the "lecture schema," such as dancing across the floor.

Enhanced Memory for Schema-Inconsistent Material. However, we sometimes show better recall for material that violates our expectations (e.g., Lampinen et al., 2000; Neuschatz et al., 2002). Specifically, people are more likely to recall schema-*inconsistent* material when that material is vivid or surprising (Brewer, 2000).

For instance, Davidson (1994) asked participants to read a variety of stories, describing well-known schemas such as "going to the movies." The results demonstrated that people were especially likely to recall schema-inconsistent events when they interrupted the normal, expected story. For example, one story described a woman named Sarah who was going to the movies. The participants were very likely to remember a schema-inconsistent sentence about a child who ran through the movie theater and smashed into Sarah. In contrast, they were less likely to remember a schema-consistent sentence about an usher tearing the movie tickets in half and giving Sarah the stubs. Incidentally, before you read further, try Demonstrations 8.6 and 8.7.

---

⑥ Demonstration 8.6

Memory for Objects

Look at the objects below for about 15 seconds. Then turn to page 272, just above the rectangle, where you will find further instructions for this demonstration.

Demonstration 8.7

Constructive Memory

Part 1

Read each sentence, count to five, answer the question, and go on to the next sentence.

Sentence	**Question**
The girl broke the window on the porch.	Broke what?
The tree in the front yard shaded the man who was smoking his pipe.	Where?
The cat, running from the barking dog, jumped on the table.	From what?
The tree was tall.	Was what?
The cat running from the dog jumped on the table.	Where?
The girl who lives next door broke the window on the porch.	Lives where?
The scared cat was running from the barking dog.	What was?
The girl lives next door.	Who does?
The tree shaded the man who was smoking his pipe.	What did?
The scared cat jumped on the table.	What did?
The girl who lives next door broke the large window.	Broke what?
The man was smoking his pipe.	Who was?
The large window was on the porch.	Where?
The tall tree was in the front yard.	What was?
The cat jumped on the table.	Where?
The tall tree in the front yard shaded the man.	Did what?
The dog was barking.	Was what?
The window was large.	What was?

Part 2

Cover the preceding sentences. Now read each of the following sentences and decide whether it is a sentence from the list in Part 1.

1. The girl who lives next door broke the window.   (old _____, new _____)

2. The tree was in the front yard.   (old _____, new _____)

3. The scared cat, running from the barking dog, jumped on the table.   (old _____, new _____)

4. The window was on the porch.   (old _____, new _____)

5. The tree in the front yard shaded the man.   (old _____, new _____)

(continued)

@ **Demonstration 8.7**

Constructive Memory   (*continued*)

6.   The cat was running from the dog.   (old _____, new _____)
7.   The tall tree shaded the man who was
       smoking his pipe.   (old _____, new _____)
8.   The cat was scared.   (old _____, new _____)
9.   The girl who lives next door broke the
       large window on the porch.   (old _____, new _____)
10.   The tall tree shaded the girl who broke
       the window.   (old _____, new _____)
11.   The cat was running from the barking dog.   (old _____, new _____)
12.   The girl broke the large window.   (old _____, new _____)
13.   The scared cat ran from the barking dog
       that jumped on the table.   (old _____, new _____)
14.   The girl broke the large window
       on the porch.   (old _____, new _____)
15.   The scared cat which broke the window on
       the porch climbed the tree.   (old _____, new _____)
16.   The tall tree in the front yard shaded the
       man who was smoking his pipe.   (old _____, new _____)

(Further instructions for Demonstration 8.6: In the box below, draw from memory the scene you saw in Demonstration 8.6. Do not look back at that photo!)

Source: Parts 1 and 2 of this demonstration are based on an example created by Jenkins, 1974; the original research was conducted by Bransford and Franks, 1971.

The Status of Schemas and Memory Selection. In 1992, Rojahn and Pettigrew conducted a meta-analysis of the research on schemas. In general, the research showed that schema-inconsistent material was somewhat more memorable. However, it would be useful to have a more recent meta-analysis that could identify factors related to the pattern of recall.

Why should we often remember schema-*inconsistent* material so accurately? A plausible explanation is that we are especially likely to remember material that attracts attention and require more effort to process. With deep, effortful processing, we will be more likely to recall that unusual material (Davis & Loftus, 2007; Lampinen et al., 2000).

However, most of the research supports another aspect of the schema approach to memory selection. When people "remember" events that never actually happened, they are likely to construct a schema-consistent event, such as a professor's reference to a previous lecture. They are not likely to construct a schema-inconsistent event, such as the professor dancing across the classroom floor.

Schemas and Boundary Extension

Now take a moment to examine the objects you drew on page 272 for Demonstration 8.6, and compare your sketch with the original photo. Does your sketch include the bottom edge of the garbage can lid—which was not present in the original photo? Does your sketch show more background surrounding each garbage can, including the top of the picket fence? If so, you've demonstrated boundary extension. **Boundary extension** refers to our tendency to remember having viewed a greater portion of a scene than was actually shown (Munger et al., 2005). We have a schema for a scene like the one depicted in Demonstration 8.6, which we could call "a photo of someone's garbage area," and our cognitive processes fill in the incomplete objects.

Notice that the other topics in this discussion of schemas are verbal; in boundary extension, however, the material is visual. Still, our schemas help us fill in missing material during a memory task.

Helene Intraub and her colleagues were the first researchers to document the boundary-extension phenomenon (e.g., Intraub, 1997; Intraub & Berkowits, 1996; Intraub et al., 1998). For example, Intraub and Berkowits (1996) showed college students a series of slides like the photo of the garbage scene in Demonstration 8.6. Each photo was shown briefly, for 15 seconds or less. Immediately afterward, the students were instructed to draw an exact replica of the original photo. The participants consistently produced a sketch that extended the boundaries beyond the view presented in the original photo. As a result, they drew more of the background that surrounded the central figure, and they also depicted a complete figure, rather than a partial one.

According to Intraub and her coauthors (1998), we comprehend a photograph by activating a *perceptual schema*. This schema features a complete central figure in the photo, and it also includes a mental representation of visual information that is just outside the boundaries of the photo. We use perceptual schemas when we look at real-life scenes, as well as photos of a scene. Notice why schemas are relevant in boundary extension: Based on our expectations, we create perceptual schemas that extend beyond the edges of the photograph and beyond the scope of our retinas (Munger et al., 2005).

The boundary-extension phenomenon also has important implications for eye-witness testimony, a topic we discussed in Chapter 5. Eyewitnesses may recall having seen portions of a suspect's face that were not really visible at the scene of the crime (Foley & Foley, 1998). In addition, after people search for a target in a crowded scene, they recall having viewed a complete target—even if it had been partially blocked by other figures (Foley et al., 2002). Apparently, the incomplete figure activates our imagery processes, so that we "fill in the blanks." Consequently, our memory stores more idealized, schema-consistent images, rather than partial figures.

Schemas and Memory Abstraction

Abstraction is a memory process that stores the meaning of a message but not the exact words. For example, you can recall much of the information about the concept "family resemblance" (pp. 248 to 249), without recalling a single sentence in its exact, original form. We tend to recall the gist or general meaning with impressive accuracy, and so our abstracted version of the passage is consistent with the original schema.

In contrast, people usually have poor word-for-word recall, or **verbatim memory,** even a few minutes after a passage has been presented (e.g., Koriat et al., 2000; Sachs, 1967). Of course, some people may need to have good verbatim memory. For instance, professional actors must remember the exact words from a Shakespeare play. But do the rest of us need verbatim memory in our everyday lives? Let's consider two approaches to the abstraction issue: the constructive approach and the pragmatic approach.

The Constructive Approach. Be sure to try Demonstration 8.7 on pages 271 and 272 before reading further. This is a simpler version of a classic study by Bransford and Franks (1971). How many sentences in Part 2 of the demonstration had you seen before? The answer is at the end of the chapter, on page 285.

Bransford and Franks (1971) asked the participants in their study to listen to sentences from several different stories. Then the participants were given a recognition test that also included new items, many of which were combinations of the earlier sentences. Nonetheless, people were convinced that they had seen these new items before. This kind of error is called a false alarm. In memory research, a **false alarm** occurs when people "remember" an item that was not originally presented. Bransford and Franks's study showed that false alarms were particularly likely for complex sentences that were consistent with the original schema, for example, "The tall tree in the front yard shaded the man who was smoking his pipe." However, the participants seldom made false alarms for sentences that violated the meaning of the earlier sentences—for example, "The scared cat that broke the window on the porch climbed the tree." More recent research shows similar findings (Chan & McDermott, 2006; Holmes et al., 1998).

Bransford and Franks (1971) proposed a constructive model of memory for prose material. According to the **constructive model of memory,** people integrate information from individual sentences in order to construct larger ideas. Later, they believe that they have already seen those complex sentences because they have combined the various facts in memory. Once sentences are fused in memory, we cannot untangle them into their original components and recall those components verbatim.

Notice that the constructive view of memory emphasizes the active nature of our cognitive processes, consistent with Theme 1 of this book. Sentences do not passively enter memory, where each is stored separately. Instead, we combine the sentences into a coherent story, fitting the related pieces together.

Constructive memory also illustrates Theme 2. Although memory is typically accurate, the errors in cognitive processing can often be traced to generally useful strategies. In real life, a useful heuristic is to fuse sentences together. However, this heuristic can lead us astray if it is applied inappropriately. As it turns out, participants in Bransford and Franks's (1971) study used a constructive memory strategy that is useful in real life but inappropriate in a study that tests verbatim memory.

The Pragmatic Approach. Murphy and Shapiro (1994) developed a different view of memory for sentences, which they call the pragmatic view of text memory. The **pragmatic view of memory** proposes that people pay attention to the aspect of a message that is most relevant to their current goals. In other words, people know that they usually need to recall the gist quite accurately, but they can ignore the specific sentences. However, if they realize that they do need to pay attention to exact wording, then their verbatim memory can be highly accurate.

Murphy and Shapiro (1994) speculated that people are particularly likely to pay attention to the specific words in a sentence if the words are part of a criticism or an insult. After all, from the pragmatic view, the exact words *do* matter if you are being insulted. In this study, participants read letters that presumably had been written by a young woman named Samantha. One group read a letter, supposedly written to her cousin Paul. The letter chatted about her new infant in a bland fashion. The letter included a number of neutral sentences such as, "It never occurred to me that I would be a mother so young" (p. 91).

A second group read a letter that was supposedly written by Samantha to her boyfriend, Arthur. Ten of the sentences that had been neutral in the bland letter to cousin Paul now appeared in a sarcastic context, though the exact words were identical. For example, the sentence, "It never occurred to me that I would be a mother so young" now referred to Arthur's infantile behavior.

Murphy and Shapiro then gave both groups a 14-item recognition test that included (a) five of the original sentences, (b) five paraphrased versions of those sentences with a slightly different form, such as, "I never thought I would be a mother at such a young age," and (c) four irrelevant sentences. Table 8.3 on page 276 shows the results.

As you can see, people rarely made the mistake of falsely "recognizing" the irrelevant sentences. However, correct recognition ("Hits") was higher for the sentences from the sarcastic condition than for the sentences in the bland condition. Furthermore, people made more false alarms for the paraphrases of the bland sentences than for the paraphrases of the sarcastic sentences.

We can compare the overall accuracy for the two conditions by subtracting the false alarms from the correct responses. As you can see, people were much more accurate in their verbatim memory for the sarcastic version (43%) than for the bland version (17%). Perhaps we are especially sensitive about emotionally threatening material, so we make an effort to recall the exact words of the sentences.

TABLE 8.3

Percentage of "Old" Judgments Made to Test Items in Murphy and Shapiro's (1994) Study.

	Story Condition	
	Bland	Sarcastic
Irrelevant sentences	4%	5%
Hits (original sentences)	71%	86%
False alarms (paraphrases)	54%	43%
Hits minus false alarms	17%	43%

Source: Murphy & Shapiro, 1994.

The Current Status of Schemas and Memory Abstraction. In reality, the constructive approach and the pragmatic approach to memory abstraction are actually quite compatible. Specifically, in many cases, we do integrate information from individual sentences so that we can construct large schemas, especially when we don't need to remember the exact words. However, in some cases, we know that the specific words do matter, and so we pay close attention to the precise wording. An actor rehearsing for a play or two people quarreling will need to remember more than just the overall gist of a verbal message.

Notice that this conclusion about remembering both general descriptions and specific information is similar to our previous conclusions about semantic memory. Specifically, your semantic memory can store both general prototypes and specific exemplar-based information.

[IN DEPTH]

Schemas and Inferences in Memory

In many cases, people use their own schemas to interpret the material they encounter, and they "remember" their own interpretation, rather than the original message. Thus, recall can contain **inferences,** or logical interpretations and conclusions that were not part of the original stimulus material (Hamilton, 2005a). In this In Depth discussion, we will consider both the classic research on this topic and the newer research demonstrating that people make inferences based on stereotypes. We'll then briefly consider the power of inferences in persuading other people.

The Classic Research on Inferences. Sir Frederick Bartlett (1932) was an important early researcher who studied people's memory for natural language material. As we've mentioned before, his theories and techniques foreshadowed the approaches of contemporary cognitive psychologists. Bartlett believed that the most interesting aspect of memory was the complex interaction between the participants' prior knowledge and the material presented during the experiment. In particular, he argued that an individual's unique interests and personal background often shape the contents of memory.

In Bartlett's (1932) best-known series of studies, he asked British students to read a Native American story called "The War of the Ghosts." They were then asked to recall the story 15 minutes later. Bartlett found that the participants tended to omit material that did not make sense from the viewpoint of a British student (for example, a portion of the story in which a ghost had attacked someone, who did not feel the wound). They also tended to shape the story into a more familiar framework, often more similar to British fairy tales.

Most relevant to our current topic, Bartlett's participants often added extra material to the story, making inferences so that the story made more sense from the British perspective. For example, part of the story describes a man who says he will not go off to war because "My relatives do not know where I have gone. But you [another man] may go with them" (Bartlett, 1932, p. 65). Participants often inserted inferences such as, "But you have no one to expect you" to explain the puzzling relationship between those two sentences (Brewer, 2000).

Bartlett also asked his participants to recall the story again, after a delay of several days. As time passed after hearing the original story, the participants borrowed more heavily from their previous knowledge and included less information from the original story.

Subsequent research confirms that schemas can influence our inferences when we are reading ambiguous or unclear material (Bransford et al., 1972; Jahn, 2004; Schacter, 2001). As Brewer (2000) emphasizes, the research on schemas and inferences demonstrates how our cognitive processes actively work to make sense out of puzzling information (Theme 1). Specifically, our top-down processes often shape our memory for complex material (Theme 5).

The research shows that background knowledge can mislead people, causing them to make systematic errors and "remember" inferences that were not actually stated. In our daily lives, however, background information is usually helpful, rather than counterproductive. For instance, our background knowledge can help us recall stories. Simple stories have definite, regular structures (Schank & Abelson, 1995). People become familiar with the basic structure of stories from their prior experiences in their culture. Then they use this structure to interpret the new stories that they hear. In general, then, this background information helps us draw correct inferences.

Research on Inferences Based on Gender Stereotypes.   The research about gender stereotypes provides further information about schemas and inferences. **Gender stereotypes** are widely shared sets of beliefs about the characteristics of females and males (J.E. Fiske, 2004; Schneider, 2004). Even when a gender stereotype is partially accurate, it cannot be applied to every individual of the specified gender (Eagly & Diekman, 2005; Jost & Hamilton, 2005). When people know someone's gender, they often make inferences about that individual's personal characteristics. For example, people usually rate men as being more competitive than women, and they rate women as being warmer than men (Eagly, 2001).

In this section, we will examine how the research methods from cognitive psychology can be used to examine people's gender stereotypes. Let's first consider one study that employs an explicit measure (recognition memory). Then we'll see how implicit measures provide additional information about gender stereotypes.

Dunning and Sherman (1997) assessed gender-based inferences by using a recognition-memory task. They instructed participants to read sentences such as, "The women at the office liked to talk around the water cooler." Later, the participants were tested for recognition memory. Specifically, participants saw a series of sentences, and they were told to respond "old" if they had previously read *exactly* the same version of the sentence earlier in the session. Otherwise, they should respond "new."

Let's look at the results for new sentences that were *consistent* with a widely held gender stereotype about women's conversations: "The women at the office liked to gossip around the water cooler." Participants responded "old" to 29% of these sentences. Other new sentences were *inconsistent* with another widely held stereotype: "The women at the office liked to talk sports around the water cooler." Participants responded "old" to only 18% of these sentences. Apparently, when people saw the original sentence, they sometimes made the stereotype-consistent inference that the women must have been gossiping. They were less likely to make the gender-inconsistent inference that the women were discussing sports.

Dunning and Sherman's (1997) recognition test is an example of an explicit memory task. As you learned in Chapter 5 (pages 137 to 139), an **explicit memory task** directly instructs participants to remember information. The participants in this study knew that their memory was being tested when they judged whether the sentences were old or new. People might guess that the researchers are measuring their gender stereotypes, and they may be aware that it's not appropriate to hold rigid stereotypes (Rudman, 2005). To reduce this problem, researchers have designed implicit memory tasks.

The goal of these implicit memory measures is to assess people's gender stereotypes without asking them directly (Fazio & Olson, 2003). Implicit memory measures are supposed to discourage people from providing socially desirable answers.

As Chapter 5 described, in an **implicit memory task,** people perform a cognitive task that does not directly ask for recall or recognition. In Chapter 5, we examined implicit tasks that assessed episodic memory, typically people's memory for words that they had seen earlier in the session. When researchers use implicit memory tasks to assess gender stereotypes, they assess people's semantic memory, their general knowledge about gender in a culture, and their tendency to make gender-consistent inferences. Let's consider two implicit memory tasks that show how gender stereotypes can affect inferences in implicit memory.

1. *Using neuroscience techniques to assess gender stereotypes.* Osterhout, Bersick, and McLaughlin (1997) assessed gender stereotypes by using a neuroscience technique. As you learned in Chapter 1, the **event-related potential (ERP) technique** records tiny fluctuations in the brain's electrical activity, in response to a stimulus. Previous researchers had tested people who were instructed to read sentences such as, "I like my coffee with cream and *dog*" (p. 273). Those researchers had discovered that the ERPs quickly changed in response to the surprising word,

To examine gender stereotypes, Osterhout and his colleagues (1997) presented some sentences that are consistent with gender stereotypes, such as, "The nurse prepared herself for the operation." These stereotype-consistent sentences did not elicit a change in the ERPs. In contrast, the ERPs changed significantly for stereotype-inconsistent sentences such as, "The nurse prepared himself for the operation." In reading the word *nurse*, people had made the gender-stereotyped inference that the nurse must be female. Consequently, the unexpected, stereotype-inconsistent word *himself* produced changes in the ERPs. In summary, this neuroscience task demonstrated implicit gender stereotypes.

2. *Using the Implicit Association Test to assess gender stereotypes.* Nosek, Banaji, and Greenwald (2002) used a very different method to assess implicit gender stereotypes, specifically the gender stereotypes that mathematics is associated with males and that the arts are associated with females. Suppose that they had asked their college-student participants (at Yale University) an explicit question: "Is math more strongly associated with males than with females?" Research with students like these demonstrates that the dominant response would be "No." After all, when students are asked an explicit question like this, they have time to be thoughtful and to recall that a "Yes" answer would not be socially appropriate.

Instead of an explicit measure, Nosek and his colleagues used the Implicit Association Test (Greenwald & Nosek, 2001; Greenwald et al., 1998; Nosek et al., 2007). The **Implicit Association Test (IAT)** is based on the principle that people can mentally pair related words together much more easily than they can pair unrelated words.

Specifically, when taking the IAT, participants sat in front of a computer screen that presented a series of words. On a typical trial—where the pairings were consistent with gender stereotypes—the participant would be told to press the key on the left if the word was related to math (e.g., *calculus* or *numbers*) or if the word was related to males (e.g., *uncle* or *son*). This same participant would press the key on the right if the word was related to the arts (e.g., *poetry* or *dance*) or if the word was related to females (e.g., *aunt* or *daughter*). Throughout the study, participants were urged to respond as quickly as possible, so that they would not consciously consider their responses. A person with strong gender stereotypes would think that math and males fit in the same category, and so would the arts and females. Therefore, their responses should be quick for this portion of the task.

Then the instructions shifted so that the pairings were inconsistent with gender stereotypes. Now, on a typical trial, the participant would press the left key for a word related to math or a word related to females. The participant would press the right key for a word related to the arts or a word related to males. People with strong gender stereotypes should have difficulty associating math terms with women and arts-related terms with men. Their responses should therefore be much slower for this portion of the task.

The results showed that the participants responded significantly faster to the stereotype-consistent pairings than to the stereotype-inconsistent pairings. In other words, math and males seem to go together, whereas the arts and females seem to go together.

In other research discussed in the same journal article, Nosek and his coauthors (2002) used the IAT to measure attitudes, as well as stereotypes. For example, one

> **⊙ Demonstration 8.8**
>
> **Using the Implicit Association Test to Assess Implicit Attitudes Toward Social Groups**
>
> Log onto the World Wide Web and visit a site sponsored by Harvard University: <https://implicit.harvard.edu/implicit/>
>   You can examine your own attitudes about gender, ethnicity, sexual orientation, people with disabilities, and elderly people. Be certain to follow the caution to make your responses as quickly as possible. More leisurely responses might assess explicit attitudes, rather than implicit attitudes.

component of the study focused on women who strongly considered themselves to be feminine and strongly associated math with being masculine. These women specifically did *not* associate themselves with mathematics, and this anti-math tendency was found even among women who were math majors! In summary, gender stereotypes are not innocent cognitive tendencies. Instead, these stereotypes can have the power to influence people's self-images and their sense of academic competence.

Psychologists have designed other implicit measures to examine gender stereotypes and other categories such as ethnicity (Correll et al., 2002; Ito et al., 2006; Reynolds et al., 2006). Furthermore, if you are interested in the connection between social psychology and cognitive psychology, you can find additional information in several useful books (Baldwin, 2005; Cacioppo et al., 2006; Dovidio et al., 2005; Hamilton, 2005b). When you have the opportunity, try Demonstration 8.8.

Implications of Inferences for Persuasion.   This material on schemas and memory interpretations can be applied to advertising and other areas that require persuasion. Suppose that an ad says, "Four out of five doctors recommend the ingredients in Gonif's brand medication." You might reasonably infer, therefore, that four out of five doctors would also recommend Gonif's medication itself—even though the ad doesn't say so.

Research suggests that people who read advertisements may jump to conclusions, "remembering" inferences that were never actually stated. For example, Harris and his colleagues (1989) asked college students to read stories that contained several advertising slogans. Some slogans made a direct claim (for example, "Tylenol cures colds"). Other slogans merely implied the same claim (for example, "Tylenol fights colds"). On a multiple-choice task that followed, people who had seen the implied-claim version often belived that they had seen the direct-claim version.

You can see why these results suggest that consumers should be careful. If an advertiser implies that a particular product has outstanding properties, make certain that you do not jump to inappropriate conclusions. You are likely to "remember" those inferences, rather than the actual, stated information.

The information about inferences and persuasion can be related to politics as well as to advertising. On January 28, 2003, President George W. Bush included this sentence in his State of the Union address: "The British government has learned that Saddam Hussein recently sought significant quantities of uranium from Africa" (Bush, 2003). This sentence persuaded many people that Iraqi scientists were constructing nuclear weapons, and the Iraq War was therefore justified.

Months later, the public discovered that this statement was not accurate, and the "evidence" had been forged. However, National Security Adviser Condoleezza Rice said that Bush's remark had been technically accurate. After all, Bush had correctly stated that the British government had indeed reported this information (The Sixteen Words, Again, 2004; Truthout, 2003). In reality, however, most of us had made the *incorrect* inference that "Saddam Hussein did indeed recently seek uranium from Africa."

After reading about the experimental evidence for humans' tendencies to draw inappropriate inferences, you might conclude that people inevitably draw conclusions based on inferences from their daily experience. However, inference making is not an obligatory process (Alba & Hasher, 1983; Wynn & Logie, 1998). Several researchers have found that people make inferences only in certain situations. In fact, people often recall material in its original form. Consistent with Theme 2, memory is often highly accurate.

Schemas and Integration in Memory

The final process in memory formation is integration. Schema theories argue that a single, integrated representation is created in memory from the information that was selected in the first phase, abstracted in a later phase, and interpreted in a still later phase (Koriat et al., 2000). In fact, some researchers argue that schemas exert a more powerful effect during the integration phase than during the earlier phases of memory (e.g., Hirt et al., 1998). Once again, however, schemas do not always operate. As we'll see, schema-consistent integration is more likely when recall is delayed and when people are performing a second, simultaneous task during recall.

Integration and Delayed Recall. A number of studies show that background knowledge may not encourage schema-consistent integration if people are tested immediately after the material is learned. However, after a longer delay, the material becomes integrated with existing schemas, and the recall is now altered.

For instance, Harris and his colleagues (1989) conducted research related to Bartlett's classic (1932) study. Harris and his coauthors asked college students in Kansas to read a story that was consistent with either U.S. culture or traditional Mexican culture. A representative story about planning a date in the traditional Mexican culture included a sentence about the young man's older sister accompanying the couple as a chaperone; the U.S. version had no chaperone. When story recall was tested 30 minutes after reading the material, the students showed no tendency for the Mexican-schema stories to shift in the direction consistent with U.S. schemas. After a two-day delay, however, the students had shifted a significant number of story details.

Integration and Limited Memory Capacity. Research also suggests that schemas are more likely to influence memory integration when memory capacity is strained during recall, but not on a relatively simple task. For example, Sherman and Bessenoff (1999) found that people committed many schema-consistent errors when they had to work on two simultaneous memory tasks. Specifically, they misremembered that pleasant words had been used to describe a priest, whereas unpleasant words had been used to describe a skinhead. In contrast, people who worked on just one memory task did not show this schema-consistent tendency. In summary, schemas often influence memory integration, especially when there is a long delay prior to recall and when memory capacity is limited (Sherman et al., 2003). However, memory integration is certainly not inevitable.

Conclusions About Schemas

In summary, schemas can influence memory in the initial selection of material, in remembering visual scenes, in abstraction, in interpretation, and even in the final process of integration. However, we must note that schemas often fail to operate in the expected fashion. For instance:

1. We often select material for memory that is *inconsistent* with our schemas.
2. We may indeed remember that we saw only a portion of an object, rather than the complete object.
3. We frequently recall the exact words of a passage as it was originally presented. (Otherwise, chorus directors would have resigned long ago.)
4. We often avoid making inappropriate inferences.
5. We may keep the elements in memory isolated from each other, rather than integrated together.
6. When we are recalling information from our real-life experiences—rather than information created by researchers—we may be more accurate (Wynn & Logie, 1998).

Yes, schemas clearly can influence memory. However, the influence is far from complete. After all, as Theme 5 states, our cognitive processes are guided by bottom-up processing, as well as top-down processing. Therefore, we select, recall, interpret, and integrate many unique features of each stimulus, in addition to the schema-consistent features that match our background knowledge.

Section Summary: *Schemas and Scripts*

1. A schema is generalized knowledge about a situation, an event, or a person; a script is a kind of schema that describes a simple, well-structured sequence of events associated with a very familiar activity.
2. According to research on scripts, we can recall the elements in a script more accurately if the script is identified at the outset.
3. Schemas may operate in the selection of memories; for example, people recall items consistent with an office schema. However, we often recall schema-inconsistent information as if that information is vivid and surprising.

4. When we remember a scene, we often extend the boundaries of the objects that had partially appeared in the scene by "remembering" them as complete objects.

5. According to the constructive model of memory, schemas encourage memory abstraction, so that the general meaning of a message is retained, even if the details are lost. According to the pragmatic view of memory, people can shift their attention to remember the exact words—when the specific words really matter. Both perspectives seem to operate, depending on the circumstances.

6. Schemas influence the inferences we make in memory; people may recall inferences that never really appeared in the original material. The research on gender stereotypes shows that people frequently make schema-consistent inferences in explicit memory (e.g., a recognition test) and in implicit memory (e.g., the ERP technique and the Implicit Association Test). People often "recall" incorrect inferences from advertisements and political messages.

7. Schemas encourage an integrated representation in memory. Research shows that people may misremember material during the integration process, so that the material is more consistent with their schemas. This tendency is especially strong if recall is delayed and if people are performing another task at the same time.

CHAPTER REVIEW QUESTIONS

1. Suppose that you read the following question on a true/false examination: "A script is a kind of schema." Describe how you would process that question in terms of the feature comparison model, the exemplar approach, the Collins and Loftus network model, and Anderson's ACT network model.

2. Think of a prototype for the category "household pet," and contrast it with a nonprototypical household pet. Compare these two animals with respect to (a) whether they would be supplied as examples of the category; (b) how quickly they could be judged after priming; and (c) the attributes that each would share with most other household pets.

3. Consider the basic-level category "dime," in contrast to the superordinate-level category "money" and the subordinate-level category "2005 dime." Discuss how the basic level has special status when we want to identify objects. Compared to basic-level categories, which part of the brain is more likely to be activated by the superordinate-level category, and which is more likely to be activated by the subordinate-level category?

4. Describe the prototype approach and the exemplar approach to semantic memory. How are they similar, and how are they different? In light of the discussion in this chapter, when would you be likely to use a prototype approach in trying to categorize an object? When would you be most likely to use the exemplar approach? In each case, give an example from your daily experience.

5. Think of some kind of information that could be represented in a diagram similar to the one in Figure 8.4 (for example, popular singers or famous novelists). Then provide examples of how the following terms could apply to this

particular diagram: spontaneous generalization, default assignment, and graceful degradation.

6. If you were instructed to describe the characteristics of the PDP approach in a 5-minute overview, what would you say? Include examples, and also be sure to describe why the approach is called *parallel distributed processing*. We discussed the topic of expertise in connection with the prototype model. Think about a specific area in which you have more expertise than a friend who is a novice. Speculate about how the two of you would differ with respect to the kind of network you have developed.

7. Describe three scripts with which you are very familiar. How would these scripts be considered heuristics, rather than exact predictors of what will happen the next time you find yourself in one of the situations described in the script?

8. You probably have a fairly clear schema of the concept "dentist's office." Focus on the discussion titled "Schemas and Memory Selection" (pp. 268 to 273) and point out the circumstances in which you would be likely to remember (a) schema-consistent material and (b) schema-inconsistent material. How might boundary extension operate when you try to reconstruct the scene you see from the dentist's chair?

9. What evidence do we have from explicit memory tasks that gender stereotypes encourage us to draw inferences that are consistent with those stereotypes? How would the demand characteristics mentioned in Chapter 7 (p. 216) be relevant to explicit memory tasks? Then discuss the two implicit memory tasks described in the In Depth discussion on inferences, and explain why they may be more effective than explicit tasks in assessing people's stereotypes.

10. Think of a schema or a script that occurs frequently in your life. Explain how that schema or script might influence your memory during five different processes: selection, boundary extension, abstraction, interpretation, and integration. Be sure to consider how memory sometimes favors schema-consistent information and sometimes favors schema-inconsistent information, as well as the cases when memory accurately reflects bottom-up processing.

KEYWORDS

semantic memory
episodic memory
category
concept
feature comparison model
defining features
characteristic features
sentence verification
  technique
typicality effect

prototype
prototype approach
prototypicality
graded structure
semantic priming effect
family resemblance
superordinate-level categories
basic-level categories
subordinate-level categories
expertise

exemplar approach
exemplar
network models
Collins and Loftus network
  model
node
link
spreading activation
ACT-R
declarative knowledge

proposition
parallel distributed processing
  (PDP) approach
connectionism
neural networks
serial search
parallel search
spontaneous generalization
default assignment
connection weights
graceful degradation

tip-of-the-tongue
  phenomenon
schema
heuristics
schema therapy
script
boundary extension
abstraction
verbatim memory
false alarm
constructive model of memory

pragmatic view of memory
inferences
gender stereotypes
explicit memory task
implicit memory task
event-related potential (ERP)
  technique
Implicit Association Test
  (IAT)

RECOMMENDED READINGS

Dovidio, J. F., Glick, P., & Rudman, L. A. (Eds.). (2005). *On the nature of prejudice: Fifty years after Allport.* Malden, MA: Blackwell. Here's a wonderful book about prejudice, stereotypes, and other biases; it includes 26 chapters by well-known researchers in the area of social cognition.

Murphy, G. L. (2002). *The big book of concepts.* Cambridge, MA: MIT Press. Topics in this book include theories of concepts, the development of conceptual knowledge, and word meaning. The tongue-in-cheek title of this book is consistent with the author's sense of humor throughout the chapters.

Pashler, H. (Ed.). (2002). *Stevens' handbook of experimental psychology* (3rd ed.). New York: Wiley. The chapters on knowledge representation and on concepts and categorization are especially relevant to the topic of general knowledge; they contain current, comprehensive information that will be useful for advanced-level students.

Saito, A. (Ed.). (2000). *Bartlett, culture and cognition.* East Sussex, England: Psychology Press. Frederick Bartlett's innovative work on schemas inspired this book, which examines anthropology issues, as well as schematic memory.

ANSWER TO DEMONSTRATION 8.7

Every sentence in Part 2 is new.

CHAPTER 9
Comprehending Language

PREVIEW

In Chapters 9 and 10, we'll examine how we process language. Specifically, Chapter 9 emphasizes language comprehension in the form of listening and reading. In contrast, Chapter 10 will emphasize language production (speaking and writing), as well as bilingualism—a topic that encompasses both language comprehension and language production.

We'll begin Chapter 9 by exploring the nature of language. In particular, we'll look at the structure of language, a brief history of psycholinguistics, several factors that influence comprehension, and some neuroscience research on language.

Next, we'll examine basic reading processes, beginning with a comparison of written and spoken language. Context is important when we need to understand the meaning of an unfamiliar word, and working memory also plays an important role in understanding sentences. This section also examines word recognition and implications for teaching reading.

The last part of Chapter 9 moves beyond small linguistic units to consider discourse, or language units that are larger than a sentence. Some important components of discourse comprehension include forming an integrated representation of a passage, drawing inferences that were not actually stated in the passage, teaching metacomprehension skills, and the relationship between test anxiety and reading comprehension. In addition, researchers in the field of artificial intelligence have designed programs that attempt to comprehend written language.

INTRODUCTION

Try to imagine a world without language. In fact, think how your life would change if you woke up tomorrow and language were forbidden. Even nonverbal gestures would be prohibited, because they are an alternate form of language (Beattie & Shovelton, 2003). Telephones, televisions, radios, newspapers, and books would all be useless. Almost all college courses would disappear. You wouldn't even be able to talk to yourself, so it would be impossible to reminisce, remind yourself about a task you must complete, or make plans for the future. Furthermore, our interpersonal and societal interactions would collapse.

Like many cognitive skills, language rarely receives the credit it deserves. After all, you simply listen to someone with a moving mouth and vocal equipment, and you understand the message this person is trying to convey. Equally effortlessly, you open your own mouth and sentences emerge almost instantaneously—an impressive testimony to the efficiency of our cognitive processes (Theme 2).

Another equally impressive characteristic of our language skills is our extraordinary ability to master thousands of words. In Chapter 8, we noted that the average North American has an estimated vocabulary of more than 20,000 to 40,000 words in his or her vocabulary (Baddeley, 1990; Saffran & Schwartz, 2003). Furthermore, the average college-educated North American has a speaking vocabulary of at least 75,000 words (Bock & Garnsey, 1998; Wingfield, 1993).

Cognitive psychologists emphasize that human language is probably one of the most complex processes to be found anywhere on our planet (Gleitman & Liberman, 1995). The domain of language includes an impressive diversity of skills. Consider just a few of the abilities that you need in order to understand a spoken sentence: encoding the sound of a speaker's voice, encoding the visual features of printed language, accessing the meaning of words, understanding the rules that determine word order, and appreciating from a speaker's intonation whether a sentence is a question or a statement. Furthermore, you manage to accomplish all these tasks while listening to a speaker who is probably producing three words each *second* (Levelt et al., 1999; Vigliocco & Hartsuiker, 2002). In fact, talking is so difficult that it should be an Olympic event—except that most humans have mastered this athletic skill (Bock & Garnsey, 1998).

In addition, the productivity of language is unlimited. For example, consider only the number of 20-word sentences that you could potentially generate. You would need 10,000,000,000,000 years—or 2,000 times the age of the earth—to say them all (Miller, 1967; Pinker, 1993).

In Chapters 9 and 10, we will discuss **psycholinguistics,** an interdisciplinary field that examines how people use language to communicate ideas (Corballis, 2006). We use language in thousands of different settings, from courtrooms to comic strips. Furthermore, language provides an excellent example of Theme 4 of this textbook, the interrelatedness of the cognitive processes. In fact, virtually every topic we have discussed so far in this book makes some contribution to language processing. To illustrate this point, try Demonstration 9.1.

⟲ Demonstration 9.1

How Other Cognitive Processes Contribute to Language

Look below at the list of chapters you have read so far. For each chapter, list at least one topic that is connected to language. The answers appear at the end of this chapter, on page 322.

Chapter 2: Perceptual Processes I: Visual and Auditory Recognition

Chapter 3: Perceptual Processes II: Attention and Consciousness

Chapter 4: Working Memory

Chapter 5: Long-Term Memory

Chapter 6: Memory Strategies and Metacognition

Chapter 7: Mental Imagery and Cognitive Maps

Chapter 8: General Knowledge

The two chapters on language should also convince you that humans are active information processors (Theme 1). Rather than passively listening to language, we actively consult our previous knowledge, use various strategies, create expectations, and draw conclusions. When we speak, we must determine what our listeners already know and what other information must be conveyed. Language is not only our most remarkable cognitive achievement, but it is also the most social of our cognitive processes.

The first of our two chapters on language focuses on language comprehension. After an introductory discussion about the nature of language, we will examine basic reading, as well as the more complex process of understanding discourse. In Chapter 10, we will switch our focus from understanding to the production of language. Chapter 10 considers two production tasks: speaking and writing. With a background in both language comprehension and language production, we can then consider bilingualism. Bilinguals—certainly the winners in any Olympic language contest—manage to communicate easily in more than one language.

THE NATURE OF LANGUAGE

Psycholinguists have developed a specialized vocabulary for language terms; let's now consider these terms. A **phoneme** (pronounced "*foe*-neem") is the basic unit of spoken language, such as the sounds *a*, *k*, and *th*. The English language has about 40 phonemes (Groome, 1999; Mayer, 2004).

In contrast, a **morpheme** (pronounced "*more*-feem") is the basic unit of meaning. For example, the word *reactivated* actually contains four morphemes: *re-*, *active,-ate*, and *-ed*. Each of those segments conveys meaning. Many morphemes can stand on their own (like *giraffe*). In contrast, some morphemes must be attached to other morphemes in order to convey their meaning. For instance, *re-* indicates a repeated action. As you might guess, the term **morphology** refers to the study of morphemes.

Another major component of psycholinguistics is syntax. **Syntax** refers to the grammatical rules that govern how we organize words into sentences (Owens, 2001). A more inclusive and familiar term, **grammar,** encompasses both morphology and syntax; it therefore examines both word structure and sentence structure (Evans & Green, 2006).

Semantics is the area of psycholinguistics that examines the meanings of words and sentences (Carroll, 2004). The related term, **semantic memory,** refers to our organized knowledge about the world. We have discussed semantic memory throughout earlier chapters of this book, but especially in Chapter 8.

An additional important term is **pragmatics,** which is our knowledge of the social rules that underlie language use; pragmatics takes into account the listener's perspective (Carroll, 2004; Tomasello, 2003). For example, think how you would define the word *syntax* to a 12-year-old child, as opposed to a college classmate. Pragmatics is an especially important topic when we consider the production of language (Chapter 10), but pragmatic factors also influence comprehension.

As you can see from reviewing the terms in this section, psycholinguistics encompasses a broad range of topics, including sounds, several levels of meaning, grammar, and social factors. We begin by noting a problem with the current research in psycholinguistics. Then we'll consider additional aspects of the nature of language: some background about the structure of language, a brief history of psycholinguistics, factors affecting comprehension, and neurolinguistics.

A Caution: Psycholinguistics Is English-Centered

In an important article, Elizabeth Bates and her coauthors (2001) emphasize a bias that operates in research about psycholinguistics. Specifically, most researchers in this discipline focus on how people understand and use English. As a result, some of the findings may apply only to English speakers, rather than to all humans. Current linguists estimate that 6,000 to 7,000 languages are spoken throughout the world, so the emphasis on just one of these languages is especially unfortunate (Fishman, 2006; Ku, 2006; Tomasello, 2003).

If your own first language is English, your ideas about language are probably English-centered. Therefore, you may react with surprise if you travel to another language community. For instance, I recall visiting Grenada, Spain, and hearing the tour guide (who appeared to be Spanish) describing the sights in Spanish and in Japanese to the tourists in her group. I'm embarrassed to report that I was startled to hear her translating Spanish into Japanese, without first passing through English.

Bates and her colleagues (2001) point out some differences among languages. For example, in English, word meaning does not depend on the relative pitch of the syllables in a word. In contrast, in Mandarin Chinese, *ma* means "mother" when the word is spoken at a single pitch. However, *ma* means "horse" when spoken in a tone that initially falls and then rises (Field, 2004).

Furthermore, Sesotho—a language spoken in southern Africa—uses the passive voice more than English does. In many languages, the nouns have a grammatical gender, although English nouns do not. Brain processing even differs as a function of a person's language. A region in the frontal lobe is activated when English speakers listen to certain complex sentences; that region does not respond when German speakers listen to the translated versions of those sentences (Bornkessel & Schlesewsky, 2006).

In summary, languages differ widely from one another on numerous dimensions (Tomasello, 2003). Clearly, psycholinguists will need to conduct extensive research in many other languages if they want to determine which linguistic principles apply universally.

Background on the Structure of Language

Before we consider the history of psycholinguistics, we need to discuss a central concept in understanding language, called phrase structure. **Phrase structure** emphasizes that we construct a sentence by using a hierarchical structure that is based on grammatical building blocks called **constituents** (Carroll, 2004). For example, suppose we have the following sentence:

The young woman carried the heavy painting.

FIGURE 9.1

An Example of Constituents.

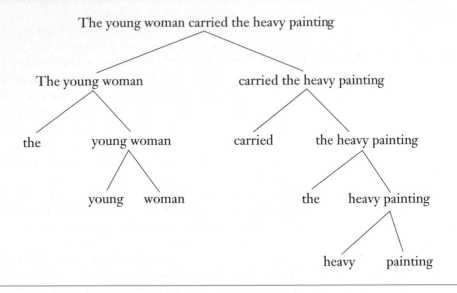

We can divide this sentence into two broad constituents: (1) the phrase that focuses on the noun—"the young woman"—and (2) the phrase that focuses on the verb—"carried the heavy painting." Each of these constituents can be further subdivided, creating a hierarchy of constituents with a diagram resembling an upside-down tree. These diagrams, like the one in Figure 9.1, help us appreciate that a sentence is not simply a chain of words, strung together like beads on a necklace. Instead, we appreciate more complicated relationships among the elements of a sentence (Owens, 2001).

We often need the entire constituent to give us cues about the meaning of the words. For example, consider the word *painting* in the sentence we just analyzed. *Painting* could be either a verb or a noun. However, from the context in which *painting* appears in the constituent *the heavy painting*, we know that the noun version is appropriate. The research indicates that people maintain a complete constituent in working memory while they process its meaning (Jarvella, 1971).

A Brief History of Psycholinguistics

Now that we have identified some central concepts in psycholinguistics, let's consider some highlights in the history of this field. Early philosophers in Greece and India debated the nature of language (Chomsky, 2000). Centuries later, both Wilhelm Wundt and William James also speculated about our impressive abilities in this area (Carroll, 2004; Levelt, 1998). However, the current discipline of psycholinguistics can be traced to the 1960s, when psycholinguists began to test whether psychological research would support the theories of Noam Chomsky (McKoon & Ratcliff, 1998). Let's consider Chomsky's theory, the reactions to his theory, and subsequent theories about language.

Chomsky's Approach. People usually think of a sentence as an orderly sequence of words that are lined up in a row on a sheet of paper. Noam Chomsky (1957) caused great excitement among psychologists and linguists by proposing that there is more to a sentence than meets the eye (or the ear). Chapter 1 of this textbook identified Chomsky's work on the psychology of language as one of the forces that led to the decline of behaviorism. The behaviorists emphasized the observable aspects of language behavior (Field, 2004). In contrast, Chomsky argued that human language abilities could be explained only in terms of a complex system of rules and principles represented in the minds of speakers (Chomsky, 2006). Chomsky is clearly one of the most influential theorists in modern linguistics (N. Smith, 2000).

Chomsky proposed that humans have innate language skills. That is, we have an inborn understanding of the abstract principles of language. As a result, children do not need to learn the basic, generalizable concepts that are universal to all languages (Chomsky, 2003, 2006; Field, 2004).

Of course, children need to learn many superficial characteristics of the language spoken in their community. For instance, children in Spanish-speaking communities will need to learn the difference between *ser* and *estar.* Spanish linguistic space is carved up somewhat differently from that of English, where children learn only one form of the verb *to be.* Still, Chomsky argues that all children have a substantial, inborn language ability. This ability allows them to produce and understand sentences they have never heard before (Belletti & Rizzi, 2002; Chomsky, 2006).

Chomsky (1975) also proposed that language is **modular;** people have a set of specific linguistic abilities that do not follow the principles of other cognitive processes, such as memory and decision making (Nusbaum & Small, 2006). We discussed a related concept, the phonetic module, in connection with speech perception on page 60. Because language is modular, Chomsky (2002, 2006) argues, young children learn complex linguistic structures many years before they master other, simpler tasks, such as mental arithmetic.

In contrast to Chomsky's theory, the standard cognitive approach argues that language is not modular. Instead, it is interconnected with other cognitive processes such as working memory. According to this alternative approach, we are skilled at language because our powerful brains can master many cognitive tasks. Language is just one of those tasks, having the same status as tasks such as memory and problem solving (Bates, 2000; Carroll, 2004; Tomasello, 2003).

In addition, Chomsky (1957, 2006) also pointed out the difference between the deep structure and the surface structure of a sentence. The **surface structure** is represented by the words that are actually spoken or written. In contrast, the **deep structure** is the underlying, more abstract meaning of a sentence (Garnham, 2005).

Two sentences may have very different surface structures, but very similar deep structures. Consider these two sentences: (1) "Sara threw the ball" and (2) "The ball was thrown by Sara." Notice that the two surface structures are different. None of the words occupies the same position in the two sentences, and three of the words in the second sentence do not even appear in the first sentence. However, "deep down," speakers of English feel that the sentences have identical core meanings (Harley, 2001).

Chomsky (1957, 2006) also pointed out that two sentences may have identical surface structures but very different deep structures; these are called **ambiguous sentences.** For example, I live outside the small town of York in rural upstate New York. One day I drove past the announcement board outside the York Town Hall, and the message said: "POP CAN DRIVE." I was puzzled: Whose father is now allowed to drive, and why had he previously been prohibited from driving? To be honest, the alternate meaning (focusing on a community fundraiser) did not occur to me until the next day.

We will discuss ambiguity in more detail later in the chapter. However, context usually helps us resolve these ambiguities. Here are three additional ambiguous sentences, each of which has two meanings:

> The shooting of the hunters was terrible.
>
> They are cooking apples.
>
> The lamb is too hot to eat.

Reactions to Chomsky's Theory. Initially, psychologists responded enthusiastically to Chomsky's ideas about grammar (Bock et al., 1992; Williams, 2005). Not all the evidence for Chomsky's theory was favorable, however. For example, the research failed to support Chomsky's prediction that people would take longer to process sentences that required numerous transformations (Carroll, 2004; Herriot, 2003). Furthermore, some of Chomsky's theories have not been tested (Agassi, 1997).

Chomsky's later theories have provided more sophisticated linguistic analyses. For example, Chomsky has placed constraints on the possible hypotheses that the language learner can make about the structure of language (Chomsky, 1981, 2000; Harley, 2001). Chomsky's newer approach also emphasizes the information contained in the individual words of a sentence. For example, the word *discuss* not only conveys information about the word's meaning, but it also specifies the requirement that *discuss* must be followed by a noun, as in the sentence, "Rita discussed the novel" (Ratner & Gleason, 1993).

Psycholinguistic Theories Emphasizing Meaning. Beginning in the 1970s, many psychologists became discouraged with Chomsky's emphasis on the grammatical aspects of language (Herriot, 2003). These psychologists began to develop theories that emphasized the human mind, rather than the structure of language (Tanenhaus, 2004; Treiman et al., 2003). They also emphasized semantics, or the *meaning* of language. In recent years, this focus on semantics has encouraged psychologists to explore how people understand the meaning of paragraphs and stories. We'll look at some of that research later in this chapter.

Several psychologists have developed theories that emphasize meaning (e.g., Kintsch, 1998; Newmeyer, 1998; Tomasello, 2003). Here, we will briefly describe one representative theory, the cognitive-functional approach to language. The **cognitive-functional approach** (also called **usage-based linguistics**) emphasizes that the function of human language in everyday life is to communicate meaning to other individuals. As the name suggests, the cognitive-functional approach also emphasizes that our cognitive processes—such as attention and memory— are intertwined with our language comprehension and language production.

Demonstration 9.2

The Cognitive-Functional Approach to Language

Imagine that you recently saw an event in which a man named Fred broke a window, using a rock. A person who was not present at the time asks you for information about the event. For each of the sentences below, construct a question that this person might have asked that would prompt you to reply with that specific wording for the sentence. For example, the brief response, "Fred broke the window" might have been prompted by the question, "What did Fred do?"

1. Fred broke the window with a rock.
2. The rock broke the window.
3. The window got broken.
4. It was Fred who broke the window.
5. It was the window that Fred broke.
6. What Fred did was to break the window.

Source: Based on Tomasello, 1998a, p. 483.

Michael Tomasello (2003) points out that young children have extremely powerful cognitive skills and social-learning skills. During the years when they are mastering language, they will hear several million adult sentences. As we'll see in Chapter 13, children analyze these sentences, and they use flexible strategies to create increasingly complex language (Kuhl, 2006).

Tomasello (1998a, 1998b) also emphasizes that adults use language strategically. Specifically, we structure our language in order to focus our listeners' attention on the information we wish to emphasize. For instance, look at Demonstration 9.2, which illustrates a concrete example of the cognitive-functional approach (Tomasello, 1998a). Notice how each of those sentences emphasizes a somewhat different perspective on the same event. You'll probably find that these different perspectives are reflected in the variety of questions you generated. In short, the cognitive-functional approach argues that people can use language creatively, in order to communicate subtle shades of meaning. We'll explore the social use of language more thoroughly in Chapter 10.

Factors Affecting Comprehension

Beginning in the 1960s, psychologists began to examine a variety of linguistic factors related to language comprehension. In general, people have difficulty understanding sentences in these four conditions:

1. If they contain negatives, such as *not*.
2. If they are in the passive rather than the active voice.

3. If they contain nested structures, with a descriptive clause in the middle of the sentence.

4. If they are ambiguous.

Negatives. A sentence in a newspaper column reads. "Georgia rejected a challenge to a referendum that had barred same-sex unions." This sentence requires several readings to understand the basic message: Will the state of Georgia prohibit same-sex unions? The research on negatives is clear-cut. If a sentence contains a negative word, such as *no* or *not,* or an implied negative (such as *rejected*), the sentence almost always requires more processing time than a similar, affirmative sentence (Williams, 2005).

In a classic study, Clark and Chase (1972) showed a picture of a star above a plus sign. Then they asked people to verify statements, such as the following:

Star is above plus. $\overset{*}{+}$

The participants responded quickly in this case, when the sentence was affirmative. They responded more slowly if the sentence contained the negative form *isn't* (for example, "Plus isn't above star"). The participants also made fewer errors with affirmative sentences than with negative sentences. Notice that these results are consistent with Theme 3 of this textbook: Our cognitive processes handle positive information better than negative information.

As you can imagine, readers' understanding decreases as the number of negative terms increases. For example, people perform only slightly better than chance when they judge sentences such as, "Few people strongly deny that the world is not flat" (Sherman, 1976, p. 145). These findings have clear-cut practical applications in numerous areas, such as education, advertising, and creating political surveys (Kifner, 1994).

The Passive Voice. As we discussed earlier, Chomsky (1957, 1965) pointed out that the active and passive forms of a sentence may differ in their surface structure, even though they have similar deep structures. However, the active form is more basic; we need to add extra words to create the passive form of a sentence.

The active form is also easier to understand (Garnham, 2005; Williams, 2005). For example, Ferreira and her coauthors (2002) asked participants to determine whether each sentence in a series was plausible or likely. The participants were highly accurate in responding "No" to sentences in the active voice, such as, "The man bit the dog." In contrast, their accuracy dropped to about 75% when the same sentences were converted to the passive voice, for example, "The dog was bitten by the man" (p. 13).

Most current writing-style manuals recommend using the active voice. For example, the current manual of the American Psychological Association (2001) points out that an active-voice sentence such as "Nuñez (2006) designed the experiment," is much more direct and vigorous than "The experiment was designed by Nuñez (2006)."

Nested Structures. A **nested structure** is a phrase that is embedded within another sentence. For example, we can take the simple sentence, "The plane leaves at 9:41," and insert the nested structure "that I want to take." We create a more structurally complex sentence: "The plane that I want to take leaves at 9:41." However, readers often experience a memory overload when they try to read a sentence that contains a nested structure (Gibson, 1998, 1999; Rayner & Clifton, 2002). You need to remember the first part of the sentence, "the plane," while you process the nested structure. Afterward, you can process the remainder of the sentence. The memory overload becomes excessive when the sentence contains several nested structures. For example, you might find yourself stranded when you try to understand the following sentence:

> The plane that I want to take when I go to Denver after he returns from Washington leaves at 9:41 in the morning.

The next time you write a paper, remember how these three factors can influence comprehension. Whenever possible, follow these guidelines: (1) Use linguistically positive sentences, rather than negative ones; (2) use active sentences, rather than passive ones; and (3) use simple sentences, rather than nested structures.

Ambiguity.   Suppose that you saw the following headline in your local newspaper: "Bombing Rocks Hope for Peace." As you might imagine, sentences are difficult to understand if they contain an ambiguous word or an ambiguous sentence structure. Recall that we mentioned ambiguous sentences in connection with Chomsky's approach to language. Now let's consider how people manage to understand these sentences.

Psychologists have designed several methods of measuring the difficulty of understanding a sentence with an ambiguous word (MacDonald, 1999; Rodd et al., 2002). For example, one method measures the amount of time that the reader pauses on a word before moving his or her eyes to the next words in the sentence (Pexman et al., 2004; Rayner et al., 2005). People typically pause longer when they are processing an ambiguous word.

Psychologists have proposed many theories to explain how listeners process an ambiguous word (Rayner & Clifton, 2002; Van Orden & Kloos, 2005). Current research supports the following explanation: When people encounter a potential ambiguity, the activation builds up for all the well-known meanings of the ambiguous item. Furthermore, people are likely to choose one particular meaning (1) if that meaning is more common than the alternate meaning and (2) if the rest of the sentence is consistent with that meaning (Morris & Binder, 2001; Rayner & Clifton, 2002; Sereno et al., 2003).

Consider this potentially ambiguous sentence: "Pat took the money to the bank." Here, the "financial institution" interpretation of *bank* would receive the most activation. After all, this is the most common interpretation of *bank*, and the context of *money* also suggests this meaning. Some minimal activation also builds up for other meanings of *bank* (as in *riverbank* and *blood bank*). However, just a fraction of a second later, these alternative meanings are suppressed, and they are no longer active (Gernsbacher et al., 2001; Rayner & Clifton, 2002). This explanation of ambiguity would be consistent with the parallel distributed processing approach.

So far, we have considered ambiguous words. However, sometimes a sentence structure is ambiguous, especially if it contains no punctuation (Rayner et al., 2003). Try reading this sentence:

1. "After the Martians invaded the town that the city bordered was evacuated." (Tabor & Hutchins, 2004, p. 432).

Did you find yourself reading along quickly, and then you were suddenly lost? You had wandered down the wrong path. An ambiguous sentence is especially difficult if you read a long string of words that seem consistent with your initial interpretation. In contrast, you can correct your initial mistake more quickly with a shorter string of words. If sentence 1 is still unclear, see if you can understand this shorter sentence:

2. "After the Martians invaded the town was evacuated." (Tabor & Hutchins, 2004, p. 432).

⊚ Demonstration 9.3

Searching for Ambiguous Language

Ambiguity occurs quite often in the English language (Rodd et al., 2002). Perhaps the best source of ambiguous words and phrases is newspaper headlines. After all, these headlines must be very brief, so they often omit the auxiliary words that could resolve the ambiguity. Here are some actual newspaper headlines that colleagues, students, and I have seen:

1. "Eye drops off shelf"
2. "Squad helps dog bite victims"
3. "British left waffles on Falkland Islands"
4. "Stolen painting found by tree"
5. "Clinton wins budget; more lies ahead"
6. "Miners refuse to work after death"
7. "Kids make nutritious snacks"
8. "Local high school dropouts cut in half"
9. "Iraqi head seeks arms"
10. "Oklahoma is among places where tongues are disappearing"

For the next few weeks, search the newspapers you normally read, looking for ambiguous headlines. Try to notice whether your first interpretation of the ambiguous portion was a correct or incorrect understanding of the phrase. If you find any particularly intriguing ambiguities, please send them to me! My address is: Department of Psychology, SUNY Geneseo, Geneseo, NY 14454.

As Rueckl (1995) observes, "Ambiguity is a fact of life. Happily, the human cognitive system is well-equipped to deal with it" (p. 501). Indeed, we can understand ambiguous sentences, just as we can understand negative sentences, sentences using the passive voice, and sentences with complex nesting. However, we typically respond more quickly and more accurately when the language we encounter is straightforward. Now that you are familiar with the concept of ambiguity, try Demonstration 9.3.

[IN DEPTH]

Neurolinguistics

Neurolinguistics is the discipline that examines how the brain processes language (Treiman et al., 2003). Research in this area has become increasingly active in recent years, and it demonstrates that the neurological basis of language is impressively complex. Let's consider three topics: aphasia, hemispheric specialization in language processing, and neuroimaging research with normal individuals.

Individuals with Aphasia. The initial investigations in neurolinguistics began in the 1800s, when early researchers studied individuals who had language disorders. In fact, before the early 1970s, almost all the information that scientists had acquired about neurolinguistics was based on people with aphasia. A person with **aphasia** has difficulty communicating, caused by damage to the speech areas of the brain. This damage is typically caused by a stroke, a tumor, or a serious infection (Saffran & Schwartz, 2003). Figure 9.2 illustrates two especially relevant regions of the brain.

Broca's area is located toward the front of the brain. Damage to Broca's area typically leads to speech that is hesitant, effortful, and grammatically simple (Dick et al., 2001; Gazzaniga et al., 2002). For example, one person with Broca's aphasia tried to describe the circumstances of his stroke:

> Alright . . . Uh . . . stroke and uh . . . I . . . huh tawanna guy . . . h . . . h . . . hot tub and . . . And the . . . two days when uh . . . Hos . . . uh . . . huh hospital and uh . . . amet . . . am . . . ambulance. (Dick et al., 2001, p. 760)

Broca's aphasia is primarily characterized by an expressive-language deficit— or trouble producing language. These symptoms make sense. Broca's region is one of the locations of the brain that manages motor movement; to produce speech, you must move your lips and tongue. However, people with Broca's aphasia may also have some trouble understanding language (Dick et al., 2001; Martin & Wu, 2005). For example, they may be unable to tell the difference between "He showed her baby the pictures" and "He showed her the baby pictures" (Jackendoff, 1994, p. 149).

Wernicke's area is located toward the back of the brain. ("Wernicke" is pronounced either "*Ver*-nih-kee" or "*Wer*-nih-kee.") Damage to Wernicke's area typically produces serious difficulties in understanding speech, as well as language production that is too wordy and confused (Harley, 2001). People with **Wernicke's aphasia** have

FIGURE 9.2

Broca's Area and Wernicke's Area: Two Regions of the Brain That Are Commonly Associated with Aphasia.

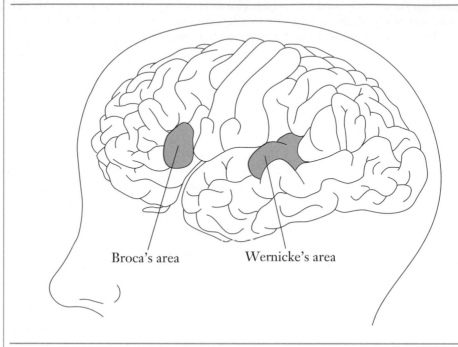

Broca's area   Wernicke's area

such severe receptive-language problems that they cannot understand basic instructions like "Point to the telephone" or "Show me the picture of the watch." In contrast to the quotation above, here's how a person with Wernicke's aphasia tried to describe the circumstances of his stroke:

> It just suddenly had a feffert and all the feffort had gone with it. It even stepped my horn. They took them from earth you know. They make my favorite nine to severed and now I'm a been habed by the uh stam of fortment of my annulment which is now forever. (Dick et al., 2001, p. 761)

The basic information about Broca's aphasia and Wernicke's aphasia has been known for about a century. However, the distinction between these two aphasias is much less clear-cut than researchers had once believed (Gazzaniga et al., 2002; Martin & Wu, 2005).

Another problem is related to an issue we emphasized earlier in the chapter, on page 291: We should not rely exclusively on English-based psycholinguistic research (Bates et al., 2001). For instance, researchers who examined aphasia in English speakers concluded that individuals with Broca's aphasia made many grammatical errors. However, these same researchers concluded that individuals with Wernicke's aphasia typically produced grammatically correct sentences.

Here is the complication: English speakers use the same grammatical form for a noun, whether it is the subject or the object of a sentence. In contrast, languages such as German and Czech add letters to the end of a noun if it is the object of a sentence, rather than the subject. Interestingly, people with Wernicke's aphasia who speak languages like German and Czech often fail to add the appropriate endings to the nouns. In short, we see that *both* kinds of aphasia can decrease a person's grammatical accuracy— once we examine some languages other than English (Dick et al., 2001).

Hemispheric Specialization.   We noted at the beginning of this In Depth section that the early researchers examined people with aphasia. These scientists also noticed that individuals with speech disorders typically had more severe damage in the left hemisphere of the brain, rather than the right hemisphere. During the mid-1900s, researchers began a more systematic study of lateralization. **Lateralization** means that each hemisphere of the brain has somewhat different functions.

If you've read about lateralization in a popular magazine—rather than an academic journal—you may have seen something like, "Language is localized in the left hemisphere of the brain." However, this statement is too strong. Yes, most neurolinguistic studies find greater activation in the left hemisphere than in the right (Bates, 2000; Grodzinsky, 2000; Scott, 2005). Still, for about 5% of right-handers and about 50% of left-handers, language is either localized in the *right* hemisphere or is processed equally by both hemispheres (Kinsbourne, 1998).

The left hemisphere does indeed perform most of the work in language processing, for the majority of people. The left hemisphere is especially skilled at speech perception; it quickly selects the most likely interpretation of a sound (Gernsbacher & Kaschak, 2003; Scott, 2005). Furthermore, the left hemisphere determines cause-and-effect relationships (Gazzaniga et al., 2002). It also excels at reading, as well as at understanding meaning and grammar (Gernsbacher & Kaschak, 2003). In addition, high-imagery sentences activate the left hemisphere (Just et al., 2004).

For many years, people thought that the right hemisphere did not play a role in language processing. However, we now know that this hemisphere does perform some tasks. For example, the right hemisphere interprets the emotional tone of a message (Gernsbacher & Kaschak, 2003; Vingerhoets et al., 2003). It also plays a role in appreciating humor (Shammi & Stuss, 1999). In general, then, the right hemisphere is responsible for more abstract language tasks (Gernsbacher & Kaschak, 2003).

The left and right hemispheres often work together on tasks such as interpreting subtle word meanings, resolving ambiguities, and combining the meaning of several sentences (Beeman & Chiarello, 1998; Beeman et al., 2000; Grodzinsky, 2006). For example, suppose that you are one of the majority of individuals for whom the left hemisphere is dominant for language. Imagine that you see this ambiguous message that I once spotted on a bumper sticker:

SOMETIMES I WAKE UP GRUMPY.
OTHER TIMES I LET HIM SLEEP IN.

On seeing the phrase, "SOMETIMES I WAKE UP GRUMPY," your left hemisphere immediately constructs a meaning in which *GRUMPY* refers to "I" (that is, the owner of the car). After reading the next sentence, "OTHER TIMES I LET HIM SLEEP IN," your right hemisphere searches for a less obvious interpretation, in which *GRUMPY* refers to another person. Fortunately, when people have normal brain functions, both hemispheres work together in a complementary fashion (Gazzaniga et al., 2002). Before you read further, try Demonstration 9.4.

⊚ Demonstration 9.4

Reading Two Sets of Sentences

A. Read the following set of sentences:

> A grandmother sat at a table.
> A young child played in a backyard.
> A mother talked on a telephone.
> A husband drove a tractor.
> A grandchild walked up to a door.
> A little boy pouted and acted bored.
> A grandmother promised to bake cookies.
> A wife looked out at a field.
> A family was worried about some crops.

B. Now read the following set of sentences:

> The grandmother sat at a table.
> The young child played in a backyard.
> The mother talked on a telephone.
> The husband drove a tractor.
> The grandchild walked up to a door.
> The little boy pouted and acted bored.
> The grandmother promised to bake cookies.
> The wife looked out at a field.
> The family was worried about some crops.

Now answer this question: The first set and the second set differ only with respect to the first word in each sentence. However, did you have a general feeling that the two sets differed in the overall meaning that they conveyed?

Source: Gernsbacher & Robertson, 2005, pp. 159-160.

Neuroimaging Research with Normal Individuals. During the past decade, researchers have increasingly used the fMRI technique to investigate language in humans. **Functional magnetic resonance imaging (fMRI)** is based on the principle that oxygen-rich blood is an index of brain activity (Cacioppo & Berntson, 2005b; Kalat, 2007; Mason & Just, 2006).

An fMRI is superior to a PET scan in detecting changes that occur very quickly. An fMRI is also safer than a PET scan, because a PET scan requires an injection of radioactive material. However, one disadvantage is that fMRI values can be inaccurate when participants move their heads even slightly (Saffran & Schwartz, 2003). You can guess, therefore, that fMRIs are more suitable for language comprehension than for language production. (Try talking without moving any portion of your head!)

Research using the fMRI technique shows that several regions of the left temporal lobe process semantic information. Therefore, processing the meaning of words is not confined to just a small region of the cortex. Furthermore, most people who have experienced damage to the left temporal lobe still understand the general meaning of a message. Typically, however, they make some relatively minor comprehension errors (Saffran & Schwartz, 2003).

In the previous discussion of hemispheric specialization, we emphasized that the right hemisphere plays an important role in language comprehension, even though the left hemisphere receives most of the publicity in the media. Morton Ann Gernsbacher and David Robertson (2005) provide a good example of the subtlety of right-hemisphere processing. Specifically, they created several sets of sentences, such as the two kinds of sentences you read in Demonstration 9.4.

The first set of sentences began with "A," whereas the second set began with "The." Would you expect such a subtle change to make a difference in the fMRI patterns? Gernsbacher and Robertson (2005) found that the two sets of sentences produced virtually identical patterns of activation in the left hemisphere. In contrast, the right hemisphere responded very differently to the two sets. As Gernsbacher and Robertson emphasize, when a series of sentences uses the word "The," it sounds more like a story in which the grandmother, the child, and other family members are connected with each other. In contrast, the string of sentences with the word "A" seems disconnected; the characters don't seem like a cohesive unit. Impressively, the right hemisphere manages to respond differently to connected language than to disconnected language. The research on longer, more sophisticated language sequences is just beginning (Mason & Just, 2006).

In summary, the neuropsychology research highlights the complexity of our language skills. We've considered studies about individuals with aphasia, information about hemispheric specialization, and fMRI research. Neurolinguists still have a distance to travel, but they have identified some important information about the coordinated brain regions that allow us to understand language.

In the first part of this chapter, we examined the basic structure of language, the history of psycholinguistics, factors affecting comprehension, and neurolinguistics. Let's summarize this background knowledge and then turn our attention to the important topic of reading.

⊚ Section Summary: *The Nature of Language*

1. Some of the central concepts in psycholinguistics are the phoneme, the morpheme, morphology, syntax, grammar, semantics, semantic memory, and pragmatics.

2. Because most psycholinguistics research focuses on English, we do not know whether the findings can be applied to other languages.

3. People use the information in constituents to determine meaning; working memory stores the constituent that people are currently processing, until they can determine its meaning.

4. According to Noam Chomsky, (a) language skills are innate in humans, (b) language is modular, and (c) the deep structure of a sentence captures its core meaning.

5. Many current psychologists emphasize the meaning of language, rather than linguistic structure; for example, the cognitive-functional approach to language emphasizes that we design our language so that listeners will pay attention to the information we want to emphasize.

6. Sentences are more difficult to understand if they (a) contain negatives, (b) use the passive voice, (c) include nested structures, and (d) are ambiguous.

7. Neurolinguistic research on adults with aphasia suggests that damage in Broca's area usually leads to difficulty in producing language, whereas damage in Wernicke's area usually leads to difficulty in understanding language; however, the distinction is not clear-cut.

8. The left hemisphere typically performs most components of language processing, such as speech perception, reading, and syntax processing; however, the right hemisphere performs tasks such as interpreting a message's emotional tone, appreciating humor, and forming connections among sentences.

9. Research using fMRIs highlights a variety of brain regions that are responsible for language-related activities; for example, this research shows that the right hemisphere can distinguish between connected language and a series of unconnected sentences.

BASIC READING PROCESSES

Reading seems so simple to competent adult readers that we forget how challenging the task is for most children (Rayner et al., 2001). Take a minute to think about the impressive variety of cognitive tasks you perform when reading a paragraph like this one. Reading requires you to use many cognitive processes we have discussed in previous chapters. For example, you must recognize letters (Chapter 2), move your eyes across the page (Chapter 3), use working memory to remember material from the sentence you are currently processing (Chapter 4), and recall earlier material that is stored in long-term memory (Chapters 5 and 6). You also need to use metacomprehension to think about the reading comprehension process (Chapter 6). In some cases, you must also construct a mental image to represent the scene of the action in the passage you are reading (Chapter 7). In addition, you must consult your semantic memory, your schemas, and your scripts when you try to understand the paragraph (Chapter 8).

In Demonstration 9.1 and throughout this book, we emphasize that the cognitive processes are interrelated (Theme 4). Reading is an important activity that requires virtually every cognitive process discussed in this textbook. Despite the complexity of the reading process, however, we are usually blissfully unaware of the cognitive effort that reading requires (Gorrell, 1999). For example we can silently identify an isolated word in 200 milliseconds, which is 1/5 of a second. In addition, we manage to read with impressive efficiency, typically at the rate of about 250 to 300 words per minute (Rayner et al., 2003; Wagner & Stanovich, 1996). Consistent with Theme 2, reading is remarkably efficient and accurate.

Here's an additional reason to admire your reading skills: In English, we do not have a one-to-one correspondence between letters of the alphabet and speech sounds. These irregular pronunciations make English more challenging than languages such as Spanish (Rayner et al., 2003).Try Demonstration 9.5 to illustrate this point. As we noted at the beginning of this chapter, most of the psycholinguistic research examines people whose language is English. We therefore cannot generalize this research to Spanish readers or readers whose language uses symbols to represent complete words (Wagner et al., 2006).

---

⑨ Demonstration 9.5

Noticing That Letters of the Alphabet Do Not Have a One-to-One Correspondence with Speech Sounds

Each of the words below has a somewhat different pronunciation for the letter sequence *ea*. Read each word aloud and notice the variety of phonemes that can be produced with those two letters.

beauty	deal	react
bread	great	séance
clear	heard	bear
create	knowledgeable	dealt

As you have demonstrated, this two-letter sequence can be pronounced in twelve different ways. Furthermore, each phoneme in the English language can be spelled in a variety of ways. Go back over this list of words and try to think of another word that has a different spelling for that phoneme. For example, the *ea(u)* phoneme in *beauty* is like the *iew* phoneme in *view*.

Source: Based on Underwood & Batt, 1996.

Let's begin this section on basic reading processes by comparing written language with spoken language. Then we'll explore how we discover the meaning of an unfamiliar word. We'll also see how working memory plays a role in reading, and then we'll consider the two pathways we use when recognizing words. A separate section in this chapter, on discourse processing, will examine how we understand larger units of language—such as sentences and stories—in both written and spoken language.

Comparing Written and Spoken Language

In Chapter 2, we explored several components of spoken language comprehension. In this section on *written* language comprehension, we encounter a somewhat different set of challenges. Reading and the comprehension of spoken language differ in important ways (Ainsworth & Greenberg, 2006; Dahan & Magnuson, 2006; Nelson et al., 2005; Rayner & Clifton, 2002; Saffran & Schwartz, 2003; Treiman et al., 2003):

1. Reading is visual and is spread out across space, whereas speech is auditory and is spread out across time.
2. Readers can control the rate of input, whereas listeners usually cannot.
3. Readers can re-scan the written input, whereas listeners must rely much more heavily on their working memory.
4. Writing is relatively standardized and error free, whereas variability, errors, sloppy pronunciation, and interfering stimuli are common in speech.
5. Writing shows discrete boundaries between words, whereas speech does not.
6. Writing is confined to the words on a page, whereas speech is supplemented by nonverbal cues and by additional auditory cues—such as stressed words and variations in pace—that enrich the linguistic message.
7. Children require elaborate teaching to master written language, whereas they learn spoken language very easily.
8. Adults who can read tend to learn new words more quickly when they appear in a written form, rather than a spoken form.

As you can imagine, these characteristics of written language have important implications for our cognitive processes. For example, we can consult the words on a page when we want to make sense out of a passage in a book—a luxury we seldom have with spoken language. Despite the differences between written and spoken language, however, both processes require us to understand words and appreciate the meaning of sentences. In fact, the research on individual differences highlights the similarity between the two comprehension processes. For adults, scores on reading comprehension tests are highly correlated with scores on oral comprehension tests; typically, the correlation is about +.90 (Rayner et al., 2001).

Demonstration 9.6

Figuring Out the Meaning of a Word from Context

Read the paragraph below. Then define, as precisely as possible, the words that are italicized.

> Two ill-dressed people—the one a tired woman of middle years and the other a tense young man—sat around a fire where the common meal was almost ready. The mother, Tanith, peered at her son through the *oam* of the bubbling stew. It had been a long time since his last *ceilidh* and Tobar had changed greatly; where once he had seemed all legs and clumsy joints, he now was well-formed and in control of his hard, young body. As they ate, Tobar told of his past year, re-creating for Tanith how he had wandered long and far in his quest to gain the skills he would need to be permitted to rejoin the company. Then all too soon, their brief *ceilidh* over, Tobar walked over to touch his mother's arm and quickly left.

Source: Based on Sternberg & Powell, 1983.

Discovering the Meaning of Unfamiliar Words

Chapter 2 examined how context aids both the visual recognition of letters and the auditory recognition of phonemes. Context also helps you recognize words. Specifically, you perceive familiar words more accurately when they are embedded within the meaningful context of a sentence (Rayner et al., 2003). Earlier in the chapter, we also saw that context helps to resolve the meaning of an ambiguous word.

In addition, context is vitally important when people want to discover the meanings of *unfamiliar* words (Rayner et al., 2003). Try Demonstration 9.6, which is an example of the passages used by Sternberg and Powell (1983) in their work on verbal comprehension.

Sternberg and Powell proposed that context can provide several kinds of information cues about the meaning of an unknown word. For instance, context can help us understand when and where this unknown item occurs. Consider the following sentence: "At dawn, the *blen* arose on the horizon and shone brightly."

This sentence contains several contextual cues that make it easy to infer the meaning of *blen*. For instance, the phrase "at dawn" provides a cue about the time at which the arising of the *blen* occurred. The word *arose* limits the possible candidates for *blen* to those things that move or appear to move. Other words and phrases in the sentence are equally helpful. With all these cues, an experienced reader can easily understand that the nonsense word *blen* is a synonym for the familiar word *sun*.

Contextual cues are especially useful if the unknown word appears in several different contexts. According to the research, words that appear in a rich context of different cues are more likely to be accurately defined (Sternberg & Powell, 1983).

As you might expect, the students in Sternberg and Powell's study showed large individual differences in their ability to use contextual cues and to provide accurate definitions for the unfamiliar words. The students who were particularly good at this task also had higher scores on tests of vocabulary, reading comprehension, and general intelligence. (Incidentally, in the passage in Demonstration 9.6, *oam* means "steam" and a *ceilidh* is a "visit.")

Reading and Working Memory

Working memory plays an important role during reading (Carpenter et al., 1995; Carroll, 2004; Martin, 2007). The research shows that readers who have a relatively large working-memory span can quickly process ambiguous sentences (Miyake et al., 1994). In addition, people with large working-memory spans are especially skilled in reading difficult passages and solving complex verbal problems (Haarmann et al., 2003; Long et al., 2006).

Working memory also helps us to understand complicated sentences (Carpenter et al., 1994, 1995; Just et al., 1996; Martin, 2007). People who can maintain many items in memory—while they unravel a sentence—are quick and accurate in understanding complex sentences such as "The reporter whom the senator attacked admitted the error."

This information about reading and working memory is an excellent illustration of Theme 4. The cognitive processes do not operate in isolation. Instead, reading skill depends heavily on other cognitive abilities, such as working memory.

Two Pathways for Reading Words

So far, our examination of reading in this textbook has emphasized how we identify alphabetical letters (Chapter 2), how our saccadic eye movements scan a line of text (Chapter 3), how we discover the meaning of an unfamiliar word, and how working memory plays a role in reading. Now we'll address an important question about reading: How do we look at a pattern of letters and actually recognize that word? For example, how do you manage to look at the eleven letters in the fourth word in this paragraph and realize that it says *examination?*

For several decades, researchers debated whether readers actually "sound out" words while reading a passage. Some researchers concluded that readers always sound out the words, and other researchers concluded that they never sound them out. In the current era, the debate is mostly resolved (Coltheart, 2005). You have probably completed enough psychology courses to guess the answer: Sometimes readers sound out the words, and sometimes they do not. In fact, the **dual-route approach to reading** specifies that skilled readers employ both a direct-access route and an indirect-access route (Coltheart, 2005; Mayer, 2004).

1. Sometimes you read a word by a **direct-access route;** you recognize this word directly through vision. That is, you look at the word *examination*, and the visual pattern is sufficient to access the word and its meaning. You are especially likely to use direct access if the word has an irregular spelling and cannot be "sounded out"—for example, the words *one* or *through*.

2. Other times, you read a word by an **indirect-access route;** you recognize this word indirectly by sounding out the word. In more detail, as soon as you see a word, you translate the ink marks on the page into some form of sound, before you can access a word and its meaning (Rayner et al., 2003; Treiman et al., 2003). You are especially likely to use indirect access if the word has a regular spelling and can be sounded out—for example, the words *ten* and *cabinet*.

Notice why this second process is indirect. According to this explanation, you must go through the intermediate step of converting the visual stimulus into a phonological (sound) stimulus. Think about whether you seem to use this intermediate step when you read. As you read this sentence, for example, do you have a speech-like representation of the words? You probably don't actually move your lips when you read, and you certainly don't say the words out loud. But do you seem to have an auditory image of what you are reading?

Let's discuss the research supporting each of these routes. Then we'll consider the implications for teaching reading to children.

Research on the Dual-Route Approach. We'll begin with a classic study that supports the direct-access route. It demonstrates that people can recognize a word visually, without paying attention to the sound of the word. Bradshaw and Nettleton (1974) showed people pairs of words that were similar in spelling, but different in sound, such as *mown–down*, *horse–worse*, and *quart–part*. In one condition, the participants were instructed to read the first word silently and then pronounce the second word out loud. Now, if they had been translating the first member of a pair into sound, the sound of *mown* would interfere with saying *down* out loud. However, the results showed that the participants experienced no hesitation in pronouncing the second word. This finding—and other similar studies—suggests that we do not silently pronounce each word during normal reading (Coltheart, 2005)

Now let's shift to the research on the indirect-access approach. Many studies suggest that we often translate visual stimuli into sound during reading (Coltheart, 2005). Furthermore, the sound coding may assist working memory, providing an additional advantage during reading (Rayner et al., 2003).

A study by Luo and his coauthors (1998) provides evidence for the indirect-access approach in adult readers. These researchers instructed college students to read a series of pairs of words and decide whether the two words were related or unrelated in meaning. A typical pair in the experimental condition was *LION–BARE*. As you know, the word *BARE* sounds the same as the word *BEAR*, which is indeed semantically related to *LION*. The students frequently made errors on these pairs, because they incorrectly judged the two words as being semantically related. This error pattern suggests that they were silently pronouncing the word pairs when they made the judgments. In contrast, they made relatively few errors on control-condition word pairs, such as *LION–BEAN*. In this word pair, the second word looked like the word *BEAR*, although it did not sound the same.

Word sounds may be especially important when children begin to read. Numerous studies demonstrate that children with high phonological awareness have superior reading skills. That is, the children who are able to identify sound patterns in a word also receive higher scores on reading achievement tests (Levy, 1999; Wagner & Stanovich, 1996).

Perhaps you're thinking that children may need to translate the printed word into sound. After all, children even move their lips when they read, but adults usually do not. Try Demonstration 9.7 and see whether you change your mind. Adults read "tongue twisters" very slowly, which indicates that—at least in some circumstances—they are indeed translating the printed words into sounds (Harley, 2001; Keller et al., 2003; Perfetti, 1996).

As we noted earlier, the dual-route approach has the definite advantage of flexibility. This approach argues that the characteristics of the reading material determine whether access is indirect or direct. For instance, you may use indirect access the first time you see a long, uncommon word; you may use direct access for a common word (Bernstein & Carr, 1996).

The dual-route approach also argues that characteristics of the reader determine whether access is indirect or direct. Beginning readers would be especially likely to sound out the words, using indirect access. Experienced readers would be especially likely to recognize the words directly from print. Adults also vary in their reading styles.

◎ Demonstration 9.7

Reading Tongue Twisters

Read each of the following tongue twisters silently to yourself:

1. The seasick sailor staggered as he zigzagged sideways.
2. Peter Piper picked a peck of pickled peppers. A peck of pickled peppers Peter Piper picked.
3. She sells seashells down by the seashore.
4. Congressional caucus questions controversial CIA-*Contra*-Crack connection.
5. Sheila and Celia slyly shave the cedar shingle splinter.

Now be honest. Could you "hear" yourself pronouncing these words as you were reading? Did you have to read them more slowly than other sentences in this book?

College students who are good readers typically use direct access, whereas college students who are relatively poor readers typically use indirect access (Jared et al., 1999).

At present, the dual-route approach seems like an intelligent compromise. The dual-route approach is also consistent with brain-imaging research (Jobard et al., 2003). Readers can identify words either directly or indirectly, depending on the characteristics of both the text and the reader.

Implications for Teaching Reading to Children. For many years, reading teachers and reading researchers debated about the most effective way to teach reading. In general, those who favored the direct-access approach also favored the whole-word approach. The **whole-word approach** argues that readers can directly connect the written word—as an entire unit—with the meaning that this word represents (Rayner et al., 2001). The whole-word approach emphasizes that the correspondence between the written and spoken codes in English is notoriously complex, as we saw in Demonstration 9.5. Supporters therefore argue that children should not learn to emphasize the way a word sounds. Instead, the whole-word approach encourages children to identify a word in terms of its context within a sentence. The problem, however, is that even skilled adult readers achieve only about 25% accuracy when they look at an incomplete sentence and guess which word is missing (Perfetti, 2003; Snow & Juel, 2005).

In contrast, people who favor the indirect-access hypothesis typically support the phonics approach. The **phonics approach** states that readers recognize words by trying to pronounce the individual letters in the word. If your grade school teachers told you to "sound it out" when you stumbled on a new word, they championed the phonics approach. The phonics approach argues that speech sound is a necessary intermediate step in reading. It also emphasizes developing young children's awareness of phonemes. According to the research, it's clear that phonics training helps children who have reading problems (McGuinness, 2004; Perfetti, 2003; Snow & Juel, 2005). For example, a meta-analysis of thirty-four studies showed that phonological training programs had a major impact on children's reading skills (Bus & van IJzendoorn, 1999).

For many years, the debate between the whole-word supporters and the phonics supporters was feverish (McGuinness, 2004; Smith, 2004). In the current decade, however, most educators and researchers support some form of a compromise: Children should be taught to use phonics to access the pronunciation of a word; they should also use context as a backup to confirm their initial hypothesis. Even the strongest phonics supporters would also agree that teachers should encourage children to recognize some words by sight alone.

Furthermore, educators typically favor some components of an approach called the whole-language approach (as opposed to the whole-word approach). According to the **whole-language approach,** reading instruction should emphasize meaning, and it should be enjoyable, to increase children's enthusiasm about learning to read. Children should read interesting stories and experiment with writing before they are expert spellers. They should also use reading throughout their classroom experiences (Luria, 2006; McGuinness, 2004; Snow & Juel, 2005).

Before we leave this section on reading, however, we need to emphasize an important point. This discussion assumes that children and adults have had the opportunity to learn how to read. In Canada and the United States, about 98% of adults have achieved basic literacy (Luria, 2006). However, the reality is that more than 800 million adults throughout the world are illiterate. Approximately two-thirds of these individuals are women. Clearly, people who cannot read face tremendous disadvantages with respect to employment, health care, and everyday communication.

⊚ Section Summary: *Basic Reading Processes*

1. Reading is a challenging cognitive task that differs from understanding spoken language in many respects. For example, readers can control the rate of input and they can re-scan the text, and writing shows clear-cut boundaries between words.

2. Readers often use a variety of contextual cues to determine the meaning of an unfamiliar word.

3. Working memory helps readers decode ambiguous sentences and understand complex sentences.

4. Working memory plays a critical role in processing ambiguous or complicated sentences.

5. The dual-route approach argues that readers sometimes recognize a word directly from the printed letters (i.e., direct access), and sometimes they convert the printed letters into a phonological code to access the word (i.e., indirect access).

6. The whole-word approach emphasizes visual recognition of words, whereas the phonics approach emphasizes sounding out the word. Most educators and researchers favor a combination of these approaches.

7. The whole-*language* approach emphasizes language meaning, as well as integrating reading throughout the curriculum.

UNDERSTANDING DISCOURSE

We began this chapter with an overview of the nature of language; that overview considered both linguistic theory and the biological basis of language. Then we explored basic reading processes. You'll notice that these topics all focus on the way we process small units of language, such as a phoneme, a letter, a word, or an isolated sentence. In your daily life, however, you are continually processing connected **discourse,** or language units that are larger than a sentence (Bamberg & Moissinac, 2003; Treiman et al., 2003). You listen to the news on the radio, you hear a friend telling a story, you follow the instructions for assembling a bookcase . . . and you read your cognitive psychology textbook.

In Chapters 1 and 8, we considered Frederick Bartlett's (1932) research, which focused on these larger linguistic units. Specifically, Bartlett demonstrated that people's recall of stories becomes more consistent with their schemas after a long delay. For the next four decades, psychologists and linguists concentrated primarily on words and isolated sentences. In fact, the topic of discourse processing was not revived until the mid-1970s (Butcher & Kintsch, 2003; Graesser et al., 2003b).

So far in this chapter, we've emphasized how context can help us understand sounds, letters, and words. Now we'll see that context also helps us comprehend larger linguistic units. As Chapter 8 explained, general background knowledge and expertise help to facilitate our conceptual understanding. Research on discourse comprehension also emphasizes the importance of expertise, scripts, and schemas (e.g., Mayer, 2004; Zwaan & Rapp, 2006). At all levels of language comprehension, we see additional evidence of Theme 5. That is, the processing of the physical stimuli (bottom-up processing) interacts with the context provided by our expectations and previous knowledge (top-down processing). This interaction is especially prominent when we form an integrated, cohesive representation of the text and when we draw inferences during reading.

Our exploration of discourse comprehension focuses on the following selected topics: (1) forming an integrated representation of the text, (2) drawing inferences during reading, (3) teaching metacomprehension skills, (4) test anxiety and discourse comprehension, and (5) artificial intelligence and reading.

Forming an Integrated Representation of the Text

Reading comprehension is much more complicated than simply fitting words and phrases together. Readers must also gather information together and remember the various concepts so that the message is both integrated and stable (Zwaan & Rapp, 2006). We should note that listeners—as well as readers—form integrated representations, remember the material, and draw inferences when they hear spoken language (e.g., Butcher & Kintsch, 2003; Marslen-Wilson et al., 1993). However, virtually all the research examines discourse processing during reading.

We use subtle cues when we form an integrated representation (Zwaan & Rapp, 2006). Look back at Demonstration 9.4 and the description of Gernsbacher and Robertson's (2005) study on pages 302–303. These researchers demonstrated that readers are attuned to subtle linguistic evidence. Specifically, readers realize that a series of sentences forms a cohesive story if all the sentences begin with the word *the*, but not when the sentences begin with *a*.

Furthermore, when we form an integrated representation, we often construct mental models of the material we are reading (Long et al., 2006; Zwaan & Rapp, 2006). In Chapter 7, for example, we saw that people construct mental models based on a written description of an environment. Similarly, readers construct internal representations that include descriptions of the characters in a story. This descriptive information may include the characters' occupations, relationships, emotional states, personal traits, goals, and actions (Carpenter et al., 1995; Trabasso et al., 1995).

Readers often need to maintain this internal representation in long-term memory for many pages of a novel (Butcher & Kintsch, 2003; Gerrig & McKoon, 2001; Kintsch, 1998). In addition, they often make inferences that go beyond the information supplied by the writer. Let's consider this topic in more detail.

Drawing Inferences During Reading

I recently read a novel called *The Kite Runner*. The novel follows two young boys grow-ing up in Kabul, Afghanistan. Amir, the protagonist, is the son of a wealthy, influential man named Baba. Amir's friend, Hassan, lives nearby in the home of Baba's servant. Readers do not need to have a sophisticated knowledge about either social class in Afghanistan or the series of tragic political wars in this country. Even before we finish the first chapter, we know that the friendship between Amir and Hassan must have an unhappy ending. Whenever we read, we activate important mental processes by going beyond the information presented on the printed page.

When we make an **inference** during reading, we draw on our world knowledge in order to activate information that is not explicitly stated in a written passage (Lea et al., 2005; Zwaan & Singer, 2003). We discussed inferences in Chapter 8 in connection with the influence of schemas on memory. People combine their information about the world with the information presented in a passage, and they draw a reasonable conclusion based on that combination. Consistent with Theme 1, people are active information processors.

Let's explore several issues that have been raised in connection with inferences dur-ing reading. First, we'll consider the constructionist view. Then we'll discuss factors that encourage inferences. Our final topic is higher-level inferences. Incidentally, try Demonstration 9.8 before you read further.

◉ Demonstration 9.8

Reading a Passage of Text

Read the following passage, and notice whether it seems to flow smoothly and logically:

1. Dick had a week's vacation due
2. and he wanted to go to a place
3. where he could swim and sunbathe.
4. He bought a book on travel.
5. Then he looked at the ads
6. in the travel section of the Sunday newspaper.
7. He went to his local travel agent
8. and asked for a plane ticket to Alaska.
9. He paid for it with his charge card.

Source: Based on Huitema et al., 1993, p. 1054.

The Constructionist View of Inferences. According to the **constructionist view of inferences,** readers usually draw inferences about the causes of events and the relationships between events. When you read a novel, for instance, you construct inferences about a character's motivations, personality, and emotions. You develop expectations about new plot developments, about the writer's point of view, and so forth (Sternberg & Ben-Zeev, 2001; Zwaan & Rapp, 2006). This perspective is a "constructionist view" because readers actively construct explanations as they integrate the current information with all the relevant information from the previous parts of the text, as well as their background knowledge (O'Brien & Myers, 1999; Zwaan & Singer, 2003). The constructionist view argues that people typically draw inferences, even when the related topics are separated by several irrelevant paragraphs.

Let's consider some research by John Huitema and his coauthors (1993), who studied brief stories like the one you read in Demonstration 9.8. The introductory material in this demonstration leads you to believe that Dick will soon be lounging on a sunny beach. You drew this inference on line 3, and this inference is contradicted five lines later, rather than in the very next sentence. The dependent variable here was the amount of time that participants had taken to read the crucial line about Dick's travel destination (line 8).

Huitema and his colleagues (1993) tested four conditions. You saw the far/inconsistent version of the story, in which several lines of text separated the sentence stating the goal from the inconsistent statement. In the near/inconsistent version, the goal and the inconsistent statement were in adjacent sentences. In the far/consistent version, several lines of text separated the goal and a consistent statement (in which Dick asked for a plane ticket to Florida—a place consistent with swimming). In the near/consistent version, the goal and the consistent statement were in adjacent sentences.

As you can see from Figure 9.3, participants in the near condition read the inconsistent version significantly more slowly than the consistent version. This finding is not surprising. However, you'll notice that participants also read the inconsistent version significantly more slowly than the consistent version in the far condition, when the relevant portions of the task were separated by four intervening lines.

The data from Huitema and his colleagues (1993) support the constructionist view. Readers clearly try to connect material within a text passage, and they consult information stored in long-term memory. During discourse processing, we try to construct a representation of the text that is internally consistent—even when irrelevant material intervenes (Klin et al., 1999; Rayner & Clifton, 2002; Underwood & Batt, 1996).

In other research, readers talk out loud about the text passages they are reading (Suh & Trabasso, 1993; Trabasso & Suh, 1993). In some of these stories, the main character had an initial goal that was blocked but later fulfilled. About 90% of the participants specifically mentioned the initial goal during their comments about the last line. Suh and Trabasso argue that readers create causal inferences in order to integrate discourse and construct a well-organized story.

Factors That Encourage Inferences. Naturally, we do not always draw inferences when we read a passage. For instance, individual differences among readers are important (Zwaan & Rapp, 2006). Readers may fail to activate information that appeared

FIGURE 9.3

Amount of Time Taken to Read the Crucial Line in the Study by Huitema and His Colleagues (1993), as a Function of the Amount of Separation Between the Goal and the Crucial Line and the Compatibility Between the Goal and the Crucial Line (consistent vs. inconsistent).

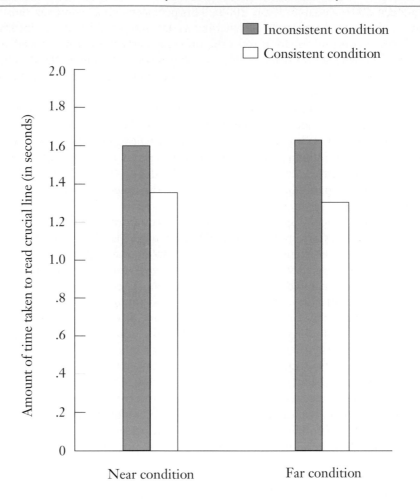

Source: Based on Huitema et al., 1993.

much earlier in the passage (Lea et al., 2005; Long et al., 2006). As you might expect, people are likely to synthesize information and draw inferences if they have a large working-memory capacity (Butcher & Kintsch, 2003; Long et al., 2006). They are also likely to draw inferences if they have excellent metacomprehension skills. These individuals are aware that they must search for connections between two seemingly unrelated sentences (Ehrlich, 1998; Mayer, 2004).

People are also likely to draw inferences if they have background information or expertise about the topic described in the text (Long et al., 2006). In fact, expertise in an area can compensate for a relatively small working-memory capacity (Butcher & Kintsch, 2003). Other research shows that people often fail to construct inferences when they are reading scientific texts (Mayer, 2004; Millis & Graesser, 1994).

This part of our discussion has focused on factors that affect inferences, and we have seen that some inferences are more probable than others. In explaining these factors, however, let's recall an important point from Chapter 8: We are sometimes just as likely to remember our inferences as to remember statements that actually occurred in the text. Our inferences blend with the text, forming a cohesive story. We often retain the gist or general meaning of a passage, forgetting that we constructed some elements that did not actually appear in the story.

Higher-Level Inferences.   Researchers are now exploring higher-level inferences, beyond the level of the paragraph. For example, different genres of books often activate different expectations. Fans of the *Harry Potter* series—and other magical stories—know that they must suspend their everyday schemas. Of course Hermione can arrange to be in two places at the same time, and of course Harry can understand conversations between snakes.

One kind of higher-level inference is based on our own preferences about the way we want a story to turn out. Perhaps you've turned the pages of a fast-paced spy novel and mentally shouted to your favorite character, "Watch out!" In fact, the research shows that readers who are involved in a story do develop strong mental preferences for a particular outcome (Allbritton & Gerrig, 1991; Rapp & Gerrig, 2006).

These mental preferences can be so strong that they can actually interfere with readers' ability to judge how the story turned out, making us pause as we try to decide whether that unhappy ending really did occur (Gerrig, 1998; Zwaan & Rapp, 2006). You may even find yourself so hopeful about a happy ending you've constructed that you need to read the final sentences several times, trying to convince yourself that the hero or heroine didn't die!

In summary, people often draw inferences when they read. They integrate material into a cohesive unit, and they are puzzled if they encounter something that contradicts the inferences they drew. People are especially likely to draw inferences if they have a large working-memory capacity or expertise. Inferences may be relatively rare in scientific texts and relatively common in novels.

Teaching Metacomprehension Skills

In the second section of this chapter, our discussion of reading instruction examined how educators can teach basic reading skills to young children. Let's now briefly consider how educators can teach older students some important metacomprehension skills.

Chapter 6 focused on the general topic of **metacognition**, which is your knowledge about your cognitive processes, as well as your control of these cognitive processes. An important part of metacognition is **metacomprehension,** a term that refers to your thoughts about comprehension.

Most young children do not have the cognitive skills to engage in metacomprehension; it's challenging enough to read individual words and sentences (Baker, 2005; Griffith & Ruan, 2005). However, older children, teenagers, and adults can contemplate their reading strategies. For instance, when you read a book, you know that you should think about your relevant background knowledge. In addition, you consider whether you should read every sentence or else skim through the details. You also know that you should monitor whether you understand the material you have just read (Griffith & Ruan, 2005; Perfetti et al., 2005). Furthermore, you sometimes become aware that your mind has wandered away from the material you are reading (Smallwood & Schooler, 2006).

In the past, educators seldom trained students to develop their metacomprehension skills (Randi et al., 2005). However, they are currently developing methods to help students benefit from these skills. For instance, teachers can instruct students in middle school to think out loud, so that they can summarize passages, make predictions about possible outcomes, and describe puzzling sections (Israel & Massey, 2005; Schreiber, 2005; Wolfe & Goldman, 2005). Let's now consider how readers' anxiety level may influence their reading skills.

Individual Differences: Test Anxiety and Reading Comprehension

According to numerous studies, people who are high in test anxiety often perform poorly on examinations (Cassady, 2004). Psychologists have usually attributed this poor performance to high levels of worry. The traditional explanation is that worry intrudes on people's consciousness, blocking them from retrieving the correct answers on a test. However, Jerrell Cassady (2004) proposes that test anxiety also decreases students' skills in understanding the information in their textbooks.

Cassady examined the link between anxiety and discourse comprehension by instructing 277 undergraduate students to read several paragraphs from a textbook, and then to read it a second time. Next, everyone completed a measure called the Cognitive Test Anxiety scale, followed by a multiple-choice test on the earlier textbook material. The students then repeated this procedure with a comparable passage from a different textbook. However, instead of the Cognitive Test Anxiety scale, the students completed a study-skills survey prior to the multiple-choice test.

Cassady found that scores on the Cognitive Test Anxiety scale were strongly correlated ($r = -.55$) with performance on the multiple-choice tests. In other words, people who are highly anxious tend to perform poorly on a reading-comprehension test. Scores on the Cognitive Test Anxiety scale were also strongly correlated ($r = -.66$) with scores on the study-skills survey. In other words, people who are highly anxious tend to report poorer study skills. However—surprisingly—study skills were not strongly correlated with recall on the multiple-choice test ($r = .24$).

In a second, similar study, Cassady (2004) found that people with high scores on the Cognitive Test Anxiety scale also made more errors in summarizing the textbook material. These people also made more errors on a test that assessed their ability to make correct inferences, based on the textbook material.

In summary, when people are highly anxious about taking tests, they may experience interference from high levels of worry. In addition, however, they perform poorly on a variety of tasks related to reading comprehension. Specifically, they make more errors than low-anxiety individuals when taking multiple-choice tests, summarizing the textbook material, and drawing inferences from that material.

Artificial Intelligence and Reading

As discussed in Chapter 1, **artificial intelligence (AI)** is the area of computer science that attempts to construct computers that can demonstrate human-like cognitive processes (Stenning et al., 2006). The goal of AI is to develop computer programs that will perform tasks that appear to be intelligent, such as language comprehension or conversations (Graesser et al., 2004; Kintsch et al., 2007; McNamara et al., 2007).

When developing AI models of language, researchers assume that computers start off with no knowledge whatsoever about natural language. **Natural language** is ordinary human language with all its sloppiness, ambiguities, and complexities. The researchers have to write into the program all the information that is necessary to make the computer behave as if it understands sentences typed on its keyboard. The program must be in the form of detailed instructions (Harley, 2001; Sobel, 2001).

The FRUMP Project. Let's consider a classic example of a computer program designed to perform reading tasks. One script-based program is called **FRUMP,** an acronym for Fast Reading Understanding and Memory Program (De Jong, 1982). The goal of FRUMP is to summarize newspaper stories, written in ordinary language. When it was developed, FRUMP could interpret about 10% of news releases issued by United Press International (Butcher & Kintsch, 2003; Kintsch, 1984). FRUMP usually worked in a top-down fashion by applying world knowledge, based on 48 different scripts.

Consider, for example, the "vehicle accident" script. The script contains information such as the number of people killed, the number of people injured, and the cause of the accident. On the basis of the "vehicle accident" script, FRUMP summarized a news article as follows: "A vehicle accident occurred in Colorado. A plane hit the ground. 1 person died." FRUMP did manage to capture the facts of the story. However, it missed the major reason that the item was newsworthy: Yes, 1 person was killed, but 21 people actually survived!

Research on script-based programs like FRUMP show that humans draw numerous inferences that artificial intelligence systems cannot access (Kintsch, 1998, 2007). We can be impressed that FRUMP and other programs can manage some language-like processes. However, consistent with Theme 2, their errors highlight the wide-ranging capabilities of human readers (Thagard, 2005).

More Recent Projects. Cognitive scientists continue to develop programs designed to understand language (Moore & Wiemer-Hastings, 2003; Shermis & Burstein, 2003; Wolfe et al., 2005). One of the most useful artificial intelligence programs was created by cognitive psychologist Thomas Landauer and his colleagues (Foltz, 2003; Landauer et al., 2007). Their program, called **latent semantic analysis (LSA),** can perform many fairly sophisticated language tasks. For instance, it can also be programmed to provide tutoring sessions in disciplines such as physics (Graesser et al., 2004).

LSA can also assess the amount of semantic similarity between two discourse segments. In fact, LSA can even be used to grade essays written by college students (Graesser et al., 2007). For example, suppose a textbook contains the following sentence: "The phonological loop responds to the phonetic characteristics of speech but does not evaluate speech for semantic content" (Butcher & Kintsch, 2003, p. 551).

Now imagine that two students are writing a short essay on working memory, for a cognitive psychology exam. With reference to that passage, Chris writes, "The rehearsal loop that practices speech sounds does not pick up meaning in words. Rather, it just reacts whenever it hears something that sounds like language." On the same exam, Pat writes, "The loop that listens to the words does not understand anything about the phonetic noises that it hears. All it does is listen for noise and then respond by practicing that noise."

LSA's analysis of those essays concluded that Chris's essay is a more accurate summary of the original text than Pat's essay. If you recall the information from Chapter 4, you'll agree with LSA's conclusion.

LSA is indeed impressive, but even its developers note that it cannot match a human grader. For instance, it cannot assess a student's creativity when writing an essay (Murray, 1998). Furthermore, all the current programs master just a small component of language comprehension. For example, LSA typically ignores syntax, whereas humans can easily detect syntax errors. In addition, LSA learns only from written text, whereas humans learn from spoken language, facial expressions, and physical gestures (Butcher & Kintsch, 2003). Once again, the artificial intelligence approach to language illustrates humans' tremendous breadth of knowledge, cognitive flexibility, understanding of syntax, and sources of information.

Section Summary: *Understanding Discourse*

1. Psycholinguists are increasingly focusing on discourse processing, or language units that are larger than a sentence.

2. Readers try to form integrated representations of discourse by using subtle cues, mental models, long-term memory, and inferences.

3. According to the constructionist view, people actively draw inferences that connect parts of the text, even though the parts may be widely separated.

4. Inferences are especially likely when people have large working-memory capacity, excellent metacomprehension skills, and expertise in the area. People also draw higher-level inferences beyond the level of the paragraph.

5. Educators are beginning to emphasize teaching metacomprehension skills to older children and teenagers.

6. Compared to people who are low in test anxiety, people who are high in test anxiety typically make more errors on multiple-choice tests, in summarizing textbook material, and in drawing inferences from a textbook.

7. An artificial intelligence program called FRUMP can create reasonably accurate summaries of newspaper stories. A more recent program called latent

semantic analysis (LSA) can assess the similarity between two passages of text. The relatively narrow scope of LSA highlights humans' competence in a wide variety of reading tasks.

CHAPTER REVIEW QUESTIONS

1. Why is language one of the most impressive human accomplishments? In what ways does it illustrate the interrelated nature of our cognitive processes?

2. The section on factors affecting comprehension emphasized that we have more difficulty understanding sentences if they are in the passive voice, instead of the active voice. Referring to the cognitive-functional approach, why would we occasionally choose to create a sentence such as "The window was broken by Fred"?

3. What does the information on aphasia, hemispheric specialization, and brain-imaging techniques tell us about the regions of the brain that play a role in understanding and producing language?

4. Context is an important concept throughout this chapter. Explain how context is important in (a) processing an ambiguous word, (b) discovering the meaning of an unfamiliar word, (c) background knowledge in understanding discourse, and (d) artificial intelligence approaches to language comprehension.

5. Throughout this chapter, we emphasized that memory contributes to language comprehension. Using the chapter outline as your guide, specify how both working memory and long-term memory are essential when we try to understand language.

6. Describe how the dual-route hypothesis explains how you recognize the words you are reading. If you can recall how you were taught to read, figure out whether that method emphasized the whole-word approach or the phonics approach.

7. Describe the constructionist view of inference discussed in the last section of this chapter. Think about several kinds of reading tasks you have performed in the last two days. Be sure to include examples other than reading your textbook. Point out how the constructionist perspective would be relevant during each discourse-processing task.

8. Review the section on metacomprehension skills, and describe how you can apply these strategies to improve your own reading skills.

9. Many parts of this chapter emphasized individual differences. Summarize this information, and speculate how individual differences might also be relevant in other aspects of language comprehension.

10. This chapter discussed both listening and reading. Compare these two kinds of language tasks. Which processes are similar, and which are different? In preparation for Chapter 10, compare speech production and writing in a similar fashion.

KEYWORDS

psycholinguistics
phoneme
morpheme
morphology
syntax
grammar
semantics
semantic memory
pragmatics
phrase structure
constituents
modular (language)
surface structure
deep structure
ambiguous sentences

cognitive-functional approach
usage-based linguistics
nested structure
neurolinguistics
aphasia
Broca's area
Broca's aphasia
Wernicke's area
Wernicke's aphasia
lateralization
functional magnetic resonance
  imaging (fMRI)
dual-route approach
  to reading
direct-access route

indirect-access route
whole-word approach
phonics approach
whole-language approach
discourse
inference
constructionist view of
  inferences
metacognition
metacomprehension
artificial intelligence (AI)
natural language
FRUMP
latent semantic analysis (LSA)

RECOMMENDED READINGS

Graesser, A. C., Gernsbacher, M. A., & Goldman, S. R. (Eds.). (2003a). *Handbook of discourse processes.* Mahwah, NJ: Erlbaum. Here's a superb handbook that includes thirteen chapters on a variety of topics related to discourse processing.

Snowling, M. J., & Hulme, C. (Eds.). (2005). *The science of reading: A handbook.* Malden, MA: Blackwell. I strongly recommend this volume, which covers topics such as word recognition, reading disorders, reading comprehension, and reading in different languages.

Traxler, M. A., & Gernsbacher, M. A. (Eds.). (2006). *Handbook of psycholinguistics* (2nd ed.). Amsterdam: Elsevier. This advanced-level handbook contains twenty-one chapters on language comprehension, in addition to other chapters on language production and language development.

Williams, J. D. (2005). *The teacher's grammar book.* Mahwah, NJ: Erlbaum. Most books on the psychology of language are difficult to understand. This was the most reader-friendly description I found for information on topics that would be useful for undergraduates who are interested in linguistics.

ANSWER TO DEMONSTRATION 9.1

Chapter 2: Visual recognition allows you to see letters and words, and auditory recognition allows you to hear phonemes and words. Chapter 3: Divided attention can permit you to take in information about two simultaneous verbal messages, whereas selective attention encourages you to pay attention to one message and ignore the other; saccadic eye movements are important in reading. Chapter 4: Working memory helps you store the stimuli (either visual or auditory) long enough to process and interpret them. Chapter 5: Long-term memory allows you to retrieve information you processed long ago. Chapter 6: The tip-of-the-tongue phenomenon means that you will sometimes be unable to access certain words, whereas metacomprehension allows you to determine whether you understand a verbal message. Chapter 7: You create mental models when you process a description about a spatial layout. Chapter 8: Semantic memory stores the meaning of words and the relationships between concepts, whereas schemas and scripts provide background knowledge for processing language. *Note:* Additional answers are also possible.

CHAPTER 10
Producing Language

PREVIEW

Chapter 9 examined language comprehension (listening and reading). In contrast, Chapter 10 focuses on language production, including speaking, writing, and bilingualism.

Our ability to produce spoken words and sentences is an impressive accomplishment. For example, we need to plan how to arrange the words in an orderly sequence within a sentence. Most of our spoken language is linguistically accurate, but we sometimes make speech errors such as slips-of-the-tongue. When we tell a story, the narrative typically follows a specific structure. The social context of speech is also crucial; for example, speakers must be certain that their conversational partners share the same background knowledge.

Writing is an important activity for college students and many professionals. Psychologists have developed a cognitive model of writing, which emphasizes working memory. Writing consists of three tasks that often overlap in time: planning, sentence generation, and revision. Novice writers typically write their ideas in a rather random order; in contrast, expert writers use metacognition to monitor their writing. One clinical application of the research focuses on writing about emotional problems.

Bilingualism is a topic that demonstrates how humans can master listening, reading, speaking, and writing in two or more languages. Therefore, the topic of bilingualism is an appropriate conclusion to our two-chapter exploration of language. Bilingual people seem to have a number of advantages over those who are monolingual. For example, they may be especially skilled on tasks where they must ignore an obvious response and focus on more subtle information. Compared with adults, children may learn to speak a second language with a less pronounced accent. However, adults and children are similar in their acquisition of vocabulary in that second language. There are also no consistent differences between adults and children with respect to their mastery of grammar in a second language. Finally, people who work as simultaneous interpreters are likely to have outstanding working-memory skills.

INTRODUCTION

Consider the number of ways in which you have produced language today. Unless you are reading this chapter very early in the morning, you may have greeted a friend, talked to someone at breakfast, spoken on the telephone, taken notes on a reading assignment, sent an e-mail, or written a reminder to yourself.

Language is probably the most social of all our cognitive processes (Turnbull, 2003). Its social nature is especially obvious when we consider language production. Except for the notes and comments we make to ourselves, we are usually producing language that is designed to influence other people (Guerin, 2003).

Now consider another aspect of language production: Every sentence that is comprehended by one person must have been produced by somebody else. If psychologists distributed their research equitably, we would know just as much about language production as we know about language comprehension. Furthermore, Chapter 10 would be just as long as Chapter 9.

However, psychologists have tended to study language comprehension, rather than language production. One reason researchers ignore language production is that they cannot typically manipulate the ideas that an individual wishes to say or write. In contrast, they can easily manipulate the text that a person hears or reads (Carroll, 2004; Fromkin & Bernstein Ratner, 1998).

Fortunately, however, psychologists are becoming somewhat more interested in the components of language production (e.g, Clark & Van Der Wege, 2002; Dell, 2005; Fowler, 2003; Meyer, 2004; Wheeldon, 2000). For example, a representative study showed that language comprehension and language production are equally likely to interfere with college students' driving ability (Kubose et al., 2005).

Let us begin by examining spoken language, and then we'll consider written language. Our final topic, bilingualism, employs all the impressive skills of both language comprehension and language production, so it will serve as the final section of these two chapters on language.

SPEAKING

Every day, most of us spend several hours telling stories, chatting, quarreling, talking on the telephone, and speaking to ourselves. Even when we listen, we produce supportive comments such as "yeah" and "mm hm" (Gardner, 2001). Indeed, speaking is one of our most complex cognitive and motor skills (Bock & Griffin, 2000; Dell, 2005). In this section of the chapter, we will first examine how we produce both individual words and sentences. Then we'll examine some common speech errors. Finally, we'll move beyond the sentence as we examine the production of discourse and the social context of speech.

Producing a Word

Like many cognitive processes, word production does not initially seem remarkable. After all, you simply open your mouth and a word emerges effortlessly. Word production becomes impressive, however, once we analyze the dimensions of the task. As we noted in Chapter 9, we can produce about two or three words each second (Levelt et al., 1999; Vigliocco & Hartsuiker, 2002). Furthermore, the average college-educated North American has a speaking vocabulary of at least 75,000 words (Bock & Garnsey, 1998; Wingfield, 1993). When you are talking, then, you must select at least two words every second from your extensive storehouse of at least 75,000 words!

Furthermore, you must choose a word accurately, so that its grammatical, semantic, and phonological information are all correct (Cutting & Ferreira, 1999; Rapp & Goldrick, 2000). As Bock and Griffin (2000) point out, many factors "complicate the journey from mind to mouth" (p. 39).

Word production is an especially active topic of research within the area of language production. An important, unresolved controversy focuses on the process of retrieving grammatical, semantic, and phonological information. Some researchers argue that speakers retrieve all three kinds of information at the same time (Damian & Martin, 1999; Saffran & Schwartz, 2003). According to this approach, for example, you look at an apple and simultaneously access the grammatical properties of *apple*, the meaning of *apple*, and the phonemes in the word *apple*.

Other researchers argue that we access each kind of information independently, with little interaction among them (Levelt et al., 1999; Pickering & Branigan, 1998; Roelofs & Baayen, 2002). For example, van Turennout and her colleagues (1998) conducted research with Dutch-speaking individuals. Dutch resembles languages such as Spanish, French, and German, in which nouns have a grammatical gender. These researchers presented pictures of objects and animals, and the participants tried to name the object as quickly as possible. Using the event-related potential technique (see pages 15 to 16), the researchers demonstrated that the speakers accessed the grammatical gender of the word about 40 milliseconds before the phonological properties of the word. These results suggest that the different kinds of information are not accessed exactly simultaneously, but with literally split-second timing.

When we produce a word, we execute elaborate motor movements of the mouth and other parts of the vocal system (Fowler, 2003). We often accompany our speech with **gestures,** which are spontaneous movements of fingers, hands, and arms (Jacobs & Garnham, 2007; McNeill, 2005). Interestingly, these motor movements of your hands can sometimes help you remember the word you want to produce (Carroll, 2004; Griffin, 2004).

In a representative study, Frick-Horbury and Guttentag (1998) read the definitions for 50 low-frequency, concrete English nouns. For example, the definition "a pendulum-like instrument designed to mark exact time by regular ticking" (p. 59) was supposed to suggest the noun *metronome*. Notice, then, that this technique resembles the tip-of-the-tongue research described in Chapter 6.

In Frick-Horbury and Guttentag's (1998) study, however, half of the participants had their hand movements restricted; they had to hold a rod with both hands. These individuals produced an average of 19 words. In contrast, the participants with unrestricted hand movements produced an average of 24 words. According to the researchers, when our verbal system is unable to retrieve a word, gestures may sometimes activate relevant information.

Other studies suggest that our eyes are often active during speech production. For example, people tend to look at an object about 1 second before naming it (Griffin, 2004; Meyer, 2004).

Producing a Sentence

Every time you produce a sentence, you must overcome the limits of your memory and attention in order to plan and deliver that sentence (Bock & Huitema, 1999; Griffin, 2004). Speech production requires a series of stages. We begin by mentally planning the **gist,** or the overall meaning, of the message we intend to generate. In other words, we begin by producing speech in a top-down fashion (Clark & Van Der Wege, 2002; Griffin & Ferreira, 2006).

During the second stage, we devise the general structure of the sentence, without selecting the exact words. In the third stage, we choose the specific words we want, abandoning other semantically similar words (Griffin & Ferreira, 2006). We also select the appropriate grammatical form, such as *eating*, rather than *eat*. In the fourth and final stage, we convert these intentions into speech by articulating the phonemes (Carroll, 2004; Treiman et al., 2003).

As you might expect, the stages of sentence production typically overlap in time. We often begin to plan the final part of a sentence before we have pronounced the first part of that sentence (Fowler, 2003; Treiman et al., 2003).

Under ideal circumstances, a speaker moves rapidly through these four stages. For instance, Griffin and Bock (2000) showed college students a simple cartoon. In less than 2 seconds, the students began to produce a description such as, "The turtle is squirting the mouse with water."

However, we often hesitate as we plan what we intend to say. English speakers often mumble an *um* or an *uh*. These pauses are longer for lengthy utterances. In general, these pauses occupy about half of our speaking time (Arnold et al., 2004; Bock, 1999; Ferreira & Engelhardt, 2006).

We often tackle an important problem when we are planning a sentence. We may have a general thought that we want to express. At other times we may have a mental image that needs to be described. These rather shapeless thoughts and images must be translated into a statement that has a disciplined, linear shape, with words following one another in time. This problem of arranging words in an ordered, linear sequence is called the **linearization problem** (Fox Tree, 2000; Griffin, 2004; Levelt, 1994). Try noticing how linearization usually occurs quite effortlessly. Consistent with Theme 2, you typically speak both rapidly and accurately. However, you may occasionally find yourself struggling, trying to describe several ideas simultaneously, at the very beginning of a description.

The speech-production process is more complex than you might initially imagine. For example, we must also plan the **prosody** of an utterance, or the "melody" of its intonation, rhythm, and emphasis (Keating, 2006; Plack, 2005; Speer & Blodgett, 2006). A speaker can use prosody to clarify an ambiguous message. For example, read the following two sentences out loud: (a) "What's that ahead in the road?" and (b) "What's that, a head in the road?" (Speer & Blodgett, 2006, p. 505). Notice how the prosody differs for these two examples.

When you actually speak a sentence, more than 100 different muscles must coordinate their interactions (Levelt, 1994). As you might expect, different languages require unique movements of the tongue, the lips, and other vocal equipment (Butcher, 2006; Harrington & Tabain, 2006). Let's now consider the nature of the speech errors we occasionally make, as well as the production of discourse that is longer than a sentence.

Speech Errors

The speech that most people produce is generally very accurate and well formed, consistent with Theme 2. In spontaneous language samples, people make an error less than once every 500 sentences (Dell, Burger, & Svec, 1997; Vigliocco & Hartsuiker, 2002).

However, some high-status speakers—including U.S. presidents—often make speech errors. For instance, the speech errors of President George W. Bush have been widely reported (e.g., Miller, 2001; Workman Publishing Company, 2007). In a talk in Washington, D.C., he announced, "This very week in 1989, there were protests in East Berlin and in Leipzig. By the end of that year, every communist dictatorship in Central America had collapsed" (November 6, 2003). Speaking on National Public Radio, President Bush said, "And there is distrust in Washington. I am surprised, frankly, at the amount of distrust that exists in this town. And I'm sorry it's the case, and I'll work hard to try to elevate it" (January 29, 2007).

Researchers have been particularly interested in the kind of speech errors called slips-of-the-tongue. **Slips-of-the-tongue** are errors in which sounds or entire words are rearranged between two or more different words. These slips of the tongue are helpful because they reveal people's extensive knowledge about the sounds, structure, and meaning of the language they are speaking (Dell et al., 2008).

Types of Slip-of-the-Tongue Errors. Gary Dell and his coauthors propose that three kinds of slips-of-the-tongue are especially common in English (Dell, 1995; Dell et al., 2008):

1. Sound errors, which occur when sounds in nearby words are exchanged—for example, *snow flurries* → *flow snurries.*
2. Morpheme errors, which occur when **morphemes** (the smallest meaningful units in language, such as *-ly* or *in-*) are exchanged in nearby words—for example, *self-destruct instruction* → *self-instruct destruction.*
3. Word errors, which occur when words are exchanged—for example, *writing a letter to my mother* → *writing a mother to my letter.*

Each of these three kinds of errors can take several forms, in addition to the exchange errors listed above. For example, people make anticipation errors (*reading list* → *leading list*), perseveration errors (*waking rabbits* → *waking wabbits*), and deletions (*same state* → *same sate*). Anticipatory errors are especially common, because we are likely to be planning ahead, rather than reflecting on the words we have already said. Errors also occur more often when the stimulus includes two consonants, such as *st* or *tr* (Schiller, 2005).

Furthermore, we are likely to create a word (e.g., *leading*), rather than a nonword (e.g., *wabbit)* when we make a slip-of-the-tongue error (Griffin & Ferreira, 2006; Rapp & Goldrick, 2000). Finally, we seldom create a word that begins with an unlikely letter sequence; an English speaker rarely creates a slip-of-the-tongue such as *dlorm* when trying to say *dorm* (Dell et al., 2000). These two principles reflect the importance of our knowledge about the English language and Theme 5's emphasis on top-down processing (Dell et al., 2008).

In almost all cases, the errors occur across items from the same category (Carroll, 2004; Clark & Van Der Wege, 2002; Fowler, 2003). For instance, in sound errors, initial consonants interchange with other initial consonants (as in the *flow snurries* example). In morpheme errors, prefixes interchange with other prefixes (as in the *self-instruct* example).

In word errors, people interchange members of the same grammatical category (as in the *mother to my letter* example). The pattern of these errors suggests that the words we are currently pronouncing are influenced by both the words we have already spoken and the words we are planning to speak (Dell, Burger, & Svec, 1997).

Dell and his colleagues propose an elaborate and comprehensive theory for speech errors that is similar to the connectionist approach and includes the concept of spreading activation (Dell, 1986, 1995, 2005; Dell, Burger & Svec, 1997; Dell et al., 1997; Dell et al., 2008). Let us consider a brief overview of how you might produce a sound error. When you are about to speak, each element of the word you are planning to say will activate the sound elements to which it is linked. For example, Figure 10.1 shows how the words in the tongue twister "She sells seashells" might activate each of the six sounds in the last word, *seashells.*

Usually, we utter the sounds that are most highly activated, and usually these sounds are the appropriate ones. However, each sound can be activated by several different words. Notice, for example, that the *sh* sound in the sound-level representation of *seashells* (that is, *seshelz*) is highly "charged" because it receives activation from the first word in the sentence, *she,* as well as the *sh* in *seashells.* As Dell (1986, 1995) emphasizes, incorrect items sometimes have activation levels that are just as high as (or higher than) the correct items. In Figure 10.1, the activation level for *sh* is just as high as the level for *s.* By mistake, a speaker may select an incorrect sound in a sentence, such as "She sells sheashells."

Dell and his colleagues argue that connectionism and spreading activation can predict the pattern of errors in both normal and aphasic speakers (Dell, 2005; Dell et al., 1997; Foygel & Dell, 2000). Basically, speakers sometimes produce sounds that have high activation levels, even though these sounds may not be correct. Try Demonstration 10.1 to determine the form and function of the slips-of-the-tongue that you typically make or hear from other speakers.

FIGURE 10.1

An Example of Dell's Model of Sound Processing in Sentence Production (simplified). See text for explanation.

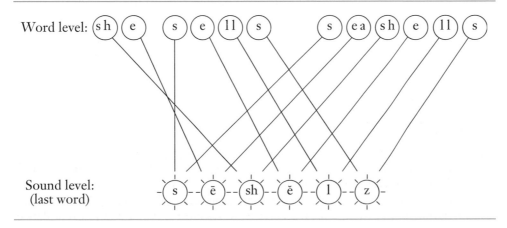

---

⑨ Demonstration 10.1

Slips-of-the-Tongue

Keep a record of all the slips-of-the-tongue that you either hear or make yourself in the next two days. Classify each slip as a sound error, morpheme error, or word error. Furthermore, decide whether the mistake is an exchange error, an anticipation error, or some other type. Also note whether the mistake occurs across items from the same category. Finally, see if you can determine why the mistake occurred, using an analysis similar to Dell's.

Producing Discourse

When we speak, we typically produce **discourse,** or language units that are larger than a sentence (Bamberg & Moissinac, 2003; Treiman et al., 2003). Unfortunately, most of the research on language production focuses on isolated words and sentences (Griffin & Ferreira, 2006).

One category of discourse is the **narrative,** the type of discourse in which someone describes a series of actual or fictional events (Griffin & Ferreira, 2006). The events in a narrative are conveyed in a time-related sequence, and they are often emotionally involving (Guerin, 2003; Schiffrin, 1994; Strömqvist & Verhoeven, 2004). Storytellers have a specific goal that must be conveyed, but they do not completely preplan the organization at the beginning of the story (H. H. Clark, 1994). Storytellers typically choose their words carefully in order to present their own actions in a favorable light (Berger, 1997; Edwards, 1997). They also try to make the story more entertaining (Dudukovic et al., 2004; Marsh & Tversky, 2004).

The format of a narrative is unusual, because it allows the speaker to "hold the floor" for an extended period. During that time, the speaker usually conveys six parts of the narrative: (1) a brief overview of the story, (2) a summary of the characters and setting, (3) an action that made the situation complicated, (4) the point of the story, (5) the resolution of the story, and (6) the final signal that the narrative is complete (for example, ". . . and so that's how I ended up traveling to Colorado with a complete stranger"). These features tend to make the story cohesive and well organized (H. H. Clark, 1994). Now that you know something about the function and structure of narratives, try Demonstration 10.2.

The Social Context of Speech

When we speak, we need to plan the content of our language. We must produce relatively error-free speech, and we must also plan the message of our discourse. In addition to these challenging assignments, we need to be attuned to the social context of speech. Language is really a social instrument (Clark & Van Der Wege, 2002; Guerin, 2003; Schober & Brennan, 2003). In fact, conversation is like a complicated dance

> ### ⑨ Demonstration 10.2
>
> #### The Structure of Narratives
>
> During the next few weeks, try to notice—in your daily conversations—what happens when someone you know begins to tell a story. First, how does the story-teller announce that she or he is about to begin the narrative? Does the structure of the narrative match the six-part sequence we discussed? Does the storyteller attempt to check whether the listeners have the appropriate background knowledge? What other characteristics do you notice that distinguish this kind of discourse from a normal conversation in which people take turns speaking?

(Clark, 1985, 1994). Speakers cannot simply utter words aloud and expect to be understood. Instead, speakers must consider their conversation partners, make numerous assumptions about those partners, and design appropriate utterances.

This complicated dance requires precise coordination. When two people enter a doorway simultaneously, they need to coordinate their motor actions. Similarly, two speakers must coordinate turn taking, they must agree on the meaning of ambiguous terms, and they must understand each other's intentions (Clark & Van Der Wege, 2002). When Helen tells Sam, "The Bakers are on their way," both participants in the conversation need to understand that this is an indirect invitation for Sam to start dinner, rather than to call the police for protection (Clark, 1985).

The knowledge of the social rules that underlie language use is called **pragmatics** (Carroll, 2004). Pragmatics focuses on how speakers successfully communicate messages to their audience. Two important topics in the research on pragmatics are common ground and an understanding of directives.

Common Ground. Suppose that a young man named Andy asks his friend Lisa, "How was your weekend?" and Lisa answers, "It was like being in Conshohocken again." Andy will understand this reply only if they share a similar understanding about the characteristics or events that took place in Conshohocken. In fact, we would expect Lisa to make this remark only if she is certain that she and Andy share the appropriate common ground (Clark & Van Der Wege, 2002; Gerrig & Littman, 1990; Stone, 2005).

Common ground occurs when conversationalists share the similar background knowledge, schemas, and experiences that are necessary for mutual understanding (Clark & Van Der Wege, 2002; Fox Tree, 2000; Hanna & Tanenhaus, 2005). To guarantee conversational coherence, the speakers need to collaborate to make certain that they share common ground with their conversational partners.

For example, speakers should make certain that their listeners are paying attention. Speakers must also avoid ambiguous statements, and they need to clarify any misunderstandings if their listeners look puzzled (Haywood et al., 2005). Speakers also use nonverbal language to clarify their message. For instance, speakers often look at or point to objects they are discussing (Bangerter, 2004; Meyer, 2004).

⊚ Demonstration 10.3

Collaborating to Establish Common Ground

For this demonstration, you need to make two photocopies of the figures below. Then cut the figures apart, keeping each sheet's figures in a separate pile and making certain the dot is at the top of each figure. Now locate two volunteers and a watch that can measure time in seconds. Your volunteers should sit across from each other or at separate tables, with their figures in front of them. Neither person should be able to see the other's figures.

Appoint one person to be the "director" and the other the "matcher." The director should arrange the figures in random order in two rows of six figures each. This person's task is to describe the first figure in enough detail so that the "matcher" is able to identify that figure and place it in Position 1 in front of him or her. The goal is for the matcher to place all twelve figures in the same order as the director's figures. They may use any kind of verbal descriptions they choose, but no gestures or imitation of body position. Record how long it takes them to reach their goal, and then make sure that the figures do match.

Ask them to try the game two more times, with the same person serving as director. Record the times again, and note whether the time decreases on the second and third trials; are the volunteers increasingly efficient in establishing common ground? Do they tend to develop a standard vocabulary (for example, "the ice skater") to refer to a given figure?

One day, our plumber called me from the hardware store, where he was trying to locate some handles for our washbowl faucet. As he described the various models over the telephone, I instantly realized that we were replicating a classic study by Clark and Wilkes-Gibbs (1986) on the collaboration process involved in establishing common ground. Demonstration 10.3 is a modification of their study, in which people worked together to arrange complex figures.

The participants in Clark and Wilkes-Gibbs's (1986) study played this game for six trials; each trial consisted of arranging all twelve figures in order. On the first trial, the director required an average of nearly four turns to describe each figure and make certain that the matcher understood the reference. (A typical "turn" consisted of a statement from the director, followed by a question or a guess from the matcher.) As Figure 10.2 shows, however, the director and the matcher soon developed a mutual shorthand, and the number of required turns decreased rapidly over trials. Just as two dancers become more skilled as they practice together at coordinating their movements, conversational partners become more skilled in communicating efficiently (Barr & Keysar, 2006).

The term **lexical entrainment** refers to this pattern that two communicators use when they create and adopt a standard term to refer to an object. According to the research, people who work together can quickly and efficiently develop lexical entrainment (Barr & Keysar, 2006; Schober & Brennan, 2003). For example, physicians often adjust their conversations according to the medical sophistication of each patient. If a patient with diabetes initially uses the term "blood sugar level," physicians are less likely to use the technical term, "blood glucose concentration (Bromme et al., 2005).

FIGURE 10.2

Average Number of Turns that Directors in Clark and Wilkes-Gibb's Study Required for Each Figure, as a Function of Trial Number.

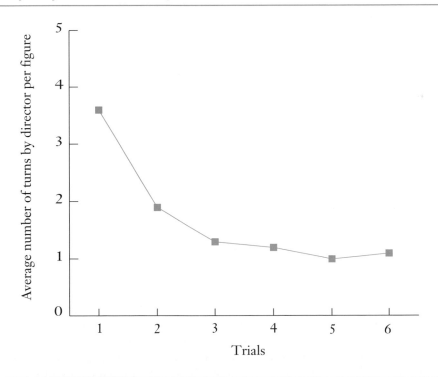

Source: Clark & Wilkes-Gibbs, 1986.

To study lexical entrainment in more detail, Bortfeld and Brennan (1997) used photos of 15 different kinds of chairs. In some cases, a student whose first language was English was paired with a student whose first language was Japanese, Chinese, or Korean. In other cases, both students spoke English as their first language. Interestingly, both kinds of student pairs showed the same degree of lexical entrainment. Both kinds of pairs soon developed names for the chairs such as "the flowered lounge chair" or "the wooden highchair." Lexical entrainment is apparently a fairly natural kind of pragmatic skill. Speakers frequently work collaboratively to agree on the names they will use in a conversation.

We have been discussing how people can establish common ground, even with strangers. However, this process is far from perfect. For example, speakers often overestimate their listeners' ability to understand a message (Barr & Keysar, 2006; Keysar & Henly, 2002; Schober & Brennan, 2003). In addition, speakers tend to assume that listeners need and want the same things the speakers themselves do (Nickerson, 2001). Also, as you might imagine, people are less likely to effectively establish common ground if they are under time pressure (Clark & Van Der Wege, 2002).

Directives. A **directive** is a sentence that requests someone to do something. In general, the most polite directives require more words (Brown & Levinson, 1987). For example, "Could you possibly by any chance lend me your car for just a few minutes?" would be considered more polite than, "Could you lend me your car?" However, some of these elaborate directives are perceived to be overly polite—even ironic—and so they may actually seem insulting (Kumon-Nakamura et al., 1995).

Speakers often state their directives in a format that anticipates potential obstacles to compliance (Gibbs, 1986, Turnbull, 2003). For instance, suppose that you missed one of your classes and you need to borrow someone's notes. You are likely to begin by asking a classmate, "Did you go to class yesterday?" You are less likely to begin by asking, "Can I borrow your notes from yesterday's class?"

Many other directives are asked in the form of an indirect request. An **indirect request** is stated like a request for information, even though it's really a request for someone to do something or to *stop* doing something (Cummings, 2005; Gibbs, 2003; Turnbull, 2003). For example, a teacher might ask a class of fifth graders, "What are you laughing at?" The teacher is not really wondering about the source of the laughter. Instead, he or she is requesting silence.

In short, speakers are typically attuned to the social context of speech. They usually work to achieve common ground, and they take care in selecting appropriate directives.

Section Summary: *Speaking*

1. Researchers conduct relatively few studies on language production, but topics such as word production are currently popular.

2. Word production is an impressive accomplishment; researchers disagree about whether grammatical, semantic, and phonological information about a word is accessed simultaneously or at different times.

3. Four stages in producing a sentence include working out the gist, formulating the general structure of the sentence, making the word choice, and articulating the phonemes; these processes overlap in time.

4. Speaking also requires speakers to overcome the linearization problem and to plan the prosody of their messages.

5. According to Dell and other researchers, slip-of-the-tongue errors occur because a speech sound other than the intended one is highly activated; researchers explain these errors in terms of a parallel distributed processing model with spreading activation.

6. A narrative is a kind of discourse that typically includes certain specified story components.

7. The pragmatic rules of speech regulate social components of speech production such as common ground (often including lexical entrainment) and the skillful use of directives (often including indirect requests).

WRITING

Writing is a task that requires virtually every cognitive process described in this text-book (Theme 4). Think about the last writing project that you completed. How did that project require letter recognition, attention, memory, imagery, background knowledge, metacognition, reading, problem solving, creativity, reasoning, and decision making?

Writing is also an important component of many people's occupations. For example, technical and professional people report that writing occupies about 30% of their typical working day (Faigley & Miller, 1982; Kellogg, 1989). As a student, you spend a major portion of your daily life taking notes on lectures and reading assignments (Piolat et al., 2005).

However, writing is one of the least understood linguistic tasks; research in this area is relatively limited (Harley, 2001; Levy & Ransdell, 1995). For example, several major handbooks in cognitive psychology and cognitive science do not even include the term *writing* in their indexes (Healy & Proctor, 2003; Pashler, 2002; Traxler & Gernsbacher, 2006; Wheeldon, 2000).

We noted earlier in this chapter that research on understanding speech is more prevalent than research on speech production. The contrast is even more dramatic when we compare written language. Reading inspires hundreds of books and research articles each year, whereas writing inspires only a handful. Even a widespread activity like composing an e-mail is seldom studied (Biorge, 2007; Finch, 2003; Oberlander & Gill, 2006; Olson & Olson, 2003).

Writing and speaking share many cognitive components. However, we are more likely to write in isolation, using more complex syntax and more extensive revisions. Writing also requires more time (Biber & Vásquez, 2008; Harley, 2001; Treiman et al., 2003). When you speak, you are more likely to refer to yourself. When speaking, you also interact more with your audience, and you have a better opportunity to establish common ground with this audience (Chafe & Danielewicz, 1987; Gibbs, 1998).

Writing consists of three phases: planning, sentence generation, and revising (Mayer, 2004). However—like the similar stages we discussed in terms of understanding and producing spoken language—these tasks often overlap in time (Kellogg, 1994, 1996; Ransdell & Levy, 1999). For example, you may be planning your overall writing strategy while you generate parts of several sentences. All components of the task are complex, and they strain the limits of attention (Kellogg, 1994, 1998; Torrance & Jeffery, 1999). In fact, a classic article on writing emphasizes that a person working on a writing assignment is "a thinker on full-time cognitive overload" (Flower & Hayes, 1980, p. 33). Still, consistent with Theme 2, we generally manage to coordinate these tasks quite skillfully when we produce written language.

Let's begin our exploration by considering a cognitive model of writing. The next section examines three phases of writing: planning, sentence generation, and revising. Then we'll emphasize the importance of metacognition throughout the writing process. Finally, we'll discuss several examples of writing in real-world settings.

A Cognitive Model of Writing

Several leading researchers have developed a model of writing that emphasizes the importance of cognitive processes. This model also includes other psychological factors (Chenoweth & Hayes, 2001; Hayes, 1996; Kellogg, 1994, 2001a, 2001b; McCutchen et al., 2008). For instance, writing is influenced by social factors, such as the audience who will read your paper (Hayes, 1996). Motor factors also influence your writing. You may write differently when using a computer rather than a pen and paper (Kellogg, 2001a).

Motivational factors are also important. For example, **self-efficacy** is your own assessment of your capabilities in a certain area. If two students are similar in writing ability, the student with high writing self-efficacy will typically produce a better paper for an academic course (Hayes, 1996; Pajares, 2003).

Working memory plays a central role in the cognitive approach to writing (McCutchen et al., 2008). In Chapter 4, we discussed Alan Baddeley's model of working memory. **Working memory** refers to the brief, immediate memory for material that we are currently processing; working memory also coordinates our ongoing mental activities. One component of working memory, the **phonological loop,** stores a limited number of sounds for a short period of time. People often talk to themselves as they generate sentences during writing—a procedure that requires the phonological loop (Kellogg, 1996). Another component of working memory, the **visuospatial sketchpad,** stores both visual and spatial information. The visuospatial sketchpad is useful when writers try to visualize the order of the sections of a paper and when they need to include figures and graphs in their paper (Kellogg, 1996).

As you may recall, the most important component of Baddeley's model of working memory is called the central executive. The **central executive** integrates information from the phonological loop, the visuospatial sketchpad, and the episodic buffer. The central executive also plays a role in attention, planning, and coordinating other cognitive activities. Because writing is such a complex task, the central executive is active in virtually every phase of the writing process (Kellogg, 1996, 1998, 2001a). For example, it coordinates the planning phase, and it is essential when we generate sentences. It also oversees the revision process. Because the central executive has a limited capacity, the writing task is especially challenging.

So far, we have discussed how writing is influenced by social factors, the physical environment, motivational forces, and working memory. Another important cognitive factor is long-term memory. Some important components of long-term memory include the writer's semantic memory, specific expertise about the topic, general schemas, and knowledge about the writing style to be used for the particular assignment (Hayes, 1996; Kellogg, 2001b; McCutchen et al., 2008). As you can see, our summary of the cognitive approach to writing provides an opportunity to review practically every topic we have discussed in the earlier chapters of this textbook!

Planning the Writing Assignment

The first stage in planning to write is to generate a list of ideas, a process called **prewriting**. Prewriting is difficult and strategic—much different from many relatively automatic language tasks (Collins, 1998; Torrance et al., 1996). As you can imagine, students differ enormously in the quality of the ideas they generate during this phase (Bruning et al., 1999). Research has shown that good writers spend more high-quality time in planning during prewriting (Hayes, 1989).

Research strongly supports the value of outlining a paper before you begin to write (Kellogg, 1994, 1998; McCutchen et al., 2008; Rau & Sebrechts, 1996). An outline may help you avoid overloaded attention. It may also help you resolve the linearization problem, which occurs in writing as well as in speaking. You've probably had the experience of beginning to write a paper, only to find that each of several interrelated ideas needs to be placed first! An outline can help you sort these ideas into an orderly, linear sequence.

⊚ Demonstration 10.4

Producing Sentences

For this exercise, you should be alone in a room, with no one else present to inhibit your spontaneity. Take a piece of paper on which you will write two sentences as requested below. For this writing task, however, say out loud the thoughts you are considering while you write each sentence. Then read the next section, on sentence generation.

1. Write one sentence to answer the question, "What are the most important characteristics that a good student should have?"
2. Write one sentence to answer the question, "What do you consider to be your strongest personality characteristics—the ones that you most admire in yourself?"

Sentence Generation During Writing

Before you read further, try Demonstration 10.4, which requires you to generate some sentences. During sentence generation, the writer must translate the general ideas developed during planning, thus creating the actual sentences of the text (Mayer, 2004).

During sentence generation, hesitant phases tend to alternate with fluent phases (Chenoweth & Hayes, 2001). Think about your own pattern when you were writing the sentences in Demonstration10.4. Did you show a similar pattern of pauses alternating with fluent writing?

Students often believe that their writing will sound more sophisticated if they use lengthy words. However, according to research by Oppenheimer (2006), people actually judge writers to be more intelligent if their essay uses shorter words.

Earlier in this chapter, we discussed slips-of-the-tongue. People also make errors when they write, whether they use a keyboard or a pen. However, writing errors are usually confined to a spelling error within a single word, whereas speaking errors often reflect switches between words (Berg, 2002).

The Revision Phase of Writing

Remember that writing is a cognitively challenging task. We cannot manage to generate sentences and revise them at the same time (Silvia, 2007). During the revision phase of writing, you should emphasize the importance of organization and coherence, so that the parts of your paper are interrelated (Britton, 1996). You'll also need to reconsider whether your paper accomplishes the goals of the assignment. The revision task *should* be time consuming. When writing their first draft, writers have numerous opportunities to make mistakes (Kellogg, 1998).

The most effective writers use flexible revision strategies, and they make substantial changes if their paper doesn't accomplish its goal (Harley, 2001). However, college students typically devote little time to revising a paper (Mayer, 2004; Torrance et al., 1996). For instance, college students in one study estimated that they had spent 30% of their writing time on revising their papers, but observation of their actual writing behavior showed that they consistently spent less than 10% of their time on revisions (Levy & Ransdell, 1995). We have seen that students' metacognitions about reading comprehension are not very accurate (Chapter 6). As we'll emphasize on page 339, students' metacognitions about the writing process also seem to be inaccurate.

As you can imagine, expert writers are especially skilled at making appropriate revisions. Hayes and his colleagues (1987) compared how first-year college students and expert writers revised a poorly written two-page letter. Most first-year students approached the text one sentence at a time. They fixed relatively minor problems with spelling and grammar, but they ignored problems of organization, focus, and transition between ideas.

The students were also more likely to judge some defective sentences as being appropriate. For example, several students found no fault with the sentence, "In sports like fencing for a long time many of our varsity team members had no previous experience anyway." Finally, the students were less likely than the expert writers to diagnose the source of a problem in a sentence. A student might say, "This sentence just doesn't sound right," whereas an expert might say, "The subject and the verb don't agree here."

One final caution about the revision process focuses on the proofreading stage. Daneman and Stainton (1993) confirmed what many of us already suspected: You can proofread someone else's writing more accurately than your own. Our extreme familiarity with what we have written helps us overlook the errors in the text. Top-down processing (Theme 5) triumphs again! Many of my students also seem to assume that the spell-check feature on their word processors will locate every mistake, but it identifies the nonwords only. It doesn't protest when you've entered the word *line*, rather than the word *life*. Furthermore, you've probably found that you cannot proofread your paper for spelling when you are focusing on the paper's content.

Metacognition and Writing

In Chapter 6, we considered the research on metamemory (your thoughts about your memory) and metacomprehension (your thoughts about your comprehension). The research on metacognition and writing is less extensive. Nevertheless, metacognitive strategies are clearly helpful at all stages of writing.

For example, novice writers typically write their thoughts—in almost random order—until their knowledge on the topic is exhausted. In contrast, expert writers try to transform the knowledge. They typically analyze potential problems in advance and plan how to solve them (Bereiter & Scardamalia, 1987; McCormick, 2003).

Writers must also monitor whether their written passage actually matches the passage they had planned to produce (McCormick, 2003). As you may recall from Chapter 6, people are often overconfident about their memory and their comprehension. Unfortunately, people also tend to be overconfident about their writing, believing that the message will be perfectly clear to other people.

Applied Psychology: Writing About Emotional Problems

In general, researchers have ignored how we write in real-world settings. However, James Pennebaker and his colleagues discovered that the writing process can be useful in clinical psychology (Pennebaker & Graybeal, 2001; Pennebaker et al., 2003). For example, when people write about a personally upsetting experience, their mental and physical health often improves. In a series of studies, these researchers invited people to come to their laboratory and write for 15 to 20 minutes a day, on three to four consecutive days. The participants in the experimental group were instructed to write about a previous traumatic experience. In contrast, the participants in the control group simply wrote about trivial topics for the same amount of time.

Pennebaker and his coauthors (2003) discovered that students in the experimental condition began to earn better grades than those in the control condition. Furthermore, unemployed adults in the experimental condition were more likely to find employment. The researchers also found that the participants in the experimental condition were more likely than those in the control condition to show improvements in their immune function, measures of stress, and other indexes of good physical health.

Interestingly, an analysis of the writing samples showed that the best predictor of physical health was the number of words that revealed cognitive activity (e.g., *understand* and *think*). In contrast, the number of words revealing emotions (e.g., *joyful* and *angry*) was not a strong predictor of physical health. Apparently, the writing experience helps people to create an understanding of the painful experience.

In related research, Erika Westling and her colleagues (2007) studied 41 HIV-positive women who participated in a writing program that lasted one month. Next, their writing samples were coded for evidence that they had discovered some meaning in their lives. Then the researchers measured the change in the women's adherence to taking their HIV-related medications (comparing their adherence before the writing program to their adherence after the writing program). The women who had written about life meaning were more likely than other women to show an improvement in taking their medication.

We tend to think of writing as a method of communicating with other people. However, the research shows that the words we write could potentially also have an important effect on our own mental health and well-being (Lepore & Smyth, 2002).

Section Summary: *Writing*

1. Writing requires numerous cognitive activities, but research on this topic is limited.

2. The cognitive model of writing emphasizes the importance of social and motivational factors, the three major components of working memory, and long-term memory.

3. Good writers spend high-quality time in planning; outlining is helpful because it helps to relieve overloaded attention.

4. When people generate sentences during writing, their fluent phases alternate with hesitant phases.

5. Expert writers are especially skilled in making appropriate revisions and in diagnosing defective sentences. Furthermore, people proofread others' writing more accurately than their own.

6. Metacognitive strategies are helpful at all stages of the writing process.

7. When people write about a personally upsetting experience, their mental and physical health often improves.

BILINGUALISM AND SECOND-LANGUAGE ACQUISITION

So far, these two chapters on language have described four impressively complicated cognitive tasks: understanding spoken language, reading, speaking, and writing. When we need to perform one of these tasks, we must coordinate our cognitive skills and social knowledge. We can marvel that human beings can manage all these tasks in one language. But then we must remind ourselves that most people throughout the world have mastered two or more languages (Schwartz & Kroll, 2006).

A **bilingual** speaker is a person who actively uses two different languages (Schwartz & Kroll, 2006). Technically, we should use the term **multilingual** to refer to someone who uses more than two languages, but psycholinguists often use the term *bilingual* to include multilinguals as well. Some bilinguals learn two languages simultaneously during childhood, an arrangement called **simultaneous bilingualism.** Other bilinguals experience **sequential bilingualism;** this person's native language is referred to as the **first language,** and the nonnative language that he or she acquires is the **second language**.

We noted in Chapter 9 that most research in psycholinguistics is English-centered. When we examine bilingualism, we must emphasize that the world has between 6,000 and 7,000 languages (Fishman, 2006; Ku, 2006). Even so, almost all of the research includes English as one of the two languages.

We need to emphasize that people do not learn a second language by simply imitating this new language. Instead, they create a new language system—called an **interlanguage**—that allows them to produce concepts, sentences, and discourse in this second language (Gass, 2006; Pienemann et al., 2005).

In this section on bilingualism, let's first discuss some background information. Then we'll note some advantages that people experience when they are bilingual. Our next topic will be an In Depth feature exploring the relationship between age of acquisition of a second language and proficiency in that second language. Finally, our Individual Differences feature will focus on simultaneous interpreters, people who have outstanding expertise in two or more languages.

Background on Bilingualism

More than half of the people in the world are at least somewhat bilingual (Schwartz & Kroll, 2006). Some people live in countries where at least two languages are commonly used. These countries include Canada, Wales, Belgium, and Switzerland. Others become bilingual because their home language is not the language used for school and business. For example, Zulu speakers in South Africa must learn English. People also become bilingual because colonization has imposed another language upon them. Still others become bilingual because they have studied another language in school, or because they grew up in homes where two languages were used routinely. In addition, immigrants moving to a new country usually need to master the language of that culture (Bialystok, 2001; Fishman, 2006; Parry, 2006).

English may be the most common language in both Canada and the United States, but many other languages are also widely used in these countries. Table 10.1 shows the ten languages most frequently "spoken at home" in the United States. Table 10.2 shows the ten languages most frequently listed as a person's "mother tongue" in Canada. As you can see from both tables, bilingualism is an important issue in the lives of many North Americans.

TABLE 10.1

Ten Languages Most Frequently Spoken at Home in the United States, Based on the 2000 U.S. Census (for people aged 5 and older).

Language	Estimated Number of Speakers[1]
English	215,200,000
Spanish	28,100,000
Chinese	2,000,000
French	1,600,000
German	1,400,000
Tagalog [2]	1,200,000
Vietnamese	1,000,000
Italian	1,000,000
Korean	900,000
Russian	700,000

Notes: (1) The number of speakers is estimated to the nearest 100,000.

(2) Tagalog is a language spoken in the Philippines.

Source: Shin & Bruno, 2003.

TABLE 10.2

Ten Languages Most Frequently Identified as the "Mother Tongue" in Canada, Based on 2006 Census.

Language	Estimated Number of Speakers
English	17,900,000
French	6,800,000
Chinese	1,000,000
Italian	500,000
German	500,000
Punjabi	400,000
Spanish	300,000
Arabic	300,000
Tagalog	200,000
Portuguese	200,000

Note: (1) The number of speakers is estimated to the nearest 100,000.

(2) Punjabi is a language spoken in India and Pakistan.

Source: Statistics Canada, 2006.

When children in North America speak a language other than English in their homes, the educational system typically pressures them to acquire English at school. Unfortunately, however, schools seldom appreciate the value of keeping a child fluent in a first language such as Korean, Arabic, or Spanish (Fishman, 2006; Pita & Utakis, 2006; Zentella, 2006). When a school values children's first language, they may actually become more fluent in English (Atkinson & Connor, 2008).

As you can imagine, the topic of bilingualism has important political and social-psychological implications, especially when educators and politicians make statements about various ethnic groups (Genesee & Gándara, 1999; Phillipson, 2000). These same social psychological forces are important when an individual wants to become bilingual. Two important predictors of success in acquiring a second language are a person's motivation and his or her attitude toward the people who speak that language (Gass & Selinker, 2001; Tokuhama-Espinosa, 2001). In fact, researchers have tried to predict how well English Canadian high school students will learn French. Research shows that the students' attitude toward French Canadians was just as important as their cognitive, language-learning aptitude (Gardner & Lambert, 1959; Lambert, 1992).

As you might expect, the relationship between attitudes and language proficiency also works in the reverse direction. Specifically, elementary school English Canadians who learned French developed more positive attitudes toward French Canadians than did children in a monolingual control group of English Canadian children (Genesee & Gándara, 1999; Lambert, 1987).

In the last decade, bilingualism has become an increasingly popular topic in psychology and linguistics. For instance, this interdisciplinary area now has its own journal, *Bilingualism: Language & Culture* and also an important handbook (Kroll & de Groot, 2005).

Furthermore, many books published in the current decade explore bilingualism and second-language learning. These books address issues such as the political aspects of bilingualism (Luria et al., 2006; Phillipson, 2000) and language pragmatics in bilingual communities (Bardovi-Harlig & Hartford, 2005; Walters, 2005). Other books examine bilingualism during different stages of life: childhood (Cenoz & Genesee, 2001; Döpke, 2001; Nelson et al., 2001; Tokuhama-Espinosa, 2001), adolescence and young adulthood (Gass & Selinker, 2001; Ohta, 2001; Silva & Matsuda, 2001), and old age (de Bot & Makoni, 2005).

Now that you have some background on bilingualism, let's consider two topics that are especially important for cognitive psychologists: (1) the advantages of bilingualism and (2) the relationship between age of acquisition and language mastery.

Advantages of Bilingualism

During the early 1900s, theorists proposed that bilingualism produced cognitive deficits because the brain must store two linguistic systems (Bialystok, 2005; Carroll, 2004). However, in the 1960s, researchers discovered that bilinguals scored higher than monolinguals on a variety of tasks, when they controlled for factors such as social class. In one of the best-known studies, for example, bilinguals were more advanced in school, they scored better on tests of first-language skills, and they showed greater mental flexibility (Lambert, 1990; Peal & Lambert, 1962).

Bilingual people have one tremendous advantage over monolinguals: They can communicate in two languages. Even 10-year-olds can translate spoken and written language with impressive accuracy (Bialystok, 2001).

In addition to gaining fluency in a second language, bilinguals seem to have a number of other advantages over monolinguals, including the following:

1. Bilinguals actually acquire more expertise in their native (first) language (Rhodes et al., 2005; van Hell & Dijkstra, 2002). For example, English-speaking Canadian children whose classes are taught in French gain greater understanding of English-language structure (Diaz, 1985; Lambert et al., 1991). Bilingual children are also more likely to realize that a word such as *rainbow* can be divided into two morphemes, *rain* and *bow* (Campbell & Sais, 1995).

2. Bilinguals are more aware that the names assigned to concepts are arbitrary (Bialystok, 1987, 1988; Cromdal, 1999; Hakuta, 1986). For example, monolingual children cannot imagine that a cow could just as easily have been assigned the name *dog*. A number of studies have examined **metalinguistics,** or knowledge about the form and structure of language. On many measures of metalinguistic skill—but not all of them—bilinguals outperform monolinguals (Bialystok, 1988, 1992, 2001; Campbell & Sais, 1995; Galambos & Goldin-Meadow, 1990; Galambos & Hakuta, 1988).

3. Bilinguals excel at paying selective attention to relatively subtle aspects of a language task, ignoring more obvious linguistic characteristics (Bialystok, 1992, 2001, 2005; Bialystok & Majumder, 1998; Cromdal, 1999). For example, Bialystok and Majumder gave third-grade children some sentences that were grammatically correct but semantically incorrect (for example, "The dog meows"). The bilingual children were more likely than the monolingual children to recognize that the sentence was grammatically correct.

4. Bilingual children are better at following complicated instructions and performing tasks where the instructions change from one trial to the next (Bialystock, 2005; Bialystok et al., 2004; Bialystok & Martin, 2004). For example, Bialystok and Martin (2004) asked preschoolers to sort some cards that featured either a blue circle, a red circle, a blue square, or a red square. The researchers first instructed them to sort the cards on one dimension (e.g., shape). Later, the researchers instructed them to sort the cards on the other dimension (e.g., color). Bilingual children were much faster in switching to the new dimension.

5. Bilinguals perform better on concept-formation tasks and on tests of nonverbal intelligence that require reorganization of visual patterns (Peal & Lambert, 1962). Bilinguals also score higher on problem-solving tasks that require them to ignore irrelevant information (Bialystok, 2001; Bialystok & Codd, 1997; Bialystok & Majumder, 1998).

6.   Bilingual children perform better than monolinguals on tests of creativity, such as thinking of a wide variety of uses for a paper clip (Hamers & Blanc, 1989; Ricciardelli, 1992).

7.   Bilingual children are more sensitive to some pragmatic aspects of language (Comeau & Genesee, 2001). For example, English-speaking children whose classes are taught in French are more aware than monolinguals that—when you speak to a blind-folded child—you need to supply additional information (Genesee et al., 1975).

Ellen Bialystok (2001, 2005) examined a wide range of bilingual advantages. She concluded that most advantages can be traced to an important factor: Bilingual children are especially skilled in selective-attention tasks where they must inhibit the most obvious response by ignoring this misleading information, focusing instead on less obvious information. Bialystok (2005) also proposes that this experience with selective attention may facilitate the development of a portion of the frontal lobe, labeled "executive attention network" in Figure 3.2 on p. 78.

The disadvantages of being bilingual are relatively minor. People who use two languages extensively may subtly alter how they pronounce some speech sounds in both languages (Gollan, Bonanni, & Montoya, 2005; Gollan, Montoya, Fennema-Notestine, & Morris, 2005). Bilinguals may also process language slightly more slowly, in comparison to monolinguals, but this disadvantage is far out-weighed by the advantages of being able to communicate effectively in two languages (Michael & Gollan, 2005).

[IN DEPTH]

Second-Language Proficiency as a Function of Age of Acquisition

A number of years ago, I met a family who had moved to the United States from Iceland and had been in their new country only a week. Both of these highly intelligent and highly educated parents had studied English in school for at least ten years. However, they clearly struggled to understand and produce conversational speech. In contrast, their 4-year-old son had already picked up a good deal of English with no formal training. When the time came to leave, the parents haltingly said their goodbyes. The 4-year-old—in unaccented English—shouted enthusiastically, "See you later, alligator!"

This anecdote raises some important questions about the relationship between the age at which you begin to learn a second language (or **age of acquisition**) and your eventual proficiency in that language. Some theorists have proposed a critical period hypothesis. According to the **critical period hypothesis**, your ability to acquire a second language is strictly limited to a specific period of your life. In fact the critical period hypothesis proposes that individuals who have already reached a specified age—perhaps early puberty—will no longer be able to acquire a new language with native-like fluency.

However, the current research evidence does not support a clear-cut, biologically based "deadline" for learning a second language. For example, several studies demonstrate that adults and older adolescents can indeed learn to speak a new language very fluently (Bialystok 2001; Birdsong, 1999; Birdsong & Molis, 2000). Many studies do report a *gradual* decline in a variety of second-language skills, as a function of age of acquisition. However, these studies do not show an abrupt drop—as predicted by the critical period hypothesis—when language learners reach a certain age (Bialystok, 2001; Hakuta et al., 2003; Wiley et al., 2005).

Even if we reject the critical period hypothesis, we still need to explore a more general issue: Do older people have more difficulty than younger people in mastering a second language? Like so many psychological controversies, the answer varies as a function of the dependent variable. As you'll see, researchers draw different conclusions, depending on whether they measure phonology, vocabulary, or grammar.

Phonology.   Research suggests that age of acquisition does influence the mastery of **phonology,** or the sounds of a person's speech. Specifically, people who acquire a second language during early childhood are more likely to pronounce words like a native speaker of that language. In contrast, those who acquire a second language during adulthood will be more likely to have a foreign accent when they speak their new language (Bialystok, 2001; Flege et al., 1999; MacKay et al., 2006).

Let's consider a study conducted by James Flege and his coauthors (1999). These researchers located 240 individuals whose native language was Korean and who immigrated to the United States when they were between the ages of 1 and 23 years. At the time of the study, all participants had lived in the United States for at least eight years.

To test phonology, Flege and his colleagues asked the participants to listen to an English sentence, and then repeat it. The phonology of each sentence was later judged by ten speakers whose native language was English. The judges used a 9-point rating scale, in which 9 represented "no accent." The judges also rated the phonology of a comparison group of twenty-four speakers whose native language was English. You can see their scores, clustered in the upper-left corner of Figure 10.3.

Now look at the corresponding data for the participants who had emigrated from Korea. As you can see, people who had arrived in the United States during childhood typically had minimal accents when speaking English. In contrast, those who had arrived as adolescents or adults usually had stronger accents. However, you'll notice a fairly smooth decline with age of acquisition, rather than the abrupt drop predicted by the critical period hypothesis (Bialystok, 2001). In later research, MacKay and his coauthors (2006) found similar results with people who had emigrated from Italy.

Vocabulary.   When the measure of language proficiency is vocabulary, age of acquisition does not seem to be related to language skills (Bialystok, 2001). Several studies reviewed by Bialystok and Hakuta (1994) reported that adults and children are equally skilled in learning words in their new language. This finding makes sense, because people continue to learn new terms in their own language throughout their lifetimes. For example, you have already learned several hundred new terms in cognitive psychology since you began this course!

FIGURE 10.3

The Average Rating for Lack of a Foreign Accent, as a Function of the Individual's Age of Arrival in the United States (9 = no accent).

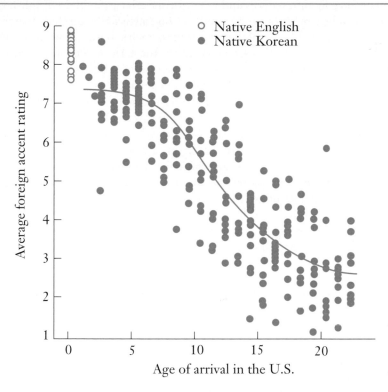

Source: Flege et al., 1999.

Grammar. The controversy about age of acquisition is strongest when we consider mastery of grammar (e.g., Bialystok, 2001; Johnson & Newport, 1989). Let's focus on the study by Flege and his coauthors (1999), which we discussed earlier in connection with phonology. These researchers also examined how the native speakers of Korean had mastered English grammar. Specifically, the researchers asked the participants to judge nine different categories of English sentences, noting whether each sentence was grammatical. Here are three representative categories, together with examples of ungrammatical sentences:

Yes/no questions: *Should have Timothy gone to the party?*

Pronouns: *Susan is making some cookies for we.*

Plurals: *Todd has many coat in his closet.*

In the initial analysis of the data, this study seemed to show that those who had learned English during childhood had better mastery of English grammar. However, Flege and his colleagues (1999) then discovered that the "early arrivers" had much more experience in U.S. schools and more formal education in the English language.

The researchers therefore conducted a second analysis, by carefully matching some of the early arrivers with some of the late arrivers. Each subgroup had an average of 10.5 years of U.S. education. In this second analysis, the early arrivers received an average score of 84% on the grammar test, virtually identical to the average score of 83% for the late arrivers. In short, once we control for years of education in the United States, age of acquisition is not related to an individual's mastery of English grammar.

The research we have cited up until now in this In Depth feature examined only the grammatical performance of people with an Asian first language. These languages are very different from English. Researchers have conducted other studies on the grammatical competence of bilinguals whose first language is Spanish or Dutch—two languages that are more similar to English. These studies do not show any consistent relationship between age of arrival and mastery of English grammar (Bahrick et al., 1994; Birdsong & Molis, 2001; Jia et al., 2002).

To understand how age of acquisition is related to competence in a second language, we will need additional research on a wider variety of first- and second-language combinations (DeKeyser & Larson-Hall, 2005). In addition, we need research in which the second language is something other than English; as we noted at the beginning of Chapter 9, the research in psycholinguistics focuses on English.

At present, though, the results suggest that age of acquisition of a second language seems to influence the speaker's accent in this new language. However, age of acquisition does not affect the speaker's mastery of vocabulary. Finally, age of acquisition affects knowledge about grammar if the two languages are very different from each other, and if the speaker has not been educated in English. However, older learners may not face a disadvantage if the two languages are similar.

As an exercise in helping you understand bilingualism, try Demonstration 10.5 at your next opportunity. Quite clearly, bilinguals and multilinguals provide the best illustration of how Theme 2 applies to language, because they manage to master accurate and rapid communication in two or more languages. Now, our Individual Differences feature will focus on the superstars of bilingualism, people who listen to speech in one language and simultaneously produce a translation in a different language.

Demonstration 10.5

Exploring Bilingualism

If you are fortunate enough to be bilingual or multilingual, you can answer these questions yourself. If you are not, locate someone you know well enough to ask the following questions:

1. How old were you when you were first exposed to your second language?

(continued)

2. Under what circumstances did you acquire this second language? For example, did you have formal lessons in this language?

3. When you began to learn this second language, did you find yourself becoming any less fluent in your native language? If so, can you provide any examples?

4. Do you think you have any special insights about the nature of language that a monolingual may not have?

5. Does the North American culture (including peer groups) discourage bilinguals from using their first language?

Individual Differences: Simultaneous Interpreters and Working Memory

If you have studied another language, you've probably had the experience of looking at a written passage in that language and writing down the English equivalent of that passage. The technical word **translation** refers to this process of translating from a text written in one language into a second written language. In contrast, the technical word **interpreting** refers to the process of translating from a spoken message in one language into a second spoken language.

Simultaneous interpreting is one of the most challenging linguistic tasks that humans can perform (Christoffels & de Groot, 2005). The task is especially complex because you must simultaneously manage three tasks.

Imagine that you are a simultaneous interpreter, listening to a person speaking in Spanish and producing the English version of that message for a group of listeners who are fluent in English but are not familiar with Spanish. You would need to manage three working-memory tasks at exactly the same time:

1. Comprehend one Spanish segment (perhaps a sentence or two).

2. Mentally transform the previous Spanish segment into English.

3. Actually speak out loud—in English—an even earlier segment.

Furthermore, you must manage to perform these cognitive gymnastics at the rate of between 100 to 200 words per minute!

It's hard to think of any other occupation that would create such a challenge for a person's working memory. Let's look at research that compares simultaneous interpreters with other bilingual individuals, on two kinds of working-memory tasks.

Ingrid Christoffels, Annette de Groot, and Judith Kroll (2006) studied three groups of bilingual people whose native language was Dutch and who were also fluent in English. These groups included 39 Dutch undergraduate students at the University of Amsterdam, 15 Dutch teachers of English who had an average of nineteen years of professional experience, and 13 Dutch simultaneous interpreters who had an average of sixteen years of professional experience. Christoffels and her colleagues hypothesized that the professional interpreters would have higher scores than the other two groups on tests of working memory. Let's consider two working-memory tasks, which the researchers called the reading-span test and the speaking-span test.

For the reading-span test, the researchers created 42 sentences in both English and Dutch. The final word of each sentence was matched for the two languages, in terms of both word length and the frequency of the word in the appropriate language. The researchers showed several series of sentences, which were two, three, four, or five sentences in length. Each sentence was shown on a screen, for half a second. At the end of each series, the participants tried to recall the last word of each of the sentences in that specific series. The participants tried this reading-span test in both English and Dutch.

For the speaking-span task, the researchers selected 42 words in both English and Dutch, matching for both word length and the frequency of the word in the appropriate language. The researchers presented several series of words, which were two, three, four, or five words in length. Each word was shown on a screen, for half a second. At the end of each series, the participants tried to produce—out loud—a grammatically correct sentence for each word in the series that they could recall. Again, the participants tried this speaking-span test in both English and Dutch.

Figure 10.4 shows that all three groups of bilinguals recalled more words in their native language of Dutch, compared to their second language of English. The more

FIGURE 10.4

Average Score on the Reading-Span Test and the Speaking Span Test, as a Function of the Language (Dutch and English) and Profession.

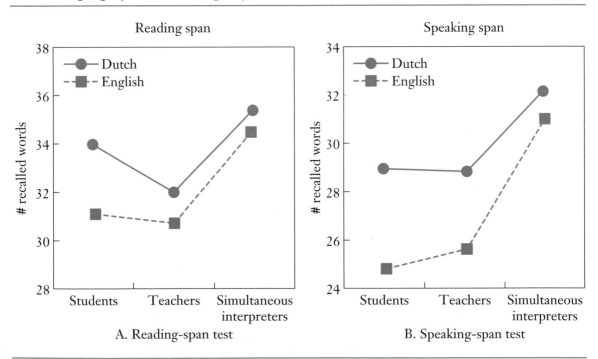

Source: Christoffels et al., 2005.

interesting comparison focuses on the three groups of people. As you can see, the simul-taneous interpreters remembered significantly more words than the other two groups, in terms of both their reading span and their speaking span.

As you know, psychologists emphasize that it's sometimes difficult to interpret sig-nificant differences between groups. In this case, we know that simultaneous interpreters perform better than either bilingual students or teachers. One possible explanation is that the experience of managing simultaneous tasks increased the working-memory skills for the simultaneous interpreters. However, another possibility is that only people with superb working-memory skills can manage to survive in a profession that requires an extremely high level of proficiency in working memory. In reality, both of these expla-nations may be correct.

Section Summary: *Bilingualism and Second-Language Acquisition*

1. Most of the world's population are at least somewhat bilingual. Many residents of Canada and the United States speak a first language other than English; chil-dren's schools may not value fluency in another language.

2. Motivation and attitudes are important determinants of bilingual skills.

3. Bilinguals have an advantage over monolinguals in their understanding of first-language structure, their awareness of the arbitrary nature of concept names, and their ability to pay attention to subtle aspects of language. Bilinguals also show superior ability to follow complex instructions, their concept formation, their creativity, and their sensitivity to pragmatics.

4. In general, bilinguals are especially skilled on selective-attention tasks in which they must inhibit the most obvious response.

5. People who acquire a second language during early childhood are less likely than adult learners to speak their new language with an accent, but adults and children are equally skilled in acquiring vocabulary. Age of acquisition is not consistently related to competency in grammar.

6. Simultaneous interpreters typically perform better than bilingual students and foreign-language teachers on two tasks that assess working memory.

CHAPTER REVIEW QUESTIONS

1. The cognitive tasks required for language production (Chapter 10) are some-what similar to the cognitive tasks required for language comprehension (Chap-ter 9). Describe some of the more complex cognitive tasks that are specifically necessary for language production, but not language comprehension.

2. Recall several conversations you have had in the last day or two. Describe how these conversations reflected the pragmatic components of speech production, such as common ground, lexical entrainment, and directives.

3. What is the linearization problem? In what way is it more relevant in language production (either speaking or writing) than it would be when you create a mental image (Chapter 7)?

4. "Language is more than simply a sequence of words." Discuss this statement with respect to language production, including topics such as gestures, prosody, and bilingualism.

5. Think of a slip-of-the-tongue that you recently made or heard in a conversation. What kind of error is this, according to Dell's classification, and how would Dell's theory explain this particular error? What slips-of-the-tongue would you be *least* likely to make?

6. How does writing differ from speaking? What cognitive tasks do these two activities share?

7. Based on the material in the section on writing, what hints could you adopt to produce a better paper the next time you begin to work on a formal writing assignment?

8. Think of another language that you would like to speak with some fluency; what factors would facilitate your mastery of that language? Describe several tasks in which bilinguals are likely to perform better than monolinguals. Which tasks would monolinguals probably perform better than bilinguals?

9. The section on bilingualism mentioned metalinguistics, or knowledge of the form and structure of language. Review this chapter, noting several topics related to metalinguistics that would be interesting to explore. Suggest several specific research projects. (For example, how would you devise a test of people's knowledge about the social context of speech?)

10. Language is perhaps the most social of our cognitive activities. Describe how social factors are relevant in our speaking and writing, as well as in bilingual interactions.

KEY WORDS

gestures
gist
linearization problem
prosody
slips-of-the-tongue
morphemes
discourse
narrative
pragmatics
common ground
lexical entrainment

directive
indirect request
self-efficacy
working memory
phonological loop
visuospatial sketchpad
central executive
prewriting
bilingual
multilingual
simultaneous bilingualism

sequential bilingualism
first language
second language
interlanguage
metalinguistics
age of acquisition
critical period hypothesis
phonology
translation
interpreting

RECOMMENDED READINGS

Bazerman, C. (Ed.) (2008). *Handbook of research on writing: History, society, school, individual, text.* Mahwah, NJ: Erlbaum. Many of the chapters in this book explore topics unrelated to psychology. However, the last thirteen chapters focus on psychological aspects of writing.

Graesser, A. C., Gernsbacher, M. A., & Goldman, S. R. (2003a). *Handbook of discourse processes.* Mahwah, NJ: Erlbaum. This handbook includes chapters on topics such as spoken discourse, indirect requests, and discourse development.

Kroll, J. F., & de Groot, A. M. (Eds.). (2005). *Handbook of bilingualism: Psycholinguistic approaches.* New York: Oxford University Press. This superb handbook includes chapters on such topics as learning foreign language vocabulary, the controversy about a critical period, and cognitive neuroscience approaches to bilingualism.

Using Problem Solving and Creativity

PREVIEW

You use problem solving when you want to reach a particular goal, but you cannot immediately figure out the best pathway to that goal. This chapter considers four aspects of problem solving: (1) understanding the problem, (2) problem-solving strategies, (3) factors that influence problem solving, and (4) creativity.

In order to understand a problem, you need to pay attention to the relevant information. Then you can represent the problem, for instance by using symbols or visual images. In some cases, people may solve a complex problem in their daily life, even though they cannot solve a similar problem on a classroom exam.

After you understand a problem, you must figure out how to solve it. Many problem-solving approaches are based on heuristics. A heuristic is a shortcut that typically produces a correct solution. One heuristic is the analogy approach, in which you solve the current problem on the basis of your experience with similar previous problems. A second approach is the means-ends heuristic, in which you break a problem into subproblems and then solve these individual subproblems. A third heuristic is the hill-climbing heuristic; at every choice point, you simply choose the alternative that seems to lead most directly toward your goal. U.S. students differ somewhat from Brazilian and Indian students in their preferences for various strategies.

The section on factors that influence problem solving emphasizes how top-down processing and bottom-up processing are both important in effective problem solving. Experts benefit by using their well-developed top-down skills. In contrast, overactive top-down processing can sometimes interfere with effective problem solving, as we'll see in the discussions of mental set and functional fixedness. An additional problem occurs when overactive top-down processing encourages stereotype threat, a problem that can decrease women's math performance. Finally, top-down processing may prevent people from solving insight problems, but it may help them solve noninsight problems.

Creativity can be defined as finding solutions that are novel, high quality, and useful. We'll discuss both a classic and a contemporary approach to creativity. Then we'll see how your motivation for working on a task may influence your creativity.

INTRODUCTION

Every day, you solve dozens of problems. For example, think about the problems you solved just yesterday. Perhaps you wanted to e-mail a student in your social psychology class, but you don't know his name or his e-mail address. Maybe you began to solve the problem of trying to organize your resources for a literature-review paper in your cognitive psychology course. Although you spent most of the day solving problems, you may have decided to relax late at night—by solving even more problems. Maybe you played computer chess or worked on a Sudoku puzzle, or you tried to help a friend who is struggling with a personal problem.

You use **problem solving** when you want to reach a certain goal, but the solution is not immediately obvious because important information is missing, and obstacles are blocking your path (D'Zurilla & Maydeu-Olivares, 2004; Leighton & Sternberg, 2003). In general, our problem-solving ability is specific to a particular domain (Kyllonen & Lee, 2005). For example, clinical psychologists must develop problem-solving strategies that can help their clients solve their real-life problems (Sternberg, 1998). Leaders of different ethnic groups—on the brink of a civil war—can participate in problem-solving workshops, developing problem-solving strategies for reaching common groups (Staub, 2003).

Every problem contains three components: (1) the initial state, (2) the goal state, and (3) the obstacles. For example, suppose that you need to reach Jim in your social psychology class. The **initial state** describes the situation at the beginning of the problem. In this case, your initial state might be, "I need to reach Jim tonight so that we can begin to work on our social psychology project . . . but I don't know his last name, his email address, or his phone number." The **goal state** is reached when you solve the problem. Here, it could be, "I have Jim's last name and his e-mail address." The **obstacles** describe the restrictions that make it difficult to proceed from the initial state to the goal state (Davidson et al., 1994; Thagard, 2005). The obstacles in this hypothetical problem might include the following: "Jim wasn't in class today," "The professor said she was going to be away this afternoon," and "We need to turn in a draft tomorrow."

Take a moment to recall a problem you have recently solved. Determine the initial state, the goal state, and the obstacles, so that you are familiar with these three concepts. Then try Demonstration 11.1.

⊚ Demonstration 11.1

Attention and Problem Solving

Suppose you are a bus driver. On the first stop you pick up 6 men and 2 women. At the second stop 2 men leave and 1 woman boards the bus. At the third stop 1 man leaves and 2 women enter the bus. At the fourth stop 3 men get on and 3 women get off. At the fifth stop, 2 men get off, 3 men get on, 1 woman gets off, and 2 women get on. What is the bus driver's name?

Source: Halpern, 2003, p. 389.

In Chapter 1, we defined the term *cognition* as the acquisition, storage, transformation, and use of knowledge. So far in this textbook, we have paid the least attention to the transformation of knowledge. However, in this chapter and in the next chapter on reasoning and decision making, we focus on how people must take the information they have acquired and transform it to reach an appropriate answer. Furthermore, both Chapters 11 and 12 can be included in the general category called "thinking." **Thinking** requires you to go beyond the information you were given, so that you can reach a goal; the goal may be a solution, a belief, or a decision (Baron, 2000).

Throughout this chapter, we will emphasize the active nature of cognitive processes in problem solving, consistent with Theme 1. When people solve problems, they seldom take a random, trial-and-error approach, blindly trying different options until they find a solution. Instead, they typically show extraordinary flexibility. They plan their attacks, often breaking a problem into its component parts and devising a strategy for solving each part. In addition, people frequently use certain kinds of strategies that are likely to produce a solution relatively quickly. People also use metacognition to monitor whether their problem-solving strategies seem to be working effectively (Hinsz, 2004; Mayer, 2004; McCormick, 2003). As this textbook emphasizes, humans do not passively absorb information from the environment. Instead, we plan our approach to problems, choosing strategies that are likely to provide useful solutions.

The first step in problem solving is understanding the problem, so let's consider this topic first. Once you understand a problem, the next step is to select a strategy for solving it; we will examine several problem-solving approaches in the second section of this chapter. Then we will examine several factors that influence effective problem solving; for example, expertise is clearly helpful, but a mental set is counterproductive. Our final topic is creativity—an area that requires finding novel solutions to challenging problems.

UNDERSTANDING THE PROBLEM

Some years ago, the companies located in a New York City skyscraper faced a major problem. The people in the building were continually complaining that the elevators moved too slowly. Numerous consultants were brought in, but the complaints only increased. When several companies threatened to move out, plans were drawn up to add an extremely expensive new set of elevators. Before reconstruction began, however, someone decided to add mirrors in the lobbies next to the elevators. The complaints stopped. Apparently, the original problem solvers had not properly understood the problem. In fact, the real problem wasn't the speed of the elevators, but the boredom of waiting for them to arrive (Thomas, 1989).

In problem-solving research, the term **understanding** means that you have constructed a mental representation of the problem, based on the information provided in the problem and your own previous experience (Robertson, 2001). In order to understand a problem, you need to construct an accurate mental representation (Fiore & Schooler, 2004; Greeno, 1991). Think about an occasion when you noticed that your mental representation did not correspond to the situation you needed to understand. I recall my mother giving her friend a recipe for homemade yogurt, which included the sentence, "Then you put the yogurt in a warm blanket." The friend looked quite alarmed, and she asked, "But isn't it awfully messy to wash the blanket out?" Unfortunately, the friend's internal representation had omitted the fact that the yogurt was in a container.

In this section of the chapter, we'll consider several topics related to understanding a problem: (1) the importance of paying attention; (2) methods of representing the problem; and (3) situated cognition, a perspective that emphasizes the role of context in understanding a problem.

Paying Attention to Important Information

To understand a problem, you need to decide which information is most relevant to the problem's solution and then attend to that information. Notice, then, that one cognitive task—problem solving—relies on other cognitive activities such as attention, memory, and decision making. This is another example of the interrelatedness of our cognitive processes (Theme 4).

Attention is important in understanding problems because attention is limited, and competing thoughts can produce divided attention (Bruning et al., 1999). For instance, Bransford and Stein (1984) presented algebra "story problems" to a group of college students. You'll remember these problems—a typical one might ask about a train traveling in one direction and a car driving in another direction. In this study, the students were asked to record their thoughts and emotions as they inspected the problem. Many students had an immediate negative reaction to the problem, such as, "Oh no, this is a mathematical word problem—I hate those things." These negative thoughts occurred frequently throughout the 5 minutes allotted to the task. They clearly distracted the students' attention away from the central task of problem solving.

Another major challenge in understanding a problem is focusing on the appropriate part (Dunbar, 1998). Researchers have found that effective problem solvers read the description of a problem very carefully, paying particular attention to inconsistencies (Mayer & Hegarty, 1996). Incidentally, if you paid attention to the bus driver riddle on page 357, you could solve it without needing to read it a second time. However, if you didn't pay attention, you can locate the answer in the first sentence of Demonstration 11.1. In summary, then, attention is a necessary initial component of understanding a problem.

Demonstration 11.2

Using Symbols in Problem Solving

Solve the following problem: Mary is 10 years younger than twice Susan's age. Five years from now, Mary will be 8 years older than Susan's age at that time. How old are Mary and Susan? (You can find the answer in the discussion of "Symbols" a little later in the text.)

Methods of Representing the Problem

As soon as the problem solver has decided which information is essential and which can be disregarded, the next step is to find a good method to represent the problem. If you choose an inappropriate method, you might not reach an effective solution to the problem (Robertson, 2001). If you can find an effective representation, you can organize the information efficiently and reduce the strain on your limited working memory. Then you'll be more likely to select a useful strategy (Leighton & Sternberg, 2003; Pretz et al., 2003; Ward & Morris, 2005).

Your representation of the problem must show the essential information that you need to solve it. Once you have selected a representation, you are likely to stay with it unless it becomes obvious that you're not making appropriate progress (Delaney et al., 2004). Some of the most effective methods of representing problems include symbols, matrices, diagrams, and visual images.

Symbols. Sometimes the most effective way to represent an abstract problem is by using symbols, as students learn to do in high school algebra (Mayer, 2004) Consider Demonstration 11.2. The usual way of solving this problem is to let a symbol such as *m*

⊚ Demonstration 11.3

Representing a Problem

Read the following information, fill in the information in the matrix, and then answer the question, "What disease does Ms. Anderson have, and in what room is she?" (The answer is at the end of the chapter.)

Five people are in a hospital. Each person has only one disease, and each has a different disease. Each person occupies a separate room; the room numbers are 101 through 105.

1. The person with asthma is in Room 101.
2. Ms. Lopez has heart disease.
3. Ms. Green is in Room 105.
4. Ms. Smith has tuberculosis.
5. The woman with mononucleosis is in Room 104.
6. Ms. Thomas is in Room 101.
7. Ms. Smith is in Room 102.
8. One of the patients, other than Ms. Anderson, has gall bladder disease.

	Room Number				
	101	102	103	104	105
Anderson					
Lopez					
Green					
Smith					
Thomas					

Source: Based on Schwartz, 1971.

represent Mary's age and a symbol such as *s* represent Susan's age. We can then "translate" each sentence into a formula. The first sentence becomes $m = 2s - 10$ and the second sentence becomes $m + 5 = s + 5 + 8$. We can then substitute for m in the second sentence and perform the necessary arithmetic. We then learn that Susan must be 18 and Mary must be 26.

A major challenge is that problem solvers often make mistakes when they try to translate words into symbols (Mayer, 2004). For example, Schoenfeld (1982) describes how calculus students were asked to rephrase simple algebra problem statements so that they were more understandable. About 10% of the rephrasings included information that directly contradicted the input, and 20% contained confusing or unintelligible information. If you misunderstand a problem, you will not translate it accurately into symbols.

One common problem in translating sentences into symbols is that the problem solver may oversimplify the sentence, thereby misrepresenting the information (Mayer, 2004; Reed, 1999). For example, Mayer and Hegarty (1996) asked college students to read a series of algebra word problems and then to recall them later. The students often misremembered the problems that contained relational statements such as, "The engine's rate in still water is 12 miles per hour more than the rate of the current." A common error was to represent this statement in a simpler form, such as, "The engine's rate in still water is 12 miles per hour."

Matrices. You can solve some problems effectively by using a **matrix,** which is a chart that shows all possible combinations of items. A matrix is an excellent way to keep track of items, particularly if the problem is complex and if the relevant information is categorical (Halpern, 2003). For example, you can solve Demonstration 11.3 most effectively by using a matrix like the one at the bottom of that demonstration.

Demonstration 11.3 is based on research by Steven Schwartz and his colleagues (Schwartz, 1971; Schwartz & Fattaleh, 1972; Schwartz & Polish, 1974). Schwartz and his co-workers found that students who represented the problem by a matrix were more

---

Demonstration 11.4

The Buddhist Monk Problem

Exactly at sunrise one morning, a Buddhist monk set out to climb a tall mountain. The narrow path was not more than a foot or two wide, and it wound around the mountain to a beautiful, glittering temple at the mountain peak.

The monk climbed the path at varying rates of speed. He stopped many times along the way to rest and to eat the fruit he carried with him. He reached the temple just before sunset. At the temple, he fasted and meditated for several days. Then he began his journey back along the same path, starting at sunrise and walking, as before, at variable speeds with many stops along the way. However, his average speed going down the hill was greater than his average climbing speed.

Prove that there must be a spot along the path that the monk will pass on both trips at exactly the same time of day. (The answer is found in Figure 11.1.)

likely to solve the problem correctly, compared to students who used alternative problem representations. The matrix method is especially suitable when the information is stable, as in Demonstration 11.3, rather than changing over time (Novick, 2006). Now try Demonstration 11.4 before you read further.

Diagrams. We know that diagrams are helpful when we want to assemble an object. For example, Novick and Morse (2000) asked students to construct origami objects—such as a miniature piano—using folded paper. People who received both a verbal description and a step-by-step diagram were much more accurate than people who received only a verbal description.

Diagrams can be useful when you want to represent a large amount of information. For example, a **hierarchical tree diagram** is a figure that uses a tree-like structure to specify various possible options in a problem. This kind of diagram is especially helpful in showing the relationship between categorized items (Novick, 2006). (Figure 6.3 on p. 174 shows a hierarchical tree diagram in a different context.)

Diagrams can represent complicated information in a clear, concrete form, so that you have more "mental space" in working memory for other problem-solving activities (Halpern, 2003; Hurley & Novick, 2006). Furthermore, students can master these aids with relatively little effort. For example, Novick and her colleagues (1999) provided students with a brief training session on matrices and hierarchical diagrams. After this training session, students were more skilled in choosing the most appropriate method for representing a variety of problems.

A diagram can also provide an additional advantage. For instance, Grant and Spivey (2003) found that diagrams attracted people's eye movements to relevant areas of the diagram, helping them solve problems more successfully.

A graph is sometimes the most effective kind of diagram for representing visual information during problem solving. Consider, for example, the Buddhist monk problem you tried to solve in Demonstration 11.4. As Figure 11.1 illustrates, we can use one line to show the monk going up the mountain on the first day. We can then use a second line to show the monk coming down the mountain several days later. The point at which the lines cross tells us the spot that the monk will pass at the same time on each of the two days. I have arbitrarily drawn the lines so that they cross at a point 900 feet up the mountain at 12 noon. However, the two paths must always cross at *some* point, even if you vary the monk's rate of ascent and descent.

Visual Images. Other people prefer to solve problems like the one about the Buddhist monk by using visual imagery. One young woman who chose a visual approach to this problem reported the following:

> I tried this and that, until I got fed up with the whole thing, but the image of that monk in his saffron robe walking up the hill kept persisting in my mind. Then a moment came when, superimposed on this image, I saw another, more transparent one, of the monk walking down the hill, and I realized in a flash that the two figures must meet at some point some time—regardless at what speed they walk and how often each of them stops. Then I reasoned out what I already knew: whether the monk descends

FIGURE 11.1

**A Graphic Representation of the Buddhist Monk Problem
in Demonstration 11.4.**

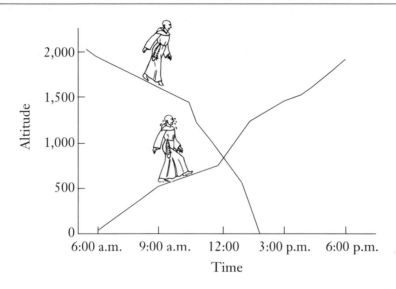

two days or three days later comes to the same; so I was quite justified in letting him descend on the same day, in duplicate so to speak. (Koestler, 1964, p. 184)

Notice that a visual image can let us escape from the boundaries of traditional, concrete representations. Good visual-imagery skills also provide an advantage when a problem requires you to construct a figure (Adeyemo, 1994; Gorman, 2006; Pylyshyn, 2006).

So far, we have considered the importance of attention in understanding problems. We've also seen that problems can be represented according to several different formats, including symbols, matrices, diagrams, and visual images. Our final topic in this section moves into a new dimension because it emphasizes the rich environmental and social context in which we understand the problems that we must solve.

Situated Cognition: The Importance of Context

In the streets of several large cities in Brazil, 10-year-old boys frequently sold candy to people passing by. Researchers studied these children, who had no formal education, yet they demonstrated a sophisticated understanding of mathematics. In addition, during that era, they were using an inflated monetary system in which a box of candy bars could sell for 20,000 Brazilian cruzeiros. Also, a seller might offer two candy bars for 500 cruzeiros, and five candy bars for 1,000 cruzeiros, so he needed to understand how to compare two ratios (Carraher et al., 1985; Robertson, 2001; Woll, 2002).

How can children understand ratio comparisons—a concept that 10-year-olds seldom learn in North American schools? Many psychologists and educators emphasize situated cognition. Supporters of the **situated-cognition approach** argue that our ability to solve a problem is tied into the specific context in which we learned to solve that problem (Lave, 1997; Robertson, 2001; Seifert, 1999). These supporters also argue that an abstract intelligence test or aptitude test often fails to reveal how competent a person would be in solving problems in real-life settings (Kyllonen & Lee, 2005).

The research on situated cognition demonstrates that ordinary people frequently succeed in figuring out which brand of a particular product is cheaper in the grocery store, even though they would fail to understand the same problem on a standardized mathematics test (Dowker, 2005; Kirshner & Whitson, 1997; Lave, 1988). It is important, however, not to overstate the advantages of situated cognition. We obviously do transfer much of our classroom knowledge to our everyday problem solving (Dowker, 2005; Reed, 1999).

The traditional cognitive approach to thinking emphasizes the processes that take place inside an individual person's head. The situated-cognition approach argues that the traditional cognitive approach is too simplistic. After all, in real life, our cognitive processes take advantage of an information-rich environment (Chrisley, 2004; Olson & Olson, 2003; Wilson, 2002). In real life, we also interact with other people, who provide information and help us clarify our cognitive processes. All these factors help us become more competent in understanding and solving problems (Glaser, 2001; Seifert, 1999).

As you can imagine, the situated-cognition perspective has important implications for education. It suggests that children should have experience in solving authentic math problems that they are likely to encounter outside a school setting. The situated-cognition perspective also suggests that college students can learn especially effectively during internships and other practical settings (Hakel, 2001; Jitendra et al., 2007).

This situated-cognition perspective is consistent with the idea that psychologists should emphasize ecological validity if they want to accurately understand cognitive processes. As noted in Chapter 1 and in Chapter 5—in connection with autobiographical memory—a study has **ecological validity** if the conditions in which the research is conducted are similar to the natural setting in which the results will be applied. For example, a study of children's mathematical skills in selling candy would have greater ecological validity than a study of children's mathematical skills on a paper-and-pencil, standardized examination.

One important principle of the situated-cognition perspective is that people learn skills within the context of a specific situation, such as a grocery store. As a consequence, they may fail to transfer these skills and use them effectively in another situation, such as a standardized math test (Anderson, Reder, & Simon, 1996; Bereiter, 1997). We will return to this problem later in the chapter, when we examine how people often fail to appreciate an analogy between previous problem-solving tasks and the problem they are currently trying to solve.

◉ Section Summary: *Understanding the Problem*

1. When you engage in problem solving, you begin with the initial state and try to overcome the obstacles in order to reach the goal state.

2. To understand a problem, you need to create an accurate mental representation of the problem.

3. Attention is relevant in problem solving because attention is limited, because competing thoughts can produce divided attention, and because problem solvers must focus their attention on the appropriate part of the problem.

4. Methods for representing problems include symbols, matrices, diagrams, and visual images.

5. According to the situated-cognition approach, we must emphasize the environmental and social context for problem solving. People can solve problems in real-life settings that they might not be able to solve in a school setting.

PROBLEM-SOLVING STRATEGIES

Once you have represented the problem, you can use many different strategies to attack it. Some strategies are very time consuming. For instance, an **algorithm** is a method that will always produce a solution to the problem, although the process can sometimes be inefficient (Sternberg & Ben-Zeev, 2001; Thagard, 2005). One example of an algorithm is a method called an **exhaustive search,** in which you try out all possible answers using a specified system. For instance, a high school student might be faced with the algebra problem in Demonstration 11.2 on an examination. The student could begin with $m = 0$ and $s = 0$ and try all possible values for m and s until the solution is reached. With such an inefficient algorithm, however, the exam would probably be over before the student solves even one problem!

Algorithms are often inefficient and unsophisticated. Other, more sophisticated methods reduce the possibilities that must be explored to find a solution. For example, suppose that you have been working on some anagrams, rearranging a string of letters to create an English word. The next anagram is LSSTNEUIAMYOUL. You might begin to solve that lengthy anagram by trying to identify the first two letters of your target word; you decide to pick out only pronounceable two-letter combinations that frequently appear at the beginning of a word. Perhaps you would reject combinations such as *LS, LT,* and *LY,* but you consider *LE, LU,* and—ideally—*SI.* This strategy would probably lead you to a solution much faster than an exhaustive search of all the more than 87 billion possible arrangements of the fourteen letters in SIMULTANEOUSLY.

The strategy of looking only for pronounceable letter combinations is an example of a heuristic. As you know from other chapters, a **heuristic** is a general rule that is usually correct. In problem solving, a heuristic is a strategy in which you ignore some alternatives and explore only those alternatives that seem especially likely to produce a solution.

We noted that algorithms such as an exhaustive search will always produce a solution, although you may grow a few years older in the process. Heuristics, in contrast, do not guarantee a correct solution. For instance, suppose you were given the anagram IPMHYLOD, and you use the heuristic of rejecting unlikely combinations of letters at the beginning of the target word. If you reject words beginning with LY, you would fail to find the correct solution, LYMPHOID. When solving a problem, you'll need to weigh the benefits of a heuristic's speed against the costs of possibly missing the correct solution.

Psychologists have conducted more research on problem solvers' heuristics than on their algorithms. One reason is that most everyday problems cannot be solved by algorithms. For example, no algorithm can be applied to the problem of discovering a classmate's name and contact information (p. 357). Furthermore, people are more likely to use heuristics than algorithms. Three of the most widely used heuristics are the analogy, the means-ends heuristic, and the hill-climbing heuristic. Let's examine these heuristics and then discuss cross-cultural factors that may be related to strategy choice.

The Analogy Approach

Every day you use analogies to solve problems. When confronted with a problem in a statistics course, for example, you refer to previous examples in your textbook. When you write a paper for your cognitive psychology course, you use many of the same strategies that were helpful when you wrote a previous paper for social psychology. When you use the **analogy** approach in problem solving, you employ a solution to a similar, earlier problem to help in solving a new one (Leighton & Sternberg, 2003). In a cross-cultural study, students in Brazil, India, and the United States were most likely to choose the analogy approach as their preferred strategy in solving problems (Güss & Wiley, 2007).

Analogies are also prominent in creative breakthroughs in domains such as art, politics, science, and engineering (Gordon, 2004; Kyllonen & Lee, 2005; Young, 2007). For example, Wilbur and Orville Wright designed some of the features of their airplanes by creating an analogy between the wings of a bird and the wings of an airplane. Specifically, they noticed that birds could control their flight patterns by making small adjustments in the orientation of their wing tips. They therefore designed airplane wing tips so that pilots could make subtle adjustments by using metal rods and gears (Weisberg, 2006).

Let's first consider the general structure of the analogy approach. Then we'll look at some of the factors that can encourage problem solvers to use the analogy approach most effectively.

The Structure of the Analogy Approach. The major challenge for people who use the analogy strategy is to determine the real problem—that is, the abstract puzzle underneath all the details. In the section on understanding the problem, we emphasized that problem solvers must peel away the irrelevant, superficial information in order to reach the core of the problem (Whitten & Graesser, 2003). Researchers use the term **problem isomorphs** to refer to a set of problems that have the same under-lying structures and solutions but different specific details.

The major barrier to using the analogy approach, however, is that people tend to focus more on the superficial content of the problem than on its abstract, underlying meaning (Bassok, 2003; Whitten & Graesser, 2003). In other words, they pay more attention to the obvious **surface features,** the specific objects and terms used in the question. Unfortunately, these problem solvers may fail to emphasize the **structural features,** the underlying core that they must understand in order to solve the prob-lem correctly. (Try Demonstration 11.5 before you read further.)

For example, Rutgers University wanted to design a system that would allow prospective students to keep track of the status of their college applications. At first, Rut-gers staff members looked only at the systems used by other universities, which were similar to their existing system in terms of surface features. Then the Rutgers staff

ⓖ Demonstration 11.5

The Hobbits-and-Orcs Problem

Try solving this problem. (The answer is at the end of the chapter.)

Three Hobbits and three Orcs arrive at the right side of a riverbank, and they all wish to cross to the left side. Fortunately, there is a boat—but unfortu-nately, the boat can hold only two creatures at one time. There is another prob-lem. Orcs are vicious creatures, and whenever there are more Orcs than Hobbits on one side of the river, the Orcs will immediately attack the Hobbits and eat them up. Consequently, you should be certain that you never leave more Orcs than Hobbits on any riverbank. How should the problem be solved? (It must be added that the Orcs, though vicious, can be trusted to bring the boat back!)

shifted their attention to structural features; they realized that they actually had a tracking problem. So they examined the system that the Federal Express company uses to track the location of its package. This system provided a highly effective solution to Rutgers' college-application problem (Ruben, 2001).

Numerous studies have demonstrated that people often fail to see the analogy between a problem they have solved and a new problem isomorph that has similar structural features (e.g., Barnett & Ceci, 2002; Hakel, 2001; Leighton & Sternberg, 2003; Lovett, 2002; Reed, 1977, 1999). As we saw in the discussion of the situated-cognition perspective (pp. 363 to 364), people often have trouble solving the same problem in a new setting; they fail to transfer their knowledge. They may also have trouble solving the same problem when it is "dressed up" with a superficially different cover story (Bassok, 2003). People with limited problem-solving skills and limited metacognitive ability are especially likely to have difficulty using analogies (Chen et al., 2004; Davidson & Sternberg, 1998).

Factors Encouraging Appropriate Use of Analogies.   In many cases, problem solvers can overcome the influence of context, and they can appropriately apply the analogy method. For instance, suppose that two problems initially seem unrelated because they have different surface characteristics. However, these two problems *do* have the same structural characteristics. If someone gives you a hint to compare the two problems, you are likely to discover the structural similarities and use the analogy approach properly (Lovett, 2002; Vander Stoep & Seifert, 1994).

People are also more likely to use the analogy strategy correctly when they try several structurally similar problems before they tackle the target problem (Bassok, 2003; Davidson & Sternberg, 1998). Furthermore, students solve statistics problems more accurately if they have been trained to sort problems into categories on the basis of structural similarities (Quilici & Mayer, 2002).

The research on using analogies to solve problems suggests that this technique can be extremely useful (Leighton & Sternberg, 2003). Furthermore, people can become more effective problem solvers if they are encouraged to emphasize structural similarities.

The Means-Ends Heuristic

The **means-ends heuristic** has two important components: (1) First, you divide the problem into a number of **subproblems**, or smaller problems, and (2) then you try to reduce the difference between the initial state and the goal state for each of the subproblems (Davies, 2005; Ormerod, 2005). The name *means-ends heuristic* is appropriate because it requires you to identify the "ends" you want and then figure out the "means" you will use to reach those ends (Feltovich et al., 2006; Ward & Morris, 2005). When problem solvers use the means-ends heuristic, they must focus their attention on the difference between the initial problem state and the goal state. Researchers emphasize that this heuristic is one of the most effective and flexible problem-solving strategies (Dunbar, 1998; Lovett, 2002).

Every day we all solve problems by using means-ends analysis. For example, several years ago, a student I knew well came running into my office saying, "Can I use your stapler, Dr. Matlin?" When I handed her the stapler, she immediately inserted the bottom edge of her skirt and deftly tacked up the hem. As she explained in a more leisurely fashion later that day, she had been faced with a problem: At 11:50, she realized that the hem of her skirt had come loose, and she was scheduled to deliver a class presentation in 10 minutes. Using the means-ends heuristic, she divided the problem into two subproblems: (1) identifying some object that could fix the hem and (2) locating that object.

When you use the means-ends heuristic to solve a problem, you can proceed in either the forward direction, from the initial state to the goal state, or backward from the goal state to the initial state (Robertson, 2001). Thus, you may solve the second subproblem prior to the first subproblem. Try noticing the kinds of problems you might solve using means-ends analysis, such as writing a term paper for a history course, solving a problem in a statistics class, or figuring out the solution to numerous everyday dilemmas. Let's now examine some research showing how people use means-ends analysis in solving problems, as well as computer-simulation investigations of this heuristic.

Research on the Means-Ends Heuristic. Research demonstrates that people do organize problems in terms of subproblems. For example, Greeno (1974) examined how people solve the Hobbits-and-Orcs problem in Demonstration 11.5. His study showed that people pause at points in the problem when they begin to tackle a subproblem and need to organize a sequence of moves. Working memory is especially active when people are planning one of these move sequences (Simon, 2001; Ward & Allport, 1997).

Sometimes the correct solution to a problem depends on moving backward and temporarily *increasing* the difference between the initial state and the goal state. For example, how did you solve the Hobbits-and-Orcs problem in Demonstration 11.5? Maybe you concentrated on *reducing* the difference between the initial state (all creatures on the right side) and the goal state (all creatures on the left side), and you therefore moved them only from right to left. If you did, you would have ignored some steps that were crucial for solving the problem, such as in Step 6 where you must move *two* creatures backward across the river to the riverbank on the right. (See the steps in the answer on pages 391–392.

Research confirms that people are reluctant to move away from the goal state—even if the correct solution depends on making this temporary detour (Robertson, 2001; R. Morris et al., 2005). In real life, as in the Hobbits-and-Orcs problem, the most effective way to move forward is sometimes to move backward temporarily.

Think about an occasion when you thought that you were almost done with an assignment, and then you discovered that your solution to an earlier subproblem had been inadequate. For example, suppose that you are writing a paper based on journal articles. Then you discover that the resources you gathered during an earlier stage were not appropriate. Now you need to move backward to that earlier subproblem and select new articles. My students tell me that this situation is particularly frustrating, especially because they need to *increase* the difference between the initial state and the goal state. In short, if we use means-ends analysis to solve a problem, we must sometimes violate a strict difference-reduction strategy.

Computer Simulation. One of the most widely discussed examples of computer simulation was devised to account for the way humans use means-ends analysis in solving problems (Baron, 1994; Stillings et al., 1995). Specifically, Allen Newell and Herbert Simon developed a theory that featured subgoals and reducing the difference between the initial state and the goal state (Newell & Simon, 1972; Simon, 1995, 1999). Let's first consider some general characteristics of computer simulation, when applied to problem solving. Then we'll briefly discuss Newell and Simon's approach, as well as more recent developments in computer simulation.

As we discussed earlier in the book, when researchers use **computer simulation,** they write a computer program that will perform a task the same way that a human would. For example, a researcher might try to write a computer program for the Hobbits-and-Orcs problem, which you tried in Demonstration 11.5. The program should make some false starts, just as a human would. The program should be no better at solving the problem than a human would be, and it also should be no worse. The researcher tests the program by having it solve a problem and noting whether the steps it takes match the steps that humans would take in solving the problem.

In 1972, Newell and Simon developed a now-classic computer simulation called General Problem Solver. **General Problem Solver (GPS)** is a program whose basic strategy is means-ends analysis. The goal of the GPS is to mimic the processes that normal humans use when they tackle these problems (Lovett, 2002; Simon, 1996). GPS has several different methods of operating, including the difference-reduction strategy.

The General Problem Solver was the first program to simulate a variety of human symbolic behaviors (Sobel, 2001; Sternberg & Ben-Zeev, 2001). As a result, GPS has had an important impact on the history of cognitive psychology. It was used to simulate how humans solve transport problems like that of the Hobbits and Orcs.

Newell and Simon eventually discarded the GPS because its generality was not as great as they had wished (Gardner, 1985). Contemporary cognitive scientists also acknowledge that people often solve **ill-defined problems,** where the goal is not obvious; means-ends analysis is therefore not useful (Sobel, 2001).

More recently, John Anderson and his colleagues have designed many computer simulations for solving problems in algebra, geometry, and computer science (Anderson et al., 1995; Anderson & Gluck, 2001). These projects are an outgrowth of Anderson's ACT theory, which was summarized in Chapter 8. These programs were originally developed to learn more about how students acquire skills in problem solving. However, these researchers have also developed "cognitive tutors" that can be used in high school mathematics classes (Anderson et al., 1995). Notice, then, that a project initially designed to examine theoretical questions can be applied to real-life situations.

The Hill-Climbing Heuristic

One of the most straightforward problem-solving strategies is called the hill-climbing heuristic. To understand this heuristic, imagine that your goal is to follow a pathway leading to the top of a hill. Just ahead, you see a fork in the path. Unfortunately, you cannot see far into the distance on either path. Because your goal is to climb upward, you select the path that has the steepest incline. Similarly, when you reach a choice point when using the **hill-climbing heuristic,** you simply select the alternative that seems to lead most directly toward your goal state (Lovett, 2002; Ward & Morris, 2005).

The hill-climbing heuristic can be useful when you do not have enough information about your alternatives—when you can see only the immediate next step (Dunbar, 1998). However, like many heuristics, the hill-climbing heuristic can lead you astray. The biggest drawback to this heuristic is that problem solvers must consistently choose the alternative that appears to lead most directly toward the goal. In doing so, they may fail to choose a less direct alternative, which may have greater long-term benefits. For example, a hillside path that seems to lead upward may quickly come to an abrupt end. The hill-climbing heuristic certainly does not guarantee that you'll end up on the top of the hill (Robertson, 2001).

Similarly, a student whose goal is to earn a high salary may decide to take a job immediately after graduating from college, although a graduate degree may yield greater long-term benefits. Sometimes the best solution to a problem requires us to move temporarily backward—away from the goal (Lovett, 2002). The major point to remember about the hill-climbing heuristic is that it encourages short-term goals, rather than long-term solutions.

Individual Differences: Cross-Cultural Comparisons in Problem-Solving Strategies

So far, the individual-differences features in your textbook have examined two main categories of topics:

1. The relationship between psychological problems and performance on a variety of cognitive tasks. These psychological problems include schizophrenia, obsessive-compulsive disorder, major depression, Attention-Deficit/Hyperactivity Disorder, and test anxiety.
2. The relationship between other personal characteristics and performance on a variety of cognitive tasks. These personal characteristics include social goals, gender, expertise, and profession.

In this chapter, our individual-differences feature belongs in the second category, because it examines the relationship between culture and problem-solving strategies. We will focus on a study by C. Dominik Güss and Brian Wiley (2007), published in *Journal of Cognition and Culture*. Güss and Wiley located 326 university students in the United States, Brazil, and India. Most students were in their early 20s. The researchers asked the students to complete a questionnaire that assessed their preferences in strategies used to solve problems.

For example, one question asked the participants how often they used each of several problem-solving strategies. Figure 11.2 shows how often the students in each group chose each of three particular strategies: analogy, means-end, or free production (that is, generating many different ideas). Güss and Wiley did not include the hill-climbing strategy in this study.

The results showed that U. S. students were slightly more likely than Brazilian and Indian students to report that they frequently used the analogy strategy. In contrast, Brazilian and Indian students were somewhat more likely than U.S. students to report that they frequently used the free-production and the means-ends strategies.

The students also rated each method in terms of its effectiveness in solving problems. According to this second measure, students in the United States gave the highest rating to the analogy method; Brazilian students preferred the means-ends strategy; and Indian students preferred the free-production strategy. However, a third measure showed that all three groups rated the analogy method as being the easiest to apply.

FIGURE 11.2

Cross-Cultural Comparisons in the Reported Frequency of Using Three Representative Strategies for Problem Solving.

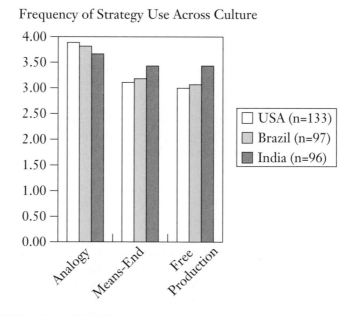

Frequency of Strategy Use Across Culture

Source: Güss & Wiley, 2007.

We need to keep in mind, however, that the cross-cultural differences in this study are relatively small. For example, the largest cross-cultural difference in Figure 11.2 is still less than half a point on a 5-point scale. We also need to remember a caution emphasized in Chapter 3: People may not have accurate insights into their cognitive processes. In particular, they may not be aware of the strategies they actually use when they encounter a problem that needs to be solved.

Section Summary: *Problem-Solving Strategies*

1. With algorithms, such as exhaustive search, the problem solver eventually reaches a solution. However, this method is often very time consuming. In contrast, heuristics are faster because they examine only a few of the alternatives; however, they do not guarantee an appropriate solution.

2. One important heuristic is the analogy approach, in which people solve a new problem by referring to an earlier problem. They may be distracted by superficial similarity, but several precautions can encourage people to emphasize structural similarity.

3. The means-ends heuristic requires dividing a problem into subproblems and then trying to reduce the difference between the initial state and the goal state for each of the subproblems. The General Problem Solver (GPS) is a computer simulation that was designed to use means-ends analysis.

4. One of the simplest problem-solving strategies is the hill-climbing heuristic; at every choice point, you select the alternative that seems to lead most directly to the goal. However, this strategy may not produce the best long-term solution.

5. University students from the United States, Brazil, and India report somewhat different patterns of usage and preference when assessing problem-solving strategies.

FACTORS THAT INFLUENCE PROBLEM SOLVING

Theme 5 of this book focuses on the interplay between bottom-up processing and top-down processing. **Bottom-up processing** emphasizes the information about the stimulus, as registered on our sensory receptors. In contrast, **top-down processing** emphasizes our concepts, expectations, and memory, which we have acquired from past experience.

As you'll see in this section, these two kinds of processing help us understand how several important factors can influence our ability to solve a problem. For example, experts use top-down processing effectively when they solve problems; they take advantage of factors such as their knowledge, memory, and strategies. In contrast, both mental set and functional fixedness can interfere with solving a problem; both of these factors rely too heavily on top-down processing. This chapter's In-Depth section also shows how stereotypes may encourage people to rely on overactive top-down processing, which leads to poor problem-solving ability. Finally, if the problem requires insight, we must also overcome overactive top-down processing in order to approach the problem from an unfamiliar perspective. In short, effective problem solving requires an ideal blend of both top-down and bottom-up processing (Theme 5).

Expertise

An individual with **expertise** demonstrates consistently exceptional performance on representative tasks for a particular area (Ericsson, 2003a, 2003b, 2006). You may recall that we discussed how experts in a particular discipline are likely to have superior long-term memory related to that discipline (Chapter 5), as well as the structure of their concepts (Chapter 8). Now we'll explore how expertise facilitates problem solving. Specifically, experts have top-down processes that allow them to perform well on many different components of problem solving in their area of expertise.

Most cognitive psychologists specify that it takes at least ten years of intense practice to gain expertise in a specific area (Ericsson, 2003b, 2006; Kellogg, 2006; Schraw, 2005). However, experts excel primarily in their own domain of expertise (Feltovich et al., 2006; Robertson, 2001). You wouldn't expect an expert musician to excel at the problem of designing an experiment in cognitive psychology!

Let's trace how experts differ from novices during several phases of problem solving. We'll begin with some of the advantages that operate in the early phases of problem solving, then explore differences in problem-solving strategies, and finally consider more general abilities, such as metacognition.

Knowledge Base.   Novices and experts differ substantially in their knowledge base, or schemas (Bransford et al., 2000; Feltovich et al., 2006; Robertson, 2001). For example, Chi (1981) found in her study of physics problem solving that the novices simply lacked important knowledge about the principles of physics. As we discussed in previous chapters, you need the appropriate schemas in order to understand a topic properly. Experts may perform especially well if they have had training in a variety of relevant settings (Barnett & Koslowski, 2002).

Memory.   Experts differ from novices with respect to their memory for information related to their area of expertise (Bransford et al., 2000; Chi, 2006; Robertson, 2001). The memory skills of experts tend to be very specific.

For example, expert chess players have much better memory than novices for various chess positions. According to one estimate, chess experts can remember about 50,000 "chunks," or familiar arrangements of chess pieces (Chi, 2006; Gobet & Simon, 1996a). Surprisingly, though, chess experts are only slightly better than novices at remembering random arrangements of the chess pieces (Gobet et al., 2004; Gobet & Simon, 1996b). In other words, experts' memory is substantially better only if the chess arrangement fits into a particular schema (Feltovich et al., 2006; Lovett, 2002).

Problem-Solving Strategies.   When experts encounter a novel problem in their area of expertise, they are more likely than novices to use the means-ends heuristic effectively (Sternberg & Ben-Zeev, 2001). That is, they divide a problem into several subproblems, which they solve in a specified order. Experts and novices also differ in the way they use the analogy approach. When solving physics problems, experts are more likely to emphasize the structural similarity between problems. In contrast, novices are more likely to be distracted by surface similarities (Chi, 2006; Leighton & Sternberg, 2003). Now try Demonstration 11.6 before you read further.

Speed and Accuracy. As you might expect, experts are much faster than novices, and they solve problems very accurately (Chi, 2006; Ericsson, 2003b). Their operations become more automatic, and a particular stimulus situation also quickly triggers a response (Bransford et al., 2000; Glaser & Chi, 1988; Robertson, 2001).

Demonstration 11.6

Mental Set

Try these two examples to see the effects of mental set.

A. Luchins's Water-Jar Problem. Imagine that you have three jars, A, B, and C. For each of the seven problems below, the capacity of the three jars is listed. You must use these jars in order to obtain the amount of liquid specified in the Goal column. You may obtain the goal amount by adding or subtracting the quantities listed in A, B, and C. (The answers can be found a little later in the text, in the discussion of mental set.)

Problem	A	B	C	Goal
1	24	130	3	100
2	9	44	7	21
3	21	58	4	29
4	12	160	25	98
5	19	75	5	46
6	23	49	3	20
7	18	48	4	22

B. A Number Puzzle. You are no doubt familiar with the kind of number puzzles in which you try to figure out the pattern for the order of numbers. Why are these numbers arranged in this order?

8, 5, 4, 9, 1, 7, 6, 3, 2, 0

The answer appears at the end of the chapter.

Source: Part A of this demonstration is based on Luchins, 1942.

On some tasks, experts may solve problems faster because they use parallel processing, rather than serial processing. As the discussion on attention in Chapter 3 noted, **parallel processing** handles two or more items at the same time. In contrast, **serial processing** handles only one item at a time. Novick and Coté (1992) discovered that experts frequently solved anagrams in less than 2 seconds. These experts typically solved the anagrams so quickly that they must have been considering several alternate solutions at the same time. In contrast, the novices solved the anagrams so slowly that they were probably using serial processing.

Metacognitive Skills. Experts are better than novices at monitoring their problem solving; you may recall that Chapter 6 discussed how self-monitoring is a component of metacognition. For example, experts seem to be better at judging the difficulty of a problem, and they are more skilled at allocating their time appropriately when solving problems (Bransford et al., 2000). In addition, they can recover relatively quickly when they realize that they have made an error (Feltovich et al., 2006).

Experts are definitely more skilled at numerous phases of problem solving and are also more skilled at monitoring their progress while working on a problem. However, experts perform poorly on one task related to metacognition. Specifically, experts underestimate the amount of time that novices will require to solve a problem in the experts' area of specialization (Hinds, 1999). In contrast, the novices are more accurate in realizing that solving the problem will be difficult!

Mental Set

Before you read further, be sure to try Demonstration 11.6, which illustrates two examples of a mental set. When problem solvers have a **mental set,** they keep trying the same solution they have used in previous problems, even though the problem could be solved by a different, easier method. If you have a mental set, you close your mind prematurely, and you stop thinking about how to solve a problem effectively (Kruglanski, 2004; Langer & Moldoveanu, 2000; Lovett, 2002).

We noted earlier that problem solving demands both top-down and bottom-up processing (Theme 5). Expertise makes *appropriate* use of top-down processing, because experts can employ their previous knowledge to solve problems both quickly and accurately. In contrast, both mental set and functional fixedness—which we'll discuss in a moment—represent *overactive* top-down processing. In both of these cases, problem solvers are so strongly guided by their previous experience that they fail to consider more effective solutions to their problems.

The classic experiment on mental set is Abraham Luchins's (1942) water-jar problem, illustrated in Part A of Demonstration 11.6. The best way to solve Problem 1 in Part A is to fill up jar B and remove one jarful with jar A and two jarfuls with jar C. Problems 1 through 5 can all be solved in this fashion, so they create a mental set for the problem solver. Most people will keep using this method when they reach Problems 6 and 7. Unfortunately, their previous learning will actually hinder their performance, because these last two problems can be solved by easier, more direct methods. For example, Problem 6 can be solved by subtracting C from A, and Problem 7 can be solved by adding C to A.

In his classic study, Luchins (1942) gave one group of participants a series of complex problems such as Problems 1 through 5 that we just discussed. He found that almost all of them persisted in using the same complex solution on later problems. In contrast, participants in a control group began right away with problems such as 6 and 7 in the demonstration. These people almost always solved these problems in the easier fashion. The same findings have been replicated in a series of three experiments by McKelvie (1990). Similarly, college students designed less creative toys if they had already seen toys that had been made by other people (Smith, 1995; Smith et al., 1993).

A mental set is related to a concept that Carol Dweck (2006) calls a "fixed mindset." If you have a **fixed mindset,** you believe that you have a certain amount of intelligence and other skills, and no amount of effort can help you perform better. You give up on trying to discover new ways to improve your abilities. In contrast, if you have a **growth mindset,** you believe that you can cultivate your intelligence and other skills. You challenge yourself to perform better, whether you are trying to learn how to play tennis, how to adjust to a new roommate, or how to perform better on your next examination in your course in cognitive psychology.

Functional Fixedness

Like a mental set, functional fixedness occurs when our top-down processing is overactive; we rely too heavily on our previous concepts, expectations, and memory. However, mental set refers to our problem-solving strategies, whereas functional fixedness refers to the way we think about physical objects. Specifically, **functional fixedness** means that the functions or uses we assign to an object tend to remain fixed or stable. As a result, we fail to think about the features of this object that might be useful in helping us solve a problem (German & Barrett, 2005; Lovett, 2002).

The classic study in functional fixedness is called Duncker's candle problem (Duncker, 1945). Imagine that you have been led to a room that contains a table. On the table are three objects: a candle, a matchbox holding some matches, and a box of thumbtacks. Your task is to find a way to attach a candle to the wall of the room so that it burns properly, using only the objects on the table. The solution requires overcoming functional fixedness by thinking flexibly. You need to realize that the matchbox can also be used for a different purpose, holding a candle, rather than just holding some matches. In fact, you can tack the empty matchbox to the wall, so that it can serve as a candle-holder.

In our everyday life, most of us have access to a variety of tools and objects, so functional fixedness does not create a significant handicap. In contrast, consider the quandary of Dr. Angus Wallace and Dr. Tom Wong. These physicians had just left on a plane for Hong Kong when they learned that another passenger was experiencing a collapsed lung. The only surgical equipment they had brought onboard was a segment of rubber tubing and a scalpel. Still, they operated on the woman and saved her life, using only this modest equipment and objects in the airplane that normally have fixed functions—a coat hanger, a knife, a fork, and a bottle of Evian water (Adler & Hall, 1995).

Interestingly, functional fixedness can even be demonstrated in cultures with little experience using manufactured objects. For example, German and Barrett (2005) showed some simple kitchen objects to adolescents living near the Amazon River in Ecuador. If the adolescents saw a spoon being used to stir rice, they later had difficulty imagining that the spoon could also serve as a bridge between two other objects.

Mental set and functional fixedness are two examples of part of Theme 2: Mistakes in cognitive processing can often be traced to a strategy that is basically very rational. It is generally a wise strategy to use the knowledge you learned in solving earlier problems to solve a current dilemma. If an old idea works well, keep using it! However, in the case of a mental set, we apply the strategy gained from past experience too rigidly and fail to notice more efficient solutions. Similarly, objects in our world normally have fixed functions. For example, we use a screwdriver to tighten a screw, and we use a coin to purchase something. In general, the strategy of using one object for one task and a second object for a different task is appropriate. Functional fixedness occurs, however, when we apply that strategy too rigidly. For example, we fail to realize that—if we don't have a screwdriver—a coin may provide a handy substitute.

IN DEPTH

Stereotypes and Problem Solving

So far, we have examined mental set and functional fixedness, two situations in which top-down processes are overactive. Let's now focus on a third situation: Our top-down processes may be overactive because our stereotypes can influence our beliefs about our own abilities. Some research on this topic has been conducted about ethnic-group stereotypes and social-class stereotypes (Crozet & Claire, 1998; Steele & Aronson, 1995). However, the most widely researched topic is gender stereotypes.

As we noted in Chapter 8, **gender stereotypes** are organized, widely shared sets of beliefs about the characteristics of females and males (Fiske, 2004; Schneider, 2004). A typical stereotype is that men are more skilled than women in solving mathematics problems. Gender stereotypes may be partially accurate, but they do not apply to every person of the specified gender. For instance, many women will score higher than the average man on any test of math problem-solving ability.

To provide a context for our discussion here, glance back at the research about inferences based on gender stereotypes. Pages 279 to 280 of Chapter 8 reported, for example, that many women do not associate themselves with mathematics, and this tendency holds true even for women who are math majors.

The Nature of Stereotype Threat. Imagine two high school seniors—Jennifer and Matthew—who are about to begin the math portion of the Scholastic Assessment Test (SAT) for the first time. Both are excellent students, with A averages in their math courses. They know that this will probably be the most important test they will ever take, because the results could determine which college they will attend. Both students are anxious, but Jennifer has an additional source of anxiety: She must struggle with the popular stereotype that, because she is a female, she should score lower than male students (Quinn & Spencer, 2001). This additional anxiety may in fact lead her to solve math problems less effectively and to earn a relatively low score on the math portion of the SAT.

In this example, Jennifer is experiencing **stereotype threat:** If you belong to a group that is hampered by a negative stereotype—and you think about your membership in that group—your performance may suffer (Hyde, 2007b; Johns et al., 2005; Steele, 1997).

Research with Asian American Females. Consider some research by Shih and her coauthors (1999), in which all of the participants were Asian American women. In North America, one stereotype is that Asian Americans are "good at math," compared to those from other ethnic groups. In contrast, as we just discussed, another stereotype is that women are "bad at math," compared to men.

Shih and her coworkers (1999) divided the Asian American women into three different conditions. Let's examine how these conditions influenced their scores on a difficult math test.

1. *Ethnicity-emphasis condition:* One group of participants were asked to indicate their ethnicity and then answer several questions about their ethnic identity. Then they took a challenging math test. These women answered 54% of the questions correctly.

2. *Control-group condition:* A second group of participants did not answer any questions beforehand. They simply took the challenging math test. These women answered 49% of the questions correctly.

3. *Gender-emphasis condition:* A third group of participants were asked to indicate their gender and then answer several questions about their gender identity. Then they took the challenging math test. These women answered only 43% of the questions correctly.

Apparently, when Asian American women are reminded of their ethnicity, they perform relatively well. However, when Asian American women are reminded of their gender, they may experience stereotype threat, and their problem-solving ability could decline. Ambady and her coauthors (2001) demonstrated this same pattern among Asian American girls enrolled in elementary and middle school.

Research with European American Females. The effects of stereotype threat have also been replicated in samples where most of the women are European American (O'Brien & Crandall, 2003; Quinn & Spencer, 2001). For instance, O'Brien and Crandall (2003) studied a group of college women taking a difficult math test. Some women were told that they would take a math test that was known to show gender differences. These women performed significantly worse than women in a second group, who were told that the math test was known to show no gender differences.

Similarly, Johns and his coauthors (2005) gave one group of students a brief description of stereotype threat. The description pointed out that any anxiety they might feel could be the results of these negative stereotypes, rather than their own actual math ability. In this condition, gender differences in math-test scores were greatly reduced.

Potential Explanations. Why should stereotype threat often lead to poorer performance? Two factors probably contribute to the problem. One factor is that stereotype threat probably produces arousal, especially because other research reported elevated blood pressure when people experienced stereotype threat (Blascovich et al., 2001; O'Brien & Crandall, 2003). High arousal is likely to interfere with working memory, especially on difficult tasks. Research shows that people may "choke under pressure" on a challenging math test. This anxiety apparently reduces the capacity of working memory (Beilock & Carr, 2005).

A second factor is that females who are taking a difficult math test may work hard to suppress the thought that they should perform poorly (Quinn & Spencer, 2001). As Chapter 3 pointed out, thought suppression requires great effort, which reduces the capacity of working memory even further.

In what way do the increased arousal and reduced working memory actually decrease women's ability to solve math problems? Quinn and Spencer (2001) proposed that these factors decrease women's abilities to construct problem-solving strategies. They studied female and male undergraduates. Half of each group completed a test with word problems; these items required strategies in order to convert the words into algebraic equations. The other half of each group completed a test with algebra problems (presented as numerical equations); these items did not require any conversion strategies. As Figure 11-3 shows, the men performed significantly better than the women on the word problems, but men and women performed similarly on the algebra problems.

At this point, you may be wondering whether gender differences appear on real-world mathematics tests, in addition to the psychology laboratory. The short answer to this question is that females tend to earn higher grades in math classes, and most standardized math tests show no substantial gender differences. During high school, however, males tend to score higher on difficult word problems and on the math portion of the SAT (Hyde, 2005, 2007a, 2007b; Matlin, 2008). These two kinds of strategy-based math questions are precisely the kind of problems that stereotype threat is likely to hinder. Before you read further, try Demonstration 11.7.

ⓢ Demonstration 11.7

Two Insight Problems

A. The Sahara Problem (based on Perkins, 2001). Suppose that you are driving a Jeep through the Sahara Desert. You see someone lying facedown in the sand. Exploring further, you see that it's a dead man. You see no tracks anywhere nearby, and there have been no recent winds to erase the tracks. You look in a pack on the man's back. What do you find?

B. The Triangle Problem. With six matches, construct four equilateral triangles. One complete match must make up one side of each triangle. The answers to these two problems appear at the end of the chapter.

FIGURE 11.3

Average Performance by Men and Women on Word Problem Test and Numerical Test.

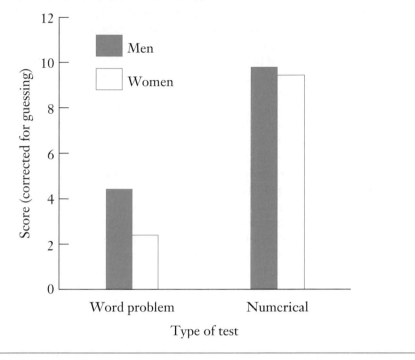

Source: Quinn & Spencer, 2001.

Insight Versus Noninsight Problems

Demonstration 11.7 illustrates two typical insight problems. When you solve an **insight problem,** the problem initially seems impossible to solve, but an alternative approach suddenly bursts into your consciousness; you immediately realize that your new solution is correct (Davidson, 2003; Johnson-Laird, 2005b; Lovett, 2002). In contrast, when you work on a **noninsight problem,** you solve the problem gradually, using your memory, reasoning skills, and a routine set of strategies (Davidson, 1995; Schooler et al., 1995). For example, Demonstration 11.1 was a noninsight problem, because you pursued the answer in a logical, step-by-step fashion, gradually solving the algebra problem.

Let's examine the nature of insight in somewhat more detail. Then we'll consider people's metacognitions when working on insight and noninsight problems.

The Nature of Insight. The concept of insight was very important to gestalt psychologists (Johnson-Laird, 2005; Lovett, 2002). As Chapters 1 and 2 noted, gestalt psychologists emphasized organizational tendencies, especially in perception and in problem solving. They argued that the parts of a problem may initially seem unrelated to one another, but a sudden flash of insight could make the parts instantly fit together into a solution (Davidson, 2003). If you solved the problems successfully in Demonstration 11.7, you experienced this feeling of sudden success.

Behaviorists rejected the concept of insight because the idea of a sudden cognitive-reorganization was not compatible with their emphasis on observable behavior. Furthermore, some contemporary psychologists prefer to think that people solve problems in a gradual, orderly fashion. These psychologists are uneasy about the sudden transformation that is suggested by the concept of insight (Metcalfe, 1998). Currently, then, some psychologists favor the concept of insight, and others reject this concept.

According to the psychologists who favor the concept of insight, people who are working on an insight problem usually hold some inappropriate assumptions when they begin to solve the problem (Chi, 2006; Ormerod et al., 2006). For example, when you began to solve Part B of Demonstration 11.7, at first you probably assumed that the six matches needed to be arranged on a flat surface. In other words, top-down processing inappropriately dominated your thinking, and you were considering the wrong set of alternatives (Ormerod et al., 2006).

In some cases, the best way to solve an insight problem is to stop thinking about this problem and do something else for a while. Many artists, scientists, and other creative people believe that incubation helps them solve problems creatively. **Incubation** is defined as a situation in which you are initially unsuccessful in solving a problem, but you are more likely to solve the problem after taking a break, rather than continuing to work on the problem without interruption (Perkins, 2001; Segal, 2004). Incubation sounds like a plausible strategy for solving insight problems (e.g., Csikszentmihalyi, 1996). Unfortunately, however, the well-controlled laboratory research shows that incubation is not consistently helpful (Perkins, 2001; Segal, 2004; Ward, 2001).

We've noted that top-down processing may prevent you from solving an insight problem. In contrast, noninsight problems—such as straight forward algebra problems—typically do benefit from top-down processing (McCormick, 2003). The strategies you learned in high school math classes offer guidance as you work, step-by-step, toward the proper conclusion of the problem.

Metacognition During Problem Solving. When you are working on a problem, how confident are you that you are on the right track? Janet Metcalfe (1986) argues that the pattern of your metacognitions differs for noninsight and insight problems. Specifically, people's confidence builds gradually for problems that do not require insight, such as standard high school algebra problems. In contrast, when people work on insight problems, they experience a sudden leap in confidence when they are close to a correct solution. In fact, the sudden rise in confidence can be used to distinguish insight from noninsight problems (Herzog & Robinson, 2005; Metcalfe & Wiebe, 1987).

Let us examine Metcalfe's (1986) research on metacognitions about insight problems. Metcalfe presented students with problems like this one:

A stranger approached a museum curator and offered him an ancient bronze coin. The coin had an authentic appearance and was marked with the date 544 B.C. The curator had happily made acquisitions from suspicious sources before, but this time he promptly called the police and had the stranger arrested. Why? (p. 624)

As students worked on this kind of insight problem, they supplied ratings every 10 seconds on a "feeling-of-warmth" scale. A rating of 0 indicated that they were completely "cold" about the problem, with no glimmer of a solution. A score of 10 meant that they were certain they had a solution.

As you can see from Figure 11.4, the participants' warmth ratings initially showed only gradual increases for the insight problems. However, their warmth ratings soared dramatically when they discovered the correct solution. If you figured out the answer to the coin question, did you experience this same sudden burst of certainty? (Incidentally, the answer to this problem is that someone who had actually lived in 544 B.C. could not possibly have used the designation "B.C." to indicate the birth of Christ half a millennium later.) Metcalfe's results have been replicated (Davidson, 1995), confirming that problem solvers typically report a dramatic increase in their confidence when they believe they have located the correct solution to an insight problem.

FIGURE 11.4

"Warmth Ratings" for Answers That Were Correct, as a Function of Time of Rating Prior to Answering.

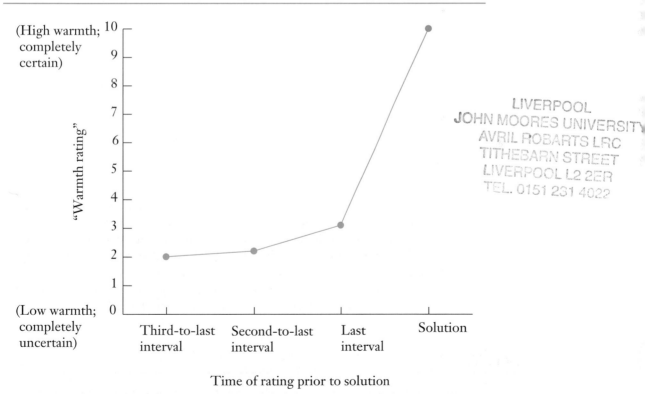

Source: Based on Metcalfe, 1986.

The potential difference between noninsight problems and insight problems suggests some strategies. You might begin to solve a problem by contemplating whether you have had previous experience with similar problems. Top-down processing will be useful when you approach a noninsight problem. From time to time, however, you should also consider whether the problem might require insight. You'll need a different approach to solve an insight problem; there are no clear rules for insight problems (Chi, 2006). However, you might try to represent the problem in a different way (Lovett, 2002; Perkins, 2001). An insight problem forces you to search for the answer "outside the box" by abandoning your customary top-down assumptions and looking for novel solutions.

Section Summary: *Factors That Influence Problem Solving*

1. Experts differ from novices with respect to their knowledge base, memory for task-related material, problem-solving strategies, speed and accuracy, and metacognitive skills.

2. Problem solving can be influenced by your mental set (in which you keep trying the same solution strategy, although another strategy would be more effective) and functional fixedness (in which you assign a fixed use to an object, although the object could be used for other tasks). In both cases, top-down processing is overactive; however, both can be traced to a basically wise strategy.

3. Stereotype threat can occur when people belong to a group that is associated with a negative stereotype; if these people think about this group membership, their performance on a test may suffer.

4. The research shows that stereotype threat is associated with Asian American and European American women; an explanation for stereotype threat may be that problem-solving strategies are hindered by factors such as high arousal and thought suppression.

5. Insight problems are solved when the answer appears suddenly; noninsight problems are solved gradually, using reasoning skills and standardized procedures. Top-down processing is overactive in the case of insight problems; it may be helpful to take a break, because incubation could operate. In contrast, top-down processing is appropriately helpful in the case of noninsight problems.

6. Research on metacognition shows that your confidence builds gradually for *noninsight* problems; in contrast, your confidence on *insight* problems is initially low, but it suddenly increases when you solve the problem.

CREATIVITY

Perhaps you breathed a sigh of relief when you finished the sections on problem solving and prepared to read a section on creativity. Problem solving sounds so routine; people who solve problems trudge along as they work out their means-ends analyses.

In contrast, creativity sounds inspired! People who think creatively often experience moments of genius, and lightbulbs frequently flash above their heads.

Truthfully, however, creativity is an area of problem solving. Creativity—like the problem-solving tasks we have already considered—requires moving from an initial state to a goal state. However, creativity is more controversial because we have no standardized definition of creativity, and the theoretical approaches are so diverse (Runco, 2007).

Creativity is a popular topic, both within and beyond psychology. Numerous books on the topic have been published in the current decade (e.g., Heilman, 2005; Kaufman & Baer, 2005, 2006; Levesque, 2001; Nettle, 2001; Perkins, 2001; Runco, 2007; Sawyer, 2003; Shavinina, 2003; Sternberg et al., 2004; Sternberg et al., 2002; Stokes, 2006; Torrance, 2000; Treflinger, 2004). Unfortunately, however, the amount of actual research on creativity has lagged behind the quantity of research on most other topics in cognitive psychology (Mayer, 1999).

Let's begin our exploration of creativity by discussing definitions, as well as two different approaches to creativity. Then we'll consider the relationship between task motivation and creativity.

Definitions

An entire chapter could be written on the variety of definitions for creativity. However, most theorists agree that novelty or originality is a necessary component of creativity (Johnson-Laird, 2005b; Runco, 2007; Weisberg, 2006). But novelty is not enough. The answer we seek must also allow us to reach some goal; it must be useful and appropriate. Suppose I asked you to creatively answer the question, "How can you roast a pig?" The nineteenth-century essayist Charles Lamb observed that one way to roast a pig would be to put it into a house and then burn down the house. The answer certainly meets the criterion of novelty, but it does not fulfill the usefulness requirement. To most theorists, then, **creativity** requires finding solutions that are novel, high quality, and useful (e.g., Boden, 2004; Feist, 2004; Sternberg & Ben-Zeev, 2001).

Although many theorists agree on the basic definition of creativity, their views differ on other characteristics. For instance, some psychologists argue that creativity is based on ordinary thinking, a process similar to our everyday problem solving (e.g., Halpern, 2003; Runco, 2007; Weisberg, 1999). In contrast, other psychologists argue that ordinary people seldom produce creative products. Instead, certain exceptional people are extraordinarily creative in their specific area of expertise, such as music, literature, or science (e.g., Feldman et al., 1994; Simonton, 2004).

Approaches to Creativity

Theorists have devised many different approaches to studying creativity. Let's consider two contrasting viewpoints. The first is Guilford's (1967) classic description of divergent production, and the second is a contemporary perspective that emphasizes the multiple necessary components of creativity (e.g., Lubart & Guignard, 2004; Sternberg & Lubart, 1995).

Divergent Production. Researchers have been interested in measuring creativity for more than a century. However, the initial scientific research is typically traced to J. P. Guilford (Plucker & Renzulli, 1999). Guilford (1967) proposed that creativity should be measured in terms of **divergent production,** or the number of different responses made to each test item. Many contemporary researchers also emphasize that creativity requires divergent thinking, rather than one single best answer (Mayer, 1999; Runco, 2007; Russ, 2001). Demonstration 11.8 shows several ways in which Guilford measured divergent production. To earn a high score, the problem solver must explore in many different directions from the initial problem state. As you can see, some items require test takers to overcome functional fixedness.

ⓢ Demonstration 11.8

Divergent Production Tests

Try the following items, which are similar to Guilford's divergent production tests.

1. Many words begin with an *L* and end with an *N*. In 1 minute, list as many words as possible that have the form *L* _____ *N*. (The words can have any number of letters between the *L* and the *N*.)

2. Suppose that people reached their final height at the age of 2, and so normal adult height would be less than 3 feet. In 1 minute, list as many consequences as possible that would result from this change.

3. Below is a list of names. They can be classified in many ways. For example, one classification would be in terms of the number of syllables: SALLY, MAYA, and HAROLD have two syllables, whereas BETH, GAIL, and JUAN have one syllable. Classify them in as many other ways as possible in 1 minute.

BETH HAROLD GAIL JUAN MAYA SALLY

4. Below are four shapes. In 1 minute, combine them to make each of the following objects: a face, a lamp, a piece of playground equipment, and a tree. Each shape may be used once, many times, or not at all in forming each object, and it may be expanded or shrunk to any size. Each shape may also be rotated.

Source: Based on Guilford, 1967.

Research on tests of divergent production has found moderate correlations between people's test scores and other judgments of their creativity (Guilford, 1967; Sternberg & O'Hara, 1999). However, the number of different ideas may not be the best measure of creativity (Nickerson et al., 1985). After all, this measure does not assess whether the solutions meet the three criteria for creativity—that solutions should be novel, high quality, and useful.

Investment Theory of Creativity. Financial experts tell us that wise investors should buy low and sell high. Similarly, Robert Sternberg and his colleagues propose that creative people, who deal in the world of ideas, also buy low and sell high (Lubart & Guignard, 2004; Lubart & Mouchiroud, 2003; Sternberg & Lubart, 1995, 1996). That is, they produce a creative idea when no one else is interested in the "investment." At a later time, when the idea has become popular, they move on to a new creative project.

What are the characteristics of these people who are wise creative investors? According to Sternberg and Lubart's **investment theory of creativity,** the essential attributes are intelligence, knowledge, motivation, an encouraging environment, an appropriate thinking style, and an appropriate personality. To work creatively, you'll need all six of these attributes. Suppose, for example, that a person qualifies in five of the characteristics, but he or she is low in intelligence. This person will probably not produce something creative (Sternberg, 2001).

Notice that the investment approach to creativity also emphasizes factors in the environment *outside* the individual. People may have creative personal attributes. However, if they lack a supportive work environment, they will not be creative in the workplace (Runco, 2007).

The investment theory of creativity is inherently appealing, particularly because it emphasizes the complex prerequisites for creative achievements (Lubart & Mouchiroud, 2003). Let's now focus on one of these six prerequisites: motivation. As you'll see, some kinds of motivation are particularly likely to enhance creativity.

Task Motivation and Creativity

Physicist Arthur Schawlow won the Nobel Prize in physics in 1981. He was once asked what factors distinguished highly creative from less creative scientists. He answered that the creative scientists are especially motivated by a curiosity that compels them to pursue the answers to a scientific puzzle (Schawlow, 1982).

An important component of creativity is **intrinsic motivation,** or the motivation to work on a task for its own sake, because you find it interesting, exciting, or personally challenging (Collins & Amabile, 1999; Eliott & Mapes, 2002; Runco, 2005). Intrinsic motivation can be contrasted with **extrinsic motivation**, or the motivation to work on a task, not because you find it enjoyable, but in order to earn a promised reward or to win a competition. As you'll see, intrinsic motivation can enhance creativity, whereas some kinds of extrinsic motivation can decrease creativity.

The Relationship Between Intrinsic Motivation and Creativity. Research demonstrates that people are likely to be most creative when they are working on a task that they truly enjoy (e.g., Amabile, 1990, 1996, 1997; Hennessey, 2000; Runco, 2005). In one study, Ruscio and his coauthors (1998) administered a standardized test of intrinsic motivation to college students. The test asked participants to rate their level of interest in three different kinds of activities: writing, art, and problem solving. Several weeks later, the students came to the laboratory, where they were asked to perform tasks in these three areas. Demonstration 11.9 is similar to the writing task, for example.

A group of trained judges then rated the students' creative projects. The results showed that the students with high intrinsic-motivation scores on the standardized test were more likely to produce a creative project.

The Relationship Between Extrinsic Motivation and Creativity. Many studies have demonstrated that students tend to produce less creative projects if they are working on these projects for external reasons (Amabile, 1990, 1994, 1997; Hennessey, 2000). For example, the American haiku you wrote in Demonstration 11.9 would probably have been less creative if you had been told that it would be evaluated by a panel of judges. When people view a task as being just a means of earning a reward, a good grade, or a positive evaluation, their extrinsic motivation is high. As a result, their intrinsic motivation often decreases. Consequently, their creativity is also likely to decrease (Hennessey, 2000; Runco, 2007).

⊚ Demonstration 11.9

Writing a Creative Poem

For this demonstration, you will write an American haiku. These instructions are similar to those that Ruscio and his colleagues supplied to the participants in their study, as follows:

> An American haiku is a five-line poem. As you can see from the sample poem below, the first line simply contains a noun, in this case the noun *ocean.* The second line has two adjectives describing the noun. The third line features three verbs related to the noun. The fourth line is a phrase of any length, which is related to the noun. The last line simply repeats the first line.

> Ocean
> Wavy, foamy
> Roll, tumble, crash
> All captured in this shell at my ear.
> Ocean

Now your task is to write a similar American haiku, featuring the noun *summer.* Take 5 minutes to write this poem.

Source: Based on Ruscio et al., 1998, p. 249.

In a representative study, for example, college students wrote less creative poems when they were told that their poems would be evaluated by a group of professional poets (Amabile, 1996). Other research confirms these findings. The effect usually holds true for both adults and children, and for both artistic creativity and verbal creativity (Amabile, 1990, 1996; Hennessey, 2000; Hennessey & Amabile, 1988).

For many years, researchers had adopted a simple perspective: Intrinsic motivation is good, and extrinsic motivation is bad. You've probably studied psychology long enough to know that no conclusions in our discipline could be that straightforward. A more detailed analysis suggests that creativity can actually be enhanced if the extrinsic factors provide useful information (Amabile, 1997; Collins & Amabile, 1999; Eisenberger & Rhoades, 2001).

In general, however, extrinsic motivation reduces your creativity when it controls and limits your options. These findings have important implications for education and for the workplace: Encourage people to work on tasks they enjoy, and select a system of external rewards that will not undermine people's creative efforts.

◉ Section Summary: *Creativity*

1. Numerous definitions have been proposed for creativity; one common definition is that creativity requires finding a solution that is novel, high quality, and useful.

2. Two approaches to creativity include (a) Guilford's measurements of divergent production and (b) Sternberg's multifactor investment theory, which proposes that creativity requires intelligence, knowledge, motivation, an encouraging environment, an appropriate thinking style, and an appropriate personality.

3. Research suggests that intrinsic motivation promotes high levels of creativity; in contrast, extrinsic motivation can reduce creativity if it controls you and limits your options.

CHAPTER REVIEW QUESTIONS

1. This chapter examined several different methods of representing a problem. Return to pages 360 to 363 and point out how each method could be used to solve a problem you have recently faced, either in college classes or in your personal life during recent weeks. In addition, identify how the situated-cognition perspective can be applied to your understanding of this problem.

2. What barriers prevent our successful use of the analogy approach to problem solving? Think of an area in which you are an expert (such as an academic subject or work-related knowledge) and point out whether you are skilled in recognizing the structural similarities shared by problem isomorphs.

3. In problem solving, how do algorithms differ from heuristics? When you solve problems, what situations encourage each of these two approaches? Describe a

situation in which the means-ends heuristic was more useful than an algorithm. Identify a time when you used the hill-climbing heuristic, and note whether it was effective in solving the problem.

4. Think of someone you know well, who is an expert in a particular area. Explain the cognitive areas in which he or she may have an advantage over a novice. When discussing this area of expertise, does this person "talk over your head" and underestimate the difficulty that other people might have in comprehending the topic?

5. How are mental set and functional fixedness related to each other, and how do they limit problem solving? Why would incubation—when it works—help in overcoming these two barriers to effective problem solving?

6. On two occasions, this chapter discussed metacognition. Discuss these two topics, and point out how metacognitive measures can help us determine which problems require insight and which do not.

7. Imagine that you are teaching seventh grade, and your students are about to take a series of standardized tests in mathematics. Assume that your students hold the stereotype that boys are better at math. Just before the test, you hear the students discussing which gender will earn a higher score. How might stereotype threat influence their performance? Describe two specific ways in which stereotype threat could influence the students' cognitive processes.

8. Think of an example of an insight problem and a noninsight problem that you have solved recently. Based on the discussion of this topic, how would these two problems differ with respect to the way in which you made progress in solving the problem and the nature of your metacognitions about your progress in problem solving.

9. We discussed the influence of the environment on problem solving in several places, in connection with (a) situated cognition, (b) the analogy approach, (c) one of the approaches to creativity, and (d) factors influencing creativity. Using this information, point out why environmental factors are important in problem solving.

10. Imagine that you are supervising ten employees in a small company. Describe how you might use the material in this chapter to encourage more effective problem solving and greater creativity. Then describe the activities you would want to avoid because they might hinder problem solving and creativity.

KEY TERMS

problem solving	understanding	algorithm
initial state	matrix	exhaustive search
goal state	hierarchical tree diagram	heuristic
obstacles	situated-cognition approach	analogy approach
thinking	ecological validity	problem isomorphs

surface features
structural features
means-ends heuristic
subproblems
computer simulation
General Problem Solver
    (GPS)
ill-defined problems
hill-climbing heuristic
bottom-up processing

top-down processing
expertise
parallel processing
serial processing
mental set
fixed mindset
growth mindset
functional fixedness
gender stereotypes
stereotype threat

insight problem
noninsight problem
incubation
creativity
divergent production
investment theory of creativity
intrinsic motivation
extrinsic motivation

RECOMMENDED READINGS

Davidson, J. E., & Sternberg, R. J. (Eds.). (2003). *The psychology of problem solving.* New York: Cambridge University Press. Here's an excellent book that includes chapters on expected topics, such as insight and analogies; however, it also features chapters on cognitive components of problem solving, such as working memory and text comprehension.

Ericsson, K. A., Charness, N., Feltovich, P. J., & Hoffman, R. R. (Eds.). (2006). *The Cambridge handbook of expertise and expert performance.* New York: Cambridge University Press. K. Anders Ericsson is the acknowledged "expert on expertise"; this handbook includes 42 chapters on theoretical, empirical, and applied aspects of expertise.

Halpern, D. F. (2003). *Thought and knowledge: An introduction to critical thinking* (4th ed.). Mahwah, NJ: Erlbaum. Diane Halpern writes clearly and engagingly about critical thinking and higher mental processes; her book includes chapters on problem solving and creativity, and she also provides a cognitive psychology approach to critical thinking.

Runco, M. A. (2007). *Creativity: Theories and themes: Research, development, and practice.* London: Elsevier Academic Press. Here's an academic book about creativity that is both comprehensive and interesting.

ANSWERS TO DEMONSTRATIONS

11.3: In the hospital room problem, Ms. Anderson has mononucleosis, and she is in Room 104.

11.5: In the Hobbits-and-Orcs problem (with R representing the right bank and L representing the left bank), here are the steps in the solution:

1. Move 2 Orcs, R to L.

2. Move 1 Orc, L to R.

3. Move 2 Orcs, R to L.

4. Move 1 Orc, L to R.

5. Move 2 Hobbits, R to L.

6. Move 1 Orc, 1 Hobbit, L to R.

7. Move 2 Hobbits, R to L.

8. Move 1 Orc, L to R.

9. Move 2 Orcs, R to L.
10. Move 1 Orc, L to R.
11. Move 2 Orcs, R to L.

11.6, B: The numbers are in alphabetical order; your mental set probably suggested that the numbers were in some mathematical sequence, not a language-based sequence.

11.7, A: The pack on the man's back contained an unopened parachute. (Other solutions would also be possible.)

11.7, B:

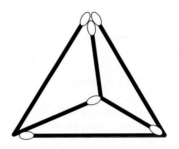

CHAPTER 12

Using Reasoning
and Decision Making

PREVIEW

This chapter considers how people perform two complex cognitive tasks: deductive reasoning and decision making. The topic of thinking includes problem solving (Chapter 11), as well as deductive reasoning and decision making.

In deductive reasoning tasks, you must draw some logical conclusions, based on the information supplied to you. This chapter focuses on conditional reasoning, using statements such as, "If today is Saturday, then Abyssinia Restaurant is open." People make several systematic errors on conditional reasoning tasks. For example, their conclusions may be influenced by their prior beliefs; they may also fail to test whether their hypotheses could be incorrect.

In decision making, we assess and choose among several alternatives; we often use three heuristics, or general strategies, to make decisions. Heuristics usually lead to the correct decision, but we sometimes apply them inappropriately.

1. When using the representativeness heuristic, we judge a sample to be likely because it looks similar to the population from which it was selected. For example, if you toss a coin six times, an outcome of six heads in a row looks very unlikely. However, sometimes we pay so much attention to representativeness that we ignore other important information such as sample size.

2. When using the availability heuristic, we estimate frequency in terms of how easily we think of examples of something. For instance, you estimate the number of corrupt politicians to be large if you can easily think of relevant examples from the news. Unfortunately, availability is often influenced by two irrelevant factors—recency and familiarity—and so this heuristic sometimes leads to decision errors.

3. When using the anchoring and adjustment heuristic, we begin by guessing a first approximation (an anchor) and then make an adjustment, based on other information. This strategy is reasonable, except that our adjustments are typically too small.

We'll also discuss how context and wording influence decisions, why people are often overconfident, and why our hindsight is often inaccurate. Then we'll see that people may actually be less happy if they have a wide variety of choices. We'll complete this chapter by exploring two current perspectives on human decision making.

INTRODUCTION

Every day, you use deductive reasoning, although you probably wouldn't spontaneously choose such a formal-sounding label. For example, suppose that Peter's syllabus for his social psychology course includes this sentence, "If you do not hand in your literature-review paper by May 10, you will fail this course." Peter does not hand in his paper by

May 10. Therefore, we draw the logical conclusion, "Peter will fail the course." Every day, you also make dozens of decisions. Should you ask Professor Adams for the letter of recommendation, or should you try Professor Sanchez?

The topics of problem solving (Chapter 11), deductive reasoning, and decision making are all interrelated, and we will note several similarities among these tasks throughout this chapter. All three topics are included in the general category called thinking. **Thinking** requires you to go beyond the information you were given; thinking also has a goal such as a solution, a decision, or a belief (Baron, 2000). In other words, you begin with several pieces of information, and you must mentally transform that information to solve a problem, to draw a conclusion on a deductive reasoning task, or to make a decision (Waltz et al., 1999).

All three thinking tasks illustrate Theme 2. This theme argues that we often use a heuristic that is typically helpful, but we overgeneralize it to inappropriate situations. Consequently, when we are engaged in a thinking task, we are likely to make a "smart mistake" (Evans, 2005, 2006; Stanovich, 2003).

Our two topics for this chapter—deductive reasoning and decision making—are clearly related. In **deductive reasoning,** you are given some specific premises, and you are asked whether those premises allow you to draw a particular conclusion, based on the principles of logic (Evans, 2004; Halpern, 2003; Johnson-Laird, 2005a). A deductive-reasoning problem provides you with all the information you need to draw a conclusion. Furthermore, the premises are either true or false, and formal logic specifies the rules you must use in order to draw conclusions (Gilhooly, 2005; Roberts & Newton, 2005; Wilhelm, 2005).

Our second topic in this chapter, **decision making,** refers to assessing and choosing among several alternatives. In contrast to deductive reasoning, decision making is much more ambiguous. Some of the information may be missing or contradictory. In addition, no clear-cut rules tell us how to proceed from the information to the conclusions. Furthermore, the consequences of that decision won't be immediately apparent, and you may need to take additional factors into account (Johnson-Laird et al., 2004; Simon et al., 2001). In fact, you may never know whether you would have been wiser to choose Professor Adams or Professor Sanchez.

In real life, the uncertainty of decision making is more common than the certainty of deductive reasoning. However, people have difficulty with both kinds of tasks, and they do not always reach the appropriate conclusions (Evans, 2004; Goodwin & Johnson-Laird, 2005).

DEDUCTIVE REASONING

One of the most common kinds of deductive reasoning tasks is called conditional reasoning. **Conditional reasoning** (or **propositional reasoning**) problems tell us about the relationship between conditions. Here's a typical conditional reasoning task:

> If a student at my college is enrolled in a course in cognitive psychology,
>   then the student must have completed a course in research methods.
> Chris has not completed a course in research methods.
> Therefore, Chris is not taking a course in cognitive psychology.

Notice that this problem tells us about the relationship between conditions, such as the relationship between enrolling in a class and the completion of a prerequisite. The kind of conditional reasoning we consider in this section explores reasoning problems that have an "if . . . then . . ." kind of structure. When researchers study conditional reasoning, they instruct people to judge whether the conclusion is valid or invalid. In the example above, the conclusion, "Chris is not taking a course in cognitive psychology" is indeed valid.

Another common kind of deductive reasoning task is called a syllogism. A **syllogism** consists of two statements that we must assume to be true, plus a conclusion. Syllogisms refer to quantities, so they use the words *all*, *none*, *some*, and other similar terms. Here's a typical syllogism:

> Some psychology majors are friendly people.
>
> Some friendly people are concerned about poverty.
>
> Therefore, some psychology majors are concerned about poverty.

When researchers study syllogisms, they instruct people to judge whether the conclusion is valid, invalid, or indeterminate. In this case, the answer is indeterminate. In fact, those psychology majors who are friendly people and those friendly people who are concerned about poverty could really be two separate populations, with no overlap whatsoever. Notice that our everyday experience encourages us to say, "Yes, the conclusion is valid," because we know that the world contains many psychology majors who are concerned about poverty! In the strict rules of deductive reasoning, however, we must conclude, "The conclusion is indeterminate."

You could take a philosophy course in logic that would spend an entire semester teaching you about the structure and solution of deductive reasoning problems like these. However, we will emphasize the cognitive factors that influence deductive reasoning. Furthermore, we will limit ourselves to conditional reasoning, a kind of deductive reasoning that students typically find more approachable. Fortunately, researchers have found that conditional reasoning tasks and syllogisms are influenced by virtually the same set of cognitive factors (Klauer et al., 2000; Leighton & Sternberg, 2003). In addition, people's performance on conditional reasoning tasks is correlated with their performance on syllogism tasks (Stanovich & West, 2000).

Let's first explore the four basic kinds of conditional reasoning tasks. Next, we'll see how reasoning is influenced by two factors: (1) whether the statements include negative information and (2) whether the problem is concrete or abstract. Then we'll discuss two cognitive errors that people often make when they solve these reasoning problems.

An Overview of Conditional Reasoning

Conditional reasoning situations occur frequently in daily life, yet these problems are surprisingly difficult to solve correctly (Evans, 2004). Let's examine the formal principles that have been devised for solving these problems.

TABLE 12.1

The Propositional Calculus: The Four Kinds of Reasoning, with Examples for the Statement, "If this is an apple, then this is a fruit."

	Portion of the Statement	
Action taken	Antecedent	Consequent
Affirm	Affirming the antecedent (valid)	Affirming the consequent (invalid)
	This is an apple; *therefore this a fruit.*	*This is a fruit;* *therefore this is an apple.*
Deny	Denying the antecedent (invalid)	Denying the consequent (valid)
	This is not an apple; *therefore this is not a fruit.*	*This is not a fruit;* *therefore this is not an apple.*

Table 12.1 illustrates **the propositional calculus,**[*] which is a system for categorizing the kinds of reasoning used in analyzing propositions or statements. Let's first introduce some basic terminology. The word **antecedent** refers to the first proposition or statement; the antecedent is contained in the "if . . ." part of the sentence. The word **consequent** refers to the proposition that comes second; it is the consequence. The consequent is contained in the "then . . ." part of the sentence. When we work on a conditional reasoning task, we can perform two possible actions: (1) We can affirm part of the sentence, saying that it is true; or (2) we can deny part of the sentence, saying that it is false.

By combining the two parts of the sentence with the two actions, we have four conditional reasoning situations:

1. **Affirming the antecedent** means that you say the "if . . ." part of the sentence is true. As shown in the upper-left corner of Table 12.1, this kind of reasoning leads to a valid, or correct, conclusion.

2. The fallacy (or error) of **affirming the consequent** means that you say the "then . . ." part of the sentence is true. This kind of reasoning leads to an invalid conclusion. Notice the upper-right corner of Table 12.1; the conclusion "This is an apple" is incorrect. After all, the item could be a pear, or a mango, or numerous other kinds of non-apple fruit.

   It's easy to see why people are tempted to affirm the consequent: In real life, we are often correct when we make this kind of reasoning error (Evans, 2000). For example, consider the two propositions, "If a person is a talented singer, then

---

[*]By tradition, the word *the* is inserted here, forming the phrase *the propositional calculus,* rather than simply *propositional calculus.*

he or she has musical abilities" and "Paula has musical abilities." It is a good bet that we can conclude Paula is indeed a talented singer. However, in logical reasoning we cannot rely on statements such as, "It's a good bet that. . . ." For example, I remember a student whose musical skills as a violinist were exceptional, yet she sang off-key.

As Theme 2 emphasizes, many cognitive errors can be traced to a heuristic, a strategy that usually works well. In this example of logical reasoning, however, "it's a good bet" is not the same as "always" (Leighton & Sternberg, 2003). In the second part of this chapter, you'll see that decision-making tasks allow us to use the concept, "it's a good bet." However, reasoning tasks require us to use the concept "always" before we conclude that the conclusion is valid.

3. The fallacy of **denying the antecedent** means that you say the "if . . ." part of the sentence is false. Denying the antecedent also leads to an invalid conclusion, as you can see from the lower-left corner of Table 12.1. Again, the item could be some fruit other than an apple.

4. **Denying the consequent** means that you say the "then . . ." part of the sentence is false. In the lower-right corner of Table 12.1, notice that this kind of reasoning leads to a correct conclusion.*

Now test yourself on the four kinds of conditional reasoning tasks by trying Demonstration 12.1. Review Table 12.1 if you have any difficulties.

Try noticing occasions when you use the two correct kinds of reasoning. Also, watch out for conclusions that are *not* valid. For example, Halpern (2003) reported an incident she heard on the evening news:

Viewers were told that if the President of the United States handled a tense situation with China well, then a tense international situation would be resolved without escalation of hostilities. The situation was resolved well (hostilities did not escalate), so the commentators concluded that the President handled the tense situation well. (p. 149)

Notice that this invalid conclusion depends on affirming the consequent.

Still, many people do manage to solve these reasoning tasks correctly. How do they succeed? According to Jonathan Evans's **heuristic-analytic theory,** people may initially use a heuristic that is quick and generally correct. However, they may then pause and switch to a more effortful analytic approach, which requires working memory and serial processing in order to realize that their initial conclusion would not necessarily be correct (Evans, 2004, 2006).

Our performance on reasoning tasks is a good example of Theme 4, which emphasizes that our cognitive processes are interrelated. For example, conditional reasoning

*If you have taken courses in research methods or statistics, you will recognize that scientific reasoning is based on the strategy of denying the consequent—that is, ruling out the null hypothesis.

---

⑨ Demonstration 12.1

The Propositional Calculus

Decide which of the following conclusions are valid and which are invalid. The answers are at the end of the chapter.

1. *Affirming the antecedent.*

   If today is Tuesday, then I have my bowling class.
   Today is Tuesday.
   Therefore, I have my bowling class.

2. *Affirming the consequent.*

   If Nereyda is a psychology major, then she is a student.
   Nereyda is a student.
   Therefore, Nereyda is a psychology major.

3. *Denying the antecedent.*

   If I am a first-year student, then I must register for next semester's classes today.
   I am not a first-year student.
   Therefore, I must not register for next semester's classes today.

4. *Denying the consequent.*

   If the judge is fair, then Susan is the winner.
   Susan is not the winner.
   Therefore, the judge is not fair.

---

relies upon working memory, especially the central-executive component of working memory that we discussed in Chapter 4 (Evans, 2006; Gilhooly, 2005). Reasoning also requires language skills (Rips, 2002; Schaeken et al., 2000; Wilhelm, 2005), and it often uses mental imagery (Evans, 2002; Goodwin & Johnson-Laird, 2005).

We would expect the cognitive burden to be especially heavy when some of the propositions contain negative terms (rather than just positive ones) and when people try to solve abstract reasoning problems (rather than concrete ones). Let's examine these two topics before we consider two cognitive tendencies that people demonstrate on conditional reasoning tasks.

Difficulties with Negative Information

Theme 3 of this book states that people can handle positive information better than negative information. As you may recall from Chapter 9, people have trouble processing sentences that contain words such as *no* or *not*. This same theme is also true for conditional reasoning tasks. For example, try the following reasoning problem:

> If today is not Friday, then we will not have a quiz today.
>
> We will not have a quiz today.
>
> Therefore, today is not Friday.

This problem is much more challenging than a similar problem that begins, "If today is Friday . . ."

Research shows that people take longer to evaluate problems that contain negative information, and they are also more likely to make errors on these problems (Garnham & Oakhill, 1994; Halpern, 2003; Noveck & Politzer, 1998). A reasoning problem is especially likely to strain our working memory if the problem involves denying the antecedent or denying the consequent. Most of us squirm when we see a reasoning problem that includes a statement like, "It is not true that today is not Friday." Furthermore, we often make errors when we translate either the initial statement or the conclusion into more accessible, positive forms.

Difficulties with Abstract Reasoning Problems

In general, people are more accurate when they solve reasoning problems that use concrete examples about everyday categories, rather than abstract, theoretical examples. For instance, you probably worked through the items in Demonstration 12.1 quite easily. In contrast, even short reasoning problems are difficult if they refer to abstract items where the characteristics are arbitrary (Evans, 2004, 2005; Manktelow, 1999; Wason & Johnson-Laird, 1972). For example, try this problem about geometric objects:

> If an object is red, then it is rectangular.
>
> This object is not rectangular.
>
> Therefore, it is not red. (Valid or invalid?)

Now check the answer to this item, located at the bottom of Demonstration 12.2 (p. 402). Other related research demonstrates we are more accurate if the propositions are high in imagery (Clement & Falmagne, 1986). Furthermore, accuracy increases when people use diagrams to make the problem more concrete (Halpern, 2003). However, we often make errors on concrete reasoning tasks if our everyday knowledge overrides the principles of logic (Evans, 2004). The belief-bias effect illustrates how this principle operates.

The Belief-Bias Effect

In our lives outside the psychology laboratory, our background knowledge helps us function well. Inside the psychology laboratory—or in a course on logic—this background information sometimes encourages us to make mistakes. For example, try the following problem (Cummins et al., 1991, p. 276):

> If my finger is cut, then it bleeds.
>
> My finger is bleeding.
>
> Therefore, my finger is cut.

In everyday life, it's a good bet that this conclusion is correct; if your finger is bleeding, then the most likely explanation is some variation on a cut. However, in the world of logic, this cut-finger problem commits the error of affirming the consequent, so it cannot be correct (Cummins et al., 1991). Similarly, your common sense probably encouraged you to decide that the conclusion was valid for the syllogism on page 396, about the psychology majors who are concerned about poverty.

The **belief-bias effect** occurs in reasoning when people make judgments based on prior beliefs and general knowledge, rather than on the rules of logic. In general, people make errors when the logic of a reasoning problem conflicts with their background knowledge (Evans & Feeney, 2004; Klauer et al., 2000; Manktelow, 1999). For example, when a conditional reasoning task is difficult, people search for additional information relevant to the situation. If the conclusion *seems* sensible, they argue that the reasoning process was correct (Evans, 2004).

The belief-bias effect is one more example of top-down processing (Theme 5). Our prior expectations help us organize our experiences and understand the world. When we see a statement that looks correct in a reasoning problem, we don't pay attention to the reasoning process that generated this statement (Stanovich, 2003). As a result, we don't question an invalid conclusion.

People vary widely in their susceptibility to the belief-bias effect. For example, people with low scores on an intelligence test are especially likely to demonstrate the belief-bias effect (Macpherson & Stanovich, 2007). People are also likely to demonstrate the belief-bias effect if they score low on a test of flexible thinking (Stanovich, 1999; Stanovich & West, 1997, 1998). These inflexible people are likely to agree with statements such as, "No one can talk me out of something I know is right."

In contrast, people who are flexible thinkers agree with statements such as "People should always take into consideration any evidence that goes against their beliefs." These people typically solve the reasoning problems correctly, without being distracted by the belief-bias effect. In general, they also tend to look more carefully at a reasoning problem, trying to determine whether the logic is faulty (Byrne et al., 2000; Johnson-Laird et al., 2000; Macpherson & Stanovich, 2007).

---

⑥ Demonstration 12.2

The Confirmation Bias

Imagine that each square below represents a card. Imagine that you are participating in a study in which the experimenter has told you that every card has a letter on one side and a number on the other side.

    You are then given this rule about these four cards: "IF A CARD HAS A VOWEL ON ONE SIDE, THEN IT HAS AN EVEN NUMBER ON THE OTHER SIDE."

    Your task is to decide which card or cards you would need to turn over in order to find out whether this rule is valid or invalid. What is your answer? The correct answer is discussed in the text.

E	J	6	7

(Incidentally, the answer to the problem about the objects on p. 401 is "valid.")
Source: The confirmation-bias task in this demonstration is based on Wason, 1968.

The Confirmation Bias

Be sure to try Demonstration 12.2 (above) before you read further. Peter Wason's (1968) selection task has inspired more research than any other deductive reasoning problem—and it has also raised many questions about whether humans are basically rational (Evans, 2004, 2005; Oswald & Grosjean, 2004). Let's first examine the original version of the selection task, and then we'll see how people typically perform better on more concrete variations of this task.

    The Standard Wason Selection Task. Demonstration 12.2 shows the original version of the selection task. Peter Wason (1968) found that people show a **confirmation bias;** they would rather try to confirm a hypothesis than try to disprove it (Kida, 2006; Krizan & Windschitl, 2007; Oswald & Grosjean, 2004). When most people try this classical selection task, they choose to turn over the *E* card. For example, one review of the literature showed that an average of 89% of research participants selected this appropriate strategy (Oaksford & Chater, 1994). This strategy allowed the participants to confirm the hypothesis by the valid method of affirming the antecedent, because this card has a vowel on it. If this *E* card has an even number on the other side, the rule is correct. If the number is odd, the rule is incorrect.

The other valid method in deductive reasoning is to deny the consequent. To accomplish this goal, you must choose to turn over the 7 card. The information about the other side of the 7 card is very valuable—just as valuable as the information about the other side of the E card. Remember that the rule is: "If a card has a vowel on its letter side, then it has an even number on its number side."

To deny the consequent in this Wason task, we need to check out a card that does *not* have an even number on its number side. (In this case, then, we must check out the 7 card.) We saw that most people—that is, 89% of the participants—are eager to affirm the antecedent. In contrast, they are reluctant to deny the consequent by searching for counterexamples. This strategy would be a wise attempt to reject a hypothesis, but people avoid this option. In a review of the literature, only 25% of research participants selected this appropriate strategy (Oaksford & Chater, 1994). Keep in mind that most participants in these selection-task studies are college students, so they should be able to master an abstract task (Evans, 2005).

You may wonder why we did not need to check on the J and the 6. If you reread the rule, you will notice that the rule did not say anything about consonants, such as J. The other side of the J could show an odd number, an even number, or even a Vermeer painting, and we wouldn't care. A review of the literature showed that most people appropriately avoided the J card. In fact, they chose it only 16% of the time (Oaksford & Chater, 1994).

The rule also does not specify what must appear on the other side of the even numbers, such as 6. However, most people select the 6 card to turn over. In fact, in a review of the literature, 62% chose this option (Oaksford & Chater, 1994). People often assume that the two parts of the rule can be switched, so that it reads, "If a card has an even number on its number side, then it has a vowel on its letter side." Thus, they make an error by choosing the 6.

Perhaps you've realized that this preference for confirming a hypothesis—rather than disproving it—corresponds to Theme 3 of this book. On the Wason selection task, we see that people who are given a choice would rather seek out positive information than negative information. We would rather know what something *is* than what it *is not*. This preference is very strong.

However, people who take time to carefully inspect the problem are more likely than impulsive people to select the two correct cards in this task (Toplak & Stanovich, 2002). Furthermore, people with high scores on the SAT exams are also more likely to provide a correct answer to this standard Wason selection task (Stanovich et al., 2004; Stanovich & West, 2000).

Variations on the Wason Selection Task. During the last two decades, researchers have tested numerous versions of the classic selection task. People choose the correct answer much more often with just a subtle change in the wording of the problem (Evans, 2002, 2004; Jackson & Griggs, 1990). People are also more accurate if they receive clear, detailed instructions about conditional reasoning strategies (Griggs, 1995; Griggs & Jackson, 1990; Platt & Griggs, 1995).

Most of the recent research focuses on versions in which the numbers and letters on the cards are replaced by concrete situations that we encounter in our everyday lives.

As you might guess, people perform much better when the task is concrete, familiar, and realistic (Evans, 2002, 2004; Hogarth, 2001; Woll, 2002).

Let's consider a classic study that demonstrates how well people can do on a concrete version of this task, rather than the standard, abstract version you saw in Demonstration 12.2. Griggs and Cox (1982) tested college students in Florida using a variation of the selection task. This task focused on the drinking age, which was then 19 in the state of Florida. This version of the Wason task was much more concrete and relevant to most college students. The participants in this study saw the following problem:

> On this task imagine that you are a police officer on duty. It is your job to ensure that people conform to certain rules. The cards in front of you have information about four people sitting at a table. On one side of a card is a person's age and on the other side of the card is what the person is drinking. Here is a rule: IF A PERSON IS DRINKING BEER, THEN THE PERSON MUST BE OVER 19 YEARS OF AGE. Select the card or cards that you definitely need to turn over to determine whether or not the people are violating the rule. (Griggs & Cox, 1982, p. 415).

The researchers presented four cards, each with one label: DRINKING A BEER, DRINKING A COKE, 16 YEARS OF AGE, and 22 YEARS OF AGE. Griggs and Cox (1982) found that 73% of the students who tried the drinking age problem made the correct selections, in contrast to 0% who tried the standard, abstract form of the selection task. Notice that Griggs and Cox's (1982) task focuses on whether people are cheating, by lying about their age.

According to subsequent research, people are especially likely to choose the correct answer when the wording of the selection task implies some kind of social contract designed to prevent people from cheating (Gigerenzer & Hug, 1992; Leighton & Sternberg, 2003; Rips, 2002).

Some theorists argue that evolution may have favored people who developed specialized skills in understanding important, adaptive problems (Barrett & Kurzban, 2006; Cosmides, 1989; Cosmides & Tooby, 1995, 2006). As a result, we humans may be especially competent in understanding the kinds of rules that are necessary for cooperative interactions in a society. For example, people can understand the societal rule that alcohol consumption is limited to individuals who are at least 19 years of age. In contrast, we may be less skilled in understanding rules that have no implications for social interactions, for example, abstract problems about cards, letters, and numbers (Evans & Over, 1996).

How can we translate the confirmation bias into real-life experiences? Try noticing your own behavior when you are searching for evidence. Do you consistently look for information that will confirm that you are right, or do you valiantly pursue ways in which your conclusion can be wrong?

The confirmation bias might sound relatively harmless. However, thousands of people die each year because our political leaders fall victim to this confirmation bias (Kida, 2006). For example, suppose that Country A wants to start a war in Country B. Country A will keep seeking support for its position. Country A will also *avoid* seeking information that its position may not be correct. Myers (2002) points out a remedy for the confirmation bias: Try to explain why another person might hold the *opposite* view. In an ideal world, the leaders of Country A should sincerely try to construct arguments against attacking Country B.

This overview of conditional reasoning does not provide much evidence for Theme 2 of this book. At least in the psychology laboratory, people are not especially accurate when they try to solve "if . . . then . . ." kinds of problems. However, the circumstances are usually more favorable in our daily lives, where problems are concrete and situations are consistent with our belief biases. Deductive reasoning is such a difficult task that we are not as efficient and accurate as we are in perception and memory—two areas in which humans are generally very competent.

⊚ Section Summary: *Deductive Reasoning*

1. Conditional reasoning focuses on "if . . . then . . ." relationships. People perform more accurately for affirmative (rather than negative) statements and for concrete (rather than abstract) problems.

2. The belief-bias effect encourages people to trust their prior knowledge, rather than the rules of logic; overactive top-down processing therefore leads to errors.

3. Furthermore, people often fall victim to the confirmation bias; they try only to confirm a hypothesis, rather than rejecting it.

4. The Wason selection task provides strong evidence for the confirmation bias; however, people are more accurate when the task describes a concrete situation that is governed by societal rules.

DECISION MAKING

When we engage in reasoning, we use established rules to draw clear-cut conclusions. In contrast, when we make decisions, we have no established rules, and we may not even know whether our decisions are correct (Klein, 1997; Tversky & Fox, 1995). Some critical information may be missing, and you may suspect that other information is not accurate. Should you apply to graduate school or get a job after college? Should you take social psychology in the morning or in the afternoon? Decision making does not provide a list of rules (such as the propositional calculus) that can help you assess the relative merits of each option. In addition, emotional factors usually influence our everyday decision making (Markman & Medin, 2002; Naqvi et al., 2006).

Decision making is an interdisciplinary field that includes research in all the social sciences, such as psychology, economics, political science, and sociology (LeBoeuf & Shafir, 2005). It also includes areas such as statistics, philosophy, medicine, and law (Markman & Medin, 2002; Simonson et al., 2001; Tetlock & Mellers, 2002).

Within the discipline of psychology, decision making inspires numerous books and articles each year. For example, many books from the current decade provide a general overview of decision making (e.g., Bazerman, 2005; Bennett & Gibson, 2006; Betsch & Haberstroh, 2005; Connolly et al., 2000; Gigerenzer & Selten, 2001; Gilovich et al., 2002; Holyoak &

Morrison, 2005; Jaeger et al., 2001; Kahneman & Tversky, 2000; Kida, 2006; Koehler & Harvey, 2004).

Other recent books consider more specific issues, such as political decision making (Cottam et al., 2004; Johnson, 2004; Jost & Sidanius, 2004), public policy decisions (Gowda & Fox, 2002), decisions in business (Henderson & Hooper, 2006), judgment during stressful situations (Hammond, 2000), intuition and decision making (Gladwell, 2005; Hogarth, 2001; Myers, 2002), decisions made by professionals (Montgomery et al., 2005), unwise decisions made by intelligent people (Sternberg, 2002), and expertise in decision making (Tetlock, 2005). In general, the research on decision making examines concrete, realistic scenarios, rather than the kind of abstract situations used in research on deductive reasoning.

This section on decision making emphasizes decision-making heuristics. As you'll recall from previous chapters, **heuristics** are general strategies that typically produce a correct solution. When we need to make a difficult decision, we use a guideline that is simple and easy to access (Kahneman & Frederick, 2005). Unfortunately, we humans often fail to appreciate the limitations of these heuristics, and so we do not always make wise decisions.

Throughout this section, you will often see the names of two researchers, Daniel Kahneman and Amos Tversky. Kahneman won the Nobel Prize in economics in 2002 for his research in decision making. (Unfortunately, Tversky had died in 1996.) Their research emphasized decision-making heuristics, an approach that connected decision making with the heuristics that we have discussed in other parts of this book.

Kahneman and Tversky proposed that a small number of heuristics guide human decision making. As they emphasized, the same strategies that normally guide us toward the correct decision may sometimes lead us astray (Kahneman & Frederick, 2002, 2005; Kahneman & Tversky, 1996). Notice that this heuristics approach is consistent with Theme 2 of this book: Our cognitive processes are usually efficient and accurate, and our mistakes can often be traced to a rational strategy.

In this part of the chapter, we will discuss many studies that illustrate errors in decision making. These errors should not lead us to conclude that humans are limited, foolish creatures. Instead, people's decision-making heuristics are well adapted to handle a wide range of problems (Hertwig & Todd, 2002; Kahneman & Tversky, 1996; Kahneman & Frederick, 2005). However, these same heuristics become a liability when they are applied too broadly, for example, when we emphasize heuristics rather than other important information.

Let us explore three classic decision-making heuristics: representativeness, availability, and anchoring and adjustment. Then, in a discussion of framing, we will consider how wording and context influence decisions. Next, the In-Depth feature explores how we are often overconfident when we make decisions. We'll also consider hindsight bias, a phenomenon related to overconfidence. In the Individual Differences feature, we'll see that people may be less happy if they typically agonize about relatively trivial decisions. Finally, we will examine some current theoretical approaches to decision making.

The Representativeness Heuristic

Here's a remarkable coincidence: Three early U.S. presidents—Adams, Jefferson, and Monroe—all died on the Fourth of July, although in different years (Myers, 2002). You have probably noticed many more personal coincidences. For example, several years ago, I was trying to locate resources on political decision making, and I found two relevant books. While recording the citations, I noticed an amazing coincidence: One was published by Stanford University Press, and the other by the University of Michigan Press (McDermott, 1998; Vertzberger, 1998). As it happened, I had earned my bachelor's degree from Stanford and my Ph.D. from the University of Michigan.

When we experience coincidences like these, we may have the sense of mystical harmony in the universe (Myers, 2002). Somehow these coincidences do not look random enough to be explained away by chance. Deaths of three presidents, for example, should be scattered randomly throughout the year, rather than occurring on the same day.

Now consider this example. Suppose that you have a regular penny with one head (H) and one tail (T), and you toss it six times. Which outcome seems most likely, T H H T H T or H H H T T T?

If you are like most people, you would guess that T H H T H T would be the most likely outcome of those two possibilities (Teigen, 2004). After all, you know that coin tossing should produce heads and tails in random order, and the order T H H T H T looks much more random than H H H T T T.

A sample looks **representative** if it is similar in important characteristics to the population from which it was selected. For instance, if a sample was selected by a random process, then that sample must look random in order for people to say it looks representative. Thus, T H H T H T is a sample that would be judged representative because it has an equal number of heads and tails (which would be the case in random coin tosses). Furthermore, T H H T H T would be judged representative because the order of the Ts and Hs looks random rather than orderly.

The research shows that we often use the **representativeness heuristic;** we judge that a sample is likely if it is similar to the population from which this sample was selected (Kahneman & Frederick, 2002; Kahneman & Tversky, 1972; Sloman, 1999). According to the representativeness heuristic, we believe that random-looking outcomes are more likely than orderly outcomes. Suppose, for example, that a cashier adds up your grocery bill, and the total is $21.97. This very random-looking outcome is a representative kind of answer, and so it looks "normal."

However, suppose that the grocery bill is $22.22. This total does not look random, and you might even be tempted to check the arithmetic. After all, addition is a process that should yield a random-looking outcome. In reality, though, a random process occasionally produces an outcome that seems nonrandom. In fact, chance alone often produces an orderly sum like $22.22, just as chance alone often produces orderly patterns like the three presidents dying on the Fourth of July.

⊚ **Demonstration 12.3**

Base Rates and Representativeness

Imagine that some psychologists have administered personality tests to 30 engineers and 70 lawyers, all people who are successful in their fields. Brief descriptions were written for each of the 30 engineers and the 70 lawyers. A sample description follows. Judge that description by indicating the probability that the person described is an engineer. Use a scale from 0 to 100.

Jack is a 45-year-old man. He is married and has four children. He is generally conservative, careful, and ambitious. He shows no interest in political and social issues and spends most of his free time on his many hobbies, which include home carpentry, sailing, and mathematical puzzles.

The probability that the man is one of the 30 engineers in the sample of 100 is _____ %.

Source: Kahneman & Tversky, 1973, p. 241.

When we make judgments about a series of coin tosses, we emphasize whether the sequence looks random. The representativeness heuristic also encourages us to make errors when we make more complex decisions, for example, about human beings. A person who is European American, wealthy, and tough on crime may seem like a "representative" U.S. Republican. However, you can probably name several Democrats who also fit that description (Kunda, 1999).

Perhaps the major problem with using the representativeness heuristic is this: This heuristic is so persuasive that we often ignore important statistical information that we *should* consider (Fischhoff, 1999; Hertwig & Todd, 2002; Kunda, 1999). Two kinds of useful statistical information are the sample size and the base rate. Be sure to try Demonstration 12.3 (above) before you read further.

Sample Size and Representativeness. When we make a decision, representativeness is such a compelling heuristic that we often fail to pay attention to sample size. For example, Kahneman and Tversky (1972) asked college students about a hypothetical small hospital, where about 15 babies are born each day, and a hypothetical large hospital, where about 45 babies are born each day. Which hospital would be more likely to report that more than 60% of the babies on a given day would be boys, or would they both be equally likely to report more than 60% boys?

The results showed that 56% of the students responded, "About the same." In other words, the majority of students thought that a large hospital and a small hospital were equally likely to report having at least 60% baby boys born on a given day. Thus, they ignored sample size.

In reality, however, sample size is an important characteristic that you should consider whenever you make decisions. A large sample is statistically more likely to reflect the true proportions in a population. In contrast, a small sample will often reveal an extreme proportion (e.g., at least 60% boy babies). However, people are often unaware that deviations from a population proportion are more likely in these small samples (Hertwig et al., 2004; Teigen, 2004).

Tversky and Kahneman (1971) point out that people often commit the **small-sample fallacy** by assuming that small samples will be representative of the population from which they are selected (Poulton, 1994). Unfortunately, the small-sample fallacy leads us to incorrect decisions.

We often commit the small-sample fallacy in social situations, as well as in relatively abstract statistics problems. For example, we may draw unwarranted stereotypes about a group of people on the basis of a small number of group members (Hamilton & Sherman, 1994). One effective way of combating inappropriate stereotypes is to become acquainted with a large number of people from the target group—for example, through exchange programs with groups of people from other countries. More generally, people can be trained to appreciate the fact that a small sample of individuals may not be representative of the entire group (Sedlmeier, 1999).

Base Rate and Representativeness.   Representativeness is such a compelling heuristic that people often ignore the **base rate,** or how often the item occurs in the population (Birnbaum, 2004; Teigen, 2004). Be sure you have tried Demonstration 12.3 on page 408 before we proceed. Using problems like the one in this demonstration, Kahneman and Tversky (1973) showed that people rely on representativeness when they are asked to judge category membership. We focus almost exclusively on whether a description is representative of members of each category. By emphasizing representativeness, we commit the **base-rate fallacy,** underemphasizing important information about base rate (Dawes, 1998; Johnson-Laird et al., 1999; Woll, 2002).

In a related study, students read the following description of a man named Rudy:

Rudy is a bit on the peculiar side. He has unusual tastes in movies and art, he is married to a performer, and he has tattoos on various parts of his body. In his spare time Rudy takes yoga classes and likes to collect 78 rpm records. An outgoing and rather boisterous person, he has been known to act on a dare on more than one occasion. What do you think Rudy's occupation most likely is? A) Farmer B) Librarian C) Trapeze Artist D) Surgeon E) Lawyer. (Swinkels, 2003, p. 120)

If people pay attention to base rates, they should select a profession that has a relatively high base rate in the population, such as a lawyer. However, most students in Swinkels's (2003) study used the representativeness heuristic, and they guessed that Rudy was a trapeze artist. The description of Rudy was highly similar to (that is, representative of) the stereotype of a trapeze artist.

You might argue, however, that the study with Rudy was unfair. After all, the base rates of the various professions were not even mentioned in the problem. Maybe the students failed to consider that lawyers are more common than trapeze artists. Well, the base rate was made very clear in Demonstration 12.3; you were told that the base rate was 30 engineers and 70 lawyers in the population. Did you make use of this base rate and guess that Jack was highly likely to be a lawyer? In Kahneman and Tversky's (1973) study using this setup, most people ignored this base-rate information and judged mostly on the basis of representativeness. In fact, this description for Jack is highly representative of our stereotype for engineers, and so people tend to guess a high percentage for the answer to the question. Now complete Demonstration 12.4 before you read further.

Kahneman and Tversky (1973) point out how their studies are related to Bayes' theorem. **Bayes' theorem** states that judgments should be influenced by two factors: the base rate and the likelihood ratio. The **likelihood ratio** assesses whether the description is more likely to apply to Population A or Population B. For example, the description in Demonstration 12.3 seems much more representative of a typical engineer than of a typical lawyer. We emphasize the likelihood ratio when answering this question, and so we reply, "Engineer." Meanwhile, we typically ignore the useful information about the base rates. Because people often ignore base rates, they are not obeying Bayes' theorem, and they can make unwise decisions.

We should emphasize, however, that the representativeness heuristic—like all the heuristics we have discussed in this book—usually helps us make a correct decision

---

◎ Demonstration 12.4

The Conjunction Fallacy

Read the following paragraph:

> Linda is 31 years old, single, outspoken, and very bright. She majored in philosophy. As a student, she was deeply concerned with issues of discrimination and social justice, and she also participated in antinuclear demonstrations.

Now rank the following options in terms of the probability of their describing Linda. Give a ranking of 1 to the most likely option and a ranking of 8 to the least likely option:

_____ Linda is a teacher at an elementary school.
_____ Linda works in a bookstore and takes yoga classes.
_____ Linda is active in the feminist movement.
_____ Linda is a psychiatric social worker.
_____ Linda is a member of the League of Women Voters.
_____ Linda is a bank teller.
_____ Linda is an insurance salesperson.
_____ Linda is a bank teller and is active in the feminist movement.

Source: From Tversky & Kahneman, 1983.

(Shepperd & Koch, 2005). Heuristics are also relatively simple to use (Hogarth & Karelaia, 2007).

In addition, some problems—and some alternative wordings of problems—produce more accurate decisions (Gigerenzer, 1998; Shafir & LeBoeuf, 2002). Furthermore, training sessions can encourage students to use base-rate information appropriately (Kruschke, 1996; Krynski & Tenenbaum, 2007; Shepperd & Koch, 2005).

You should also be alert for other everyday examples of the base-rate fallacy. For instance, one study of pedestrians killed at intersections showed that 10% were killed when crossing at a signal that said "walk." In contrast, only 6% were killed when crossing at a signal that said "stop" (Poulton, 1994). Does that mean that—for your own safety—you should cross the street only when the signal says "stop"? But think about the base rates: Many more people cross the street when the signal says "walk."

The Conjunction Fallacy and Representativeness. Be sure to try Demonstration 12.4 on page 410 before you read further. Now inspect your answers. Which did you rank more likely—that Linda is a bank teller, or that Linda is a bank teller and is active in the feminist movement?

Tversky and Kahneman (1983) presented the "Linda" problem and another similar problem to three groups of people. One was a "statistically naïve" group of undergraduates. The "intermediate-knowledge" group consisted of first-year graduate students who had taken one or more courses in statistics. The "statistically sophisticated" group consisted of doctoral students in a decision science program who had taken several advanced courses in statistics. In each case, the participants were asked to rank all eight statements according to their probability, with the rank of 1 assigned to the most likely statement.

Figure 12.1 shows the average rank for each of the three groups for the two critical statements: (1) "Linda is a bank teller" and (2) "Linda is a bank teller and is active in the feminist movement." Notice that the people in all three groups thought that the second statement would be more likely than the first.

Think for a moment why this conclusion is mathematically impossible. According to the **conjunction rule**, the probability of the conjunction of two events cannot be larger than the probability of either of its constituent events. In the Linda problem, the conjunction of the two events—bank teller and feminist—cannot occur more often than either event by itself—for instance, being a bank teller. Consider some other situations where the conjunction rule operates. For example, the number of murders last year in Detroit cannot be greater than the number of murders last year in Michigan (Kahneman & Frederick, 2005).

As we saw earlier in this section, representativeness is such a powerful heuristic that people often ignore useful statistical information, such as sample size and base rate. Apparently, they also ignore the mathematical implications of the conjunction rule (Kahneman & Frederick, 2005).

When most people try the "Linda problem," they commit the **conjunction fallacy:** They judge the probability of the conjunction of two events to be greater than the probability of a constituent event. Tversky and Kahneman (1983) trace the conjunction

FIGURE 12.1

The Influence of Type of Statement and Level of Statistical Sophistication on Likelihood Rankings. Low numbers on the ranking indicate that people think the event is more likely an incorrect decision.

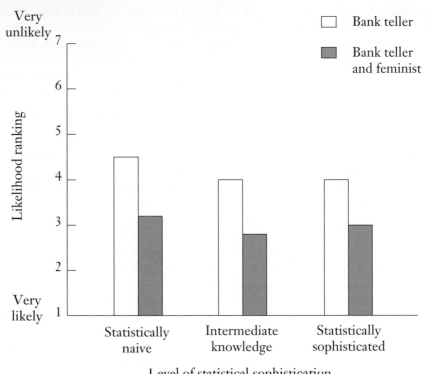

Source: Based on Tversky & Kahneman, 1983.

fallacy to the representativeness heuristic. They argue that people judge the conjunction of "bank teller" and "feminist" to be more likely than the simple event "bank teller," because "feminist" is a characteristic that is very representative of (that is, similar to) someone who is single, outspoken, bright, a philosophy major, concerned about social justice, and an antinuclear activist. A person with these characteristics doesn't seem likely to become a bank teller. However, she seems highly likely to be a feminist. By adding the extra detail of "feminist" to "bank teller," we have made the description seem more representative and plausible—even though that description is statistically less likely (Swoyer, 2002).

Psychologists are intrigued with the conjunction fallacy, especially because it demonstrates that people can ignore one of the most basic principles of probability theory. The results for the conjunction fallacy have been replicated many times, with generally consistent findings (Ben-Zeev, 2002; Fisk, 2004; Kahneman & Frederick, 2005). For example, the probability of "spilling hot coffee" seems greater than the probability of "spilling coffee" (Moldoveanu & Langer, 2002) . . . until you identify the conjunction fallacy.

Before we discuss a second decision-making heuristic, let's briefly review the representativeness heuristic. We use the representativeness heuristic when we make decisions based on whether a sample looks similar in important characteristics to the population from which it is selected. The representativeness heuristic is so appealing that we tend to ignore other important characteristics that we *should* consider, such as sample size and base rate. We also fail to realize that the probability of two events occurring together (for example, bank teller and feminist) needs to be smaller than the probability of just one of those events (for example, bank teller). In summary, the representativeness heuristic is basically helpful in our daily lives, but we sometimes use it inappropriately (Ben-Zeev, 2002).

The Availability Heuristic

A second important heuristic that people use in making decisions is availability. You use the **availability heuristic** when you estimate frequency or probability in terms of how easy it is to think of relevant examples of something (Hertwig et al., 2005; Tversky & Kahneman, 1973). In other words, people judge frequency by assessing whether they can easily retrieve relevant examples from memory or whether this memory retrieval is difficult.

The availability heuristic is generally helpful in everyday life. For example, suppose that someone asked you whether your college had more students from Illinois or more from Idaho. You have probably not memorized these geography statistics, so you would be likely to answer the question in terms of the relative availability of examples of Illinois students and Idaho students. Perhaps your memory has stored the names of dozens of Illinois students, and so you can easily retrieve their names ("Jessica, Akiko, Bob . . ."). Perhaps your memory has stored only one name of an Idaho student, so it's difficult to think of examples of this category. Because examples of Illinois students were relatively easy to retrieve, you conclude that your college has more Illinois students. In general, then, this availability heuristic is a relatively accurate method for making decisions about frequency.

As you'll recall, a heuristic is a general strategy that is typically accurate. The availability heuristic is accurate as long as availability is correlated with true, objective frequency—and it usually is. However, the availability heuristic can lead to errors. As we will see in a moment, several factors can influence memory retrieval, even though they are not correlated with true, objective frequency (Kunda, 1999). These factors can bias availability, and so they therefore decrease the accuracy of our decisions. We will see that recency and familiarity—both factors that influence memory—can potentially distort availability. Figure 12.2 illustrates how these two factors can contaminate the relationship between true frequency and availability.

Let's make certain that you understand how availability differs from representativeness. When we use the representativeness heuristic, we are given a specific example (such as T H H T H T or Linda the bank teller). We then make judgments about

FIGURE 12.2

The Relationship Between True Frequency and Estimated Frequency, with Recency and Familiarity as "Contaminating" Factors.

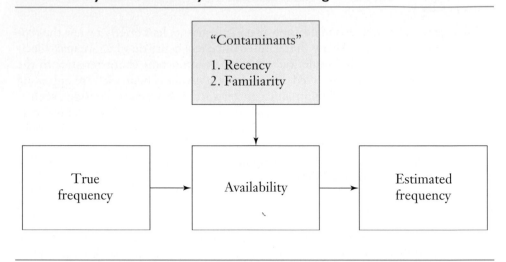

whether the specific example is *similar* to the general category that it is supposed to represent (such as coin tosses or philosophy majors concerned about social justice). In contrast, when we use the availability heuristic, we are given a general category, and we must *recall* the specific examples (such as examples of Illinois students). Then we make decisions based on whether the specific examples come easily to mind. So here is a way to remember the two heuristics:

1. If the problem is based on a judgment about *similarity*, you are dealing with the representativeness heuristic.
2. If the problem requires you to *remember examples*, you are dealing with the availability heuristic.

We'll begin our exploration of availability by considering two factors that can bias availability—recency and familiarity. Next, we'll consider the recognition heuristic, an instance of the availability heuristic in which our decisions are usually *accurate*. Then we will examine a consequence of availability, called illusory correlations. Finally, we will see how availability operates when people try to imagine an event in the future.

Recency and Availability. As you know from Chapters 4, 5, and 6, memory for items generally declines with the passage of time. Thus, you recall the more recent items more accurately. In other words, more recent items are more available. As a result, we judge recent items to be more likely than they really are. For example, take yourself back to 2007 and 2008, following the violent shootings at two U.S. universities. If you had been asked to estimate the frequency of violence on university campuses, you probably would have provided a high estimate.

Research on the availability heuristic has important implications for clinical psychology. According to MacLeod and Campbell (1992), when people were encouraged to recall pleasant events from their past, they later judged pleasant events to be more likely in their future. In contrast, when people were encouraged to recall unpleasant events, they later judged unpleasant events to be more likely in their future. Psychotherapists might encourage depressed clients to envision a more hopeful future by having them recall and focus on previous pleasant events.

Familiarity and Availability. The familiarity of the examples—as well as their recency—can also produce a distortion in frequency estimation. For instance, people who know many divorced individuals often provide higher estimates of national divorce rates than do people who have rarely encountered divorce (Kozielecki, 1981). Similarly, physicians often judge a disease to be especially dangerous if it is discussed frequently in medical journals (Christensen-Szalanski et al., 1983). This tendency operates, even if the disease is not very serious. People who are not physicians show a similar bias related to diseases frequently mentioned in newspapers (Hertwig et al., 2005).

Journalists and news reporters overexpose us to some events and underexpose us to others (Fox & Farmer, 2002; Hertwig et al., 2005; Reber, 2004). For example, they tell us about violent events such as fires and murders much more often than less dramatic (and more common) causes of death. One hundred times as many people die from diseases as are murdered, yet the newspapers carry three times as many articles about murders.

According to research conducted in Canada, the United States, and China, the media can even influence people's estimates of a country's population (Brown, Cui & Gordon, 2002; Brown & Siegler, 1992). For example, Brown and Siegler (1992) conducted a study during an era when El Salvador was frequently mentioned in the news because of U.S. intervention in Latin America. In contrast, Indonesia was seldom mentioned. Brown and Siegler found that the students' estimates for the population of these two countries were similar, even though the population of Indonesia was about 35 times as large as the population of El Salvador.

Try asking a friend to estimate the population of Israel (population = 6,000,000) and Bulgaria (population = 7,600,000). How about Iraq (population = 24,000,000) and Nepal (population = 25,900,000)? Are your friend's estimates for these two pairs of countries distorted by the frequency of media coverage?

The media can also influence viewers' ideas about the prevalence of different points of view (Ivins, 1999). For instance, the media often give similar coverage to several thousand protesters and to several dozen counter-protestors. Notice whether you can spot the same tendency in current news broadcasts. Do the media currently create our cognitive realities?

Try Demonstration 12.5, which is a modification of a highly influential study by Tversky and Kahneman (1973). See whether your friends respond according to the familiarity of the examples, rather than true frequency. Tversky and Kahneman presented people with lists of 39 names. A typical list might contain the names of 19 famous

> ## Demonstration 12.5
>
> ### Familiarity and Availability
>
> Read this list of names to several friends. After you have finished the entire list, ask your friends to estimate whether there were more men or women listed. Do not allow them to answer, "About the same." (In reality, 14 women's names and 15 men's names are listed.)
>
> | | |
> |---|---|
> | Louisa May Alcott | Maya Angelou |
> | John Dickson Carr | Virginia Woolf |
> | Alice Walker | Robert Lovett |
> | Thomas McGuane | Judy Blume |
> | Laura Ingalls Wilder | George Nathan |
> | Frederick Rolfe | Allan Nevins |
> | Edward George Lytton | Jane Austen |
> | Danielle Steel | Henry Crabb Robinson |
> | Michael Drayton | Joseph Lincoln |
> | Toni Morrison | Emily Brontë |
> | Hubert Selby, Jr. | Arthur Hutchinson |
> | Sue Grafton | James Hunt |
> | Agatha Christie | Joyce Carol Oates |
> | Richard Watson Gilder | Brian Hooker |
> | Harriet Beecher Stowe | |

women and 20 less famous men. After hearing the list, participants were asked to judge whether the list contained more men's names or more women's names. About 80% of the participants in this condition erroneously guessed that there were more women's names on the list. The relatively familiar names were apparently more available, even though women's names were objectively less frequent. Similar results have been obtained in replications (McKelvie, 1997; Reber, 2004).

The Recognition Heuristic. We have frequently emphasized that the decision-making heuristics are generally helpful and accurate. However, most of the examples have emphasized that judgment accuracy is hindered by factors such as recency and familiarity. Let's discuss a special case of the availability heuristic, called the recognition heuristic; when you use the recognition heuristic, you are likely to make an accurate decision (Goldstein & Gigerenzer, 2002; Newell & Shanks, 2004; Volz et al., 2006).

Suppose that someone asks you which of two Italian cities has the larger population, Milan or Modena. Most U.S. students have heard of Milan, but they do not recognize the name of a nearby city called Modena. The **recognition heuristic** typically operates when you must compare the relative frequency of two categories; if you recognize one category, but not the other, you conclude that the recognized category has the higher frequency. In this case, you would—correctly—respond that Milan has the greater population. Keep this example of *correct* decision making in mind as you read the remainder of this chapter.

Illusory Correlation and Availability. So far, we have seen that availability—or the ease with which examples come to mind—is typically a useful heuristic. However, this heuristic can become "contaminated" by factors such as recency and familiarity, leading to inappropriate decisions about the true frequency of an event. Now we turn to a third topic, to see how the availability heuristic can contribute to a cognitive error called an illusory correlation.

The word *illusory* means deceptive or unreal, and a correlation is a statistical relationship between two variables. Therefore, an **illusory correlation** occurs when people believe that two variables are statistically related, even though there is no real evidence for this relationship. According to numerous studies, we often believe that a certain group of people tends to have certain kinds of characteristics, even though an accurate tabulation would show that the relationship is not statistically significant (Fiedler, 2004; Fiedler & Walther, 2004; Hamilton et al., 1993).

Think of some stereotypes that arise from illusory correlations. These illusory correlations may either have no basis in fact or much less basis than is commonly believed. For example, consider the following illusory correlations: Females have poor math skills, people on welfare are cheaters, gay males and lesbians have psychological problems, and so forth.

According to the **social cognition approach**, we form stereotypes by means of our normal cognitive processes; motivational factors are less relevant. In the case of illusory correlations, an important cognitive factor is the availability heuristic (Reber, 2004; Stroessner & Plaks, 2001). You may recall that Chapter 8 discussed how gender stereotypes are related to schemas, another important cognitive factor.

Chapman and Chapman (1967) performed a classic investigation of illusory correlation. They showed that people created illusory correlations between a person's psychiatric symptoms (e.g., suspiciousness) and a drawing that the person had presumably made (e.g., a drawing of someone with exaggerated eyes). Even though the symptoms were paired *completely at random* with the drawings, people thought that they had detected a systematic relationship. Chapman and Chapman (1969) also found that students formed an illusory correlation between people's reported sexual orientation and their responses on an inkblot test.

Theorists have proposed a variety of alternate cognitive explanations for illusory correlations, including unevenly distributed attention and characteristics of the memory trace (e.g., Kunda, 1999; Stroessner & Plaks, 2001). However, let's explore in more detail how the availability heuristic might help to explain illusory correlations.

When we try to determine whether two variables are related to each other, we really need to consider the data about four categories in a matrix. For example, suppose

Table 12.2

A Matrix Showing Hypothetical Information About Sexual Orientation and Psychological Problems

	Number in Each Category	
	Gay people	Straight people
People with psychological problems	6	8
People without psychological problems	54	72
Totals	60	80

that we want to determine whether people who are lesbians or gay males are more likely than heterosexuals to have psychological problems.* Imagine, for example, that researchers gathered the data in Table 12.2. These data show that 6 out of 60 gay people (or 10%) have psychological problems, and 8 out of 80 straight people (also 10%) have psychological problems. We should therefore conclude that sexual orientation is not related to psychological problems.

Unfortunately, however, people typically pay the most attention to only one cell in the matrix, especially if the two characteristics are statistically less frequent (Hamilton et al., 1993; Kunda, 1999; Stroessner & Plaks, 2001). In this example, some people notice only the six gay people who have psychological problems, ignoring the important information in the other three cells.

People with an established bias against gay people might be especially likely to pay attention to this cell. Furthermore, they will continue to look for information that confirms their hypothesis that gay people have problems. You'll recall from the discussion of conditional reasoning that people would rather try to confirm a hypothesis than try to disprove it, consistent with Theme 3.

Try applying the information about illusory correlations to some stereotype that you hold. Notice whether you tend to focus on only one cell in the matrix, ignoring the other three. Have you specifically tried to *disconfirm* the stereotypes? Also, notice how politicians and the media often base their arguments on illusory correlations (Myers, 2002). For example, they may focus on the number of welfare recipients with fraudulent claims. This number is meaningless unless we know additional information, such as the number of welfare recipients *without* fraudulent claims.

Let us review what we've discussed about the availability heuristic, in which we estimate frequency or probability in terms of how easily we can think of examples of

---

*Although some people believe in this illusory correlation, the research does not show a consistent relationship between sexual orientation and psychological problems (e.g., Garnets, 2004; Kurdek, 2004; Morris & Hart, 2003; Rothblum & Factor, 2001).

something. This heuristic is generally accurate in our daily lives, and people are able to estimate relative frequency with impressive accuracy (Sedlmeier et al., 1998). However, availability can be contaminated by two factors that are not related to objective frequency—recency and familiarity. This information suggests a specific precaution for situations in which you make frequency judgments: Ask yourself whether you are giving a special advantage to a category of items that occurred more recently or that are somehow more familiar (Kunda, 1999). According to the recognition heuristic, however, we are reasonably accurate in judging relative frequency, for example, in guessing which of two cities has the larger population. Finally, we saw that availability helps to create illusory correlations, another error in decision making.

The Anchoring and Adjustment Heuristic

In mid-December, 2007, a snowstorm gripped Boston, dumping about 10″ of snow on the city and the surrounding region. People left work to go home early, because they knew that the snowfall would be relatively heavy. I spoke with people who ordinarily commuted to their home in 45 minutes when the weather was clear. As they began driving, they made adjustments in this estimated commute time. After all, snow makes the drive more challenging, so they thought the commute might take up to 90 minutes. However, they demonstrated the anchoring and adjustment heuristic, because the snow was falling much faster than usual. Furthermore, many drivers had abandoned their cars, clogging the narrow streets even further. In fact, some of them arrived home 3 to 4 hours later. Clearly, they had not made large enough adjustments to their initial time estimate. (Try Demonstration 12.6 when convenient, but try Demonstration 12.7 before you read further.)

According to the **anchoring and adjustment heuristic**—also known as the **anchoring effect**—we begin with a first approximation—an **anchor**—and then we make adjustments to that number on the basis of additional information (Kida, 2006; Mussweiler et al., 2004; Tversky & Kahneman, 1982). This heuristic often leads to a reasonable answer, just as the representativeness and availability heuristics often lead to reasonable answers. However, people typically rely too heavily on the anchor, and their adjustments are too small.

The anchoring and adjustment heuristic illustrates once more that people tend to endorse their current hypotheses or beliefs, rather than trying to question them (Baron, 2000; Kida, 2006). They emphasize top-down processing, consistent with Theme 5. We've seen several other examples of this tendency in the present chapter:

1. *The belief-bias effect:* We rely too heavily on our established beliefs.
2. *The confirmation bias:* We prefer to confirm a current hypothesis, rather than to reject it.
3. *The illusory correlation:* We rely too strongly on one well-known cell in a data matrix, failing to seek information about the other three cells.

Let's begin by considering some research on the anchoring and adjustment heuristic. Then we will see how this heuristic can be applied to estimating confidence intervals.

> ### ◎ Demonstration 12.6
>
> **The Anchoring and Adjustment Heuristic**
>
> Copy the two multiplication problems listed below on separate pieces of paper. Show Problem A to at least five friends, and show Problem B to at least five other friends. In each case, ask the participants to estimate the answer within 5 seconds.
>
> A. 8 X 7 X 6 X 5 X 4 X 3 X 2 X 1
>
> B. 1 X 2 X 3 X 4 X 5 X 6 X 7 X 8
>
> Now tally the answers separately for the two problems, listing the answers from smallest to largest. Calculate the median for each problem. (If you have an uneven number of participants, the median is the answer in the middle of the distribution—with half larger and half smaller. If you have an even number of participants, take the average between the two answers in the middle of the distribution.)

> ### ◎ Demonstration 12.7
>
> **Estimating Confidence Intervals**
>
> For each of the following questions, answer in terms of a range, rather than a single number. Specifically, you should supply a 98% confidence interval, which is the range within which you expect the correct answer to fall. For example, suppose you answer a question by supplying a 98% confidence interval that is 2,000 to 7,000. This means that you think there is only a 2% chance that the real answer is either less than 2,000 or more than 7,000. The correct answers can be found at the end of the chapter on page 438.
>
> 1. What percentage of the voting-age population in Canada voted in the 2000 federal election?
> 2. What percentage of the voting-age population in the United States voted in the 2000 federal election?
> 3. What percentage of U.S. college graduates reported that they smoked at least one cigarette during the previous month?
> 4. What was the estimated population of Texas in 2003?
> 5. What is the area of France, in square miles?
> 6. How many people in Canada had at least a bachelor's degree, as of 2001?
> 7. How much money had the United States spent on the War in Iraq, as of May 1, 2008?
> 8. What is the current literacy rate in Cuba?
>
> *(continued)*

9. What was the year of birth for Sojourner Truth, the Black female abolitionist?

10. How many political refugees were reported worldwide, as of 2003?

Source: All questions are based on information in the *World Almanac and Book of Facts* (2005), Statistics Canada (2008), and National Priorities Project (2008).

Research on the Anchoring and Adjustment Heuristic. Demonstration 12.6 illustrates the anchoring and adjustment heuristic. In a classic study, high school students were asked to estimate the answers to these two multiplication problems (Tversky & Kahneman, 1982). The students were allowed only 5 seconds to respond. The results showed that the two problems generated widely different answers. If the first number in this sequence was 8, a relatively large number, the median of their estimates was 2,250. (That is, half the students estimated higher than 2,250, and half estimated lower.) In contrast, if the first number was 1, a small number, their median estimate was only 512.

Furthermore, both groups anchored too heavily on the initial impression that every number in the problem was only a single digit, because both estimates were far too low: The correct answer for both problems is 40,320. Did the anchoring and adjustment heuristic influence the people you tested?

The anchoring and adjustment heuristic is so powerful that it operates even when the anchors are obviously arbitrary or impossibly extreme (e.g., a person living to the age of 140). It also operates for both novices and experts (Englich & Mussweiler, 2001; Kida, 2006; Mussweiler et al., 2004; Tversky & Kahneman, 1974).

Researchers have not developed precise explanations for the anchoring and adjustment heuristic. However, one likely mechanism is that the anchor restricts the search for relevant information in memory. Specifically, people concentrate their search on information relatively close to the anchor (Pohl et al., 2003).

Let's consider some applications of the basic anchoring and adjustment heuristic. Then we'll see how the anchoring and adjustment heuristic encourages us to make errors when we estimate confidence intervals.

Applications of the Anchoring and Adjustment Heuristic. The anchoring and adjustment heuristic is not confined to situations in which we estimate numbers. In fact, it often operates when we make judgments about other people (Kruglanski, 2004; Kunda, 1999).

For example, let's suppose that you hold a stereotype about people who belong to a particular group, such as people who live in a region of the United States or students who have a particular major. When you meet someone from that group, you often rely on your stereotype in order to create an initial anchor. Then you consider the unique characteristics of that particular individual, and you make some adjustments. However, you may not make sufficiently large adjustments away from that initial anchor. In terms of Theme 5, you probably rely too heavily on top-down processing, and not enough on bottom-up processing.

The anchoring and adjustment heuristic has numerous applications in everyday life (Mussweiler et al., 2004). For example, Englich and Mussweiler (2001) studied anchoring effects in courtroom sentencing. Trial judges with an average of fifteen years of experience listened to a typical legal case. The role of the prosecutor was played by a person who was introduced as a computer science student. This student was obviously a novice in terms of legal experience, so his judgments should not be taken seriously. However, when the "prosecutor" demanded a sentence of 34 months, these experienced judges recommended a sentence of 36 months. When the same "prosecutor" demanded a sentence of 12 months, the judges recommended 28 months. (Be sure to try Demonstration 12.7 on page 420 before you read further.)

Estimating Confidence Intervals. We use anchoring and adjustment when we estimate a single number. We also use this heuristic when we estimate **confidence intervals,** or ranges within which we expect a number to fall a certain percentage of the time. For example, you might guess that the 98% confidence interval for the number of students at a particular college is 3,000 to 5,000. This guess would mean that you think there is a 98% chance that the population is between 3,000 and 5,000.

Demonstration 12.7 tested the accuracy of your estimates for various kinds of numerical information. Check page 438 to see how many of your confidence-interval estimates included the correct answer. Suppose that a large number of people were to answer a large number of questions. Then we would expect their confidence intervals to include the correct answer about 98% of the time—assuming that their estimation techniques are correct. However, studies have shown that people provide

---

⊚ Demonstration 12.8

The Framing Effect and Background Information

Try the following two problems:

Problem 1
Imagine that you decided to see a play and you paid $20 for the admission price of one ticket. As you enter the theater, you discover that you have lost the ticket. The theater keeps no record of ticket purchasers, so the ticket cannot be recovered. Would you pay $20 for another ticket for the play?

Problem 2
Imagine that you have decided to buy a ticket for a play where the admission price of one ticket is $20. As you enter the theater, you discover that you have lost a $20 bill. Would you still pay $20 for a ticket for the play?

Source: Based on Tversky & Kahneman, 1981.

98% confidence intervals that actually include the correct answer only about 60% of the time (Block & Harper, 1991; Fischhoff, 1982; Tversky & Kahneman, 1974). In other words, the confidence intervals that we estimate are definitely too narrow (Hoffrage, 2004).

Tversky and Kahneman (1974) point out how the anchoring and adjustment heuristic is relevant when we make confidence-interval estimates. We first provide a best estimate and use this figure as an anchor. Then we make adjustments upward and downward from this anchor to construct the confidence-interval estimate. However, our adjustments are often too small.

For example, perhaps you initially guessed that the percentage of U.S. voters in the 2000 elections was 75%. You might then say that your confidence interval was between 65% and 85%. This range is too narrow, because you may have made a large error in your original estimate. Again, we establish our anchor, and we do not wander far from it in the adjustment process (Kruglanski, 2004). When we shut our minds to new evidence, we rely too heavily on top-down processing.

An additional problem is that most people don't really understand confidence intervals. For instance, when you estimated the confidence intervals in Demonstration 12.7,

---

⊚ Demonstration 12.9

The Framing Effect and the Wording of a Question

Try the following two problems:

Problem 1
Imagine that the United States is preparing for the outbreak of an unusual Asian disease, which is expected to kill 600 people. Two alternative programs to combat the disease have been proposed. Assume that the exact scientific estimate of the consequences of the programs are as follows:

> If Program A is adopted, 200 people will be saved.

> If Program B is adopted, there is a one-third probability that 600 people will be saved, and a two-thirds probability that no people will be saved.

> Which program would you favor?

Problem 2
Now imagine the same situation, with these two alternatives:

> If Program C is adopted, 400 people will die.

> If Program D is adopted, there is a one-third probability that nobody will die, and a two-thirds probability that 600 people will die.

> Which program would you favor?

Source: Based on Tversky & Kahneman, 1981.

did you emphasize to yourself that each confidence interval should be so wide that there was only a 2% chance of the actual number being larger or smaller than this interval? Teigen and Jørgensen (2005) found that college students tend to think that 90% confidence intervals are associated with an estimated certainty of only about 50%. Juslin and his coauthors (2007) also argue that people make errors because they do not understand that statistics about a sample are different from statistics about a population.

Let's review the last of the three major decision-making heuristics. When we use the anchoring and adjustment heuristic, we begin by guessing a first approximation or anchor. Then we make adjustments to that anchor. This heuristic is generally useful, but we typically fail to make large enough adjustments. The anchoring and adjustment heuristic can be applied to a variety of areas, such as stereotyping and legal studies. The anchoring and adjustment heuristic also accounts for our errors when we estimate confidence intervals; we usually supply ranges that are far too narrow, given the degree of uncertainty they should reflect.

In order to overcome potential biases from the anchoring and adjustment heuristic, think carefully about your initial estimate. Then ask yourself whether you are paying enough attention to the unique features of this specific situation that might require large adjustments away from your initial anchor.

The Framing Effect

When I was writing this chapter on decision making, I took a break to read the mail that had just arrived. I opened an envelope from an organization I support, called "The Feminist Majority." The letter pointed out that in a previous year, right-wing organizations had introduced legislation in 17 state governments that would eliminate affirmative action programs for women and people of color. This figure surprised and saddened me; apparently the anti–affirmative action supporters had more influence than I had imagined! And then I realized that the framing effect might be operating. Perhaps, at that very moment, other people throughout the United States were opening their mail from organizations that endorsed the other perspective. Perhaps their letter pointed out that their organization—and others with a similar viewpoint—had *failed* to introduce legislation in 33 state governments. Yes, a fairly subtle change in the wording of a sentence can produce a very different emotional reaction! Are political organizations perhaps hiring cognitive psychologists?

The **framing effect** demonstrates that the outcome of a decision can be influenced by two factors: (1) the background context of the choice and (2) the way in which a question is worded (or framed). However, before we discuss these two factors, be sure you have tried Demonstration 12.8, which appeared on page 422.

Background Information and the Framing Effect. Take a moment to read Demonstration 12.8 once more. Notice that the amount of money is $20 in both cases. If decision makers were perfectly "rational," they would respond identically to both problems (Kida, 2006; Shafir & Tversky, 1995; Stanovich, 1999). However, the decision frame differs for the two situations, so they seem psychologically different from each other.

We frequently organize our mental expense accounts according to topics. Specifically, we view going to the theater as a transaction in which the cost of the ticket is exchanged for the experience of seeing a play. If you buy another ticket, the cost of seeing that play has increased to a level that many people find unacceptable. When Kahneman and Tversky (1984) asked people what they would do in the case of Problem 1, only 46% said that they would pay for another ticket.

In contrast, in Problem 2, people didn't tally the lost $20 bill in the same account as the cost of a ticket. In this second case, people viewed the lost $20 as being generally irrelevant to the ticket. In Kahneman and Tversky's (1984) study, 88% of the participants said that they would purchase the ticket in Problem 2. In other words, the background information provides different frames for the two problems, and the specific frame strongly influences the decision. Now, before you read further, be sure that you have tried Demonstration 12.9, which appeared on page 423.

The Wording of a Question and the Framing Effect. In Chapter 11, we saw that people often fail to realize that two problems may share a deep-structure similarity. In other words, people are distracted by the differences in the surface structure of the problems. We will see that people are also distracted by differences in surface structure when they make decisions between various options.

Tversky and Kahneman (1981) tested college students in both Canada and the United States, using Problem 1 in Demonstration 12.9; notice that both choices emphasize the number of lives that would be *saved*. They found that 72% of their participants chose Program A, and only 28% chose Program B. Notice that the participants in this group were "risk averse." That is, they preferred the certainty of saving 200 lives, rather than the risky prospect of a one-in-three possibility of saving 600 lives. Notice, however, that the benefits of Programs A and B in Problem 1 are statistically identical.

Now inspect your answer to Problem 2, in which both choices emphasize the number of lives that would be *lost* (that is, the number of deaths). Tversky and Kahneman (1981) presented this problem to a different group of students from the same colleges that they had tested with Problem 1. Only 22% favored Program C, but 78% favored Program D. Here the participants were "risk taking"; they preferred the two-in-three chance that 600 would die, rather than the guaranteed death of 400 people. Again, however, the benefits of the two programs are statistically equal. Furthermore, notice that Problem 1 and Problem 2 have identical deep structures. The only difference is that the outcomes are described in Problem 1 in terms of the lives saved, but in Problem 2 in terms of the lives lost.

The way that a question is framed—lives saved or lives lost—has an important effect on people's decisions (Kida, 2006). This framing changes people from focusing on the possible gains (lives saved) to focusing on the possible losses (lives lost). In the case of Problem 1, we tend to prefer the certainty of having 200 lives saved, so we avoid the option where it's possible that no lives will be saved. In the case of Problem 2, however, we tend to prefer the risk that nobody will die (even though there is a good chance that 600 will die); we avoid the option where 400 face certain death. Tversky and Kahneman (1981) chose the name **prospect theory** to refer to people's tendencies to think about possible gains as being different from possible losses. Specifically:

1. When dealing with possible *gains* (for example, lives saved), people tend to *avoid* risks.
2. When dealing with possible *losses* (for example, lives lost), people tend to *seek* risks.

Numerous studies have replicated the general framing effect, and the effect is typically quite strong (Halpern, 2003; Isen, 2000; Kida, 2006; Rohrbaugh & Shanteau, 1999; Shafir & Tversky, 1995; Stanovich, 1999). For instance, the framing effect is common among statistically sophisticated people as well as statistically naive people, and the magnitude of the effect is relatively large. Furthermore, Mayhorn and his colleagues (2002) found framing effects among older adults, as well as among students in their 20s.

The framing effect also has an important impact on consumer behavior. In one classic study, for example, Johnson (1987) discovered that people are much more likely to prefer ground beef that is labeled "80% lean," rather than "20% fat."

Many studies have also examined how framing influences medical decisions (e.g., Linville et al., 1993; Rothman & Salovey, 1997). For example, Jasper and his colleagues (2001) discovered an important application of the framing effect when healthcare professionals provide information about drug-related risks. These researchers monitored a telephone counseling service in Toronto, Canada, that provided information to women who were already pregnant or planned to become pregnant.

As you know, women need to be careful to avoid taking certain medications during pregnancy. When a woman called the counseling service with a question about taking a drug to counteract allergies, she was randomly assigned to one of two groups. Women in one group heard a message that was framed in terms of a possible problem: "In every pregnancy, there is a 1–3% chance that a woman will give birth to a child who has a major birth defect. This drug has not been shown to change that." Women in the other group heard a message that was framed in terms of a healthy outcome: "In every pregnancy, there is a 97–99% chance that a woman will give birth to a child who does not have a major birth defect. This drug has not been shown to change that" (p. 1237).

Several days after calling, the researchers contacted the women and asked them to rate their likelihood of taking the allergy medication. The women in the first group (birth defect) rated their own personal risk as being relatively high, compared to women in the second group (no birth defect).

Huber and her colleagues (1987) examined the general framing effect. They concluded that decision making often depends on whether the choice is presented as "Is the pitcher half empty, or is the pitcher half full?" This area of research confirms Theme 4 of this textbook; the cognitive processes are indeed interrelated. In this case, descriptive language has an important influence on decision making.

Let's review the framing effect. Background information can influence decisions; we do not make choices in a vacuum, without knowledge about the world. In addition, the wording of the question can influence decisions. Specifically, people avoid risks when the wording implies gains, and they seek risks when the wording implies losses.

The research on framing suggests some practical advice: When you are making an important decision, try rewording the description of this decision. For example, suppose that you need to decide whether to accept a particular job offer. Ask yourself how you would feel about having this job, and then ask yourself how you would feel about *not* having this job.

| IN DEPTH |

Overconfidence About Decisions

So far, we have seen that decisions can be influenced by three decision-making heuristics: the representativeness heuristic, the availability heuristic, and the anchoring and adjustment heuristic. Furthermore, the framing effect demonstrates that both background information and wording can encourage us to make unwise decisions.

Given these sources of error, people should realize that their decision-making skills are nothing to boast about. Unfortunately, however, the research shows that people are frequently overconfident (Hoffrage, 2004; Johnson, 2004; Kida, 2006; Krizan & Windschitl, 2007). **Overconfidence** means that people's confidence judgments are higher than they should be, based on their actual performance on the task.

We have already discussed two examples of overconfidence in decision making in this chapter. In an illusory correlation, people are confident that two variables are related, when in fact the relationship is either weak or nonexistent. In anchoring and adjustment, people are so confident in their estimation abilities that they supply very narrow confidence intervals for these estimates.

Overconfidence is a characteristic of other cognitive tasks, in addition to decision making. For example, Chapter 5 noted that people are often overconfident about the accuracy of their eyewitness testimony. Furthermore, Chapter 6 pointed out that people are typically overconfident about how well they understood material they had read, even when they answered many questions incorrectly. Let's consider research on several aspects of overconfidence; then we'll discuss several factors that help to create overconfidence.

General Studies on Overconfidence. A variety of studies show that humans are overconfident in many decision-making situations. For example, people are overconfident about how long a person with a fatal disease will live, which firms will go bankrupt, and whether the defendant is guilty in a court trial (Kahneman & Tversky, 1995). People consistently have more confidence in their own decisions than in predictions that are based on statistically objective measurements.

People are also overconfident in estimating their future performance, based on judgments about their current performance (Bjork, 1999). In addition, people tend to overestimate their social skills, creativity, leadership abilities, and a wide range of academic skills (Kahneman & Renshon, 2007; Matlin, 2004; Matlin & Stang, 1978). In addition, physicists, economists, and other researchers are overconfident that their theories are correct (Trout, 2002).

We need to emphasize, however, that individuals differ widely with respect to overconfidence (Steel, 2007). For example, a large-scale study showed that 77% of the student participants were overconfident about their accuracy in answering general-knowledge questions like those in Demonstration 12.7. Still, these results tell us that 23% were either on target or underconfident (Stanovich, 1999).

Let's consider two research areas in which overconfidence has been extensively documented. As you'll see, politicians are often overconfident about the decisions they make. Furthermore, if we explore an area that is personally more familiar, students are usually overconfident that they will complete their academic projects on time.

Overconfidence in Political Decision Making. Even very bright politicians can make unwise personal decisions—for example, Bill Clinton's sexual relationship with White House intern Monica Lewinsky. Powerful politicians often make irrational decisions that most ordinary citizens would avoid (Halpern, 2002; Sternberg, 2002).

Let's shift to the decisions that politicians make about international policy—decisions that can affect thousands of people. Unfortunately, political leaders seldom think systematically about the risks involved in important decisions. For instance, they often fail to consider the risks involved in (a) invading another country, (b) continuing a war that they cannot win, and (c) leaving the other country in a better political situation following the war. In an international conflict, each side tends to overestimate its own chances of success (Johnson, 2004; Kahneman & Renshon, 2007; Kahneman & Tversky, 1995).

When politicians need to make a decision, they are also overconfident that their data are accurate. I wrote this chapter in January, 2008, several years after U.S. citizens learned that our country went to war with Iraq because our political leaders were overconfident that Iraq had owned weapons of mass destruction.

For instance, Vice President Dick Cheney had stated on August 26, 2002, "There is no doubt that Saddam Hussein now has weapons of mass destruction." President George W. Bush had declared on March 17, 2003, "Intelligence gathered by this and other governments leaves no doubt that the Iraq regime continues to possess and conceal some of the most lethal weapons ever devised." However, it is now clear that crucial information had been a forgery, and these weapons did not exist (Tavris & Aronson, 2007).

Researchers have created methods for reducing overconfidence about decisions. For example, a program called Tactical Decision Making Under Stress encourages military decision makers to carefully consider alternative hypotheses. One component in this program is a strategy called the crystal-ball technique (Cannon-Bowers & Salas, 1998; Cohen et al., 1998). The **crystal-ball technique** asks decision makers to imagine that a completely accurate crystal ball has determined that their favored hypothesis is actually *incorrect;* the decision makers must therefore search for alternative explanations for the outcome. They must also find reasonable evidence to support these alternative explanations. If the Bush administration had used the crystal-ball technique, for example, they would have been instructed to describe several reasons why Saddam Hussein could *not* have weapons of mass destruction.

Unfortunately, political leaders are apparently not currently using methods like the crystal-ball technique to make important political decisions. As Griffin and Tversky (2002) point out,

> It can be argued that people's willingness to engage in military, legal, and other costly battles would be reduced if they had a more realistic assessment of their chances of success. We doubt that the benefits of overconfidence outweigh its costs. (p. 249)

Students' Overconfidence About Completing Projects on Time. Are you surprised to learn that students are often overly optimistic about how quickly they can complete a project (Buehler et al., 1994, 2002)? In reality, this overconfidence applies to most humans.

According to the **planning fallacy,** people typically underestimate the amount of time (or money) required to complete a project; they also estimate that the task will be relatively easy to complete (Buehler et al., 2002). Notice why this fallacy is related to overconfidence: If you are overconfident in decision making, you will estimate that your paper for cognitive psychology will take only 10 hours to complete, and you can easily finish it on time if you start next Tuesday.

Shelley Taylor and her colleagues (1998) explored the planning fallacy by studying how college students worked on academic projects. They asked students at the University of California at Los Angeles to select an academic project—such as a short paper—that needed to be completed during the next week.

One group of students in this study received instructions in "process simulation." They were told to envision every step in the process of completing the project, such as gathering the materials, organizing the project's basic structure, and so forth. These students were instructed to rehearse the simulations for 5 minutes each day during the following week. Students in the control condition did not use any simulation. The results of the study showed that 41% of the students in the process-simulation condition finished on time, in contrast to only 14% of those in the control group.

The planning fallacy has been replicated in several studies in the United States, Canada, and Japan. How can we explain people's overconfidence that they will complete a task on time? One factor is that people create an optimistic scenario that represents the ideal way in which they will make progress on a project. This scenario fails to consider the large number of problems that can arise (Buehler et al., 2002). People also recall that they completed similar tasks relatively quickly in the past (Roy & Christenfeld, 2007; Roy et al., 2005). In addition, they estimate that they will have more free time in the future, compared to the free time they have right now (Zauberman & Lynch, 2005). In other words, people use the anchoring and adjustment heuristic, and they do not make large enough adjustments to their original scenario based on other useful information.

When students use process simulation—as in the study by Taylor and her coauthors (1998)—they apparently regulate their behavior so that it is somewhat more consistent with their original idealistic estimation of the completion time. However, only 41% of students in this condition actually completed their projects on time. Even process simulation cannot come close to eliminating the planning fallacy!

Reasons for Overconfidence. We have seen many examples demonstrating that people tend to be overconfident about the correctness of their decisions. This overconfidence arises from errors during many different stages in the decision-making process:

1. People are often unaware that their knowledge is based on very tenuous and uncertain assumptions and on information from unreliable or inappropriate sources (Bishop & Trout, 2002; Carlson, 1995; Johnson, 2004).
2. Examples confirming our hypotheses are readily available, whereas we resist searching for counterexamples (Baron, 1998; Idson et al., 2001; Sanbonmatsu et al., 1998).

You'll recall from the discussion of deductive reasoning that people persist in confirming their current hypothesis, rather than looking for negative evidence.

3. People have difficulty recalling the other possible hypotheses, and decision making depends on memory (Theme 4). If you cannot recall the competing hypotheses, you will be overly confident about the hypothesis you have endorsed (Trout, 2002).

4. Even if people manage to recall the other possible hypotheses, they do not treat them seriously. The choice once seemed ambiguous, but the alternatives now seem trivial (Kida, 2006; Simon et al., 2001).

5. When people make decisions as a group, they sometimes engage in groupthink (Deutsch, 2005; Janis, 1972; Kerr & Tindale, 2004; Kruglanski, 2004). **Groupthink** can occur when a cohesive group is so concerned about reaching a unanimous decision that members ignore potential problems, and they are overconfident that their decision will have a favorable outcome.

When people are overconfident in a risky situation, the outcome can often produce disasters, deaths, and widespread destruction. The term **my-side bias** describes the overconfidence that one's own view is correct in a confrontational situation (Baron, 1998; Toplak & Stanovich, 2002). Conflict often arises when individuals (or groups or nations) each fall victim to my-side bias. They are so confident that their position is correct that they cannot consider the possibility that their opponent's position may be at least partially correct. If you find yourself in conflict with someone, try to overcome my-side bias and determine whether some part of the other person's position may have merit.

More generally, try to reduce the overconfidence bias when you face an important decision. Review the five points listed above, and determine whether your confidence is appropriately justified.

The Hindsight Bias

In the preceding In-Depth feature, we discussed how people are overconfident about predicting events that will happen in the future. In contrast, **hindsight** refers to our judgments about events that already happened in the past. The **hindsight bias** occurs when an event has happened, and we say that the event had been inevitable; we had actually "known it all along."

In other words, the hindsight bias reflects our overconfidence that we could have predicted a particular outcome (Kida, 2006; Pohl, 2004b; Sanna & Schwarz, 2006). The hindsight bias demonstrates that we often reconstruct the past so that it matches our present knowledge (Schacter, 2001).

Research About the Hindsight Bias. The hindsight bias can operate for the judgments we make about people. For example, Linda Carli (1999) asked students to read a two-page story about a young woman named Barbara and her relationship with

Jack, a man she had met in graduate school. The story, told from Barbara's viewpoint, provided background information about Barbara, her interactions with Jack, and their growing relationship. Half of the students read a version that had a tragic ending, in which Jack rapes Barbara. The other half read a version with a happy ending, in which

---

⊚ **Demonstration 12.10**

Decision-Making Style

1	2	3	4	5	6	7

Completely disagree   Completely agree

Using the scale above, answer each of the following questions:

1. Whenever I'm faced with a choice, I try to imagine what all the other possibilities are, even ones that aren't present at the moment.

2. Whenever I make a choice, I try to get information about how the other alternatives turned out.

3. When I am in the car listening to the radio, I often check other stations to see if something better is playing, even if I am relatively satisfied with what I'm listening to.

4. When I watch TV, I channel surf, often scanning through the available options even while attempting to watch one program.

5. I treat relationships like clothing: I expect to try a lot on before finding the perfect fit.

6. I often find it difficult to shop for a gift for a friend.

7. Renting videos or DVDs is really difficult. I'm always struggling to pick the best one.

8. When shopping, I have a hard time finding clothing that I really love.

9. I'm a big fan of lists that attempt to rank things (the best movies, the best singers, the best athletes, the best novels, etc.).

10. I find that writing is very difficult, even if it's just writing a letter to a friend, because it's so hard to word things just right. I often do several drafts of even simple things.

11. No matter what I do, I have the highest standards for myself.

12. I never settle for second best.

13. I often fantasize about living in ways that are quite different from my actual life.

Source: Schwartz, et al., 2002.

Jack proposes marriage to Barbara. The two versions were identical, except for the ending.

After reading the story, each student then completed a true/false memory test. This test examined recall for the facts of the story, but it also included questions about information that had not been mentioned in the story. Some of these questions were consistent with a stereotyped version of a rape scenario (e.g., "Barbara met many men at parties"). Other questions were consistent with a marriage-proposal scenario (e.g., "Barbara wanted a family very much").

The results of Carli's (1999) study confirmed the hindsight bias. People who read the version about the rape said that they could have predicted Barbara would be raped. Similarly, people who read the marriage-proposal version said that they could have predicted Jack would propose to Barbara. (Remember that the two versions were actually *identical*, except for the final ending.) Furthermore, each group committed systematic errors on the memory test; each group recalled items that were consistent with the ending they had read, even though this information had not appeared in the story.

Carli's (1999) research helps us understand why many people "blame the victim" following a tragic event such as a rape. In reality, that individual's earlier actions may have been perfectly appropriate. However, people often search the past for reasons why a victim deserved that outcome. As we've seen in Carli's research, people may even "reconstruct" some reasons that did not occur.

The hindsight bias has been demonstrated in a number of different studies, though the effect is not always strong (e.g., Agans & Shaffer, 1994; Cannon & Quinsey, 1995; Harley et al., 2004; Koriat et al., 2006; Pohl, 2004b). The bias has also been documented in North America, Europe, Asia, and Australia (Pohl et al., 2002). According to the research, doctors show the hindsight bias when guessing a medical diagnosis (Dehn & Erdfelder, 1998). We also demonstrate this bias in our everyday experiences. For example, people display the hindsight bias when making judgments about the amount of sugar, butter, and fruit juice in a variety of foods (Pohl et al., 2003).

Explanations for the Hindsight Bias. Despite all the research, the explanations for the hindsight bias are not clear (Pohl, 2004b). One likely cognitive explanation is that people might use anchoring and adjustment (Hawkins & Hastie, 1990; Pohl, 2004b). After all, they have been told that a particular outcome actually happened—that it was 100% certain. Therefore, they use this 100% value as the anchor in estimating the likelihood that they would have predicted the answer, and then they do not adjust their certainty downward as much as they should.

We also noted in discussing Carli's (1999) study that people may misremember past events so that those events are consistent with current information; these events help to justify the outcome. Did the results of Carli's study about the tragic versus the upbeat story ending surprise me? Of course not . . . I knew it all along!

Let's now shift topics so that we can examine some research on individual differences. Be sure that you have tried Demonstration, 12.10 on page 431, before you read further.

Individual Differences: Decision-Making Style and Psychological Well-Being

Think back to the last time you needed to buy something in a fairly large store in the United States or Canada. Let's say that you needed to buy a shirt. Did you carefully inspect every shirt that seemed to be the right size, and then reconsider the top contenders before buying the shirt? **Maximizers** are people who have a **maximizing decision-making style;** they tend to examine as many options as possible. The task becomes even more challenging as the number of options increases.

In contrast, did you look through an assortment of shirts until you found one that was good enough to meet your standards, even if it isn't the best possible shirt? **Satisficers** are people who have a **satisficing decision-making style;** they tend to settle for something that is satisfactory.* Satisficers are not concerned about a potential shirt in another location that might be even better (Schwartz, 2004; Schwartz et al., 2002).

Now look at your answers to Demonstration 12.10, and add up the total number of points. If your total is 65 or higher, you are in the "maximizer" region of the scale. If your total is 40 or lower, you are in the "satisficer" region of the scale. (Scores between 41 and 64 are in the intermediate region.)

Barry Schwartz and his coauthors (2002) gave the questionnaire in Demonstration 12.10 to a total of 1,747 individuals, including college students in the United States and Canada, as well as groups such as healthcare professionals and people waiting at a train station. The researchers also administered several other measures. One of these was a measure of regret following a choice. It included such items as "Whenever I make a choice, I try to get information about how the other alternatives turned out" and "When I think about how I'm doing in life, I often assess opportunities I have passed up" (p. 1182). Schwartz and his colleagues found a significant correlation (r = +.52) between people's scores on the maximizing–satisficing scale and their score on the regret scale. Those who were maximizers tended to experience more regret.

The researchers also found a significant correlation (r = +.34) between people's scores on the maximizing–satisficing scale and their score on a standard scale of depressive symptoms, the Beck Depression Inventory. The maximizers tended to experience more depression. Keep in mind that these data are correlational, and they do not necessarily demonstrate that a maximizing decision-making style actually *causes* depression. However, it seems likely that people pay a price for their extremely careful decision-making style. They keep thinking about how their choice might not have been ideal, so they experience regret. The research by Schwartz and his coauthors (2002) suggests that this regret contributes to a person's more generalized depression.

---

*Herbert Simon (1955) was the first to discuss the concept of satisficing, or choosing a good-enough option—rather than maximizing—when making a decision.

Keep in mind that people may be maximizers when making some choices and satisficers when making other choices. Furthermore, choices about your education, profession, and romantic partner should obviously require much more effort and time than decisions connected with shopping for clothing.

An interesting conclusion from Schwartz's (2004) book is that having an abundance of choices certainly doesn't make the maximizers any happier. In fact, if they are relatively wealthy, they will need to make even more choices about their purchases, leading to even greater regret about the items that they did not buy.

Current Perspectives on Decision Making

In this final part of the chapter, let's briefly consider some current theoretical perspectives focusing on decision making. Gerd Gigerenzer is a researcher at the Max Planck Institute for Human Development in Germany. Gigerenzer and his colleagues admit that people are not perfectly rational decision makers, especially under time pressure. Still, they point out that people can do relatively well when they are given a fair chance on decision-making tasks. For example, we saw on pages 416 to 417 that the recognition heuristic is reasonably accurate. Other research shows that people answer questions more accurately in naturalistic settings and if the questions focus on frequencies, rather than probabilities (e.g., Gigerenzer, 2004, 2006a, 2006b; Goldstein & Gigerenzer, 2002; Todd & Gigerenzer, 2000, 2007).

Peter Todd and Gerd Gigerenzer (2007) devised a term called **ecological rationality** to describe how people create a wide variety of heuristics to help them make useful, adaptive decisions in the real world. This point resembles the observation that Brazilian children accurately solve math problems when selling candy in the streets, but not in a classroom (Carraher et al., 1985; Woll, 2002). Similarly, people typically make wise decisions, if we examine the specific characteristics of the environment in which they live.

For example, only 28% of U.S. residents become potential organ donors, in contrast to 99.9% of French residents. Todd and Gigerenzer (2007) suggest that both groups are using a simple **default heuristic;** specifically, if there is a default option, people will choose it. In the United States, you typically have to sign up to become an organ donor. Therefore, the majority of U.S. residents—using the default heuristic—remain in the non-donor category. In France, you are an organ donor unless you specifically opt out of the donor program. Therefore, the majority of French residents—using the default heuristic—remain in the donor category.

Furthermore, people bring their world knowledge into the research laboratory, where researchers often design the tasks to specifically contradict their schemas. For example, do you *really* believe that Linda wouldn't be a feminist (p. 410), given her long-time commitment to social justice?

Meanwhile, Daniel Kahneman and his colleagues have explored a new approach to heuristics called attribution substitution. **Attribute substitution** operates when someone asks you to make a judgment, and you don't know the answer; in this case, you substitute an answer to a similar but easier question (Kahneman, 2003; Kahneman & Frederick, 2002, 2005; Newell et al., 2007).

Kahneman and Frederick (2005) offer an example of attribute substitution. Suppose that someone asks you what percent of long-distance relationships break up within one year. Frankly, I don't know anyone who has the data to answer this question accurately. Therefore, most of us would answer this difficult question by substituting an easier question, specifically, "How easily do examples come to mind of long-distance relationships that have broken up?" This substitution is an application of the availability heuristic, and we make a similar substitution for the representativeness heuristic (Kahneman, 2003; Kahneman & Frederick, 2002, 2005).

The two approaches—one proposed by Gigerenzer and one by Kahneman—may seem fairly different. However, both approaches suggest that decision-making heuristics generally serve us well in the real world. Furthermore, we can become more effective decision makers by realizing the limitations of these important strategies (Kahneman & Tversky, 1996, 2000).

◉ Section Summary: *Decision Making*

1. Decision-making heuristics are typically helpful in our daily lives; however, we can make errors in decision making when we overemphasize heuristics and underemphasize the unique features of the current decision.

2. According to the representativeness heuristic, we judge that a sample is likely if it resembles the population from which it was selected (for example, the sample should look random if it was gathered by random selection).

3. We are so impressed by representativeness that we tend to ignore important statistical information such as the size of the sample and the base rates in the population; furthermore, the conjunction fallacy can be traced to the representativeness heuristic.

4. According to the availability heuristic, we estimate frequency or probability in terms of how easily we can remember examples of something. The availability heuristic produces errors when biasing factors such as recency and familiarity influence availability. However, a related phenomenon—called the recognition heuristic—helps us make accurate decisions about relative frequency.

5. The availability heuristic helps to explain the phenomenon of illusory correlation, which is related to stereotypes.

6. According to the anchoring and adjustment heuristic, we establish an anchor and then make adjustments based on other information; the problem is that these adjustments are usually too small.

7. We also use the anchoring and adjustment heuristic when we estimate confidence intervals. We begin with a single best estimate, and then we make very small adjustments on either side of that estimate; however, this confidence interval is often too narrow.

8. The way in which a question is framed can influence our decisions; background information can influence our decisions inappropriately. The framing effect

also applies to wording. When the wording implies gains, we tend to avoid risks; when the wording implies losses, we tend to seek out risks.

9. People are frequently overconfident about their decisions. For instance, political decision makers may risk lives when they are overconfident. In addition, college students tend to be overconfident about the estimated completion time for projects.

10. In the hindsight bias, people know the outcome of an event, and they are overly optimistic that they could have predicted that specific outcome before it actually happened.

11. Satisficers make decisions quickly; in contrast, maximizers agonize over their decisions, which may lead to regret and depressive symptoms.

12. Gerd Gigerenzer and his colleagues emphasize that humans are reasonably skilled at making decisions in natural settings, using a wide variety of heuristics.

13. According to the recent approaches developed by Kahneman and his colleagues, we often use attribute substitution; when we do not know the answer to a question, we substitute an answer to a similar, easier question.

CHAPTER REVIEW QUESTIONS

1. Describe the basic differences between deductive reasoning and decision making. Provide at least one example from your daily life that illustrates each of these cognitive processes. Why can both of them be categorized as "thinking"?

2. To make certain that you understand conditional reasoning, begin with this sentence: "If today is Monday, the art museum is closed." Apply the four conditional reasoning situations (the propositional calculus) to this sentence, and point out which are valid and which are invalid.

3. What factors influence our accuracy when we work on conditional reasoning tasks? Give an example of each of these factors, based on your own experience.

4. Many of the errors that people make in reasoning can be traced to overreliance on previous knowledge or overactive top-down processes. Discuss this point, and then relate it to the anchoring and adjustment heuristic.

5. Throughout this chapter, you have seen many examples of a general cognitive tendency: We tend to accept the status quo (or the currently favored hypothesis), without sufficiently exploring other options. Describe how this statement applies to deductive reasoning and to several kinds of decision-making tasks.

6. Describe which heuristic is represented in each of the following everyday errors: (a) Someone asks you whether cardinals or robins are more common, and you make this decision based on the number of birds of each kind that you have seen this winter. (b) One of your classes has 30 students, including two people named Matthew and three named Jessica, which seems too coincidental to be due to chance alone. (c) You estimate the number of bottles of soda you will

need for the Fourth of July picnic based on the Christmas party consumption, taking into account the fact that the weather will be warmer in July.

7. In the case of the representativeness heuristic, people fail to take into account two important factors that should be *emphasized*. In the case of the availability heuristic, people take into account two important factors that should be *ignored*. Discuss these two statements, with reference to the information in this chapter. Give examples of each of these four kinds of errors.

8. Describe the variety of ways in which people tend to be overconfident in their decision making. Think of relevant examples from your own experience. Then point out how you can avoid the planning fallacy when you face a deadline for a class assignment.

9. Think of a recent example from the news in which a politician made a decision for which he or she was criticized by news commentators. How could overconfidence have led to this unwise decision? Why might the hindsight bias be relevant here? What cognitive processes might the news commentators be using to make the decision seem more foolish than it might actually have been?

10. Imagine that you have been hired by your local high school district to create a course in critical thinking. Review the chapter and make fifteen to twenty suggestions (each only one sentence long) about precautions that should be included in such a program.

KEYWORDS

thinking
deductive reasoning
decision making
conditional reasoning
propositional reasoning
syllogism
the propositional calculus
antecedent
consequent
affirming the antecedent
affirming the consequent
denying the antecedent
denying the consequent
heuristic-analytic theory
belief-bias effect
confirmation bias
heuristics
representative

representativeness heuristic
small-sample fallacy
base rate
base-rate fallacy
Bayes' theorem
likelihood ratio
conjunction rule
conjunction fallacy
availability heuristic
recognition heuristic
illusory correlation
social cognition approach
anchoring and adjustment
  heuristic
anchoring effect
anchor
confidence intervals
framing effect

prospect theory
overconfidence
crystal-ball technique
planning fallacy
groupthink
my-side bias
hindsight
hindsight bias
maximizers
maximizing decision-making
  style
satisficers
satisficing decision-making
  style
ecological rationality
default heuristic
attribute substitution

RECOMMENDED READINGS

Pohl, R. (2004a). *Cognitive illusions: Handbook on fallacies and biases in thinking, judgment, and memory.* Hove, UK: Psychology Press. I strongly recommend this book, which is designed for students enrolled in courses in cognitive psychology. It includes 22 chapters on topics such as the confirmation bias, the availability heuristic, and overconfidence.

Schwartz, B. (2004). *The paradox of choice: Why more is less: How the culture of abundance robs us of satisfaction.* New York: HarperCollins. Schwartz's book explores the topic of maximizers and satisficers, discussed in this chapter's Individual Differences feature. The book goes beyond decision making to examine our cultural values.

Stanovich, K. E. (2003). The fundamental computational biases of human cognition: Heuristics that (sometimes) impair decision making and problem solving. In J. E. Davidson & R. J. Sternberg (Eds.), *The psychology of problem solving* (pp. 291–342). New York: Cambridge University Press. Stanovich's chapter provides an interesting and clear approach to deductive reasoning, and it also examines some relevant aspects of decision making.

Tavris, C., & Aronson, E. (2007). *Mistakes were made (but not by me): Why we justify foolish beliefs, bad decisions, and hurtful acts.* Orlando, FL: Harcourt. Here's an excellent book, written by two prominent psychologists, which examines the human tendency to avoid taking responsibility for making inappropriate decisions.

ANSWERS TO DEMONSTRATION 12.1

1. valid
2. invalid
3. invalid
4. valid

ANSWERS TO DEMONSTRATION 12.7

1. 72% voted
2. 41% voted
3. 14% of college graduates
4. 22,119,000 people
5. 211,000 square miles
6. 3,688,000 people
7. $518 billion dollars
8. 97% literacy rate
9. 1797 was her year of birth.
10. 11,900,000 political refugees

Did most of your confidence intervals include the correct answers, or were these confidence intervals too broad?

CHAPTER 13

Developing Cognitive Abilities

PREVIEW

In this chapter, we'll examine how cognitive processes develop in several areas we've discussed in earlier chapters. Rather than discussing many topics briefly, we will explore three topics in detail: memory, metamemory, and language. One purpose of this chapter is to inform you how humans develop in these three important areas. You'll see that some skills improve as children mature to adulthood, and some decline as adults reach old age. However, many skills show less change than you might expect. A second purpose of this chapter is to encourage you to review some important concepts that were introduced earlier in the book. As you know from Chapter 6, you'll learn more effectively if you spread your learning over time. You can now refresh your memory about concepts that you initially learned several weeks ago.

According to recent research, even young infants can remember people, objects, and events. For example, young infants can remember how to activate a mobile by using a kicking motion that they learned several weeks earlier. Children's long-term recognition memory is surprisingly accurate, but their working memory and long-term recall memory are considerably less accurate than in adults. Young children also fail to use memory strategies spontaneously when they want to remember something. When conditions are ideal, children can provide accurate eyewitness testimony. Errors are more likely if children are young, if they heard misinformation, and if they have mental retardation.

Elderly adults are somewhat similar to young adults when the tasks require straightforward working memory, implicit memory, or recognition memory. However, they have more difficulty on tasks that require complex working memory, prospective memory, or explicit recall (for instance, remembering people's names).

Children's metamemory skills improve as they grow older. For example, young children are wildly overconfident about their memory accuracy, whereas older children and adults are more accurate. Elderly adults and young adults have similar beliefs about memory tasks. However, elderly adults tend to be more overconfident about the accuracy of their memory.

With respect to language development, young infants are remarkably competent in perceiving speech sounds and other important components of language. As children mature, their language skills increase dramatically in areas such as word meaning, grammatical relationships, and the pragmatic aspects of language.

INTRODUCTION

Consider the following conversation between a mother and her 2 1/2-year-old child:

Child: Why that boy go home?
Mother: Because his mother thought he was tired.
Child: Why he tired?

Mother: Because he hasn't slept all day.
Child: Why he not sleep?
Mother: Because they went to a party.
Child: Why they go to party?
Mother (exasperated): Because! (Karmiloff & Karmiloff-Smith, 2001, p. 102)

This interaction captures the considerable language skills of young children. It also illustrates Theme 1 of this textbook, because children actively pursue information (Gauvain, 2001; Gelman & Brenneman, 2004). In fact, parents—such as this mother—may occasionally wish that children were less persistent in their pursuit of knowledge. However, the interaction also illustrates that children's syntax is not yet fully developed. As a 4-year-old boy remarked to his mother one morning, "You know, I thought I'd be a grown-up by now. . . . It sure is taking a long time!" (Rogoff, 1990, p. 3). As we will see in this chapter, the boy is certainly correct. Obviously, 4-year-olds have mastered some components of memory and language. However, they still need to develop their skills in areas such as memory performance, memory strategies, metacognition, syntax, and pragmatics.

Most cognitive psychology textbooks limit their discussion of cognitive development to infancy and childhood. This textbook emphasizes the **lifespan approach to development,** which argues that developmental changes continue beyond young adulthood; we continue to change and adapt throughout our entire lives (Smith & Baltes, 1999; Whitbourne, 2008). As you will see, some cognitive skills decline during the aging process, but many other capabilities remain stable.

A lifespan approach to cognitive development is important in North America, because about 13% of Canadian residents and 12% of U.S. residents are 65 years of age or older (Statistics Canada, 2008; *World Almanac and Book of Facts,* 2005). Fortunately, an increasing number of psychologists are focusing their research on elderly individuals (Birren & Schroots, 2001).

When we study the cognitive abilities of infants, children, and elderly adults, the research problems are even more complex than when we study young adults. For example, how can young infants convey what they know, given their limited language and motor skills? With creative research techniques, however, researchers can partially overcome these limitations and discover that even young infants can understand information about the people and objects in their world (e.g., Holmes & Teti, 2005; Mandler, 2004a; Rovee-Collier & Cuevas, 2008).

Research with elderly individuals presents a different set of methodological problems (Boker & Bisconti, 2006; Salthouse, 2000; Whitbourne, 2008). Hundreds of studies have compared the cognitive performance of young, healthy college students with the performance of elderly people whose health, self-confidence, education, and familiarity with technology are relatively poor. Furthermore, college students are much more likely than elderly adults to have recent experiences with memorizing material and taking tests.

Notice the problem: Suppose that a poorly controlled memory study determines that young adults recall 25% more items than elderly adults. Perhaps the superior performance of the young adults should be attributed to confounding variables—such as health or education—rather than to the aging process itself. In general, researchers believe that confounding variables can explain a substantial portion of the differences in cognitive performance. However, researchers have identified some age-related differences that persist, even when they eliminate confounding variables (Baltes et al., 1999; Rabbitt, 2002; Whitbourne, 2008).

This chapter focuses on cognitive development in three areas: memory, metacognition, and language. I specifically organized this textbook so that the final chapter would encourage you to review the major concepts from three important areas within cognitive psychology. As you'll also learn, infants and young children possess cognitive skills that you might not have suspected. In addition, you'll see that elderly people are much more cognitively competent than the popular stereotype suggests.

THE LIFESPAN DEVELOPMENT OF MEMORY

We have examined memory in many parts of this textbook. Chapters 4, 5, and 6 focused specifically on memory, and the remaining chapters often discussed the contribution of memory to other cognitive processes. Now we will examine how memory develops from infancy—the first two years of life—and childhood through old age.

Memory in Infants

Try to picture an infant who is about 4 months old—not yet old enough to sit upright without support. Would you expect that this baby would recognize his or her mother or remember how to make a mobile move? Several decades ago, psychologists believed that infants as young as 4 months of age could not remember anything for more than a brief period (Gelman, 2002). Of course, we cannot expect young infants to demonstrate sophisticated memory feats because regions of the cortex most relevant to working memory and long-term memory are not yet fully developed (Bauer, 2004; Kagan & Herschkowitz, 2005).

Furthermore, early researchers underestimated infants' memory capacities because of methodological problems. Fortunately, developmental psychologists have recently devised several research methods to test infants' ability to remember people and objects. This research shows that infants have greater memory capabilities than you might expect. For example, we now know that a 6-month-old can create an association between two objects, even if he or she has never previously seen the objects together at the same time (Cuevas et al., 2006). Indeed, Theme 2—which emphasizes cognitive competence—certainly applies to infants, as well as children and adults.

One way to assess infants' memory is to see whether they imitate an action after a delay (e.g., Learmonth et al., 2004, 2005; Mandler, 2004a; Nelson, 2006). Let's consider three other research topics: (1) infants' attention patterns, (2) recognizing mother, and (3) conjugate reinforcement with a mobile. As you'll see, babies can demonstrate substantial memory ability, even during their first month of life.

Attention Patterns. Researchers can measure infants' memory by noticing how long they spend paying attention to a particular stimulus (e.g., Cohen & Cashon, 2003;

Luo et al., 2003). Let's consider a recent study, which explored the own-race bias in infants. As Chapter 5 noted, the **own-race bias** refers to people's tendency to identify members of their own ethnic group relatively accurately, in contrast to members of another ethnic group (Brigham et al., 2007; Meissner et al., 2005; Walker & Hewstone, 2006). Sangrigoli and de Schonen (2004) located photos of White and Asian women's faces. The two sets of photos were matched in terms of characteristics such as the women's age.

Sangrigoli and de Schonen tested 3-month-old White babies by repeatedly presenting one photo until the baby looked at it only half as long as on the initial trials. Then the researchers presented a pair of photos, side by side: (1) the familiar photo and (2) a photo of an unfamiliar woman from the same racial category. The results showed that babies who had initially seen a White woman later looked longer at the unfamiliar White woman than at the familiar White woman. These data indicate that the babies could tell the difference between the two White faces. In contrast, babies who had initially seen an Asian woman later looked equally long at the unfamiliar Asian woman and the familiar Asian woman, indicating that the babies could *not* tell the difference between the two Asian faces. These findings are intriguing; if you were a researcher, what additional questions would you like to explore?

Recognizing Mother. Research on visual recognition shows that even 3-day-olds can distinguish their mother from a stranger (Rovee-Collier et al., 2001; Slater & Butterworth, 1997; Walton et al., 1992).

Infants' ability to recognize their mother's voice is especially remarkable (Siegler et al., 2003). For example, Kisilevsky and her coauthors (2003) tested infants about one or two weeks *before* they were born. Specifically, these researchers approached women who were receiving prenatal care at a hospital in China, to ask about testing their infants' voice-recognition ability prior to birth. If the mother agreed, the researchers presented either the mother's voice reading a Chinese poem or a female stranger's voice reading the same poem. Impressively, the infant's heart rate changed more when hearing their mother's voice than when hearing the stranger's voice.

Conjugate Reinforcement. Obviously, young infants cannot verbally tell us that they remember something they saw earlier. Carolyn Rovee-Collier and her colleagues designed a nonverbal measure to assess infant memory. They have continued to use this conjugate reinforcement technique in their extensive program of research on infant memory (Rovee-Collier & Cuevas, 2008). In the **conjugate reinforcement technique,** a mobile hangs above a young infant's crib; a ribbon connects the infant's ankle and the mobile, so that the infant's kicks will make the mobile move (see Figure 13.1).

This game is especially appealing to 2- to 6-month-old infants. After several minutes, they begin to kick rapidly and pump up the mobile; then they lie quietly and watch parts of the mobile move. As the movement dies down, they typically shriek and then kick vigorously, thereby pumping it up again. In operant conditioning terms, the response is a foot kick, and the reinforcement is the movement of the mobile (Barr et al., 2005; Rovee-Collier & Cuevas, 2008).

FIGURE 13.1

The Conjugate Reinforcement Setup in Rovee-Collier's Research.

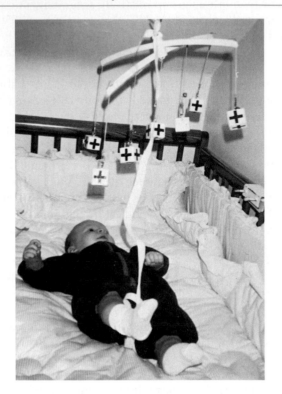

Let's see how the conjugate reinforcement technique can be used to assess infant memory. All the training and testing take place in the infant's crib at home, so that measurements are not distorted by the infant's reactions to the new surroundings. For a 3-minute period at the beginning of the first session, the experimenter takes a baseline measure. During this time, the ribbon is connected from the infant's ankle to an "empty" mobile stand, rather than to the mobile. Thus, the experimenters can measure the amount of spontaneous kicking that occurs in the presence of the mobile, before the infant learns how to make the mobile move (Rovee-Collier, 1999; Rovee-Collier & Barr, 2002).

Next, the experimenter moves the ribbon so that it runs from the baby's ankle to the stand from which the mobile is hung. The babies are allowed 9 minutes to discover that their kicks can activate the mobile; this is the acquisition phase. The infants typically receive two training sessions like this, spaced 24 hours apart. At the end of the second training session, the ribbon is unhooked and returned to the empty stand for 3 minutes in order to measure what the infants remember; this is the immediate retention test.

Researchers then measure long-term memory after 1 to 42 days have elapsed. The mobile is once again hung above the infant's crib, with the ribbon hooked to the empty

stand. If the infant recognizes the mobile and recalls how kicking had produced movement, then he or she will soon produce the foot-kick response. Notice, then, that Rovee-
Collier devised a clever way to "ask" infants if they remember how to activate the
mobile. She also devised an objective method for assessing long-term memory, because
she can compare two measures: (1) the number of kicks produced in the immediate
retention test and (2) the number of kicks produced following the delay.

Rovee-Collier later devised a second operant conditioning task that is more appealing to infants between the ages of 6 and 18 months. In this second task, older infants learn
to press a lever in order to make a miniature train move along a circular track. By combining
information from the two tasks, researchers can trace infant memory from 2 months
through 18 months of age (Hsu & Rovee-Collier, 2006; Rovee-Collier & Barr, 2002).

Figure 13.2 shows how much time can pass before infants no longer show significant recall for the relevant task. For example, 6-month-olds can recall how to move

FIGURE 13.2

**The Maximum Duration for Which Different Groups of Infants
Demonstrated Significant Retention.** In this study, 2- to 6-month-old infants kicked to
activate a mobile, and 6- to 18-month-old infants pressed a lever to activate a train.

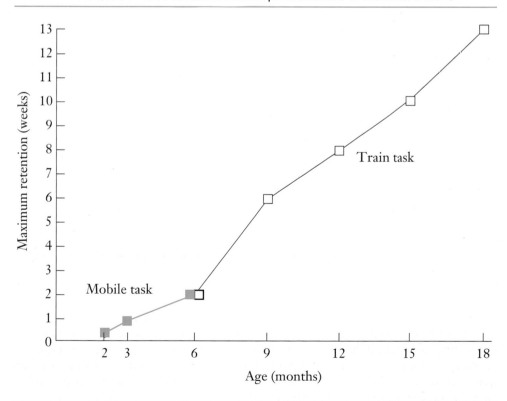

Source: Rovee-Collier, 1999.

the mobile and also how to move the train, even after a two-week delay. This research demonstrates that long-term retention shows a steady, linear improvement during the first 18 months of life (Hsu & Rovee-Collier, 2006).

Several decades ago, researchers thought that infant memory was extremely limited. However, Rovee-Collier and her coworkers have demonstrated that infants can remember actions, even after a substantial delay. Furthermore, infant memory and adult memory are influenced by many of the same factors (Rovee-Collier & Barr, 2002; Rovee-Collier & Cuevas, 2008; Rovee-Collier et al., 2001).

For example, you saw in Chapter 5 that context sometimes influences adult memory. Context effects are even stronger for infants. Rovee-Collier and her colleagues (1985) used the conjugate reinforcement technique to test 3-month-old infants whose cribs were lined with a fabric that had a distinctive, colorful pattern. The infants' recall was excellent when they were tested after a seven-day delay. However, another group of infants was tested with the same mobile and the same delay—but with a different crib liner. This second group of infants showed no retention whatsoever! Without the proper environmental context, infants' memories decline sharply (Rovee-Collier & Hayne, 2000).

You'll also recall from Chapter 5 (pp. 152–154) that young adults' eyewitness testimony for details of an accident was less accurate if they learned new, contradictory information—about a stop sign, rather than a yield sign—after witnessing the events. Similarly, Rovee-Collier and her coauthors (1993) measured "eyewitness testimony" in 3-month-olds. Immediately after the infants had learned how to produce movement in one particular mobile, they were shown a different mobile for just 3 minutes. When the researchers later tested the infants' long-term memory, they showed significantly less recall for the original mobile than did infants in a control group, who had seen no second mobile. Infants—like adults—recall an event less accurately if they have been exposed to postevent information (Gulya et al., 2002).

In additional research, Rovee-Collier and her associates have discovered numerous other similarities between infant and adult memory. For example, you may recall the **spacing effect** from Chapter 6; students learn most effectively if their practice is distributed over time, rather than if they learn the material all at once (p. 170). A number of studies have now demonstrated that infants also remember better with distributed practice (Barr et al., 2005; Bearce & Rovee-Collier, 2006).

Furthermore, infants show a levels-of-processing effect, with better recall for items that were processed at a deep level (Adler et al., 1998; Rovee-Collier et al., 2001). As you can see, researchers have designed several creative techniques, which allow them to discover that many principles of adult memory are also relevant for infants who have not yet reached their first birthday.

In summary, infants demonstrate memory on a number of tasks. For example, young infants—like adults—show the own-race bias in identifying faces. Even newborns can recognize their mother's voice. Furthermore, 6-month-olds can remember how to activate a mobile after a two-week delay, and some of the same factors that influence an adult's memory also influence an infant's memory.

Memory in Children

We have seen that researchers need to be extremely inventive when they study infant memory. By using the conjugate reinforcement technique, imitation tasks, and other creative methods, they have concluded that infants' memory is reasonably impressive.

It's much easier to assess children's memory, because children can respond verbally. However, the task is still challenging. Young children may have trouble understanding task instructions, and they may not recognize letters of the alphabet or printed words. With these problems in mind, let's consider five topics: (1) children's working memory, (2) their long-term memory, (3) their memory strategies, (4) their eyewitness testimony, and (5) the relationship between children's intelligence and the accuracy of their eyewitness testimony.

Children's Working Memory. Working memory is often measured in terms of memory span, or the number of items that can be correctly recalled in order, immediately after presentation. Memory spans improve dramatically during childhood (Gathercole et al., 2005; Hitch, 2006; Schneider, 2002; Zoelch et al., 2005). According to one estimate, for example, a 2-year-old can recall an average of two numbers in a row, whereas a 9-year-old can recall six (Kail, 1992).

As you saw in Chapter 4, Alan Baddeley (2006) and other theorists propose that adult working memory has three especially important components, the central executive, the phonological loop, and the visuospatial sketchpad. Susan Gathercole and her colleagues (2004) found that this same structural model also applies to the working memory of children as young as 4 and continuing through adolescence.

As you might expect, children's working-memory skills are correlated with their performance in school. For instance, children with high scores on phonological working memory are likely to excel in reading, writing, and listening (Alloway et al., 2005). Similarly, children with high scores on visuospatial working memory are likely to excel in mathematics (Gathercole & Pickering, 2000; Hitch, 2006).

Now let's turn our attention to long-term memory in children. Later, we'll see how older children's use of memory strategies helps to explain the improvement in their memory performance.

Children's Long-Term Memory. With respect to long-term memory, children typically have excellent recognition memory but poor recall memory (e.g., Flavell et al., 2002; Howe, 2000; Howe et al., 2000; Schneider & Bjorklund, 1998). In a classic study, Myers and Perlmutter (1978) administered research tasks similar to those in Demonstration 13.1, using 2- and 4-year-old children. To test recognition, the researchers showed children 18 objects. Then they presented 36 items, including the 18 previous objects and 18 new objects. The 2-year-olds recognized an impressive 80% of the items, and the 4-year-olds recognized about 90% of the items.

Myers and Perlmutter (1978) also tested different groups of children for their ability to *recall* nine objects. The 2-year-olds recalled only about 20% of the items, and the 4-year-olds recalled about 40% of the items. Recall memory seems to require the

---

⊚ Demonstration 13.1

Age Differences in Recall and Recognition

In this study, you will need to test a college-age person and a preschool child. You should reassure the child's parents that you are simply testing memory as part of a class project.

You will be examining both recall and recognition in this demonstration. First, assemble twenty common objects, such as a pen, pencil, piece of paper, leaf, stick, rock, book, key, apple, and so on. Place the objects in a box or cover them with a cloth.

You will use the same testing procedure for both people, although the preschool child will require more extensive explanation. Remove ten objects in all, one at a time. Show each object for about 5 seconds and then conceal it again. After all ten objects have been shown, ask each person to recall as many of the objects as possible. Do not provide feedback about the correctness of the responses. After recall is complete, test for recognition. Remove one object at a time, randomly presenting the old objects mixed in sequence with new objects. In each case, ask whether the object is old or new.

Count the number of correct recalls and the number of correct recognitions for each person. You should find that they both show a similarly high level of performance on the recognition measures.

---

active use of memory strategies. As you'll see later in this section, these strategies are not developed until middle childhood (Schneider & Bjorklund, 1998). Let's now consider two more specific issues: (1) autobiographic memory for events from childhood and (2) children's source monitoring.

1. *Autobiographical memory and early childhood.* Several researchers have instructed older children and adults to think back on their early experiences. In general, people typically do not describe events that had occurred in their own lives before they were about 2 or 3 years old, a phenomenon called **childhood amnesia** (Bauer, 2005b; Howe, 2000, 2003).

Rubin (2000) located previous research in which adolescents and adults had been instructed to recall autobiographical memories from the first ten years of their lives. As you can see in Figure 13.3, people seldom report events that happened when they were younger than 3.

The concept of childhood amnesia would be surprising, however, given our discussion of the impressive memory skills that 1-year-old infants demonstrate (Rovee-Collier & Cuevas, 2008). We also know that 2-year-old children frequently describe an event that occurred several weeks or months ago, so they must be able to store verbal memories for substantial periods of time (Gauvain, 2001; Ornstein & Haden, 2001).

At present, then, the concept of childhood amnesia is controversial. For example, according to Carolyn Rovee-Collier and Kimberly Cuevas (2008), infants have memories that are qualitatively similar to the memories of adults. Patricia Bauer (2005a,

FIGURE 13.3

The Proportion of Memories Supplied by Adolescents and Adults That Occurred for Each Year, 1 to 10 Years of Age.

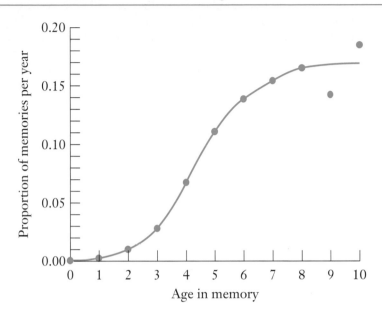

Source: Based on studies examined by Rubin, 2000.

2005b) also questions the concept of childhood amnesia, but she is somewhat less optimistic. She reviews the research on deferred imitation and concludes that long-term memory becomes reasonably strong when children are about 20 months old. Her data suggest that children who are 24 months of age can verbally describe events that they had experienced 4 months earlier.

However, other researchers support the concept of infantile amnesia. They argue that children younger than 2 do not have a well-organized sense of who they are (Fivush & Nelson, 2004; Goodman & Melinder, 2007; Howe, 2000, 2003). Therefore, they may have difficulty encoding and retrieving a series of events connected with themselves (Newcombe et al., 2000).

The answer to the question of infantile amnesia probably lies somewhere in the middle ground. Recall accuracy for events prior to 3 years of age probably depends on whether children receive "reminders" about an earlier event and whether the children are allowed to demonstrate their recall nonverbally, rather than in cohesive verbal descriptions.

2. *Children's source monitoring.* You may recall that Chapter 5 discussed **source monitoring,** which is the process of trying to decide which memories or beliefs are real and which are simply imagined. In general, children younger than 7 years of age have more difficulty than adults in distinguishing between reality and fantasy (Ratner et al., 2000;

Ratner et al., 2001; Sluzenski et al., 2004). For example, I know an extremely bright child who had participated in an imaginary trip to the moon one day at school. Later that day, she insisted to her parents that she really had visited the moon.

Research by Mary Ann Foley, Hilary Horn Ratner, and their colleagues has systematically clarified the conditions in which young children are most likely to make source-monitoring errors. For example, Foley and Ratner (1998) asked one group of 6-year-olds to perform specific physical activities, such as making a motion like an airplane. A second group of 6-year-olds was instructed to imagine how specific physical activities would feel (for example: "Try to imagine what it would actually feel like to do that"). A third group was instructed to visualize themselves performing each specific physical activity (for example: "Try to picture what you look like . . .").

According to the results, when children had actually *performed* an action, they seldom reported that they had simply imagined it. In contrast, when children had simply *imagined* an action, they often reported that they had actually performed it. This bias was especially likely for children in the second group. In other words, the children who made the most source-monitoring errors were those who had imagined how it would feel to make airplane movements; they often convinced themselves that they had actually circled around the room.

Other research on source monitoring shows that children sometimes recall that they performed a task, when the task had actually been performed by another person with whom they had been collaborating (Foley, Ratner, & House, 2002; Ratner et al., 2002). Apparently, children between the ages of 4 and 6 can watch another person at work, and they anticipate the steps in the project. Later, they become confused, and their memory of *thinking* about the project becomes transformed into a memory of actually *completing* the project. As you might guess, children's source monitoring is especially poor if they are questioned a long time after the original event (Sluzenski et al., 2004).

Children's Memory Strategies. So far, our exploration of children's memory has demonstrated that young children are fairly similar to adults in recognizing items. However, children are much less accurate than adults in terms of recall and source monitoring. Adults have another advantage: When they want to remember something that must be recalled at a later time, they often use memory strategies. One important reason young children have relatively poor recall is that they cannot use memory strategies effectively (Bransford et al., 2000; DeHart et al., 2004).

Memory strategies are intentional, goal-oriented activities that we use to improve our memories. Young children may not realize that strategies can be helpful. Furthermore, some young children may not use the strategies effectively, a problem called **utilization deficiency** (Pressley & Hilden, 2006; Schneider et al., 2004). As a result, the strategies may not improve their recall (Bjorklund et al., 1997; Ornstein et al., 2006; Schneider, 2002).

In contrast, older children typically realize that strategies are helpful. In addition, they choose their strategies more carefully and use them more consistently. Also, older children often use a variety of strategies when they need to learn several items, and they may monitor how they use these strategies (Coyle & Bjorklund, 1997; Schneider, 1998). As a result, older children can recall items with reasonable accuracy. Let's survey three major kinds of memory strategies: rehearsal, organization, and imagery.

1. *Rehearsal*, or merely repeating items over and over, is not a particularly effective strategy, but it may be useful for maintaining items in working memory. Research suggests that 4- and 5-year-olds do not spontaneously rehearse material they want to remember (Flavell et al., 1966; Gathercole et al., 1994). However, 7-year-olds do use rehearsal strategies, often silently rehearsing several words together (Gathercole, 1998; Schneider & Bjorklund, 1998).

Another important point is that younger children often benefit from rehearsal strategies, even though they do not use these strategies spontaneously (e.g., Bjorklund et al., 1997; Flavell et al., 2002; Gathercole, 1998). As we will see later, in the section on metacognition, young children often fail to realize that they could improve their memory performance by using strategies.

2. *Organizational strategies*, such as categorizing and grouping, are often helpful for adults, as we saw in Chapter 6. However, many young children do not spontaneously group similar items together to aid memorization (Flavell et al., 2002; Ornstein et al., 2006; Pressley & Hilden, 2006; Schneider et al., 2004). Try Demonstration 13.2 on page 452; are the children in your sample reluctant to adopt an organizational strategy?

This demonstration is based on a classic study by Moely and her colleagues (1969), in which children studied pictures from four categories: animals, clothing, furniture, and vehicles. During the 2-minute study period, they were told that they could rearrange the pictures in any order they wished. Younger children rarely moved the pictures next to other similar pictures, but older children frequently organized the pictures into categories. The researchers specifically urged other groups of children to organize the pictures. Even the younger children saw that the organizational strategy was useful, and this strategy increased their recall.

3. *Imagery*, a topic discussed in Chapters 6 and 7, is an extremely useful device for improving memory in adults. Research shows that even 6-year-olds can be trained to use visual imagery effectively (Foley et al., 1993; Howe, 2006). However, young children usually do not use imagery spontaneously. In fact, the spontaneous use of imagery does not develop until adolescence. Even most college students do not use this helpful strategy often enough (Pressley & Hilden, 2006; Schneider & Bjorklund, 1998).

In short, preschool children are unlikely to use memory strategies in a careful, consistent fashion. In fact, as we have suggested here—and will further discuss in connection with metamemory—young children seldom appreciate that they *need* to use memory strategies (Ornstein et al., 2006; Schneider, 1999). However, as children develop, they learn how to use memory strategies such as rehearsal, organization, and (eventually) imagery. In addition, they exert more effort to use these memory strategies, rather than merely trusting that they will remember important material (Bransford et al., 2000; Kuhn, 2000; Ornstein et al., 2006).

It's also worth mentioning that teachers can help children by showing them how to use age-appropriate memory strategies. Furthermore, teachers can use spaced rather than massed presentation (see p. 170) in the classroom to improve their students' recall (Seabrook et al., 2005).

ⓢ Demonstration 13.2

Organizational Strategies in Children

Make a photocopy of the pictures on this page and use scissors to cut them apart. In this study you will test a child between the ages of 4 and 8; ideally, it would be interesting to test children of several different ages. Arrange these pictures in random order in a circle facing the child. Instruct him or her to study the pictures so that they can be remembered later. Mention that the pictures can be rearranged in any order. After a 2-minute study period, remove the pictures and ask the child to list as many items as possible. Notice two things in this demonstration: (1) Does the child spontaneously rearrange the items at all during the study period? (2) Does the child show clustering during recall, with similar items appearing together?

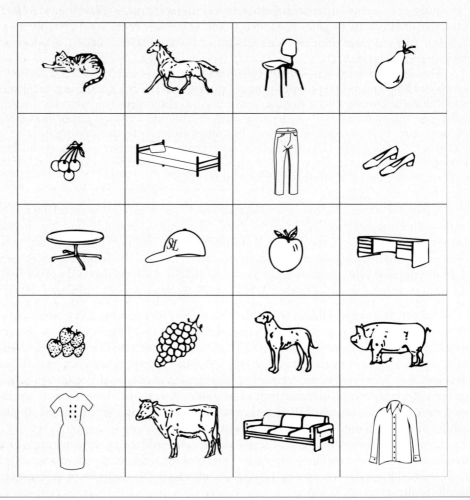

Children's Eyewitness Testimony. So far, we have examined children's working memory, long-term memory, and memory strategies. We've seen that young children's performance in those three areas is definitely inferior when compared with adults' performance. All three of these factors have implications for an applied area of cognition, the accuracy of their eyewitness testimony. As you might guess, older children provide much more accurate eyewitness testimony than younger children (Melnyk et al., 2007; Powell et al., 2003; Schneider, 2002).

A real-life court case inspired Michelle Leichtman and Stephen Ceci (1995) to conduct an experiment. In the original court case, a 9-year-old girl had provided eyewitness testimony, and it seemed likely that both stereotypes and suggestions could have influenced her report. Leichtman and Ceci's study explored the impact of these two factors.

Leichtman and Ceci tested 176 preschoolers, assigning each child to one of four conditions. In the control condition, a stranger named Sam Stone visited the classroom, strolling around and making several bland comments for a period of about 2 minutes. In the stereotype condition, a research assistant presented one story each week to the children for three weeks prior to Sam Stone's visit. Each story emphasized that Sam Stone was nice but very clumsy and bumbling. In the suggestion condition, children had no information about Sam Stone prior to his visit. However, during interviews after his visit, the interviewer provided two *incorrect* suggestions—that Sam Stone had ripped a book and that he had spilled a chocolate drink on a white teddy bear. Finally, in the stereotype-plus-suggestion condition, children were exposed to both the stereotype before Sam Stone's visit and the incorrect suggestions afterward.

Ten weeks after Sam Stone's classroom visit, a new interviewer—whom no child had previously met—asked what Sam Stone had done during his visit. As a key part of the interview, the children were asked whether they had actually seen Sam Stone tear up the book and spill chocolate on the teddy bear. Figure 13.4 shows the percentage of children in each condition who said they had witnessed at least one of these two events.

Notice, first of all, that children in the control group were highly accurate; only 5% of the younger children and none of the older children claimed to have witnessed something that Sam Stone had not actually done. In other words, children can provide valid eyewitness testimony if they do not receive misleading information, either before or after the target event (Bruck & Ceci, 1999; Bruck et al., 1997; Schneider, 2002).

As Figure 13.4 also shows, however, a worrisome number of children claimed that they had actually witnessed these actions if the researchers had established a previous stereotype. Even more of the younger children claimed that they had actually witnessed the actions if they had received inaccurate suggestions after the event. The most alarming data came from the younger children who had received both the stereotype and the suggestions. Almost half of the younger children falsely reported that they had seen Sam Stone damage either the book or the teddy bear.

Other research confirms that the accuracy of children's eyewitness testimony is influenced by the child's age, stereotyping, and misleading suggestions (Melnyk et al., 2007; Memon et al., 2006; Roebers et al., 2004; Roebers et al., 2005). As you might imagine, social factors can also have a major impact. For example, children make more errors when interviewers ask questions in a highly emotional tone or when the interviewer uses complex language (Bruck & Ceci, 1999; Imhoff & Baker-Ward, 1999; Melnyk et al., 2007).

FIGURE 13.4

The Effects of Stereotypes and Suggestions on Young Children's Eyewitness Testimony.   Graph shows the percentage who reported actually seeing events that had not occurred.

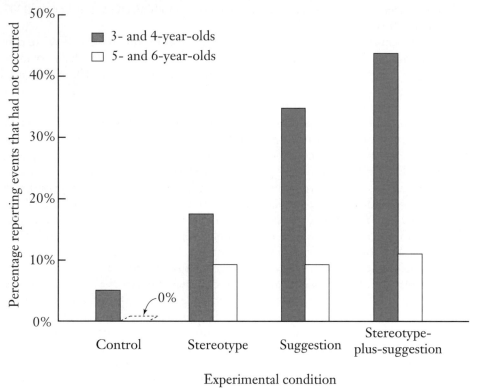

Source: Based on Leichtman & Ceci, 1995.

In addition, children are extremely reluctant to say, "I don't know" when an adult asks a question (Bruck & Ceci, 1999). Furthermore, children are likely to change their statements if someone cross-examines them, and this tendency is stronger among 5- and 6-year-olds than among 9- and 10-year-olds (Zajac & Hayne, 2006).

Individual Differences: Children's Intelligence and Eyewitness Testimony

So far, this chapter has focused on typically developing children, and we have seen that the accuracy of children's eyewitness testimony increases as they grow older. What happens for children with mental retardation? Lucy Henry and Gisli Gudjonsson (2007) studied children in England, who were either enrolled in special schools for children

TABLE 13.1

The Number of Correct Items Supplied by Children in Free Recall.

	Average Age of Child	
Category of Children	9 Years 2 Months	12 Years 8 Months
Children with intellectual disability	7.2 items	13.6 items
Typically developing children	18.9 items	34.5 items

Source: Henry & Gudjonsson, 2007.

with mental retardation or enrolled in mainstream schools. In each group, they tested children who were an average of either 9 years 2 months old or 12 years 8 months old.

All the children saw a 3-minute video clip that featured four children pulling up to a gas station in a car, filling up the car with gas, and driving off without paying for the gas. Each child then performed a short irrelevant task, and then the researcher asked the child to describe as much as possible about the video. The recall narrative was scored in terms of the total number of correct items supplied by the child. As Table 13.1 shows, older children recalled more items than the younger children, and this difference was especially strong in the typically developing children.

Henry and Gudjonson (2007) also asked some specific misleading questions, for example, about the color of the police car, when there was no police car. In this case, the older children made the same number of errors as the younger children; however, within each age group, the typically developing children made fewer errors.

In summary, then, typically developing children provided a great number of correct answers and a smaller number of errors in response to misleading questions. However, the authors point out that there was only a short delay period between seeing the event and providing eyewitness testimony. Further research would need to include a longer delay, consistent with real-life eyewitness-testimony situations.

IN DEPTH

Memory in Elderly People

The popular stereotype for elderly people is that they may be pleasant, but they are typically forgetful and cognitively incompetent (Cuddy & Fiske, 2002; Hess et al., 2003; Levy & Banaji, 2002). Consider the following example of the way people judge cognitive errors made by elderly people (Hulicka, 1982). A 78-year-old woman served a meal to her guests, and the meal was excellent, except that she had used bleach instead of vinegar in the salad dressing. Her concerned relatives attributed the error to impaired memory and general intellectual decline, and they discussed placing her in a nursing home. As it turned out, someone else had placed the bottle of bleach in the cupboard where the vinegar was kept. Understandably, the woman had reached for the wrong bottle, which was similar in size, shape, and color to the vinegar bottle.

Some time later, the same people were guests in another home. A young woman in search of hair spray reached into a bathroom cabinet and found a can of the correct size and shape. She proceeded to drench her hair with Lysol. In this case, however, no one suggested that the younger woman should be institutionalized; they merely teased her about her absentmindedness.

In mainstream North American culture, people often believe that elderly people have substantial cognitive deficits. As a result, an incident may be considered humorous in a younger person; however, the same incident provides evidence of incompetence in an older person. Unfortunately, the stereotype about forgetful older adults can have important consequences, so that elderly people actually remember less information (Hess, 2005; Hess et al., 2003; Hess et al., 2004; Zacks & Hasher, 2006).

During the current decade, research on age-related changes in memory has increased dramatically, and we now have a wide variety of review articles and books (e.g., Bialystok & Craik, 2006; Birren & Schaie, 2001; Dixon & Cohen, 2003; Erber, 2005; Graf & Ohta, 2002; Light, 2000; Park & Schwarz, 2000; Tulving & Craik, 2000; Whitbourne, 2008). The picture that emerges suggests large individual differences and complex developmental trends in various components of memory (Fabiani & Wee, 2001; Light, 2000; Whitbourne, 2008). Let us consider the research on working memory and long-term memory in elderly people; then we will examine some potential explanations for the memory changes during aging.

Working Memory in Elderly People.   How well do elderly people perform on tasks requiring working memory, when they need to retain information in memory for less than a minute? If you have taken several previous psychology courses, you know that your professors and your textbooks frequently use the phrase, "It all depends on . . . ." In the case of working memory, factors such as the nature of the task determine whether we find age similarities or age differences (Craik, 2006).

In general, we find age similarities when the task is relatively straightforward and requires simple storage. In contrast, we typically find age differences when the task is complicated and requires manipulation of information (Bäckman et al., 2001; Craik, 2006; Park & Payer, 2006; Whitbourne, 2008; Zacks & Hasher, 2006).

For example, younger and older adults perform similarly on a standard digit-span test of working memory. On these tasks, people are instructed to recall a list of numbers in order (Bäckman et al., 2001; Dixon & Cohen, 2003; Fabiani & Wee, 2001).

In contrast, age differences are substantial on a working-memory task in which people must either ignore irrelevant information or perform two simultaneous tasks (Carstensen, 2007; Kramer & Kray, 2006; Oberauer et al., 2003; Park & Payer, 2006). For instance, in one study, people were given short lists of unrelated words, with the instructions to report the words in correct alphabetical order (Craik, 1990). On this complex task, the average young participant reported 3.2 correct items on the alphabetical-order task, whereas the average elderly participant reported only 1.7 correct items.

Another example of the complex nature of working memory comes from Stine and her coauthors (1989), who tested people's recall for spoken English. When the sentences had normal syntax and were spoken at a normal rate, the younger and older participants performed similarly. In contrast, when the words were in random order and the speech rate was much faster than normal, the younger participants recalled about twice as many items. We should keep in mind, then, that elderly people often perform well on the tasks they are most likely to encounter in everyday life.

Long-Term Memory in Elderly People. Do elderly people differ from younger adults in their long-term memory? Once again, the answer is, "It all depends on . . . ." In general, elderly people perform quite well on tests of semantic memory (Zacks & Hasher, 2006). They also tend to perform quite well on tasks they can do relatively automatically (Economou et al., 2006; Little et al., 2004). However, age differences emerge on more complex tasks. In this discussion of long-term memory, let's consider four topics: (1) prospective memory, (2) implicit memory; (3) explicit recognition memory, and (4) explicit recall memory.

1. *Prospective memory.* Chapter 6 discussed **prospective memory,** or remembering to do something in the future. In general, older adults have difficulty on many prospective-memory tasks. (Craik, 2006; Einstein & McDaniel, 2004). For example, one prospective-memory task—high in ecological validity—simulates a shopping task. Participants saw a list of items they were supposed to purchase. For example, when they saw an image of a fast-food restaurant, they were supposed to "buy" a hamburger. On these tasks, younger adults successfully completed a greater number of tasks than the older adults (Farrimond et al., 2006; McDermott & Knight, 2004).

Compared to young adults, older adults generally make more errors on prospective-memory tasks. These results make sense, because prospective memory relies heavily on working memory. People need to keep reminding themselves to do the relevant task, and older adults often show a decline in working memory.

In contrast, older adults perform relatively accurately when they have an environmental cue, such as a book placed near the door, reminding them to take it to the library (Craik, 2006; Einstein & McDaniel, 2004). Occasionally, older adults even perform more accurately than younger adults, for example, when instructed to take a certain medicine on a daily basis (Park & Hedden, 2001; Park et al., 1999).

2. *Implicit Memory.* Chapter 5 discussed the difference between explicit and implicit memory tasks. As explained in that chapter, participants in an **explicit memory task** are specifically instructed to remember information that they have previously learned (for example, to recognize or recall information). In contrast, an **implicit memory task** requires the participants to perform a perceptual or cognitive task (for example, to complete a series of word fragments); past experience with the material facilitates their performance on the task.

In a representative study, Light and her colleagues (1995) measured implicit memory in terms of the time participants required to read a letter sequence that was either familiar or unfamiliar. People demonstrated implicit memory if they read a familiar sequence faster than an unfamiliar sequence. On this implicit memory task, adults between the ages of 64 and 78 performed as well as did the younger adults, who were between the ages of 18 and 24.

Other research on implicit memory shows either similar performance by older and younger adults, or else just a slight deficit for older adults (e.g., Bäckman et al., 2001; Craik, 2006; Economou et al., 2006; Whitbourne, 2008; Zacks & Hasher, 2006). Thus, age differences are minimal when the memory task does not require effortful remembering.

3. *Explicit Recognition Memory.* A number of research papers and reviews of the literature argue that long-term recognition memory declines either slowly or not at all as people grow older (Burke, 2006; Erber, 2005; Moulin et al., 2007). For example, one study on recognition memory found that 20-year-olds correctly recognized 67% of words that had been presented earlier; the 70-year-olds recalled a nearly identical 66% of the words (Intons-Peterson et al., 1983).

4. *Explicit Recall Memory.* So far, our discussion of long-term memory has shown that elderly people have difficulty with prospective memory, but they perform reasonably well on two kinds of long-term memory tasks: implicit memory and explicit-recognition memory. Let us now turn to performance on explicit *recall* tasks. In general, performance on these measures decreases slowly throughout later adulthood, and the age differences are more substantial (Dixon & Cohen, 2003; Wingfield & Kahana, 2002; Zacks & Hasher, 2006).

In a representative study, Dunlosky and Hertzog (1998a) asked participants to learn pairs of unrelated English words. They reported that the 20-year-old participants recalled an average of 20% more of the items than did the 70-year-old participants. In other research, older people made more errors in recalling names, recalling details of historical events, and remembering stories (Cohen, 1993; Cohen et al., 1994; Zacks & Hasher, 2006).

However, elderly individuals differ widely in their performance on long-term recall tasks. For example, people with low verbal ability and little education are especially likely to show a decline in recall during the aging process. In contrast, age differences are minimal for people who have high verbal ability and are highly educated (Bäckman et al., 2001; Manly et al., 2003; Rabbitt, 2002).

Lynn Hasher and her coauthors have explored another variable to add to the list of "It all depends on. . ." factors: the time of day when people's memory is tested (Hasher et al., 2002; Yoon, May, & Hasher, 2000; Zacks & Hasher, 2006). Specifically, older adults tend to function well—compared to younger adults—when they are tested in the morning. In contrast, older adults make substantially more memory errors than younger adults when they are tested in the afternoon.

Notice how the research on long-term memory obeys the "It all depends on. . ." principle. Elderly people are fairly similar to younger people in implicit memory and explicit recognition memory. Even when we examine an area in which age differences are more prominent—such as explicit recall—we cannot draw a simple conclusion, because highly verbal, well-educated elderly people are less likely to show deficits. Elderly people can also perform relatively well when tested in the morning.

In other words, memory deficits are far from universal among elderly people. In fact, Zacks and Hasher (2006) end their chapter on aging and long-term memory with the following statement: "Taken together, these recent findings suggest that we may have seriously underestimated the memory abilities of older adults" (p. 174).

Explanations for Age Differences in Memory. We have examined a complex pattern of age-related memory effects. As you might expect, this complex pattern of effects requires a complex explanation, rather than just one straightforward cause.

Research in cognitive neuroscience demonstrates some changes in brain structures during normal aging. Remember that explicit recall memory is especially likely to show a deficit. From a neuroscience perspective, this makes sense, because explicit recall relies on a complex network of many different brain structures. These structures include the frontal and parietal regions of the cortex and many subcortical structures. Because these parts of the brain must work together, explicit recall memory can be disrupted if one component of the network is not functioning appropriately. Furthermore, many of these brain structures are known to decrease in volume during normal aging (Einstein & McDaniel, 2004; Moulin et al., 2007).

However, it is not yet clear how these biological changes in the brain actually correspond to psychological processes (Grady & Craik, 2000). Let's look at several psychological processes that might help to explain the pattern of changes in memory performance during normal aging. To account for these changes, we probably need to rely on several mechanisms, because no single explanation is sufficient (Moulin et al., 2007).

1. *Difficulty paying attention.* In general, the research suggests that elderly adults are more likely than younger adults to have difficulty paying attention. Elderly people often comment that they have more difficulty concentrating on a task (Craik, 2006; Mueller-Johnson & Ceci, 2007). In fact, when elderly adults work on a standard memory task, they perform about the same as when young adults work on a memory task that requires divided attention (Craik, 2006; Naveh-Benjamin et al., 2007; Naveh-Benjamin et al., 2005).

2. *Ineffective use of memory strategies.* Elderly people could have impaired memory because they use memory strategies and metamemory less effectively. Some research suggests that elderly adults construct fewer chunks in working memory, compared to younger adults (Naveh-Benjamin et al., 2007). As you may recall from Chapter 4, a **chunk** is a memory unit that consists of several components that are strongly associated with one another (Cowan et al., 2004). However, many studies conclude that elderly and young adults are similar in their use of other memory strategies in long-term memory (Dunlosky & Hertzog, 1998; Light, 2000). Still, a problem in working memory could lead to errors in prospective memory and explicit recall memory.

3. *The contextual-cues hypothesis.* As we saw earlier, elderly people perform relatively well on recognition tasks. Contextual cues are present on recognition tasks; researchers present an item, and the participant reports whether he or she had seen it previously. In contrast, contextual cues are absent on explicit recall tasks; instead, these recall tasks require people to use effortful, deliberate processing.

Young adults are relatively skilled in remembering contextual cues, such as where they were and what date it was when they heard a particular news item (Grady & Craik, 2000; Light, 2000). These contextual cues may boost the accuracy of a young adult's explicit recall. In contrast, elderly adults recall fewer contextual cues. Therefore, elderly adults must rely on effortful, deliberate processing in order to retrieve the information, and the explicit-recall task is more difficult for them.

4. *Cognitive slowing.* A final explanation is one that has been acknowledged for decades: Elderly people often experience **cognitive slowing,** or a slower rate of responding on cognitive tasks (e.g., Bunce & Macready, 2005; Einstein & McDaniel, 2004; Salthouse, 2002). The cognitive-slowing explanation can account for some of the age-related differences in memory, but it cannot fully explain why elderly people function relatively well on some other memory tasks.

In summary, we currently have several hypotheses that each explain some portion of the memory differences between older and younger adults. Perhaps researchers will develop a more refined version of several of these hypotheses, or they may propose additional hypotheses. At this point, we currently have a complex set of findings about memory in elderly individuals, but no comprehension explanation for these results.

Section Summary: *The Lifespan Development of Memory*

1. The lifespan approach to development emphasizes that changes and adaptations continue throughout the lifespan, from infancy through old age.

2. Psychologists interested in the development of cognition encounter methodological problems in their research, particularly when they study infants and elderly people.

3. Research demonstrates that 3-day-olds can recognize their mothers' face and voice. Older infants can recall how to move a mobile—following a delay of several days—when they are tested with the conjugate reinforcement technique; infant memory is influenced by many factors—such as context effects and the spacing effect—that are also important in adulthood.

4. Compared to adults, children have reduced working memory; children have reasonably strong recognition memory, but poor recall memory.

5. The concept of childhood amnesia is controversial, but most people cannot recall events that occurred prior to the age of 2 or 3. In general, children have poor source monitoring.

6. As children grow older, they increasingly use memory strategies such as rehearsal and organization; by adolescence, they can also use imagery appropriately.

7. Under ideal circumstances, children's eyewitness reports can be trustworthy, but their reports may be unreliable when they are young or when they have been supplied with stereotypes and suggestive questions.

8. Children's eyewitness testimony is also influenced by characteristics of the interview, such as complex language and cross-examination.

9. Compared to others in their age group, children with mental retardation tend to recall fewer items on an eyewitness-testimony task; they also make more errors following misleading information.

10. As adults grow older, their working memory remains intact for some tasks, but it is limited if the task is complicated or it requires manipulation of information.

11. With respect to long-term memory in adulthood, age differences are relatively large for prospective memory tasks; in contrast, age differences are relatively small for implicit memory tasks and for explicit recognition tasks.

12. Age differences on explicit recall tasks are more substantial, but the deficits depend on a variety of factors. For instance, elderly individuals perform relatively well if they have high verbal ability, if they are highly educated, or if they are tested early in the day.

13. Cognitive neuroscience research shows changes in the brain structure of elderly individuals. Potential psychological explanations for age-related memory changes during adulthood include (a) difficulty paying attention, (b) ineffective use of memory strategies, (c) the contextual-cues hypothesis, and (d) cognitive slowing.

THE LIFESPAN DEVELOPMENT OF METAMEMORY

As we discussed in Chapter 6, **metacognition** is your knowledge about your cognitive processes—or your thoughts about thinking. Two important kinds of metacognition are **metamemory** (for example, realizing that you need to use a strategy to remember someone's name) and **metacomprehension** (for example, trying to decide whether you understood that definition of *metacognition*). Unfortunately, researchers seldom examine metacomprehension in children, and they essentially ignore metacomprehension in elderly people. Consequently, this section focuses on the relatively narrow topic of metamemory.

Metamemory in Children

The first research on metacognition in children was conducted more than thirty years ago (Pressley, 2005). In fact, the first major research in metacognition focused on children rather than on college students (Flavell, 1971). Flavell argued that young children have relatively poor metacognitive skills. For example, they seldom monitor their memory, language, problem solving, or decision making (Flavell, 1979). More recent research about children's metacognition has focused on a topic called theory of mind. **Theory of mind** refers to people's ideas on how their minds work and on their beliefs about other people's thoughts (e.g., Flavell et al., 2000; Schneider et al., 2005; Taylor, 2005).

In the present discussion of children's metamemory, we will focus on children's beliefs about how their memory works, their awareness that effort is necessary, and their judgments about their own memory performance. Then we'll discuss how metamemory is related to memory performance.

Children's Understanding of How Memory Works. An important component of metamemory is your knowledge about how memory works. Demonstration 13.3 includes some questions about this aspect of metamemory. Even young children, 3 and 4 years of age, know that a small set of pictures can be remembered better than a large set (Schneider & Pressley, 1997).

However, children often have unsophisticated ideas about how their memories work. For example, 7-year-olds are not yet aware that words are easier to remember when they are related to one another, rather than randomly selected (Joyner & Kurtz-Costes, 1997; Moynahan, 1978; Schneider & Pressley, 1997). Furthermore, when young children are taught to use a memory strategy, they often fail to realize that the strategy

---

⊚ Demonstration 13.3

Metamemory in Adults and Children

Ask a child the questions listed below. (Ideally, try to question several children of different ages.) Compare the accuracy and/or the completeness of the answers with your own responses. Note that some questions should be reworded so that the level is appropriate for the individuals you are testing.

1. A child will be going to a party tomorrow, and she wants to remember to bring her skates. What kinds of things can she do to help her to remember them?

2. Suppose that I were to read you a list of words. How many words do you think you could recall in the correct order? (Then read the following list and count the number of words correctly recalled. Use only part of the list for young children.)

   cat rug chair leaf sky book apple pencil house teacher

3. Two children want to learn the names of some flowers. One child learned the names last month but forgot them. The other child never learned the names. Who will have an easier time in learning the names?

4. Suppose that you memorize somebody's address. Will you remember it better after 2 minutes have passed or after two days have passed?

5. Two children want to remember some lists of words. One child has a list of 10 words, and the other has a list of 5 words. Which child will be more likely to remember all the words on the list correctly?

6. Two children are reading the same paragraph. The teacher tells one child to remember all the sentences in the paragraph and repeat them word for word. The teacher tells the other child to remember the main ideas of the paragraph. Which child will have an easier job?

actually improved their memory performance (Bjorklund, 2005). If children don't know how their memories work, they won't know how to plan effective study strategies (Bjorklund, 2005; Bransford et al., 2000; Schneider, 2002).

Children's Awareness That Effort Is Necessary. Another important component of metamemory is the awareness that—if you really want to remember something—you need to make an effort (Joyner & Kurtz-Costes, 1997; Bjorklund, 2005; Schneider, 2002). However, young children do not appreciate this principle. In addition, they are even more likely than adults to keep studying information that they already know (Schneider & Bjorklund, 1998). Furthermore, they are not accurate in judging whether they have successfully committed some information to memory. They typically report to the experimenter that they have satisfactorily memorized a list, yet they recall little on a test (Pressley & Hilden, 2006).

In addition, children often fail to realize that they need to make an effort to use a memory strategy. However, they are more likely to successfully use a memory strategy if they have received instructions about why the strategy should help their memory (Pressley & Hilden, 2006).

Older children also have naive ideas about the effort required in memorization. I recall a visit from an 11-year-old in our neighborhood who had been memorizing some information about the U.S. Constitution. My husband asked her how she was doing and whether she would like him to quiz her on the material. She replied that she knew the material well, but he could quiz her if he wanted. Her recall turned out to be minimal for both factual and conceptual information. She had assumed that by allowing her eyes to wander over the text several times, the material had magically worked its way into her memory.

Of course, magical thinking is not limited to children. If your high school courses were relatively easy for you, perhaps you reached college before you realized that you need effortful processing in order to retain difficult material (Schneider, 2002).

Children's Judgments About Their Memory Performance. In general, young children are unrealistically optimistic when they assess their memory performance. In contrast, older children are somewhat more accurate (Keast et al., 2007; Pressley & Hilden, 2006; Yussen & Levy, 1975).

For example, Claudia Roebers and her colleagues (2004) gathered measures of metamemory as part of their larger study on children's eyewitness testimony. Children between the ages of 5 and 10 years of age watched a live magic show, which lasted 8 minutes. One week later, an interviewer met with each child individually and asked a series of 56 questions about the show. A typical question was, "Where did the magician get the bag from?" (p. 326). After answering each question, children rated how confident they were that their answer had been correct. Specifically, they used a rating scale consisting of five cartoon faces. The facial expressions varied from a very frowning face ("very unsure," corresponding to a rating of 1) to a very smiling face ("very sure," corresponding to a rating of 5).

Figure 13.5 shows the results. As you can see, when children answered a question correctly, all three age groups were very sure that their answer had been correct.

FIGURE 13.5

Average Level of Confidence for Questions Answered Correctly and Questions Answered Incorrectly. (1 = Very Unsure; 5 = Very Sure)

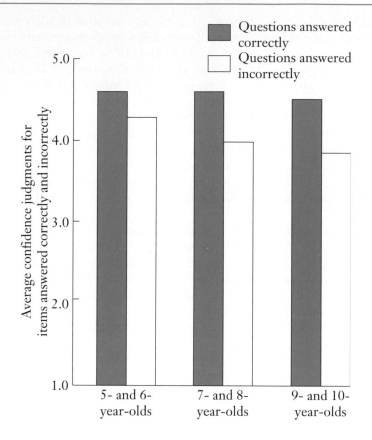

Source: Roebers et al., 2004.

When they answered a question incorrectly, they should have circled either the very frowning face or the somewhat frowning face. However, notice that the children were highly confident that their answer had been correct. Even the oldest children in the study judged that their erroneous answers were accurate.

As children grow up, they become less confident about their answers that happen to be incorrect. However, as we saw in Chapter 6, even college students typically over-estimate the total number of correct answers that they had supplied on a memory test (Koriat, 2007; Koriat & Bjork, 2005, 2006a, 2006b).

Children's Metamemory: The Relationship Between Metamemory and Memory Performance. Let us summarize several observations from this chapter that are related to memory in young children:

1. Their metamemory is faulty; they do not realize that they need to make an effort to memorize, and they also do not realize how little they can remember.
2. They do not spontaneously use helpful memory strategies.
3. Relative to older children, their memory performance is poor.

Does a causal relationship link these three observations? Perhaps the three are related in this fashion:

Metamemory → Strategy use → Memory performance

According to this argument, when children have poor metamemory, they will not be aware that they must use strategies to commit material to memory. If they do not use strategies, then their memory performance will be poor.

We have some evidence that metamemory is related to strategy use (Bjorklund, 2005; Flavell et al., 2002; Ornstein et al., 2006). For example, children with more sophisticated metacognitive abilities are more likely to report using memory strategies. They are also somewhat more likely to use these strategies effectively (Alexander & Schwanenflugel, 1994; Justice et al., 1997; Taylor, 2005). In addition, we have extensive evidence to support the second link in the chain. As we saw on page 451, children's strategy use is related to memory performance.

So, metamemory is linked to strategy use, and strategy use is linked to memory performance. Is there a relationship between the two ends in that chain—that is, metamemory and memory performance? Analysis of the research shows that the correlation between metamemory and memory performance is moderate (Ornstein et al., 2006; Schneider, 2002; Schneider & Pressley, 1997).

It makes sense that the correlation is not stronger. An important limiting factor is that it's difficult to test children's metamemory, because they haven't yet developed the sophisticated vocabulary necessary to describe their mental states (Joyner & Kurtz-Costes, 1997; Schneider, 1999; Sodian, 2005). Furthermore, children may know that memory strategies would be helpful, and yet they do not actually use them. After all, even bright college students may have finely tuned metamemory skills; however, they may lack either the time or the desire to actually use some potentially useful memory strategies.

In summary, we can conclude that metamemory is moderately related to memory performance (Schneider, 2002). Consequently, the proposed causal sequence (Metamemory → Strategy use → Memory performance) could account for a substantial portion of the improvement in memory performance as children grow older.

Metamemory in Elderly People

Research on metacognition in elderly people is limited almost exclusively to the topic of metamemory (Dixon & Cohen, 2003). Many other components of metacognition are still unexplored. For example, we know very little about elderly people's thoughts about their comprehension (that is, their metacomprehension) or their thoughts about problem solving. Our discussion of metacognition in elderly individuals is therefore restricted to the area of metamemory. Let's consider three components of metamemory that are relevant for elderly people.

1. *Beliefs about memory.* Older and younger adults share similar beliefs about the properties of memory tasks (Light, 1996; Salthouse, 1991). Both groups have the same fundamental knowledge about how memory works, which strategies are most effective, and what kinds of material can be remembered most readily (Hertzog et al., 1999).

2. *Memory monitoring.* On some tasks, older and younger adults are equally skilled in monitoring their memory performance (Bieman-Copland & Charness, 1994; Hertzog & Dixon, 1994). For example, the two groups are similar in their ability to predict—on an item-by-item basis—which items they can recall at a later time (Connor et al., 1997). Older and younger adults are also similar with respect to selecting the most difficult items for further study (Dunlosky & Hertzog, 1997). The two groups also perform equally well in judging their accuracy when answering general-knowledge questions and when deciding whether a particular item is old or new (Dodson et al., 2007).

However, older adults are more likely than younger adults to be overconfident on some memory tasks (e.g., Dunlosky & Hertzog, 1998; Perfect, 1997; Salthouse, 1991). For example, Chad Dodson and his colleagues (2007) studied adults whose average age was 67 and college students whose average age was 21. The older adults were more likely than the young adults to overestimate their overall performance on a test of memory for specific details about a recent event.

3. *Awareness of memory problems.* Elderly people are likely to report problems with their everyday memory, especially on explicit recall tasks such as remembering names and phone numbers (Dunlosky & Hertzog, 1998; Kester et al., 2002; Rendell et al., 2005). They are also likely to say that their memory failures have increased over the years. Based on the research we reviewed on explicit-recall memory in elderly individuals, these reports are probably accurate.

The problem is that the popular stereotype about elderly people's poor memory may encourage elderly individuals to think that memory decline is inevitable. As a result, many elderly people will not try to develop helpful memory strategies (Hess, 2005; Hess et al., 2003; Kester et al., 2002). In contrast, some elderly people are high in **memory self-efficacy**, or the belief in their own potential to perform well on memory tasks. They think that it's important to keep developing their memory. As a result, they are likely to perform relatively well (Dixon & Cohen, 2003; Zacks & Hasher, 2006).

In summary, our examination of metamemory has revealed that elderly adults and young adults are similar in some respects (Craik et al., 1995; Dodson et al., 2007; Light, 2000). We saw earlier in this section that young children's metamemory is less accurate than young adults' metamemory. In contrast, elderly adults do not experience an overwhelming metamemory impairment, and they remain quite competent on some metamemory tasks.

◉ Section Summary: *The Lifespan Development of Metacognition*

1. Young children have some knowledge of the factors that influence memory, and their knowledge increases as they mature.

2. Young children are not aware that they must make an effort to learn a list of items, and they cannot accurately judge when they have mastered the material.

3. Older children and adults are much more accurate than younger children in judging their accuracy on a memory task; younger children tend to be extremely overconfident.

4. To some extent, children's deficits in metamemory partly explain their poor performance on memory tasks: As children grow older, their metamemory improves, leading to increased strategy use, in turn producing better memory performance.

5. Elderly adults and young adults have similar beliefs about memory tasks. They also have a similar ability to monitor their memory on an item-by-item basis; however, on some tasks, elderly adults are more likely to overestimate their overall performance.

6. Elderly people report an increase in the frequency of some memory problems, an assessment that is probably correct. When elderly people believe that a memory decline is inevitable, they may not try to develop useful memory strategies.

THE DEVELOPMENT OF LANGUAGE

"Mama!" (8 months old)

"Wash hair." (1 year, 4 months old)

"Don't tickle my tummy, Mommy!" (1 year, 11 months old)

"My Grandma gave me this dolly, Cara. My Grandma is my Mommy's Mommy. I have another Grandma, too. She's my Daddy's Mommy. And Aunt Elli is my Daddy's sister." (2 years, 9 months old)

These selections from the early language of my daughter Sally are typical of children's remarkable achievements during language acquisition. Individual children differ in the rate at which they master language (e.g., Bloom & Gleitman, 1999; Fernald &

Marchman, 2006; Tomasello, 2003, 2006). Still, within a period of two to three years, all normal children progress from one-word utterances to complex discourse. In fact, by the age of 5, most children produce sentences that resemble adult speech (Gleitman & Bloom, 1999; Kuhl, 2000).

Language acquisition is often considered to be the most spectacular of human accomplishments (Thompson & Madigan, 2005; Tomasello, 2006). Therefore, as you might expect, children's linguistic skills clearly exemplify Theme 2. For instance, the average 6-year-old can speak between about 10,000 and 14,000 words. To acquire a vocabulary this large, children must learn about seven new words each day from the time they start speaking until their sixth birthday (Carroll, 2008; Wellman, 2000). If you are not impressed by a 14,000-word vocabulary, consider how much effort high school students must exert to acquire 1,000 words in a foreign language—and those 6-year-old language learners are only waist-high!

However, language acquisition includes much more than the simple acquisition of new words. For example, children combine these words into phrases that they have never heard before, such as, "My dolly dreamed about toys" (2 years, 2 months).

Researchers have typically ignored developmental changes in language during late adulthood, although some new research is beginning to emerge (e.g., Charness et al., 2001; de Bot & Makoni, 2005; Hillis, 2002; Kemper, 2006; Stine-Morrow et al., 2006; Whitbourne, 2008). Our discussion of language development will therefore be limited to infancy and childhood.

Language in Infants

Let's begin by considering how young infants perceive the sounds of speech. Then we will look at their early skill in understanding language, as well as their language production. Finally, we'll see how infants' language acquisition is encouraged by the language that adults use in interacting with them.

Speech Perception in Infancy. To acquire language, infants must be able to distinguish between **phonemes,** or the smallest sound units in a language. However, the ability to make distinctions is only half of the struggle. Infants must also be able to group together the sounds that are phonetically equivalent. For example, infants must be able to recognize that the sounds *b* and *p* are different from each other. They must also recognize that the sound *b*, spoken by the deepest bass voice, is the same as the sound *b*, spoken by the highest soprano voice (Jusczyk & Luce, 2002; Saffran et al., 2006).

If you have recently observed a baby who is younger than 6 months old, you might have been tempted to conclude that the baby's mastery of language was roughly equivalent to that of a tennis shoe. Until the early 1970s, psychologists were not much more optimistic. However, more than thirty years of research have demonstrated that infants' speech perception is surprisingly advanced. Infants can perceive almost all the speech-sound contrasts used in language, either at birth or within the first few weeks of life (Houston, 2005; Jusczyk & Luce, 2002; Todd et al., 2006). They can also recognize similarities, an important early stage in the understanding of language. Infants' abilities are highly conducive to language learning (Flavell et al., 2002; Saffran et al., 2006; Werker & Tees, 1999).

Peter Eimas and his coauthors (1971) were among the first to discover infants' capacity for speech perception. In their study, 1- to 4-month-old infants sucked on rubber nipples, in order to produce a specific phoneme. After a number of presentations, infants showed habituation. **Habituation** occurs after a stimulus has been presented frequently; the response rate gradually decreases and then remains low. Presumably, this sound is now too boring, and it is not worth the hard work of frequent sucking.

After the infant had habituated to the first sound, Eimas and his colleagues presented a different speech sound. For example, an infant who had shown habituation to *bah* was suddenly presented with a highly similar sound, *pah*. These infants quickly showed dishabituation. Now, when *pah* was presented, they suddenly started sucking vigorously once more. In contrast, a control group of infants showed no dishabituation when they continued to hear the *bah* sound; their response rate remained low. This technique revealed that infants respond at different rates to different speech sounds, and so they must be able to perceive the difference between them.

In some cases, young infants are even better than older infants and adults in making phonemic distinctions. For example, infants raised in English-speaking homes can make distinctions between phonemic contrasts that are important in Hindi, a language spoken in India. In Hindi, the *t* sound is sometimes made by placing the tongue against the back of the teeth and sometimes by placing the tongue farther back along the roof of the mouth. In contrast, English does not distinguish between these two *t* sounds. However, Werker and Tees (1984) demonstrated that English-environment infants can distinguish between these phonemes with about 95% accuracy when they are 6 to 8 months old. Their accuracy drops to about 70% at 8 to 10 months of age, and to about 20% at 10 to 12 months of age.

Apparently, young infants may be able to appreciate phonetic distinctions in all languages. Later, however, they reorganize their perceptual categories so that they focus on the important distinctions they hear in their own language (Kuhl, 2000; Saffran et al., 2006; Todd et al., 2006).

Can older infants and adults actually relearn those distinctions that they could make when they were younger? Patricia Kuhl (2004) studied 9-month-old infants who were raised in an English speaking environment. She arranged for these infants to interact—individually—with an adult woman who was speaking with the infant in Mandarin Chinese. These infants later demonstrated that they could discriminate between two phoneme distinctions found in Mandarin. However, other 9-month-old infants watched—individually—a videotape of the same adult woman, speaking in Mandarin. These infants could not master the distinction. Furthermore, adults can also learn to appreciate the phonetic distinctions from other languages, but adults require extensive training (Kuhl, 2006).

However, let's return to the newborns. According to other research on speech perception, newborns can discriminate between two languages that have different rhythms, such as English and Italian (Saffran et al., 2006). Furthermore, research by Bosch & Sebastián-Gallés (2001) focused on children being raised in bilingual homes where the parents spoke two rhythmically similar languages, Spanish and Catalan (a language spoken in the region near Barcelona, Spain). Impressively, 4-month-olds could discriminate between these two languages! This discrimination skill helps infants to keep these two languages from being confused with each other (Saffran et al., 2006).

Language Comprehension in Infancy. The research on speech perception in infancy has been active for several decades. In contrast, researchers have been slower to explore how infants master the more complex aspects of language comprehension, beyond the level of the phoneme. However, we now have information about young infants' comprehension skills in a variety of areas: (1) recognizing important words, (2) discriminating between grammatical words and words that emphasize meaning, (3) understanding the correspondence between a speaker's facial expression and the emotional tone of the speaker's voice, and (4) appreciating semantic concepts.

1. *Recognizing important words.* Interestingly, infants between the ages of 4 and 5 months can already recognize the sound patterns in their own name. Specifically, Mandel and her colleagues (1995) found that infants are likely to turn their heads to look at a location from which their own name is spoken. In contrast, they seldom turn their heads when a different name is spoken that is similar in length and accented syllable (e.g., *Megan* for an infant named *Rachel*).

Young infants also understand a few selected words (Saffran et al., 2006). For example, Tincoff and Jusczyk (1999) showed 6-month-olds two videos placed next to each other. One video showed the infant's mother, and the other showed the infant's father. Meanwhile, the researchers presented either the word *mommy* or the word *daddy*. When *mommy* was presented, the infants looked longest at the video of their mother; when *daddy* was presented, they looked longest at the video of their father. However, the infants' concepts are not yet generalized to other adults. In a second study, these researchers used videos of unfamiliar males and females. The infants showed no preference for looking at the gender-appropriate stranger when hearing the words "mommy" and "daddy" (Tincoff & Jusczyk, 1999).

2. *Discriminating between grammatical words and meaning words.* Infants can also distinguish between more abstract categories of words (Saffran ct al., 2006; Shi & Werker, 2001; Walley, 2005). Specifically, 6-month-olds prefer to listen to nouns and verbs that convey meaning (e.g., *mommy*, *play*, and *cookie*), rather than words that serve a grammatical function (e.g., *in*, *the*, and *that's*).

3. *Understanding the correspondence between sound and sight.* Infants also appreciate another component of language comprehension: the emotional tone of spoken language (Flavell et al., 2002). For example, Walker-Andrews (1986) played recordings of either a happy voice or an angry voice to 7-month-old infants. Meanwhile, the infants saw a pair of films—one of a happy speaker and one of an angry speaker—projected side-by-side. The mouth region of the faces was covered so that the infants could not rely on lip movements to match the voice with the film. Consequently, the infants had to look for emotional cues only in the speaker's cheeks and eyes, and not in their mouths.

The results of Walker-Andrews's (1986) study showed that infants who heard a happy voice tended to watch the happy face, whereas infants who heard an angry voice tended to watch the angry face. In other words, even young infants appreciate that facial expression must correspond with vocal intonation.

4. *Appreciating semantic concepts.* So far, we've seen that infants respond when they hear their own names. They also prefer to hear "meaning words," instead of "grammar words." In addition, they know that sight and sound must be linked together.

According to research by Jean Mandler and her colleagues, infants demonstrate even more remarkable skills when we consider their concepts about objects. For example, by the age of 9 months, infants can distinguish between toy birds and toy airplanes that are visually very similar (Mandler, 1997, 2004a, 2004b; Mandler & McDonough, 1993). At about the same age, they can distinguish between animate objects, which move by themselves, and inanimate objects, which cannot move independently (Mandler, 2003, 2004a, 2007).

In other research, McDonough and Mandler (1998) showed 9-month-old infants a dog drinking from a cup and a car giving a doll a ride. The researchers then handed the infants some new objects from two categories—such as a cat and an anteater for the animal category and a truck and a forklift for the vehicle category. The infants showed the appropriate imitation patterns for the new objects, even for the relatively unfamiliar ones. That is, they showed the anteater drinking, whereas they showed the forklift giving the doll a ride. Infants therefore have the ability to generalize across a category such as "animal" or "vehicle" (Mandler, 2003, 2004a).

As children mature, their categories become more refined. For example, 14-month-old children watched a researcher give a dog a drink from a cup. Then the researcher handed the cup to a child, together with a different dog, a cat, an unfamiliar mammal, and a bird. Children chose to give the cup to the mammals, but they avoided giving the cup to the bird (Mandler, 2004a, 2004b). By their actions, young children reveal their sophisticated knowledge about categories: "Land animals can drink from a cup, but birds cannot."

In Chapter 8, we saw that our conceptual ability allows us to categorize similar objects together and to make inferences based on these categories According to Mandler and her colleagues, this skill begins to develop before a child's first birthday.

The word *infant* originally meant "not speaking." In a moment we'll see that the language production of infants is certainly limited. However, their speech perception and language comprehension are impressively sophisticated, even when they are only a few months old.

Language Production in Infancy. The early vocalizations of infants pass through a series of stages. By about 2 months of age, infants begin to make **cooing** noises, sounds that involve vowels such as *oo*. By about 6 months they have developed **babbling,** a vocalization that uses both consonants and vowels, often repeating sounds in a series such as *dadada* (Flavell et al., 2002; Trevarthen, 2004). By about 10 months of age, these vocalizations begin to sound like the infant's native language (Bates et al., 2001; DeHart et al., 2004; Thompson & Madigan, 2005). This observation coincides with infants' decreased ability to discriminate between phonemes that are irrelevant in their native language (Kuhl, 2004; Werker & Tees, 1999); we discussed this phenomenon on page 469.

The first attempts at intentional communication occur at about 8 to 10 months of age, when babies begin to produce actions designed to capture the attention of other people. They may hand an object to an adult or point to an object. They may also

---

┌───┐

⊚ **Demonstration 13.4**

Producing Child-Directed Speech

Locate a doll that resembles an infant as closely as possible in features and size. Select a friend who has had experience with infants, and ask him or her to imagine that the doll is a niece or nephew who just arrived with parents for a first visit. Encourage your friend to interact with the "baby" in a normal fashion. Observe your friend's language for qualities such as pitch, variation in pitch, vocabulary, sentence length, repetition, and intonation. Also observe any nonverbal communication. What qualities are different from the language used with adults?

└───┘

repeat an action—such as clapping—that has attracted attention in the past (Herriot, 2004; Taylor, 2005; Tomasello, 2003). Let's now consider the nature of the language that adults provide to infants.

Adults' Language to Infants.   Infants learn language quickly because of their impressive auditory skills, their memory capacity, and their receptivity to language. In addition, most infants receive superb assistance from their parents and other adults. Adults tend to make language acquisition somewhat simpler by adjusting their language when speaking with the children. The term **child-directed speech** refers to the language spoken to children. Child-directed speech uses repetition, simple vocabulary and syntax, a slow pace, a high pitch, exaggerated changes in pitch, and exaggerated facial expressions (Fernald & Marchman, 2006; Kuhl, 2006; Trevarthen, 2004). Demonstration 13.4 illustrates child-directed speech (DeHart, 1989).

Motherese is a term that was previously used for child-directed speech. However, this gender-biased term neglects the fact that many fathers, other adults, and older children speak "motherese" to infants and young children (DeHart et al., 2004; Gleitman & Bloom, 1999). In reality, though, many fathers who are secondary caregivers do seem to be less "tuned in" to their offspring's communication needs, and their speech to infants tends to be more like their speech to adults. Also, when fathers do not understand something spoken by their children, they usually respond with a nonspecific question, such as, "What?" In contrast, mothers make more specific requests for clarification, such as, "Where should I put the Raggedy Andy?" (DeHart et al., 2004; Tomasello et al., 1990).

Obviously, it would be interesting to study the language patterns of fathers who are primary caregivers, as well as mothers who are secondary caregivers. Most psychological gender differences are minimal when researchers eliminate confounding variables such as the number of hours spent in caregiving (Hyde, 2007a; Matlin, 2008).

Research in a variety of language communities throughout the world shows that adults typically use a different language style when speaking to infants and young children than when speaking to older people. However, these communities differ in the specific nature of this child-directed speech (Fernald & Marchman, 2006). In general the features of child-directed language help young language learners understand the meaning and structure of language.

However, mothers who are psychologically depressed do not use all the useful features of child-directed language, such as the exaggerated changes in pitch. Babies of depressed mothers may therefore have a disadvantage in terms of language-learning opportunities, unless other caretakers provide sufficient child-directed language (Kaplan et al., 2002).

Language in Children

Sometime around their first birthday, most infants throughout the world speak their first word. Let's look at the characteristics of these initial words, as well as the words spoken by older children. Then we will consider children's grammar, specifically morphology and syntax. Finally, we will examine how children master pragmatics, or the social rules of language.

Words. Although children typically produce their first word when they are about 1 year of age, the vocabulary size for normal 1-year-old children ranges from 0 to about 50 words (Bates et al., 2001; Thompson & Madigan, 2005). A child's first words usually refer to people, objects, and their own activities (Bloom, 2001; Waxman, 2002). These first concepts may be quite different from the standard adult version. For example, the concept of "animal" may simply refer to any objects that begin to move by themselves (Mandler, 2006).

Word production increases rapidly. By the time children are 20 months old, they produce an average of about 180 words. By 28 months, the average is about 380 words (de Boysson-Bardies, 1999; Woodward & Markman, 1998). Children's vocabulary growth is especially rapid if caregivers frequently read to them and if caregivers frequently talk about activities they are doing with the child (Patterson, 2002; Rollins, 2003).

Children's comprehension of words also increases rapidly (Rollins, 2003). For example, when they hear a particular word, they quickly direct their attention to the appropriate object (Fernald et al., 1998). Children can also learn the meaning of some words by overhearing them in other people's conversations (Akhtar et al., 2001). In general, children understand more words than they can produce (de Boysson-Bardies, 1999).

Children's memory skills also improve rapidly during this period, which boosts both their language production and their language comprehension (Baddeley et al., 1998; MacWhinney, 1998). This interrelationship between memory and language is an example of Theme 4 of this textbook.

Another factor that helps children learn new words is called **fast mapping,** or using context to make a reasonable guess about a word's meaning after just one or two exposures (Bloom, 2001; Mandler, 2004b). Chapter 9 emphasized that adults are guided by the context in which a word appears. Fast mapping demonstrates that context is also critically important for young children.

In a study on fast mapping, Heibeck and Markman (1987) showed preschoolers a series of paired objects. For each pair, the researcher asked the children to locate one item. The request specifically used one familiar term and one unfamiliar term, such as, "Bring me the chartreuse one. Not the blue one, the chartreuse one." Other requests used familiar and unfamiliar terms for shape and texture, as well as color. The children understood the requests, bringing the appropriate object with the unfamiliar label. When tested several minutes later, even 2-year-olds remembered the unfamiliar terms. Children with large vocabularies are especially skilled in using fast mapping (Kuczaj, 1999).

Young children may apply a newly learned label to a category that is either too broad or too narrow. An **overextension** is the use of a word to refer to other objects in addition to objects that adults would consider appropriate (Bloom, 2000; Donaldson, 2004; Flavell et al., 2002). For example, when my daughter Beth was 1 year old, she used the word *baish* to refer initially to her blanket. Then she later applied the term to a diaper, a diaper pin, and a vitamin pill. Often an object's shape or function is important in determining overextensions. However, sometimes—as in the case of the vitamin pill—word usage can wander away from the original meaning.

Children around the age of 2 often produce overextensions for words such as *dog* and *ball*. For example, one child produced the name *dog* for nine species of dog and one toy dog—all correct answers. However, he also used the word *dog* for two bears, a wolf, a fox, a doe, a rhinoceros, a hippopotamus, and a fish—all overextensions. Some overextensions occur when a child does not yet know the correct word for an unfamiliar item (Mandler, 2004a; Taylor, 2005). Few 2-year-olds have ever seen a rhinoceros or a hippopotamus. However, in many cases, a child may be confused about the exact differences between two concepts, such as a tulip versus a daffodil.

Children may also supply an **underextension,** using a word in a narrower sense than adults do (Bloom, 2000; Taylor, 2005). For example, they may apply the name *doggie* only to the family pet. Older children may refuse to believe that the word *animal* could apply to insects such as a praying mantis (Anglin, 1997).

Morphology. Children initially use the simple form of a word in every context—for example, "girl run," rather than "girl runs." However, they soon begin to master how to add on **morphemes** (basic units of meaning, which include endings such as -*s* and -*ed*, as well as simple words such as *run*). **Morphology** is the study of these basic units of meaning.

Children appreciate morphology at a young age. For example, 15-month-olds pay significantly greater attention to phrases with appropriate morphology, such as, "Grandma is singing," than to phrases with inappropriate morphology, such as, "Grandma can singing" (Santelmann & Jusczyk, 1998).

After children have learned many words with regular plurals and past tenses—like *girls* and *kicked*—they progress to a more advanced understanding of morphology. At this point, they sometimes create their own regular forms, such as *mouses* and *runned*, although typically children are surprisingly accurate (Bates et al., 2001). These errors show that language acquisition is not simply a matter of imitating the words produced by parents, because parents seldom produce mistakes such as *mouses* and *runned* (Stromswold, 1999).

The tendency to add the most customary morphemes to create new forms of irregular words is called **overregularization.** (Keep in mind, then, that *overextension* refers to the tendency to broaden a word's meaning inappropriately, whereas *overregularization* refers to the tendency to add regular morphemes inappropriately.) Later still, children learn that many words have regular plurals and past tenses, but some words have irregular forms, such as *mice* and *ran* (Flavell et al., 2002; McDonald, 1997).

Theorists have developed several different explanations of children's overregularizations. One approach is based on parallel distributed processing, which we discussed in previous chapters. According to the **parallel distributed processing (PDP)** framework (Chapter 8), cognitive processes can be understood in terms of networks that link groups of neuron-like units.

This PDP framework proposes that the language system keeps a tally of the morpheme patterns for forming past tenses (McClelland & Seidenberg, 2000; Rumelhart & McClelland,1986, 1987). The language system notes that -*ed* is the statistically most likely pattern. Accordingly, young children generalize this ending to new verbs. The child therefore forms inappropriate past tenses, such as *runned*, *growed*, *goed*, and *eated*. The PDP approach argues that a child does not need to consult an internal set of rules to make these overregularizations. Instead, patterns of excitation within neural networks can account for the phenomenon.

Gary Marcus (1996) has proposed an alternative explanation for overregularization. According to Marcus's **rule-and-memory theory,** children learn a general rule for past-tense verbs, which specifies that they must add -*ed*; however, they also store in memory the past tenses for many irregular verbs. English has about 200 verbs with irregular past tenses, so young children would store only the most common of these irregular verbs (Kagan & Herschkowitz, 2005; Marcus, 1996).

Marcus's theory also proposes that children who remember an irregular form will consistently use it, rather than applying the default "add-*ed*" rule. As children gather more expertise about language, they gradually replace the overregularized words with the appropriate past-tense verbs. Marcus (1996) applied his theory to a sample of more than 11,000 past-tense verbs generated by children, and he found that specific components of the theory predicted the patterns of overregularization. He also observed a linear decrease in the number of overregularizations, from 4% among preschoolers to 1% among fourth graders.

Syntax. At about 18 to 24 months of age, the average child begins to combine two words—usually after acquiring between 50 and 100 words (de Boysson-Bardies, 1999; Flavell et al., 2002; Tomasello, 2006). An important issue that arises at this point is **syntax,** or the grammatical rules that govern how words can be combined into sentences. As children struggle with syntax, their rate of combining words is initially slow. However, it increases rapidly after the age of 2 (de Villiers & de Villiers, 1999). Another factor that probably contributes to this rapid increase in word combinations is the growing capacity of working memory.

Children's two-word utterances express many different kinds of relationships, such as possessor–possession ("Mama dress"), action–object ("Eat cookie"), and agent–action ("Teddy fall"). Furthermore, a two-word phrase can have different meanings in different contexts. "Daddy sock" may signify that the father is putting the child's sock on her foot, or that a particular sock belongs to the father (de Villiers & de Villiers, 1999). Many of these utterances, such as "me going" may not be grammatically correct, but they obviously convey the message (Tomasello, 2006).

After children have reached the two-word stage, they begin to fill in the missing words and word endings, and they also improve their word order. "Baby cry" becomes

"The baby is crying," for example. By 3 1/2 years of age, most children are reasonably accurate with respect to both morphology and syntax (Bates & Goodman, 1997). Their sentences also express more complex concepts such as causality and time sequences (Bloom, 1998).

We need to emphasize that language learning is an active process, consistent with Theme 1 of this book. Children learn language by actively constructing their own speech. They produce phrases that adults would never say, such as "Allgone sticky," "Bye-bye hot," and "More page" (Rogers, 1985). Children's speech is far richer than a simple imitation of adult language.

As children grow increasingly skilled in producing sophisticated language, they also grow increasingly skilled in understanding it. Consider, for example, how a child comes to understand the sentence, "Pat hit Chris." How does the child know who is the actor in that sentence and who is the recipient of the action? In English, the word order of the sentence is the most important cue, and children use this information appropriately (Hirsh-Pasek & Golinkoff, 1996). We might be tempted to assume that word order is similarly helpful in all languages. However, young children learning Turkish or Polish use the endings of words—rather than word-order information—to decode the meaning of sentences (Weist, 1985).

Children seem to be clever strategists who can use whatever syntax cues are available in their language. Furthermore, children usually realize that the purpose of language is to communicate with others. Therefore, it's no surprise that they try to produce language that adults can comprehend (Baldwin & Meyer, 2007).

Pragmatics. As we discussed in Chapter 10, the knowledge of the social rules that underlie language use is called **pragmatics** (Carroll, 2004). Research on pragmatics focuses on how speakers successfully communicate messages to their audience.

Children must learn what should be said (and what should *not* be said) in certain circumstances (Pan et al., 2000). They also need to understand that they should use different language styles when speaking to their parents, their teachers, their peers, and younger children (Bjorklund, 2005; Taylor, 2005). They must learn that two speakers need to coordinate a conversation by taking turns and by being a responsive listener.

Every family has its stories about children's wildly inappropriate remarks to elderly relatives, friendly neighbors, and complete strangers. A student in my child development class described an example of a pragmatic violation. Her family was attending a church service, and her 4-year-old brother noticed that their father was starting to fall asleep during the sermon. So the little boy stood up on the church pew and announced in a loud voice, "Be quiet everyone! My daddy is trying to sleep!" As you can imagine, everyone reacted more strongly to the fact that the child had broken a pragmatic rule than to the fact that he had tried to help his dozing daddy.

Another pragmatic skill that children learn is to adapt their language to the listener. For instance, they must determine whether their listener has the appropriate background information about a topic (Pan & Snow, 1999; Siegal, 1996). Until the early 1970s, psychologists believed that children's language ignored the listener's level of understanding.

However, an important study by Shatz and Gelman (1973) showed that children often make appropriate adjustments. These researchers found that 4-year-olds modified their speech substantially when the listener was a 2-year-old, rather than a peer or an adult. Specifically, the 4-year-olds described a toy to their 2-year-old listeners using short, simple utterances. However, when describing the toy to another 4-year-old or an adult, their utterances were much longer and more complex. Even 2-year-olds tend to modify their language when speaking to their infant siblings (Dunn & Kendrick, 1982). If you know any young preschoolers, you may wish to repeat Demonstration 13.4 with them. Children clearly understand some of the social aspects of language before they enter kindergarten.

Children also learn to take turns in a conversation. Sophisticated turn taking requires each speaker to anticipate when the conversational partner will complete his or her remark. This requirement demands an impressive knowledge of language structure (Siegal, 1996; Snow, 1999). Young children have longer gaps in turn taking than adults do, perhaps because they are not as skilled in anticipating the completion of a remark. As children mature, they also learn how to use phrases such as "and then" to signal that they plan to continue talking, so that the listener must not interrupt (Pan & Snow, 1999).

The next time you observe two adults conversing, notice how the listener responds to the speaker by smiling, gazing, and other gestures of interest. In one study, researchers recorded these kinds of listener responses in young children who were discussing with an adult such topics as toys, a popular film, and siblings (Miller et al., 1985). All these listener responses were more abundant in the older children. For example, 8% of 3-year-olds said "uh-hum" at some point while the adult was speaking, in contrast to 50% of 5-year-olds. Furthermore, only 67% of 3-year-old listeners nodded their heads, in contrast to 100% of 5-year-olds. Thus, children learn how to be pragmatically skilled listeners, as well as speakers (Snow, 1999).

Infants and children seem to be specially prepared to notice and interact socially (Wellman & Gelman, 1992). Children are eager to master language and to become active participants in ongoing conversations. This enthusiasm about learning language encourages children to master the words, morphemes, syntax, and pragmatics of speech.

Throughout this chapter, we have seen examples of the early competence of infants and children. For instance, young infants are remarkably skilled at remembering faces and distinguishing speech sounds. These early skills foreshadow the impressive cognitive skills that adults exhibit (Theme 2). Furthermore, children's active, inquiring interactions with the people, objects, and concepts in their world (Theme 1) help them develop memory, metamemory, and language. Finally, the research on the cognitive skills of elderly people reveals some specific deficits. However, many cognitive abilities remain both accurate and active throughout the life span.

Section Summary: *The Development of Language*

1. Research with infants reveals their remarkable speech perception abilities. For example, infants can perceive the difference between two similar phonemes, discriminate between two similar languages, recognize important

words, understand the correspondence of sound and sight, and appreciate semantic concepts.

2. During late infancy, babbling begins to resemble the language in the infant's environment, and the infant attempts intentional communication. The child-friendly language that parents use with infants encourages their verbal development.

3. Young children rapidly acquire new words from context (fast mapping), but their word usage shows both overextensions and underextensions.

4. During language acquisition, children show overregularization, adding regular morphemes to words that have irregular plurals and past tenses.

5. Between the ages of 18 and 24 months, children begin active efforts to master syntax by combining words.

6. Young children often violate pragmatic rules. As children mature, however, they adapt their language to the listener, and they develop turn-taking strategies. They also learn how listeners are supposed to respond to speakers.

CHAPTER REVIEW QUESTIONS

1. Prior to the 1970s, psychologists were pessimistic about the cognitive skills of infants and young children. Since then, however, psychologists have become more optimistic. If you wanted to impress someone with infants' and children's cognitive skills, what would you describe about their memory, metacognition, and language abilities?

2. Part of the difficulty with infant research is designing experiments that reveal an infant's true abilities. Describe how researchers have developed experimental procedures so that they can discover infants' skills in memory and language.

3. Compare children, young adults, and elderly people with respect to working memory, implicit memory, explicit recognition memory, and explicit recall memory. Be sure to list factors that might influence your conclusions.

4. Describe the proposed explanation for children's memory performance, which focuses on memory strategies and metamemory. Discuss the evidence for this explanation, including information on the correlation between metamemory and memory performance.

5. Suppose that the outcome of an important court case in your community depends on the eyewitness testimony of a young child. What factors would encourage you to trust the child's report? What factors would make you question the child's accuracy?

6. In general, what kinds of memory tasks are especially difficult for elderly people? What explanations can best account for memory deficits in elderly individuals? How might overconfidence and stereotypes about older adults explain these difficulties?

7. This chapter describes children's metamemory and strategy use. What could a third-grade teacher do to encourage students' memory skills? What should this teacher know about children's metacognitive ability?

8. In 1985, Branthwaite and Rogers commented that being a child is like being a spy who is trying to break a code to discover how the world works. Apply this idea to the development of word meaning, morphology, word order, and pragmatic rules.

9. Describe some of the pragmatic rules of language that are important in our culture. How does the mastery of these rules change as children develop?

10. Consider the information about cognitive processes in this chapter. Are infants as different from young adults as you had originally thought? Do any of the findings on elderly people surprise you, or do they match your original impressions?

ONE LAST TASK

To review this book as comprehensively as possible, try this final task: On separate sheets of paper, list each of the five themes of this book. Then skim through each chapter, noting on the appropriate sheet each time a theme is mentioned. You can check the completeness of your lists by consulting the entries for Theme 1, 2, 3, 4, and 5 in the subject index. After completing your lists, try to synthesize the material within each of the five themes.

KEYWORDS

lifespan approach to
  development
own-race bias
conjugate reinforcement
  technique
spacing effect
childhood amnesia
source monitoring
memory strategies
utilization deficiency
prospective memory
explicit memory task
implicit memory task

chunk
cognitive slowing
metacognition
metamemory
metacomprehension
theory of mind
memory self-efficacy
phonemes
habituation
cooing
babbling
child-directed speech
motherese

fast mapping
overextension
underextension
morphemes
morphology
overregularization
parallel distributed
  processing (PDP)
rule-and-memory theory
syntax
pragmatics

RECOMMENDED READINGS

Bialystok, E., & Craik, F. I. M. (Eds.). (2006). *Lifespan cognition: Mechanisms of change*. New York: Oxford University Press. Here's an excellent book that focuses on both childhood and old age, exploring topics such as brain changes, working memory, long-term memory, and language.

Bjorklund, D. F. (2005). *Children's thinking: Cognitive development and individual differences* (4th ed.). Belmont,

CA: Thomson Wadsworth. This interesting textbook includes chapters about standard topics such as memory and language, but it also provides information about less familiar topics, such as problem solving, spatial cognition, and social cognition.

Kuhn, D., & Siegler, R. (Eds.). (2006). *Handbook of child psychology* (6th ed., Vol. 2: *Cognition, perception and language*). Hoboken, NJ: Wiley. The multivolume *Handbook of child psychology* has been a standard resource for more than seventy years. In addition to chapters on infants' language, children's language, and memory strategies, you can read about nonverbal communication, problem solving, and mathematical understanding.

Mandler, J. M. (2004a). *The foundations of mind: Origins of conceptual thought.* New York: Oxford University Press. This superb book provides a cohesive theory, based on an in-depth investigation of infants' and young children's semantic concepts.

Whitbourne, S. K. (2008). *Adult development and aging: Biopsychosocial perspectives* (3rd ed.). Hoboken, NJ: Wiley. Susan Whitbourne, a prominent gerontology researcher, provides a clear overview of the research about memory and language in older adults; she also explores related topics such as perception, health, and social interactions.

◎ Glossary

abstraction A memory process that stores the meaning of a message without storing the exact words and grammatical structures.

acoustic confusions Confusion involving similar-sounding stimuli, resulting in memory errors.

ACT-R (Automatic Components of Thought-Rational) A series of network models that attempts to account for all of cognition, including memory, learning, spatial cognition, language, reasoning, and decision making.

ADHD *See* attention-deficit/hyperactivity disorder (ADHD).

affirming the antecedent In conditional reasoning, this phrase means that one is saying that the "if . . ." part of the sentence is true. This kind of reasoning leads to a valid, or correct, conclusion.

affirming the consequent In conditional reasoning, this phrase means that one is saying that the "then . . ." part of the sentence is true. This kind of reasoning leads to an invalid conclusion.

age of acquisition In psycholinguistics, the age at which a person begins to learn a second language.

AI *See* artificial intelligence (AI).

alerting attention network In the cerebral cortex, the system responsible for sensitivity and alertness to new stimuli; it also keeps a person alert and vigilant for long periods of time.

algorithm A method that will always produce a solution to the problem, although the process may be inefficient.

alignment heuristic In cognitive maps, a heuristic by which people tend to remember a series of geographic structures as being more lined up than they really are.

ambiguous figure-ground relationship In gestalt psychology, the situation in which the figure and the ground reverse from time to time, so that the figure becomes the ground and then becomes the figure again.

ambiguous sentences Sentences that have identical surface structures but very different deep structures.

amnesia Severe deficits in episodic memory.

analog code In imagery, a mental representation that closely resembles the physical object. Also called a *depictive representation* or a *pictorial representation*.

analogy approach In problem solving, the approach that uses a solution to a similar, earlier problem to help solve a new one.

anchor In decision making, the first approximation in the anchoring and adjustment heuristic.

anchoring and adjustment heuristic A decision-making heuristic in which people begin with a first approximation (an anchor) and then make adjustments to that number on the basis of additional information. Typically, people rely too heavily on the anchor, and their adjustments are too small. This is called *anchoring effect.*

anchoring effect *See* anchoring and adjustment heuristic.

antecedent In conditional reasoning, the proposition or statement that comes first; the antecedent is contained in the "if . . ." part of the sentence.

anterograde amnesia A loss of memory for events that occurred after brain damage.

aphasia Damage to the speech area of the brain, which produces difficulty in communication.

approach social goals Style of interacting with other people that emphasizes close relationships.

artificial intelligence (AI) The branch of computer science that explores human cognitive processes by creating computer models that accomplish the same tasks that humans do.

Atkinson-Shiffrin model The proposal that memory can be understood as a sequence of discrete steps, in which information is transferred from one cognitive storage area to another.

attention A concentration of mental activity.

attention-deficit/hyperactivity disorder (ADHD) A psychological disorder characterized by inattention, hyperactivity, and impulsivity.

attribute substitution In decision making, a situation in which people do not know the answer to a question. In this case, they substitute an answer to a similar but easier question.

autobiographical memory Memory for events and topics related to one's own everyday life.

availability heuristic A decision-making heuristic in which frequency or probability is estimated in terms of how easy it is to think of relevant examples of something.

avoidance social goals A style of interacting with other people by avoiding close relationships.

babbling The early vocalization of infants that uses both consonants and vowels, often repeating sounds in a series (for example, *dadada*).

base rate The frequency of occurrence of an item in the population.

base-rate fallacy In decision making, an error in which people underemphasize important information about base rate.

basic-level categories In the prototype approach to semantic memory, a moderately specific category level.

Bayes' theorem The rule that judgments should be influenced by two factors: base rate and the likelihood ratio. In decision making, people tend to overemphasize the likelihood ratio and underemphasize the base rate.

behaviorist approach A theoretical perspective that focuses only on objective, observable reactions. Behaviorism emphasizes the environmental stimuli that determine behavior.

belief-bias effect A situation in reasoning when people make judgments based on prior beliefs and general knowledge, rather than on the rules of logic.

betrayal trauma A child's adaptive response when a trusted parent or caretaker betrays him or her by sexual abuse. The child depends on this adult and must actively forget about the abuse in order to maintain an attachment to the adult.

bilingual A term describing a person who actively uses two different languages in his or her everyday life.

binding problem A problem in human vision that stems from the fact that important features of an object (such as shape and color) are not represented as a unified whole by the visual system.

blindsight The condition in which an individual with a damaged visual cortex claims not to be able to see an object, yet can accurately report some characteristics of that object.

bottleneck theories The theories of attention that propose that a narrow passageway in human information processing can limit the quantity of information to which people can pay attention. When one message is flowing through the bottleneck, other messages must be left behind.

bottom-up processing The kind of cognitive processing that emphasizes the importance of information from the stimuli registered on sensory receptors.

boundary extension The tendency to "remember" having viewed a greater portion of a scene than was actually shown.

brain lesions The destruction of brain tissue caused by strokes, tumors, or accidents.

Broca's aphasia Damage to Broca's area of the brain, characterized by an expressive-language deficit—that is, trouble producing language. People with Broca's aphasia may also have some trouble understanding language.

Broca's area An area in the front of the brain; damage to this area produces speech that is hesitant, labored, and grammatically simple.

categorical perception A phenomenon in which people report hearing a clear-cut phoneme (e.g., a clear-cut *b* or a clear-cut *p*), even though they actually heard a sound halfway between two speech sounds (e.g., halfway between *b* and *p*).

category A set of objects that belong together.

central executive In Baddeley's working-memory model, this component of memory integrates information from the phonological loop, the visuospatial sketchpad, the episodic buffer, and long-term memory. The central executive also plays a major role in focusing attention, planning strategies, coordinating behavior, and suppressing irrelevant information.

cerebral cortex The outer layer of the brain that is primarily responsible for cognitive processes.

change blindness The inability to detect change in an object or a scene.

characteristic features In semantic memory, those attributes that are merely descriptive but are not essential.

child-directed speech The kind of language spoken to children, including repetition, simple vocabulary and syntax, slow pace, a high pitch, exaggerated changes in pitch, and exaggerated facial expressions.

childhood amnesia The inability of older children and adults to recall events that occurred in their own lives before they were about 2 or 3 years old.

chunk The basic unit of short-term memory, consisting of several components that are strongly associated with one another.

chunking A memory organizational strategy in which several small units are combined into larger units.

coarticulation The variability in phoneme pronunciation that occurs because the shape of the mouth is influenced by the previous phoneme and the following phoneme.

cocktail party effect The situation in which, when paying close attention to one conversation, a person can often notice if his or her name is mentioned in a nearby conversation.

cognition Mental activities involving the acquisition, storage, transformation, and use of knowledge.

cognitive approach A theoretical orientation that emphasizes people's knowledge and their mental processes.

cognitive-functional approach A theory that the function of human language is to communicate meaning to other individuals. Also called *usage-based linguistics.*

cognitive map A mental representation of the external environment that surrounds a person.

cognitive neuroscience The field that examines how cognitive processes can be explained by the structure and function of the brain.

cognitive psychology (1) A synonym for cognition. (2) The cognitive approach to psychology; a theoretical approach that emphasizes people's knowledge and their mental processes.

cognitive science An interdisciplinary field that examines questions about the mind. Cognitive science includes the disciplines of cognitive psychology, neuroscience, artificial intelligence, philosophy, linguistics, anthropology, sociology, and economics.

cognitive slowing In elderly people, a slower rate of responding on cognitive tasks, compared to young adults.

Collins and Loftus network model The proposal that semantic memory is organized in terms of netlike structures with many interconnections; after information is retrieved, activation spreads to related concepts.

common ground A situation in which conversational partners share similar background knowledge, schemas, and experiences that are necessary for mutual understanding.

compulsion Repetitive behaviors that are designed to reduce the anxiety produced by obsessive thoughts or images.

computer metaphor The perspective that cognitive processes work like a computer—in other words, like a complex, multipurpose machine that processes information quickly and accurately.

computer modeling. *See* computer simulation.

computer simulation A computer system that resembles human performance on a specific cognitive task. Also called *computer modeling.*

concept The mental representation of a category.

conditional reasoning A kind of deductive reasoning that concerns the relationship between conditions, using an "if . . ., then . . ." format. Also known as propositional reasoning.

confidence intervals In decision making, the estimated range within which a number is expected to fall a certain percentage of the time.

confirmation bias In reasoning, the phenomenon that people would rather try to confirm a hypothesis than try to disprove it.

conjugate reinforcement technique An infant-memory research technique in which a mobile is placed above an infant's crib with a ribbon connecting the infant's ankle and the mobile, so that the infant's kicks make the mobile move.

conjunction fallacy In decision making, the erroneous judgment that the probability of the conjunction of two events is greater than the probability of either constituent event occurring alone.

conjunction rule In decision making, a rule stating that the probability of a conjunction of two events cannot be larger than the probability of either of its constituent events.

connection weights In the parallel distributed processing approach, the weighted connections (links) between neuron-like units, or nodes, of a network. Connection weights determine how much activation one unit can pass on to another unit.

connectionism The model proposing that cognitive processes can be understood in terms of networks that link together neuron-like units, and that many operations can proceed simultaneously rather than one step at a time. Also known as the *parallel distributed processing (PDP) approach.*

consciousness An awareness of the external world, as well as thoughts and emotions about one's internal world.

consequent In conditional reasoning, the proposition that follows the antecedent; it is the consequence.

consistency bias During recall, the tendency to exaggerate the consistency between past and present feelings and beliefs. As a result, memory of the past may be distorted.

constituents In psycholinguistics, the grammatical building blocks on which the hierarchical structure of sentence construction is based.

constructionist view of inferences The concept that readers usually draw inferences about the causes of events and the relationships between events.

constructive model of memory The model by which people integrate information from individual sentences in order to construct larger ideas.

constructivist approach In memory, the perspective that people construct knowledge by integrating what they know, so that their understanding of an event or topic is coherent and makes sense.

control processes In the Atkinson-Shiffrin model, intentional strategies—such as rehearsal—that people use to improve their memory.

cooing The early vocalization of infants that involves vowels such as *oo*.

creativity In problem solving, the process of finding a solution that is novel, high quality, and useful.

critical period hypothesis In psycholinguistics, the argument that second language acquisition is strictly limited to a specific period. Individuals who have already reached a specified age (e.g., early puberty) will no longer be able to acquire a new language with native-like fluency.

cross-race effect *See* own-race bias.

crystal-ball technique A decision-making technique in which people imagine that a completely accurate crystal ball has determined that their favored hypothesis is actually incorrect; the decision makers must therefore search for alternative explanations for the outcome.

decision making The thought process for assessing and choosing among several alternatives.

declarative knowledge One's knowledge about facts and things.

deductive reasoning The reasoning process in which specific premises are given, and a person decides whether those premises allow a particular logical conclusion to be drawn. In reasoning, the premises are either true or false, and formal logic specifies the rules for drawing conclusions.

deep structure In language, the underlying, more abstract meaning of a sentence.

default assignment In parallel distributed processing, the act of filling in missing information about a specific item by making a best guess, based on information about similar items.

default heuristic A decision-making heuristic which states that, if there is a default option, people will typically choose it.

defining features In semantic memory, those attributes that are necessary to the meaning of the item.

demand characteristics The cues that might convey the experimenter's hypothesis to a participant in research.

denying the antecedent In conditional reasoning, this phrase means that one is saying that the "if . . ." part of the sentence is false. Denying the antecedent leads to an invalid conclusion.

denying the consequent In conditional reasoning, this phrase means that one is saying that the "then . . ." part of the sentence is false. This kind of reasoning leads to a correct conclusion.

depictive representation In imagery, a mental representation that closely resembles the physical object. Also called a *pictorial representation* or *analog code*.

depth-of-processing approach The proposal that deep, meaningful kinds of information processing lead to more permanent retention than shallow, sensory kinds of processing. Also known as the *levels-of-processing approach*.

descriptive representation In imagery, an abstract, language-like mental representation, in a form that is neither visual nor spatial; this mental representation does not physically resemble the original stimulus. Also called a *propositional code*.

desirable difficulties A learning situation that is somewhat challenging, but not too difficult. This situation enhances long-term recall.

dichotic listening (pronounced "die-*kot*-ick") The experience of listening simultaneously to two different stimuli, one in each ear.

direct-access route In language, the hypothesis that readers can recognize words directly from printed letters. That is, the visual pattern of the word is sufficient to locate information about word meaning from semantic memory.

directive In language, a sentence that requests someone to do something; polite directives usually require more words.

discourse Long passages of spoken and written language; language units that are larger than a sentence.

dissociation In cognitive neuroscience, a pattern that occurs (a) when a variable has large effects on Test A performance, but little or no effect on Test B performance or (b) when a variable has one kind of effect on Test A performance, and the opposite effect on Test B performance. Dissociation is similar to the concept of statistical interaction.

distal stimulus In perception, the actual object that is "out there" in the environment—for example, a cell phone sitting on a desk.

distinctive feature A characteristic, or component, of a visual stimulus.

distinctiveness In connection with recall from memory, a situation in which one memory trace is different from all other memory traces.

distributed attention The kind of perceptual processing that allows people to register features automatically, using parallel processing and registering all features simultaneously. Roughly equivalent to automatic processing, this processing is relatively effortless.

distributed-practice effect In memory, the research finding that people learn more if they spread their learning trials over time, rather than learning the material all at once. Also known as the *spacing effect*.

divergent production A measurement of creativity in terms of the number of varied responses made to each test item.

divided-attention tasks Tasks in which people must attend to two or more simultaneous messages, responding to each appropriately.

dual-route approach to reading The hypothesis that readers sometimes recognize a word directly through the visual route, and sometimes recognize a word indirectly through the sound route ("sounding out" words while reading a passage).

ecological rationality The observation that people create a wide variety of heuristics to help them make useful, adaptive decisions in the real world.

ecological validity A principle stating that the conditions in which research is conducted should be similar to the natural setting to which the results will be applied.

elaboration A processing style in memory acquisition that requires rich processing in terms of meaning and interconnected concepts.

emotion In psychological terms, a reaction to a specific stimulus.

emotional Stroop task In clinical psychology, a technique in which people are instructed to look at a list of words (related to a possible psychological disorder) and name the color of ink for each word.

empirical evidence Scientific evidence obtained by careful observation and experimentation.

encoding The initial acquisition of information. During encoding, information is embedded in memory.

encoding-specificity principle The principle stating that recall is better if the retrieval context is similar to the encoding context. In contrast, forgetting often occurs when the two contexts do not match.

episodic buffer In Baddeley's working-memory model, the episodic buffer serves as a temporary storehouse for combining information from the phonological loop, the visuospatial sketchpad, and long-term memory. The episodic buffer manipulates information, for example, to interpret an earlier experience.

episodic memory People's memory for events that happened to them; the memories describe episodes in life.

ERP *See* event-related potential (ERP) technique.

event-related potential (ERP) technique A neuroscience technique that records the small, brief fluctuations in the brain's electrical activity, in response to a stimulus.

executive attention network In the cerebral cortex, the system handling the kind of attention used when a task features conflict (e.g., on the Stroop task).

exemplar In semantic memory, the specific examples of a concept stored in memory.

exemplar approach In semantic memory, the argument that people first learn some specific examples of a concept, and then classify each new stimulus by deciding how closely it resembles those specific examples.

exhaustive search In semantic memory, the specific type of algorithm, trying all possible answers, using a specified system.

experimenter expectancy The situation in which the researcher's biases and expectations can influence the outcome of an experiment.

expertise Consistently exceptional performance on representative tasks in a particular area, typically achieved by deliberate practice for at least 10 years.

explicit memory task A memory task in which participants are specifically instructed to retrieve information that they have previously learned (for example, to recognize or recall information).

external memory aid Any device, external to the person, that facilitates memory in some way.

extrinsic motivation The motivation to work on a task in order to earn a promised reward or to win a competition.

false alarm In memory research, the phenomenon in which people "remember" an item that was not originally presented.

false-memory perspective The approach whose supporters argue that many recovered memories are actually incorrect memories; that is, they are constructed stories about events that never occurred.

family resemblance In the prototype approach to semantic memory, the notion that each example has at least one attribute in common with some other example of the concept.

fast mapping The ability of children, when learning new words, to use context to make a reasonable guess about a word's meaning after just one or two exposures.

feature-analysis theories In perception, the object-recognition theories proposing that a visual stimulus is composed of a small number of characteristics, each of which is called a distinctive feature.

feature comparison model An approach to semantic memory in which concepts are stored in memory according to a list of necessary features or characteristics.

feature-integration theory A theory of attention proposing that people sometimes look at a scene using distributed attention, with all parts of the scene processed simultaneously; on other occasions, they use focused attention, with each item in the scene processed one at a time.

feeling of knowing In memory, the prediction about whether one could correctly recognize the correct answer to a question.

figure In gestalt psychology, when two areas share a common boundary, the figure has a distinct shape with clearly defined edges. In contrast, the ground forms the background.

first language A bilingual person's native language.

first-letter technique A memory strategy in which the first letter of each word to be remembered is used to compose a word or sentence.

fixations The period between saccadic movements (about 50 milliseconds) in which the visual system acquires the information that is useful for reading.

fixed mindset The belief that one has a certain amount of intelligence and other skills, so that no amount of effort will improve performance.

flashbulb memory Memory of a situation in which a person first learned of a very surprising and emotionally arousing event.

fMRI *See* functional magnetic resonance imaging (fMRI).

focused attention In feature-integration theory, the kind of perceptual processing that requires serial processing, in which more complex objects are identified one at a time.

foresight bias The tendency to overestimate the number of correct answers on a future test.

fovea In vision, the center of the retina, which has better acuity than other retinal regions.

framing effect A phenomenon in which the outcome of a decision is influenced by either of two factors: (1) the background context of the choice or (2) the way in which a question is worded (framed).

FRUMP (Fast Reading Understanding and Memory Program) A script-based computer program designed to perform reading tasks.

functional fixedness In problem solving, a phenomenon in which top-down processing is overactive; the functions or uses assigned to objects tend to remain fixed or stable.

functional magnetic resonance imaging (fMRI) A neuroscience procedure in which a research participant reclines with his or her head surrounded by a large magnet. This magnetic field that is created produces changes in oxygen atoms. A scanning device records these oxygen atoms while the participant performs a cognitive task.

gender stereotypes The organized, widely shared set of beliefs about the characteristics of females and males. Gender stereotypes may be partially accurate, but they do not apply to every person of the specified gender.

general mechanism approaches In psycholinguistics, the proposal that humans use the same neural mechanisms to process both speech sounds and nonspeech sounds, and that speech perception is a learned ability.

General Problem Solver (GPS) A computer program whose basic problem-solving strategy is means-ends analysis. The goal of the GPS is to mimic normal human problem solving.

geons In vision, a shortened version of the phrase "geometrical ions." In the recognition-by-components theory, the basic assumption is that a given view of an object can be represented as an arrangement of simple 3-D shapes or geons.

gestalt (pronounced "geh-*shtahlt*") The term for recognition that is based on an overall quality that transcends the individual elements.

gestalt psychology (pronounced "geh-*shtahlt*") The theoretical approach which emphasizes that humans have basic tendencies to organize what they see, and that the whole is greater than the sum of its parts.

gestures Spontaneous movements of fingers, hands, and arms.

gist In psycholinguistics, the overall, intended meaning of the message.

goal state In problem solving, the state reached when the problem is solved.

GPS *See* General Problem Solver (GPS).

graceful degradation In the parallel distributed processing approach, the brain's ability to provide partial memory, when complete memory is not possible.

graded structure In the prototype approach to semantic memory, the organization of members within a category, beginning with the most representative or prototypical members and continuing on through the category's nonprototypical members.

grammar The study of word structure and sentence structure.

ground In gestalt psychology, the ground is the region that is behind the figure, forming the background.

groupthink In group decision making, a cohesive group may be so concerned about reaching a unanimous decision that members ignore potential problems, and they are overconfident that their decision is correct.

growth mindset The belief that one can cultivate intelligence and other skills to enhance performance.

habituation A decrease in response rate that occurs when a stimulus is presented frequently.

heuristic A general strategy that usually produces a correct solution, for example, in language, problem solving, and decision making.

heuristic-analytic theory In solving reasoning tasks, people may initially use a quick heuristic. However, they then pause and switch to a more effortful analytic approach, realizing that their initial conclusion may be incorrect.

hierarchical tree diagram In problem solving, a figure that uses a tree-like structure to specify various possible options in a problem.

hierarchy A memory organizational strategy in which items are arranged in a series of classes, from the most general classes to the most specific.

hill-climbing heuristic In problem solving, a strategy of choosing—at each choice point—the alternative that seems to lead most directly toward the goal.

hindsight In decision making, judgments about events that have already happened in the past.

hindsight bias The tendency for people to falsely report that they would have accurately predicted an outcome, even if they had not known about that outcome

in advance. People report that they had actually "known it all along."

hippocampus Brain structure underneath the cortex that is important in many learning and memory tasks.

holistic A term describing recognition based on overall shape and structure, rather than on individual elements.

IAT *See* Implicit Association Test (IAT).

iconic memory The kind of brief memory that allows an image of a visual stimulus to persist for about 200 to 400 milliseconds after the stimulus has disappeared. Also known as *visual sensory memory*.

ill-defined problems Problems in which the goal is not obvious.

illusory conjunction An inappropriate combination of features (for example, combining one object's shape with a nearby object's color).

illusory contours A visual illusion, in which people see edges even though they are not physically present in the stimulus. Also called *subjective contours*.

illusory correlation A situation in which people believe that two variables are statistically related, even though there is no real evidence for this relationship.

imagery Mental representations of stimuli that are not physically present.

imagery debate Controversy about whether mental images resemble language (using a propositional code) or perception (using an analog code).

Implicit Association Test (IAT) A test of stereotyping, based on the principle that people can mentally pair related words together much more quickly than they can pair unrelated words.

implicit memory task A memory task in which participants see the material; later, during the testing phase, participants complete a cognitive task that does not directly ask for recall or recognition. However, previous experience with the material facilitates performance on this task.

inattentional blindness The inability to notice a new object that appears suddenly and unexpectedly when a person is paying attention to other events in a scene.

incubation A situation in which people are initially unsuccessful in solving a problem, but they become more likely to solve the problem after taking a break, rather than working without interruption.

indirect-access route A hypothesis about reading, which states that people must first translate the letters on the page into sound before locating information about a word's meaning.

indirect request In language, a request for someone to do something or to stop doing something, presented like a request for information.

infantile amnesia *See* childhood amnesia.

inferences Logical interpretations and conclusions that were never part of the original stimulus material. In reading, the activation of information that is not explicitly stated in a written passage.

information-processing approach An approach in cognitive psychology which argues that (1) mental processes can be compared with the operations of a computer, and (2) information progresses through the system in a series of stages, one step at a time.

initial state In problem solving, a description of the situation at the beginning of a problem.

insight problem A problem that initially seems impossible to solve, but a correct alternative suddenly enters a person's mind.

interlanguage The new language system created when learning a second language.

interpreting The process of translating from a spoken message in one language into a second spoken language.

intrinsic motivation The motivation to work on a task for its own sake, because it is interesting, exciting, or personally challenging.

introspection The process of systematically analyzing one's own sensations and reporting them as objectively as possible.

investment theory of creativity A theory in which the essential attributes of creativity are intelligence, knowledge, motivation, an encouraging environment, an appropriate thinking style, and an appropriate personality.

ironic effects of mental control The way people's efforts backfire when they attempt to control their consciousness or try to eliminate a particular thought.

keyword method A memory strategy in which the learner identifies an English word (the keyword) that sounds similar to the new word; then an image is created that links the keyword with the meaning of the new word.

landmark effect In a mental map, the general tendency to provide shorter estimates of distance when traveling to a landmark, rather than to a nonlandmark.

latent semantic analysis (LSA) An artificial intelligence program designed to perform many language tasks and to assess the amount of semantic similarity between two words or two discourse segments. LSA can be used to provide tutoring sessions in specific disciplines and to grade essays.

lateralization The concept indicating that the two hemispheres of the brain have somewhat different functions.

levels of processing The observation that recall accuracy is improved when information is processed at a deep level, rather than at a shallow level.

levels-of-processing approach The proposal that deep, meaningful kinds of information processing lead to more permanent retention than shallow, sensory kinds of processing. Also known as the *depth-of-processing approach*.

lexical entrainment In language, the process of selecting descriptive words, which occurs when two communicators create and adopt a standardized term to refer to an object.

lifespan approach to development The developmental perspective that people continue to change and adapt throughout their entire lives, from infancy to old age.

likelihood ratio In decision making, the assessment of whether a description is more likely to apply to population A or population B.

linearization problem In language, the problem of arranging words in an ordered, linear sequence.

link In the Collins and Loftus network model, the element that connects a particular concept node with another concept node.

long-term memory The large-capacity memory that contains one's memory for experiences and information that have accumulated over a lifetime.

LSA *See* latent semantic analysis (LSA).

major depression A psychological disorder characterized by sadness, discouragement, and hopelessness, accompanied by fatigue and little interest in leisure activities.

massed learning Learning material all at once, rather than spreading learning trials over time.

matrix In problem solving, a chart that shows all possible combinations of items.

maximizers Decision makers who tend to examine as many options as possible when making a choice.

maximizing decision-making style Decision making in which as many options as possible are examined. The task becomes more challenging as the number of options increases.

McGurk effect A phenomenon in which visual information influences speech perception, when individuals integrate both visual and auditory information.

means-ends heuristic A problem-solving strategy in which a person first divides the problem into a number of subproblems and then tries to reduce the difference between the initial state and the goal state for each subproblem.

memory The process of maintaining information over time.

memory self-efficacy A person's belief in his or her potential to perform well on memory tasks.

memory strategies Deliberate, goal-oriented mental activities used to improve encoding and retrieval.

mental set A mental rut or mindless rigidity that blocks effective problem solving.

meta-analysis technique A statistical method for synthesizing numerous studies on a single topic into one statistical index that shows whether a variable has a statistically significant effect.

metacognition Knowledge and thoughts about one's own cognitive processes, as well as control of those cognitive processes.

metacomprehension Knowledge and thoughts about one's own reading comprehension and language comprehension.

metalinguistics Knowledge and thoughts about the form and structure of language.

metamemory Knowledge and thoughts about one's own memory.

method of loci (pronounced "*low*-sigh") A memory strategy in which items to be learned are associated with a series of physical locations, arranged in a specific sequence. During recall, a person reviews the locations in order to retrieve the items.

mindfulness A flexible approach to the world, with a sensitivity to new things and an appreciation for new ways of approaching a problem.

mnemonics (pronounced "ni-*mon*-icks") The use of mental strategies to improve memory.

modular In language, a term describing the proposal that people have a set of specific linguistic abilities that do not follow the principles of other cognitive processes, such as memory and decision making.

mood A general, long-lasting emotional experience.

mood congruence A phenomenon demonstrating that memory is better when the material to be remembered is congruent with a person's current mood.

morpheme (pronounced "*more*-feem") The basic unit of meaning in language.

morphology The study of the basic units of meaning in language.

motherese The kind of language used by adult caretakers when speaking to children, currently called *child-directed speech*.

multilingual A term describing someone who uses more than two languages.

multimodal approach A theory of memory improvement that emphasizes a comprehensive approach to memory problems (for example, attention to physical and mental problems, as well as a variety of memory strategies).

my-side bias In decision making, the general tendency to be overconfident that one's own view is correct in a confrontational situation.

narrative The type of discourse in which someone describes a series of events, either actual or fictional. The events in a narrative are described in a time-related sequence, and they are often emotionally involving.

narrative technique A memory organizational method that creates stories to link a series of words together.

natural language Ordinary human language, as found in everyday life, which includes errors, complexities, and ambiguities.

nested structure In language, a phrase that is embedded within sentence.

network model A model of semantic memory that proposes a netlike organization of concepts in memory, with many interconnections. The meaning of a particular concept depends on the concepts to which it is connected.

neural networks The model proposing that cognitive processes can be understood in terms of networks that link together neuron-like units; in addition, many operations can proceed simultaneously rather than one step at a time. Also known as the *parallel distributed processing (PDP) approach*.

neurolinguistics The discipline that examines how the brain processes language.

neuron The basic cell in the nervous system.

90-degree angle heuristic In mental maps, the heuristic that angles in a mental map are remembered as being closer to 90 degrees than they really are.

node In the parallel distributed processing approach, the location of each neural activity; nodes are interconnected in a complex fashion with many other nodes. In the Collins and Loftus network model of semantic memory, each concept can be represented as a node, or location in the network; links connect nodes to form a network.

noninsight problem A problem that is solved gradually, using memory, reasoning skills, and a routine set of strategies.

object permanence The knowledge that an object exists, even when it is temporarily out of sight.

object recognition The process of identifying a complex arrangement of sensory stimuli.

obsession A persistent thought or image that is intrusive or inappropriate, causing extreme anxiety.

obsessive-compulsive disorder (OCD) A psychological disorder characterized by recurrent obsessions or compulsions that are recognized as excessive, uncontrollable, and time consuming.

obstacles In problem solving, the restrictions that make it difficult to proceed from the initial state to the goal state.

OCD *See* obsessive-compulsive disorder (OCD).

operational definition A precise definition that specifies exactly how researchers will measure a concept.

organization In memory, the attempt to bring systematic order to the material to be learned; often used to refer to a category of memory strategies.

orienting attention network In the cerebral cortex, the system responsible for the kind of attention required for visual search, in which a person must shift attention around to various spatial locations.

other-race effect *See* own-race bias.

overconfidence People's tendency to be overly optimistic about the accuracy of their performance, for example, on a memory or decision-making task.

overextension Children's use of a word to refer to other objects, in addition to objects that adults would consider appropriate.

overregularization The tendency to add regular morphemes inappropriately (for example, *mouses* or *runned*).

own-race bias The phenomenon in which people are generally more accurate in identifying members of their own ethnic group than members of another ethnic group.

parallel distributed processing (PDP) approach The model proposing that cognitive processes can be understood in terms of networks that link together neuron-like units; the model states that many operations proceed simultaneously, rather than one at a time. Also known as *connectionism* and *neural networks*.

parallel processing A type of cognitive processing in which a person can handle many signals at the same time, as opposed to *serial processing*.

parallel search A type of information processing in which a person considers all attributes of a visual scene simultaneously.

pattern recognition The process of identifying a complex arrangement of sensory stimuli.

PDP *See* parallel distributed processing (PDP) approach.

perception The use of previous knowledge to gather and interpret the stimuli registered by the senses.

perceptual span In reading, the number of letters and spaces that can be perceived during a visual fixation.

PET scan *See* positron emission tomography (PET scan).

phobic disorder An excessive fear of a specific object.

phoneme (pronounced "*foe*-neem") The basic unit of spoken language.

phonemic restoration In auditory perception, the phenomenon in which people fill in sounds that are missing by using context as a cue.

phonetic module A hypothetical special-purpose neural mechanism in humans that specifically facilitates speech perception, rather than other kinds of auditory perception. Also known as *speech module*.

phonics approach An approach to reading that states that people recognize words by trying to pronounce the individual letters in the word. The phonics approach emphasizes that speech sound is a necessary intermediate step in reading.

phonological loop In Baddeley's working-memory model, the storage device for a limited number of sounds for a short period of time.

phonology Speech sounds of a language.

phrase structure In psycholinguistics, an approach that emphasizes the hierarchical structure of sentences, based on grammatical building blocks called constituents.

PI *See* proactive interference (PI).

pictorial representation A mental representation that closely resembles the physical object. Also called a *depictive representation* or an *analog code*.

planning fallacy In decision making, people's underestimation of the amount of time or money required to complete a project; they also incorrectly estimate that the task will be relatively easy to complete.

Pollyanna principle In memory and other cognitive processes, the principle that pleasant items are usually processed more efficiently and more accurately than less pleasant items.

positivity effect A phenomenon demonstrating that people tend to rate past events more positively with the passage of time.

positron emission tomography (PET scan) A procedure in which researchers measure blood flow by injecting the participant with a radioactive chemical just before the participant performs a cognitive task.

post-event misinformation effect A phenomenon in which people first view an event, and then they receive misleading information about the event; later, they mistakenly recall the misleading information, rather than the event they actually saw.

pragmatic view of memory In language comprehension, the proposition that people strategically pay attention to the aspect of a message that is most relevant to their current goals.

pragmatics The social rules that underlie language use. Pragmatics takes into account the listener's perspective and focuses on how speakers successfully communicate messages to their audience.

prewriting The first stage in planning to write, which requires generating a list of ideas.

primacy effect In a serial-position curve, the enhanced recall for items at the beginning of a list, which presumably occurs because people rehearse early items more than other items.

primary visual cortex The portion of the cerebral cortex that is concerned with basic processing of visual stimuli. Located in the occipital lobe of the brain.

proactive interference (PI) A concept stating that people have trouble learning new material because previously learned material keeps interfering with new learning.

problem isomorphs In problem solving, a set of problems with the same underlying structures and solutions, but with different specific details.

problem solving The use of strategies to reach a goal in which the solution is not immediately obvious because important information is missing.

procedural memory A person's memory about how to do something.

proposition The smallest unit of knowledge that can be judged either true or false.

propositional calculus In logical reasoning, a system for categorizing the kinds of reasoning used in analyzing propositions or statements.

propositional code In imagery, an abstract, language-like mental representation, in a form that is neither visual nor spatial; this mental representation does not physically resemble the original stimulus. Also called a *descriptive representation*.

propositional reasoning A kind of deductive reasoning that concerns the relationship between conditions, using an "if . . ., then . . ." format. Also known as *conditional reasoning*.

prosody The "melody," or intonation, rhythm and emphasis of speech.

prosopagnosia (pronounced "pro-soap-ag-*know*-zhia") A condition in which people cannot recognize human faces visually, though they perceive other objects relatively normally.

prospect theory A theory that refers to people's tendencies to think differently about possible gains versus possible losses. When dealing with possible gains, people tend to avoid risks. When dealing with possible losses, people tend to seek risks.

prospective memory A memory task in which one remembers to do something in the future, as opposed to retrospective memory.

prototype In semantic-memory theory, the idealized item that is most typical and representative of the category.

prototype approach An approach to semantic memory in which a person decides whether an item belongs to a category by comparing that item with a prototype.

prototypicality The degree to which members of a category are prototypical.

proximal stimulus In perception, the information registered on one's sensory receptors (for example, the image on the retina created by the cell phone sitting on a desk).

psycholinguistics An interdisciplinary field that examines how people use language to communicate ideas.

pure AI The branch of computer science that seeks to design a program that will accomplish a task as efficiently as possible.

recall In memory, the reproduction of items that had been learned at an earlier time.

recency effect In a serial-position curve, the enhanced accuracy for the final items in a series of stimuli, which presumably occurs because the items are still in working memory.

recognition In memory, the identification of items that had been presented at an earlier time.

recognition-by-components theory In perception, the proposal that a specific view of an object can be represented as an arrangement of simple 3-D shapes called geons. Also known as the *structural theory*.

recognition heuristic A decision-making heuristic in which a person compares the relative frequency of two categories. If one category is recognized, but not the other, the person concludes that the recognized category has the higher frequency.

recovered-memory perspective The approach whose supporters argue that memories of childhood sexual abuse can be forgotten for many years and then recovered at a later time, often prompted by a specific event or by encouragement from a therapist.

regressions In reading, the eye movements in which the eye returns to earlier material in the sentence.

rehearsal In memory, the repetition of information to be learned.

release from proactive interference A memory phenomenon in which proactive interference is reduced when a person switches to a new stimulus category, leading to increased recall.

repetition priming task A memory task in which recent exposure to a word increases the likelihood that this word will later come to mind, when one is given a cue that could evoke many words.

representative In decision making, a type of sample that is similar in important characteristics to the population from which it was selected; for example, if a sample was selected by a random process, then that sample must look random to be considered representative.

representativeness heuristic A decision-making heuristic by which a sample is judged to be likely if it is similar to the population from which it was selected.

retina In vision, the inside back portion of the eye, containing millions of different kinds of neurons that register and transmit visual information from the outside world.

retrieval In memory, the process of locating information and accessing that information.

retroactive interference In memory, the process in which people have trouble recalling old material because recently learned, new material keeps interfering with old memories.

retrograde amnesia A loss of memory for events that occurred prior to brain damage.

retrospective memory A memory task in which one recalls previously learned information, as opposed to prospective memory.

rotation heuristic In cognitive maps, the heuristic by which a figure that is slightly tilted will be remembered as being either more vertical or more horizontal than it really is.

rule-and-memory theory In language development, the theory that children learn a general rule for past-tense verbs that specifies that they must add *-ed*; however, they also store in memory the past tenses for some irregular verbs.

saccadic eye movement (pronounced "suh-*cod*-dik") In reading, the kind of eye movement that brings the center of the retina into position over the words to be read.

satisficers Decision makers who tend to settle for something that is satisfactory, even if it may not be ideal.

satisficing decision-making style Decision making in which people tend to settle for something that is good enough to meet their standard, even if it may not be ideal.

schema (pronounced "*skee*-muh") Generalized knowledge or expectation, which is distilled from past experiences with an event, an object, or a person. Schemas frequently guide memory recall.

schema therapy In clinical psychology, an approach to help a client develop appropriate new schemas that can replace the maladaptive schemas developed early in life.

schizophrenia A psychological disorder characterized by severely disordered thoughts. People with schizophrenia do not show intense emotion, and they may have hallucinations.

script A simple, well-structured sequence of events—in a specified order—associated with a highly familiar activity; a script is one category of schema.

second language A bilingual individual's nonnative language.

selective-attention task A task in which people must respond selectively to certain kinds of information while ignoring other information.

self-efficacy A self-assessment of one's own capabilities in a certain area.

self-reference effect The enhancement of long-term memory by relating the material to one's personal experiences.

semantic memory A person's factual, organized knowledge about the world, including knowledge about word meanings.

semantic priming effect The tendency for people to respond faster to an item if it was preceded by an item with similar meaning.

semantics The area of psycholinguistics that examines the meanings of words and sentences.

sensory memory A large-capacity storage system that records and briefly stores information from each of the senses with reasonable accuracy.

sentence verification technique A research method in which people see simple sentences, and they must consult their stored semantic knowledge to determine whether the sentences are true or false.

sequential bilingualism A term referring to bilingual people who acquire a second, nonnative language after they have learned their native language.

serial position effect The U-shaped relationship between a word's position in a list and its probability of recall.

serial processing A type of cognitive processing in which only one item is handled at a given time, and one step must be completed before proceeding to the next step.

serial search A type of information processing in which only one item is processed at a time.

shadow In attention research, the process of repeating a message heard in one ear during a dichotic listening task.

short-term memory The kind of memory that contains only the small amount of information that a person is actively using. At present, most people prefer the term, "working memory."

simultaneous bilingualism A term referring to bilingual people who learn two languages simultaneously during childhood.

single-cell recording technique A neuroscience technique in which researchers study the characteristics of an animal's brain and nervous system by inserting an electrode next to a single neuron.

situated-cognition approach An approach that examines how the ability to solve a problem is tied to the specific context in which a person learned to solve that problem.

situative perspective *See* situated-cognition approach.

slips-of-the-tongue Speech errors in which sounds or entire words are rearranged between two or more different words.

small-sample fallacy The incorrect assumption that small samples will be representative of the population from which they were selected.

social cognition approach The perspective that stereotypes are formed by means of normal cognitive processes, which rely on strategies such as the availability heuristic.

social cognitive neuroscience The field that uses neuroscience to examine how cognitive processes are used in one's interactions with other people.

social goals Style of interacting with other people, in terms of friendships and other interpersonal relationships.

source monitoring The process of trying to identify the origin of memories and beliefs in order to decide which memories or beliefs are real and which ones are simply imagined.

spaced learning In memory, the situation in which the learning trials are spread over time, rather than learning material all at once.

spacing effect In memory, the research finding that people learn more if they spread their learning trials over time, rather than learning the material all at once. Also known as the *distributed-practice effect*.

spatial cognition A broad area that includes how people construct cognitive maps, how they remember the world they navigate, and how they keep track of objects in a spatial array.

spatial framework model In spatial cognition, a model emphasizing that the above-below dimension is more prominent in spatial thinking than the front-back dimension or the right-left dimension.

special mechanism approach In psycholinguistics, an approach stating that humans are born with a specialized cognitive device for decoding speech stimuli. As a result, people process speech sounds more quickly and accurately than other auditory stimuli. Also known as the *speech-is-special approach*.

speech-is-special approach In psycholinguistics, an approach stating that humans are born with a specialized cognitive device for decoding speech stimuli. As a result, people process speech sounds more quickly and accurately than other auditory stimuli. Also known as the *special mechanism approach*.

speech module A hypothetical special-purpose neural mechanism in humans that specifically facilitates speech perception, rather than other kinds of auditory perception. Also known as *phonetic module*.

speech perception In hearing, the translation of sound vibrations into a sequence of sounds that the listener perceives to be speech.

spontaneous generalization In parallel distributed processing, the inferences that people draw—based on individual cases—about general information that they have never learned.

spreading activation In semantic memory, the process in which, when the name of a concept is mentioned, the node representing that concept is activated, and the activation expands from that node to other nodes to which it is connected.

stereotype threat A source of anxiety when a person's membership in a group is hampered by a negative stereotype; this anxiety produces performance problems.

Stroop effect The observation that people take much longer to name the color of a stimulus when it is used in printing an incongruent word than when it appears as a solid patch of color.

structural features In problem solving, the abstract, underlying core of a problem.

structural theory In perception, the proposal that a given view of an object can be represented as an arrangement of simple 3-D shapes called geons. Also known as the *recognition-by-components theory*.

subjective contours A visual illusion, in which people see edges even though they are not physically present in the stimulus. Also called *illusory contours*.

subordinate-level categories In the prototype approach to semantic memory, the lower-level or more specific category levels.

subproblems The smaller problems that a person creates by subdividing a target problem, in order to facilitate problem solving.

subvocalization Silent pronunciation of words.

superordinate-level categories In the prototype approach to semantic memory, the higher-level or more general category levels.

surface features In problem solving, the superficial content of the problem to be solved.

surface structure In language, the words that are actually spoken or written.

syllogism A deductive reasoning task consisting of two statements that are assumed to be true, plus a conclusion.

symmetry heuristic In cognitive maps, the heuristic that people remember figures to be more symmetrical and regular than they truly are.

syntax The grammatical rules that govern how words can be organized into sentences.

template A specific perceptual pattern stored in memory.

template-matching theory In pattern recognition, the theory stating that a stimulus is compared with a set of templates, or specific patterns stored in memory. After comparison, the person notes the template that matches most closely.

testing effect The observation that test taking boosts long-term recall for academic material.

Theme 1 Cognitive processes are active, rather than passive.

Theme 2 Cognitive processes are remarkably efficient and accurate.

Theme 3 Cognitive processes handle positive information better than negative information.

Theme 4 Cognitive processes are interrelated with one another; they do not operate in isolation.

Theme 5 Many cognitive processes rely on both bottom-up and top-down processing.

theory of mind In cognitive development, people's ideas of how their minds work and their beliefs about other people's thoughts.

thinking The cognitive process of going beyond the information given, so that one can reach a goal such as a solution, a decision, or a belief.

tip-of-the-tongue phenomenon The subjective feeling that people have of being confident that they know the target word for which they are searching, yet they cannot recall this word.

top-down processing The kind of cognitive processing that emphasizes the influence of concepts, expectations, and memory.

total time hypothesis In memory, the proposition that the amount learned depends on the total time devoted to learning.

translation Process of translating from a text written in one language into a second written language.

typicality effect Using the sentence verification technique, a research finding that people reach decisions faster when an item is a typical member of a category, rather than an unusual member.

underextension The use of words, by children, in a narrower sense than adults would use them.

underlying structure *See* deep structure.

understanding In problem solving, the mental representation of a problem, based on the information provided in the problem and one's own previous experience.

unilateral neglect In perception, a spatial deficit for one half of the visual field.

usage-based linguistics A theory that the function of human language is to communicate meaning to other individuals. Also called the *cognitive-functional approach*.

utilization deficiency The failure to apply memory strategies, especially common in children.

verbatim memory Word-for-word memory, as opposed to recall of the "gist" or general meaning.

viewer-centered approach In perception, the model proposing that a small number of views of 3-D objects are stored in memory, rather than just one view.

visual sensory memory *See* iconic memory.

visuospatial sketchpad In Baddeley's working-memory model, the component that processes both visual and spatial information. This sketchpad stores visual information, including information that has been encoded from verbal stimuli; it also allows a person to create a mental map from a complex scene.

Wernicke's aphasia (pronounced "*Ver*-nih-keez" or "*Wer*-nih-keez") Damage to Wernicke's area of the brain, which produces severe receptive-language problems, including failure to understand basic instructions, as well as language production that is too wordy and confused.

Wernicke's area (pronounced "*Ver*-nih-keez" or "*Wer*-nih-keez") An area toward the back of the brain;

damage to this area causes serious difficulties in understanding speech, as well as language production that is too wordy and confused.

whole-language approach A movement within education suggesting that reading instruction should emphasize meaning, and it should be enjoyable. In addition, children should read interesting stories, experiment with writing before they are expert spellers, and use reading throughout the classroom.

whole-word approach An approach to reading stating that people can directly connect the written word with the word's meaning. The whole-word approach argues against "sounding out" an unfamiliar word. Instead, readers should identify the word in terms of its context within a sentence.

word superiority effect In perception, a phenomenon in which a single letter can be identified more accurately and more rapidly when it appears in a meaningful word than when it appears by itself or in a meaningless string of unrelated letters.

working memory The brief, immediate memory for material that is currently being processed; a portion of working memory also coordinates ongoing mental activities. Working memory was previously called *short-term memory*.

working-memory approach According to Baddeley, immediate memory is a multipart system that temporarily holds and manipulates information when people perform cognitive tasks.

References

Abelson, R. P. (1981). Psychological status of the script concept. *American Psychologist, 36,* 715–729.

Adeyemo, S. A. (1994). Individual differences in thinking and problem solving. *Personality and Individual Differences, 17,* 117–124.

Adler, J., & Hall, C. (1995, June 5). Surgery at 33,000 feet. *Newsweek,* p. 36.

Adler, S. A., Gerhardstein, P., & Rovee-Collier, C. (1998). Levels-of-processing effects in infant memory? *Child Development, 69,* 280–294.

Adler, T. (1991, July). Memory researcher wins Troland award. *APA Monitor,* pp. 12–13.

Agans, R. P., & Shaffer, L. S. (1994). The hindsight bias: The role of the availability heuristic and perceived risk. *Basic and Applied Social Psychology, 15,* 439–449.

Agassi, J. (1997). The novelty of Chomsky's theories. In D. M. Johnson & C. E. Erneling (Eds.), *The future of the cognitive revolution* (pp. 136–148). New York: Oxford University Press.

Ainsworth, W., & Greenberg, S. (2006). Auditory processing of speech. In S. Greenberg & W. A. Ainsworth (Eds.), *Listening to speech: An auditory perspective* (pp. 3–17). Mahwah, NJ: Erlbaum.

Akhtar, N., Jipson, J., & Callanan, M. A. (2001). Learning words through overhearing. *Child Development, 72,* 416–430.

Alba, J. W., & Hasher, L. (1983). Is memory schematic? *Psychological Bulletin, 93,* 203–231.

Alexander, J. M., & Schwanenflugel, P. J. (1994). Strategy regulation: The role of intelligence, metacognitive attributions, and knowledge base. *Developmental Psychology, 30,* 709–723.

Allbritton, D. W., & Gerrig, R. J. (1991). Participatory responses in text understanding. *Journal of Memory and Language, 30,* 603–626.

Allen, G. L. (2004). Preface: Routes of human spatial memory research. In G. L. Allen (Ed.), *Human spatial memory: Remembering where* (pp. xiii-xx). Mahwah, NJ: Erlbaum.

Alloway, T. P., et al. (2005). Working memory and phonological awareness as predictors of progress towards early learning goals at school entry. *British Journal of Developmental Psychology, 23,* 417–426.

Alter, J. (2000, July 3). A reckoning on death row. *Newsweek,* p. 31.

Alvarez, G. A., & Cavanaugh, P. (2004). The capacity of visual short-term memory is set both by visual information load and by number of objects. *Psychological Science, 15,* 106–111.

Amabile, T. M. (1990). Within you, without you: The social psychology of creativity, and beyond. In M. A. Runco & R. S. Albert (Eds.), *Theories of creativity* (pp. 61–91). Newbury Park, NY: Sage.

Amabile, T. M. (1994). The "atmosphere of pure work": Creativity in research and development. In W. R. Shadish & S. Fuller (Eds.), *The social psychology of science* (pp. 316–328). New York: Guilford.

Amabile, T. M. (1996). *Creativity in context: Update to the social psychology of creativity.* Boulder, CO: Westview.

Amabile, T. M. (1997). Motivating creativity in organizations: On doing what you love and loving what you do. *California Management Review, 40,* 39–58.

Ambady, N., Shih, M., Kim, A., & Pittinsky, T. L. (2001). Stereotype susceptibility in children: Effects of identity activation on quantitative performance. *Psychological Science, 12,* 385–390.

American Psychiatric Association. (2000). *Diagnostic and statistical manual of mental disorders* (4th edition, text revision). Washington, DC: Author.

American Psychological Association. (2001). *Publication manual of the American Psychological Association* (5th ed.). Washington, DC: Author.

Amir, N., & Selvig, A. (2005). Implicit memory tasks in clinical research. In A. Wenzel & D. C. Rubin (Eds.), *Cognitive methods and their application to clinical research* (pp. 153–171). Washington, DC: American Psychological Association.

Anastasi, J. S., & Rhodes, M. G. (2003). Evidence for an own-age bias in face recognition. *North American Journal of Psychology, 8,* 237–252.

Anderson, J. R. (1983). *The architecture of cognition.* Cambridge, MA: Harvard University Press.

Anderson, J. R. (1990). *The adaptive character of thought.* Hillsdale, NJ: Erlbaum.

Anderson, J. R. (2000). *Learning and memory: An integrated approach* (2nd ed.). New York: Wiley.

Anderson, J. R., Douglass, S., & Qin, Y. (2005). How should a theory of learning and cognition inform instruction? In A. F. Healy (Ed.), *Experimental cognitive psychology and its applications* (pp. 47–59).

Washington DC: American Psychological Association.

Anderson, J. R., & Gluck, K. A. (2001). What role do cognitive architectures play in intelligent tutoring systems? In S. M. Carver & D. Klahr (Eds.), *Cognition and instruction: Twenty-five years of progress* (pp. 227–261). Mahwah, NJ: Erlbaum.

Anderson, J. R., Reder, L. M., & Lebiere, C. (1996). Working memory: Activation limitations on retrieval. *Cognitive Psychology, 30*, 221–256.

Anderson, J. R., Reder, L. M., & Simon, H. A. (1996). Situated learning and education. *Educational Researcher, 25*, 5–11.

Anderson, J. R., & Schooler, L. J. (2000). The adaptive nature of memory. In E. Tulving & F. I. M. Craik (Eds.), *The Oxford handbook of memory* (pp. 557–581). New York: Oxford University Press.

Anderson, J. R., & Schunn, C. D. (2000). Implications of the ACT-R learning theory: No magic bullets. In R. Glaser (Ed.), *Advances in instructional psychology* (Vol. 5, pp. 1–33). Mahwah, NJ: Erlbaum.

Anderson, J. R., et al. (2004). An integrated theory of mind. *Psychological Review, 111*, 1036–1060.

Anderson, M. C. (2001). Active forgetting: Evidence for functional inhibition as a source of memory failure. In J. J. Freyd & A. P. DePrince (Eds.), *Trauma and cognitive science* (pp. 185–210). New York: Haworth.

Anderson, R. E. (1998). Imagery and spatial representation. In W. Bechtel & G. Graham (Eds.), *A companion to cognitive science* (pp. 204–211). Malden, MA: Blackwell.

Anglin, J. M. (1997). *Word, object, and conceptual development.* New York: Norton.

Arnold, J. E., Tanenhaus, M. K., Altman, R. J., & Fagnano, M. (2004). The old and thee, uh, new: Disfluency and reference resolution. *Psychological Science, 15*, 578–582.

Ashby, F. G., Prinzmetal, W., Ivry, R., & Maddox, W. T. (1996). A formal theory of feature binding in object perception. *Psychological Review, 103*, 165–192.

Atkinson, D., & Connor, U. (2008). Multilingual writing development. In C. Bazerman (Ed.), *Handbook of research on writing: History, society, school, individual, text* (pp. 515–532). Mahwah, NJ: Erlbaum.

Atkinson, R. C., & Shiffrin, R. M. (1968). Human memory: A proposed system and its control processes. In K. W. Spence & J. T. Spence (Eds.), *The psychology of learning and motivation: Advances in research and theory* (Vol. 2, pp. 89–105). New York: Academic Press.

Awh, E., et al. (1999). Rehearsal in spatial working memory: Evidence from neuroimaging. *Psychological Science, 10*, 433–437.

Baars, B. J. (1997). *In the theater of consciousness.* New York: Oxford University Press.

Baars, B. J., & Newman, J. B. (Eds.). (2002). *Essential sources in the scientific study of consciousness.* Cambridge, MA: MIT Press.

Baars, B. J., Newman, J., & Taylor, J. G. (1998). Neuronal mechanisms of consciousness: A relational global-workplace framework. In S. R. Hameroff, A. W. Kaszniak, & A. C. Scott (Eds.), *Toward a science of consciousness II: The second Tucson discussion and debates* (pp. 269–278). Cambridge, MA: MIT Press.

Bäckman, L., Small, B. J., & Wahlin, A. (2001). Aging and memory: Cognitive and biological perspectives. In J. E. Birren & K. W. Schaie (Eds.), *Handbook of the psychology of aging* (5th ed., pp. 349–377). San Diego: Academic Press.

Baddeley, A. D. (1986). *Working memory.* Oxford, UK: Clarendon.

Baddeley, A. D. (1990). *Human memory: Theory and practice.* Boston: Allyn and Bacon.

Baddeley, A. D. (1994). The magical number seven: Still magic after all these years? *Psychological Review, 101*, 353–356.

Baddeley, A. D. (1995). Working memory. In M. S. Gazzaniga (Ed.), *The cognitive neurosciences* (pp. 755–764). Cambridge, MA: MIT Books.

Baddeley, A. D. (1997). *Human memory: Theory and practice* (Rev. ed.). East Sussex, UK: Psychology Press.

Baddeley, A. D. (1999). *Essentials of human memory.* East Sussex, UK: Psychology Press.

Baddeley, A. D. (2000a). Short-term and working memory. In E. Tulving & F. I. M. Craik (Eds.), *The Oxford handbook of memory* (pp. 77–92). New York: Oxford University Press.

Baddeley, A. D. (2000b). The episodic buffer: A new component of working memory? *Trends in Cognitive Sciences, 4*, 417–423.

Baddeley, A. D. (2001). Is working memory still working? *American Psychologist, 56*, 849–864.

Baddeley, A. D. (2003). Working memory and language: An overview. *Journal of Communication Disorders, 36*, 189–208.

Baddeley, A. D. (2004). Memory and context. In R. L. Gregory (Ed.), *The Oxford companion to the mind* (2nd ed., pp. 571–572). New York: Oxford University Press.

Baddeley, A. D. (2006). Working memory: An overview. In S. J. Pickering (Ed.), *Working memory and education* (pp. 3–31). Burlington, MA: Elsevier.

Baddeley, A. D., & Andrade, J. (1998). Working memory and consciousness: An empirical approach. In M. A. Conway, S. E. Gathercole, & C. Cornoldi (Eds.), *Theories of memory II* (pp. 1–24). Hove, UK: Psychology Press.

Baddeley, A. D., Gathercole, S., & Papagno, C. (1998). The phonological loop as a language learning device. *Psychological Review, 105*, 158–173.

Baddeley, A. D., Grant, S., Wight, E., & Thomson, N. (1973). Imagery and visual working memory. In P. M. A. Rabbitt & S. Dornic (Eds.), *Attention and performance V* (pp. 205–217). London: Academic Press.

Baddeley, A. D., & Hitch, G. J. (1974). Working memory. In G. Bower (Ed.), *Recent advances in learning and memory* (Vol. 8, pp. 47–90). New York: Academic Press.

Baddeley, A. D., Thomson, N., & Buchanan, M. (1975). Word length and the structure of short-term memory. *Journal of Verbal Learning and Verbal Behavior, 14*, 575–589.

Baddeley, A. D., Wilson, B. A., & Watts, F. N. (Eds.). (1995). *Handbook of memory disorders*. Chichester, UK: Wiley.

Bahrick, H. P. (2005). The long-term neglect of long-term memory: Reasons and remedies. In A. F. Healy (Ed.), *Experimental cognitive psychology and its applications* (pp. 89–100). Washington DC: American Psychological Association.

Bahrick, H. P., & Hall, L. K. (2005). The importance of retrieval failures to long-term retention: A metacognitive explanation of the spacing effect. *Journal of Memory and Language, 52*, 566–577.

Bahrick, H. P., Hall, L. K., & Dunlosky, J. (1993). Reconstructive processing of memory content for high versus low test scores and grades. *Applied Cognitive Psychology, 7*, 1–10.

Bahrick, H. P., et al. (1994). Fifty years of language maintenance and language dominance in bilingual Hispanic immigrants. *Journal of Experimental Psychology: General, 123*, 264–283.

Baker, J. M. C., & Dunlosky, J. (2006). Does momentary accessibility influence metacomprehension judgments? The influence of study-judgment lags on accessibility effects. *Psychonomic Bulletin & Review, 13*, 60–65.

Baker, K. D. (1999). Personal communication.

Baker, L. (2005). Developmental differences in metacognition: Implications for metacognitively oriented reading instruction. In S. E. Israel, C. C. Block, K. L. Bauserman, & K. Kinnucan-Welsch (Eds.), *Metacognition in literacy learning: Theory, assessment, instruction, and professional development* (pp. 61–79). Mahwah, NJ: Erlbaum.

Balch, W. R. (2006a). Encouraging distributed study: A classroom experiment on the spacing effect. *Teaching of Psychology, 33*, 249–252.

Balch, W. R. (2006b). Introducing psychology students to research methodology: A word-pleasantness experiment. *Teaching of Psychology, 33*, 132–134.

Baldwin, D., & Meyer, M. (2007). How inherently social is language? In E. Hoff & M. Shatz (Eds.), *Blackwell handbook of language development* (pp. 87–106). Malden, MA: Blackwell.

Baldwin, M. W. (Ed.). (2005). *Interpersonal cognition*. New York: Guilford.

Baldwin, M. W., & Dandeneau, S. D. (2005). Understanding and modifying the relational schemas underlying insecurity. In M. W. Baldwin (Ed.), *Interpersonal cognition* (pp. 33–61). New York: Guilford.

Baltes, P. B., Staudinger, U. M., & Lindenverger, U. (1999). Lifespan psychology: Theory and application to intellectual functioning. *Annual Review of Psychology, 50*, 471–507.

Bamberg, M., & Moissinac, L. (2003). Discourse development. In A. C. Graesser, M. A. Gernsbacher, & S. R. Goldman (Eds.), *Handbook of discourse processes* (pp. 395–437). Mahwah, NJ: Erlbaum.

Bangerter, A. (2004). Using pointing and describing to achieve joint focus of attention in dialogue. *Psychological Science, 15*, 415–419.

Barash, D. P. (2006, July 14). I am, therefore I think. *Chronicle of Higher Education*, pp. B9–B10.

Bardovi-Harlig, K., & Hartford, B. S. (Eds.). (2005). *Interlanguage pragmatics: Exploring institutional talk*. Mahwah, NJ; Erlbaum.

Bargh, J., & Ferguson, M. J. (2000). Beyond behaviorism: On the automaticity of higher mental processes. *Psychological Bulletin, 126*, 925–945.

Barnes, J. B. (2004). Aristotle. In R. L. Gregory (Ed.), *The Oxford companion to the mind* (2nd ed., pp. 45–46). New York: Oxford University Press.

Barnett, R. C., & Rivers, C. (2004). *Same difference: How gender myths are hurting our relationships, our children, and our jobs*. New York: Basic Books.

Barnett, S. M., & Ceci, S. J. (2002). When and where do we apply what we learn? A taxonomy for far transfer. *Psychological Bulletin, 128*, 612–637.

Barnett, S. M., & Koslowski, B. (2002). Adaptive expertise: Effects of type of experience and the level of theoretical understanding it generates. *Thinking and Reasoning, 8,* 237–267.

Baron, J. (1994). *Thinking and deciding* (2nd ed.). New York: Cambridge University Press.

Baron, J. (1998). *Judgment misguided: Intuition and error in public decision making.* New York: Oxford University Press.

Baron, J. (2000). *Thinking and deciding* (3rd ed.). New York: Cambridge University Press.

Barr, D. J., & Keysar, B. (2006). Perspective taking and the coordination of meaning in language use. In M. J. Traxler & M. A. Gernsbacher (Eds.), *Handbook of psycholinguistics* (2nd ed., pp. 901–938). Amsterdam: Elsevier.

Barr, R., Rovee-Collier, C., & Campanella, J. (2005). Retrieval protracts deferred imitation by 6-month-olds. *Infancy, 7,* 263–283.

Barrett, H. C., & Kurzban, R. (2006). Modularity in cognition: Framing the debate. *Psychological Review, 113,* 628–647.

Barsalou, L. W. (1990). On the indistinguishability of exemplar memory and abstraction in category representation. In T. K. Srull & R. S. Wyer (Eds.), *Advances in social cognition* (Vol. 3, pp. 61–88). Hillsdale, NJ: Erlbaum.

Barsalou, L. W. (1992). Frames, concepts, and conceptual fields. In A. Lehrer & E. F. Kittay (Eds.), *Frames, fields, and contrasts* (pp. 21–74). Hillsdale, NJ: Erlbaum.

Barsalou, L. W. (1993). Flexibility, structure, and linguistic vagary in concepts: Manifestations of a compositional system of perceptual symbols. In A. F. Collins, S. E. Gathercole, M. A. Conway, & P. E. Morris (Eds.), *Theories of memory* (pp. 29–101). Hove, UK: Erlbaum.

Barsalou, L. W. (2003). Situated simulation in the human conceptual system. *Language and Cognitive Processes, 18,* 513–562.

Bartlett, F. C. (1932). *Remembering: An experimental and social study.* Cambridge, UK: Cambridge University Press.

Baruss, I. (2003). *Alterations of consciousness: An empirical analysis for social scientists.* Washington, DC: American Psychological Association.

Bassok, M. (2003). Analogical transfer in problem solving. In J. E. Davidson & R. J. Sternberg (Eds.), *The psychology of problem solving* (pp. 343–369). New York: Cambridge University Press.

Bates, E. (2000). On the nature and nurture of language. In R. Levi-Montalcini et al. (Eds.), *Frontiere della biologia* [Frontiers of biology]. Rome: Giovanni Trecanni.

Bates, E., Devescovi, A., & Wulfeck, B. (2001). Psycholinguistics: A cross-language perspective. *Annual Review of Psychology, 52,* 369–396.

Bates, E., & Goodman, J. C. (1997). On the inseparability of grammar and the lexicon: Evidence from acquisition, aphasia and real-time processing. *Language and Cognitive Processes, 12,* 507–584.

Bauer, B., & Jolicoeur, P. (1996). Stimulus dimensionality effects in mental rotation. *Journal of Experimental Psychology: Human Perception and Performance, 22,* 82–94.

Bauer, P. J. (2004). Getting explicit memory off the ground: Steps toward construction of a neurodevelopmental account of changes in the first two years of life. *Developmental Review, 24,* 347–373.

Bauer, P. J. (2005a). Developments in declarative memory: Decreasing susceptibility to storage failure over the second year of life. *Psychological Science, 16,* 41–47.

Bauer, P. J. (2005b). New developments in the study of infant memory. In D. M. Teti (Ed.), *Handbook of research methods in developmental science* (pp. 467–488). Malden, MA: Blackwell.

Bayliss, D. M., Jarrold, C., Baddeley, A. D., & Leigh, E. (2005). Differential constraints on the working memory and reading abilities of individuals with learning difficulties and typically developing children. *Journal of Experimental Child Psychology, 92,* 76–99.

Bazerman, C. (Ed.) (2008). *Handbook of research on writing: History, society, school, individual, text.* Mahwah, NJ: Erlbaum.

Bazerman, M. H. (Ed.). (2005). *Negotiation, decision making and conflict management* (Vols. 1–3). Northampton, MA: Edward Elgar Publishing.

Bearce, K. H., & Rovee-Collier, C. (2006). Repeated priming increases memory accessibility in infants. *Journal of Experimental Child Psychology, 93,* 357–376.

Beardsley, T. (1997, August). The machinery of thought. *Scientific American,* 78–83.

Beattie, G., & Shovelton, H. (2004). Body language. In R. L. Gregory (Ed.), *The Oxford companion to the mind* (2nd ed., pp. 111–112). New York: Oxford University Press.

Bechtel, W., Abrahamsen, A., & Graham, G. (1998). The life of cognitive science. In W. Bechtel & G. Graham (Eds.), *A companion to cognitive science* (pp. 2–104). Malden, MA: Blackwell.

Beck, M. R., Angelone, B. L., & Levin, D. T. (2004). Knowledge about the probability of change affects change detection performance. *Journal of Experimental Psychology: Human Perception and Performance, 30*, 778–791.

Bediou, B., et al. (2005). Effects of emotion and identity on facial affect processing in schizophrenia. *Psychiatric Research, 133*, 149–157.

Beeman, M., Bowden, E. M., & Gernsbacher, M. A. (2000). Right and left hemisphere cooperation for drawing predictive and coherence inferences during normal story comprehension. *Brain and Language, 71*, 310–336.

Beeman, M., & Chiarello, C. (1998). Concluding remarks: Getting the whole story right. In M. Beeman & C. Chiarello (Eds.), *Right hemisphere language comprehension: Perspectives from cognitive neuroscience* (pp. 377–389). Mahwah, NJ: Erlbaum.

Beilock, S. I., & Carr, T. H. (2005). When high-powered people fail: Working memory and "choking under pressure" in math. *Psychological Science, 16*, 101–105.

Belletti, A., & Rizzi, L. (2002). Editors' introduction: Some concepts and issues in linguistic theory. In A. Belletti & L. Rizzi (Eds.), *On nature and language* (pp. 1–44). Cambridge, UK: Cambridge University Press.

Bellezza, F. S. (1984). The self as a mnemonic device: The role of internal cues. *Journal of Personality and Social Psychology, 47*, 506–516.

Bellezza, F. S. (1992). Recall of congruent information in the self-reference task. *Bulletin of the Psychonomic Society, 30*, 275–278.

Bellezza, F. S. (1996). Mnemonic method to enhance storage and retrieval. In E. Bjork & R. Bjork (Eds.), *Memory* (pp. 345–380). San Diego: Academic Press.

Bellezza, F. S., & Hoyt, S. K. (1992). The self-reference effect and mental cueing. *Social Cognition, 10*, 51–78.

Beni, R. D., Pazzaglia, F., & Gardini, S. (2006). The role of mental rotation and age in spatial perspective-taking tasks: When age does not impair perspective-taking performance. *Applied Cognitive Psychology, 20*, 807–821.

Bennett, M. D., & Gibson, J. M. (2006). *A field guide to good decisions.* Westport, CT: Praeger.

Bentin, S., et al. (2002). Priming visual face-processing mechanisms: Electrophysiological evidence. *Psychological Science, 13*, 190–193.

Ben-Zeev, T. (2002). If "ignorance makes us smart," then does reading books make us less smart? [Review of *Simple heuristics that make us smart*]. *Contemporary Psychology, 47*, 653–656.

Bereiter, C. (1997). Situated cognition and how to overcome it. In D. Kirshner & J. A. Whitson (Eds.), *Situated cognition: Social, semiotic, and psychological perspectives* (pp. 281–300). Mahwah, NJ: Erlbaum.

Bereiter, C., & Scardamalia, M. (1987). *The psychology of written composition.* Hillsdale, NJ: Erlbaum.

Berg, T. (2002). Slips of the typewriter key. *Applied Psycholinguistics, 23*, 185–207.

Berger, C. R. (1997). Producing messages under uncertainty. In J. O. Greene (Ed.), *Message production* (pp. 221–224). Mahwah, NJ: Erlbaum.

Berliner, L., & Briere, J. (1999). Trauma, memory, and clinical practice. In L. M. Williams & V. L. Banyard (Eds.), *Trauma & memory* (pp. 3–18). Thousand Oaks, CA: Sage.

Bernstein, D. M., Laney, C., Morris, E. K., & Loftus, E. F. (2005). False memories about food can lead to food avoidance. *Social Cognition, 23*, 11–34.

Bernstein, S. E., & Carr, T. H. (1996). Dual-route theories of pronouncing printed words: What can be learned from concurrent task performance? *Journal of Experimental Psychology: Learning, Memory, and Cognition, 22*, 86–116.

Betsch, T., & Haberstroh, S. (Eds.). (2005). *The routines of decision making.* Mahwah, NJ: Erlbaum.

Bialystok, E. (1987). Words as things: Development of word concept by bilingual children. *Studies in Second Language Acquisition, 9*, 133–140.

Bialystok, E. (1988). Levels of bilingualism and levels of linguistic awareness. *Developmental Psychology, 24*, 560–567.

Bialystok, E. (1992). Selective attention in cognitive processing: The bilingual edge. In R. J. Harris (Ed.), *Language processing in bilingual children* (pp. 501–513). Amsterdam: Elsevier.

Bialystok, E. (2001). *Bilingualism in development: Language, literacy, & cognition.* New York: Cambridge University Press.

Bialystok, E. (2005). Consequences of bilingualism for cognitive development. In Kroll, J. F., & de Groot, A. M. (Eds.). (2005). *Handbook of bilingualism: Psycholinguistic approaches* (pp. 417–432). New York: Oxford University Press.

Bialystok, E., & Codd, J. (1997). Cardinal limits: Evidence from language awareness and bilingualism for developing concepts of number. *Cognitive Development, 12*, 85–106.

Bialystok, E., & Craik, F. I. M. (Eds.). (2006). *Lifespan cognition: Mechanisms of change.* New York: Oxford University Press.

Bialystok, E., Craik, F. I. M., Klein, R., & Viswanatha, M. (2004). Bilingualism, aging, and cognitive control: Evidence from the Simon Task. *Psychology and Aging, 19,* 290–303.

Bialystok, E., & Hakuta, K. (1994). *In other words: The science and psychology of second-language acquisition.* New York: Basic Books.

Bialystok, E., & Majumder, S. (1998). The relationship between bilingualism and the development of cognitive processes in problem solving. *Applied Psycholinguistics, 19,* 69–85.

Bialystok, E., & Martin, M. (2004). Attention and inhibition in bilingual children: Evidence from the dimensional change card sort task. *Developmental Science, 7,* 325–339.

Biber, D., & Vásquez, C. (2008). Writing and speaking. In C. Bazerman (Ed.), *Handbook of research on writing: History, society, school, individual, text* (pp. 535–548). Mahwah, NJ: Erlbaum.

Biederman, I. (1990). Higher-level vision. In E. N. Osherson, S. M. Kosslyn, & J. M. Hollerbach (Eds.), *An invitation to cognitive science* (Vol. 2, pp. 41–72). Cambridge, MA: MIT.

Biederman, I. (1995). Visual object recognition. In S. F. Kosslyn & D. N. Osherson (Eds.), *An invitation to cognitive science* (2nd ed., pp. 121–165). Cambridge, MA: MIT Press.

Bieman-Copland, S., & Charness, N. (1994). Memory knowledge and memory monitoring in adulthood. *Psychology and Aging, 9,* 287–302.

Billman, D. (1996). Structural biases in concept learning: Influences from multiple functions. *Psychology of Learning and Motivation, 35,* 283–321.

Binder, J., & Price, C. J. (2001). Functional neuroimaging of language. In R. Cabeza & A. Kingstone (Eds.), *Handbook of functional neuroimaging of cognition* (pp. 187–251). Cambridge, MA: MIT Press.

Biorge, A. K. (2007). Power distance in English lingua franca email communication. *International Journal of Applied Linguistics, 17,* 60–80.

Birdsong, D. (1999). Introduction: Whys and whynots of the critical period hypothesis for second language acquisition. In D. Birdsong (Ed.), *Critical period hypothesis* (pp. 161–181). Mahwah, NJ: Erlbaum.

Birdsong, D., & Molis, M. (2001). On the evidence for maturational constraints in second-language acquisition. *Journal of Memory and Language, 44,* 235–249.

Birnbaum, M. H. (2004). Base rates in Bayesian inference. In R. F. Pohl (Eds.). *Cognitive illusions: A handbook on fallacies and biases in thinking, judgement, and memory* (pp. 43–60). Hove, UK: Psychology Press.

Birren, J. E., & Schaie, K. W. (2001). (Eds.). *Handbook of the psychology of aging* (5th ed.). San Diego, CA: Academic Press.

Birren, J. E., & Schroots, J. J. F. (2001). History of geropsychology. In J. E. Birren & K. W. Schaie (Eds.), *Handbook of the psychology of aging* (5th ed., pp. 3–28). San Diego: Academic Press.

Bishop, M. A., & Trout, J. D. (2002). 50 years of successful predictive modeling should be enough. *Lessons for Philosophy of Science, 69,* S197–S208.

Bjork, E. L., & Bjork, R. A. (1988). On the adaptive aspects of retrieval failure in autobiographical memory. In M. M. Gruneberg, P. E. Morris, & R. N. Sykes (Eds.), *Practical aspects of memory* (Vol. 2). London: Academic Press.

Bjork, E. L., Bjork, R. A., & MacLeod, M. D. (2005). Types and consequences of forgetting: Intended and unintended. In L.-G. Nilsson & Nobuo Ohta (Eds.), *Memory and society: Psychological perspectives* (pp. 134–158). New York: Psychology Press.

Bjork, R. A. (1999). Assessing our own competence: Heuristics and illusions. In D. Gopher & A. Koriat (Eds.), *Attention and performance XVII* (pp. 435–459). Cambridge, MA: MIT Press.

Bjork, R. A., & Richardson-Klavehn, A. (1987). On the puzzling relationship between environmental context and human memory. In C. Izawa (Ed.), *Current issues in cognitive processes* (pp. 313–344). Hillsdale, NJ: Erlbaum.

Bjorklund, D. F. (2005). *Children's thinking: Cognitive development and individual differences* (4th ed.). Belmont, CA: Thomson Wadsworth.

Bjorklund, D. F., Miller, P. H., Coyle, T. R., & Slawinski, J. L. (1997). Instructing children to use memory strategies: Evidence of utilization deficiencies in memory training studies. *Developmental Review, 17,* 411–441.

Blascovich, J., Spencer, S. J., Quinn, D., & Steele, C. (2001). African Americans and high blood pressure: The role of stereotype threat. *Psychological Science, 12,* 225–229.

Block, R. A., & Harper, D. R. (1991). Overconfidence in estimation: Testing the anchoring-and-adjustment hypothesis. *Organizational Behavior and Human Decision Processes, 49,* 188–207.

Bloom, F. E., & Lazerson, A. (1988). *Brain, mind, and behavior* (2nd ed.). New York: Freeman.

Bloom, L. (1998). Language acquisition in its developmental context. In W. Damon (Ed.), *Handbook of child psychology: Cognition, perception, and language* (5th ed., Vol. 2, pp. 309–370). New York: Wiley.

Bloom, L. C., & Mudd, S. A. (1991). Depth of processing approach to face recognition: A test of two theories. *Journal of Experimental Psychology: Learning, Memory, and Cognition, 17,* 556–565.

Bloom, P. (2000). *How children learn the meanings of words.* Cambridge, MA: MIT Press.

Bloom, P. (2001). Précis of *How children learn the meaning of words. Behavioral and Brain Sciences, 24,* 1095–1103.

Bloom, P., & Gleitman, L. (1999). Word meaning, acquisition of. In R. A. Wilson & F. C. Keil (Eds.), *The MIT encyclopedia of the cognitive sciences* (pp. 434–438). Cambridge, MA: MIT Press.

Bluck, S., & Habermas, T. (2001). Extending the study of autobiographical memory: Thinking back about life across the life span. *Review of General Psychology, 5,* 135–147.

Bock, K. (1999). Language production. In R. A. Wilson & F. C. Keil (Eds.), *The MIT encyclopedia of the cognitive sciences* (pp. 453–456). Cambridge, MA: MIT Press.

Bock, K., & Garnsey, S. M. (1998). Language processing. In W. Bechtel & G. Graham (Eds.), *A companion to cognitive science* (pp. 226–234). Malden, MA: Blackwell.

Bock, K., & Griffin, Z. M. (2000). Producing words: How mind meets mouth. In L. Wheeldon (Ed.), *Aspects of language production* (pp. 7–47). Philadelphia: Psychology Press.

Bock, K., & Huitema, J. (1999). Language production. In S. Garrod & M. J. Pickering (Eds.), *Language processing* (pp. 365–388). East Sussex, UK: Psychology Press.

Bock, K., Loebell, H., & Morey, R. (1992). From conceptual roles to structural relations: Bridging the syntactic cleft. *Psychological Review, 99,* 150–171.

Boden, M. (2004). Artificial intelligence (AI). In R. L. Gregory (Ed.), *The Oxford companion to the mind* (2nd ed., pp. 59–61). New York: Oxford University Press.

Boden, M. A. (2004). *The creative mind: Myths and mechanisms* (2nd ed.). New York: Routledge.

Bodenhausen, G. V., Macrae, C. N., & Hugenberg, K. (2003). Social cognition. In I. B. Weiner (Ed.), *Handbook of psychology* (Vol. 5, pp. 257–282). Hoboken, NJ: Wiley.

Bohanek, J. G., Fivush, R., & Walker, E. (2005). Memories of positive and negative emotional events. *Applied Cognitive Psychology, 19,* 51–66.

Boker, S. M., & Bisconti, T. L. (2006). Dynamical systems modeling for aging research. In C. S. Bergeman & S. M. Boker (Eds.), *Methodological issues in aging research* (pp. 185–229). Mahwah, NJ: Erlbaum.

Bond, Z. S. (2005). Slips of the ear. In D. B. Pisoni & R. E. Remez (Eds.), *The handbook of speech perception* (pp. 290–310). Malden, MA: Blackwell.

Boot, W. E., Brockmole, J. R., & Simons, D. J. (2005). Attention capture is modulated in dual-task situations. *Psychonomic Bulletin & Review, 12,* 662–668.

Bornkessel, I., & Schlesewsky, M. (2006). The extended argument dependency model: A neurocognitive approach to sentence comprehension across languages. *Psychological Review, 113,* 787–821.

Bortfeld, H., & Brennan, S. E. (1997). Use and acquisition of idiomatic expressions in referring by native and non-native speakers. *Discourse Processes, 23,* 119–147.

Bosch, L., & Sebastián-Gallés, N. (2001). Early language differentiation in bilingual infants. In J. Cenoz & F. Genesee (Eds.), *Trends in bilingual acquisition* (pp. 71–93). Amsterdam: Benjamins.

Bower, G. H. (1998). An associative theory of implicit and explicit memory. In M. A. Conway, S. E. Gathercole, & C. Cornoldi (Eds.), *Theories of memory* (Vol. 2, pp. 25–60). Hove, UK: Psychology Press.

Bower, G. H. (2000). A brief history of memory research. In E. Tulving & F. I. M. Craik (Eds.), *The Oxford handbook of memory* (pp. 3–32). New York: Oxford University Press.

Bower, G. H., & Clark, M. C. (1969). Narrative stories as mediators for serial learning. *Psychonomic Science, 14,* 181–182.

Bower, G. H., Clark, M. C., Lesgold, A. M., & Winzenz, D. (1969). Hierarchical retrieval schemes in recall of categorized word lists. *Journal of Verbal Learning and Verbal Behavior, 8,* 323–343.

Bower, G. H., & Forgas, J. P. (2000). Affect, memory, and social cognition. In E. Eich et al. (Eds.), *Cognition and emotion* (pp. 87–168). New York: Oxford University Press.

Bower, G. H., & Springston, F. (1970). Pauses as recoding points in letter series. *Journal of Experimental Psychology, 83,* 421–430.

Bower, G. H., & Winzenz, D. (1970). Comparison of associative learning strategies. *Psychonomic Science, 20,* 119–120.

Bradshaw, J. L., & Nettleton, N. C. (1974). Articulatory inference and the MOWN-DOWN heterophone effect. *Journal of Experimental Psychology, 102,* 88–94.

Brainerd, C. J., & Reyna, V. F. (2005). *The science of false memory*. New York: Oxford University Press.

Brandimonte, M. A., & Gerbino, W. (1996). When imagery fails: Effects of verbal recoding on accessibility of visual memories. In C. Cornoldi et al. (Eds.), *Stretching the imagination: Representation and transformation in mental imagery* (pp. 31–76). New York: Oxford University Press.

Brandimonte, M. A., Hitch, G. J., & Bishop, D. V. M. (1992). Influence of short-term memory codes on visual image processing: Evidence from image transformation tasks. *Journal of Experimental Psychology: Learning, Memory, and Cognition, 18*, 157–165.

Brandt, K. R., Cooper, L. M., & Dewhurst, S. A. (2005). Expertise and recollective experience: Recognition memory for familiar and unfamiliar academic subjects. *Applied Cognitive Psychology, 19*, 1113–1125.

Bransford, J. D., Barclay, J. R., & Franks, J. J. (1972). Sentence memory: A constructive versus interpretive approach. *Cognitive Psychology, 3*, 193–209.

Bransford, J. D., Brown, A. L., & Cocking, R. R. (2000). *How people learn: Brain, mind, experience, and school* (expanded edition). Washington, DC: National Academy Press.

Bransford, J. D., & Franks, J. J. (1971). Abstraction of linguistic ideas. *Cognitive Psychology, 2*, 331–350.

Bransford, J. D., Franks, J. J., Morris, C. D., & Stein, B. S. (1979). Some general constraints on learning and memory research. In L. S. Cermak & F. I. M. Craik (Eds.), *Levels of processing in human memory* (pp. 331–354). Hillsdale, NJ: Erlbaum.

Bransford, J. D., & Stein, B. S. (1984). *The IDEAL problem solver*. New York: Freeman.

Branthwaite, A., & Rogers, D. (1985). Introduction. In A. Branthwaite & D. Rogers (Eds.), *Children growing up* (pp. 1–2). Milton Keynes, UK: Open University Press.

Bressler, S. L. (2002). Understanding cognition through large-scale cortical networks. *Current Directions in Psychological Science, 11*, 57–61.

Brewer, N., Weber, N., & Semmler, C. (2005). Eyewitness identification. In N. Brewer & K. D. Williams (Eds.), *Psychology and law: An empirical perspective* (pp. 177–221). New York: Guilford.

Brewer, W. F. (2000). Bartlett's concept of the schema and its impact on theories of knowledge representation in contemporary cognitive psychology. In A. Saito (Ed.), *Bartlett, culture and cognition* (pp. 69–89). East Sussex, UK: Psychology Press.

Brewer, W. F., & Treyens, J. C. (1981). Role of schemata in memory for places. *Cognitive Psychology, 13*, 207–230.

Brigham, J. C., Bennett, L. B., Meissner, C. A., & Mitchell, T. L. (2007). The influence of race on eyewitness memory. In R. C. L. Lindsay, D. F. Ross, J. D. Read, & M. P. Toglia (Eds.), *Handbook of eyewitness psychology* (Vol. 2, pp. 257–281). Mahwah, NJ: Erlbaum.

Britton, B. K. (1996). Rewriting: The arts and sciences of improving expository instructional text. In C. Michael Levy & S. Ransdell (Eds.), *The science of writing: Theories, methods, individual differences, and applications* (pp. 323–345). Mahwah, NJ: Erlbaum.

Broadbent, D. E. (1958). *Perception and communication*. New York: Pergamon.

Bromme, R., Jucks, R., & Wagner, T. (2005). How to refer to 'diabetes'? Language in online health advice. *Applied Cognitive Psychology, 19*, 569–586.

Brooks, L. R. (1968). Spatial and verbal components of the act of recall. *Canadian Journal of Psychology, 22*, 349–368.

Brown, A. S. (1991). A review of the tip-of-the-tongue experience. *Psychological Bulletin, 109*, 204–233.

Brown, A. S. (2002). Consolidation theory and retrograde amnesia in humans. *Psychonomic Bulletin and Review, 9*, 403–425.

Brown, A. S., Bracken, E., Zoccoli, S., & Douglas, K. (2004). Generating and remembering passwords. *Applied Cognitive Psychology, 18*, 641–651.

Brown, C. H., & Sinnott, J. M. (2006). Cross-species comparisons of vocal perception. In S. Greenberg & W. A. Ainsworth (Eds.), *Listening to speech: An auditory perspective* (pp. 183–201). Mahwah, NJ: Erlbaum.

Brown, J. (1958). Some tests of the decay theory of immediate memory. *Quarterly Journal of Experimental Psychology, 10*, 12–21.

Brown, J. (2004). Memory: Biological basis. In R. L. Gregory (Ed.), *The Oxford companion to the mind* (2nd ed., pp. 564–568). New York: Oxford University Press.

Brown, N. R., Cui, X., & Gordon, R. D. (2002). Estimating national populations: Cross-cultural differences and availability effects. *Applied Cognitive Psychology, 16*, 811–827.

Brown, N. R., & Siegler, R. S. (1992). The role of availability in the estimation of national populations. *Memory & Cognition, 20*, 406–412.

Brown, P., & Levinson, S. C. (1987). *Politeness: Some universals of language usage*. Cambridge, UK: Cambridge University Press.

Brown, R., & Kulik, J. (1977). Flashbulb memories. *Cognition, 5*, 73–99.

Brown, R., & McNeill, D. (1966). The "tip of the tongue" phenomenon. *Journal of Verbal Learning and Verbal Behavior, 5*, 325–377.

Brown, S. C., & Craik, F. I. M. (2000). Encoding and retrieval of information. In E. Tulving & F. I. M. Craik (Eds.), *The Oxford handbook of memory* (pp. 93–108). New York: Oxford University Press.

Brown, T. L., Gore, C. L., & Carr, T. H. (2002). Visual attention and word recognition in Stroop color naming: Is word recognition "automatic"? *Journal of Experimental Psychology: General, 131*, 220–240.

Bruce, V., Green, P. R., & Georgeson, M. A. (2003). *Visual perception* (4th ed.). Hove, UK: Psychology Press.

Bruce, V., Henderson, A., Newman, C., & Burton, A. M. (2001). Matching identities of familiar and unfamiliar faces caught on CCTV images. *Journal of Experimental Psychology: Applied, 7*, 207–218.

Bruck, M., & Ceci, S. J. (1999). The suggestibility of children's memory. *Annual Review of Psychology, 50*, 419–439.

Bruck, M., Ceci, S. J., & Melnyk, L. (1997). External and internal sources of variation in the creation of false reports in children. *Learning and Individual Differences, 9*, 289–316.

Bruner, J. (1997). Will cognitive revolutions ever stop? In D. M. Johnson & C. E. Erneling (Eds.), *The future of the cognitive revolution* (pp. 279–292). New York: Oxford University Press.

Bruning, R. H., Schraw, G. J., & Ronning, R. R. (1999). *Cognitive psychology and instruction* (3rd ed.). Upper Saddle River, NJ: Prentice Hall.

Bruno, L., Zarrinpar, A., & Kosslyn, S. M., (2003). Do separate processes identify objects as exemplars versus members of basic-level categories? Evidence from hemispheric specialization. *Brain and Cognition, 53*, 15–27.

Bryant, D. J. (1998). Human spatial concepts reflect regularities of the physical world and human body. In P. Olivier & K. Gapp (Eds.), *Representation and processing of spatial expressions* (pp. 215–230). Mahwah, NJ: Erlbaum.

Bryant, D. J., & Tversky, B. (1999). Mental representations of perspective and spatial relations from diagrams and models. *Journal of Experimental Psychology: Learning, Memory, and Cognition, 25*, 137–156.

Bryant, D. J., Tversky, B., & Franklin, N. (1992). Internal and external spatial frameworks for representing described scenes. *Journal of Memory and Language, 31*, 74–98.

Buckner, R. L., & Logan, J. M. (2001). Functional neuroimaging methods: PET and fMRI. In R. Cabeza & A. Kingstone (Eds.), *Handbook of functional neuroimaging of cognition* (pp. 27–48). Cambridge, MA: MIT Press.

Buckner, R. L., & Petersen, S. E. (1998). Neuroimaging. In W. Bechtel & G. Graham (Eds.), *A companion to cognitive science* (pp. 413–424). Malden, MA: Blackwell.

Buehler, R., Griffin, D., & Ross, M. (1994). Exploring the "planning fallacy." Why people underestimate their task completion times. *Journal of Personality and Social Psychology, 67*, 366–381.

Buehler, R., Griffin, D., & Ross, M. (2002). Inside the planning fallacy: The causes and consequences of optimistic time predictions. In T. Gilovich, D. Griffin, & D. Kahneman (Eds.), *Heuristics and biases: The psychology of intuitive judgment* (pp. 250–270). New York: Cambridge University Press.

Bull, R., & Espy, K. A. (2006). Working memory, executive functioning, and children's mathematics. In S. J. Pickering (Ed.), *Working memory and education* (pp. 93–123). Burlington, MA: Elsevier.

Bunce, D., & Macready, A. (2005). Processing speed, executive function, and age differences in remembering and knowing. *Quarterly Journal of Experimental Psychology, 58A*, 155–168.

Bundesen, C., & Habekost, T. (2005). Attention. In K. Lamberts & R. L. Goldstone (Eds.), *Handbook of cognition*. Thousand Oaks, CA: Sage.

Bundesen, C., Habekost, T., & Kyllingsbæk, S. (2005). A neural theory of visual attention: Bridging cognition and neurophysiology. *Psychological Review, 112*, 291–328.

Burgess, C., & Lund, K. (2000). The dynamics of meaning in memory. In E. Dietrich & A. B. Markman (Eds.), *Cognitive dynamics: Conceptual and representational change in humans and machines* (pp. 117–156). Mahwah, NJ: Erlbaum.

Burke, D. M. (2006). Representation and aging. In E. Bialystok & F. I. M. Craik (Eds.), *Lifespan cognition: Mechanisms of change* (pp. 193–206). New York: Oxford University Press.

Burns, D. J. (2006). Assessing distinctiveness: Measures of item-specific and relational processing. In R. R. Hunt & J. B. Worthen (Eds.), *Distinctiveness and memory* (pp. 109–130). New York: Oxford University Press.

Burton, A. M., Wilson, S., Cowan, M., & Bruce, V. (1999). Face recognition in poor-quality video: Evidence from security surveillance. *Psychological Science, 10*, 243–248.

Bus, A. G., & van IJzendoorn, M. H. (1999). Phonological awareness and early reading: A meta-analysis of experimental training studies. *Journal of Educational Psychology, 91*, 403–414.

Bush, G. W. (2003, January 28). *State of the Union.* Retrieved August 15, 2007, from www.whitehouse.gov/new/release/2003/01/20030128-19.html

Bushman, B. J. (1998). Effects of television violence on memory for commercial messages. *Journal of Experimental Psychology: Applied, 4*, 291–307.

Bushman, B. J. (2003, August). *If the television program bleeds, memory for advertisement recedes.* Paper presented at the annual meeting of the American Psychological Association.

Bushman, B. J. (2005). Violence and sex in television programs do not sell products in advertisements. *Psychological Science, 16*, 702–708.

Bushman, B. J., & Huesmann, L. R. (2001). Effects of televised violence on aggression. In D. G. Singer & J. L. Singer (Eds.), *Handbook of children and the media* (pp. 223–254). Thousand Oaks, CA: Sage.

Butcher, A. (2006). Australian Aboriginal languages: Consonant-salient phonologies and the "Place-of-articulation imperative." In J. Harrington & M. Tabain (Eds.), *Speech production: Models, phonetic processes, and techniques* (pp. 1–10). New York: Psychology Press.

Butcher, K. R., & Kintsch, W. (2003). Text comprehension and discourse processing. In A. F. Healy & R. W. Proctor (Eds.), *Handbook of psychology* (Vol. 4, pp. 575–595). Hoboken, NJ: Wiley.

Byrne, R. M. J., Espino, O., & Santamaria, C. (2000). Counterexample availability. In W. Schaecken, G. DeVooght, A. Vandierendonck, & G. d'Ydewalle (Eds.), *Deductive reasoning and strategies* (pp. 97–110). Mahwah, NJ: Erlbaum.

Cabe, P. A., Walker, M. H., & Williams, M. (1999). Newspaper advice column letters as teaching cases for developmental psychology. *Teaching of Psychology, 26*, 128–131.

Cacioppo, J. T., & Berntson, G. G. (Eds.). (2005a). *Social neuroscience: Key readings.* New York: Psychology Press.

Cacioppo, J. T., & Berntson, G. G. (2005b). Volume overview: Analyses of the social brain through the lens of human brain imaging. In J. T. Cacioppo & G. G. Berntson (Eds.), *Social neuroscience: Key readings* (pp. 1–17). New York: Psychology Press.

Cacioppo, J. T., Visser, P. S., & Pickett, C. L. (Eds.). (2006). *Social neuroscience: People thinking about thinking people.* Cambridge, MA: MIT Press.

Cain, K. (2006). Children's reading comprehension: The role of working memory in normal and impaired development. In S. J. Pickering (Ed.), *Working memory and education* (pp. 61–91). Burlington, MA: Elsevier.

Calkins, M. W. (1910). The teaching of elementary psychology in colleges supposed to have no laboratory. *Psychological Monographs, 124 (Whole No. 51)*, 41–53.

Campbell, R., & Sais, E. (1995). Accelerated metalinguistic (phonological) awareness in bilingual children. *British Journal of Developmental Psychology, 13*, 61–68.

Cannon, C. K., & Quinsey, V. L. (1995). The likelihood of violent behaviour: Predictions, postdictions, and hindsight bias. *Canadian Journal of Behavioral Science, 27*, 92–106.

Cannon-Bowers, J. A., & Salas, E. (Eds.). (1998). *Making decisions under stress: Implications for individuals and team training.* Washington, DC: American Psychological Association.

Caplan, P. J., & Caplan, J. B. (1999). *Thinking critically about research on sex and gender* (2nd ed.). New York: Longman.

Caramazza, A., & Miozzo, M. (1997). The relation between syntactic and phonological knowledge in lexical access: Evidence from the "tip-of-the-tongue" phenomenon. *Cognition, 69*, 309–343.

Carli, L. L. (1999). Cognitive reconstruction, hindsight, and reactions to victims and perpetrators. *Personality and Social Psychology Bulletin, 25*, 966–979.

Carlson, E. R. (1995). Evaluating the credibility of sources: A missing link in the teaching of critical thinking. *Teaching of Psychology, 22*, 39–41.

Carney, R. N., & Levin, J. R. (2001). Remembering the names of unfamiliar animals: Keywords as keys to their kingdom. *Applied Cognitive Psychology, 15*, 133–143.

Carpenter, P. A., & Just, M. A. (1999). Computational modeling of high-level cognition versus hypothesis testing. In R. J. Sternberg (Ed.), *The nature of cognition* (pp. 245–293). Cambridge, MA: MIT Press.

Carpenter, P. A., Just, M. A., & Reichle, E. D. (2000). Working memory and executive function: Evidence from neuroimaging. *Current Opinion in Neurobiology, 10*, 195–199.

Carpenter, P. A., Miyake, A., & Just, M. A. (1994). Working memory constraints in comprehension. In M. A. Gernsbacher (Ed.), *Handbook of psycholinguistics* (pp. 1075–1122). San Diego: Academic Press.

Carpenter, P. A., Miyake, A., & Just, M. A. (1995). Language comprehension: Sentence and discourse processing. *Annual Review of Psychology, 46*, 91–120.

Carpenter, S. K., & DeLosh, E. L. (2005). Application of the testing and spacing effects to name learning. *Applied Cognitive Psychology, 19,* 619–636.

Carr, W., & Roskos-Ewoldsen, B. (1999). Spatial orientation by mental transformation. *Psychological Research/Psychologische Forschung, 62,* 36–47.

Carraher, T. N., Carraher, D. W., & Schliemann, A. D. (1985). Mathematics in the streets and in schools. *British Journal of Developmental Psychology, 3,* 21–29.

Carroll, D. W. (2004). *Psychology of language* (4th ed.). Belmont, CA: Wadsworth.

Carroll, D. W. (2008). *Psychology of language* (5th ed.). Belmont, CA: Thomson Wadsworth.

Carson, S. H., & Langer, E. J. (2006). Mindfulness and self-acceptance. *Journal of Rational-Emotive and Cognitive Behavior Therapy, 24,* 29–34.

Carstensen, L. L. (2007, Winter). Growing old or living long: Take your pick. *Issues in Science and Technology,* pp. 41–50.

Cassady, J. (2004). The impact of cognitive test anxiety on text comprehension and recall in the absence of external evaluative pressure. *Applied Cognitive Psychology, 18,* 311–325.

Castelli, P., et al. (2006). Evaluating eyewitness testimony in adults and children. In I. B. Weiner & A. K. Hess (Eds.), *The handbook of forensic psychology* (3rd ed., pp. 243–304). Hoboken, NJ: Wiley.

Ceballo, R. (1999). Negotiating the life narrative: A dialogue with an African American social worker. *Psychology of Women Quarterly, 23,* 309–321.

Ceci, S. J., & Liker, J. K. (1986). A day at the races: A study of IQ, expertise, and cognitive complexity. *Journal of Experimental Psychology: General, 115,* 255–266.

Cenoz, J., & Genesee, F. (Eds.). (2001). *Trends in bilingual acquisition.* New York: John Benjamins.

Cepeda, N. J., et al. (2006). Distributed practice in verbal recall tasks: A review and quantitative synthesis. *Psychological Bulletin, 132,* 354–380.

Chafe, W., & Danielewicz, J. (1987). Properties of spoken and written language. In R. Horowitz & S. J. Samuels (Eds.), *Comprehending oral and written language* (pp. 83–113). San Diego: Academic Press.

Chalmers, D. (2007). The hard problem of consciousness. In M. Velmans & S. Schneider (Eds.), *The Blackwell companion to consciousness* (pp. 225–235). Malden, MA: Blackwell.

Chambers, D., & Reisberg, D. (1985). Can mental images be ambiguous? *Journal of Experimental Psychology: Human Perception and Performance, 11,* 317–328.

Chan, J. C. K., & McDermott, K. B. (2006). Remembering pragmatic inferences. *Applied Cognitive Psychology, 20,* 633–639.

Chapman, L. J., & Chapman, J. P. (1967). Genesis of popular but erroneous psychodiagnostic observations. *Journal of Abnormal Psychology, 72,* 193–204.

Chapman, L. J., & Chapman, J. P. (1969). Illusory correlations as an obstacle to the use of valid psychodiagnostic signs. *Journal of Abnormal Psychology, 74,* 271–280.

Chapman, P., & Underwood, G. (2000). Forgetting near-accidents: The roles of severity, culpability and experience in the poor recall of dangerous driving situations. *Applied Cognitive Psychology, 14,* 31–44.

Charness, N., Parks, D. C., & Sabel, B. A. (2001). *Communication, technology, and aging: Opportunities and challenges for the future.* New York: Springer.

Chen, E. Y. H., & Berrios, G. E. (1998). The nature of delusions: A hierarchical neural network approach. In D. J. Stein & J. Ludik (Eds.). *Neural networks and psychopathology* (pp. 167–188). Cambridge, England: Cambridge University Press.

Chen, Z., Mo, L., & Honomichl, R. (2004). Having the memory of an elephant: Long-term retrieval and the use of analogues in problem solving. *Journal of Experimental Psycholgoy: General, 133,* 415–433.

Chenoweth, N. A., & Hayes, J. R. (2001). Fluency in writing. *Written Communication, 18,* 80–98.

Cherry, C. (1953). Some experiments on the recognition of speech with one and with two ears. *Journal of the Acoustical Society of America, 25,* 975–979.

Chi, M. T. H. (1981). Knowledge development and memory performance. In M. Friedman, J. P. Das, & N. O'Connor (Eds.), *Intelligence and learning* (pp. 221–230). New York: Plenum.

Chi, M. T. H. (2000). Self-explaining expository texts: The dual processes of generating inferences and repairing mental models. In R. Glaser (Ed.), *Advances in instructional psychology* (Vol. 5, pp. 161–238). Mahwah, NJ: Erlbaum.

Chi, M. T. H. (2006). Two approaches to the study of experts' characteristics. In K. A. Ericsson, N. Charness, P. J. Feltovich, & R. R. Hoffman (Eds.), *The Cambridge handbook of expertise and expert performance* (pp. 21–30). New York: Cambridge University Press.

Chi, M. T. H., & Ohlsson, S. (2005). Complex declarative learning. In K. J. Holyoak & R. G. Morrison (Eds.), *The Cambridge handbook of thinking and reasoning* (pp. 371–399). New York: Cambridge University Press.

Chipman, S. F. (2004). Research on the women and mathematics issue: A personal case history. In A. M. Gallagher & J. C. Kaufman (Eds.), *Gender differences in mathematics: An integrative psychological approach* (pp. 1–24). New York: Cambridge University Press.

Chomsky, N. (1957). *Syntactic structures.* The Hague: Mouton.

Chomsky, N. (1965). *Aspects of the theory of syntax.* Cambridge, MA: MIT Press.

Chomsky, N. (1975). *Reflections on language.* New York: Pantheon.

Chomsky, N. (1981). *Lectures on government and binding.* Dordrecht, Netherlands: Foris.

Chomsky, N. (2000). *New horizons in the study of language and mind.* Cambridge, England: Cambridge University Press.

Chomsky, N. (2002). *On nature and language.* Cambridge, England: Cambridge University Press.

Chomsky, N. (2004). Language: Chomsky's theory. In R. L. Gregory (Ed.), *The Oxford companion to the mind* (2nd ed., pp. 511–513). New York: Oxford University Press.

Chomsky, N. (2006). *Language and mind* (3rd ed.). New York: Cambridge University Press.

Chrisley, R. (2004). Artificial intelligence (AI). In R. L. Gregory (Ed.), *The Oxford companion to the mind* (2nd ed., pp. 61–63). New York: Oxford University Press.

Christensen-Szalanski, J. J. J., et al. (1983). The effect of journal coverage on physicians' perception of risk. *Journal of Applied Psychology, 68,* 278–284.

Christoffels, I. K., & de Groot, A. M. B. (2005). Simultaneous interpreting: A cognitive perspective. In J. F. Kroll & A. M. B. de Groot (Eds.), *Handbook of bilingualism: Psycholinguistic approaches* (pp. 454–479). New York: Oxford University Press.

Christoffels, I. K., de Groot, A. M. B., & Kroll, J. F. (2006). Memory and language skills in simultaneous interpreters: The role of expertise and language proficiency. *Journal of Memory and Language, 54,* 324–345.

Christopher, G., & MacDonald, J. (2005). The impact of clinical depression on working memory. *Cognitive Neuropsychiatry, 10,* 379–399.

Chun, M. M., & Marois, R. (2002). The dark side of visual attention. *Current Opinion in Neurobiology, 12,* 184–189.

Chun, M. M., & Wolfe, J. M. (2001). Visual attention. In E. B. Goldstein (Ed.), *Blackwell handbook of perception* (pp. 272–310). Malden, MA: Blackwell.

Clark, D. A. (2005). *Intrusive thoughts in clinical disorders: Theory, research, and treatment.* New York: Guilford Press.

Clark, D. A., & O'Connor, K. (2005). Thinking is believing: Ego-dystonic intrussive thoughts in obsessive-compulsive disorder. In D. A. Clark (Ed.), *Intrusive thoughts in clinical disorders: Theory, research, and treatment* (pp. 145–174). New York: Guilford Press.

Clark, H. H. (1985). Language use and language users. In G. Lindzey & E. Aronson (Eds.), *Handbook of social psychology* (2nd ed., Vol. 2, pp. 179–231). New York: Random House.

Clark, H. H. (1994). Discourse in production. In M. A. Gernsbacher (Ed.), *Handbook of psycholinguistics* (pp. 985–1021). San Diego: Academic Press.

Clark, H. H., & Chase, W. G. (1972). On the process of comparing sentences against pictures. *Cognitive Psychology, 3,* 472–517.

Clark, H. H., & Van Der Wege, M. M. (2002). Psycholinguistics. In D. Medin (Ed.), *Stevens' handbook of experimental psychology* (3rd ed., Vol. 2, pp. 209–259). New York: Wiley.

Clark, H. H., & Wilkes-Gibbs, D. (1986). Referring as a collaborative process. *Cognition, 22,* 1–39.

Cleary, M., & Pisoni, D. B. (2001). Speech perception and spoken word recognition: Research and theory. In E. B. Goldstein (Ed.), *Blackwell handbook of perception* (pp. 499–534). Malden, MA: Blackwell.

Clement, C. A., & Falmagne, R. J. (1986). Logical reasoning, world knowledge, and mental imagery: Interconnections in cognitive processes. *Memory & Cognition, 14,* 299–307.

Clump, M. A. (2006). An active learning classroom activity for the "Cocktail Party Phenomenon." *Teaching of Psychology, 33,* 51–53.

Cohen, G. (1993). Memory and ageing. In G. M. Davies & R. H. Logie (Eds.), *Memory in everyday life* (pp. 419–446). Amsterdam: North-Holland.

Cohen, G., Conway, M. A., & Maylor, E. A. (1994). Flashbulb memories in older adults. *Psychology and Aging, 9,* 454–463.

Cohen, J. D., & Schooler, J. W. (1997). Science and sentience: Some questions regarding the scientific investigation of consciousness. In J. D. Cohen & J. W. Schooler (Eds.), *Scientific approaches to consciousness* (pp. 3–10). Mahwah, NJ: Erlbaum.

Cohen, J. D., Usher, M., & McClelland, J. C. (1998). A PDP approach to set size effects within the Stroop task: Reply to Kanne, Balota, Spieler, and Faust (1998). *Psychological Review, 105,* 188–194.

Cohen, L. B., & Cashon, C. H. (2003). Infant perception and cognition. In R. M. Lerner, M. A. Easterbrooks, & J. Mistry (Eds.), *Handbook of psychology* (Vol. 6, pp. 65–89). Hoboken, NJ: Wiley.

Cohen, M. S., Freeman, J. T., & Thompson, B. (1998). Critical thinking skills in tactical decision making: A model and training strategy. In J. A. Cannon-Bowers & E. Salas (Eds.), *Making decisions under stress: Implications for individual and team training* (pp. 155–189). Washington, DC: American Psychological Association.

Collins, M. A., & Amabile, T. M. (1999). Motivation and creativity. In R. J. Sternberg (Ed.), *Handbook of creativity* (pp. 297–312). New York: Cambridge University Press.

Collins, A. M., & Loftus, E. F. (1975). A spreading-activation theory of semantic memory. *Psychological Review, 82,* 407–428.

Collins, D. (2008). *Personal Communication.*

Collins, J. L. (1998). *Strategies for struggling writers.* New York: Guilford.

Coltheart, M. (2005). Modeling reading: The dual-route approach. In J. Snowling & C. Hulme (Eds.), *The science of reading: A handbook* (pp. 6–23). Malden, MA: Blackwell.

Comeau, L., & Genesee, F. (2001). Bilingual children's repair strategies during dyadic communication. In J. Cenoz & F. Genesee (Eds.), *Trends in bilingual acquisition* (pp. 231–256). New York: John Benjamins.

Connolly, T., Arkes, H. R., & Hammond, K. R. (Eds.). (2000). *Judgment and decision making: An interdisciplinary reader* (2nd ed.) New York: Cambridge University Press.

Connor, L. T., Dunlosky, J., & Hertzog, C. (1997). Age-related differences in absolute but not relative metamemory accuracy. *Psychology and Aging, 12,* 50–71.

Connor-Greene, P. A. (2000). Making connections: Evaluating the effectiveness of journal writing in enhancing student learning. *Teaching of Psychology, 27,* 44–46.

Conrad, R., & Hull, A. J. (1964). Information, acoustic confusion, and, memory span. *British Journal of Psychology, 55,* 432–439.

Conway, A. R. A., Cowan, N., & Bunting, M. F. (2001). The cocktail party phenomenon revisited: The importance of working memory capacity. *Psychonomic Bulletin & Review, 8,* 331–335.

Conway, A. R. A., et al. (Eds.). (2007). *Variation in working memory.* New York: Oxford University Press.

Conway, M. A. (2001). Sensory-perceptual episodic memory and its context: Autobiographical memory. *Philosophical Transactions of the Royal Society of London, 356,* 1375–1384.

Conway, M. A., & Fthenaki, A. (2000). Disruption and loss of autobiographical memory. In F. Boller & J. Grafman (Eds.), *Handbook of neuropsychology* (2nd ed., Vol. 2, pp. 281–312). Amsterdam: Elsevier.

Cook, G. I., Marsh, R. L., & Hicks, J. L. (2005). Associating a time-based prospective memory task with an expected context can improve or impair intention completion. *Applied Cognitive Psychology, 19,* 345–360.

Cooper, L. A., & Lang, J. M. (1996). Imagery and visual-spatial representations. In E. L. Bjork & R. A. Bjork (Eds.), *Memory* (pp. 129–164). San Diego: Academic Press.

Corballis, M. C. (2006). Language. In K. Pawlik & G. d'Ydewalle (Eds.), *Psychological concepts: An international historical perspective* (pp. 197–221). New York: Psychology Press.

Coren, S. (2003). Sensation and perception. In D. F. Freedheim (Ed.), *Handbook of psychology* (Vol. 1: The history of psychology, pp. 85–108). Hoboken, NJ: Wiley.

Coren, S., Ward, L. M., & Enns, J. T. (2004). *Sensation and perception* (6th ed.). Hoboken, NJ: Wiley.

Corkin, S. (1984). Lasting consequences of bilateral medial temporal lobe excision. *Neuropsychologia, 6,* 255–265.

Cornoldi, C. (1998). The impact of metacognitive reflection on cognitive control. In G. Mazzoni & T. O. Nelson (Eds.), *Metacognition and cognitive neuropsychology* (pp. 139–159). Mahwah, NJ: Erlbaum.

Cornoldi, C., & Vecchi, T. (2003). *Visuo-spatial working memory and individual differences.* New York: Psychology Press.

Correll, J., Park, B., Judd, C. M., & Wittenbrink, B. (2002). The police officer's dilemma: Using ethnicity to disambiguate potentially threatening individuals. *Journal of Personality and Social Psychology, 83,* 1314–1329.

Cosmides, L. (1989). The logic of social exchange: Has natural selection shaped how humans reason? Studies with the Wason selection task. *Cognition, 31,* 187–276.

Cosmides, L., & Tooby, J. (1995). From function to structure: The role of evolutionary biology and computational theories in cognitive neuroscience. In M. Gazzaniga (Ed.), *The cognitive neurosciences* (pp. 1199–1210). Cambridge, MA: MIT Press.

Cosmides, L., & Tooby, J. (2006). Evolutionary psychology, moral heuristics, and the law. In G. Gigerenzer & C. Engel (Eds.), *Heuristics and the law* (pp. 175–205). Cambridge, MA: MIT Press.

Cottam, M., Dietz-Uhler, B., Mastors, E., & Preston, T. (2004). *Introduction to political psychology.* Mahwah, NJ: Erlbaum.

Cowan, N. (2001). The magical number 4 in short-term memory: A reconsideration of mental storage capacity. *Behavioral and Brain Sciences, 24,* 87–185.

Cowan, N. (2003). Working-memory capacity limits in a theoretical context. In C. Izawa & N. Ohta (Eds.), *Human learning and memory: Advances in theory and application.* Mahwah, NJ: Erlbaum.

Cowan, N. (2005). *Working memory capacity.* New York: Psychology Press.

Cowan, N., Chen, Z., & Rouder, J. N. (2004). Constant capacity in an immediate serial-recall task: A logical sequel to Miller (1956). *Psychological Society, 15,* 634–640.

Cowan, N., Johnson, T. D., & Saults, J. S. (2005). Capacity limits in list item recognition: Evidence from proactive interference. *Memory, 13,* 293–299.

Cowan, N., Morey, C. C., Chen, Z., & Bunting, M. F. (2007). What do estimates of working memory capacity tell us? In N. Osaka & R. Logie (Eds), *Working memory: Behavioural & neural correlates.* New York: Oxford University Press.

Cowan, N., & Wood, N. L. (1997). Constraints on awareness, attention, processing, and memory: Some recent investigations with ignored speech. *Consciousness and Cognition, 6,* 182–203.

Coward, L. A., & Sun, R. (2004). Criteria for an effective theory of consciousness and some preliminary attempts. *Consciousness and Cognition, 13,* 268–301.

Cox, W. M., Fadardi, J. S., & Pothos, E. M. (2006). The addiction-Stroop test: Theoretical considerations and procedural recommendations. *Psychological Bulletin, 132,* 443–476.

Coyle, T. R., & Bjorklund, D. F. (1997). Age differences in, and consequences of, multiple- and variable-strategy use on a multitrial sort-recall task. *Developmental Psychology, 33,* 372–380.

Craik, F. I. M. (1990). Changes in memory with normal aging: A functional view. In R. J. Wurtman (Ed.), Advances in neurology: Vol. 51. *Alzheimer's disease* (pp. 201–205). New York: Raven.

Craik, F. I. M. (1999). Levels of encoding and retrieval. In B. H. Challis & B. M. Velichkovsky (Eds.), *Stratification in cognition and consciousness* (pp. 97–104). Philadelphia: John Benjamins.

Craik, F. I. M. (2006). Age-related changes in human memory: Practical consequences. In L.-G. Nilsson & N. Ohta (Eds.), *Memory and society: Psychological perspectives* (pp. 175–191). New York: Psychology Press.

Craik, F. I. M., & Lockhart, R. S. (1972). Levels of processing: A framework for memory research. *Journal of Verbal Learning and Verbal Behavior, 11,* 671–684.

Craik, F. I. M., Anderson, N. D., Kerr, S. A., & Li, K. Z. H. (1995). Memory changes in normal ageing. In A. D. Baddeley, B. A. Wilson, & F. N. Watts (Eds.), *Handbook of memory disorders* (pp. 211–241). Chichester, England: Wiley.

Craik, F. I. M., & Tulving, E. (1975). Depth of processing and the retention of words in episodic memory. *Journal of Experimental Psychology: General, 104,* 268–294.

Craik, F. I. M., et al. (1999). In search of the self: A positron emission tomography study. *Psychological Science, 10,* 26–34.

Cranberg, L. D., & Albert, M. L. (1988). The chess mind. In L. K. Obler & D. Fein (Eds.), *The exceptional brain: Neuropsychology of talent and special abilities* (pp. 156–190). New York: Guilford.

Craver-Lemley, C., Arterberry, M. E., & Reeves, A. (1999). "Illusory" illusory conjunctions. The conjoining of features of visual and imagined stimuli. Journal of Experimental Psychology: *Human Perception and Performance, 25,* 1036–1049.

Craver-Lemley, C., & Reeves, A. (1987). Visual imagery selectively reduces vernier acuity. *Perception, 16,* 599–614.

Craver-Lemley, C., & Reeves, A. (1992). How visual imagery interferes with vision. *Psychological Review, 99,* 633–649.

Cromdal, J. (1999). Childhood bilingualism and metalinguistic skills: Analysis and control in young Swedish-English bilinguals. *Applied Psycholinguistics, 20,* 1–20.

Crozet, J., & Claire, T. (1998). Extending the concept of stereotype threat to social class: The intellectual underperformance of students from low socioeconomic backgrounds. *Personality and Social Psychology Bulletin, 24,* 588–594.

Csikszentmihalyi, M. (1996). *Creativity: Flow and the psychology of discovery and invention.* New York: HarperCollins.

Cuddy, A. J. C., & Fiske, S. T. (2002). Doddering but dear: Process, content, and function in stereotyping of older persons. In T. D. Nelson (Ed.), *Ageism: Stereotyping and prejudice against older persons* (pp. 3–26). Cambridge, MA: MIT Press.

Cuevas, K., Rovee-Collier, C., & Learmonth, A. E. (2006). Infants form associations between memory representations of stimuli that are absent. *Psychological Science, 17,* 543–549.

Cummings, L. (2005). *Pragmatics: A multidisciplinary perspective.* Mahwah, NJ: New Jersey.

Cummins, D. D., Lubart, T., Alksnis, O., & Rist, R. (1991). Conditional reasoning and causation. *Memory & Cognition, 19,* 274–282.

Cutting, J. C., & Ferreira, V. S. (1999). Semantic and phonological information flow in the production lexicon. *Journal of Experimental Psychology: Learning, Memory, and Cognition, 25,* 318–344.

Dahan, D., & Magnuson, J. S. (2006). Spoken word recognition. In M. J. Traxler & M. A. Gernsbacher (F.ds.), *Handbook of psycholinguistics* (2nd ed., pp. 249–283). Amsterdam: Elsevier.

Damian, M. F., & Martin, R. C. (1999). Semantic and phonological codes interact in a single word production. *Journal of Experimental Psychology: Learning, Memory, and Cognition, 25,* 345–361.

Daneman, M. F., & Hannon, B. (2001). Using working memory theory to investigate the construct validity of multiple-choice reading comprehension tests such as the SAT. *Journal of Experimental Psychology: General, 130,* 208–223.

Daneman, M. F., & Stainton, M. (1993). The generation effect in reading and proofreading. *Reading and Writing: An Interdisciplinary Journal, 5,* 297–313.

D'Argembeau, A., Comblain, C., & Van Der Linden, M. (2003). Phenomenal characteristics of autobiographical memories for positive, negative, and neutral events. *Applied Cognitive Psychology, 17,* 281–294.

Darwin, C. J., Turvey, M. T., & Crowder, R. G. (1972). An auditory analogue of the Sperling partial report procedure: Evidence for brief auditory storage. *Cognitive Psychology, 3,* 255–267.

Davelaar, E. J., Haarmann, H. J., Goshen-Gottstein, Y., & Usher, M. (2006). Semantic similarity dissociates short-from long-term effects: Testing a neurocomputational model of list memory. *Memory & Cognition, 34,* 323–334.

Davelaar, E. J., et al. (2005). The demise of short-term memory revisited: Empirical and computational investigations of recency effects. *Psychological Review, 112,* 3–42.

Davidson, D. (1994). Recognition and recall of irrelevant and interruptive atypical actions in script-based stories. *Journal of Memory and Language, 33,* 757–775.

Davidson, D. (2006). Memory for bizarre and other unusual events: Evidence from script research. In R. R. Hunt & J. B. Worthen (Eds.), Distinctiveness and memory (pp. 157–179). New York: Oxford University Press.

Davidson, J. E. (1995). The suddenness of insight. In R. J. Sternberg & J. E. Davidson (Eds.), *The nature of insight* (pp. 125–155). Cambridge, MA: MIT Press.

Davidson, J. E. (2003). Noninsights about insightful problem solving. In J. E. Davidson & R. J. Sternberg (Eds.), *The psychology of problem solving* (pp. 149–175). New York: Cambridge University Press.

Davidson, J. E., Deuser, R., & Sternberg, R. J. (1994). The role of metacognition in problem solving. In J. Metcalfe & A. P. Shimamura (Eds.), *Metacognition: Knowing about knowing* (pp. 207–226). Cambridge, MA: MIT Press.

Davidson, J. E., & Sternberg, R. J. (1998). Smart problem solving: How metacognition helps. In D. J. Hacker, J. Dunlosky, & A. C. Graesser (Eds.), *Metacognition in educational theory and practice* (pp. 47–65). Mahwah, NJ: Erlbaum.

Davidson, J. E., & Sternberg, R. J. (Eds.). (2003). *The psychology of problem solving.* New York: Cambridge University Press.

Davies, M. (1999). Consciousness. In R. A. Wilson & F. C. Keil (Eds.), *The MIT encyclopedia of the cognitive sciences* (pp. 190–193). Cambridge, MA: MIT Press.

Davies, S. P. (2005). Planning and problem solving in well-defined domains. In R. Morris & G. Ward (Eds.), *The cognitive psychology of planning* (pp. 35–51). Hove, UK: Psychology Press.

Davis, D., & Friedman, R. D. (2007). Memory for conversation: The orphan child of witness memory researchers. In M. P. Toglia, J. D. Read, D. F. Ross, & R. C. L. Lindsay (Eds.), *Handbook of eyewitness psychology* (Vol. 1, pp. 3–52). Mahwah, NJ: Erlbaum.

Davis, D., & Loftus, E. F. (2007). Internal and external sources of misinformation in adult witness memory. In M. P. Toglia, J. D. Read, D. F. Ross, & R. C. L. Lindsay (Eds.), *Handbook of eyewitness psychology* (Vol. 1, pp. 195–237). Mahwah, NJ: Erlbaum.

Davis, M. H., Marslen-Wilson, W. D., & Gaskell, M. G. (2002). Leading up the lexical garden path: Segmentation and ambiguity in spoken word recognition. *Journal of Experimental Psychology: Human Perception and Performance, 28,* 218–244.

Dawes, R. M. (1998). Behavioral decision making and judgment. In D. T. Gilbert, S. T. Fiske, & G. Lindzey (Eds.), *The handbook of social psychology* (4th ed., Vol. 1, pp. 497–548). Boston: McGraw-Hill.

De Beni, R., & Moe, A. (2003). Presentation modality effects in studying passages. Are mental images always effective? *Applied Cognitive Psychology, 17,* 309–324.

de Bot, K., & Makoni, S. (2005). *Language and aging in multilingual contexts.* Clevedon, England: Multilingual Matters.

de Boysson-Bardies, B. (1999). *How language comes to children: From birth to two years.* Cambridge, MA: MIT Press.

Defeldre, A.-C. (2005). Inadvertent plagiarism in everyday life. *Applied Cognitive Psychology, 19,* 1033–1040.

Dehaene, S. (Ed.). (2001). *The cognitive neuroscience of consciousness.* Cambridge, MA: MIT Press.

Dehaene, S., & Naccache, L. (2001). Towards a cognitive neuroscience of consciousness: Basic evidence and a workspace framework. In S. Dehaene (Ed.), *The cognitive neuroscience of consciousness* (pp. 1–37). Cambridge, MA: MIT Press.

Dehaene, S., et al. (2006). Conscious, preconscious, and subliminal processing: A testable taxonomy. *Trends in Cognitive Sciences, 10,* 204–211.

DeHart, G. B. (1989). *Personal communication.*

DeHart, G. B., Sroufe, L. A., & Cooper, R. G. (2004). *Child development: Its nature and course* (5th ed.). New York: McGraw Hill.

Dehn, D. M., & Erdfelder, E. (1998). What kind of bias is hindsight bias? *Psychological Research, 61,* 735–746.

De Jong, G. (1982). Skimming stories in real time: An experiment in integrated understanding. In W. Lehnert & M. H. Ringle (Eds.), *Natural language processing.* Hillsdale, NJ: Erlbaum.

De Jong, P. F. (2006). Understanding normal and impaired reading development: A working memory perspective. In S. J. Pickering (Ed.), *Working memory and education* (pp. 33–60). Burlington, MA: Elsevier.

DeKeyser, R., & Larson-Hall, J. (2005). What does the critical period really mean? In Kroll, J. F., & de Groot, A. M. (Eds.), *Handbook of bilingualism: Psycholinguistic approaches* (pp. 88–108). New York: Oxford University Press.

Delaney, P. F., Ericsson, K. A., & Knowles, M. E. (2004). Immediate and sustained effects of planning in a problem-solving task. *Journal of Experimental Psychology: Learning, Memory, and Cognition, 30,* 1219–1234.

Dell, G. S. (1986). A spreading-activation theory of retrieval in sentence production. *Psychological Review, 93,* 283–321.

Dell, G. S. (1995). Speaking and misspeaking. In L. R. Gleitman & M. Liberman (Eds.), *Language* (pp. 183–208). Cambridge, MA: MIT Press.

Dell, G. S. (2005). Language production, lexical access, and aphasia. In G. Houghton (Ed.), *Connectionist models in cognitive psychology* (pp. 373–401). New York: Psychology Press.

Dell, G. S., Burger, L. K., & Svec, W. R. (1997). Language production and serial order: A functional analysis and a model. *Psychological Review, 104,* 123–147.

Dell, G. S., Reed, K. D., Adams, D. R., & Meyer, A. S. (2000). Speech errors, phonotactic constraints, and implicit learning: A study of the role of experience in language production. *Journal of Experimental Psychology: Learning, Memory, and Cognition, 26,* 1355–1367.

Dell, G. S., Warker, J. A., & Whalen, C. A. (2008). Speech errors and the implicit learning of phonological sequences. In E. Morsella, J. A. Bargh, & P. M. Gollwitzer (Eds.), *The psychology of action.* Oxford University Press.

Dell, G. S., et al. (1997). Lexical access in aphasic and nonaphasic speakers. *Psychological Review, 104,* 801–838.

Denis, M., & Kosslyn, S. M. (1999a). Does the window *really* need to be washed? More on the mental scanning paradigm. *Cahiers de Psychologie Cognitive, 18,* 593–616.

Denis, M., & Kosslyn, S. M. (1999b). Scanning visual mental images: A window on the mind. *Cahiers de Psychologie Cognitive, 18,* 409–465.

Denis, M., Mellet, E., & Kosslyn, S. M. (2004). Neuroimaging of mental imagery: An introduction. *European Journal of Cognitive Psychology, 16,* 625–630.

DePrince, A. P., & Freyd, J. J. (2004). Forgetting trauma stimuli. *Psychological Science, 15,* 488–492.

D'Esposito, M., Zarahn, E., & Aguirre, G. K. (1999). Event-related functional MRI: Implications for cognitive psychology. *Psychological Bulletin, 125,* 155–164.

Deubel, H., O'Regan, J. K., & Radach, R. (2000). Attention, information processing, and eye movement control. In A. Kennedy, R. Radach, D. Heller, & J. Pyne (Eds.), *Reading as a perceptual process* (pp. 355–374). Amsterdam: Elsevier.

Deutsch, M. (2005). Commentary on morality, decision making, and collateral casualties. *Peace and Conflict: Journal of Peace Psychology, 11,* 63–66.

de Villiers, J. G., & de Villiers, P. A. (1999). Language development. In M. H. Bornstein & M. E. Lamb

(Eds.), *Developmental psychology: An advanced textbook* (4th ed., pp. 313–373). Mahwah, NJ: Erlbaum.

Devlin, A. S. (2001). *Mind and maze: Spatial cognition and environmental behavior*. Westport, CT: Praeger.

deWinstanley, P. A., & Bjork, R. A. (2002). Successful lecturing: Presenting information in ways that engage effective processing. In D. F. Halpern & M. D. Hakel (Eds.), *Applying the science of learning to university teaching and beyond* (pp. 19–31). San Francisco: Jossey-Bass.

Diana, R. A., & Reder, L. M. (2004). Visual and verbal metacognition: Are they really different? In D. T. Levin (Ed.), *Thinking and seeing: Visual metacognition in adults and children* (pp. 187–201). Cambridge, MA: MIT Press.

Diaz, R. M. (1985). Bilingual cognitive development: Addressing three gaps in current research. *Child Development, 56*, 1376–1388.

Dick, F., et al. (2001). Language deficits, localization, and grammar: Evidence for a distributive model of language breakdown in aphasic patients and neurologically intact individuals. *Psychological Review, 108*, 759–788.

Dickinson, S. J. (1999). Object representation and recognition. In E. Lepore & Z. Pylyshyn (Eds.), *What is cognitive science?* (pp. 172–207). Malden, MA: Blackwell.

Diehl, R. L., Lotto, A. J., & Holt, L. L.(2004). Speech perception. *Annual Review of Psychology, 55*, 149–179.

Diwadkar, V. A., Carpenter, P. A., & Just, M. A. (2000). Collaborative activity between parietal and dorso-lateral prefrontal cortex in dynamic spatial working memory revealed by fMRI. *NeuroImage, 12*, 85–99.

Dixon, R. A., & Cohen, A. L. (2003). Cognitive development in adulthood. In R. M. Lerner, M. A. Easterbrooks, & J. Mistry (Eds.), *Handbook of psychology* (Vol. 6, pp. 443–461). Hoboken, NJ: Wiley.

Djordjevic, J., Zatorre, R. J., & Jones-Cotman, M. (2004). The mind's nose: Effects of odor and visual imagery on odor detection. *Psychological Science, 15*, 143–148.

Dodd, B., & Campbell, R. (1986). *Hearing by eye: The psychology of lip reading*. London: Erlbaum.

Dodson, C. S., Bawa, S., & Krueger, L. F. (2007). Aging, metamemory, and high-confidence errors: A misrecollection account. *Psychology and Aging, 22*, 122–133.

Dominowski, R. L. (2002). *Teaching undergraduates*. Mahwah, NJ: Erlbaum.

Donaldson, M. (2004). Language: Learning word meanings. In R. L. Gregory (Ed.), *The Oxford companion to the mind* (2nd ed., pp. 513–515). New York: Oxford University Press.

Donderi, D. C. (2006). Visual complexity: A review. *Psychological Bulletin, 132*, 73–97.

Döpke, S. (Ed.). (2001). *Cross-linguistic structures in simultaneous bilingualism*. New York: John Benjamins.

Douglass, A. B., & Steblay, N. (2006). Memory distortion in eyewitnesses: A meta-analysis of the post-identification feedback effect. *Applied Cognitive Psychology, 20*, 859–869.

Dovidio, J. F., Glick, P., & Rudman, L. A. (Eds.). (2005). *On the nature of prejudice: Fifty years after Allport*. Malden, MA: Blackwell.

Dowker, A. (2005). *Individual differences in arithmetic: Implications for psychology, neuroscience and education*. Hove, UK: Psychology Press.

Drieghe, D., Brysbaert, M., Desmet, T., & DeBaecke, C. (2004). Word skipping in reading: On the interplay of linguistic and visual factors. In R. Radach, A. Kennedy, & K. Rayner (Eds.), *Eye movements and information processing during reading* (pp. 79–103). Hove, UK: Psychology Press.

Dror, I. E., & Kosslyn, S. M. (1994). Mental imagery and aging. *Psychology and Aging, 9*, 90–102.

Dudukovic, N. M., Marsh, E. J., & Tversky, B. (2004). Telling a story or telling it straight: The effects of entertaining versus accurate retellings on memory. *Applied Cognitive Psychology, 18*, 125–143.

Dunbar, K. (1998). Problem solving. In W. Bechtel & G. Graham (Eds.), *A companion to cognitive science* (pp. 289–298). Malden, MA: Blackwell.

Duncan, J. (1999). Attention. In R. A. Wilson & F. C. Keil (Eds.), *The MIT encyclopedia of the cognitive sciences* (pp. 39–41). Cambridge, MA: MIT Press.

Duncan, J., et al. (2000). A neural basis for general intelligence. *Science, 289*, 457–460.

Duncker, K. (1945). On problem solving. *Psychological Monographs, 58* (Whole No. 270).

Dunlosky, J., & Hertzog, C. (1997). Older and younger adults use a functionally identical algorithm to select items for restudy during multitrial learning. *Journal of Gerontology: Psychological Sciences, 52B*, P178–P186.

Dunlosky, J., & Hertzog, C. (1998). Aging and deficits in associative memory: What is the role of strategy production? *Psychology and Aging, 13*, 597–607.

Dunlosky, J., Rawson, K. A., & McDonald, S. L. et al. (2002). Influence of practice tests on the accuracy of predicting memory performance for paired associates, sentences, and text material. In T. J. Perfect & B. L. Schwartz (Eds.), *Applied metacognition* (pp. 68–92). Cambridge, UK: Cambridge University Press.

Dunlosky, J., Rawson, K. A., & Middleton, E. L. (2005). What constrains the accuracy of metacomprehension judgments? Testing the transfer-appropriate-monitoring and accessibility hypotheses. *Journal of Memory and Language, 52*, 551–565.

Dunn, J., & Kendrick, C. (1982). The speech of two- and three-year-olds to infant siblings: "Baby talk" and the context of communication. *Journal of Child Language, 9*, 579–595.

Dunning, D. (2005). *Self-insight: Roadblocks and detours on the path to knowing thyself.* New York: Psychology Press.

Dunning, D., Johnson, K., Ehrlinger, J., & Kruger, J. (2003). Why people fail to recognize their own incompetence. *Current Directions in Psychological Science, 12*, 83–87.

Dunning, D., & Sherman, D. A. (1997). Stereotypes and tacit inference. *Journal of Personality and Social Psychology, 73*, 459–471.

Dweck, C. S. (2006). *Mindset: The new psychology of success.* New York: Random House.

Dysart, J. E., & Lindsay, R. C. L. (2007). The effects of delay on eyewitness identification accuracy: Should we be concerned? In R. C. L. Lindsay, D. F. Ross, J. D. Read, & M. P. Toglia (Eds.), *Handbook of eyewitness psychology* (Vol. 2, pp. 361–376). Mahwah, NJ: Erlbaum.

D'Zurilla, T. J, & Maydeu-Olivares, A. (2004). Social problem solving: Theory and assessment. In E. C. Chang, T. J. D'Zurilla, & L. J. Sanna (Eds.), *Social problem solving: Theory, research, and training* (pp. 11–27). Washington, DC: American Psychological Association.

Eagly, A. H. (2001). Social role theory of sex differences and similarities. In J. Worell (Ed.), *Encyclopedia of women and gender* (pp. 1069–1078). San Diego: Academic Press.

Eagly, A. H., & Diekman, A. B. (2005). What is the problem? Prejudice as an attitude-in-context. In J. F. Dovidio, P. Glick, & L. A. Rudman (Eds.), *On the nature of prejudice: Fifty years after Allport* (pp. 19–35). Malden, MA: Blackwell.

Easton, A., & Emery, N. J. (Eds.). (2005). *The cognitive neuroscience of social behaviour* (pp. 1–16). New York: Psychology Press.

Economou, A., Simos, P. G., & Papanicolaou, A. C. (2006). Age-related memory decline. In A. C. Papanicolaou (Ed.), *The amnesias: A clinical textbook of memory disorders* (pp. 57–74). New York: Oxford University Press.

Edelman, G. M. (2005). *Wider than the sky: The phenomenal gift of consciousness.* New Haven: Yale University Press.

Edwards, D. (1997). *Discourse and cognition.* London: Sage.

Ehrlich, M. (1998). Metacognitive monitoring in the processing of anaphoric devices in skilled and less skilled comprehenders. In C. Cornoldi & J. Oakhill (Eds.), *Reading comprehension difficulties: Processes and interventions* (pp. 221–249). Mahwah, NJ: Erlbaum.

Eich, E. (1995). Mood as a mediator of place dependent memory. *Journal of Experimental Psychology: General, 124*, 293–308.

Eimas, P. D., Siqueland, E. R., Jusczyk, P., & Vigorito, J. (1971). Speech perception in infants. *Science, 171*, 303–306.

Einstein, G. O., & McDaniel, M. A. (1996). Retrieval processes in prospective memory: Theoretical approaches and some new empirical findings. In M. Brandimonte, G. O. Einstein, & M. A. McDaniel (Eds.), *Prospective memory: Theory and applications* (pp. 115–141). Mahwah, NJ: Erlbaum.

Einstein, G. O., & McDaniel, M. A. (2004). *Memory fitness: A guide for successful aging.* New Haven, CT: Yale University Press.

Einstein, G. O., et al. (2003). Forgetting of intentions in demanding situations is rapid. *Journal of Experimental Psychology: Applied, 9*, 147–162.

Eisen, M. L., Quas, J. A., & Goodman, G. S. (Eds.). (2002). *Memory and suggestibility in the forensic interview.* Mahwah, NJ: Erlbaum.

Eisenberger, R., & Rhoades, L. (2001). Incremental effects of rewards on creativity. *Journal of Personality and Social Psychology, 81*, 728–741.

Eliott, A. J., & Mapes, R. R. (2002). Enhancing the yield. [Review of the book *Intrinsic and extrinsic motivation: The search for optimal motivation and performance*]. *Contemporary Psychology, 47*, 200–202.

Elliott, E. M., & Cowan, N. (2001). Habituation to auditory distractors in a cross-modal, color-word interference task. *Journal of Experimental Psychology: Learning, Memory, and Cognition, 27*, 654–667.

Emery, N. J., & Easton, A. (2005). Introduction: What is social cognitive neuroscience (SCN)? In A. Easton & N. J. Emery (Eds.), *The cognitive neuroscience of social behaviour* (pp. 1–16). New York: Psychology Press.

Emmorey, K., Klima, E., & Hickok, G. (1998). Mental rotation within linguistic and non-linguistic domains in users of American Sign Language. *Cognition, 68*, 221–246.

Endsley, M. R. (2006). Expertise and situation awareness. In K. A. Ericsson, N. Charness, P. J. Feltovich, & R. R. Hoffman (Eds.), *The Cambridge handbook of expertise and expert performance* (pp. 633–651). New York: Cambridge University Press.

Engbert, R., Nuthman, A., Richter, E. M., & Kliegl, R. (2005). SWIFT: A dynamic model of saccade generation during reading. *Psychological Review, 112,* 777–813.

Engelkamp, J. (1998). *Memory for actions.* Hove, UK: Psychology Press.

Engle, R. W. (2002). Working memory capacity as executive attention. *Current Directions in Psychological Science, 11,* 19–23.

Engle, R. W., & Conway, A. R. A. (1998). Working memory and comprehension. In R. H. Logie & K. J. Gilhooly (Eds.), *Working memory and thinking* (pp. 67–91). Hove, UK: Psychology Press.

Engle, R. W., & Kane, M. J. (2004). Executive attention, working memory capacity, and a two-factor theory of cognitive control. *Psychology of Learning and Motivation, 44,* 145–199.

Engle, R. W., & Oransky, N. (1999). Multi-store versus dynamic models of temporary storage in memory. In R. J. Sternberg (Ed.), *The nature of cognition* (pp. 515–555). Cambridge, MA: MIT Press.

Englich, B., & Mussweiler, T. (2001). Sentencing under uncertainty: Anchoring effects in the courtroom. *Journal of Applied Social Psychology, 31,* 1535–1551.

Epstein, R. (2004). Watson, John Broadus. In R. L. Gregory (Ed.), *The Oxford companion to the mind* (2nd ed., pp. 942–943). New York: Oxford University Press.

Erber, J. T. (2005). *Aging and older adulthood.* Belmont, CA: Thomson Wadsworth.

Erickson, M. A., & Kruschke, J. K. (1998). Rules and exemplars in category learning. *Journal of Experimental Psychology: General, 127,* 107–140.

Erickson, M. A., & Kruschke, J. K. (2002). Rule-based extrapolation in perceptual categorization. *Psychonomic Bulletin & Review, 9,* 160–168.

Ericsson, K. A. (2003a). Exceptional memorizers: Made, not born. *TRENDS in Cognitive Psychology, 7,* 233–235.

Ericsson, K. A. (2003b). The search for general abilities and basic capacities: Theoretical implications from the modifiability and complexity of mechanisms mediating expert performance. In R. J. Sternberg & E. L. Grigorenko (Eds.), *The psychology of abilities, competencies, and expertise* (pp. 93–125). New York: Cambridge University Press.

Ericsson, K. A. (2003c). Valid and non-reactive verbalization of thoughts during performance of tasks. *Journal of Consciousness Studies, 10,* 1–8.

Ericsson, K. A. (2004). Deliberate practice and the acquisition and maintenance of expert performance in medicine and related domains, *Academic Medicine, 79,* S70–S81.

Ericsson, K. A. (2006). An introduction to *Cambridge handbook of expertise and expert performance:* Its development, organization and content. In K.A. Ericsson, N. Charness, P. J. Feltovich, & R. R. Hoffman (Eds.), *The Cambridge handbook of expertise and performance* (pp. 3–19). New York: Cambridge University Press.

Ericsson, K. A., Charness, N., Feltovich, P. J., & Hoffman, R. R. (2006). *The Cambridge handbook of expertise and expert performance.* New York: Cambridge University Press.

Ericsson, K. A., Delaney, P. F., Weaver, G., & Mahadevan, R. (2004). Uncovering the structure of a memorist's "basic" memory capacity." *Cognitive Psychology, 49,* 191–237.

Ericsson, K. A., & Kintsch, W. (1995). Long-term working memory. *Psychological Review, 102,* 211–245.

Ericsson, K. A., & Lehmann, A. C. (1996). Expert and exceptional performance: Evidence of maximal adaptation to task constraints. *Annual Review of Psychology, 47,* 273–305.

Esgate, A., & Groome, D. (2005). *An introduction to applied cognitive psychology.* Hove, UK: Psychology Press.

Evans, J. St. B. T. (2000). What could and could not be a strategy in reasoning. In W. Schaeken, G. DeVooght, A. Vandierendonck, & G. d'Ydewalle (Eds.), *Deductive reasoning and strategies* (pp. 1–22). Mahwah, NJ: Erlbaum.

Evans, J. St. B. T. (2002). Logic and human reasoning: An assessment of the deduction paradigm. *Psychological Bulletin, 128,* 978–996.

Evans, J. St. B. T. (2004). Biases in deductive reasoning. In R. F. Pohl (Eds.), *Cognitive illusions: A handbook on fallacies and biases in thinking, judgement, and memory* (pp. 127–144). Hove, UK: Psychology Press.

Evans, J. St. B. T. (2005). Insight and self-insight in reasoning and decision making. In V. Girotto & P. N. Johnson-Laird (Eds.), *The shape of reason: Essays in honour of Paolo Legrenzi* (pp. 27–47). Hove, UK: Psychology Press.

Evans, J. St. B. T. (2006). The heuristic-analytic theory of reasoning: Extension and evaluation. *Psychonomic Bulletin & Review, 13,* 378–395.

Evans, J. St. B. T., & Feeney, A. (2004). The role of prior belief in reasoning. In J. P. Leighton & R. J. Sternberg (Eds.), *The nature of reasoning* (pp. 78–102). New York: Cambridge University Press.

Evans, J. St. B. T., & Over, D. E. (1996). *Rationality and reasoning*. Hove, UK: Psychology Press.

Evans, V., & Green, M. (2006). *Cognitive linguistics: An introduction*. Mahwah, NJ: Erlbaum.

Eysenck, M. W., & Keane, M. T. (2005). *Cognitive psychology: A student's handbook*. Hove, UK: Psychology Press.

Fabiani, M., & Wee, E. (2001). Age-related changes in working memory and frontal lobe function: A review. In C. A. Nelson & M. Luciana (Eds.), *Handbook of developmental cognitive neuroscience* (pp. 473–488). Cambridge, MA: MIT Press.

Faigley, L., & Miller, T. P. (1982). What we learn from writing on the job. *College English, 44,* 557–559.

Falsetti, S. A., Monnier, J., & Resnick, H. S. (2005). Intrusive thoughts in postraumatic stress disorder. In D. A. Clark (Ed.), *Intrusive thoughts in clinical disorders: Theory, research, and treatment* (pp. 30–53). New York: Guilford Press.

Fan, J., et al. (2002). Testing the efficiency and independence of attentional networks. *Journal of Cognitive Neuroscience, 14,* 340–347.

Farah, M. J. (2000a). *The cognitive neuroscience of vision*. Malden, MA: Blackwell.

Farah, M. J. (2000b). The neural bases of mental imagery. In M. S. Gazzaniga (Ed.), *The new cognitive neurosciences* (2nd ed., pp. 961–974). Cambridge, MA: MIT Press.

Farah, M. J. (2001). Consciousness. In B. Rapp (Ed.), *The handbook of cognitive neuropsychology* (pp. 159–182). Philadelphia: Psychology Press.

Farah, M. J. (2002). Emerging ethical issues in neuroscience. *Nature Neuroscience, 5, 1123.*

Farah, M. J. (2004). *Visual agnosia* (2nd ed.). Cambridge, MA: MIT Press.

Farrimond, S., Knight, R. G., & Titov, N. (2006). The effects of aging on remembering intentions: Performance on a simulated shopping task. *Applied Cognitive Psychology, 20,* 533–555.

Fazio, R. H., & Olson, M. A. (2003). Implicit measures in social cognition research: Their meaning and use. *Annual Review of Psychology, 54,* 297–327.

Fehr, B. (2005). The role of prototypes in interpersonal cognition. In M. W. Baldwin (Ed.), *Interpersonal cognition* (pp. 180–205). New York: Guilford.

Feist, G. J. (2004). The evolved fluid specificity of human creative talent. In R. J. Sternberg, E. L. Grigorenko, & J. L. Singer (Eds.), *Creativity: From potential to realization* (pp. 57–82). Washington, DC: American Psychological Association.

Feist, G. J. (2006). Why the studies of science need a psychology of science. *Review of General Psychology 10,* 183–187.

Feldman, D. H., Csikszentmihalyi, M., & Gardner, H. (1994). *Changing the world: A framework for the study of creativity*. Westport, CT: Praeger.

Feltovich, P. J., Prietula, M. J., & Ericsson, K. A. (2006). Studies of expertise from psychological perspectives. In K. A. Ericsson, N. Charness, P. J. Feltovich, & R. R. Hoffman (Eds.), *The Cambridge handbook of expertise and expert performance* (pp. 41–67). New York: Cambridge University Press.

Ferguson, E. L., & Hegarty, M. (1994). Properties of cognitive maps constructed from texts. *Memory & Cognition, 22,* 455–473.

Fernald, A., & Marchman, V. A. (2006). Language learning in infancy. In M. J. Traxler & M. A. Gernsbacher (Eds.), *Handbook of psycholinguistics* (2nd ed., pp. 1027–1071). Amsterdam: Elsevier.

Fernald, A., et al. (1998). Rapid gains in speed of verbal processing by infants in the 2nd year. *Psychological Science, 9,* 228–231.

Fernandez-Duque, D., & Johnson, M. L. (2002). Cause and effect theories of attention: The role of conceptual metaphors. *Review of General Psychology, 6,* 153–165.

Ferreira, F., Bailey, G. D., & Ferraro, V. (2002). Good-enough representation in language comprehension. *Current Directions in Psychological Science, 11,* 11–15.

Ferreira, F., & Engelhardt, P. E. (2006). Syntax and production. In M. J. Traxler & M. A. Gernsbacher (Eds.), *Handbook of psycholinguistics* (2nd ed., pp. 61–91). Amsterdam: Elsevier.

Fiedler, K. (2004). Illusory correlation. In R. Pohl (Ed.), *Cognitive illusions: Handbook on fallacies and biases in thinking, judgment, and memory* (pp. 97–114). Hove, UK: Psychology Press.

Fiedler, K., Nickel, S., Asbeck, J., & Pagel, U. (2003). Mood and the generation effect. *Cognition and Emotion, 17,* 585–608.

Fiedler, K., & Walther, E. (2004). *Stereotyping as inductive hypothesis testing*. Hove, UK: Psychology Press.

Field, J. (2004). *Psycholinguistics: The key concepts*. New York: Routledge.

Fields, A. W., & Shelton, A. L. (2006). Individual skill differences and large-scale environmental learning. *Journal of Experimental Psychology: Learning, Memory, and Cognition, 32*, 506–315.

Finch, G. (2003). *Word of mouth: A new introduction to language and communication.* New York: Palgrave.

Findlay, J. M., & Gilchrist, I. D. (2001). Visual attention: The active vision perspective. In M. Jenkin & L. Harris (Eds.), *Vision and attention* (pp. 83–103). New York: Springer-Verlag.

Findlay, J. M., & Walker, R. (1999). A model of saccade generation based on parallel processing and competitive inhibition. *Behavioral and Brain Sciences, 22*, 661–721.

Finke, R. A., Pinker, S., & Farah, M. J. (1989). Reinterpreting visual patterns in mental imagery. *Cognitive Science, 13*, 51–78.

Finstad, K., Bink, M., McDaniel, M., & Einstein, G. O. (2006). Breaks and task switches in prospective memory. *Applied Cognitive Psychology, 20*, 705–712.

Fiore, S., & Schooler, J. W. (2004). Process mapping and shared cognition: Teamwork and the development of shared problem models. In E. Salas & S. M. Fiore (Eds.), *Team cognition: Understanding the factors that drive process and performance* (pp. 133–152). Washington, DC: American Psychological Association.

Fischhoff, B. (1982). Debiasing. In D. Kahneman, P. Slovic, & A. Tversky (Eds.), *Judgment under uncertainty: Heuristics and biases* (pp. 422–444). New York: Cambridge University Press.

Fischhoff, B. (1999). Judgment heuristics. In R. A. Wilson & F. C. Keil (Eds.), *The MIT encyclopedia of the cognitive sciences* (pp. 423–425). Cambridge, MA: MIT Press.

Fisher, D. L., & Pollatsek, A. (2007). Novice driver crashes: Failure to divide attention or failure to recognize risks. In A. F. Kramer, D. A. Wiegmann, & A. Kirlik (Eds.), *Attention: From theory to practice* (pp. 134–153). New York: Oxford University Press.

Fishman, J. A. (2006). The new linguistic order. In H. Luria, D. M. Seymour, & T. Smoke (Eds.), *Language and linguistics in context: Readings and applications for teachers* (pp. 175–189). Mahwah, NJ: Erlbaum.

Fisk, J. E. (2004). Conjunction fallacy. In R. Pohl (Ed.), *Cognitive illusions: Handbook on fallacies and biases in thinking, judgment, and memory* (pp. 23–42) Hove, UK: Psychology Press.

Fiske, S. T. (2004). *Social beings: A core motives approach to social psychology.* Hoboken, NJ: Wiley.

Fivush, R., & Nelson, K. (2004). Culture and language in the emergence of autobiographical memory. *Psychological Science, 15*, 573–577.

Flavell, J. H. (1971). First discussant's comments. What is memory development the development of? *Human Development, 14*, 272–278.

Flavell, J. H. (1979). Metacognition and cognitive monitoring. *American Psychologist, 34*, 906–911.

Flavell, J. H., Beach, D. R., & Chinsky, J. M. (1966). Spontaneous verbal rehearsal in a memory task as a function of age. *Child Development, 37*, 283–299.

Flavell, J. H., Green, F. L., & Flavell, E. R. (2000). Development of children's awareness of their own thoughts. *Journal of Cognition and Development, 1*, 97–112.

Flavell, J. H., Miller, P. H., & Miller, S. A. (2002). *Cognitive development* (4th ed.). Upper Saddle River, NJ: Prentice-Hall.

Flege, J. E., Yeni-Komshiam, G. H., & Liu, S. (1999). Age constraints on second-language acquisition. *Journal of Memory and Language, 41*, 78–104.

Flores d'Arcais, G. B. (1988). Language perception. In F. J. Newmeyer (Ed.), *Linguistics: The Cambridge survey* (Vol. 3, pp. 97–123). Cambridge, UK: Cambridge University Press.

Flower, L. S., & Hayes, J. R. (1980). The dynamics of composing: Making plans and juggling constraints. In L. W. Gregg & E. R. Steinberg (Eds.), *Cognitive processes in writing* (pp. 31–50). Hillsdale, NJ: Erlbaum.

Foley, M. A., Belch, C., Mann, R., & McLean, M. (1999). Self-referencing: How incessant the stream? *American Journal of Psychology, 112*, 73–96.

Foley, M. A., & Foley, H. J. (1998). A study of face identification: Are people looking beyond disguises? In M. J. Intons-Peterson & D. L. Best (Eds.), *Memory distortions and their prevention* (pp. 29–47). Mahwah, NJ: Erlbaum.

Foley, M. A., Foley, H. J., Durley, J. R., & Maitner, A. T. (2006). Anticipating partners' responses: Examining item and source memory following interactive exchanges. *Memory & Cognition, 34*, 1539–1547.

Foley, M. A., Foley, H. J., & Korenman, L. M. (2002). Adapting a memory framework (source monitoring) to the study of closure processes. *Memory & Cognition, 30*, 412–422.

Foley, M. A., & Ratner, H. H. (1998). Distinguishing between memories for thoughts and deeds: The role of prospective processing in children's source monitoring. *British Journal of Developmental Psychology, 16*, 465–484.

Foley, M. A., Ratner, H. H., & House, A. T. (2002). Anticipation and source-monitoring errors: Children's memory for collaborative activities. *Journal of Cognition and Development, 3,* 385–414.

Foley, M. A., Wilder, A., McCall, R., & Van Vorst, R. (1993). The consequences for recall of children's ability to generate interactive imagery in the absence of external supports. *Journal of Experimental Child Psychology, 56,* 173–200.

Foltz, P. W. (2003). Quantitative cognitive models of text and discourse processing. In A. C. Graesser, M. A. Gernsbacher, & S. R. Goldman (Eds.), *Handbook of discourse processes* (pp. 487–523). Mahwah, NJ: Erlbaum.

Forgas, J. P. (2001). The Affect Infusion Model (AIM): An integrative theory of mood effects on cognition and judgment. In L. L. Martin & G. L. Clore (Eds.), *Theories of mood and cognition* (pp. 99–134). Mahwah, NJ: Erlbaum.

Forster, K. I. (1981). Priming and the effects of sentence and lexical contexts on naming time: Evidence for autonomous lexical processing. *Quarterly Journal of Experimental Psychology, 33A,* 465–495.

Fowler, C. A. (2003). Speech production and perception. In A. F. Healy & R. W. Proctor (Eds.), *Handbook of psychology* (Vol. 4, pp. 237–266). Hoboken, NJ: Wiley.

Fowler, C. A., & Galantucci, B. (2005). The relation of speech perception and speech production. In D. B. Pisoni & R. E. Remez (Eds.), *The handbook of speech perception* (pp. 633–652). Malden, MA: Blackwell.

Fox, E. (Ed.). (2005). *Visual social cognition.* Hove, UK: Psychology Press.

Fox, J. C., & Farmer, R. (2002). A behavioral approach to political advertising research. In R. Gowda & J. C. Fox (Eds.), *Judgments, decisions, and public policy* (pp. 199–217). New York: Cambridge University Press.

Fox Tree, J. E. (2000). Coordinating spontaneous talk. In L. Wheeldon (Ed.), *Aspects of language production* (pp. 375–406). Hove, UK: Psychology Press.

Foygel, D., & Dell, G. S. (2000). Models of impaired lexical access in speech production. *Journal of Memory and Language, 43,* 182–216.

Fraley, R. C. (2007). A connectionist approach to the organization and continuity of working models of attachment. *Journal of Personality, 75,* 1157–1180.

Franconeri, S. I., Hollingworth, A., & Simons, D. J. (2005). Do new objects capture attention? *Psychological Science, 16,* 275–281.

Franklin, N., & Tversky, B. (1990). Searching imagined environments. *Journal of Experimental Psychology: General, 119,* 63–76.

Franklin, S. (1995). *Artificial minds.* Cambridge, MA: MIT Press.

Freedheim, D. F. (Ed.). (2003). *Handbook of psychology* (Vol. 1: The history of psychology, pp. 465–481). Hoboken, NJ: Wiley.

Freyd, J. J. (1996). *Betrayal trauma: The logic of forgetting childhood abuse.* Cambridge, MA: Harvard University Press.

Freyd, J. J. (1998). Science in the memory debate. *Ethics & Behavior, 8,* 101–113.

Freyd, J. J., & DePrince, A. A. (Eds.). (2001). *Trauma and cognitive science.* New York: Haworth.

Freyd, J. J., & Quina, K. (2000). Feminist ethics in the practice of science: The contested memory controversy as an example. In M. M. Brabeck (Ed.), *Practicing feminist ethics in psychology* (pp. 101–123). Washington, DC: American Psychological Association.

Frick-Horbury, D., & Guttentag, R. E. (1998). The effects of restricting hand gesture production on lexical retrieval and free recall. *American Journal of Psychology, 111,* 43–62.

Friedman, A., Brown, N. R., & McGaffey, A. P. (2002). A basis for bias in geographical judgments. *Psychonomic Bulletin & Review, 9,* 151–159.

Friedman, A., & Montello, D. R. (2006). Global-scale location and distance estimates: Common representations and strategies in absolute and relative judgments. *Journal of Experimental Psychology: Learning, Memory, and Cognition, 32,* 333–346.

Friedman, A., Spetch, M. L., & Ferrey, A. (2005). Recognition by humans and pigeons of novel views of 3–D objects and their photographs. *Journal of Experimental Psychology: General, 134,* 149–162.

Friedman, A., et al. (2005). Cross-cultural similarities and differences in North Americans' geographic location judgments. *Psychonomic Bulletin & Review, 12,* 1054–1060.

Frishman, L. J. (2001). Basic visual processes. In E. B. Goldstein (Ed.), *Blackwell handbook of perception* (pp. 53–91). Malden, MA: Blackwell.

Frith, C., & Rees, G. (2004). Brain imaging: The methods. In R. L. Gregory (Ed.), *The Oxford companion to the mind* (2nd ed., pp. 131–133). New York: Oxford University Press.

Fromkin, V. A., & Bernstein Ratner, N. (1998). Speech production. In J. Berko-Gleason & N. Bernstein

Ratner (Eds.), *Psycholinguistics* (2nd ed., 309–346). Fort Worth: Harcourt Brace.

Fuchs, A. H., & Milar, K. J. (2003). Psychology as a science. In D. F. Freedheim (Ed.), *Handbook of psychology* (Vol. 1: *The history of psychology*, pp. 1–26). Hoboken, NJ: Wiley.

Furnham, A., & Bradley, A. (1997). Music while you work: The differential distraction of background music on the cognitive test performance of introverts and extraverts. *Applied Cognitive Psychology, 11,* 445–455.

Fuster, J. M. (2003). *Cortex and mind: Unifying cognition.* New York: Oxford University Press.

Galambos, S. J., & Goldin-Meadow, S. (1990). The effects of learning two languages on levels of metalinguistic awareness. *Cognition, 34,* 1–56.

Galambos, S. J., & Hakuta, K. (1988). Subject-specific and task-specific characteristics of metalinguistic awareness in bilingual children. *Applied Psycholinguistics, 9,* 141–162.

Gallagher, M., & Nelson, R. J. (2003). *Handbook of psychology* (Vol. 3, pp. ix–xviii). Hoboken, NJ: Wiley.

Gallo, D. A. (2006). *Associative illusions of memory.* New York: Psychology Press.

Ganellen, R. J., & Carver, C. S. (1985). Why does self-reference promote incidental encoding? *Journal of Experimental Social Psychology, 21,* 284–300.

Ganis, G., Thompson, W. L., & Kosslyn, S. M. (2004). Brain areas underlying visual mental imagery and visual perception: An fMRI study. *Cognitive Brain Research, 20,* 226–241.

García-Mira, R., & Real, J. E. (2005). Environmental perception and cognitive maps. *International Journal of Psychology, 40,* 1–2.

Gardner, H. (1985). *The mind's new science: A history of the cognitive revolution.* New York: Basic Books.

Gardner, R. (2001). *When listeners talk: Response tokens and listener stance.* Philadelphia: John Benjamins.

Gardner, R. C., & Lambert, W. E. (1959). Motivational variables in second-language acquisition. *Canadian Journal of Psychology, 13,* 266–272.

Garnets, L. D. (2004). Life as a lesbian: What does gender have to do with it? In J. C. Chrisler, C. Golden, & P. D. Rozee (Eds.), *Lectures on the psychology of women* (3rd ed., pp. 171–186). New York: Boston.

Garnham, A. (2005). Language comprehension. In K. Lamberts & R. L. Goldstone (Eds.), *Handbook of cognition* (pp. 241–254). Thousand Oaks, CA: Sage.

Garnham, A., & Oakhill, J. (1994). *Thinking and reasoning.* Oxford, UK: Blackwell.

Gass, S. M. (2006). Fundamentals of second language acquisition. In H. Luria, D. M. Seymour, & T. Smoke (Eds.), *Language and linguistics in context: Readings and applications for teachers* (pp. 43–59). Mahwah, NJ: Erlbaum.

Gass, S. M., & Selinker, L. (2001). *Second language acquisition: An introductory course* (2nd ed.). Mahwah, NJ: Erlbaum.

Gathercole, S. E. (1998). The development of memory. *Journal of Child Psychology and Psychiatry, 39,* 3–27.

Gathercole, S. E., Adams, A., & Hitch, G. J. (1994). Do young children rehearse? An individual-differences analysis. *Memory & Cognition, 22,* 201–207.

Gathercole, S. E., & Baddeley, A. D. (1993). *Working memory and language.* Hove, UK : Erlbaum.

Gathercole, S. E., Lamont, E., & Alloway, T. P. (2006). Working memory in the classroom. In S. J. Pickering (Ed.), *Working memory and education* (pp. 219–240). Burlington, MA: Elsevier.

Gathercole, S. E., & Pickering, S. J. (2000). Working memory deficits in children with low achievement in the national curriculum at 7 years of age. *British Journal of Educational Psychology, 70,* 177–194.

Gathercole, S. E., Pickering, S. J., Ambridge, B., & Wearing, H. (2004). The structure of working memory from 4 to 15 years of age. *Developmental Psychology, 40,* 177–190.

Gathercole, S. E., Pickering, S. J., Knight, C., & Stegmann, Z. (2004). Working memory skills and educational attainment: Evidence from national curriculum assessments at 7 and 14 years of age. *Journal of Applied Psychology, 18,* 1–16.

Gauvain, M. (2001). *The social context of cognitive development.* New York: Guilford.

Gazzaniga, M. S., Ivry, R. B., & Mangun, G. R. (2002). *Cognitive neuroscience: The biology of the mind* (2nd ed.). New York: Norton.

Geiselman, R. E., & Glenny, J. (1977). Effects of imagining speakers' voices on the retention of words presented visually. *Memory & Cognition, 5,* 499–504.

Geisler, W. S., & Super, B. J. (2000). Perceptual organization of two-dimensional patterns. *Psychological Review, 107,* 677–708.

Gelman, R. (2002). Cognitive development, In H. Pashler (Ed.), *Stevens' handbook of experimental psychology* (Vol. 2, pp. 533–550). New York: Wiley.

Gelman, R., & Brenneman, K. (2004). Science learning pathways for young children. *Early Childhood Research Quarterly, 19,* 150–158.

Genesee, F., & Gándara, P. (1999). Bilingual education programs: A cross-national perspective. *Journal of Social Issues, 55,* 665–685.

Genesee, F., Tucker, R., & Lambert, W. E. (1975). Communication skills of bilingual children. *Child Development, 46,* 1010–1014.

Geng, J. J., & Behrmann, M. (2003). Selective visual attention and visual search: Behavioral and neural mechanisms. In D. E. Irwin & B. H. Ross (Eds.), *The psychology of learning and motivation* (pp. 157–191). San Diego, CA: Academic Press.

Gennaro, R. J., Herrmann, D. J., & Sarapata, M. (2005). Aspects of the unity of consciousness and everyday memory failures. *Consciousness and Cognition, 15,* 372–385.

German, T. P., & Barrett, H. C. (2005). Functional fixedness in a technologically sparse culture. *Psychological Science, 16,* 1–5.

Gernsbacher, M. A., & Kaschak, M. P. (2003). Neuroimaging studies of language production and comprehension. *Annual Review of Psychology, 54,* 91–114.

Gernsbacher, M. A., & Robertson, D. A. (2005). Watching the brain comprehend discourse. In A. F. Healy (Ed.), *Experimental cognitive psychology and its applications* (pp. 157–167). Washington, DC: American Psychological Association.

Gernsbacher, M. A., Robertson, R. R. W., & Werner, N. K. (2001). The costs and benefits of meaning. In D. S. Gorfein (Ed.), *On the consequences of meaning selection: Perspectives on resolving lexical ambiguity* (pp. 119–137). Washington, DC: American Psychological Association.

Gerrie, M. P., Garry, M., & Loftus, E. F. (2005). False memories. In N. Brewer & K. D. Williams (Eds.), *Psychology and law: An empirical perspective* (pp. 222–253). New York: Guilford.

Gerrig, R. J. (1998). *Experiencing narrative words.* Boulder, CO: Westview Press.

Gerrig, R. J., & Littman, M. L. (1990). Disambiguation by community membership. *Memory & Cognition, 18,* 331–338.

Gerrig, R. J., & McKoon, G. (2001). Memory processes and experiential continuity. *Psychological Science, 12,* 81–85.

Gibbs, R. W., Jr. (1986). What makes some indirect speech acts conventional? *Journal of Memory and Language, 25,* 181–196.

Gibbs, R. W., Jr. (1998). The varieties of intentions in interpersonal communication. In S. R. Fussell & R. J. Kreuz (Eds.), *Social and cognitive approaches to interpersonal communications* (pp. 19–37). Mahwah, NJ: Erlbaum.

Gibbs, R. W., Jr. (2003). Nonliteral speech acts in text and discourse. In A. C. Graesser, M. A. Gernsbacher, & S. R. Goldman (Eds.), *Handbook of discourse processes* (pp. 357–393). Mahwah, NJ: Erlbaum.

Gibson, E. J. (1969). *Principles of perceptual learning and development.* New York: Prentice Hall.

Gibson, E. J. (1998). Linguistic complexity: Locality of syntactic dependencies. *Cognition, 68,* 1–76.

Gibson, E. J. (1999). The dependency locality theory: A distance-based theory of linguistic complexity. In Y. Miyashita, A. P. Marantz, & W. O'Neil (Eds.), *Image, language, brain.* Cambridge, MA: MIT Press.

Gigerenzer, G. (1998). Ecological intelligence: An adaptation for frequencies. In D. D. Cummins & C. Allen (Eds.), *The evolution of mind* (pp. 9–29). New York: Oxford University Press.

Gigerenzer, G. (2004). Striking a blow for sanity in theories of rationality. In M. Augier & J. G. March (Eds.), *Models of a man: Essays in memory of Herbert A. Simon* (pp. 389–409). Cambridge, MA: MIT Press.

Gigerenzer, G. (2006a). Bounded and rational. In R. J. Stainton (Ed.), *Contemporary debates in cognitive science* (pp. 115–133). Oxford, UK: Blackwell.

Gigerenzer, G. (2006b). Heuristics. In G. Gigerenzer & C. Engel (Eds.), *Heuristics and the law* (pp. 17–44). Cambridge, MA: MIT Press.

Gigerenzer, G., & Hug, K. (1992). Domain-specific reasoning: Social contracts, cheating, and perspective change. *Cognition, 43,* 127–171.

Gigerenzer, G., & Selten, R. (Eds.). (2001). *Bounded rationality: The adaptive toolbox.* Cambridge, MA: MIT Press.

Gilbert, S. (2002). *Improving memory: Understanding and preventing age-related memory loss.* Boston: Harvard Health Publications.

Gilhooly, K. J. (2005). Working memory and strategies in reasoning. In M. J. Roberts & E. J. Newton (Eds.), *Methods of thought: Individual differences in reasoning strategies* (pp. 57–80). Hove, UK: Psychology Press.

Gillam, B., & Chan, W. M. (2002). Grouping has a negative effect on both subjective contours and perceived occlusion at T-junctions. *Psychological Science, 13,* 279–283.

Gillihan, S. J., & Farah, M. J. (2005). Is self special? A critical review of evidence from experimental psychology and cognitive neuroscience. *Psychological Bulletin, 131,* 76–97.

Gilovich, T., Griffin, D., & Kahneman, D. (2002). *Heuristics and biases: The psychology of intuitive judgment*. New York: Cambridge University Press.

Gladwell, M. (2005). *Blink: The power of thinking without thinking*. New York: Little Brown.

Glaser, R. (2001). Progress then and now. In S. M. Carver & D. Klahr (Eds.), *Cognition and instruction: Twenty-five years of progress* (pp. 493–507). Mahwah, NJ: Erlbaum.

Glaser, R., & Chi, M. T. H. (1988). Overview. In M. T. H. Chi, R. Glaser, & M. J. Farr (Eds.), *The nature of expertise* (pp. xv–xxxvi). Hillsdale, NJ: Erlbaum.

Gleitman, L., & Bloom, P. (1999). Language acquisition. In R. A. Wilson & F. C. Keil (Eds.), *The MIT encyclopedia of the cognitive sciences* (pp. 434–438). Cambridge, MA: MIT Press.

Gleitman, L., & Liberman, M. (1995). The cognitive science of language: Introduction. In l. Gleitman & M. Liberman (Eds.), *Language: An invitation to cognitive science* (2nd ed., pp. xix–xxxviii). Cambridge, MA: MIT Press.

Glenberg, A. M., Sanocki, T., Epstein, W., & Morris, C. (1987). Enhancing calibration of comprehension. *Journal of Experimental Psychology: General, 116*, 119–136.

Glicksohn, J. (1994). Rotation, orientation, and cognitive mapping. *American Journal of Psychology, 107*, 39–51.

Gluck, M. A., & Myers, C. E. (2001). *Gateway to memory: An introduction to neural network modeling of the hippocampus and learning*. Cambridge, MA: MIT Press.

Gobet, F., de Voogt, A., & Retschitzki, J. (2004). *Moves in mind: The psychology of board games*. Hove, UK: Psychology Press.

Gobet, F., & Simon, H. A. (1996a). Recall of random and distorted chess positions: Implications for the theory of expertise. *Memory & Cognition, 24*, 493–503.

Gobet, F., & Simon, H. A. (1996b). Recall of rapidly presented random chess positions is a function of skill. *Psychonomic Bulletin & Review, 3*, 159–163.

Goldberg, E. (2001). *The executive brain: Frontal lobes and the civilized mind*. New York: Oxford University Press.

Goldsmith, M., Koriat, A., & Pansky, A. (2005). Strategic regulation of grain size in memory reporting over time. *Journal of Memory and Language, 52*, 050–525.

Goldstein, D. G., & Gigerenzer, G. (2002). Models of ecological rationality: The recognition heuristic. *Psychological Review, 109*, 75–90.

Goldstein, E. B. (2007). *Sensation and perception* (7th ed.). Belmont, CA: Wadsworth.

Goldstone, R. L., & Kersten, A. (2003). Concepts and categorization. In I. B. Weiner (Ed.), *Handbook of psychology* (Vol. 4). Hoboken, NJ: Wiley.

Gollan, T. H., & Acenas, L.-A. R. (2004). What is a TOT? Cognate and translation effects on tip-of-the-tongue states in Spanish-English and Tagalog-English bilinguals. *Journal of Experimental Psychology: Learning, Memory, and Cognition, 29*, 1095–1105.

Gollan, T. H., Bonanni, M. P., & Montoya, R. I. (2005). Proper names get stuck on bilingual and monolingual speakers' tip of the tongue equally often. *Neuropsychology, 19*, 278–287.

Gollan, T. H., Montoya, R. I., Fennema-Notestine, C., & Morris, S. K. (2005). Bilingualism affects picture naming but not picture classification. *Memory & Cognition, 33*, 1220–1234.

Goodman, G. S., & Melinder, A. (2007). The development of autobiographical memory: A new model. In S. Magnussen & T. Helstrup (Eds.), *Everyday memory* (pp. 111–135). New York: Psychology Press.

Goodman, G. S., & Paz-Alonso, P. M. (2006). Trauma and memory: Normal versus special memory mechanisms. In B. Uttl, N. Ohta, & A. L. Siegenthaler (Eds.), *Memory and emotion: Interdisciplinary perspectives* (pp. 234–257). Malden, MA: Blackwell.

Goodman, G. S., et al. (2003). A prospective study of memory for child sexual abuse: New findings relevant to the repressed-memory controversy. *Psychological Science, 14*, 113–118.

Goodman, G. S., et al. (2007). Memory illusions and false memories in the real world. In S. Magnussen & T. Helstrup (Eds.), *Everyday memory* (pp. 157–182). New York: Psychology Press.

Goodwin, G. P. & Johnson-Laird, P. N., (2005). Reasoning about relations. *Psychological Review, 112*, 468–493.

Gordon, A. S. (2004). *Strategy representation: An analysis of planning knowledge*. Mahwah, NJ: Erlbaum.

Gordon, I. E. (2004). *Theories of visual perception* (3rd ed.). Hove, UK: Psychology Press.

Gordon, R., Franklin, N., & Beck, J. (2005). Wishful thinking and source monitoring. *Memory & Cognition, 33*, 418–438.

Gorman, M. E. (2006). Scientific and technological thinking. *Review of General Psychology, 10*, 113–129.

Gorrell, P. (1999). Sentence processing. In R. A. Wilson & F. C. Keil (Eds.), *The MIT encyclopedia of the cognitive sciences* (pp. 748–751). Cambridge, MA: MIT Press.

Gowda, R., & Fox, J. C. (Eds.). (2002). *Judgments, decisions, and public policy*. New York: Cambridge University Press.

Grady, C. L., & Craik, F. I. M. (2000). Changes in memory processing with age. *Current Opinion in Neurobiology, 10*, 224–231.

Graesser, A. C., Gernsbacher, M. A., & Goldman, S. R. (Eds.). (2003a). *Handbook of discourse processes*. Mahwah, NJ: Erlbaum.

Graesser, A. C., Gernsbacher, M. A., & Goldman, S. R. (2003b). Introduction to the handbook of discourse processes. In A. C. Graesser, M. A. Gernsbacher, & S. R. Goldman (Eds.), *Handbook of discourse processes* (pp. 1–23). Mahwah, NJ: Erlbaum.

Graesser, A. C., et al. (2004). AutoTutor: A tutor with dialogue in natural language. *Behavior Research Methods, Instruments, & Computers, 36*, 180–192.

Graesser, A. C., et al. (2007). Using LSA in AutoTutor: Learning through mixed-initiative dialogue in natural language. In T. K. Landauaer, D. S. McNamara, S. Dennis, & W. Kintsch (Eds.), *Handbook of latent semantic analysis* (pp. 243–262). Mahwah, NJ: Erlbaum.

Graf, M., Kaping, D., & Bülthoff, H. H. (2005). Orientation congruency effects for familiar objects: Coordinate transformations in object recognition. *Psychological Science, 16*, 214–221.

Graf, P., & Ohta, N. (2002). *Lifespan development of human memory*. Cambridge, MA: MIT Press.

Grainger, J., & Jacobs, A. M. (2005). Pseudoword context effects on letter perception: The role of word misperception. *European Journal of Cognitive Psychology, 17*, 289–318.

Grant, E. R., & Spivey, M. J. (2003). Eye movements and problem solving: Guiding attention guides thought. *Psychological Science, 14*, 462–466.

Greenberg, S., & Ainsworth, W. A. (Eds.). (2006). *Listening to speech: An auditory perspective*. Mahwah, NJ: Erlbaum.

Greeno, J. G. (1974). Hobbits and Orcs: Acquisition of a sequential concept. *Cognitive Psychology, 6*, 270–292.

Greeno, J. G. (1991). A view of mathematical problem solving in school. In M. U. Smith (Ed.), *Toward a unified theory of problem solving* (pp. 69–98). Hillsdale, NJ: Erlbaum.

Greenwald, A. G., McGee, D. E., & Schwartz, J. L. K. (1998). Measuring individual differences in implicit cognition: The Implicit Association Test. *Journal of Personality and Social Psychology, 74*, 1464–1480.

Greenwald, A. G., & Nosek, B. A. (2001). Health of the Implicit Association Test at age 3. *Zeitschrift für Experimentelle Psychologie, 48*, 85–93.

Greenwald, A. G., et al. (2002). A unified theory of implicit attitudes, stereotypes, self-esteem, and self-concept. *Psychological Review, 109*, 3–25.

Gregory, R. L. (2004a). Perception. In R. L. Gregory (Ed.), *The Oxford companion to the mind* (2nd ed., pp. 707–710). New York: Oxford University Press.

Gregory, R. L. (2004b). Piaget and education. In R. L. Gregory (Ed.), *The Oxford companion to the mind* (2nd ed., pp. 732–733). New York: Oxford University Press.

Griffin, D., & Tversky, A. (2002). The weighing of evidence and the determinants of confidence. In T. Gilovich, D. Griffin, & D. Kahneman (Eds.), *Heuristics and biases: The psychology of intuitive judgment* (pp. 230–249). New York: Cambridge University Press.

Griffin, Z. M. (2004). Why look? Reasons for eye movements related to language production. In J. M. Henderson & F. Ferreira (Eds.), *The interface of language, vision, and action: Eye movements and the visual world* (pp. 213–247). New York: Psychology Press.

Griffin, Z. M., & Bock, K. (2000). What the eyes say about speaking. *Psychological Science, 11*, 274–279.

Griffin, Z. M., & Ferreira, V. S. (2006). Properties of spoken language production. In M. J. Traxler & M. A. Gernsbacher (Eds.), *Handbook of psycholinguistics* (2nd ed., pp. 505–527). Amsterdam: Elsevier.

Griffith, P. L., & Ruan, J. (2005). What is metacognition and what should be its role in literacy instruction? In S. E. Israel, C. C. Block, K. L. Bauserman, & K. Kinnucan-Welsch (Eds.), *Metacognition in literacy learning: Theory, assessment, instruction, and professional development* (pp. 3–18). Mahwah, NJ: Erlbaum.

Griggs, R. A. (1995). The effects of rule clarification, decision justification, and selection instruction on Wason's abstract selection task. In S. E. Newstead & J. St. B. T. Evans (Eds.), *Perspectives on thinking and reasoning: Essays in honour of Peter Wason*. Hove, UK: Erlbaum.

Griggs, R. A., & Cox, J. R. (1982). The elusive thematic-materials effect in Wason's selection task. *British Journal of Psychology, 73*, 407–420.

Griggs, R. A., & Jackson, S. L. (1990). Instructional effects on responses in Wason's selection task. *British Journal of Psychology, 81*, 197–204.

Grill-Spector, K., & Kanwisher, N. (2005). Visual recognition: As soon as you know it is there, you know what it is. *Psychological Science, 16*, 152–160.

Grodzinsky, Y. (2000). The neurology of syntax: Language use without Broca's area. *Behavioral and Brain Sciences, 23*, 1–71.

Grodzinsky, Y. (2006). A blueprint for a brain map of syntax. In Y. Grodzinsky & K. Amunts (Eds.), *Broca's region* (pp. 83–107). New York: Oxford University Press.

Groninger, L. D. (1971). Mnemonic imagery and forgetting. *Psychonomic Science, 23,* 161–163.

Groninger, L. D. (2000). Face-name mediated learning and long-term retention: The role of images and imagery processes. *American Journal of Psychology, 113,* 199–219.

Groome, D. (1999). *An introduction to cognitive psychology: Processes and disorders.* Hove, UK: Psychology Press.

*Grossberg, S. (2000). The complementary brain: Unifying brain dynamics and modularity. *Trends in Cognitive Sciences, 4,* 233–245.

Grossberg, S. (2003a). Filling-in the forms: Surface and boundary interactions in visual cortex. In L. Pessoa & P. DeWeerd (Eds.), *Filling-in: From perceptual completion to skill learning* (pp. 13–37). New York: Oxford University Press.

Grossberg, S. (2003b). Resonant neural dynamics of speech perception. *Journal of Phonetics, 31,* 423–445.

Grossberg, S., Govindarajan, K. K., Wyse, L. L., & Cohen, M. A. (2004). ARTSTREAM: A neural network model of auditory scene analysis and source segregation. *Neural Networks, 17,* 511–536.

Guerin, B. (2003). Language use as social strategy: A review and an analytic framework for the social sciences, *Review of General Psychology, 7,* 251–298.

Guilford, J. P. (1967). *The nature of human intelligence.* New York: McGraw-Hill.

Gulya, M., Rossi-George, A., & Rovee-Collier, C. (2002). Dissipation of retroactive interference in human infants. *Journal of Experimental Psychology: Animal Behavior Processes, 28,* 151–162.

Gunter, B., Furman, A., & Pappa, E. (2005). Effects of television violence on memory for violent and nonviolent advertising. *Journal of Applied Social Psychology, 35,* 1680–1697.

Gurung, R. A. R. (2003). Pedagogical aids and student performance. *Teaching of Psychology, 30,* 92–95.

Gurung, R. A. R. (2004). Pedagogical aids: Learning enhancers or dangerous detours? *Teaching of Psychology, 31,* 164–166.

Güss, C. D., & Wiley, B. (2007). Metacognition of problem-solving strategies in Brazil, India, and the United States. *Journal of Cognition and Culture, 7,* 1–25.

Guynn, M. J., McDaniel, M. A., & Einstein, G. O. (1998). Prospective memory: When reminders fail. *Memory & Cognition, 26,* 287–298.

Haarmann, H. J., Davelaar, E. J., & Usher, M. (2003). Individual differences in semantic short-term memory capacity and reading comprehension. *Journal of Memory and Language, 48,* 320–345.

Haberlandt, K. (1999). *Human memory: Exploration and application.* Boston: Allyn and Bacon.

Hahn, U., & Chater, N. (1997). Concepts and similarity. In K. Lamberts & D. Shanks (Eds.), *Knowledge, concepts and categories* (pp. 43–92). Cambridge, MA: MIT Press.

Hakel, M. D. (2001). Learning that lasts. *Psychological Science, 12,* 433–434.

Hakuta, K. (1986). *Mirror of language: The debate on bilingualism.* New York: Basic Books.

Hakuta, K., Bialystok, E., & Wiley, E. (2003). Critical evidence: A test of the critical-period hypothesis for second-language acquisition. *Psychological Science, 14,* 31–38.

Hall, J., et al. (2004). Social cognition and face processing and schizophrenia. *British Journal of Psychiatry, 185,* 169–170.

Halpern, D. F. (2002). Sex, lies, and audiotapes: The Clinton-Lewinsky scandal. In R. J. Sternberg (Ed.), *Why smart people can be so stupid* (pp. 106–123). New Haven, CT: Yale University Press.

Halpern, D. F. (2003). *Thought and knowledge: An introduction to critical thinking* (4th ed.). Mahwah, NJ: Erlbaum.

Halpern, D. F., & Collaer, M. L. (2005). Sex differences in visuospatial abilities. In P. Shah & A. Miyake (Eds.), *The Cambridge handbook of visuospatial thinking* (pp. 170–212). New York: Cambridge University Press.

Hamers, J. F., & Blanc, M. H. A. (1989). *Bilinguality and bilingualism.* Cambridge, UK: Cambridge University Press.

Hamilton, D. L. (2005a). Social cognition: An introductory overview. In D. L. Hamilton (Ed.), *Social cognition: Key readings* (pp. 1–36). New York: Psychology Press.

Hamilton, D. L. (Ed.). (2005b). *Social cognition: Key readings.* New York: Psychology Press.

Hamilton, D. L., & Sherman, J. W. (1994). Stereotypes. In R. S. Wyer, Jr., & T. K. Srull (Eds.), *Handbook of social cognition* (2nd ed., Vol. 2, pp. 1–68). Hillsdale, NJ: Erlbaum.

Hamilton, D. L., Stroessner, S. J., & Mackie, D. M. (1993). The influence of affect on stereotyping: The case of illusory correlations. In D. M. Mackie & D. L. Hamilton (Eds.), *Affect, cognition, and stereotyping:*

Interactive processes in group perception (pp. 39–61). San Diego: Academic Press.

Hammond, K. R. (2000). *Judgment under stress.* New York: Oxford University Press.

Hampton, J. A. (1997a). Conceptual combination. In K. Lamberts & D. Shanks (Eds.), *Knowledge, concepts, and categories* (pp. 133–159). Cambridge, MA: MIT Press.

Hampton, J. A. (1997b). Psychological representation of concepts. In M. A. Conway (Ed.), *Cognitive models of memory* (pp. 81–110). Cambridge, MA: MIT Press.

Han, S.-H., & Kim, M.-S. (2004). Visual search does not remain efficient when executive working memory is working. *Psychological Science, 15,* 623–628.

Hanna, J. E., & Tanenhaus, M. K. (2005). The use of perspective during referential interpretation. In J. C. Trueswell & M. K. Tanenhaus (Eds.), *Approaches to studying world-situated language use* (pp. 133–152). Cambridge, MA: Bradford.

Harley, E. M., Carlsen, K. A., & Loftus, G. R. (2004). The "saw-it-all-along" effect: Demonstrations of visual hindsight bias. *Journal of Experimental Psychology: Learning, Memory, and Cognition, 30,* 960–968.

Harley, T. A. (2001). *The psychology of language: From data to theory* (2nd ed.). East Sussex, UK: Psychology Press.

Harrington, J., & Tabain, M. (2006). Introduction. In J. Harrington & M. Tabain (Eds.), *Speech production: Models, phonetic processes, and techniques* (pp. 1–10). New York: Psychology Press.

Harris, C. R., & Pashler, H. (2004). Attention and the processing of emotional words and names: Not so special after all. *Psychological Science, 15,* 171–178.

Harris, R. J., Sardarpoor-Bascom, F., & Meyer, T. (1989). The role of cultural knowledge in distorting recall for stories. *Bulletin of the Psychonomic Society, 27,* 9–10.

Harvey, A. G. (2005). Unwanted intrusive thoughts in insomnia. In D. A. Clark (Ed.), *Intrusive thoughts in clinical disorders: Theory, research, and treatment* (pp. 86–118). New York: Guilford Press.

Hasher, L., Chung, C., May, C. P., & Foong, N. (2002). Age, time of testing, and proactive interference. *Canadian Journal of Experimental Psychology, 56,* 200–207.

Hasher, L., Lustig, C., & Zacks, R. (2007). Inhibitory mechanisms and the control of attention. In A. R. A. Conway et al. (Eds.), *Variations in working memory* (pp. 227–249). New York: Oxford University Press.

Hassin, R. R. (2005). Nonconscious control and implicit working memory. In R. R. Hassin, J. E. Uleman, & J. A. Bargh (Eds.), *The new unconscious* (pp. 196–222). New York: Oxford University Press.

Hassin, R. R., Uleman, J. S., & Bargh, J. A. (2005). *The new unconscious.* New York: Oxford University Press.

Hawkins, S. A., & Hastie, R. (1990). Hindsight: Biased judgments of past events after the outcomes are known. *Psychological Bulletin, 107,* 311–327.

Hay, J. F., & Jacoby, L. L. (1996). Separating habit and recollection: Memory slips, process dissociations, and probability matching. *Journal of Experimental Psychology: Learning, Memory, and Cognition, 22,* 1323–1335.

Hayes, J. R. (1989). Writing research: The analysis of a very complex task. In D. Klahr & K. Kotovsky (Eds.), *Complex information processing: The impact of Herbert A. Simon* (pp. 209–234). Hillsdale, NJ: Erlbaum.

Hayes, J. R. (1996). A new framework for understanding cognition and affect in writing. In C. M. Levy & S. Randsell (Eds.), *The science of writing: Theories, methods, individual differences, and applications* (pp. 1–27). Mahwah, NJ: Erlbaum.

Hayes, J. R., et al. (1987). Cognitive processes in revision. In S. Rosenberg (Ed.), *Advances in psycholinguistics: Vol. 2. Reading, writing, and languages processing.* Cambridge, UK: Cambridge University Press.

Haywood, S. J., Pickering, M. J., & Branigan, H. P. (2005). Do speakers avoid ambiguities during dialogue? Psychological Science, 16, 362–366.

Hayworth, K. J., & Biederman, I. (2006). Neural evidence for intermediate representations in object recognition. *Vision Research, 46,* 4024–4031.

Hazeltine, R. E., Prinzmetal, W., & Elliott, K. (1997). If it's not there, where is it? Locating illusory conjunctions. *Journal of Experimental Psychology: Human Perception and Performance, 23,* 263–277.

Healy, A. F., & Proctor, R. W. (Eds.). (2003). *Handbook of psychology* (Vol. 4.). Hoboken, NJ: Wiley.

Hearst, E. (1991). Psychology and nothing. *American Scientist, 79,* 432–443.

Heibeck, T. H., & Markman, E. M. (1987). Word learning in children: An examination of fast mapping. *Child Development, 58,* 1021–1034.

Heilman, K. M. (2005). *Creativity and the brain.* New York: Psychology Press.

Heit, E., & Barsalou, L. W. (1996). The instantiation principle in natural categories. *Memory, 4,* 413–451.

Henderson, D. R., & Hooper, C. L. (2006). *Making great decisions in business and life.* Chicago Park, CA: Chicago Park Press.

Henderson, J. M. (Ed.). (2005). *Real-world scene perception.* Hove, UK: Psychology Press.

Henderson, J. M., & Ferreira, F. (Eds.). (2004a). *The interface of language, vision, and action: Eye movements and the visual world.* New York: Psychology Press.

Henderson, J. M., & Ferreira, F. (2004b). Scene perception for psycholinguists. In J. M. Henderson & F. Ferreira (Eds.), *The interface of language, vision, and action: Eye movements and the visual world* (p. 1–58). New York: Psychology Press.

Henderson, J. M., & Hollingworth, A. (2003). Global transsaccadic change blindness during scene perception. *Psychological Science, 14,* 493–497.

Henderson, Z., Bruce, V., & Burton, A. M. (2001). Matching the faces of robbers captured on video. *Applied Cognitive Psychology, 15,* 445–464.

Hennessey, B. A. (2000). Rewards and creativity. In C. Sansone & J. M. Harackiewicz (Eds.), *Intrinsic and extrinsic motivation: The search for optimal motivation and perormance* (pp. 55–78). San Diego, CA: Academic Press.

Hennessey, B. A., & Amabile, T. M. (1988). The conditions of creativity. In R. J. Sternberg (Ed.), *The nature of creativity: Contemporary psychological perspectives* (pp. 11–38). New York: Cambridge University Press.

Henry, L. A., & Gudjonsson, G. H. (2007). Individual and developmental differences in eyewitness recall and suggestibility in children with intellectual disabilities. *Applied Cognitive Psychology, 21,* 361–381.

Hernandez-García, L., Wager, T., & Jonides, J. (2002). Functional brain imaging. In H. Pashler & J. Wixted (Eds.), *Stevens' handbook of experimental psychology* (3rd ed., Vol. 4, pp. 175–221), New York: Wiley.

Herriot, P. (2004). Language development in children. In R. L. Gregory (Ed.), *The Oxford companion to the mind* (2nd ed., pp. 519–521). New York: Oxford University Press.

Herrmann, D. J. (1991). *Super memory.* Emmaus, PA: Rodale.

Herrmann, D.J., & Gruneberg, M. (2006). Memory failures in the workplace and in everyday life. In W. Karwowski (Ed.), *International encyclopedia of ergonomics and human factors* (2nd ed.). Boca Raton, FL: CRC Press.

Herrmann, D. J., Gruneberg, M. et al. (2006). Memory failures and their causes in everyday life. In L.-G. Nilsson & Nobuo Ohta (Eds.), *Memory and society: Psychological perspectives* (pp. 251–268). New York: Psychology Press.

Herrmann, D. J, Raybeck, D., & Gruneberg, M. (2002). *Improving memory and study skills.* Kirkland, WA: Hogrefe & Huber.

Herrmann, D. J., Yoder, C. Y., Gruneberg, M., & Payne, D. G. (2006). *Applied cognitive psychology: A textbook.* Mahwah, NJ: Erlbaum.

Hertwig, R., Barron, G., Weber, E. U., & Erev, I. (2004). Decisions from experience and the effect of rare events in risky choice. *Psychological Science, 15,* 534–539.

Hertwig, R., Pachur, T., & Kurzenhäuser, S. (2005). Judgments of risk frequencies: Tests of possible cognitive mechanisms. *Journal of Experimental Psychology: Learning, Memory, and Cognition, 31,* 621–642.

Hertwig, R., & Todd, P. M. (2002). Heuristics. In V. S. Ramachandran (Ed.), *Encyclopedia of the human brain* (Vol. 2, pp. 449–460). San Diego, Academic Press.

Hertzog, C., & Dixon, R. A. (1994). Metacognitive development in adulthood and old age. In J. Metcalfe & A. P. Shimamura (Eds.), *Metacognition: Knowing about knowing* (pp. 227–251). Cambridge, MA: MIT Press.

Hertzog, C., Dunlosky, J., Robinson, E. A., & Kidder, D. P. (2003). Encoding fluency is a cue used for judgments about learning. *Journal of Experimental Psychology: Learning, Memory, and Cognition, 29,* 22–34.

Hertzog, C., Lineweaver, T. T., & McGuire, C. L. (1999). Beliefs about memory and aging. In F. Blanchard-Fields & T. M. Hess (Eds.), *Social cognition and aging* (pp. 43–68). New York: Academic Press.

Herzog, C., & Robinson, A. E. (2005). Metacognition and intelligence. In O. Wilhelm & R. W. Engle (Eds.), *Handbook of understanding and measuring intelligence* (pp. 101–123). Thousand Oaks: Sage.

Hess, T. M. (2005). Memory and aging in context. *Psychological Bulletin, 131,* 383–406.

Hess, T. M., Auman, C., Colcombe, S. J., & Rahhal, T. A. (2003). The impact of stereotype threat on age differences in memory performance. *Journal of Gerontology Psychological Sciences, 58B,* P3–P11.

Hess, T. M., Hinson, J. T., & Statham, J. A. (2004). Explicit and implicit stereotype activation effects on memory: Do age and awareness moderate the impact of priming? *Psychology and Aging, 19,* 495–505.

Heth, C. D., Cornell, E. H., & Flood, T. L. (2002). Self-ratings of sense of direction and route reversal performance. *Applied Cognitive Psychology, 16,* 309–324.

Higbee, K. L. (1999). 25 years of memory improvement: The evolution of a memory-skills course. *Cognitive Technology, 4,* 38–42.

Hillis, A. E. (Ed.). (2002). *The handbook of adult language disorders.* New York: Psychology Press.

Hinds, P. J. (1999). The curse of expertise: The effects of expertise and debiasing methods on predictions of novice performance. *Journal of Experimental Psychology: Applied, 5,* 205–211.

Hinsz, V. B. (2004). Metacognition and mental models in groups: An illustration with metamemory of group recognition memory. In E. Salas & S. M. Fiore (Eds.), *Team cognition: Understanding the factors that drive process and performance* (pp. 33–58). Washington, DC: American Psychological Association.

Hirsh-Pasek, K., & Golinkoff, R. M. (1996). *The origins of grammar: Evidence from early language comprehension.* Cambridge, MA: MIT Press.

Hirt, E. R., McDonald, H. E., & Markman, K. D. (1998). Expectancy effects in reconstructive memory: When the past is just what we expected. In S. J. Lynn & K. M. McConkey (Eds.), *Truth in memory* (pp. 62–89). New York: Guilford.

Hirtle, S. C., & Jonides, J. (1985). Evidence of hierarchies in cognitive maps. *Memory & Cognition, 13,* 208–217.

Hirtle, S. C., & Mascolo, M. F. (1986). Effect of semantic clustering on the memory of spatial locations. *Journal of Experimental Psychology: Learning, Memory, and Cognition, 12,* 182–189.

Hitch, G. J. (2006). Working memory in children: A cognitive approach. In E. Bialystok & F. I. M. Craik (Eds.), *Lifespan cognition: Mechanisms of change* (pp. 112–127). New York: Oxford University Press.

Hoerl, C. (2001). The phenomenology of episodic recall. In C. Hoerl & T. McCormack (Eds.), *Time and memory: Issues in philosophy and psychology* (pp. 315–355). New York: Oxford University Press.

Hoffrage, U. (2004). Overconfidence. In R. Pohl (Ed.), *Cognitive illusions: Handbook on fallacies and biases in thinking, judgment, and memory.* Hove, UK: Psychology Press.

Hogarth, R. M. (2001). *Educating intuition.* Chicago: University of Chicago Press.

Hogarth, R. M., & Karelaia, N. (2007). Heuristic and linear models of judgment: Matching rules and environments. *Psychological Review, 114,* 733–758.

Holden, C. (2003). Deconstructing schizophrenia. *Science, 299,* 333–335.

Hollingworth, A. (2004). Constructing visual representations of natural scenes. The roles of short- and long-term visual memory. *Journal of Experimental Psychology: Human Perception and Performance, 30,* 519–537.

Hollingworth, A. (2006a). Scene and position specificity in visual memory for objects. *Journal of Experimental Psychology: Learning, Memory, and Cognition, 32,* 58–69.

Hollingworth, A. (2006b). Visual memory for natural scenes: Evidence from change detection and visual search. *Visual Cognition, 14,* 781–807.

Hollingworth, A., & Henderson, J. M. (2004). Sustained change blindness to incremental scene rotation: A dissociation between explicit change detection and visual memory. *Perception and Psychophysics, 66,* 800–807.

Hollingworth, H. (1910). The oblivescence of the disagreeable. *Journal of Philosophy, Psychology and Scientific Methods, 7,* 709–714.

Holmes, A., & Teti, D. M. (2005). Developmental science and the experimental method. In D. M. Teti (Ed.), *Handbook of research methods in developmental science* (pp. 66–80). Malden, MA: Blackwell.

Holmes, J. B., Waters, H. S., & Rajaram, S. (1998). The phenomenology of false memories: Episodic content and confidence. *Journal of Experimental Psychology: Learning, Memory, and Cognition, 24,* 1026–1040.

Holyoak, K. J. & Morrison. R. G. (Eds.). (2005). *The Cambridge handbook of thinking and reasoning.* New York: Cambridge University Press.

Hong, Y., Morris, M. W., Chiu, C., & Benet-Martínez, V. (2000). Multicultural minds: A dynamic constructivist approach to culture and cognition. *American Psychologist, 55,* 709–720.

Honig, E. (1997). Striking lives: Oral history and the politics of memory. *Journal of Women's History, 9,* 139–157.

Houston, D. M. (2005). Speech perception in infants. In D. B. Pisoni & R. E. Remez (Eds.), *The handbook of speech perception* (pp. 417–448). Malden, MA: Blackwell.

Howe, M. L. (2000). *The fate of early memories.* Washington, DC: American Psychological Association.

Howe, M. L. (2003). Memories from the cradle. *Current Directions in Psychological Science, 12,* 62–65.

Howe, M. L. (2006). Distinctiveness effects in children's memory. In R. R. Hunt & J. B. Worthen (Eds.), *Distinctiveness and memory.* New York: Oxford University Press.

Howe, M. L., Courage, M. L., Vernescu, R., & Hunt, M. (2000). Distinctiveness effects in children's long-term retention. *Developmental Psychology, 36,* 778–792.

Howes, M. B. (2007). *Human memory: Structures and images.* Thousand Oaks, CA: Sage.

Hsu, V. C., & Rovee-Collier, C. (2006). Memory reactivation in the second year of life. *Infant Behavior & Development, 29,* 91–107.

Hubel, D. H. (1982). Explorations of the primary visual cortex, 1955–1978. *Nature, 299,* 515 524.

Hubel, D. H., & Wiesel, T. N. (1965). Receptive fields of single neurons in two nonstriate visual areas (18 and 19) of the cat. *Journal of Neurophysiology, 28*, 229–289.

Hubel, D. H., & Wiesel, T. N. (1979). Brain mechanisms and vision. *Scientific American, 241* (3), 150–162.

Hubel, D. H., & Wiesel, T. N. (2005). *Brain and visual perception: The story of a 25–year collaboration.* New York: Oxford University Press.

Huber, V. L., Neale, M. A., & Northcraft, G. B. (1987). Decision bias and personnel selection strategies. *Organizational Behavior and Human Decision Processes, 40*, 136–147.

Huettel, S. A., Song, A. W., & McCarthy, G. (2004). *Functional magnetic resonance imaging.* Sunderland, MA: Sinauer.

Huitema, J. S., Dopkins, S., Klin, C. M., & Myers, J. L. (1993). Connecting goals and actions during reading. *Journal of Experimental Psychology: Learning, Memory, and Cognition, 19*, 1053–1060.

Hulicka, I. M. (1982). Memory functioning in late adulthood. In F. I. M. Craik & S. Trehub (Eds.), *Advances in the study of communication and affect* (Vol. 8, pp. 331–351). New York: Plenum.

Hulme, C., et al. (2004). Abolishing the word-length effect. *Journal of Experimental Psychology: Learning, Memory, and Cognition, 30*, 98–106.

Hulme, C., et al. (2006). The distinctiveness of the word-length effect. *Journal of Experimental Psychology, 32*, 586–594.

Humphreys, G. W., & Riddoch, M. J. (2001). The neuropsychology of visual object and space perception. In E. B. Goldstein (Ed.), *Blackwell handbook of perception* (pp. 204–236). Malden, MA: Blackwell.

Hunt, R. R. (2006). The concept of distinctiveness in memory research. In R. R. Hunt & J. B. Worthen (Eds.), *Distinctiveness and memory* (pp. 3–25). New York: Oxford University Press.

Hunt, R. R., & Worthen, J. B. (Eds.). (2006). *Distinctiveness and memory.* New York: Oxford University Press.

Hunter, I. M. L. (2004a). James, William. In R. L. Gregory (Ed.), *The Oxford companion to the mind* (2nd ed., pp. 492–494). New York: Oxford University Press.

Hunter, I. M. L. (2004b). Mnemonics. In R. L. Gregory (Ed.), *The Oxford companion to the mind* (2nd ed., 610–612). New York: Oxford University Press.

Hurley, S. M., & Novick, L. R. (2006). Context and structure: The nature of students' knowledge about three spatial diagram representations. *Thinking & Reasoning, 12*, 281–308.

Hyde, J. S. (2005). The gender similarities hypothesis. *American Psychologist, 60*, 581–592.

Hyde, J. S. (2007a). *Half the human experience: The psychology of women.* Boston: Houghton Mifflin.

Hyde, J. S. (2007b). New directions in the study of gender similarities and differences. *Current Directions, 16*, 259–263.

Hyde, J. S. (2007c). Women in science: Gender similarities in abilities and sociocultural forces. In S. J. Ceci & W. M. Williams (Eds.), *Why aren't more women in science?* (pp. 131–145). Washington, DC: American Psychological Association.

Hyman, I. E., Jr., Husband, T. H., & Billings, F. J. (1995). False memories of childhood experiences. *Applied Cognitive Psychology, 9*, 181–197.

Hyman, I. E., Jr., & Kleinknecht, E. E. (1999). False childhood memories: Research, theory, and applications. In L. M. Williams & V. L. Banyard (Eds.), *Trauma & memory* (pp. 175–188). Thousand Oaks, CA: Sage.

Hyman, I. E., Jr., & Loftus, E. F. (2002). False childhood memories and eyewitness memory errors. In M. L. Eisen, J. A. Quas, & G. S. Goodman (Eds.), *Memory and suggestibility in the forensic interview* (pp. 63–84). Mahwah, NJ: Erlbaum

Iannuzzi, P., Strichart, S. S., & Mangrum, C. T., II. (1998). *Teaching study skills and strategies in college.* Boston: Allyn and Bacon.

Idson, L. C., Krantz, D. H., Osherson, D., & Bonini, N. (2001). The relation between probability and evidence judgment: An extension of support theory. *Journal of Risk and Uncertainty, 22*, 227–249.

Imhoff, M. C., & Baker-Ward, L. (1999). Preschoolers' suggestibility: Effects of developmentally appropriate language and interviewer supportiveness. *Journal of Applied Developmental Psychology, 20*, 407–429.

Intons-Peterson, M. J. (1983). Imagery paradigms: How vulnerable are they to experimenters' expectations? *Journal of Experimental Psychology: Learning, Memory, and Cognition, 10*, 699–715.

Intons-Peterson, M. J., Russell, W., & Dressel, S. (1992). The role of pitch in auditory imagery. *Journal of Experimental Psychology: Human Perception and Performance, 18*, 233–240.

Intraub, H. (1997). The representation of visual scenes. *TRENDS in Cognitive Sciences, 1*, 217–222.

Intraub, H. (1999). Understanding and remembering briefly glimpsed pictures: Implications for visual scanning and memory. In V. Coltheart (Ed.), *Fleeting memories: Cognition of brief visual stimuli* (pp. 47–70). Cambridge, MA: MIT Press.

Intraub, H., & Berkowits, D. (1996). Beyond the edges of a picture. *American Journal of Psychology, 109,* 581–598.

Intraub, H., Gottesman, C. V., & Bills, A. J. (1998). Effects of perceiving and imagining scenes on memory for pictures. *Journal of Experimental Psychology: Learning, Memory, and Cognition, 24,* 186–201.

Irwin, D. E. (2003). Eye movements and visual cognitive suppression. *The Psychology of Learning and Motivation, 42,* 265–293.

Irwin, D. E. (2004). Fixation location and fixation duration as indices of cognitive processing. In J. M. Henderson & F. Ferreira (Eds.), *The interface of language, vision, and action: Eye movements and the visual world* (pp. 105–133). New York: Psychology Press.

Irwin, D. E., & Zelinsky, G. J. (2002). Eye movements and scene perception: Memory for things observed. *Perception & Psychophysics, 64,* 882–895.

Isen, A. M. (2000). Positive affect and decision making. In M. Lewis & J. M. Haviland-Jones (Eds.), *Handbook of emotions* (2nd ed., pp. 417–435). New York: Guilford.

Ishai, A., & Sagi, D. (1995). Common mechanisms of visual imagery and perception. *Science, 268,* 1772–1774.

Isikoff, M., & Lipper, T. (2003, July 21). A spy takes the bullet. *Newsweek,* pp. 24–25.

Israel, S. E., & Massey, D. (2005). Metacognitive think-aloud: Using a gradual release model with middle school students. In S. E. Israel, C. C. Block, K. L. Bauserman, & K. Kinnucan-Welsch (Eds.), *Metacognition in literacy learning: Theory, assessment, instruction, and professional development* (pp. 183–198). Mahwah, NJ: Erlbaum.

Ito, T. A., Urland, G. R., Willadsen-Jensen, E., & Correll, J. (2006). The social neuroscience of stereotyping and prejudice: Using event-related brain potentials to study social perception. In J. T. Cacioppo, P. S. Visser, & C. L. Pickett (Eds.), *Social neuroscience: People thinking about thinking people* (pp. 189–208). Cambridge, MA: MIT Press.

Ivins, M. (1999, December 20). Media coverage of WTO was simplistic nonsense. *Liberal Opinion,* p. 12.

Izaute, M., Chambres, P., & Larochelle, S. (2002). Feeling-of-knowing for proper names. *Canadian Journal of Experimental Psychology, 56,* 263–272.

Izawa, C. (Ed.). (1999). *On human memory: Evolution, progress, and reflections on the 30th anniversary of the Atkinson-Shiffrin model.* Mahwah, NJ: Erlbaum.

Jackendoff, R. (1994). *Patterns in the mind.* New York: Basic Books.

Jackendoff, R. (1997). *The architecture of the language faculty.* Cambridge, MA: MIT Press.

Jackson, S. L., & Griggs, R. A. (1990). The elusive pragmatic reasoning schemas effect. *Quarterly Journal of Experimental Psychology, 42A,* 353–373.

Jacobs, N., & Garnham, A. (2007). The role of conversational hand gestures in a narrative task. *Journal of Memory and Language, 56,* 291–303.

Jacoby, L. L., Yonelinas, A. P., & Jennings, J. M. (1997). The relation between conscious and unconscious (automatic) influences: A declaration of independence. In J. D. Cohen & J. W. Schooler (Eds.), *Scientific approaches to consciousness* (pp. 13–47). Mahwah, NJ: Erlbaum.

Jaeger, C. C., Renn, O., Rosa, E. A., & Webler, T. (2001). *Risk, uncertainty, and rational action.* London: Earthscan.

Jahn, G. (2004). Three turtles in danger: Spontaneous construction of causally relevant spatial situation models. *Journal of Experimental Psychology: Learning, Memory, and Cognition, 30,* 969–987.

Jain, A. K., & Duin, R. P. W. (2004). Pattern recognition. In R. L. Gregory (Ed.), *The Oxford companion to the mind* (2nd ed., p. 698–703). New York: Oxford University Press.

James, L. E., & Burke, D. M. (2000). Phonological priming effects on words retrieval and tip-of-the-tongue experiences in young and older adults, *Journal of Experimental Psychology: Learning, Memory, and Cognition, 26,* 1378–1391.

James, L. E., & MacKay, D. G. (2001). H.M., word knowledge, and aging: Support for a new theory of long-term retrograde amnesia. *Psychological Science, 12,* 485–492.

James, W. (1890). *The principles of psychology.* New York: Henry Holt.

Janis, I. (1972). *Victims of groupthink.* Boston: Houghton Mifflin.

Jared, D., Levy, B. A., & Rayner, K. (1999). The role of phonology in the activation of word meanings during reading: Evidence from proofreading and eye movements. *Journal of Experimental Psychology: General, 128,* 219–264.

Jarrold, C., & Bayliss, D. M. (2007). Variation in working memory due to typical and atypical development. In A. R. A. Conway et al. (Eds.), *Variations in working memory* (pp. 134–161). New York: Oxford University Press.

Jarvella, R. J. (1971). Syntactic processing of connected speech. *Journal of Verbal Learning and Verbal Behavior, 10*, 409–416.

Jasper, J. D., et al. (2001). Effects of framing on teratogenic risk perception in pregnant women. *Lancet, 358*, 1237–1238.

Jenkins, J. J. (1974). Remember that old theory of memory? Well, forget it. *American Psychologist, 29*, 785–795.

Jenkins, W., & McDowall, J. (2001). Implicit memory and depression: An analysis of perceptual and conceptual processes. *Cognition and Emotion, 15*, 803–812.

Jia, G., Aaronson, D., & Wu, Y. (2002). Long-term language attainment of bilingual immigrants: Predictive variables and language group differences. *Applied Psycholinguistics, 23*, 599–621.

Jitendra, A. K., et al. (2007). A comparison of single and multiple strategy instruction on third-grade students' mathematical problem solving. *Journal of Educational Psychology, 99*, 115–127.

Jobard, G., Crivello, E., & Tzourio-Mazoyer, N. (2003). Evaluation of the dual route theory of reading: A meta-analysis of 35 neuroimaging studies. *Neuroimage, 20*, 693–712.

Johansson, P., et al. (2006). How something can be said about telling more than we can know: On choice blindness and introspection. *Consciousness and Cognition, 15*, 673–692.

Johns, M., Schmader, T., & Martens, A. (2005). Knowing is half the battle: Teaching stereotype threat as a means of improving women's math performance. *Psychological Science, 16*, 175–179.

Johnson, D. D. P. (2004). *Overconfidence and war: The havoc and glory of positive illusions.* Cambridge, MA: Harvard University Press.

Johnson, J. S., & Newport, E. L. (1989). Critical effects in second language learning: The influence of maturational state on the acquisition of English as a second language. *Cognitive Psychology, 21*, 60–99.

Johnson, K. E., & Mervis, C. B. (1997). Effects of varying levels of expertise on the basic level of categorization. *Journal of Experimental Psychology: General, 126*, 248–277.

Johnson, M. H., & Bolhuis, J. J. (2000). Predispositions in perceptual and cognitive development. In J. J. Bolhuis (Ed.), *Brain, perception, memory* (pp. 68–84). New York: Oxford University Press.

Johnson, M. K. (1996). Fact, fantasy, and public policy. In D. J. Herrmann et al. (Eds.), *Basic and applied memory research theory in context* (Vol. 1, pp. 83–103). Mahwah, NJ: Erlbaum.

Johnson, M. K. (1997). Identifying the origin of mental experience. In M. S. Myslobodsky (Ed.), *The mythomanias: The nature of deception and self-deception* (pp. 133–180). Mahwah, NJ: Erlbaum.

Johnson, M. K. (1998). Individual and cultural reality monitoring. *Annals of the American Academy of Political and Social Science, 560*, 179–193.

Johnson, M. K. (2002, October). Reality monitoring: Varying levels of analysis. *APS Observer*, pp. 8, 28–29.

Johnson, M. K., & Raye, C. L. (2000). Cognitive and brain mechanisms of false memories and beliefs. In D. L. Schachter & E. Scarry (Eds.), *Memory, brain, and belief* (pp. 35–86). Cambridge, MA: Harvard University Press.

Johnson, R. D. (1987). Making judgments when information is missing: Inferences, biases, and framing effects. *Acta Psychologica, 66*, 69–72.

Johnson-Laird, P. N. (2005a). Mental models and thought. In K. J. Holyoak & R. G. Morrison (Eds.), *The Cambridge handbook of thinking and reasoning* (pp. 185–208) New York: Cambridge University Press.

Johnson-Laird, P. N. (2005b). The shape of problems. In V. Girotto & P. N. Johnson-Laird (Eds.), *The shape of reason: Essays in honour of Paolo Legrenzi* (pp. 3–26). Hove, UK: Psychology Press.

Johnson-Laird, P. N., Girotto, V., & Legrenzi, P. (2004). Reasoning from inconsistency to consistency. *Psychological Review, 111*, 640–661.

Johnson-Laird, P. N., Savary, F., & Bucciarelli, M. (2000). Strategies and tactics in reasoning. In W. Schaeken, G. DeVooght, A. Vandierendonck, & G. d'Ydewalle (Eds.), *Deductive reasoning and strategies* (pp. 209–240). Mahwah, NJ: Erlbaum.

Johnson-Laird, P. N., et al. (1999). Naive probability: A mental model theory of extensional reasoning. *Psychological Review, 106*, 62–88.

Jolicoeur, P., & Kosslyn, S. M. (1985a). Demand characteristics in image scanning experiments. *Journal of Mental Imagery, 9*, 41–50.

Jolicoeur, P., & Kosslyn, S. M. (1985b). Is time to scan visual images due to demand characteristics? *Memory & Cognition, 13*, 320–332.

Jones, D. M., Macken, W. J., & Nicholls, A. P. (2004). The phonological store of working memory: Is it phonological and is it a store? *Journal of Experimental Psychology, Learning, Memory, and Cognition, 30*, 656–674.

Jones, J. (1999). *The psychotherapist's guide to human memory.* New York: Basic Books.

Joormann, J., & Siemer, M. (2004). Memory accessibility, mood regulation, and dysphoria: Difficulties in repairing sad mood with happy memories? *Journal of Abnormal Psychology, 113,* 179–188.

Jordan, T. R., & Bevan, K. M. (1994). Word superiority over isolated letters: The neglected case of forward masking. *Memory & Cognition, 22,* 133–144.

Jost, J. T., & Hamilton, D. L. (2005). Stereotypes in our culture. In J. F. Dovidio, P. Glick, & L. A. Rudman (Eds.), *On the nature of prejudice: Fifty years after Allport* (pp. 208–224). Malden, MA: Blackwell.

Jost, J. T., & Sidanius, J. (2004). *Political psychology: Key readings.* New York: Psychology Press.

Joyner, M. H., & Kurtz-Costes, B. (1997). Metamemory development. In N. Cowan & C. Hulme (Eds.), *The development of memory in childhood* (pp. 275–300). East Sussex, UK: Psychology Press.

Jusczyk, P. W. , & Luce, P. A. (2002). Speech perception. In H. Pashler (Ed.), *Stevens' handbook of experimental psychology* (3rd ed., Vol. 1, pp. 493–536). New York: Wiley.

Juslin, P., Winman, A., & Hansson, P. (2007). The naïve intuitive statistician: A naïve sampling model of intuitive confidence intervals. *Psychological Review, 114,* 678–703.

Just, M. A., Carpenter, P. A., & Keller, T. A. (1996). The capacity theory of comprehension: New frontiers of evidence and arguments. *Psychological Review, 103,* 773–780.

Just, M. A., et al. (2001). Interdependence of nonoverlapping cortical systems in dual cognitive tasks. *NeuroImage, 14,* 417–426.

Just, M. A., et al. (2004). Imagery in sentence comprehension: An fMRI study. *NeuroImage, 21,* 112–124.

Justice, E. M., Baker-Ward, L., Gupta, S., & Jannings, L. R. (1997). Means to the goal of remembering: Developmental changes in awareness of strategy use-performance relations. *Journal of Experimental Child Psychology, 65,* 293–314.

Kagan, J., & Herschkowitz, N. (2005). *A young mind in a growing brain.* Mahwah, NJ: Erlbaum.

Kahneman, D. (2003). A perspective on judgment and choice: Mapping bounded rationality. *American Psychologist, 58,* 697–720.

Kahneman, D., & Frederick, S. (2002). Representativeness revisited: Attribute substitution in intuitive judgment. In T. Gilovich, D. Griffin, & D. Kahneman (Eds.), *Heuristics and biases: The psychology of intuitive judgment* (pp. 49–81). New York: Cambridge University Press.

Kahneman, D., & Frederick, S. (2005). A model of heuristic judgment. In K. J. Holyoak. & R. G. Morrison (Eds.), *The Cambridge handbook of thinking and reasoning* (pp. 267–293). New York: Cambridge University Press.

Kahneman, D., & Renshon, J. (2007, January/February). Why hawks win. *Foreign Policy,* pp. 34–38.

Kahneman, D., & Tversky, A. (1972). Subjective probability: A judgment of representativeness. *Cognitive Psychology, 3,* 430–454.

Kahneman, D., & Tversky, A. (1973). On the psychology of prediction. *Psychological Review, 80,* 237–251.

Kahneman, D., & Tversky, A. (1984). Choices, values, and frames. *American Psychologist, 39,* 341–350.

Kahneman, D., & Tversky, A. (1995). Conflict resolution: A cognitive perspective. In K. Arrow et al. (Eds.), *Barriers to conflict resolution* (pp. 44–60). New York: Norton.

Kahneman, D., & Tversky, A. (1996). On the reality of cognitive illusions. *Psychological Review, 103,* 582–591.

Kahneman, D., & Tversky, A. (2000). *Choice, values, and frames.* New York: Cambridge University Press.

Kail, R. (1992). Development of memory in children. In L. R. Squire (Ed.), *Encyclopedia of learning and memory* (pp. 99–102). New York: Macmillan.

Kalat, J. W. (2007). *Biological psychology* (9th ed.) Belmont, CA: Thomson Wadsworth.

Kanwisher, N., Downing, P., Epstein, R., & Kourtzi, Z. (2001). Functional neuroimaging of visual recognition. In R. Cabeza & A. Kingstone (Eds.), *Handbook of funtional neuroimaging of cognition* (pp. 110–151). Cambridge, MA: MIT Press.

Kaplan, P. S., Bachorowski, J., Smoski, M. J., & Hudenko, W. J. (2002). Infants of depressed mothers, although competent learners, fail to learn in response to their own mothers' infant-directed speech. *Psychological Science, 13,* 268–271.

Karatekin, C. (2004). A test of the integrity of the components of Baddeley's model of working memory in attention-deficit/hyperactivity disorder (ADHD). *Journal of Child Psychology and Psychiatry, 45,* 912–926.

Karmiloff, K., & Karmiloff-Smith, A. (2001). *Pathways to language: From fetus to adolescent.* Cambridge, MA: Harvard University Press.

Kashima, Y., et al. (2007). Connectionism and self: James, Mead, and the stream of enculturated consciousness. *Psychological Inquiry, 18,* 2007, 73–96.

Kaufman, J. C., & Baer, J. (Eds.). (2005). *Creativity across domains: Faces of the muse.* Mahwah, NJ: Erlbaum.

Kaufman, J. C., & Baer, J. (Eds.). (2006). *Creativity and reason in cognitive development*. New York: Cambridge University Press.

Kaufman, N. J., Randlett, A. L., & Price, J. (1985). Awareness of the use of comprehension strategies in good and poor college readers. *Reading Psychology, 6*, 1–11.

Kayaert, G., Biederman, I., & Vogels, R. (2003). Shape tuning in macaque inferior temporal cortex. *Journal of Neuroscience, 23*, 3016–3027.

Keast, A., Brewer, N., & Wells, G. L. (2007). Children's metacognitive judgments in an eyewitness identification task. *Journal of Experimental Child Psychology, 97*, 286–314.

Keating, P. A. (2006). Phonetic encoding of prosodic structure. In J. Harrington & M. Tabain (Eds.), *Speech production: Models, phonetic processes, and techniques* (pp. 167–186). New York: Psychology Press.

Keehner, M., et al. (2006). Learning a spatial skill for surgery: How the contributions of abilities change with practice. *Applied Cognitive Psychology, 20*, 487–503.

Keil, F. C. (2003). Categorization, causation and the limits of understanding. *Language and Cognitive Processes, 18*, 663–692.

Keller, T. A., Carpenter, P. A., & Just, M. A. (2003). Brain imaging of tongue-twister sentence comprehension: Twisting the tongue and the brain. *Brain and Language, 84*, 189–203.

Kelley, C. M., & Jacoby, L. L. (2000). Recollection and familiarity: Process-dissociation. In E. Tulving & F. I. M. Craik (Eds.), *The Oxford handbook of memory* (pp. 215–228). New York: Oxford University Press.

Kellogg, R. T. (1989). Idea processors: Computer aids for planning and composing text. In B. K. Britton & S. M. Glynn (Eds.), *Computer writing environments: Theory, research, and design* (pp. 57–92). Hillsdale, NJ: Erlbaum.

Kellogg, R. T. (1994). *The psychology of writing*. New York: Oxford University Press.

Kellogg, R. T. (1996). A model of working memory in writing. In C. M. Levy & S. Ransdell (Eds.), *The science of writing: Theories, methods, individual differences, and applications* (pp. 57–71). Mahwah, NJ: Erlbaum.

Kellogg, R. T. (1998). Components of working memory in text production. In M. Torrance & G. C. Jeffery (Eds.), *The cognitive demands of writing: Processing capacity and working memory effects in text production*. Amsterdam: Amsterdam University Press.

Kellogg, R. T. (2001a). Competition for working memory among writing processes. *American Journal of Psychology, 114*, 175–191.

Kellogg, R. T. (2001b). Long-term working memory in text production. *Memory & Cognition, 29*, 43–52.

Kellogg, R. T. (2006). Professional writing expertise. In K. A. Ericsson, N. Charness, P. J. Feltovich, & R. R. Hoffman (Eds.), *The Cambridge handbook of expertise and performance* (pp. 389–402). New York: Cambridge University Press.

Kelly, F., & Grossberg, S. (2000). Neural dynamics of 3-D surface perception: Figure-ground separation and lightness perception. *Perception & Psychophysics, 62*, 1596–1618.

Kemp, R., Towell, N., & Pike, G. (1997). When seeing should not be believing: Photographs, credit cards, and fraud. *Journal of Applied Psychology, 11*, 211–222.

Kemper, S. (2006). Language and adulthood. Aging and attention. In E. Bialystok & F. I. M. Craik (Eds.), *Lifespan cognition: Mechanisms of change* (pp. 223–238). New York: Oxford University Press.

Kennedy, Q., Mather, M., & Carstensen, L. (2004). The role of motivation in the age-related positivity effect in autobiographical memory. *Psychological Science, 15*, 208–214.

Kerr, N. L., & Tindale, R. S. (2004). Group performance and decision making. *Annual Review of Psychology, 55*, 623–655.

Kersten, D., Mamassian, P., & Yuille, A. (2004). Object perception as Bayesian inference. *Annual Review of Psychology, 55*, 271–304.

Kerstholt, J. H., Jansen, N. J. M., Van Amelsvoort, A. G., & Broeders, A. P. A. (2006). Earwitnesses: Effects of accent, retention and telephone. *Applied Cognitive Psychology, 20*, 187–197.

Kester, J. D., Benjamin, A. S., Castel, A. D., & Craik, F. I. M. (2002). Memory in elderly people. In A. D. Baddeley, M. D. Kopelman, & B. A. Wilson (Eds.), *The handbook of memory disorders* (2nd ed., pp. 543–567). New York: Wiley.

Keysar, B., & Henly, A. S. (2002). Speakers' overestimation of their effectiveness. *Psychological Science, 13*, 207–212.

Kida, T. (2006). *Don't believe everything you think: The 6 basic mistakes we make in thinking*. Amherst, NY: Prometheus Books.

Kifner, J. (1994, May 20). Pollster finds error on Holocaust doubts. *New York Times* (Late New York Edition), p. A12.

Kihlstrom, J. F. (1998). Exhumed memory. In S. J. Lynn & K. M. McConkey (Eds.), *Truth in memory* (pp. 3–31). New York: Guilford.

Kihlstrom, J. F., & Cork, R. C. (2007). Consciousness and anesthesia. In M. Velmans & S. Schneider (Eds.), *The Blackwell companion to consciousness* (pp. 628–640). Malden, MA: Blackwell.

Kihlstrom, J. F., Dorfman, J., & Park, L. (2007). Implicit and explicit memory and learning. In M. Velmans & S. Schneider (Eds.), *The Blackwell companion to consciousness* (pp. 526–539). Malden, MA: Blackwell.

Kimball, D. R., & Holyoak, K. K. (2000). Transfer and expertise. In E. Tulving & F. I. M. Craik (Eds.), *The Oxford handbook of memory* (pp. 109–122). New York: Oxford University Press.

Kinsbourne, M. (1998). The right hemisphere and recovery from aphasia. In B. Stemmer & H. A. Whitaker (Eds.), *Handbook of neurolinguistics* (pp. 385–392). San Diego: Academic Press.

Kintsch, W. (1984). Approaches to the study of the psychology of language. In T. G. Bever, J. M. Carroll, & L. A. Miller (Eds.), *Talking minds: The study of language in cognitive science* (pp. 111–145). Cambridge, MA: MIT Press.

Kintsch, W. (1998). *Comprehension: A paradigm for cognition.* New York: Cambridge University Press.

Kintsch, W. (2007). Meaning in context. In T. K. Landauaer, D. S. McNamara, S. Dennis, & W. Kintsch (Eds.), *Handbook of latent semantic analysis* (pp. 89–105). Mahwah, NJ: Erlbaum.

Kintsch, W., & Buschke, H. (1969). Homophones and synonyms in short-term memory. *Journal of Experimental Psychology, 80,* 403–407.

Kintsch, W., McNamara, D. S., Dennis, S., & Landauer, T. K. (2007). LSA and meaning in theory and application. In T. K. Landauaer, D. S. McNamara, S. Dennis, & W. Kintsch (Eds.), *Handbook of latent semantic analysis* (pp. 467–479). Mahwah, NJ: Erlbaum.

Kintsch, W., et al. (1999). Models of working memory. In A. Miyake & P. Shah (Eds.), *Models of working memory: Mechanisms of active maintenance and executive control* (pp. 412–441). New York: Cambridge University Press.

Kircher, T. T. J., et al. (2000). Towards a functional neuroanatomy of self processing: Effects of faces and words. *Cognitive Brain Research, 10,* 133–144.

Kirsh, S. J. (2006). *Children, adolescents, and media violence: A critical look at the research.* Thousand Oaks, CA: Sage.

Kirshner, D., & Whitson, J. A. (1997). Editors' introduction to situated cognition: Social, semiotic, and psychological perspectives. In D. Kirshner & J. A. Whitson (Eds.), *Situated cognition: Social, semiotic, and psychological perspectives* (pp. 1–16). Mahwah, NJ: Erlbaum.

Kisilevsky, B. S., et al. (2003). Effects of experience on fetal voice recognition. *Psychological Science, 14,* 220–224.

Kitchin, R., & Blades, M. (2002). *The cognition of geographic space.* London: Tauris.

Kizilbash, A. H., Vanderploeg, R. D., & Curtiss, G. (2002). The effects of depression and anxiety on memory performance. *Archives of Clinical Neuropsychology, 17,* 57–67.

Klauer, K. C., Musch, J., & Naumer, B. (2000). On belief bias in syllogistic reasoning. *Psychological Review, 107,* 852–884.

Klein, G. (1997). Naturalistic decision making: Where are we going? In C. E. Zsambok & G. Klein (Eds.), *Naturalistic decision making* (pp. 383–397). Mahwah, NJ: Erlbaum.

Klein, I., et al. (2004). Retinotopic organization of visual mental images as revealed by functional magnetic resonance imaging. *Cognitive Brain Research, 22,* 26–31.

Klein, S. B., & Kihlstrom, J. F. (1986). Elaboration, organization, and the self-reference effect in memory. *Journal of Experimental Psychology: General, 115,* 26–38.

Kliegl, R., Grabner, E., Rolfe, M., & Engbert, R. (2004). Length, frequency, and predictability effects of words on eye movements in reading. In R. Radach, A. Kennedy, & K. Rayner (Eds.), *Eye movements and information processing during reading* (pp. 262–284). Hove, UK: Psychology Press.

Klin, C. M., Guzmán, A. E., & Levine, W. H. (1999). Prevalence and persistence of predictive inferences. *Journal of Memory and Learning, 40,* 593–604.

Knott, R., & Marslen-Wilson, W. (2001). Does the medial temporal lobe bind phonological memories? *Journal of Cognitive Neuroscience, 13,* 593–609.

Knouse, L. E., Paradise, M. J., & Dunlosky, J. (2006). Does ADHD in adults affect the relative accuracy of metamemory judgments? *Journal of Attention Disorders, 10,* 160–170.

Knowlton, B. (1997). Declarative and nondeclarative knowledge: Insights from cognitive neuroscience. In K. Lamberts & D. Shanks (Eds.), *Knowledge, concepts and categories* (pp. 215–246). Cambridge, MA: MIT Press.

Koehler, D. J., & Harvey, N. (Eds.). (2004). *The Blackwell handbook of judgment and decision making.* Oxford, UK: Blackwell.

Koestler, A. (1964). *The act of creation.* London: Hutchinson.

Koriat, A. (1997). Monitoring one's own knowledge during study: A cue-utilization approach to judgments of learning. *Journal of Experimental Psychology: General, 126,* 349–370.

Koriat, A. (2000). Control processes in remembering. In E. Tulving & F. I. M. Craik (Eds.), *The Oxford handbook of memory* (pp. 333–346). New York: Oxford University Press.

Koriat, A. (2007). Metacognition and consciousness. In P. D. Zelazo, M. Moscovitch, & E. Thompson (Eds.), *The Cambridge handbook of consciousness* (pp. 289–325). Cambridge, UK: Cambridge University Press.

Koriat, A., & Bjork, R. A. (2005). Illusions of competence in monitoring one's knowledge during study. *Journal of Experimental Psychology: Learning, Memory, and Cognition, 31*, 187–194.

Koriat, A., & Bjork, R. A. (2006a). Illusions of competence during study can be remedied by manipulations that enhance learners' sensitivity to retrieval conditions at test. *Memory & Cognition, 34*, 959–972.

Koriat, A., & Bjork, R. A. (2006b). Mending metacognitive illusions: A comparison of mnemonic-based and theory-based procedures. *Journal of Experimental Psychology: Learning, Memory, and Cognition, 32*, 1133–1145.

Koriat, A., Fiedler, K., & Bjork, R. A. (2006). Inflation of conditional predictions. *Journal of Experimental Psychology: General, 135*, 429–447.

Koriat, A., Goldsmith, M., & Pansky, A. (2000). Toward a psychology of memory accuracy. *Annual Review of Psychology, 51*, 481–537.

Koriat, A., & Helstrup, T. (2007). Metacognitive aspects of memory. In S. Magnussen & T. Helstrup (Eds.), *Everyday memories* (pp. 251–274). New York: Psychology Press.

Koriat, A., Levy-Sadot, R., Edry, E., & de Marcas, S. (2003). What do we know about what we cannot remember? Accessing the semantic attributes of words that cannot be recalled. *Journal of Experimental Psychology: Learning, Memory, and Cognition, 29*, 1095–1105.

Kornell, N., & Metcalfe, J. (2006). Study efficacy and the region of proximal learning framework. *Journal of Experimental Psychology: Learning, Memory, and Cognition, 37*, 609–622.

Kosslyn, S. M. (1983). *Ghosts in the mind's machine: Creating and using images in the brain*. New York: Norton.

Kosslyn, S. M. (2001). Visual consciousness. *Advances in Consciousness Research, 8*, 79–103.

Kosslyn, S. M. (2004). Mental imagery: Depictive accounts. In R. L. Gregory (Ed.), *The Oxford companion to the mind* (pp. 585–587). New York: Oxford University Press.

Kosslyn, S. M., Alpert, N. M., & Thompson, W. L. (1995). Identifying objects at different levels of hierarchy: A positron emission tomography study. *Human Brain Mapping, 3*, 107–132.

Kosslyn, S. M., Ball, T. M., & Reiser, B. J. (1978). Visual images preserve metric spatial information: Evidence from studies of image scanning. *Journal of Experimental Psychology: Human Perception & Performance, 4*, 47–60.

Kosslyn, S. M., Ganis, G., & Thompson, W. L. (2001). Neural foundations of imagery. *Nature Reviews/Neuroscience, 2*, 635–642.

Kosslyn, S. M., Ganis, G., & Thompson, W. L. (2003). Mental imagery: Against the nihilistic hypothesis. *TRENDS in Cognitive Sciences, 7*, 109–111.

Kosslyn, S. M., Ganis, G., & Thompson, W. L. (2004). Mental imagery:: Depictive accounts. In R. L. Gregory (Ed.), *The Oxford companion to the mind* (pp. 585–587). New York: Oxford University Press.

Kosslyn, S. M., Seger, C., Pani, J. R., & Hillger, L. A. (1990). When is imagery used in everyday life? A diary study. *Journal of Mental Imagery, 14*, 131–152.

Kosslyn, S. M., & Thompson, W. L. (2000). Shared mechanisms in visual imagery and visual perception: Insights from cognitive neurosciences. In M. S. Gazzaniga (Ed.), *The new cognitive neurosciences* (2nd ed., pp. 975–985). Cambridge, MA: MIT Press.

Kosslyn, S. M., Thompson, W. L., & Ganis, G. (2006). *The case for mental imagery*. New York: Oxford University Press.

Kosslyn, S. M., Thompson, W. L., Wraga, M., & Alpert, N. M. (2001). Imagining rotation by endogenous versus exogenous forces: Distinct neural mechanisms. *Cognitive Neuroscience and Neuropsychology, 12*, 2519–2525.

Kosslyn, S. M., et al. (1996). Individual differences in cerebral blood flow in Area 17 predict the time to evaluate visualized letters. *Journal of Cognitive Neuroscience, 8*, 78–82.

Kosslyn, S. M., et al. (2002). Bridging psychology and biology: The analysis of individuals in groups. *American Psychologist, 57*, 341–351.

Kozielecki, J. (1981). *Psychological decision theory*. Warsaw, Poland: Polish Scientific Publishers.

Kramer, A. F., & Kray, J. (2006). Aging and attention. In E. Bialystok & F. I. M. Craik (Eds.), *Lifespan cognition: Mechanisms of change* (pp. 57–69). New York: Oxford University Press.

Krizan, Z., & Windschitl, P. D. (2007). The influence of outcome desirability on optimism. *Psychological Bulletin, 133*, 95–121.

Kroll, J. F., & de Groot, A. M. (Eds.). (2005). *Handbook of bilingualism: Psycholinguistic approaches.* New York: Oxford University Press.

Krueger, L. E. (1992). The word-superiority effect and phonological recoding. *Memory & Cognition, 20,* 685–694.

Kruglanski, A. W. (2004). *The psychology of closed mindedness.* New York: Psychology Press.

Kruschke, J. K. (1996). Base rates in category learning. *Journal of Experimental Psychology: Learning, Memory, and Cognition, 22,* 3–26.

Krynski, R. R., & Tenenbaum, J. B. (2007). The role of causality in judgments under uncertainty. *Journal of Experimental Psychology: General, 136,* 430–450.

Ku, R. J.-S. (2006). Confessions of an English professor: Globalization and the anxiety of the (standard) English practice. In H. Luria, D. M. Seymour, & T. Smoke (Eds.), *Language and linguistics in context: Readings and applications for teachers* (pp. 377–384). Mahwah, NJ: Erlbaum.

Kubose, T. T., et al. (2005). The effects of speech production and speech comprehension on simulated driving performance. *Applied Cognitive Psychology, 20,* 43–63.

Kubose, T. T., et al. (2006). The effects of speech production and speech comprehension on simulated driving performance. *Applied Cognitive Psychology, 20,* 43–64.

Kubovy, M., Epstein, W., & Gepshtein, S. (2003). Foundations of visual perception. In A. F. Healy & R. W. Proctor (Eds.), *Handbook of psychology* (Vol. 4, pp. 87–121). Hoboken, NJ: Wiley.

Kuczaj, S. A. (1999). The world of words: Thoughts on the development of a lexicon. In M. Barrett (Ed.), *The development of language* (pp. 133–159). Hove, UK: Psychology Press.

Kuhl, P. K. (1994). Learning and representation in speech and language. *Current Opinion in Neurobiology, 4,* 812–822.

Kuhl, P. K. (2000). Language, mind, and brain: Experience alters perception. In M. Gazzaniga (Ed.), *The new cognitive neurosciences* (pp. 99–115). Cambridge, MA: MIT Press.

Kuhl, P. K. (2004). Early language acquisition: Cracking the speech code. *Nature Reviews: Neuroscience, 5,* 831–843.

Kuhl, P. K. (2006). A new view of language acquisition. In H. Luria, D. M. Seymour, & T. Smoke (Eds.), *Language and linguistics in context: Readings and applications for teachers* (pp. 29–41). Mahwah, NJ: Erlbaum.

Kuhn, D. (2000). Metacognitive development. *Current Directions in Psychological Science, 9,* 178–181.

Kuhn, D., & Siegler, R. (Eds.). (2006). *Handbook of child psychology* (6th ed., Vol. 2: *Cognition, perception and language*). Hoboken, NJ: Wiley.

Kumon-Nakamura, S., Glucksberg, S., & Brown, M. (1995). How about another piece of pie: The allusional pretense theory of discourse irony. *Journal of Experimental Psychology: General, 124,* 3–21.

Kunda, Z. (1999). *Social cognition: Making sense of people.* Cambridge, MA: MIT Press.

Kurdek, L. A. (2004). Are gay and lesbian cohabiting couples *really* different from heterosexual married couples? *Journal of Marriage & Family, 66,* 880–900.

Kvavilashvili, L., Mirani, J., Schlagman, S., & Kornbrot, D. E. (2003). Comparing flashbulb memories of September 11 and the death of Princess Diana: Effects of time delays and nationalities. *Applied Cognitive Psychology, 17,* 1017–1031.

Kyllonen, P. C., Lee, S. (2005). Assessing problem solving in context. In O. Wilhelm & R. W. Engle (Eds.), *Handbook of understanding and measuring intelligence* (pp. 11–25). Thousand Oaks, CA: Sage.

LaBerge, D. (1995). *Attentional processing: The brain's art of mindfulness.* Cambridge, MA: Harvard University Press.

Lachter, J., Forster, K. I., & Ruthruff, E. (2004). Forty-five years after Broadbent (1958): Still no identification without attention. *Psychological Review, 111,* 880–913.

Laeng, B., Zarrinpar, A., & Kosslyn, S. M. (2003). Do separate processes identify objects as exemplars versus members of basic-level categories? Evidence from hemispheric specialization. *Brain and Cognition, 53,* 15–27.

Lakoff, G. (1987). *Women, fire and dangerous things: What categories reveal about the mind.* Chicago: University of Chicago Press.

Lambert, W. E. (1987). The effects of bilingual and bicultural experiences on children's attitudes and social perspectives. In P. Homel, M. Palij, & D. Aaronson (Eds.), *Childhood bilingualism: Aspects of linguistic, cognitive, and social development* (pp. 197–228). Hillsdale, NJ: Erlbaum.

Lambert, W. E. (1990). Persistent issues in bilingualism. In B. Harley, P. Allen, J. Cummins, & M. Swain (Eds.), *The development of second language proficiency* (pp. 201–218). Cambridge, UK: Cambridge University Press.

Lambert, W. E. (1992). Challenging established views on social issues. *American Psychologist, 47,* 533–542.

Lambert, W. E., Genesee, F., Holobow, N., & Chartrand, L. (1991). *Bilingual education for majority English-speaking children.* Montreal: McGill University, Psychology Department.

Lampinen, J. M., Beike, D. R., & Behrend, D. A. (2004). The self and memory: It's about time. In D. R. Beike, J. M., & Behrend (Eds.), *The self and memory* (pp. 255–262). New York: Psychology Press.

Lampinen, J. M., Copeland, S. M., & Neuschatz, J. S. (2001). Recollection of things schematic: Room schemas revisited. *Journal of Experimental Psychology: Learning, Memory, & Cognition, 27,* 1211–1222.

Lampinen, J. M., Faries, J. M., Neuschatz, J. S., & Toglia, M. P. (2000). Recollections of things schematic: The influence of scripts on recollective experience. *Applied Cognitive Psychology, 14,* 543–554.

Landauer, T. K., & Dumais, S. T. (1997). A solution to Plato's problem: The latent semantic analysis theory of acquisition, induction, and representation of knowledge. *Psychological Review, 104,* 211–240.

Landauer, T. K., McNamara, D. S., Dennis, S., & Kintsch, W. (Eds.). (2007). *Handbook of latent semantic analysis.* Mahwah, NJ: Erlbaum.

Langer, E. J. (2000). Mindful learning. *Current Directions in Psychological Science, 9,* 220–223.

Langer, E. J., & Moldoveanu, M. (2000). The construct of mindfulness. *Journal of Social Issues, 56,* 1–9.

Lappin, J. S., & Craft, W. D. (2000). Foundations of spatial vision: From retinal images to perceived shapes. *Psychological Review, 107,* 6–38.

Larsen, A., & Bundesen, C. (1996). A template-matching pandemonium recognizes unconstrained handwritten characters with high accuracy. *Memory & Cognition, 24,* 136–143.

Laszlo, E., Artigiani, R., Combs, A., & Csányi, V. (1996). *Changing visions: Human cognitive maps, past, present, and future.* Westport, CT: Praeger.

Lave, J. (1988). *Cognition in practice: Mind, mathematics, and culture in everyday life.* New York: Cambridge University Press.

Lave, J. (1997). What's special about experiments as contexts for thinking. In M. Cole, Y. Engeström, & O. Vasquez (Eds.), *Mind, culture, and activity* (pp. 56–69). New York: Cambridge University Press.

Lavie, N. (2007). Attention and consciousness. In M. Velmans & S. Schneider (Eds.), *The Blackwell companion to consciousness* (pp. 489–503). Malden, MA: Blackwell.

Lea, R. B., Mulligan, E. J., & Walton, J. L. (2005). Accessing distant premise information: How memory feeds reasoning. *Journal of Experimental Psychology: Learning, Memory, and Cognition, 31,* 387–395.

Leahey, T. H. (2003). Cognition and learning. In D. F. Freedheim (Ed.), *Handbook of psychology* (Vol. 1: *The history of psychology,* pp. 109–133). Hoboken, NJ: Wiley.

Learmonth, A. E., Lamberth, R., & Rovee-Collier, C. (2004). Generalization of deferred imitation during the first year of life. *Journal of Experimental Child Psychology, 88,* 297–318.

Learmonth, A. E., Lamberth, R., & Rovee-Collier, C. (2005). The social context of imitation in infancy. *Journal of Experimental Child Psychology, 91,* 297–314.

LeBoeuf, R. A., & Shafir, E. B. (2005). Decision making. In K. J. Holyoak & R. G. Morrison (Eds.), *The Cambridge handbook of thinking and reasoning* (pp. 243–263) New York: Cambridge University Press.

Leek, E. C. (2005). Category-specific semantic memory impairments: What can connectionist simulations reveal about the organization of conceptual knowledge? In G. Houghton (Ed.), *Connectionist models in cognitive psychology* (pp. 175–214). New York: Psychology Press.

Leichtman, M. D., & Ceci, S. J. (1995). The effects of stereotypes and suggestions on preschoolers' reports. *Developmental Psychology, 31,* 568–578.

Leighton, J. P., & Sternberg, R. J. (2003). Reasoning and problem solving. In A. F. Healy & R. W. Proctor (Eds.), *Handbook of psychology* (Vol. 4, pp. 623–648). Hoboken, NJ: Wiley.

Leippe, M., & Eisenstadt, D. (2007). Eyewitness confidence and the confidence-accuracy relationship in memory for people. In R. C. L. Lindsay, D. F. Ross, J. D. Read, & M. P. Toglia (Eds.), *Handbook of eyewitness psychology* (Vol. 2, pp. 377–425). Mahwah, NJ: Erlbaum.

Lepore, S. J., & Smyth, J. M. (Eds.). (2002). *The writing cure: How expressive writing promotes health and emotional well-being.* Washington, DC: American Psychological Association.

Levelt, W. J. M. (1994). The skill of speaking. In P. Bertelson, P. Eelen, & G. d'Ydewalle (Eds.), *International perspectives on psychological science* (Vol. 1, pp. 89–103). Hove, UK: Erlbaum.

Levelt, W. J. M. (1998). The genetic perspective in psycholinguistics or where do spoken words come from? *Journal of Psycholinguistic Research, 27,* 167–180.

Levelt, W. J. M., Roelofs, A., & Meyer, A. S. (1999). A theory of lexical access in speech production. *Behavioral and Brain Sciences, 22,* 1–75.

Levesque, L. C. (2001). *Breakthrough creativity: Achieving top performance using the eight creative talents.* Palo Alto, CA: Davies-Black.

Levin, D. T. (2004a). Introduction. In D. T. Levin (Ed.), *Thinking and seeing: Visual metacognition in adults and children* (pp. 1–11). Cambridge, MA: MIT Press.

Levin, D. T. (Ed.).(2004b). *Thinking and seeing: Visual metacognition in adults and children.* Cambridge, MA: MIT Press.

Levine, D. S. (2002). Neural network modeling. In H. Pashler (Ed.), *Stevens' handbook of experimental psychology* (3rd ed., Vol. 4, pp. 223–269). New York: Wiley.

Levine, L. J., & Bluck, S. (2004). Painting with broad strokes: Happiness and the malleability of event memory. *Cognition and Emotion, 18,* 559–574.

Levine, L. J., & Burgess, S. L. (1997). Beyond general arousal: Effects of specific emotions on memory. *Social Cognition, 15,* 157–181.

Levy, B., & Banaji, M. R. (2002). Implicit ageism. In T. D. Nelson (Ed.), *Ageism: Stereotyping and prejudice against older persons* (pp. 49–75). Cambridge, MA: MIT Press.

Levy, B. A. (1999). Whole words, segments, and meaning: Approaches to reading education. In R. M. Klein & P. McMullen (Eds.), *Converging methods for understanding reading and dyslexia* (pp. 77–110). Cambridge, MA: MIT Press.

Levy, C. M., & Ransdell, S. (1995). Is writing as difficult as it seems? *Memory & Cognition, 23,* 767–779.

Levy, J., Pashler, H., & Boer, E. (2006). Central interference in driving: Is there any stopping the psychological refractory period? *Psychological Science, 17,* 228–235.

Lewandowsky, S., & Li, S.-C. (1995). Catastrophic interference in neural networks: Causes, solutions, and data. In F. N. Dempster & C. J. Brainerd (Eds.), *Interference and inhibition in cognition* (pp. 329–361). San Diego: Academic Press.

Liberman, A. M. (1996). *Speech: A special code.* Cambridge, MA: MIT Press.

Liberman, A. M., & Mattingly, I. G. (1989). A specialization for speech perception. *Science, 243,* 489–494.

Lieberman, M. D. (2007). Social cognitive neuroscience: A review of core processes. *Annual Review of Psychology, 58,* 259–259.

Light, L. L. (1996). Memory and aging. In E. L. Bjork & R. A. Bjork (Eds.), *Memory* (2nd ed., pp. 443–490). San Diego: Academic Press.

Light, L. L. (2000). Memory changes in adulthood. In S. H. Qualls & N. Abeles (Eds.), *Psychology and the aging revolution* (pp. 73–97). Washington, DC: American Psychological Association.

Light, L. L., La Voie, D., & Kennison, R. (1995). Repetition priming of nonwords in young and older adults. *Journal of Experimental Psychology: Learning, Memory, and Cognition, 21,* 327–346.

Lindsay, R. C. I., et al. (Eds.). (2007). *Handbook of eyewitness psychology: Vol. 2: Memory for events.* Mahwah, NJ: Erlbaum.

Linville, P. W., Fischer, G. W., & Fischhoff, B. (1993). AIDS risk perceptions and decision biases. In J. B. Pryor & G. D. Reeder (Eds.), *The social psychology of HIV infection* (pp. 5–38). Hillsdale, NJ: Erlbaum.

Little, D. M., Prentice, K. J., & Wingfield, A. (2004). Adult age differences in judgments of semantic fit. *Applied Psycholinguistics, 25,* 135–142.

Liversedge, S. P., & Findlay, J. M. (2000). Saccadic eye movements and cognition. *Trends in Cognitive Sciences, 4,* 6–14.

Lobley, K. J., Baddeley, A. D., & Gathercole, S. E. (2005). Phonological similarity effects in verbal complex span. *The Quarterly Journal of Experimental Psychology, 58A,* 1462–1478.

Lockhart, R. S. (2000). Methods of memory research. In E. Tulving & F. I. M. Craik (Eds.), *The Oxford handbook of memory* (pp. 45–57). New York: Oxford University Press.

Lockhart, R. S. (2001). Commentary: Levels of processing and memory theory. In M. Naveh-Benjamin, M. Moscovitch, & H. L. Roediger, III (Eds.), *Perspectives on human memory and cognitive aging: Essays in honour of Fergus Craik* (pp. 99–102). New York: Psychology Press.

Loftus, E. F., & Guyer, M. J. (2002a, May/June). Who abused Jane Doe? (Part 1). *Skeptical Inquirer,* pp. 24–32.

Loftus, E. F., & Guyer, M. J. (2002b, July/August). Who abused Jane Doe? (Part 2). *Skeptical Inquirer,* pp. 37–40.

Loftus, E. F., Miller, D. G., & Burns, H. J. (1978). Semantic integration of verbal information into visual memory. *Journal of Experimental Psychology: Human Learning and Memory, 4,* 19–31.

Logan, G. D. (2002). An instance theory of attention and memory. *Psychological Review, 109,* 376–400.

Logan, G. D. (2004). Cumulative progress in formal theories of attention. *Annual Review of Psychology, 55,* 207–234.

Logie, R. H. (1995). *Visuo-spatial working memory.* Hove, UK: Erlbaum.

Logie, R. H. (2003). Spatial and visual working memory: A mental workspace. *The Psychology of Learning and Motivation, 42,* 37–78.

Logie, R. H., & Della Sala, S. (2005). Disorders of visuospatial working memory. In P. Shah & A. Miyaki (Eds.), *The Cambridge handbook of visuospatial thinking* (pp. 81–120). New York: Cambridge University Press.

Long, D. L., Johns, C. L., & Morris, P. E. (2006). Comprehension ability in mature readers. In M. J. Traxler & M. A. Gernsbacher (Eds.), *Handbook of psycholinguistics* (2nd ed., pp. 801–833). Amsterdam: Elsevier.

Long, G. M., & Toppino, T. C. (2004). Enduring interest in perceptual ambiguity: Alternating views of reversible figures. *Psychological Bulletin, 130,* 748–768.

Lord, R. C., Hanges, P. J., & Godfrey, E. G. (2003). Integrating neural networks into decision-making and motivational theory: Rethinking VIE theory. *Canadian Psychology/Psychologie canadienne, 44,* 21–38.

Lovelace, E. A. (1984). Metamemory: Monitoring future recallability during study. *Journal of Experimental Psychology: Learning, Memory, and Cognition, 10,* 756–766.

Lovelace, E. A. (1996). *Personal communication.*

Lovett, M. C. (2002). Problem solving. In D. Medin (Ed.), *Stevens' handbook of experimental psychology* (pp. 317–362). New York: Wiley.

Lubart, T. L., & Guignard, J.-H. (2004). The generality-specificity of creativity: A multivariate approach. In R. J. Sternberg, E. L. Grigorenko, & J. L. Singer (Eds.), *Creativity: From potential to realization* (pp. 43–56). Washington, DC: American Psychological Association.

Lubart, T. L., & Mouchiroud, C. (2003). Creativity: A source of difficulty in problem solving. In J. E. Davidson & R. J. Sternberg (Eds.), *The psychology of problem solving* (pp. 127–148). New York: Cambridge University Press.

Luchins, A. S. (1942). Mechanization in problem solving. *Psychological Monographs, 54* (Whole No. 248).

Luck, S. J., & Vecera, S. P. (2002). Attention. In H. Pashler (Ed.), *Stevens' handbook of experimental psychology* (3rd ed., Vol. 1, pp. 235–286). New York: Wiley.

Luo, C. R., Johnson, R. A., & Gallo, D. A. (1998). Automatic activation of phonological information in reading: Evidence from the semantic relatedness decision task. *Memory & Cognition, 26,* 833–843.

Luo, Y., Baillargeon, R., Brueckner, L., & Munakata, Y. (2003). Reasoning about a hidden object after a delay: Evidence for robust representations in 5-month-old infants. *Cognition, 88,* B23–B32.

Luria, H. (2006). Introduction to Unit III: Literacy and education in a globalized world. In H. Luria, D. M. Seymour, & T. Smoke (Eds.), *Language and linguistics in context: Readings and applications for teachers* (pp. 233–242). Mahwah, NJ: Erlbaum.

Luria, H., Seymour, D. M. & Smoke, T. (Eds.). (2006). *Language and linguistics in context: Readings and applications for teachers.* Mahwah, NJ: Erlbaum.

Lustig, C., & Hasher, L. (2001a). Implicit memory is not immune to interference. *Psychological Bulletin, 127,* 618–628.

Lustig, C., & Hasher, L. (2001b). Implicit memory is vulnerable to proactive interference. *Psychological Science, 12,* 408–412.

Lustig, C., Matell, M. S., & Meck, W. H. (2005). Not "just" coincidence: Frontal-striatal interactions in working memory and interval timing. *Memory, 13,* 441–448.

Lynch, E. B., Coley, J. D., & Medin, D. L. (2000). Tall is typical: Central tendency, ideal dimensions, and graded category structure among tree experts and novices. *Memory & Cognition, 28,* 41–50.

Lynn, S. J., & McConkey, K. M. (Eds.). (1998). *Truth in memory.* New York: Guilford.

MacDonald, M. C. (1999). Distributional information in language comprehension, production, and acquisition: Three puzzles and a moral. In B. MacWhinney (Ed.), *The emergence of language* (pp. 177–196). Mahwah, NJ: Erlbaum.

MacKay, D. (2004). Information theory. In R. L. Gregory (Ed.), *The Oxford companion to the mind* (2nd ed., pp. 456–467). New York: Oxford University Press.

MacKay, I. R. A., Flege, J. E., & Imai, S. (2006). Evaluating the effects of chronological age and sentence duration on degree of perceived foreign accent. *Applied Psycholinguistics, 27,* 153–183.

MacLeod, C. (2005). The Stroop task in clinical research. In A. Wenzel & D. C. Rubin (Eds.), *Cognitive methods and their application to clinical research* (pp. 41–62). Washington, DC: American Psychological Association.

MacLeod, C., & Campbell, L. (1992). Memory accessibility and probability judgments: An experimental evaluation of the availability heuristic. *Journal of Personality and Social Psychology, 63,* 890–902.

MacLeod, C., & MacLeod, C. (2005). The Stroop task: Indirectly measuring concept activation. In A. Wenzel & D. C. Rubin (Eds.), *Cognitive methods and their application to clinical research* (pp. 13–16). Washington, DC: American Psychological Association.

MacLeod, C. M. (2005). The Stroop task in cognitive research. In A. Wenzel & D. C. Rubin (Eds.), *Cognitive methods and their application to clinical research* (pp. 17–40). Washington, DC: American Psychological Association.

MacLin, O. H., & Malpass, R. S. (2001). Racial categorization of faces: The ambiguous race face effect. *Psychology, Public Policy, and Law, 7,* 98–118.

Macpherson, R., & Stanovich, K. E. (2007). Cognitive ability, thinking dispositions, and instructional set as predictors of critical thinking. *Learning and Individual Differences, 17,* 115–127.

Macrae, C. N., et al. (2004). Medial prefrontal activity predicts memory for self. *Cerebral Cortex, 14,* 647–654.

MacWhinney, B. (1998). Models of the emergence of language. *Annual Review of Psychology, 49,* 199–227.

Madigan, S., & O'Hara, R. (1992). Short-term memory at the turn of the century: Mary Whiton Calkins's memory research. *American Psychologist, 47,* 170–174.

Magnussen, S., et al. (2006). What people believe about memory. *Memory, 14,* 595–613.

Maier, N. R. F. (1931). Reasoning in humans: II. The solution of a problem and its appearance in consciousness. *Journal of Comparative Psychology, 12,* 181–194.

Maki, R. H. (1998). Test predictions over text material. In D. J. Hacker, J. Dunlosky, & H. C. Graesser (Eds.), *Metacognition in educational theory and practice* (pp. 117–144). Mahwah, NJ: Erlbaum.

Maki, R. H., & Berry, S. L. (1984). Metacomprehension of text material. *Journal of Experimental Psychology: Learning, Memory, and Cognition, 10,* 663–679.

Maki, R. H., Jonas, D., & Kallod, M. (1994). The relationship between comprehension and metacomprehension ability. *Psychonomic Bulletin & Review, 1,* 126–129.

Maki, R. H., & McGuire, M. J. (2002). Metacognition for text: Findings and implications for education. In T. J. Perfect & B. L. Schwartz (Eds.), *Applied metacognition* (pp. 39–67). Cambridge, UK: Cambridge University Press.

Maki, R. H., & Serra, M. (1992). The basis of test prediction for text material. *Journal of Experimental Psychology: Learning, Memory, and Cognition, 18,* 116–126.

Maki, R. H., Shields, M., Wheeler, A. E., & Zacchilli, T. L. (2005). Individual differences in absolute and relative metacomprehension accuracy. *Journal of Educational Psychology, 97,* 723–731.

Maki, W. S., & Maki, R. H. (2000). Evaluation of a web-based introductory psychology course: II. Contingency management to increase use of on-line study aids. *Behavior Research Methods, Instruments & Computers, 32,* 240–245.

Mandel, D. R., Jusczyk, P. W., & Pisoni, D. B. (1995). Infants' recognition of the sound patterns of their own names. *Psychological Science, 6,* 314–317.

Mandler, G. (1985). *Cognitive psychology: An essay in cognitive science.* Hillsdale, NJ: Erlbaum.

Mandler, J. M. (1997). Development of categorization: Perceptual and conceptual categories. In G. Bremner, A. Slater, & G. Butterworth (Eds.), *Infant development: Recent advances.* Hove, UK: Erlbaum.

Mandler, J. M. (2003). Conceptual categorization. In D. Rakison & L. M. Oakes (Eds.), *Early category and concept development.* New York: Oxford University Press.

Mandler, J. M. (2004a). *The foundations of mind: Origins of conceptual thought.* New York: Oxford University Press.

Mandler, J. M. (2004b). Thought before language. *TRENDS in Cognitive Science, 8,* 508–524.

Mandler, J. M. (2006). Actions organize the infant's world. In K. Hirsh-Pasek & R. M. Golinkoff (Eds.), *Action meets word: How children learn verbs* (pp. 111–133). New York: Oxford University Press.

Mandler, J. M. (2007). The conceptual foundations of animals and artifacts. In E. Margolis & S. Laurence (Eds.), *Creations of the mind: Theories of artifacts and their representation.* Oxford, UK: Clarendon.

Mandler, J. M., & McDonough, L. (1993). Concept formation in infancy. *Cognitive Development, 8,* 291–318.

Manktelow, K. (1999). *Reasoning and thinking.* East Sussex, UK: Psychology Press.

Manly, J. J., Touradji, P., Tang, M., & Stern, Y. (2003). Literacy and memory decline among ethnically diverse elders. *Journal of Clinical and Experimental Neuropsychology, 25,* 680–690.

Mäntylä, T. (1997). Recollections of faces: Remembering differences and knowing similarities. *Journal of Experimental Psychology: Learning, Memory, and Cognition, 23,* 1203–1216.

Marcus, G. F. (1996). Why do children say "breaked"? *Current Directions in Psychological Science, 5,* 81–85.

Marian, V., & Fausey, C. M. (2006). Language-dependent memory in bilingual learning. *Applied Cognitive Psychology, 20,* 1025–1047.

Markman, A. B. (1999). *Knowledge representation*. Mahwah, NJ: Erlbaum.

Markman, A. B. (2002). Knowledge representation. In D. Medin (Ed.), *Stevens' handbook of experimental psychology* (3rd ed., Vol. 2, pp. 165–208). New York: Wiley.

Markman, A. B., & Gentner, D. (2001). Thinking. *Annual Review of Psychology, 52*, 223–247.

Markman, A. B., & Medin, D. L. (2002). Decision making. In D. Medin (Ed.), *Stevens' handbook of experimental psychology* (3rd ed., Vol. 2, pp. 413–466). New York: Wiley.

Markman, A. B., & Ross, B. H. (2003). Category use and category learning. *Psychological Bulletin, 129*, 592–613.

Marsh, E. J., & Tversky, B. (2004). Spinning the stories of our lives. *Applied Cognitive Psychology, 18*, 491–503.

Marsh, R. L., Hicks, J. L., & Hancock, T. W. (2000). On the interaction of ongoing cognitive activity and the nature of an event-based intention. *Applied Cognitive Psychology, 14*, S29–S41.

Marsh, R. L., Hicks, J. L., & Landau, J. D. (1998). An investigation of everyday prospective memory. *Memory & Cognition, 26*, 633–643.

Marsh, R. L., Landau, J. D., & Hicks, J. L. (1997). Contributions of inadequate source monitoring to unconscious plagiarism during idea generation. *Journal of Experimental Psychology: Learning, Memory, and Cognition, 23*, 886–897.

Marsh, R. L., et al. (2007). Memory for intention-related material presented in a to-be-ignored channel. *Memory & Cognition, 35*, 1197–1204.

Marslen-Wilson, W. D., Tyler, L. K., & Koster, C. (1993). Integrative processes in utterance resolution. *Journal of Memory and Language, 32*, 647–666.

Martin, E. (1967). *Personal communication*.

Martin, F., Baudouin, J., Tiberghien, G., & Franck, N. (2005). Processing emotional expression and facial identity in schizophrenia. *Psychiatry Research, 134*, 43–53.

Martin, R. C. (2007). Semantic short-term memory, language processing, and inhibition. In A. S. Meyer, L. R. Wheeldon, & A. Krott (Eds.), *Automaticity and control in language processing* (pp. 161–191). New York: Psychology Press.

Martin, R. C., & Wu, D. H. (2005). The cognitive neuropsychology of language. In K. Lamberts & R. L. Goldstone (Eds.), *Handbook of cognition* (pp. 382–404). Thousand Oaks, CA: Sage.

Martinussen, R., Hayden, J., Hogg-Johnson, S., & Tannock, R. (2005). A meta-analysis of working memory impairments in children with attention-deficit/hyperactivity disorder. *Journal of the American Academy of Child and Adolescent Psychology, 44*, 377–384.

Mason, R. A., & Just, M. A. (2006). Neuroimaging contributions to the understanding of discourse processes. In M. J. Traxer & M. A. Gernsbacher (Eds.), *Handbook of psycholinguistics* (2nd ed., pp. 765–799). New York: Academic Press.

Masoura, E., & Gathercole, S. E. (2005). Contrasting contributions of phonological short-term memory and long-term knowledge to vocabulary learning in a foreign language. *Memory, 13*, 422–429.

Massaro, D. W. (1998). *Perceiving talking faces*. Cambridge, MA: MIT Press.

Massaro, D. W. (1999), Speechreading: Illusion or window into pattern recognition. *Trends in Cognitive Sciences, 3*, 310–317.

Massaro, D. W., Cohen, M. M., & Smeele, P. M. T. (1995). Cross-linguistic comparisons in the integration of visual and auditory speech. *Memory & Cognition, 23*, 113–131.

Massaro, D. W., & Cole, R. (2000, August). From "speech is special" to talking heads in language learning. *Proceedings of Integrating Speech Technology in the (Language) Learning and Assistive Interface*, pp. 153–161. New York: Association for Computer Machinery.

Massaro, D. W., & Stork, D. G. (1998). Speech recognition and sensory integration. *American Scientist, 86*, 236–244.

Mast, F., Kosslyn, S. M., & Berthoz, A. (1999). Visual mental imagery interferes with allocentric orientation judgements. *NeuroReport, 10*, 3549–3553.

Mather, G. (2006). *Foundations of perception*. Hove, UK: Psychology Press.

Mather, M. (2006). Why memories may become more positive as people age. In B. Uttl, N. Ohta, & A. L. Siegenthaler (Eds.), *Memory and emotion: Interdisciplinary perspectives* (pp. 135–158). Malden, MA: Blackwell.

Matlin, M. W. (2004). Pollyanna Principle. In R. Pohl (Ed.), *Cognitive illusions: Handbook on fallacies and biases in thinking, judgment, and memory* (pp. 255–272). Hove, UK: Psychology Press.

Matlin, M. W. (2008). *The psychology of women* (6th ed.). Belmont, CA: Thomson Wadsworth.

Matlin, M. W., & Foley, H. J. (1997). *Sensation and perception* (4th ed.). Boston: Allyn and Bacon.

Matlin, M. W., & Stang, D. J. (1978). *The Pollyanna Principle: Selectivity in language, memory, and thought*. Cambridge, MA: Schenkman.

Mayer, R. E. (1999). Fifty years of creativity research. In R. J. Sternberg (Ed.), *Handbook of creativity* (pp. 449–460). New York: Cambridge University Press.

Mayer, R. E. (2003). Memory and information processing. In W. M. Reynolds & G. E. Miller (Eds.), *Handbook of psychology* (Vol. 7, pp. 47–57). Hoboken, NJ: Wiley.

Mayer, R. E. (2004). Teaching of subject matter. *Annual Review of Psychology, 55,* 715–744.

Mayer, R. E., & Hegarty, M. (1996). The process of understanding mathematical problems. In R. J. Sternberg & T. Ben-Zeev (Eds.), *The nature of mathematical thinking* (pp. 29–53). Mahwah, NJ: Erlbaum.

Mayhorn, C. B., Fisk, A. B., & Whittle, J. D. (2002). Decisions, decisions: Analysis of age, cohort, and time of testing on framing of risky decision options. *Human Factors, 44,* 515–521.

Maynard, A. M. (2006). *Personal communication.*

Maynard, A. M., Maynard, D. C., & Rowe, K. A. (2004). Exposure to the fields of psychology: Evaluation of an introductory psychology project. *Teaching of Psychology, 31,* 37–40.

McAdams, D. P. (2004). The redemptive self: Narrative identity in America today. In D. R. Beike, J. M., & Behrend (Eds.), *The self and memory* (pp. 95–115). New York: Psychology Press.

McAdams, S., & Drake, C. (2002). Auditory perception and cognition. In S. Yantis (Ed.), *Stevens' handbook of experimental psychology* (3rd ed., Vol. 1, pp. 397–452). New York: Wiley.

McClelland, J. L. (1981). Retrieving general and specific knowledge from stored knowledge of specifics. *Proceedings of the Third Annual Conference of the Cognitive Science Society,* 170–172.

McClelland, J. L. (1995). Constructive memory and memory distortions: A parallel-distributed processing approach. In D. L. Schacter (Ed.), *Memory distortion: How minds, brains, and societies reconstruct the past* (pp. 71–89). Cambridge, MA: Harvard University Press.

McClelland, J. L. (1999). Cognitive modeling, connectionist. In R. A. Wilson & F. C. Keil (Eds.), *The MIT encyclopedia of the cognitive sciences* (pp. 137–139). Cambridge, MA: MIT Press.

McClelland, J. L. (2000). Connectionist models of memory. In E. Tulving & F. I. M. Craik (Eds.), *The Oxford handbook of memory* (pp. 583–597). New York: Oxford University Press.

McClelland, J. L., & Rogers, T. T. (2003). The parallel distributed processing approach to semantic cognition. *Nature Reviews, 4,* 310–322.

McClelland, J. L., & Rumelhart, D. E. (Eds.). (1986). *Parallel distributed processing: Explorations in the microstructure of cognition* (Vol. 2). Cambridge, MA: MIT Press.

McClelland, J. L., Rumelhart, D. E., & Hinton, G. E. (1986). The appeal of parallel distributed processing. In D. E. Rumelhart, J. L. McClelland, & the PDP Research Group (Eds.), *Parallel distributed processing* (Vol. 1, pp. 3–44). Cambridge, MA: MIT Press.

McClelland, J. L., & Seidenberg, M. S. (2000). Why do kids say *goed* and *brang? Science, 287,* 47–48.

McCormick, C. B. (2003). Metacognition and learning. In W. M. Reynolds & G. E. Miller (Eds.), *Handbook of psychology* (Vol. 7, pp. 79–102). Hoboken, NJ: Wiley.

McCutchen, D., Teske, P., & Bangston, C. (2008). In C. Bazerman (Ed.), *Handbook of research on writing: History, society, school, individual, text* (pp. 451–470). Mahwah, NJ: Erlbaum.

McDaniel, M. A., & Einstein, G. O. (2000). Strategic and automatic processes in prospective memory retrieval: A multiprocess framework. *Applied Cognitive Psychology, 14,* S127–S144.

McDaniel, M. A., & Einstein, G. O. (2005). Material appropriate difficulty: A framework for determining when difficulty is desirable for improving learning. In A. F. Healy (Ed.), *Experimental cognitive psychology and its applications* (pp. 73–85). Washington, DC: American Psychological Association.

McDaniel, M. A., & Einstein, G. O. (2007). *Prospective memory: An overview and synthesis of an emerging field.* Thousand Oaks, CA: Sage.

McDaniel, M. A., Einstein, G. O., Graham, T., & Rall, E. (2004). Delaying execution of intentions: Overcoming the costs of interruptions. *Applied Cognitive Psychology, 18,* 533–547.

McDaniel, M. A., Waddill, P. J., & Shakesby, P. S. (1996). Study strategies, interest, and learning from text: The application of material appropriate processing. In D. J. Herrmann et al. (Eds.), *Basic and applied memory research: Practical applications* (Vol. 1, pp. 385–397). Mahwah, NJ: Erlbaum.

McDermott, K., & Knight, R. G. (2004). The effects of aging on a measure of prospective remembering using naturalistic stimuli. *Applied Cognitive Psychology, 18,* 349–362.

McDermott, R. (1998). *Risk taking in international politics: Prospect theory in American foreign policy.* Ann Arbor: University of Michigan.

R45

McDonald, J. L. (1997). Language acquisition: The acquisition of linguistic structure in normal and special populations. *Annual Review of Psychology, 48*, 215–241.

McDonald, S. A., & Shillcock, R. C. (2003). Eye movements reveal the on-line computation of lexical probabilities during reading. *Psychological Science, 14*, 648–652.

McDonough, L., & Mandler, J. M. (1998). Inductive generalization in 9- and 11-month-olds. *Developmental Science, 1*, 227–232.

McDougall, S., & Gruneberg, M. (2002). What memory strategy is best for examinations in psychology? *Applied Cognitive Psychology, 16*, 451–458.

McGovern, T. V., & Brewer, C. L. (2003). Undergraduate education. In D. F. Freedheim (Ed.), *Handbook of psychology* (Vol. 1: *The history of psychology*, pp. 465–481). Hoboken, NJ: Wiley.

McGuinness, D. (2004). *Early reading instruction: What science really tells us about how to teach reading.* Cambridge, MA: Bradford.

McGurk, H., & McDonald, J. (1976). Hearing lips and seeing voices. *Nature, 264*, 746–748.

McKelvie, S. J. (1990). Einstellung: Luchins' effect lives on. *Journal of Social Behavior and Personality, 5*, 105–121.

McKelvie, S. J. (1997). The availability heuristic: Effects of fame and gender on the estimated frequency of male and female names. *Journal of Social Psychology, 137*, 63–78.

McKelvie, S. J., Sano, E. K., & Stout, D. (1994). Effects of colored separate and interactive pictures on cued recall. *Journal of General Psychology, 12*, 241–251.

McKone, E. (2004). Isolating the special component of face recognition: Peripheral identification and a Mooney face. *Journal of Experimental Psychology: Learning, Memory, and Cognition, 30*, 181–197.

McKoon, G., & Ratcliff, R. (1998). Memory-based language processing: Psycholinguistic research in the 1990s. *Annual Review of Psychology, 49*, 25–42.

McNally, R. J. (2003). Recovered memories of trauma: A view from the laboratory. *Current Directions in Psychological Science, 12*, 32–35.

McNamara, D. S., Cai, Z., & Louwerse, M. M. (2007). Optimizing LSA measures of cohesion. In T. K. Landauer, D. S. McNamara, Dennis, S., & Kintsch, W. (Eds.), *Handbook of latent semantic analysis* (pp. 379–425). Mahwah, NJ: Erlbaum.

McNamara, D. S., & Shapiro, A. M. (2005). Multimedia and hypermedia solutions for promoting metacognitive engagement, coherence, and learning. *Journal of Educational Computing Research, 33*, 1–29.

McNamara, T. P. (2005). *Semantic priming: Perspectives from memory and word recognition.* New York: Psychology Press.

McNamara, T. P., & Diwadkar, V. A. (1997). Symmetry and asymmetry of human spatial memory. *Cognitive Psychology, 34*, 160–190.

McNamara, T. P., & Holbrook, J. B. (2003). The native mind: Biological categorization and reasoning in development across cultures. *Psychological Review, 111*, 960–983.

McNeil, J. E., & Warrington, E. K. (1993). Prosopagnosia: A face-specific disorder. *Quarterly Journal of Experimental Psychology, 46A*, 1–10.

McNeill, D. (2005). *Gesture and thought.* Chicago: University of Chicago Press.

McQueen, J. M. (2005). Speech perception. In K. Lamberts & R. L. Goldstone (Eds.), *Handbook of cognition* (pp. 255–275). London, UK: Sage.

Medin, D. L., & Atran, S. (2004). The native mind: Biological categorization and reasoning in development and across cultures. *Psychological Review, 111*, 960–983.

Medin, D. L., Lynch, E. B., & Solomon, K. O. (2000). Are there kinds of concepts? *Annual Review of Psychology, 51*, 121–147.

Medin, D. L., & Rips, L. J. (2005). Concepts and categories: Memory, meaning and metaphysics. In K. J. Holyoak & R. G. Morrison (Eds.), *The Cambridge handbook of thinking and reasoning* (pp. 37–72). New York: Cambridge University Press.

Meeter, M., Eijsackers, E. V., & Mulder, J. L. (2006). Retrograde amnesia for autobiographical memories and public events in mild and moderate Alzheimer's disease. *Journal of Clinical and Experimental Neuropsychology, 28*, 914–927.

Meeter, M., & Murre, J. M. J. (2004). Consolidation of long-term memory: Evidence and alternatives. *Psychological Bulletin, 130*, 843–857.

Meissner, C. A., & Brigham, J. C. (2001). Thirty years of investigating the own-race bias in memory for faces: A meta-analytic review. *Psychology, Public Policy, & Law, 7*, 3–35.

Meissner, C. A., Brigham, J. C., & Butz, D. A. (2005). Memory for own- and other-race faces: A dual-process approach. *Applied Cognitive Psychology, 19*, 545–567.

Melnyk, L., Crossman, A. M., Scullin, M. H. (2007). The suggestibility of children's memory. In M. Toglia, J. D. Read, D. F. Ross, & R. C. L. Lindsay (Eds.), *Handbook of eyewitness psychology* (Vol. 1, pp. 401–451). Mahwah, NJ: Erlbaum.

Memon, A., Holliday, R., & Hill, C. (2006). Pre-event stereotypes and misinformation effects in young children. *Memory, 14,* 104–114.

Mendola, J. (2003). Contextual shape processing in human visual cortex: Beginning to fill-in the blanks. In L. Pessoa & P. De Weerd (Eds.), *Filling-in: From perceptual completion to cortical reorganization* (pp. 38–58). New York: Oxford University Press.

Mervis, C. B., Catlin, J., & Rosch, E. (1976). Relationships among goodness-of-example, category norms, and word frequency. *Bulletin of the Psychonomic Society, 7,* 283–284.

Metcalfe, J. (1986). Premonitions of insight predict impending error. *Journal of Experimental Psychology: Learning, Memory, and Cognition, 12,* 623–634.

Metcalfe, J. (1998). Insight and metacognition. In G. Mazzoni & T. O. Nelson (Eds.), *Metacognition and cognitive neuropsychology* (pp. 181–197). Mahwah, NJ: Erlbaum.

Metcalfe, J. (2000). Metamemory. In E. Tulving & F. I. M. Craik (Eds.), *The Oxford handbook of memory* (pp. 197–211). New York: Oxford University Press.

Metcalfe, J. (2002). Is study time allocated selectively to a region of proximal learning? *Journal of Experimental Psychology: General, 131,* 349–363.

Metcalfe, J., & Wiebe, D. (1987). Intuition in insight and noninsight problem solving. *Memory & Cognition, 15,* 238–246.

Meyer, A. S. (2004). The use of eye tracking in studies of sentence generation. In J. M. Henderson & F. Ferreira (Eds.), *The interface of language, vision, and action: Eye movements and the visual world* (p. 191–211). New York: Psychology Press.

Michael, E. B., & Gollan, T. H. (2005). Being and becoming bilingual: Individual differences and consequences for language production. In J. F. Kroll & A. M. B. de Groot (Eds.), *Handbook of bilingualism: Psycholinguistic approaches* (pp. 389–407). New York: Oxford University Press.

Michie, D. (2004). Computer chess. In R. L. Gregory (Ed.), *The Oxford companion to the mind* (2nd ed., pp. 196–199). New York: Oxford University Press.

Miller, G. A. (1956). The magical number seven, plus or minus two: Some limits on our capacity for processing information. *Psychological Review, 63,* 81–97.

Miller, G. A. (1967). The psycholinguists. In G. A. Miller (Ed.), *The psychology of communication* (pp. 70–92). London, UK: Penguin.

Miller, G. A. (1979). *A very personal history.* Address to Cognitive Science Workshop, Massachusetts Institute of Technology, Cambridge, MA.

Miller, L. C., Lechner, R. E., & Rugs, D. (1985). Development of conversational responsiveness: Preschoolers' use of responsive listener cues and relevant comments. *Developmental Psychology, 21,* 473–480.

Miller, M. C. (2001). *The Bush dyslexicon.* New York: Norton.

Milliken, B., Joordens, S., Merikle, P. M., & Seiffert, A. E. (1998). Selective attention: A reevaluation of the implications of negative priming. *Psychological Review, 105,* 203–229.

Millis, K. K., & Graesser, A. C. (1994). The time-course of constructing knowledge-based inferences for scientific texts. *Journal of Memory and Language, 33,* 583–599.

Milner, B. (1966). Amnesia. In C. W. M. Whitty & O. L. Zangwill (Eds.), *Amnesia following operation on the temporal lobes* (pp. 109–133). London, UK: Butterworth.

Milton, F., & Wills, A. J. (2004). The influence of stimulus properties on category construction. *Journal of Experimental Psychology: Learning, Memory, and Cognition, 30,* 407–415.

Miozzo, M., & Caramazza, A. (1997). Retrieval of lexical-syntactic features in tip-of-the-tongue states. *Journal of Experimental Psychology: Learning, Memory, and Cognition, 23,* 1410–1423.

Mitchell, K. J., & Johnson, M. K. (2000). Source monitoring: Attributing mental experiences. In E. Tulving & F. I. M. Craik (Eds.), *The Oxford handbook of memory* (pp. 179–195). New York: Oxford University Press.

Miyake, A. (Ed.). (2001). Individual differences in working memory: Introduction to the special section. *Journal of Experimental Psychology: General, 130,* 163–168.

Miyake, A., Just, M. A., & Carpenter, P. A. (1994). Working memory constraints on the resolution of lexical ambiguity: Maintaining multiple interpretations in neutral contexts. *Journal of Memory and Language, 33,* 175–202.

Miyake, A., & Shah, P. (Eds.). (1999a). *Models of working memory: Mechanisms of active maintenance and executive control.* New York: Cambridge University Press.

Miyake, A., & Shah, P. (1999b). Toward unified theories of working memory. In A. Miyake & P. Shah (Eds.), *Models of working memory: Mechanisms of active maintenance and executive control* (pp. 442–481). New York: Cambridge University Press.

Moar, I., & Bower, G. H. (1983). Inconsistency in spatial knowledge. *Memory & Cognition, 11,* 107–113.

Moely, B. E., Olson, F. A., Halwes, T. G., & Flavell, J. H. (1969). Production deficiency in young children's clustered recall. *Developmental Psychology, 1,* 26–34.

Moldoveanu, M., & Langer, E. (2002). When "stupid" is smarter than we are. In R. J. Sternberg (Ed.), *Why smart people can be so stupid* (pp. 212–231). New Haven, CT: Yale University Press.

Montgomery, H., Lipshitz, R., & Brehmer, B. (Eds.). (2005). *How professionals make decisions.* Mahwah, NJ: Erlbaum.

Montello, D. R. (2005). Navigation. In P. Shah & A. Miyake (Eds.), *The Cambridge handbook of visuospatial thinking* (pp. 257–294). New York: Cambridge University Press.

Montello, D. R., Waller, D., Hegarty, M., & Richardson, A. E. (2004). Spatial memory of real environments, virtual environments, and maps. In G. L. Allen (Ed.), *Human spatial memory: Remembering where* (pp. 251–285). Mahwah, NJ: Erlbaum.

Moore, J. D., & Wiemer-Hastings, P. (2003). Discourse in computational linguistics and artificial intelligence. In A. C. Graesser, M. A. Gernsbacher, & S. R. Goldman (Eds.), *Handbook of discourse processes* (pp. 439–485). Mahwah, NJ: Erlbaum.

Moray, N. (1959). Attention in dichotic listening: Affective cues and the influence of instructions. *Quarterly Journal of Experimental Psychology, 11,* 56–60.

Morey, C. C., & Cowan, N. (2004). When visual and verbal memories compete: Evidence of cross-domain limits in working memory. *Psychonomic Bulletin & Review, 11,* 296–301.

Morey, C. C., & Cowan, N. (2005). When do visual and verbal memories conflict? The importance of working-memory load and retrieval. *Journal of Experimental Psychology: Learning, Memory, and Cognition, 31,* 703–713.

Morris, J. F., & Hart, S. (2003). Defending claims about mental health. In M. R. Stevenson & J. C. Cogan (Eds.), *Everyday activism: A handbook for lesbian, gay, and bisexual people and their allies* (pp. 57–78). New York: Routledge.

Morris, P. E., et al. (2005). Strategies for learning proper names: Expanding retrieval practice, meaning and imagery. *Applied Cognitive Psychology, 19,* 779–798.

Morris, R., Kotitsa, M., & Bramham, J. (2005). Planning in patients with focal brain damage: From simple to complex task performance. In In R. Morris & G. Ward (Eds.), *The cognitive psychology of planning* (pp. 153–198). Hove, UK: Psychology Press.

Morris, R. K., & Binder, K. S. (2001). What happens to the unselected meaning of an ambiguous word in skilled reading? In D. S. Gorfein (Ed.), *On the consequences of meaning selection: Perspectives on resolving lexical ambiguity* (pp. 139–153). Washington, DC: American Psychological Association.

Morrison, A. P. (2005). Psychosis and the phenomenon of unwanted intrusive thoughts. In D. A. Clark (Ed.), *Intrusive thoughts in clinical disorders: Theory, research, and treatment* (pp. 175–198). New York: Guilford.

Morrison, R. G. (2005). Thinking in working memory. In K. J. Holyoak & R. G. Morrison (Eds.), *The Cambridge handbook of thinking and reasoning* (pp. 457–473). New York: Cambridge University Press.

Moscovitch, M., & Craik, F. I. M. (1976). Depth of processing, retrieval cues, and uniqueness of encoding as factors in recall. *Journal of Verbal Learning and Verbal Behavior, 15,* 447–458.

Most, S. B., Scholl, B. J., Clifford, E. R., & Simons, D. J. (2005). What you see is what you set: Sustained inattentional blindness and the capture of awareness. *Psychological Review, 112,* 217–242.

Most, S. B., et al. (2001). How not to be seen: The contribution of similarity and selective ignoring to sustained inattentional blindness. *Psychological Science, 12,* 9–17.

Moulin, C. J. A., Thompson, R. G., Wright, D. B., & Conway, M. A. (2007). Eyewitness memory in older adults. In M. P. Toglia, J. D. Read, D. F. Ross, & R. C. L. Lindsay (Eds.), *Handbook of eyewitness psychology* (Vol. 1, pp. 627–646). Mahwah, NJ: Erlbaum.

Moynahan, E. D. (1978). Assessment and selection of paired associate strategies: A developmental study. *Journal of Experimental Child Psychology, 26,* 257–266.

Mueller, T. (2005, December 12). Your move: How computer chess programs are changing the game. *New Yorker,* pp. 62–69.

Mueller-Johnson, K., & Ceci, S. J. (2007). The elderly eyewitness: A review and prospectus. In M. P. Toglia, J. D. Read, D. F. Ross, & R. C. L. Lindsay (Eds.), *Handbook of eyewitness psychology* (Vol. 1, pp. 577–605). Mahwah, NJ: Erlbaum.

Müller, H. J., & Krummenacher, J. (2006). Visual search and selective attention. *Visual Cognition, 14,* 389–410.

Munakata, Y., & McClelland, J. L. (2003). Connectionist models of development. *Developmental Science,* 413–429.

Munger, M. P., Owens, T. R., & Conway, J. E. (2005). Are boundary extension and representational momentum related? *Visual Cognition, 12,* 1041–1056.

Murphy, G. L. (2002). *The big book of concepts.* Cambridge, MA: MIT Press.

Murphy, G. L., & Shapiro, A. M. (1994). Forgetting of verbatim information in discourse. *Memory & Cognition, 22,* 85–94.

Murray, B. (1998, August). The latest techno tool: Essay-grading computers. *APA Monitor,* p. 43.

Murray, L. A., Whitehouse, W. G., & Alloy, L. B. (1999) Mood congruence and depressive deficits in memory: A forced-recall analysis, *Memory, 7,* 175–196.

Mussweiler, T., Englich, B., & Strack, F. (2004). Anchoring effects. In R. Pohl (Ed.), *Cognitive illusions: Handbook on fallacies and biases in thinking, judgment, and memory* (pp. 183–200). Hove, UK: Psychology Press.

Myers, D. G. (2002). *Intuition: Its powers and perils.* New Haven, CT: Yale University Press.

Myers, D. G. (2007). Teaching psychological science through writing. *Teaching of Psychology, 34,* 77–84.

Myers, N. A., & Perlmutter, M. (1978). Memory in the years from two to five. In P. A. Ornstein (Ed.), *Memory development in children* (pp. 191–218). Hillsdale, NJ: Erlbaum.

Nairne, J. S. (2002). Remembering over the short-term: The case against the standard model. *Annual Review of Psychology, 53,* 53–81.

Nairne, J. S. (2005). The functionalist agenda in memory. In A. F. Healy (Ed.), *Experimental cognitive psychology and its applications* (pp. 115–126). Washington DC: American Psychological Association.

Naqvi, N., Shiv, B., & Bechara, A. (2006). The role of emotion in decision making: A cognitive neuroscience perspective. *Current Directions in Psychological Science, 15,* 260–264.

National Priorities Project. (2008). Bringing the federal budget home. Retrieved May 9, 2008 from http://www.national priorities.org/costofwar_home

Naveh-Benjamin, M., & Ayres, T. J. (1986). Digit span, reading rate, and linguistic relativity. *Quarterly Journal of Experimental Psychology, 38,* 739–751.

Naveh-Benjamin, M., Cowan, N., Kilb, A., & Chen, Z. (2007). Age-related differences in immediate serial recall: Dissociating chunk formation and capacity. *Memory & Cognition, 35,* 724–737.

Naveh-Benjamin, M., Craik, F. I. M., Guez, J., & Dori, H. (1998). Effects of divided attention on encoding and retrieval processes in human memory: Further support for an asymmetry. *Journal of Experimental Psychology: Learning, Memory, & Cognition, 24,* 1091–1104.

Naveh-Benjamin, M., Craik, F. I. M., Guez, J., & Kreuger, S. (2005). Divided attention in younger and older adults: Effects of strategy and relatedness on memory performance and secondary task costs. *Journal of Experimental Psychology: Learning, Memory, and Cognition, 31,* 520–537.

Neath, I., Brown, G. D. A., Poirier, M., & Fortin, C. (2005). Short-term and working memory: Past, progress, and prospects. *Memory, 13,* 225–235.

Neisser, U. (1967). *Cognitive psychology.* New York: Appleton.

Neisser, U. (1994). Multiple systems: A new approach to cognitive theory. *European Journal of Cognitive Psychology, 6,* 225–241.

Neisser, U. (2003). New directions for flashbulb memories: Comments on the ACP special issue. *Applied Cognitive Psychology, 17,* 1149–1155.

Neisser, U., & Libby, L. K. (2000). Remembering life experiences. In E. Tulving & F. I. M. Craik (Eds.), *The Oxford handbook of memory* (pp. 315–332). New York: Oxford University Press.

Nelson, J. R., Balass, M., & Perfetti, C. A. (2005). Differences between written and spoken input in learning new words. *Written Language and Literacy, 8,* 101–120.

Nelson, K. (2006). Development of representation in childhood. In E. Bialystok & F. I. M. Craik (Eds.), *Lifespan cognition: Mechanisms of change* (pp. 178–192). New York: Oxford University Press.

Nelson, K., Aksu-Koc, A., & Johnson, C. (Eds.). (2001). *Children's language: Interactional contributions to language development* (Vol. 11). Mahwah, NJ: Erlbaum.

Nelson, T. O. (1996). Consciousness and metacognition. *American Psychologist, 51,* 102–116.

Nelson, T. O. (1999). Cognition versus metacognition. In R. J. Sternberg (Ed.), *The nature of cognition* (pp. 625–641). Cambridge, MA: MIT Press.

Nelson, T. O., Dunlosky, J., Graf, A., & Narens, L. (1994). Utilization of metacognitive judgments in the allocation of study during multitrial learning. *Psychological Science, 5,* 207–213.

Nelson, T. O., & Leonesio, R. J. (1988). Allocation of self-paced study time and the "labor-in-vain effect." *Journal of Experimental Psychology: Learning, Memory, and Cognition, 14,* 676–686.

Nettle, D. (2001). *Strong imagination: Madness, creativity, and human nature.* New York: Oxford University Press.

Neuschatz, J. S., et al. (2002). The effect of memory schemata on memory and the phenomenological experience of naturalistic situations. *Applied Cognitive Psychology, 16,* 687–708.

Neuschatz, J. S., et al. (2007). False memory research: History, theory, and applied implications. In M. P. Toglia, J. D. Read, D. F. Ross, & R. C. L. Lindsay (Eds.), *Handbook of eyewitness psychology* (Vol. 1, pp. 239–260). Mahwah, NJ: Erlbaum.

Newcombe, N. S. (2002). Spatial cognition. In D. Medin (Ed.), *Stevens' handbook of experimental psychology* (3rd ed., Vol. 2, pp. 113–163). New York: Wiley.

Newcombe, N. S. (2006, March 3). A plea for spatial literacy. *Chronicle of Higher Education*, p. B20.

Newcombe, N. S., & Huttenlocher, J. (2000). *Making space: The development of spatial representation and reasoning.* Cambridge, MA: MIT Press.

Newcombe, N. S., et al. (2000). Remembering early childhood: How much, how, and why (or why not). *Current Directions in Psychological Science, 9,* 55–58.

Newell, A., & Simon, H. A. (1972). *Human problem solving.* Englewood Cliffs, NJ: Prentice-Hall.

Newell, B. R., Lagnado, D. A., & Shanks, D. R. (2007). *Straight choices: The psychology of decision making.* Hove, UK: Psychology Press.

Newell, B. R., & Shanks, D. R. (2004). On the role of recognition in decision making. *Journal of Experimental Psychology: Learning, Memory, and Cognition, 30,* 923–935.

Newman, S. D., Just, M. A., & Carpenter, P. A. (2002). The synchronization of the human cortical working memory network. *NeuroImage, 15,* 810–822.

Newmeyer, F. J. (1998). *Language form and language function.* Cambridge, MA: MIT Press.

Ng, W.-K., & Lindsay, R. C. L. (1994). Cross-race facial recognition: Failure of the contact hypothesis. *Journal of Cross-Cultural Psychology, 25,* 217–232.

Nicholls, M. E. R., Searle, D. A., & Bradshaw, J. L. (2004). Read my lips. *Psychological Science, 15,* 138–141.

Nickerson, R. S. (2001). The projective way of knowing: A useful heuristic that sometimes misleads. *Current Directions in Psychological Science, 10,* 168–176.

Nickerson, R. S., Perkins, D. N., & Smith, E. E. (1985). *The teaching of thinking.* Hillsdale, NJ: Erlbaum.

Nisbett, R. E., & Wilson, T. D. (1977). Telling more than we can know: Verbal reports on mental processes. *Psychological Review, 84,* 231–259.

Noice, T., & Noice, H. (1997). *The nature of expertise in professional acting: A cognitive view.* Mahwah, NJ: Erlbaum.

Nosek, B. A., Banaji, M. R., & Greenwald, A. G. (2002). Math = male, me = female, therefore math ≠ me. *Journal of Personality and Social Psychology, 83,* 44–59.

Nosek, B. A., Greenwald, A. G., & Banaji, M. R. (2007). The Implicit Association Test at age 7: A methodological

and conceptual review. In J. A. Bargh (Ed.), *Social psychology and the unconscious: The automaticity of higher mental processes* (pp. 265–292). New York: Psychology Press.

Nosofsky, R. M., & Palmeri, T. J. (1998). A rule-plus-exception model for classifying objects in continuous-dimension spaces. *Psychonomic Bulletin & Review, 5,* 345–369.

Noveck, I. A., & Politzer, G. (1998). Leveling the playing field: Investigating competing claims concerning relative inference difficulty. In M. D. S. Braine & D. P. O'Brien (Eds.), *Mental logic* (pp. 367–384). Mahwah, NJ: Erlbaum.

Novick, L. R. (2003). At the forefront of thought: The effect of media exposure on airplane typicality. *Psychonomic Bulletin & Review, 10,* 971–974.

Novick, L. R. (2006). Understanding spatial diagram structure: An analysis of hierarchies, matrices, and networks. *The Quarterly Journal of Experimental Psychology, 59,* 1826–1856.

Novick, L. R., & Coté, N. (1992). *The nature of expertise in anagram solution.* Proceedings of the Fourteenth Annual Conference of the Cognitive Science Society (pp. 450–455). Hillsdale, NJ: Erlbaum.

Novick, L. R., Hurley, S. M., & Francis, M. (1999). Evidence for abstract, schematic knowledge of three spatial diagram representations. *Memory & Cognition, 27,* 288–308.

Novick, L. R., & Morse, D. L. (2000). Folding a fish, making a mushroom: The role of diagrams in executing assembly procedures. *Memory & Cognition, 28,* 1242–1256.

Nusbaum, H. C., & Small, S. L. (2006). In J. T. Caciaoppi, P. S. Vissr, & C. L. Pickett (Eds.), *Social neuroscience: People thinking about thinking people.* (pp. 131–165). Cambridge, MA: MIT Press.

Nyberg, L., & McIntosh, A. R. (2001). Functional neuroimaging: Network analysis. In R. Cabeza & A. Kingstone (Eds.), *Handbook of functional neuroimaging of cognition* (pp. 49–72). Cambridge, MA: MIT Press.

Oakes, S., & North, A. C. (2006). The impact of background musical tempo and timbre congruity upon ad content recall and affective response. *Applied Cognitive Psychology, 20,* 505–520.

Oaksford, M., & Chater, N. (1994). A rational analysis of the selection task as optimal data selection. *Psychological Review, 101,* 608–631.

Oberauer, K., Süss, H.-M., Wilhelm, O., & Sander, N. (2007). Individual differences in working memory capacity and reasoning ability. In A. R. A. Conway et al. (Eds.), *Variations in working memory* (pp. 49–75). New York: Oxford University Press.

Oberauer, K., Wendland, M., & Kliegl, R. (2003). Age differences in working memory—the roles of storage and selective access. *Memory & Cognition, 31*, 563–569.

Oberlander, J. & Gill, A. J. (2006). Language with character: A stratified corpus comparison of individual differences in e-mail communication. *Discourse Processes, 42*, 239–270.

O'Brien, E. J., & Myers, J. L. (1999). Text comprehension: A view from the bottom up. In S. Goldman et al. (Eds.), *Narrative comprehension, causality, and coherence: Essays in honor of Tom Trabasso* (pp. 35–53). Mahwah, NJ: Erlbaum.

O'Brien, L. T., & Crandall, C. S. (2003). Stereotype threat and arousal: Effects on women's math performance. *Personality and Social Psychology Bulletin, 29*, 782–789.

Ohta, A. S. (2001). *Second language acquisition processes in the classroom: Learning Japanese.* Mahwah, NJ: Erlbaum.

Olesen, P. J., Westerberg, H., & Klingberg, T. (2004). Increased prefrontal and parietal activity after training of working memory. *Nature Neuroscience, 7*, 75–79.

Olivetti Belardinelli, M., et al. (2004). Intermodal sensory image generation: An fMRI analysis. *European Journal of Cognitive Psychology, 16*, 729–752.

Olson, G. M., & Olson, J. S. (2003). Human-computer interaction: Psychological aspects of the human use of computing. *Annual Review of Psychology, 54*, 491–516.

Olson, K. R., Lambert, A. J., Zacks, J. M. (2004). Graded structure and the speed of category verification: On the moderating effects of anticipatory control for social vs. non-social categories. *Journal of Experimental Social Psychology, 40*, 239–246.

Oppenheimer, D. M. (2006). Consequences of erudite vernacular utilized irrespective of necessity: Problems with using long words needlessly. *Applied Cognitive Psychology, 20*, 139–156.

O'Reilly, R. C., & Munakata, Y. (2000). *Computational explorations in cognitive neuroscience: Understanding the mind by simulating the brain.* Cambridge, MA: MIT Press.

Ormerod, T. C. (2005). Planning and ill-defined problems. In R. Morris & G. Ward (Eds.), *The cognitive psychology of planning* (pp. 53–70). Hove, UK: Psychology Press.

Ormerod, T. C., Chronicle, E. P., & MacGregor, J. V. (2006). The remnants of insight. *Proceedings of the Annual Cognitive Science Society Conference*, Vancouver, CA.

Ornstein, P. A., & Haden, C. A. (2001). *Memory* development or the *development* of memory? *Current Directions in Psychological Science, 10*, 202–205.

Ornstein, P. A., Haden, C. A., & Elischberger, H. B. (2006). Children's memory development: Remembering the past and preparing for the future. In E. Bialystok & F. I. M. Craik (Eds.), *Lifespan cognition: Mechanisms of change* (pp. 143–161). New York: Oxford University Press.

Osterhout, L., Bersick, M., & McLaughlin, J. (1997). Brain potentials reflect violations of gender stereotypes. *Memory & Cognition, 25*, 273–285.

Oswald, M. E., & Grosjean, S. (2004). Confirmation bias. In R. Pohl (Ed.), *Cognitive illusions: Handbook on fallacies and biases in thinking, judgment, and memory* (pp. 77–96). Hove, UK: Psychology Press.

Owens, R. E., Jr. (2001). *Language development: An introduction.* Boston: Allyn and Bacon.

Paas, F., & Kester, L. (2006). Learner and information characteristics in the design of powerful learning environments. *Applied Cognitive Psychology, 20*, 281–285.

Paivio, A. (1978). Comparison of mental clocks. *Journal of Experimental Psychology: Human Perception and Performance, 4*, 61–71.

Paivio, A. (1995). Imagery and memory. In M. S. Gazzaniga (Ed.), *The cognitive neurosciences* (pp. 977–986). Cambridge, MA: MIT Press.

Pajares, F. (2003). Self-efficacy beliefs, motivation, and achievement in writing: A review of the literature. *Reading & Writing Quarterly, 19*, 139–158.

Palmer, S. E. (1999). *Vision science: Photons to phenomenology.* Cambridge, MA: MIT Press.

Palmer, S. E. (2002). Perceptual organization in vision. In S. Yantis (Ed.), *Stevens' handbook of experimental psychology* (3rd ed., Vol. 1, pp. 177–234). New York: Wiley.

Palmer, S. E. (2003). Visual perception of objects. In A. F. Healy & R. W. Proctor (Eds.), *Handbook of psychology* (Vol. 4, pp. 179–211). Hoboken, NJ: Wiley.

Pan, B. A., Perlmann, R. Y., & Snow, C. E. (2000). Food for thought: Dinner table as a context for observing parent-child discourse. In L. Menn & N. B. Ratner (Eds.), *Methods for studying language production* (pp. 205–224). Mahwah, NJ: Erlbaum.

Pan, B. A., & Snow, C. E. (1999). The development of conversational and discourse skills. In M. Barrett (Ed.), *The development of language* (pp. 229–249). Hove, UK: Psychology Press.

Pansky, A. & Koriat, A. (2004). The basic-level convergence effect on memory distortions. *Psychological Science, 15*, 52–59.

Pansky, A., Koriat, A., & Goldsmith, M. (2005). Eyewitness recall and testimony. In N. Brewer & K. D. Williams (Eds.), *Psychology and law: An empirical perspective* (pp. 93–150). New York: Guilford.

Parasuraman, R., & Greenwood, P. (2007). Individual differences in attention and working memory: A molecular genetic approach. In A. F. Kramer, D. A. Wiegmann, & A. Kirlik (Eds.), *Attention: From theory to practice* (pp. 59–72). New York: Oxford University Press.

Park, D. C., & Hedden, T. (2001). Working memory and aging. In M. Naveh-Benjamin, M. Moscovitch, & H. L. Roediger, III (Eds.), *Perspectives on human memory and cognitive aging: Essays in honour of Fergus Craik* (pp. 148–169). New York: Psychology Press.

Park, D. C., & Payer, D. (2006). Working memory across the adult lifespan. In E. Bialystok & F. I. M. Craik (Eds.), *Lifespan cognition: Mechanisms of change* (pp. 128–142). New York: Oxford University Press.

Park, D. C., & Schwarz, N. (2000). *Cognitive aging.* Philadelphia: Psychology Press.

Park, D. C., et al. (1999). Medication adherence in rheumatoid arthritis patients: Older is wiser. *Journal of the American Geriatric Society, 47*, 172–183.

Parks, T. (2004). Iconic image. In R. L. Gregory (Ed.), *The Oxford companion to the mind* (2nd ed., p. 425). New York: Oxford University Press.

Parrott, W. G., & Spackman, M. P. (2000). Emotion and memory. In M. Lewis & J. M. Haviland-Jones (Eds.), *Handbook of emotions* (2nd ed., pp. 476–490). New York: Guilford.

Parry, K. (2006). People and language. In H. Luria, D. M. Seymour, & T. Smoke (Eds.), *Language and linguistics in context: Readings and applications for teachers* (pp. 153–168). Mahwah, NJ: Erlbaum.

Pashler, H. (Ed.). (2002). *Stevens' handbook of experimental psychology* (3rd ed.). New York: Wiley.

Pashler, H., & Johnston, J. C. (1998). Attention limitations in dual-task performance. In H. Pashler (Ed.), *Attention* (pp. 155–189). East Sussex, UK: Psychology Press.

Pashler, H., Rohrer, D., Cepeda, N. J., & Carpenter, S. K. (2007). Enhancing learning and retarding forgetting: Choice and consequences. *Psychonomic Bulletin and Review,14*, 187–193.

Pashler, H., & Wixted, J. (Eds.). (2002). *Stevens' handbook of experimental psychology* (3rd ed., Vol. 4, pp. 223–269), New York: Wiley.

Pasternak, T., Bisley, J. W., & Calkins, D. (2003). Visual processing in the primate brain. In M. Gallagher & R. J. Nelson (Eds.), *Handbook of psychology* (Vol. 3, pp. 139–185). Hoboken, NJ: Wiley.

Pastore, R. E., Li, X.-F., & Layer, J. K. (1990). Categorical perception of nonspeech chirps and bleats. *Perception & Psychophysics, 48*, 151–156.

Pasupathi, M. (2001). The social construction of the personal past and its implications for adult development. *Psychological Bulletin, 127*, 651–672.

Patel, A. D., et al. (1998). Processing syntactic relations in language and music: An event-related potential study. *Journal of Cognitive Neuroscience, 10*, 717–733.

Patterson, J. L. (2002). Relationships of expressive vocabulary to frequency of reading and television experience among bilingual toddlers. *Applied Psycholinguistics, 23*, 493–508.

Payne, D. G., & Wenger, M. J. (1992). Improving memory through practice. In D. J. Herrmann, H. Weingartner, A. Searleman, & C. McEvoy (Eds.), *Memory improvement: Implications for memory theory* (pp. 187–209). New York: Springer-Verlag.

Payne, D. G., et al. (1999). Memory applied. In T. Durso et al. (Eds). *Handbook of applied psychology* (pp. 83–113). New York: Wiley.

Peal, E., & Lambert, W. E. (1962). The relation of bilingualism to intelligence. *Psychological Monographs*, 546.

Pear, J. J. (2001). *The science of learning.* Philadelphia: Psychology Press

Pennebaker, J. W., & Graybeal, A. (2001). Patterns of natural language use: Disclosure, personality, and social integration. *Current Directions in Psychological Science, 10*, 90–93.

Pennebaker, J. W., Mehl, M. R., & Niederhoffer, K. G. (2003). Psychological aspects of natural language use: Our words, ourselves. *Annual Review of Psychology, 54*, 547–577.

Penrod, S. D., & Cutler, B. (1999). Preventing mistaken convictions in eyewitness identification trials: The case against traditional safeguards. In R. Roesch, S. D. Hart, & J. R. P. Ogloff (Eds.), *Psychology and law: The state of the discipline.* New York: Kluwer Academic/Plenum Publishers.

Perfect, T. J. (1997). Memory aging as frontal lobe dysfunction. In M. A. Conway (Ed.), *Cognitive models of memory* (pp. 315–339). Cambridge, MA: MIT Press.

Perfect, T. J. (2004). The role of self-rated ability in the accuracy of confidence judgements in eyewitness memory and general knowledge. *Applied Cognitive Psychology, 18,* 157–168.

Perfect, T. J., & Schwartz, B. L. (Eds.). (2002). *Applied metacognition.* Cambridge, UK: Cambridge University Press

Perfetti, C. A. (1996). *Reading: Universals and particulars across writing systems.* Paper presented at the convention of the Eastern Psychological Association, Philadelphia.

Perfetti, C. A. (2003). The universal grammar of reading. *Scientific Studies of Reading, 7,* 3–24.

Perfetti, C. A., Landi, N., & Oakhill, J. (2005). The acquisition of reading comprehension skill. In M. J. Snowling & C. Hulme (Eds.), *The science of reading: A handbook* (pp. 227–250). Oxford, UK: Blackwell.

Perkins, D. (2001). *The Eureka Effect: The art and logic of breakthrough thinking.* New York: Norton.

Peterson, L. R., & Peterson, M. (1959). Short-term retention of individual verbal items. *Journal of Experimental Psychology, 58,* 193–198.

Pexman, P. M., Hino, Y., & Lunker, S. J. (2004). Semantic ambiguity and the process of generating meaning from print. *Journal of Experimental Psychology: Learning, Memory, and Cognition, 30,* 1252–1270.

Pezdek, K. (2003a). Event memory and autobiographical memory for the events of September 11, 2001. *Applied Cognitive Psychology, 17,* 1033–1045.

Pezdek, K. (Ed.). (2003b). Memory and cognition for the events of September 11, 2001 [Special issue]. *Applied Cognitive Psychology, 17* (9).

Pezdek, K., Finger, K., & Hodge, D. (1997). Planting false childhood memories: The role of event plausibility. *Psychological Science, 8,* 437–441.

Pezdek, K., & Taylor, J. (2002). Memory for traumatic events in children and adults. In M. L. Eisen, J. A. Quas, & G. S. Goodman (Eds.), *Memory and suggestibility in the forensic interview* (pp. 165–183). Mahwah, NJ: Erlbaum.

Phillips, W. D. (1995). *Personal communication.*

Phillipson, R. (Ed.). (2000). *Rights to language: Equity, power, and education.* Mahwah, NJ: Erlbaum.

Pickering, M. J., & Branigan, H. P. (1998). The representation of verbs: Evidence from syntactic priming in language production. *Journal of Memory and Language, 39,* 633–651.

Pickering, S. J. (2006a). Assessment of working memory in children, In S. J. Pickering (Ed.), *Working memory and education* (pp. 241–271). Burlington, MA: Elsevier.

Pickering, S. J. (2006b). Introduction. In S. J. Pickering (Ed.), *Working memory and education* (pp. xv–xxii). Burlington, MA: Elsevier.

Pickering, S. J. (Ed.) (2006c). *Working memory and education.* Burlington, MA: Elsevier.

Pickford, R. W., & Gregory, R. L. (2004). Bartlett, Sir Frederic Charles. In R. L. Gregory (Ed.), *The Oxford companion to the mind* (2nd ed., pp. 86–87). New York: Oxford University Press.

Pickrell, J. E., Bernstein, D. M., & Loftus, E. E. (2004). Misinformation effect. In R. Pohl (Ed.), *Cognitive illusions: Handbook on fallacies and biases in thinking, judgment, and memory* (pp. 345–361) Hove, UK: Psychology Press.

Pienemann, M., Di Biase, B., Kawaguchi, S., & Håkansson, G. (2005). Processing constraints on L1 transfer. In J. F. Kroll & A. M. B. de Groot (Eds.), *Handbook of bilingualism: Psycholinguistic approaches* (pp. 128–153). New York: Oxford University Press.

Pinker, S. (1985). Visual cognition: An introduction. In S. Pinker (Ed.), *Visual cognition* (pp. 1–63). Cambridge, MA: MIT Press.

Pinker, S. (1993). The central problem for the psycholinguist. In G. Harman (Ed.), *Conceptions of the human mind* (pp. 59–84). Hillsdale, NJ: Erlbaum.

Pinker, S. (1997). *How the mind works.* New York: Norton.

Pinker, S. (2002). *The blank slate: The modern denial of human nature.* New York: Viking.

Pinker, S., & Prince, A. (1999). The nature of human concepts: Evidence from an unusual source. In R. Jackendoff, P. Bloom, & K. Winn (Eds.), *Language, logic, and concepts* (pp. 221–261). Cambridge, MA: MIT Press.

Piolat, A., Olive, T., & Kellogg, R. T. (2005). Cognitive effort during note taking. *Applied Cognitive Psychology, 19,* 291–312.

Pisoni, D. B., & Remez, R. E. (Eds.). (2005). *The handbook of speech perception.* Malden, MA: Blackwell.

Pita, M. D., & Utakis, S. (2006). Educational polity for the transnational Dominican community. In H. Luria, D. M. Seymour, & T. Smoke (Eds.), *Language and linguistics in context: Readings and applications for teachers* (pp. 333–341). Mahwah, NJ: Erlbaum.

Plack, C. J. (2005). *The sense of hearing.* Mahwah, NJ: Erlbaum.

Plant, E. A., Ericsson, K. A., Hill, L., & Asberg, K. (2005). Why study time does not predict grade point average across college students: Implications of deliberate practice for academic performance. *Contemporary Educational Psychology, 30,* 96–116.

Platt, R. D., & Griggs, R. A. (1995). Facilitation and matching bias in the abstract selection task. *Thinking and Reasoning, 1,* 55–70.

Plucker, J. A., & Renzulli, J. S. (1999). Psychometric approaches to the study of human creativity. In R. J. Sternberg (Ed.), *Handbook of creativity* (pp. 35–61). New York: Cambridge University Press.

Pohl, R. F. (Ed.). (2004a). *Cognitive illusions: Handbook on fallacies and biases in thinking, judgment, and memory.* Hove, UK: Psychology Press.

Pohl, R. F. (2004b). Hindsight bias. In R. Pohl (Ed.), *Cognitive illusions: Handbook on fallacies and biases in thinking, judgment, and memory* (pp. 363–378). Hove, UK: Psychology Press.

Pohl, R. F., Bender, M., & Lachmann, G. (2002). Hindsight bias around the world. *Experimental Psychology, 49,* 270–282.

Pohl, R. F., Schwarz, S., Sczesny, S., & Stahlberg, D. (2003). Hindsight bias in gustatory judgments. *Experimental Psychology, 50,* 107–115

Polk, T. A., et al. (2002). Neural specialization for letter recognition. *Journal of Cognitive Neuroscience, 14,* 145–159.

Posner, M. I. (2004). Progress in attention research. In M. I Posner (Ed.), *Cognitive neuroscience of attention* (pp. 3–9). New York: Guilford.

Posner, M. I., & DiGirolamo, G. J. (2000a). Attention in cognitive neuroscience: An overview. In M. S. Gazzaniga (Ed.), *The new cognitive neurosciences* (2nd ed., pp. 623–621). Cambridge, MA: MIT Press.

Posner, M. I., & DiGirolamo, G. J. (2000b). Cognitive neuroscience: Origins and promise. *Psychological Bulletin, 126,* 873–889.

Posner, M. I., & Rothbart, M. K. (2007a). *Educating the human brain.* Washington, DC: American Psychological Association.

Posner, M. I., & Rothbart, M. K. (2007b). Research on attention networks as a model for the integration of psychological science. *Annual Review of Psychology, 58,* 1–23.

Potter, M. C. (1999). Understanding sentences and scenes: The role of conceptual short-term memory. In V. Coltheart (Ed.), *Fleeting memories: Cognition of brief visual stimuli* (pp. 13–46). Cambridge, MA: MIT Press.

Poulton, E. C. (1994). *Behavioral decision theory: A new approach.* Cambridge, UK: Cambridge University Press.

Powell, M. B., Thomson, D. M., & Ceci, S. J. (2003). Children's memory of recurring events: Is the first event always the best remembered? *Applied Cognitive Psychology, 17,* 127–146.

Press, B. (2004, February 9). It's official: No weapons of mass destruction. *Liberal Opinion,* p. 4.

Pressley, M. (1996). Personal reflections on the study of practical memory in the mid-1990s: The complete cognitive researcher. In D. J. Herrmann et al. (Eds.), *Basic and applied memory research: Practical applications* (Vol. 2, pp. 19–33). Mahwah, NJ: Erlbaum.

Pressley, M. (2005). Final reflections: Metacognitive instructional practice. In S. E. Israel, C. C. Block, K. L. Bauserman, & K. Kinnucan-Welsch (Eds.), *Metacognition in literacy learning* (pp. 391–411). Mahwah, NJ: Erlbaum.

Pressley, M., & Ghatala, E. S. (1988). Delusions about performance on multiple-choice comprehension tests. *Reading Research Quarterly, 23,* 454–464.

Pressley, M., & Hilden, K. (2006). Cognitive strategies. In D. Kuhn & R. Siegler (Eds.), *Handbook of child psychology* (6th ed., Vol. 2, pp. 511–556). Hoboken, NJ: Wiley.

Pressley, M., Levin, J. R., & Ghatala, E. S. (1984). Memory strategy monitoring in adults and children. *Journal of Verbal Learning and Verbal Behavior, 23,* 270–288.

Pressley, M., Levin, J. R., & Ghatala, E. S. (1988). Strategy-comparison opportunities promote long-term strategy use. *Contemporary Educational Psychology, 13,* 157–168

Pretz, J. E., Naples, A. J., & Sternberg, R. J. (2003). Recognizing, defining, and representing problems. In J. E. Davidson & R. J. Sternberg (Eds.), *The psychology of problem solving* (pp. 3–30). New York: Cambridge University Press.

Pringle, H. L., Kramer, A. F., & Irwin, D. E. (2004). Individual differences in the visual representation of scenes. In D. T. Levin (Ed.), *Thinking and seeing: Visual metacognition in adults and children* (pp. 165–185). Cambridge, MA: MIT Press.

Protopapas, A. (1999). Connectionist modeling of speech perception. *Psychological Bulletin, 125,* 410–436.

Puce, A., & Perrett, D. (2005). Electrophysiology and brain imaging of biological motion. In J. T. Cacioppo & G. G. Berntson (Eds.), *Social neuroscience: Key readings* (pp. 115–129). New York: Psychology Press.

Purdon, C. (2005). Unwanted intrusive thoughts: Present status and future directions. In D. A. Clark (Ed.), *Intrusive thoughts in clinical disorders: Theory, research, and treatment* (pp. 226–244). New York: Guilford Press.

Purdon, C., Rowa, K., & Antony, M. M. (2005). Thought suppression and its effects on thought frequency, appraisal and mood state in individuals with obsessive-compulsive disorder. *Behavior Research and Therapy, 43*, 93–108.

Purves, D., & Lotto, R. B. (2003). *Why we see what we do*. Sunderland, MA: Sinauer.

Pylyshyn, Z. W. (1984). *Computation and cognition*. Cambridge, MA: MIT Press.

Pylyshyn, Z. W. (2003). Return of the mental image: Are there pictures in the brain? *TRENDS in Cognitive Sciences, 7*, 113–118.

Pylyshyn, Z. W. (2004). Mental imagery. In R. L. Gregory (Ed.), *The Oxford companion to the mind* (pp. 582–585). New York: Oxford University Press.

Pylyshyn, Z. W. (2006). *Seeing and visualizing: It's not what you think*. Cambridge, MA: MIT Press.

Pynte, J., Kennedy, A., & Ducrot, S. (2004). The influence of parafoveal typographical errors on eye movements in reading. In R. Radach, A. Kennedy, & K. Rayner (Eds.), *Eye movements and information processing during reading* (pp. 178–202). Hove, UK: Psychology Press.

Quilici, J. L., & Mayer, R. E. (2002). Teaching students to recognize structural similarities between statistics word problems. *Applied Cognitive Psychology, 16*, 325–342.

Quinlan, P. T. (Ed.). (2003a). *Connectionist models of development: Developmental processes in real and artificial neural networks*. Hove, UK: Psychology Press.

Quinlan, P. T. (2003b). Visual feature integration theory: Past, present, and future. *Psychological Bulletin, 129*, 643–673.

Quinn, D. M., & Spencer, S. J. (2001). The interference of stereotype threat with women's generation of mathematical problem-solving strategies. *Journal of Social Issues, 57*, 55–71.

Quinn, P. C., et al. (2002). Development of form similarity as a Gestalt grouping principle in infancy. *Psychological Science, 13*, 320–328.

Raaijmakers, J. G. W., & Shiffrin, R. M. (2002). Models of memory. In D. Medin (Ed.), *Stevens' handbook of experimental psychology* (3rd ed., pp. 43–76). New York: Wiley.

Rabbitt, P. (2002). Aging and cognition. In H. Pashler (Ed.), *Stevens' handbook of experimental psychology* (3rd ed., Vol. 4, pp. 793–860). New York: Wiley.

Rachlin, H. (2002). A framework for scientific psychology [Review of the book, *The new behaviorism: Mind, mechanism, and society*]. *Contemporary Psychology, 47*, 360–361.

Rachlinski, J. J. (2004). Misunderstanding ability, misallocating responsibility. In D. T. Levin (Ed.), *Thinking and seeing: Visual metacognition in adults and children* (pp. 251–276). Cambridge, MA: MIT Press.

Radach, R., & Kennedy, A. (2004). Theoretical perspectives on eye movements in reading: Past controversies, current issues, and an agenda for future research. In R. Radach, A. Kennedy, & K. Rayner (Eds.), *Eye movements and information processing during reading* (pp. 3–26). Hove, UK: Psychology Press.

Radach, R., Kennedy, A., & Rayner, K. (Eds.). (2004a). *Eye movements and information processing during reading*. Hove, UK: Psychology Press.

Radach, R., Kennedy, A., & Rayner, K. (2004b). Preface. In R. Radach, A. Kennedy, & K. Rayner (Eds.), *Eye movements and information processing during reading* (pp. 1–2). Hove, UK: Psychology Press.

Raichle, M. E. (2001). Functional neuroimaging: A historical and physiological perspective. In R. Cabeza & A. Kingstone (Eds.), *Handbook of functional neuroimaging of cognition* (pp. 3–26). Cambridge, MA: MIT Press.

Randi, J., Grigorenko, E. L., & Sternberg, R. J. (2005). Revisiting definitions of reading comprehension: Just what is reading comprehension anyway? In S. E. Israel, C. C. Block, K. L. Bauserman, & K. Kinnucan-Welsch (Eds.), *Metacognition in literacy learning: Theory, assessment, instruction, and professional development* (pp. 19–39). Mahwah, NJ: Erlbaum.

Ransdell, S., & Levy, C. M. (1999). Writing, reading, and speaking memory spans and the importance of resource flexibility. In M. Torrance & G. C. Jeffery (Eds.), *The cognitive demands of writing: Processing capacity and working memory in text production* (pp. 99–113). Amsterdam: Amsterdam University Press.

Rapp, B., & Goldrick, M. (2000). Discreteness and interactivity in spoken word production. *Psychological Review, 107*, 460–499

Rapp, D. N., & Gerrig, R. J. (2006). Predilections for narrative outcomes: The impact of story contexts and reader preferences. *Journal of Memory and Language, 54*, 54–67.

Rapp, D. N., & Taylor, H. A. (2004). Interactive dimensions in the construction of mental representations for text. *Journal of Experimental Psychology: Learning, Memory, and Cognition, 30*, 988–1001.

Rasmussen, E. B. (2006). Expanding your coverage of neuroscience: An interview with Michael Gazzaniga *Teaching of Psychology, 33*, 212–215.

Ratcliff, R. (1990). Connectionist models of recognition memory: Constraints imposed by learning and forgetting functions. *Psychological Review, 97,* 285–308.

Ratner, H. H., Foley, M. A., & Gimpert, N. (2000). Person perspectives on children's memory and learning: What do source-monitoring failures reveal? In K. Roberts & M. Blades (Eds.), *Children's source monitoring.* Mahwah, NJ: Erlbaum.

Ratner, H. H., Foley, M. A., & Gimpert, N. (2002). The role of collaborative planning in children's source-monitoring errors and learning. *Journal of Experimental Child Psychology, 81,* 44–73.

Ratner, H. H., Foley, M. A., & McCaskill, P. (2001). Understanding children's activity memory: The role of outcomes. *Journal of Experimental Child Psychology, 79,* 162–191.

Ratner, N. B., & Gleason, J. B. (1993). An introduction to psycholinguistics: What do language users know? In J. B. Gleason & N. B. Ratner (Eds.), *Psycholinguistics.* Fort Worth: Harcourt Brace Jovanovich.

Rau, P. S., & Sebrechts, M. M. (1996). How initial plans mediate the expansion and resolution of options in writing. *Quarterly Journal of Experimental Psychology, 49A,* 616–638.

Rayner, K. (1998). Eye movements in reading and information processing: 20 years of research. *Psychological Bulletin, 124,* 372–422.

Rayner, K., & Clifton, C., Jr. (2002). Language processing. In D. Medin (Ed.), *Stevens' handbook of experimental psychology* (3rd ed., Vol. 2, pp. 261–316). New York: Wiley.

Rayner, K., & Johnson, R. L. (2005). Letter-by-letter acquired dyslexia is due to the serial encoding of letters. *Psychological Science, 16,* 530–534.

Rayner, K., Juhasz, B. J., & Pollatsek, A. (2005). Eye movements during reading. In J. Snowling & C. Hulme (Eds.), *The science of reading: A handbook* (pp. 61–78). Malden, MA: Blackwell.

Rayner, K., & Liversedge, S. P. (2004). Visual and linguistic processing during eye fixations in reading. In J. M. Henderson & F. Ferreira (Eds.), *The interface of language, vision, and action: Eye movements and the visual world* (pp. 59–104). New York: Psychology Press.

Rayner, K., Liversedge, S. P., & White, S. J. (2006). Eye movements when reading disappearing text: The importance of the word to the right of fixation. *Vision Research, 46,* 310–323.

Rayner, K., Pollatsek, A., & Starr, M. S. (2003). Reading. In I. B. Weiner (Ed.), *Handbook of psychology* (Vol. 4, pp. 549–574). Hoboken, NJ: Wiley.

Rayner, K., Warren, T., Juhasz, B. J., & Liversedge, S. P. (2004). The effect of plausibility on eye movements in reading. *Journal of Experimental Psychology: Learning, Memory, and Cognition, 30,* 1290–1301.

Rayner, K., White, S. J., Johnson, R. L., & Liversedge, S. P. (2006). Raeding wrods with jumbled lettres: There is a cost. *Psychological Science, 17,* 192–193.

Rayner, K., et al. (2001). How psychological science informs the teaching of reading. *Psychological Science in the Public Interest, 2,* 31–74.

Read, J. D., & Connolly, D. A. (2007). The effects of delay on long-term memory for witnessed events. In M. P. Toglia, J. D. Read, D. F. Ross, & R. C. L. Lindsay (Eds.), *Handbook of eyewitness psychology* (Vol. 1, pp. 117–155). Mahwah, NJ: Erlbaum.

Read, S. J., & Urada, D. I. (2003). A neural network simulation of the outgroup homogenity effect. *Personality and Social Psychology Review, 7,* 146–169.

Reber, R. (2004). Availability. In R. Pohl (Ed.), *Cognitive illusions: Handbook on fallacies and biases in thinking, judgment, and memory.* Hove, UK: Psychology Press.

Recarte, M., & Nunes, L. M. (2000). Effects of verbal and spatial-imagery tasks on eye fixations while driving. *Journal of Experimental Psychology: Applied, 6,* 31–43.

Reed, S. K. (1974). Structural descriptions and the limitations of visual images. *Memory & Cognition, 2,* 329–336.

Reed, S. K. (1977). Facilitation of problem solving. In N. J. Castellan, Jr., D. B. Pisoni, & G. R. Potts (Eds.). *Cognitive theory* (Vol. 2, pp. 3–20). Hillsdale, NJ: Erlbaum.

Reed, S. K. (1999). *Word problems: Research and curriculum reform.* Mahwah, NJ: Erlbaum.

Rehder, B., & Hoffman, A. B. (2005). Thirty-something categorization results explained: Selective attention, eyetracking, and models of category learning. *Journal of Experimental Psychology: Learning Memory, and Cognition, 31,* 811–929.

Reicher, G. M. (1969). Perceptual recognition as a function of meaningfulness of stimuli material. *Journal of Experimental Psychology, 81,* 275–280.

Reichle, E. D., & Laurent, P. A. (2006). Using reinforcement learning to understand the emergence of "intelligent" eye-movement behavior during reading. *Psychological Review, 113,* 390–408.

Reichle, E. D., Pollatsek, A., Fisher, D. L., & Rayner, K. (1998). Toward a model of eye movement control in reading. *Psychological Review, 105,* 125–157.

Reisberg, D., & Heuer, F. (2005). Visuospatial images. In P. Shah & A. Miyake (Eds.), *The Cambridge handbook of visuospatial thinking* (pp. 35–80). New York: Cambridge University Press.

Reisberg, D., Pearson, D. G., & Kosslyn, S. M. (2003). Intuitions and introspections about imagery: The role of imagery experience in shaping an investigator's theoretical views. *Applied Cognitive Psychology, 17,* 147–160.

Remnick D. (2003, July 28). Faith-based intelligence. *New Yorker,* pp. 27–29.

Rendell, P. G., Castel, A. D., & Craik, F. I. M. (2005). Memory for proper names in old age: A disproportionate impairment? *Quarterly Journal of Experimental Psychology, 58A,* 54–71.

Rensink, R. A. (2002). Change detection. *Annual Review of Psychology, 53,* 245–277.

Rensink, R. A., O'Regan, J. K., & Clark, J. J. (1997). To see or not to see: The need for attention to perceive changes in scenes. *Psychological Science, 8,* 368–373.

Reuter-Lorenz, P. A., & Jonides, J. (2007). The executive is central to working memory: Insights from age, performance, and task variations. In A. R. A. Conway et al. (Eds.), *Variations in working memory* (pp. 250–271). New York: Oxford University Press.

Reyna, V. F., Mills, B., Estreada, S., & Brainerd, C. J. (2007). False memory in children: Data, theory, and legal implications. In M. P. Toglia, J. D. Read, D. F. Ross, & R. C. L. Lindsay (Eds.). *Handbook of eyewitness psychology* (Vol. 1, pp. 479–507). Mahwah, NJ: Erlbaum.

Reynolds, D. J., Garnham, A., & Oakhill, J. (2006). Evidence of immediate activation of gender information from a social role name. *Quarterly Journal of Experimental Psychology, 59,* 886–903.

Rhodes, R. L., Ochoa, S. H., & Ortiz, S. O. (2005). *Assessing culturally and linguistically diverse students: A practical guide.* New York: Guilford.

Ricciardelli, L. A. (1992). Creativity and bilingualism. *Journal of Creative Behavior, 26,* 242–259.

Riccio, D. C., Millin, P. M., & Gisquet-Verrier, P. (2003). Retrograde amnesia: Forgetting back. *Current Directions in Psychological Science, 12,* 41–44.

Richardson, J. T. E. (1996a). Evolving concepts of working memory. In J. T. E. Richardson et al. (Eds.), *Working memory and human cognition* (pp. 3–30). New York: Oxford University Press.

Richardson, J. T. E. (1996b). Evolving issues in working memory. In J. T. E. Richardson et al. (Eds.), *Working memory and human cognition* (pp. 120–148). New York: Oxford University Press.

Richardson, J. T. E. (1999). *Imagery.* East Sussex, UK: Psychology Press.

Richardson-Klavehn, A., & Gardiner, J. M. (1998). Depth-of-processing effects on priming in stem completion: Tests of the voluntary-contamination, conceptual-processing, and lexical-processing hypotheses. *Journal of Experimental Psychology: Learning, Memory, and Cognition, 24,* 593–609.

Riddoch, M. J., & Humphreys, G. W. (2001). Object recognition. In B. Rapp (Ed.), *The handbook of cognitive neuropsychology* (pp. 45–74). Philadelphia: Psychology Press.

Rinck, M. (2005). Spatial situation models. In P. Shah & A. Miyake (Eds.), *The Cambridge handbook of visuospatial thinking* (pp. 334–382). New York: Cambridge University Press.

Rips, L. J. (2002). Reasoning. In D. Medin (Ed.), *Stevens' handbook of experimental psychology* (3rd ed., Vol. 2, pp. 363–411). New York: Wiley.

Robbins, S. B., et al. (2004). Do psychosocial and study skill factors predict college outcomes? A meta-analysis. *Psychological Bulletin, 130,* 261–282.

Roberts, M. J., & Newton, E. J. (2005). Introduction: Individual differences in reasoning strategies. In M. J. Roberts & E. J. Newton (Eds.), *Methods of thought: Individual differences in reasoning strategies* (pp. 1–9). Hove, UK: Psychology Press.

Robertson, S. I. (2001). *Problem solving.* East Sussex, UK: Psychology Press.

Robins, R. W., Gosling, S. D., & Craik, K. H. (1999). An empirical analysis of trends in psychology. *American Psychologist, 54,* 117–128.

Rodd, J., Gaskell, G., & Marslen-Wilson, W. (2002). Making sense of semantic ambiguity: Semantic competition in lexical access. *Journal of Memory and Language, 46,* 245–266.

Roebers, C. M., Gelhar, T., & Schneider, W. (2004). "It's magic!" The effects of presentation modality on children's event memory, suggestibility, and confidence judgments. *Journal of Experimental Child Psychology, 87,* 320–335.

Roebers, C. M., & Schneider, W. (2000). The impact of misleading questions on eyewitness memory in children and adults. *Applied Cognitive Psychology, 14,* 509–526.

Roebers, C. M., Schwarz, S., & Neumann, R. (2005). Social influence and children's event recall and suggestibility. *European Journal of Developmental Psychology, 2,* 47–69.

Roediger, H. L., III. (1996). Prospective memory and episodic memory. In M. Brandimonte, G. O. Einstein,

& M. A. McDaniel (Eds.), *Prospective memory: Theory and applications* (pp. 149–155). Mahwah, NJ: Erlbaum.

Roediger, H. L., III. (2000). Why retrieval is the key process in understanding human memory. In E. Tulving (Ed.), *Memory, consciousness, and the brain* (pp. 52–75). Philadelphia: Psychology Press.

Roediger, H. L., III, & Amir, N. (2005). Implicit memory tasks: Retention without conscious recollection. In A. Wenzel & D. C. Rubin (Eds.), *Cognitive methods and their application to clinical research* (pp. 121–127). Washington, DC: American Psychological Association.

Roediger, H. L., III, & Gallo, D. A. (2001). Levels of processing: Some unanswered questions. In M. Naveh-Benjamin, M. Moscovitch, & H. L. Roediger, III (Eds.), *Perspectives on human memory and cognitive aging: Essays in honour of Fergus Craik* (pp. 28–47). New York: Psychology Press.

Roediger, H. L., III, & Gallo, D. A. (2004). Associative memory illusions. In R. Pohl (Ed.), *Cognitive illusions: Handbook on fallacies and biases in thinking, judgment, and memory* (pp. 309–326). Hove, UK: Psychology Press.

Roediger, H. L., III, Gallo, D. A., & Geraci, L. (2002). Processing approaches to cognition: The impetus from the levels-of-processing framework. *Memory, 10,* 319–332.

Roediger, H. L., III, & Guynn, M. J. (1996). Retrieval processes. In E. L. Bjork & R. A. Bjork (Eds.), *Memory* (pp. 197–236). San Diego: Academic Press.

Roediger, H. L., III, & Karpicke, J. D. (2006a). The power of testing memory: Basic research and implications for educational practice. *Perspectives on Psychological Science, 1,* 181–210.

Roediger, H. L., III, & Karpicke, J. D. (2006b). Test-enhanced learning: Taking memory tests improves long-term retention, *Psychological Science, 17,* 249–255.

Roediger, H. L., III, & Marsh, E. J. (2003). Episodic and autobiographical memory. In A. H. Healy & R. W. Proctor (Eds.), *Handbook of psychology* (Vol. 4, pp. 475–497).

Roediger, H. L., III, Marsh, E. J., & Lee, S. C. (2002). Kinds of memory. In D. Medin (Ed.), *Stevens' handbook of experimental psychology* (3rd ed., pp. 1–41). New York: Wiley.

Roediger, H. L., III, & McDermott, K. B. (1995). Creating false memories: Remembering words not presented in lists. *Journal of Experimental Psychology: Learning, Memory, and Cognition, 21,* 803–814.

Roediger, H. L., III, & McDermott, K. B. (2000). Distortions of memory. In E. Tulving & F. I. M. Craik (Eds.), *The Oxford handbook of memory* (pp. 149–162). New York: Oxford University Press.

Roelofs, A., & Baayen, H. (2002). Morphology by itself in planning the production of spoken words. *Psychonomic Bulletin & Review, 9,* 132–138.

Rogers, D. (1985). Language development. In A. Branthwaite & D. Rogers (Eds.), *Children growing up* (pp. 82–93). Milton Keynes, UK: Open University Press.

Rogers, T. B., Kuiper, N. A., & Kirker, W. S. (1977). Self-reference and the encoding of personal information. *Journal of Personality and Social Psychology, 35,* 677–688.

Rogers, T. T. & McClelland, J. L. (2004). *Semantic cognition: A parallel distributed processing approach.* Cambridge, MA: MIT Press.

Rogoff, B. (1990). *Apprenticeship in thinking: Cognitive development in social context.* New York: Oxford University Press.

Rohrbaugh, C. C., & Shanteau, J. (1999). Context, process, and experience: Research on applied judgment and decision making. In F. T. Durso et al. (Eds.), *Handbook of applied cognition* (pp. 115–139). New York: Wiley.

Rohrer, D., & Taylor, K. (2006). The effects of overlearning and distributed practice on the retention of mathematics knowledge. *Applied Cognitive Psychology, 20,* 1209–1224.

Rojahn, K., & Pettigrew, T. F. (1992). Memory for schema-relevant information: A meta-analytic resolution. *British Journal of Social Psychology, 31,* 81–109.

Rollins, P. R. (2003). Caregivers' contingent comments to 9-month-old infants: Relationships with later language. *Applied Psycholinguistics, 24,* 221–234.

Rolls, E. T. (2004). Neural networks in the brain. In R. L. Gregory (Ed.), *The Oxford companion to the mind* (2nd ed., pp. 639–641). New York: Oxford University Press.

Rolls, E. T., & Tovee, M. J. (1995). Sparseness of the neuronal representation of stimuli in the primate temporal visual cortex. *Journal of Neurophysiology, 73,* 713–726.

Rosch, E. H. (1973). Natural categories. *Cognitive Psychology, 4,* 328–350.

Rosch, E. H. (1975). The nature of mental codes for color categories. *Journal of Experimental Psychology: Human Perception and Performance, 1,* 303–322.

Rosch, E. H., & Mervis, C. B. (1975). Family resemblances: Studies in the internal structure of categories. *Cognitive Psychology, 7,* 573–605.

Rosch, E. H., et al. (1976). Basic objects in natural categories. *Cognitive Psychology, 8,* 382–439.

Rose, S. P. R. (2004). Memory: Biological basis. In R. L. Gregory (Ed.), *The Oxford companion to the mind* (2nd ed., pp. 564–568). New York: Oxford University Press.

Rosen, R. D., et al. (2007). *Bad President.* New York: Workman.

Rosen, V. M., & Engle, R. W. (1997). The role of working memory capacity in retrieval. *Journal of Experimental Psychology: General, 126,* 211–227.

Rosenblum, L. D. (2005). Primacy of multimodal speech perception. In D. B. Pisoni & R. E. Remez (Eds.), *The handbook of speech perception* (pp. 51–78). Malden, MA: Blackwell.

Roskos-Ewoldsen, B., McNamara, T. P., Shelton, A. L., & Carr, W. (1998). Mental representations of large and small spatial layouts are orientation dependent. *Journal of Experimental Psychology: Learning, Memory, and Cognition, 24,* 215–226.

Ross, B. H., & Makin, V. S. (1999). Prototype versus exemplar models in cognition. In R. J. Sternberg (Ed.), *The nature of cognition* (pp. 205–241). Cambridge, MA: MIT Press.

Rothblum, E. D., & Factor, R. (2001). Lesbians and their sisters as a control group. *Psychological Science, 12,* 63–69.

Rothman, A. J., & Salovey, P. (1997). Shaping perceptions to motivate healthy behavior: The role of message framing. *Psychological Bulletin, 121,* 3–19.

Rouw, R., Kosslyn, S. M., & Hamel, R. (1997). Detecting high-level and low-level properties in visual images and visual precepts. *Cognition, 63,* 209–226.

Rovee-Collier, C. K. (1999). The development of infant memory. *Current Directions in Psychological Science, 8,* 80–85.

Rovee-Collier, C. K., & Barr, R. (2002). Infant cognition. In H. Pashler (Ed.), *Stevens' handbook of experimental psychology* (Vol. 4, pp. 693–791). New York: Wiley.

Rovee-Collier, C. K., Borza, M. A., Adler, S. A., & Boller, K. (1993). Infants' eyewitness testimony: Effects of postevent information on a prior memory representation. *Memory & Cognition, 21,* 267–279.

Rovee-Collier, C. K. & Cuevas, K. (2008). The development of infant memory. In M. Courage & N. Cowan (Eds.), *The development of memory in childhood.* Hove, UK: Psychology Press.

Rovee-Collier, C. K., Griesler, P. C., & Earley, L. A. (1985). Contextual determinants of retrieval in three-month-old infants. *Learning and Motivation, 16,* 139–157.

Rovee-Collier, C., & Hayne, H. (2000). Memory in infancy and early childhood. In E. Tulving & F. I. M. Craik (Eds.), *The Oxford handbook of memory* (pp. 267–282). New York: Oxford University Press.

Rovee-Collier, C., Hayne, H., & Colombo, M. (2001). *The development of implicit and explicit memory.* Philadelphia: John Benjamins Publishing Company.

Roy, M. M., & Christenfeld, N. J. S. (2007). Bias in memory predicts bias in estimation of future task duration. *Memory & Cognition, 35,* 557–564.

Roy, M. M., Christenfeld, N. J. S., & McKenzie, C. R. M. (2005). Underestimating the duration of future events: Memory incorrectly used or memory bias? *Psychological Review, 131,* 738–756.

Royden, C. S., Wolfe, J. M., & Klempen, N. (2001). Visual search asymmetries in motion and optic flow fields. *Perception & Psychophysics, 63,* 436–444.

Ruben, B. D. (2001, July 13). We need excellence beyond the classroom. *Chronicle of Higher Education,* pp. B15–16.

Rubin, D. C. (2000). The distribution of early childhood memories. *Memory, 8,* 265–269.

Rubin, E. (1915/1958). Synoplevede Figurer [Figure and ground]. In D. C. Beardslee & M. Wertheimer (Eds.), *Readings in perception* (pp. 194–203). Princeton, NJ: Van Nostrand.

Rudman, L. A. (2005). Rejection of women? Beyond prejudice as antipathy. In J. F. Dovidio, P. Glick, & L. A. Rudman (Eds.), *On the nature of prejudice: Fifty years after Allport* (pp. 106–120). Malden, MA: Blackwell.

Rueckl, J. G. (1995). Ambiguity and connectionist networks: Still settling into a solution—comment on Joordens and Besner (1994). *Journal of Experimental Psychology: Learning, Memory, and Cognition, 21,* 501–508

Rueckl, J. G., & Oden, G. C. (1986). The integration of contextual and featural information during word identification. *Journal of Memory and Language, 25,* 445–460.

Rumelhart, D. E., & McClelland, J. L. (1986). On learning the past tenses of English verbs. In J. L. McClelland & D. E. Rumelhart (Eds.), *Parallel distributed processing: Explorations in the microstructure of cognition* (Vol. 2, pp. 216–271). Cambridge, MA: MIT Press.

Rumelhart, D. E., & McClelland, J. L. (1987). Learning the past tenses of English verbs: Implicit rules or parallel distributed processing? In B. MacWhinney (Ed.), *Mechanisms of language acquisition* (pp. 195–248). Hillsdale, NJ: Erlbaum.

Rumelhart, D. E., McClelland, J. L., & the PDP Research Group (Eds.). (1986). *Parallel distributed processing* (Vol. 1). Cambridge, MA: MIT Press.

Runco, M. A. (2005). Motivation, competence, and creativity. In A. J. Elliot & C. S. Dweck (Eds.), *Handbook of competence and motivation* (pp. 609–623). New York: Guilford.

Runco, M. A. (2007). *Creativity: Theories and themes: Research, development, and practice.* London: Elsevier Academic Press.

Rundus, D. (1971). Analysis of rehearsal processes in free recall. *Journal of Experimental Psychology, 89,* 63–77.

Ruscio, J., Whitney, D. M., & Amabile, T. M. (1998). Looking inside the fishbowl of creativity: Verbal and behavioral predictors of creative performance. *Creativity Research Journal, 11,* 243–263.

Russ, S. W. (2001). Writing creatively: How to do it. [Review of the book *Writing in flow: Keys to enhanced creativity*] *Contemporary Psychology, 46,* 181–182.

Ryan, L., & Eich, E. (2000). Mood dependence and implicit memory. In E. Tulving (Ed.), *Memory, consciousness, and the brain* (pp. 91–105). Philadelphia: Psychology Press.

Sachs, J. (1967). Recognition memory for syntactic and semantic aspects of a connected discourse. *Perception & Psychophysics, 2,* 437–442.

Saffran, E. M., & Schwartz, M. F. (2003). Language. In I. B. Weiner (Ed.), *Handbook of psychology* (Vol. 4, pp. 595–636). Hoboken, NJ: Wiley.

Saffran, J. B., Werker, J. F., & Werner, L. A. (2006). The infant's auditory world: Hearing, speech, and the beginnings of language. In D. Kuhn & R. Siegler (Eds.), *Handbook of child psychology* (6th ed., Vol. 2, pp. 58–108). Hoboken, NJ: Wiley.

Saito, A. (Ed.). (2000). *Bartlett, culture and cognition.* East Sussex, UK: Psychology Press.

Salthouse, T. A. (1991). *Theoretical perspectives on cognitive aging.* Hillsdale, NJ: Erlbaum.

Salthouse, T. A. (2000). Psychological assumptions in cognitive aging research. In F. I. M. Craik & T. A. Salthouse (Eds.), *The handbook of aging and cognition* (2nd ed.). Mahwah, NJ: Erlbaum.

Salthouse, T. A. (2002). Age-related effects on memory in the context of age-related effects on cognition. In P. Graf & N. Ohta (Eds.), *Lifespan development of human memory* (pp. 139–158). Cambridge, MA: MIT Press.

Samuel, A. G., & Ressler, W. H. (1986). Attention within auditory word perception: Insights from the phonemic restoration illusion. *Journal of Experimental Psychology: Human Perception and Performance, 12,* 70–79.

Sanbonmatsu, D. M., Posavac, S. S., Kardes, F. R., & Mantel, S. P. (1998). Selective hypothesis testing. *Psychonomic Bulletin & Review, 5,* 197–220.

Sangrigoli, S., & de Schonen, S. (2004). Recognition of own-face and other-race faces by three-month-old infants. *Journal of Child Psychology and Psychiatry, 45,* 1219–1227.

Sanna, L. J., & Schwarz, N. (2006). Metacognitive experiences and human judgment: The case of hindsight bias and its debiasing. *Current Directions in Psychological Science, 15,* 172–176.

Santelmann, L. M., & Jusczyk, P. W. (1998). Sensitivity to discontinuous dependencies in language learners: Evidence for limitations in processing space. *Cognition, 69,* 105–134.

Sawyer, R. K. (2003). *Group creativity: Music, theater, collaboration.* Mahwah, NJ: Erlbaum.

Saylor, M. M., & Baldwin, D. A. (2004). Action analysis and change blindness: Possible links. In D. T. Levin (Ed.), *Thinking and seeing: Visual metacognition in adults and children* (pp. 37–56). Cambridge, MA: MIT Press.

Schacter, D. L. (1999). The seven sins of memory: Insights from psychology and cognitive neuroscience. *American Psychologist, 54,* 182–203.

Schacter, D. L. (2001). *The seven sins of memory.* Boston: Houghton Mifflin.

Schacter, D. L., & Badgaiyan, R. D. (2001). Neuroimaging of priming: New perspectives on implicit and explicit memory. *Current Directions in Psychological Science, 10,* 1–4.

Schacter, D. L., Church, B., & Treadwell, J. (1994). Implicit memory in amnesic patients: Evidence for spared auditory priming. *Psychological Science, 5,* 20–25.

Schacter, D. L., Norman, K. A., & Koustaal, W. (1998). The cognitive neuroscience of constructive memory. *Annual Review of Psychology, 49,* 289–318.

Schacter, D. L., & Wiseman, A. L. (2006). Reducing memory errors: The distinctiveness heuristic. In R. R. Hunt & J. B. Worthen (Eds.), *Distinctiveness and memory* (pp. 89–107). New York: Oxford University Press.

Schaefer, E. G., & Laing, M. L. (2000). 'Please, remind me. . .': The role of others in prospective remembering. *Applied Cognitive Psychology, 14,* S-99-S114.

Schaeken, W., DeVooght, G., Vandierendonck, A., & d'Ydewalle, G. (2000). Strategies and tactics in deductive reasoning. In W. Schaeken, G. DeVooght, A. Vandierendonck, & G. d'Ydewalle (Eds.), *Deductive reasoning and strategies* (pp. 301–309). Mahwah, NJ: Erlbaum.

Schall, J. D. (2004). On building a bridge between brain and behavior. *Annual Review of Psychology, 55,* 23–50.

Schank, R. C., & Abelson, R. P. (1977). *Scripts, plans, goals, and understanding.* Hillsdale, NJ: Erlbaum.

Schank, R. C., & Abelson, R. P. (1995). Knowledge and memory: The real story. In R. S. Wyer, Jr. (Ed.), *Knowledge and memory: The real story* (pp. 1–85). Hillsdale, NJ: Erlbaum.

Schawlow, A. (1982, Fall). Going for the gaps. *Stanford Magazine,* 42.

Schiffrin, D. (1994). Making a list. *Discourse Processes, 17,* 377–406.

Schiller, N. O. (2005). Verbal self-monitoring. In A. Cutler (Ed.), *Twenty-first century psycholinguistics: Four cornerstones* (pp. 245–261). Mahwah, NJ: Erlbaum.

Schmidt, S. R. (2006). Emotion, significance, distinctiveness, and memory. In R. R. Hunt & J. B. Worthen (Eds.), *Distinctiveness and memory* (pp. 47–64). New York: Oxford University Press.

Schmolck, H., Buffalo, E. A., & Squire, L. R. (2000). Memory distortions develop over time: Recollections of the O.J. Simpson trial verdict after 15 and 32 months. *Psychological Science, 11,* 39–45.

Schneider, D. J. (2004). *The psychology of stereotyping.* New York: Guilford.

Schneider, W. (1998). The development of procedural metamemory in childhood and adolescence. In G. Mazzoni & T. O. Nelson (Eds.), *Metacognition and cognitive neuropsychology* (pp. 1–21). Mahwah, NJ: Erlbaum.

Schneider, W. (1999). The development of metamemory in children. In D. Gopher & A. Koriat (Eds.), *Attention and performance XVII* (pp. 487–514). Cambridge, MA: MIT Press.

Schneider, W. (2002). Memory development in childhood. In In U. Goswami (Ed.), *Blackwell handbook of childhood cognitive development* (pp. 236–256). Malden, MA: Blackwell.

Schneider, W., & Bjorklund, D. F. (1998). Memory. In D. Kuhn & R. S. Siegler (Eds.), *Handbook of child psychology* (5th ed., Vol. 2, pp. 467–521). New York: Wiley.

Schneider, W., & Pressley, M. (1997). *Memory development: Between two and twenty* (2nd ed.). Mahwah, NJ: Erlbaum.

Schneider, W., Kron, V., Hünnerkopf, M., & Krajewsi, K. (2004). The development of young children's memory strategies: First findings from the Würzburg Longitudinal Memory Study. *Journal of Experimental Child Psychology, 88,* 191–209.

Schneider, W., Schumann-Hengsteler, R., & Sodian, B. (Eds.). (2005). *Young children's cognitive development: Interrelationships among executive functioning, working memory, verbal ability, and theory of mind.* Mahwah, NJ: Erlbaum.

Schneider, W., & Shiffrin, R. M. (1977). Controlled and automatic information processing: I. Detection, search, and attention. *Psychological Review, 84,* 1–66.

Schober, M. F., & Brennan, S. E. (2003). Processes of interactive spoken discourse: The role of the partner. In A. C. Graesser, M. A. Gernsbacher, & S. R. Goldman (Eds.), *Handbook of discourse processes* (pp. 123–164). Mahwah, NJ: Erlbaum.

Schoenfeld, A. H. (1982). Some thoughts on problem-solving research and mathematics education. In F. K. Lester & J. Garofalo (Eds.), *Mathematical problem solving: Issues in research* (pp. 27–37). Philadelphia: The Franklin Institute.

Scholl, B. J., Simons, D. J., & Levin, D. T. (2004). "Change blindness" blindness: An implicit measure of a metacognitive error. In D. T. Levin (Ed.), *Thinking and seeing: Visual metacognition in adults and children* (pp. 145–165). Cambridge, MA: MIT Press.

Schooler, J. W. (2001). Discovering memories of abuse in the light of meta-awareness. In J. J. Freyd & A. P. DePrince (Eds.), *Trauma and cognitive science* (p. 105–136). New York: Haworth.

Schooler, J. W., & Eich, E. (2000). Memory for emotional events. In E. Tulving & F. I. M. Craik (Eds.), *The Oxford handbook of memory* (pp. 379–392). New York: Oxford University Press.

Schooler, J. W., Fallshore, M., & Fiore, S. M. (1995). Epilogue: Putting insight into perspective. In R. J. Sternberg & J. E. Davidson (Eds.), *The nature of insight* (pp. 559–587). Cambridge, MA: MIT Press.

Schooler, J. W., Reichle, E. D., & Halpern, D. V. (2004). Zoning out while reading: Evidence for dissociations between experience and metaconsciousness. In D. T. Levin (Ed.), *Thinking and seeing: Visual metacognition in adults and children* (pp. 204–226). Cambridge, MA: MIT Press.

Schooler, L. J., & Hertwig, R. (2005). How forgetting aids heuristic inference. *Psychological Review, 112,* 610–628.

Schrauf, R. W., & Rubin, D. C. (2001). Effects of voluntary immigration on the distribution of autobiographical memory over the lifespan. *Applied Cognitive Psychology, 15,* S75–S88.

Schraw, G. (1994). The effect of metacognitive knowledge on local and global monitoring. *Contemporary Educational Psychology, 19,* 143–154.

Schraw, G. (2005). An interview with K. Anders Ericsson. *Educational Psychology Review, 17,* 389–412.

Schreiber, F. J. (2005). Metacognition and self-regulation in literacy. In S. E. Israel, C. C. Block, K. L. Bauserman, & K. Kinnucan-Welsch (Eds.), *Metacognition in literacy learning: Theory, assessment, instruction, and professional development* (pp. 215–239). Mahwah, NJ: Erlbaum.

Schwartz, A. L., & Kroll, J. F. (2006). Language processing in bilingual speakers. In M. J. Traxler & M. A. Gernsbacher (Eds.), *Handbook of psycholinguistics* (2nd ed., pp. 967–999). Amsterdam: Elsevier.

Schwartz, B. (2004). *The paradox of choice: Why more is less: How the culture of abundance robs us of satisfaction.* New York: HarperCollins.

Schwartz, B., et al. (2002). Maximizing versus satisficing: Happiness is a matter of choice. *Journal of Personality and Social Psychology, 83,* 1178–1197.

Schwartz, B. L. (1999). Sparkling at the end of the tongue: The etiology of tip-of-the-tongue phenomenology. *Psychonomic Bulletin & Review, 6,* 379–393.

Schwartz, B. L. (2002). *Tip-of-the-tongue states: Phenomenology, mechanism, and lexical retrieval.* Mahwah, NJ: Erlbaum.

Schwartz, B. L., Benjamin, A. S., & Bjork, R. A. (1997). The inferential and experiential bases of metamemory. *Current Directions in Psychological Science, 6,* 132–137.

Schwartz, B. L., & Perfect, T. J. (2002). Introduction: Toward an applied metacognition. In T. J. Perfect & B. L. Schwartz (Eds.), *Applied metacognition* (pp. 15–38). Cambridge, UK: Cambridge University Press.

Schwartz, B. L., & Smith, S. M. (1997). The retrieval of related information influences tip-of-the-tongue states. *Journal of Memory and Language, 36,* 68–86.

Schwartz, B. L., Travis, D. M., Castro, A. M., & Smith, S. M. (2000). The phenomenology of real and illusory tip-of-the-tongue states. *Memory & Cognition, 28,* 18–27.

Schwartz, S. H. (1971). Modes of representation and problem solving: Well evolved is half solved. *Journal of Experimental Psychology, 91,* 347–350.

Schwartz, S. H., & Fattaleh, D. (1972). Representation in deductive problem solving: The matrix. *Journal of Experimental Psychology, 95,* 343–348.

Schwartz, S. H., & Polish, J. (1974). The effect of problem size on representation in deductive problem solving. *Memory & Cognition, 2,* 683–686.

Schwarz, N. (1995). Social cognition: Information accessibility and use in social judgment. In E. E. Smith & D. N. Osherson (Eds.), *Thinking* (2nd ed., pp. 345–376). Cambridge, MA: MIT Press.

Schwarz, N. (2001). Feelings as information: Implications for affective influences on information processing. In L. L. Martin & G. L. Clore (Eds.), *Theories of mood and cognition* (pp. 159–176). Mahwah, NJ: Erlbaum.

Scott, S. K. (2005). The neurobiology of speech perception. In A. Cutler (Ed.), *Twenty-first century psycholinguistics: Four cornerstones* (pp. 141–156). Mahwah, NJ: Erlbaum.

Seabrook, R., Brown, G. D. A., & Solity, J. E. (2005). Distributed and massed practice: From laboratory to classroom. *Applied Cognitive Psychology, 19,* 107–122.

Searleman, A., & Herrmann, D. (1994). *Memory from a broader perspective.* New York: McGraw-Hill.

Sedlmeier, P. (1999). *Improving statistical reasoning: Theoretical models and practical implications.* Mahwah, NJ: Erlbaum.

Sedlmeier, P., Hertwig, R., & Gigerenzer, G. (1998). Are judgments of the positional frequencies of letters systematically biased due to availability? *Journal of Experimental Psychology: Learning, Memory, and Cognition, 24,* 754–770.

Segal, E. (2004). Incubation in insight problem solving. *Creativity Research Journal, 16,* 141–148.

Segal, S. J., & Fusella, V. (1970). Influence of imaged pictures and sounds on detection of visual and auditory signals. *Journal of Experimental Psychology, 83,* 458–464.

Seifert, C. M. (1999). Situated cognition and learning. In R. A. Wilson & F. C. Keil (Eds.), *The MIT encyclopedia of the cognitive sciences* (pp. 767–769). Cambridge, MA: MIT Press.

Semmler, C., & Brewer, N. (2006). Postidentification feedback effects on face recognition confidence: Evidence for metacognitive influences. *Applied Cognitive Psychology, 20,* 895–916.

Serences, J. T., et al. (2005). Coordination of voluntary and stimulus-driven control in human cortex. *Psychological Science, 16,* 114–122.

Sereno, S. C., Brewer, C. C., & O'Donnell, P. J. (2003). Context effects in word recognition: Evidence for early interactive processing. *Psychological Science, 14,* 328–333.

Shafir, E. B., & LeBoeuf, R. A. (2002). Rationality. *Annual Review of Psychology, 53,* 491–517.

Shafir, E. B., & Tversky, A. (1995). Decision making. In E. E. Smith & D. N. Osherson (Eds.), *Thinking* (pp. 77–100). Cambridge, MA: MIT Press.

Shah, P., & Miyake, A. (Eds.) (2005). *The Cambridge handbook of visuospatial thinking.* New York: Cambridge University Press.

Shammi, P., & Stuss, D. T. (1999). Humour appreciation: A role of the right frontal lobe. *Brain, 122,* 657–666.

Shanks, D. R. (1997). Representation of categories and concept in memory. In M. A. Conway (Ed.), *Cognitive models of memory* (pp. 111–146). Cambridge, MA: MIT Press.

Sharps, M. J., Price, J. L., & Williams, J. K. (1994). Spatial cognition and gender: Instructional and stimulus influences on mental image rotation performance. *Psychology of Women Quarterly, 18,* 413–425.

Sharps, M. J., & Wertheimer, M. (2000). Gestalt perspectives on cognitive science and on experimental psychology. *Review of General Psychology, 4,* 315–336.

Shatz, M., & Gelman, R. (1973). The development of communication skills: Modifications in the speech of young children as a function of listener. *Monographs of the Society for Research in Child Development, 38* (2, Serial No. 152).

Shavinina, L. V. (Ed.). (2003). *The international handbook on innovation.* Oxford, UK: Elsevier Science.

Shelton, A. L. (2004). Putting spatial memories into perspective: Brain and behavioral evidence for representational differences. In G. L. Allen (Ed.), *Human spatial memory: Remembering where* (pp. 309–327). Mahwah, NJ: Erlbaum.

Shelton, A. L., & Gabrieli, J. D. E. (2004). Neural correlates of individual differences in spatial learning strategies. *Neuropsychology, 18,* 442–449.

Shelton, A. L., & McNamara, T. P. (2004). Orientation and perspective dependence in route and survey learning. *Journal of Experimental Psychology: Learning, Memory, and Cognition, 30,* 158–170.

Shepard, R. N., & Chipman, S. (1970). Second-order isomorphism of internal representation: Shapes of states. *Cognitive Psychology, 1,* 1–17.

Shepard, R. N., & Metzler, J. (1971). Mental rotation of three-dimensional objects. *Science, 171,* 701–703.

Shepperd, J. A., & Koch, E. J. (2005). Pitfalls in teaching judgment heuristics. *Teaching of Psychology, 32,* 43–46.

Sherman, J. W., & Bessenoff, G. R. (1999). Stereotypes as source-monitoring cues: On the interaction between episodic and semantic memory. *Psychological Science, 10,* 106–110.

Sherman, J. W., Groom, C. J., Ehrenberg, K., & Klauer, K. C. (2003). Bearing false witness under pressure: Implicit and explicit components of stereotype-driven memory distortions. *Social Cognition, 21,* 213–246.

Sherman, M. A. (1976). Adjectival negation and the comprehension of multiply negated sentences. *Journal of Verbal Learning and Verbal Behavior, 15,* 143–157.

Shermis, M. D., & Burstein, J. (Eds.). (2003). *Automated essay scoring: A cross-disciplinary perspective.* Mahwah, NJ: Erlbaum.

Shi, R., & Werker, J. F. (2001). Six-month-old infants' preference for lexical words. *Psychological Science, 12,* 70–75.

Shiffrin, R. M., & Schneider, W. (1977). Controlled and automatic human information processing: II. Perceptual learning, automatic attending, and a general theory. *Psychological Review, 84,* 127–190.

Shih, M., Pittinsky, T. L., & Ambady, N. (1999). Stereotype susceptibility: Identity salience and shifts in quantitative performance. *Psychological Science, 10,* 80–83.

Sholl, M. J., Kenny, R. J., & Della Porta, K. A. (2006). Allocentric-heading recall and its relation to self-reported sense-of-direction. *Journal of Experimental Psychology: Learning, Memory, and Cognition, 32,* 516–533.

Siegal, M. (1996). Conversation and cognition. In R. Gelman & T. K. Au (Eds.), *Perceptual and cognitive development* (pp. 243–282). San Diego: Academic Press.

Siegler, R. S., DeLoache, J., & Eisenberg, N. (2003). *How children develop.* New York: Worth.

Sillito, A. M. (2004). Visual system: Organization. In R. L. Gregory (Ed.), *The Oxford companion to the mind* (2nd ed., pp. 931–936). New York: Oxford University Press.

Silva, T., & Matsuda, P. K. (Eds.). (2001). *Landmark essays on ESL writing.* Mahwah, NJ: Erlbaum.

Silvia, P. J. (2007). *How to write a lot.* Washington, DC: American Psychological Association.

Simon, D., Pham, L. B., Le, Q. A., & Holyoak, K. J. (2001). The emergence of coherence over the course of decision making. *Journal of Experimental Psychology: Learning, Memory, and Cognition, 27,* 1250–1260.

Simon, H. A. (1955). A behavioral model of rational choice. *Quarterly Journal of Economics, 69,* 99–118.

Simon, H. A. (1995). Technology is not the problem. In P. Baumgartner & S. Payr (Eds.), *Speaking minds: Interviews with twenty eminent cognitive scientists* (pp. 231–248). Princeton, NJ: Princeton University Press.

Simon, H. A. (1996). *The sciences of the artificial* (3rd ed.). Cambridge, MA: MIT Press.

Simon, H. A. (1999). Problem solving. In R. A. Wilson & F. C. Keil (Eds.), *The MIT encyclopedia of the cognitive sciences* (pp. 674–676). Cambridge, MA: MIT Press.

Simon, H. A. (2001). Learning to research about learning. In S. M. Carver & D. Klahr (Eds.), *Cognition and instruction: Twenty-five years of progress* (pp. 205–226). Mahwah, NJ: Erlbaum.

Simon, H. A., & Gobet, F. (2000). Expertise effects in memory recall: Comment on Vicente and Wang (1998). *Psychological Review, 107,* 593–600.

Simons, D. J., & Chabris, C. F. (1999). Gorillas in our midst: Sustained inattentional blindness for dynamic events. *Perception, 28,* 1059–1074.

Simons, D. J., Chabris, C. F., Schnur, T., & Levin, D. T. (2002). Evidence for preserved representations in change blindness. *Consciousness and Cognition, 11,* 78–97.

Simons, D. J., & Levin, D. T. (1997a). Change blindness. *TRENDS in Cognitive Sciences, 1,* 261–267.

Simons, D. J., & Levin, D. T. (1997b). Failure to detect changes to unattended objects. *Investigative Ophthalmology and Visual Science, 38,* S707.

Simons, D. J., & Levin, D. T. (1998). Failure to detect changes to people during a real-world interaction. *Psychonomic Bulletin & Review, 5,* 644–649.

Simonson, I., et al. (2001). Consumer research: In search of identity. *Annual Review of Psychology, 52,* 249–275.

Simonton, D. K. (2004). Creativity as a constrained stochastic process. In R. J. Sternberg, E. L. Grigorenko, & J. L. Singer (Eds.), *Creativity: From potential to realization* (pp. 83–101). Washington, DC: American Psychological Association.

Sims, V. K., & Mayer, R. E. (2002). Domain specificity of spatial expertise: The case of video game players. *Applied Cognitive Psychology, 16,* 97–115.

Singer, J. L. (2006). *Imagery in psychotherapy.* Washingon, DC: American Psychological Association.

The Sixteen Words, Again. (2004, July 21). *The Washington Post,* p. A18.

Skinner, B. F. (2004). Behaviorism, B. F. Skinner on. In R. L. Gregory (Ed.), *The Oxford companion to the mind* (2nd ed., pp. 90–92). New York: Oxford University Press.

Slater, A., & Butterworth, G. (1997). Perception of social stimuli: Face perception and imitation. In G. Brenner, A. Slater, & G. Butterworth (Eds.), *Infant development: Recent advances* (pp. 223–245). Hove, UK: Psychology Press.

Sloman, S. A. (1999). Rational versus arational models of thought. In R. J. Sternberg (Ed.), *The nature of cognition* (pp. 557–585). Cambridge, MA: MIT Press.

Sloman, S. A., Love, B. C., & Ahn, W. (1998). Feature centrality and conceptual coherence. *Cognitive Science, 22,* 189–228.

Sluzenski, J., Newcombe, N., & Ottinger, W. (2004). Changes in reality monitoring and episodic memory in early childhood. *Developmental Science, 7,* 225–245.

Smallwood, J., & Schooler, J. W. (2006). The restless mind. *Psychological Bulletin, 132,* 946–958.

Smith, E. E. (1978). Theories of semantic memory. In W. K. Estes (Ed.), *Handbook of learning and cognitive processes* (Vol. 6). Hillsdale, NJ: Erlbaum.

Smith, E. E. (2000). Neural bases of human working memory. *Current Directions in Psychological Science, 9,* 45–49.

Smith, E. E., & Jonides, J. (1997). Working memory: A view from neuroimaging. *Cognitive Psychology, 33,* 5–42.

Smith, E. E., & Jonides, J. (1998). Neuroimaging analyses of human working memory. *Proceedings of the National Academy of Science, 95,* 12061–12068.

Smith, E. E., & Jonides, J. (1999). Storage and executive processes in the frontal lobes. *Science, 283,* 1657–1660.

Smith, E. E., Patalano, A. L., & Jonides, J. (1998). Alternative strategies of categorization. *Cognition, 65,* 167–196.

Smith, E. E., Shoben, E. J., & Rips, L. J. (1974). Structure and process in semantic memory: A featural model for semantic decisions. *Psychological Review, 81,* 214–241.

Smith, F. (2004). *Understanding reading: A psycholinguistic analysis of reading and learning to read* (6th ed.). Mahwah, NJ: Erlbaum.

Smith, J., & Baltes, P. B. (1999). Life-span perspectives on development. In M. H. Bornstein & M. E. Lamb (Eds.), *Developmental psychology: An advanced textbook* (4th ed., pp. 47–720). Mahwah, NJ: Erlbaum.

Smith, J. D. (2002). Exemplar theory's predicted typicality gradient can be tested and disconfirmed. *Psychological Science, 13,* 437–442.

Smith, N. (2000). Foreword. In N. Chomsky (Ed.) *On nature and language* (pp. 1–44). Cambridge, UK: Cambridge University Press.

Smith, R. E. (2006). Adult age differences in episodic memory: Item-specific, relational, and distinctive processing. In R. R. Hunt & J. B. Worthen (Eds.),

Distinctiveness and memory (pp. 259–289). New York: Oxford University Press.

Smith, S. M. (1995). Fixation, incubation, and insight in memory and creative thinking. In S. M. Smith, T. B. Ward, & R. A. Finke (Eds.), *The creative cognition approach* (pp. 135–156). Cambridge, MA: MIT Press.

Smith, S. M., & Gleaves, D. H. (2007). Recovered memories. In M. P. Toglia, J. D. Read, D. F. Ross, & R. C. L. Lindsay (Eds.), *Handbook of eyewitness psychology* (Vol. 1, pp. 299–320). Mahwah, NJ: Erlbaum.

Smith, S. M., Glenberg, A., & Bjork, R. A. (1978). Environmental context and human memory. *Memory & Cognition, 6,* 342–353.

Smith, S. M., Ward, T. B., & Schumacher, J. S. (1993). Constraining effects of examples in a creative generation task. *Memory & Cognition, 21,* 837–845.

Smith, S. M., et al. (2003). Eliciting and comparing false and recovered memories: An experimental approach. *Applied Cognitive Psychology, 17,* 251–279.

Smyth, M. M., Collins, A. F., Morris, P. E., & Levy, P. (1994). *Cognition in action* (2nd ed.). Hove, UK: Erlbaum.

Smyth, M. M., Morris, P. E., Levy, P., & Ellis, A. W. (1987). *Cognition in action*. Hillsdale, NJ: Erlbaum.

Snow, C. E. (1999). Social perspectives on the emergence of language. In B. MacWhinney (Ed.), *The emergence of language* (pp. 257–276). Mahwah, NJ: Erlbaum.

Snow, C. E., & Juel, C. (2005). Teaching children to read: What do we know about how to do it? In M. J. Snowling & C. Hulme (Eds.), *The science of reading: A handbook* (pp. 501–520). Malden, MA: Blackwell.

Snowling, M. J., & Hulme, C. (Eds.). (2005). *The science of reading: A handbook*. Malden, MA: Blackwell.

Sobel, C. P. (2001). *The cognitive sciences: An interdisciplinary approach*. Mountain View, CA: Mayfield.

Sodian, B. (2005). Theory of mind—the case for conceptual development. In W. Schneider, R. Schumann-Hengsteler, & B. Sodian (Eds.), *Young children's cognitive development* (pp. 95–130). Mahwah, NJ: Erlbaum.

Son, L. K., & Metcalfe, J. (2000). Metacognitive and control strategies in study-time allocation. *Journal of Experimental Psychology: Learning, Memory, and Cognition, 26,* 204–221.

Son, L. K., & Schwartz, B. L. (2002). The relation between metacognitive monitoring and control. In T. J. Perfect & B. L. Schwartz (Eds.), *Applied metacognition* (pp. 15–38). Cambridge, UK: Cambridge University Press.

Sparing, R., et al. (2002). Visual cortex excitability increases during visual mental imagery—a TMS study in healthy human subjects. *Brain Research, 938,* 92–97.

Speer, S., & Blodgett, A. (2006). Prosody. In M. J. Traxler & M. A. Gernsbacher (Eds.), *Handbook of psycholinguistics* (2nd ed., pp. 505–527). Amsterdam: Elsevier.

Sperling, G. (1960). The information available in brief visual presentations. *Psychological Monographs, 74,* 1–29.

Sporer, S. L. (1991). Deep—deeper—deepest? Encoding strategies and the recognition of human faces. *Journal of Experimental Psychology: Learning, Memory, and Cognition, 17,* 323–333.

Staddon, J. (2001). *The new behaviorism: Mind, mechanism, and society.* Philadelphia: Psychology Press.

Stanovich, K. E. (1999). *Who is rational? Studies of individual differences in reasoning.* Mahwah, NJ: Erlbaum.

Stanovich, K. E. (2003). The fundamental computational biases of human cognition: Heuristics that (sometimes) impair decision making and problem solving. In J. E. Davidson & R. J. Sternberg (Eds.), *The psychology of problem solving* (pp. 291–342). New York: Cambridge University Press.

Stanovich, K. E., Sá. W. C., & West, R. F. (2004). Individual differences in thinking, reasoning, and decision making. In J. P. Leighton & R. J. Sternberg (Eds.), *The nature of reasoning* (pp. 375–409). New York: Cambridge University Press.

Stanovich, K. E., & West, R. F. (1981). The effect of sentence processing on ongoing word recognition: Tests of a two-process theory. *Journal of Experimental Psychology: Human Perception and Performance, 7,* 658–672.

Stanovich, K. F., & West, R. F. (1983). On priming by a sentence context. *Journal of Experimental Psychology: General, 112,* 1–36.

Stanovich, K. E., & West, R. F. (1997). Reasoning independently of prior belief and individual differences in actively open-minded thinking. *Journal of Educational Psychology, 89,* 342–357.

Stanovich, K. E., & West, R. F. (1998). Individual differences in rational thought. *Journal of Experimental Psychology: General, 127,* 161–188.

Stanovich, K. E., & West, R. F. (2000). Individual differences in reasoning: Implications for the rationality debate? *Behavioral and Brain Sciences, 23,* 645–726.

Starr, M. S., & Inhoff, A. W. (2004). Attention allocation to the right and left of a fixated word: Use of information from multiple words during reading. In R. Radach, A. Kennedy, & K. Rayner (Eds.), *Eye movements and information processing during reading* (pp. 203–225). Hove, UK: Psychology Press.

Statistics Canada. (2008). *Canadian statistics.* Retrieved May 8, 2008, from http://www.statcan.ca/english/

Staub, E. (2003). *The psychology of good and evil: Why children, adults, and groups help and harm others.* New York: Cambridge University Press.

Steel, P. (2007). The nature of procrastination: A meta-analytic and theoretical review of quintessential self-regulatory failure. *Psychological Bulletin, 133,* 65–94.

Steele, C. M. (1997). A threat in the air: How stereotypes shape intellectual identity and performance. *American Psychologist, 52,* 613–629.

Steele, C. M., & Aronson, J. (1995). Stereotype threat and the intellectual test performance of African Americans. *Journal of Personality and Social Psychology, 69,* 797–811.

Stenning, K., Lascarides, A., & Calder, J. (2006). *Introduction to cognition and communication.* Cambridge, MA: MIT Press.

Sternberg, R. J. (1998). A balance theory of wisdom. *Review of General Psychology, 2,* 347–365.

Sternberg, R. J. (1999). A dialectical basis for understanding the study of cognition. In R. J. Sternberg (Ed.), *The nature of cognition* (pp. 51–78). Cambridge, MA: MIT Press.

Sternberg, R. J. (2001). What is the common thread of creativity? *American Psychologist, 56,* 360–362.

Sternberg, R. J. (2002). Smart people are not stupid, but they sure can be foolish. In R. J. Sternberg (Ed.), *Why smart people can be so stupid* (pp. 232–242). New Haven, CT: Yale University Press.

Sternberg, R. J., & Ben-Zeev, T. (2001). *Complex cognition: The psychology of human thought.* New York: Oxford University Press.

Sternberg, R. J., Grigorenko, E. L., & Singer, J. L. (Eds.). (2004). *Creativity: From potential to realization.* Washington, DC: American Psychological Association.

Sternberg, R. J., Kaufman, J. C., Pretz, J. E. (2002). *The creativity conundrum: A propulsion model of kinds of creative contributions.* New York: Psychology Press.

Sternberg, R. J., & Lubart, T. I. (1995). *Defying the crowd: Cultivating creativity in a culture of conformity.* New York: Free Press.

Sternberg, R. J., & Lubart, T. I. (1996). Investing in creativity. *American Psychologist, 51,* 677–688.

Sternberg, R. J., & O'Hara, L. A. (1999). Creativity and intelligence. In R. J. Sternberg (Ed.), *Handbook of creativity* (pp. 251–272). New York: Cambridge University Press.

Sternberg, R. J., & Powell, J. S. (1983). Comprehending verbal comprehension. *American Psychologist, 38,* 878–893.

Stevens, A., & Coupe, P. (1978). Distortions in judged spatial relations. *Cognitive Psychology, 10,* 422–437.

Stillings, N. A., et al. (1995). *Cognitive science: An introduction* (2nd ed.). Cambridge, MA: MIT Press.

Stine, E. L., Wingfield, A., & Poon, L. W. (1989). Speech comprehension and memory through adulthood: The roles of time and strategy. In L. W. Poon, D. C. Rubin, & B. A. Wilson (Eds.), *Everyday cognition in adulthood and later life* (pp. 195–221). New York: Cambridge University Press.

Stine-Morrow, E. A. L., Miller, L. M. S., & Hertzog, C. (2006). Aging and self-regulated language processing. *Psychological Bulletin, 132,* 582–606.

Stokes, P. D. (2006). *Creativity from constraints: The psychology of breakthrough.* New York: Springer.

Stone, M. (2005). Communicative intentions and conversational processes in human-human and human-computer dialogue. In J. C. Trueswell & M. K. Tanenhaus (Eds.), *Approaches to studying world-situated language use* (pp. 39–69). Cambridge, MA: Bradford.

Strachman, A., & Gable, S. L. (2006). What you want (and do not want) affects what you see (and do not see): Avoidance social goals and social events. *Personality and Social Psychology Bulletin, 32,* 1446–1458.

Strayer, D. L., & Drews, F. A. (2007). Multitasking in the automobile. In A. F. Kramer, D. A. Wiegmann, & A. Kirlik (Eds.), *Attention: From theory to practice* (pp. 121–133). New York: Oxford University Press.

Strayer, D. L., Drews, F. A., & Johnston, W. A. (2003). Cell phone-induced failures of visual attention during simulated driving. *Journal of Experimental Psychology: Applied, 9,* 23–32.

Stroessner, S. J., & Plaks, J. E. (2001). Illusory correlation and stereotype formation: Tracing the arc of research over a quarter century. In G. B. Moskowitz (Ed.), *Cognitive social psychology* (pp. 247–259). Mahwah, NJ: Erlbaum.

Strömqvist, S., & Verhoeven, L. (2004). Typological and contextual perspectives on narrative development. In S. Strömqvist, & L. Verhoven, (2004). *Relating events in narrative* (Vol. 2, pp. 1–4). Mahwah, NJ: Erlbaum.

Stromswold, K. (1999). Cognitive and neural aspects of language acquisition. In E. Lepore & Z. Pylyshyn (Eds.), *What is cognitive science?* (pp. 356–400). Malden, MA: Blackwell.

Stroop, J. R. (1935). Studies of interference in serial verbal reactions. *Journal of Experimental Psychology, 18,* 643–662.

Stuss, D. T., Binns, M. A., Murphy, K. J., & Alexander, M. P. (2002). Dissociations within the anterior attentional system: Effects of task complexity and irrelevant information on reaction time speed and accuracy. *Neuropsychology, 16*, 500–513.

Styles, E. A. (2005). *Attention, perception, and memory: An integrated introduction.* Hove, UK: Psychology Press.

Styles, E. A. (2006). *The psychology of attention* (2nd ed.). New York: Psychology Press.

Suh, S., & Trabasso, T. (1993). Inferences during reading: Converging evidence from discourse analysis, talk-aloud protocols, and recognition priming. *Journal of Memory and Language, 32*, 279–300.

Sutherland, R., & Hayne, H. (2001). The effect of post-event information on adults' eyewitness reports. *Applied Cognitive Psychology, 15*, 249–263.

Suzuki-Slakter, N. S. (1988). Elaboration and metamemory during adolescence. *Contemporary Educational Psychology, 13*, 206–220.

Swanson, H. L. (2005). Working memory, intelligence, and learning disabilities. In O. Wilhelm & R. W. Engle (Eds.), *Handbook of understanding and measuring intelligence* (pp. 409–429). Thousand Oaks, CA: Sage.

Swinkels, A. (2003). An effective exercise for teaching cognitive heuristics. *Teaching of Psychology, 30*, 120–122.

Swoyer, C. (2002). Judgment and decision making: Extrapolations and applications. In R. Gowda & J. C. Fox (Eds.), *Judgments, decisions, and public policy* (pp. 9–45). New York: Cambridge University Press.

Symons, C. S., & Johnson, B. T. (1997). The self-reference effect in memory: A meta-analysis. *Psychological Bulletin, 121*, 371–394.

Tabor, W., & Hutchins, S. (2004). Evidence for self-organized sentence processing: Digging-in effects. *Journal of Experimental Psychology: Learning, Memory, and Cognition, 30*, 431–450.

Talarico, J. M., LaBar, K. S., & Rubin, D. C. (2004). Emotional intensity predicts autobiographical memory experience. *Memory & Cognition, 32*, 1118–1132.

Talarico, J. M., & Rubin, D. C. (2003). Confidence, not consistency, characterizes flashbulb memories. *Psychological Science, 14*, 455–461.

Talarico, J. M., & Rubin, D.C. (2007). Flashbulb memories are special after all; in phenomenology, not accuracy. *Applied Cognitive Psychology, 21*, 557–578.

Tanaka, J. W., & Curran, T. (2001). A neural basis for expert object recognition. *Psychological Science, 12*, 43–47.

Tanaka, J. W., & Farah, M. J. (1993). Parts and wholes in face recognition. *Quarterly Journal of Experimental Psychology, 46A*, 225–245.

Tanenhaus, M. K. (2004). On-line sentence processing: Past, present, and future. In M. Carreiras & C. Clifton, Jr. (Eds.), *The on-line study of sentence comprehension: Eyetracking, ERPs and beyond* (pp. 371–393). New York: Psychology Press.

Tarr, M. J., & Vuong, Q. C. (2002). Visual object recognition. In S. Yantis (Ed.), *Stevens' handbook of experimental psychology* (3rd ed., Vol. 1, pp. 287–314). New York: Wiley.

Tavris, C., & Aronson, E. (2007). *Mistakes were made (but not by me): Why we justify foolish beliefs, bad decisions, and hurtful acts* Orlando, FL: Harcourt.

Taylor, H. A. (2005). Mapping the understanding of understanding maps. In P. Shah & A. Miyake (Eds.), *The Cambridge handbook of visuospatial thinking* (pp. 295–333). New York: Cambridge University Press.

Taylor, H. A., Naylor, S. J., & Chechile, N. A. (1999). Goal-specific influences on the representation of spatial perspective. *Memory & Cognition, 27*, 309–319.

Taylor, L. M. (2005). *Introducing cognitive development.* New York: Psychology Press.

Taylor, S. E., Phan, L. B., Rivkin, I. D., & Armor, D. A. (1998). Harnessing the imagination: Mental simulation, self-regulation, and coping. *American Psychologist, 53*, 429–439.

Teasdale, J. D., et al. (1995). Stimulus-independent thought depends on central executive resources. *Memory & Cognition, 23*, 551–559.

Teigen, K. H. (2004). Judgment by representativeness. In R. Pohl (Ed.), *Cognitive illusions: Handbook on fallacies and biases in thinking, judgment, and memory* (pp. 165–182). Hove, UK: Psychology Press.

Teigen, K. H., & Jørgensen, M. (2005). When 90% confidence intervals are 50% certainty. *Applied Cognitive Psychology, 19*, 455–475.

Tetlock, P. E. (2005). *Expert political judgment: How good is it? How can we know?* Princeton, NJ: Princeton University Press.

Tetlock, P. E., & Mellers, B. A. (2002). The great rationality debate. *Psychological Science, 13*, 94–99.

Thagard, P. (2005). *Mind: Introduction to cognitive science* (2nd ed.). Cambridge, MA: MIT Press.

Thiede, K. W., Dunlosky, J., Griffin, T. D., & Wiley, J. (2005). Understanding the delayed-keyword effect on metacomprehension accuracy. *Journal of Experimental Psychology: Learning, Memory, and Cognition, 31*, 1267–1280

Thomas, J. C. (1989). Problem solving by human-machine interaction. In K. J. Gilhooly (Ed.), *Human and machine problem solving* (pp. 317–362). New York: Plenum.

Thomas, R. D. (1998). Learning correlations in categorization tasks using large, ill-defined categories. *Journal of Experimental Psychology: Learning, Memory, and Cognition, 24,* 119–143.

Thompson, C. P., Skowronski, J. J., Larsen, S. F., & Betz, A. (1996). *Autobiographical memory: Remembering what and remembering when.* Mahwah, NJ: Erlbaum.

Thompson, R. F. (2005). In search of memory traces. *Annual Review of Psychology, 56,* 1–23.

Thompson, R. F., & Madigan, S. A. (2005). *Memory: The key to consciousness.* Washington, DC: Joseph Henry Press.

Thompson, W. L., & Kosslyn, S. M. (2000). Neural systems activated during visual mental imagery: A review and meta-analyses. In A. W. Toga & J. C. Mazziotta (Eds.), *Brain mapping: The systems* (pp. 535–560). San Diego, CA: Academic Press.

Thorndyke, P. W. (1981). Distance estimation from cognitive maps. *Cognitive Psychology, 13,* 526–550.

Tincoff, R., & Jusczyk, P. W. (1999). Some beginnings of word comprehension in 6-month-olds. *Psychological Science, 10,* 172–175.

Tippett, L. J., McAuliffe, S., & Farah, M. J. (1995). Preservation of categorical knowledge in Alzheimer's disease: A computational account. In R. A. McCarthy (Ed.), *Semantic knowledge and semantic representations* (pp. 519–533). East Sussex, UK: Erlbaum.

Todd, N. P. M., Lee, C. S., & O'Boyle, D. J. (2006). A sensorimotor theory of speech perception: Implications for learning, organization, and recognition. In S. Greenberg & W. A. Ainsworth (Eds.), *Listening to speech: An auditory perspective* (pp. 351–373). Mahwah, NJ: Erlbaum.

Todd, P. M., & Gigerenzer, G. (2000). Précis of *Simple heuristics that make us smart. Behavioral and Brain Sciences, 23,* 727–780,

Todd, P. M., & Gigerenzer, G. (2007). Environments that make us smart: Ecological rationality. *Current Directions in Psychological Science, 126,* 167–171.

Toglia, M. P., et al. (Eds.). (2007). *Handbook of eyewitness psychology: Vol. 1: Memory for events.* Mahwah, NJ: Erlbaum.

Tokuhama-Espinosa, T. (2001). *Raising multilingual children: Foreign language acquisition and children.* Westport, CT: Bergin & Garvey.

Tolan, G. A., & Tehan, G. (2005). Is spoken duration a sufficient explanation of the word length effect? *Memory, 13,* 372–379.

Tolin, D. A., Abramowitz, J. S., Przeworski, A., & Foa, E. B. (2002). Thought suppression in obsessive-compulsive disorder. *Behaviour Research and Therapy, 40,* 1255–1274.

Tomasello, M. (1998a). Cognitive linguistics. In W. Bechtel & G. Graham (Eds.), *A companion to cognitive science* (pp. 477–487). Malden, MA: Blackwell.

Tomasello, M. (1998b). Introduction: A cognitive-functional perspective on language structure. In M. Tomasello (Ed.), *The new psychology of language: Cognitive and functional approaches to language structure* (pp. vii–xxiii). Mahwah, NJ: Erlbaum.

Tomasello, M. (2003). *Constructing a language: A usage-based theory of language acquisition.* Cambridge, MA: Harvard University Press.

Tomasello, M. (2006). Acquiring linguistic constructions. In D. Kuhn & R. Siegler (Eds.), *Handbook of child psychology* (6th ed., Vol. 2, pp. 255–298). Hoboken, NJ: Wiley.

Tomasello, M., Conti-Ramsden, G., & Ewert, B. (1990). Young children's conversations with their mothers and fathers: Differences in breakdown and repair. *Journal of Child Language, 17,* 115–130.

Toms, M., Morris, N., & Foley, P. (1994). Characteristics of visual interference with visuospatial working memory. *British Journal of Psychology, 85,* 131–144.

Toplak, M. E., & Stanovich, K. E. (2002). The domain specificity and generality of disjunctive reasoning: Searching for a generalizable critical thinking skills. *Journal of Educational Psychology, 94,* 197–209.

Toppino, T. C., & Long, G. M. (2005). Top-down and bottom-up processes in the perception of reversible figures: Toward a hybrid model. In N. Ohta, C. M. MacLeod, & B. Uttl (Eds.), *Dynamic cognitive processes* (pp. 37–58). Tokyo: Springer-Verlag.

Torrance, E. P. (Ed.). (2000). *On the edge and keeping on the edge.* Westport, CT: Ablex.

Torrance, M., & Jeffery, G. (1999). Writing processes and cognitive demands. In M. Torrance & G. C. Jeffery (Eds.), *The cognitive demands of writing: Processing capacity and working memory in text production* (pp. 1–11). Amsterdam: Amsterdam University Press.

Torrance, M., Thomas, G. V., & Robinson, E. J. (1996). Finding something to write about: Strategic and automatic processes in idea generation. In C. M. Levy & S. Ransdell (Eds.), *The science of writing:*

Theories, methods, individual differences, and applications (pp. 189–205). Mahwah, NJ: Erlbaum.

Towse, J. N., & Hitch, G. J. (2007). Variation in working memory due to normal development. In A. R. A. Conway et al. (Eds.), *Variations in working memory* (pp. 109–133). New York: Oxford University Press.

Trabasso, T., & Suh, S. (1993). Understanding text: Achieving explanatory coherence through on-line inferences and mental operations in working memory. *Discourse Processes, 16,* 3–34.

Trabasso, T., Suh, S., Payton, P., & Jain, R. (1995). Explanatory inferences and other strategies during comprehension and their effect on recall. In R. F. Lorch & E. J. O'Brien (Eds.), *Sources of coherence in reading* (pp. 219–239). Hillsdale, NJ: Erlbaum.

Trafimow, D., & Wyer, R. S., Jr. (1993). Cognitive representation of mundane social events. *Journal of Personality and Social Psychology, 64,* 365–376.

Traxler, M. A., & Gernsbacher, M. A. (Eds.). (2006). *Handbook of psycholinguistics* (2nd ed.). Amsterdam: Elsevier.

Treflinger, D. J. (Ed.). (2004). *Creativity and giftedness.* Thousand Oaks, CA: Sage.

Treiman, R., Clifton, C., Jr., Meyer, A. S., & Wurm, L. H. (2003). Language comprehension and production. In A. F. Healy & R. W. Proctor (Eds.), *Handbook of psychology* (Vol. 4, pp. 527–547). Hoboken, NJ: Wiley.

Treisman, A. (1964). Monitoring and storage of irrelevant messages and selective attention. *Journal of Verbal Learning and Verbal Behavior, 3,* 449–459.

Treisman, A. (1986, November). Features and objects in visual processing. *Scientific American, 255* (5), 114B–125.

Treisman, A. (1990). Visual coding of features and objects: Some evidence from behavioral studies. In National Research Council (Ed.), *Advances in the modularity of vision: Selections from a symposium on frontiers of visual science* (pp. 39–61). Washington, DC: National Academy Press.

Treisman, A. (1993). The perception of features and objects. In A. Baddeley & L. Weiskrantz (Eds.), *Attention: Selection, awareness, and control* (pp. 5–35). Oxford, UK: Clarendon

Treisman, A. (2003, Fall/Winter). Eminent women in psychology. *The General Psychologist, 38*(3), 44–45.

Treisman, A., & Gelade, G. (1980). A feature-integration theory of attention. *Cognitive Psychology, 12,* 97–136.

Treisman, A., & Schmidt, H. (1982). Illusory conjunction in the perception of objects. *Cognitive Psychology, 14,* 107–141.

Treisman, A., & Souther, J. (1985). Search asymmetry: A diagnostic for preattentive processing of separable features. *Journal of Experimental Psychology: General, 114,* 285–310.

Treisman, A., & Souther, J. (1986). Illusory words: The roles of attention and of top-down constraints in conjoining letters to form words. *Journal of Experimental Psychology: Human Perception and Performance, 12,* 3–17.

Treisman, A., Viera, A., & Hayes, A. (1992). Automatic and preattentive processing. *American Journal of Psychology, 105,* 341–362.

Trevarthen, C. (2004). In R. L. Gregory (Ed.), *The Oxford companion to the mind* (2nd ed., pp. 455–464). New York: Oxford University Press.

Trout, J. D. (2001). The biological basis of speech: What to infer from talking to the animals. *Psychological Review, 108,* 523–549.

Trout, J. D. (2002). Scientific explanation and the sense of understanding. *Philosophy of Science, 69,* 212–233.

Truthout. (2003). *White House credibility defense shifting.* Retrieved September 1, 2003, from http://truthout.org/docs.

Tsang, P. S. (2007). The dynamics of attention and aging. In A. F. Kramer, D. A. Wiegmann, & A. Kirlik (Eds.), *Attention: From theory to practice* (pp. 170–184). New York: Oxford University Press.

Tuckey, M. R., & Brewer, N. (2003). How schemas affect eyewitness memory over repeated retrieval attempts. *Applied Cognitive Psychology, 17,* 855–880.

Tuckman, B. W. (2003). The effect of learning and motivation strategies training on college students' achievement. *Journal of College Student Development, 44,* 430–437.

Tulving, E. (2002). Episodic memory: From mind to brain. *Annual Review of Psychology, 53,* 1–25.

Tulving, E., & Craik, F. I. M. (Eds.). (2000). *The Oxford handbook of memory.* New York: Oxford University Press.

Tulving, E., & Rosenbaum, S. (2006). What do explanations of the distinctiveness effect need to explain? In R. R. Hunt & J. B. Worthen (Eds.), *Distinctiveness and memory* (pp. 407–423). New York: Oxford University Press.

Turnbull, W. (2003). *Language in action: Psychological models of conversation.* New York: Psychology Press.

Tversky, A., & Fox, C. R. (1995). Weighing risk and uncertainty. *Psychological Review, 102,* 269–283.

Tversky, A., & Kahneman, D. (1971). Belief in the law of small numbers. *Psychological Bulletin, 76,* 105–110.

Tversky, A., & Kahneman, D. (1973). Availability: A heuristic for judging frequency and probability. *Cognitive Psychology, 5,* 207–232.

Tversky, A., & Kahneman, D. (1974). Judgments under uncertainty: Heuristics and biases. *Science, 185,* 1124–1131.

Tversky, A., & Kahneman, D. (1981). The framing of decisions and the psychology of choice. *Science, 211,* 453–458.

Tversky, A., & Kahneman, D. (1982). Judgment under uncertainty: Heuristics and biases. In D. Kahneman, P. Slovic, & A. Tversky (Eds.), *Judgment under uncertainty: Heuristics and biases* (pp. 3–20). New York: Cambridge University Press.

Tversky, A., & Kahneman, D. (1983). Extensional versus intuitive reasoning: The conjunction fallacy in probability judgment. *Psychological Review, 90,* 293–315.

Tversky, B. (1981). Distortions in memory for maps. *Cognitive Psychology, 13,* 407–433.

Tversky, B. (1991). Spatial mental models. *The Psychology of Learning and Motivation, 27,* 109–145.

Tversky, B. (1997). Spatial constructions. In N. L. Stein, P. A. Ornstein, B. Tversky, & C. Brainerd (Eds.), *Memory for everyday and emotional events* (pp. 181–208). Mahwah, NJ: Erlbaum.

Tversky, B. (1998). Three dimensions of spatial cognition. In M. A. Conway, S. E. Gathercole, & C. Cornoldi (Eds.), *Theories of memory* (Vol. 2, pp. 259–275). East Sussex, UK: Psychology Press.

Tversky, B. (1999). Talking about space [Review of the book *Representation and processing of spatial expressions*]. *Contemporary Psychology, 44,* 39–40.

Tversky, B. (2000a). Levels and structure of spatial knowledge. In S. M. Freundschuh & R. Kitchin (Eds.), *Cognitive mapping: Past, present, and future* (pp. 24–43). New York: Routledge.

Tversky, B. (2000b). Remembering spaces. In E. Tulving & F. I. M. Craik (Eds.), *The Oxford handbook of memory* (pp. 363–378). New York: Oxford University Press.

Tversky, B. (2005a). Functional significance of visuospatial representations. In P. Shah & A. Miyake (Eds.), *The Cambridge handbook of visuospatial thinking* (pp. 1–34). New York: Cambridge University Press.

Tversky, B. (2005b). Visuospatial reasoning. In K. J. Holyoak & R. G. Morrison (Eds.), *The Cambridge handbook of thinking and reasoning* (pp. 209–240). New York: Cambridge University Press.

Tversky, B., & Lee, P. U. (1998). How space structures language. In C. Freska, C. Habel, & K. F. Wender (Eds.), *Spatial cognition* (pp. 157–175). New York: Springer.

Tversky, B., Morrison, J. B., Franklin, N., & Bryant, D. J. (1999). Three spaces of spatial cognition. *Professional Geographer, 51,* 516–524.

Tversky, B., & Schiano, D. J. (1989). Perceptual and conceptual factors in distortions in memory for graphs and maps. *Journal of Experimental Psychology: General, 118,* 387–398.

Tversky, B., Zacks, J. M., & Lee, P. (2004). Events by hands and feet. *Spatial Cognition and Computation, 4,* 5–14.

Uchanski, R. M. (2005). Clear speech. In D. B. Pisoni & R. E. Remez (Eds.), *The handbook of speech perception* (pp. 207–235). Malden, MA: Blackwell.

Uhlhaas, P. J., & Silverstein, S. M. (2005). Perceptual organization in schizophrenia spectrum disorders: Empirical research and theoretical implications. *Psychological Bulletin, 131,* 618–632.

Underwood, G., & Batt, V. (1996). *Reading and understanding: An introduction to the psychology of reading.* Cambridge, MA: Blackwell.

U.S. Census Bureau. (2006). *Statistical abstract of the United States: 2005–2006.* Washington, DC: Author.

Uttl, B., Ohta, N., & Siegenthaler, A. L. (Eds.). (2006). *Memory and emotion: Interdisciplinary perspectives.* Malden, MA: Blackwell.

Uttl, B., Siegenthaler, A. L., & Ohta, N. (2006). Memory and emotion from interdisciplinary perspectives. In B. Uttl, N. Ohta, & A. L. Siegenthaler (Eds.), *Memory and emotion: Interdisciplinary perspectives* (pp. 11–12). Malden, MA: Blackwell.

Vander Stoep, S. W., & Seifert, C. M. (1994). Problem solving, transfer, and thinking. In P. R. Pintrich, D. R. Brown, & C. E. Weinstein (Eds.), *Student motivation, cognition, and learning: Essays in honor of Wilbert J. McKeachie* (pp. 27–49). Hillsdale, NJ: Erlbaum.

van Hell, J. G., & Dijkstra, T. (2002). Foreign language knowledge can influence native language performance in exclusively native contexts. *Psychonomic Bulletin & Review, 9,* 780–789.

Van Orden, G. C., & Kloos, H. (2005). The question of phonology and reading. In M. J. Snowling & C. Hulme (Eds.), *The science of reading: A handbook* (pp. 61–78). Malden, MA: Blackwell.

Van Overschelde, J. P., Rawson, K. A., Dunlosky, & Hunt, R. R. (2005). Distinctive processing underlies skilled memory. *Psychological Science, 16,* 358–361.

Van Overwalle, F., & Labiouse, C. (2004). A recurrent connectionist model of person impression formation. *Personality and Social Psychology Review, 8,* 28–61.

Van Rooy, D. et al. (2003). A recurrent connectionist model of group biases. *Psychological Review, 110,* 536–563.

van Turennout, M., Hagoort, P., & Brown, C. M. (1998). Brain activity during speaking: From syntax to phonology in 40 milliseconds. *Science, 280,* 572–574.

Van Wallendael, L. R., & Kuhn, J. C. (1997). Distinctiveness is in the eye of the beholder: Cross-racial differences in perceptions of faces. *Psychological Reports, 80,* 35–39.

Vecera, S. P. (1998). Visual object representation: An introduction. *Psychobiology, 26,* 281–308.

Vecera, S. P., & O'Reilly, R. C. (1998). Figure-ground organization and object recognition processes: An interactive account. *Journal of Experimental Psychology: Human Perception and Performance, 24,* 441–462.

Velmans, M., & Schneider, S. (2007). *The Blackwell companion to consciousness.* Malden, MA: Blackwell.

Vertzberger, Y. Y. I. (1998). *Risk taking and decision making: Foreign military intervention decisions.* Stanford, CA: Stanford University Press.

Vicente, K. J., & Wang, J. H. (1998). An ecological theory of expertise effects in memory recall. *Psychological Review, 105,* 33–57.

Vigliocco, G., & Hartsuiker, R. J. (2002). The interplay of meaning, sound, and syntax in sentence production. *Psychological Bulletin, 128,* 442–472.

Viney, W., & King, D. B. (2003). *A history of psychology: Ideas and context* (3rd ed.). Boston: Allyn and Bacon.

Vingerhoets, G., Berckmoes, C., & Stroobant, N. (2003). Cerebral hemodynamics during discrimination of prosodic and semantic emotion in speech studied by transcranial Doppler ultrasonography. *Neuropsychology, 17,* 93–99.

Volz, K. G., et al. (2006). Why you think Milan is larger than Modena: Neural correlates of the recognition heuristic. *Journal of Cognitive Neuroscience, 18,* 1924–1936.

Voyer, D., Nolan, C., & Voyer, S. (2000). The relation between experience and spatial performance in men and women. *Sex Roles, 43,* 891–915.

Vroomen, J., & de Gelder, B. (1997). Activation of embedded words in spoken word recognition. *Journal of Experimental Psychology: Human Perception and Performance, 23,* 710–720.

Wade, K. A., Garry, M., Read, J. D., & Lindsay, D. S. (2002). A picture is worth a thousand lies: Using false photographs to create false childhood memories. *Psychonomic Bulletin and Review, 9,* 597–603.

Wagner, M. (2006). *The geometries of visual space.* Mahwah, NJ: Erlbaum.

Wagner, R. K., Piasta, S. B., & Torgesen, J. KI. (2006). Learning to read. In M. J. Traxler & M. A. Gernsbacher (Eds.), *Handbook of psycholinguistics* (2nd ed., pp. 1111–1142). Amsterdam: Elsevier.

Wagner, R. K., & Stanovich, K. E. (1996). Expertise in reading. In K. A. Ericsson (Ed.), *The road to excellence: The acquisition of expert performance in the arts and sciences, sports, and games* (pp. 189–225). Mahwah, NJ: Erlbaum.

Walker, I., & Hulme, C. (1999). Concrete words are easier to recall than abstract: Evidence for a semantic contribution to short-term serial recall. *Journal of Experimental Psychology: Learning, Memory, & Cognition, 25,* 1256–1271.

Walker, P. M., & Hewstone, M. (2006). A perceptual discrimination investigation of the own-race effect and intergroup experience. *Applied Cognitive Psychology, 20,* 461–475.

Walker, W. R., Vogl, R. J., & Thompson, C. P. (1997). Autobiographical memory: Unpleasantness fades faster than pleasantness over time. *Applied Cognitive Psychology, 11,* 399–413.

Walker, W. R., et al. (2003). On the emotions that accompany autobiographical memories: Dysphoria disrupts the fading affect bias. *Cognition and Emotion, 17,* 703–724.

Walker-Andrews, A. S. (1986). Intermodal perception of expressive behaviors: Relation of eye and voice? *Developmental Psychology, 22,* 373–377.

Walley, A. C. (2005). Speech perception in childhood. In D. B. Pisoni & R. E. Remez (Eds.), *The handbook of speech perception* (pp. 449–468). Malden, MA: Blackwell.

Walters, J. (2005). *Bilingualism: The sociopragmatic-psycholinguistic interface.* Mahwah, NJ: Erlbaum.

Walton, G. E., Bower, N. J., & Bower, T. G. R. (1992). Recognition of familiar faces by newborns. *Infant Behavior and Development, 15,* 265–269.

Waltz, J. A., et al. (1999). A system for relational reasoning in human prefrontal cortex. *Psychological Science, 10,* 119–125.

Wang, G., Tanaka, K., & Tanifuji, M. (1996). Optical imaging of functional organization in the monkey inferotemporal cortex. *Science, 272,* 1665–1668.

Ward, A. (2004). *Attention: A neuropsychological approach*. New York: Psychology Press.

Ward, G., & Allport, A. (1997). Planning and problem-solving using the five-disc tower of London task. *Quarterly Journal of Experimental Psychology, 50A*, 49–78.

Ward, G., Avons, S. E., & Melling, L. (2005). Serial position curves in short-term memory: Functional equivalence across modalities. *Memory, 13*, 308–317.

Ward, G., & Morris, R. (2005). Introduction to the psychology of planning. In R. Morris & G. Ward (Eds.), *The cognitive psychology of planning* (pp. 1–34). Hove, UK: Psychology Press.

Wright, R. D., & Ward, L. M. (2008). *Orienting of attention*. New York: Oxford University Press.

Ward, T. B. (2001). Creative cognition, conceptual combination, and the creative writing of Stephen R. Donaldson. *American Psychologist, 56*, 350–354.

Warren, R. M. (2006). The relation of speech perception to the perception of nonverbal auditory patterns. In S. Greenberg & W. A. Ainsworth (Eds.), *Listening to speech: An auditory perspective* (pp. 333–349). Mahwah, NJ: Erlbaum.

Warren, R. M., & Warren, R. P. (1970, December). Auditory illusions and confusions. *Scientific American, 223* (6), 30–36.

Warrington, E. K., & Weiskrantz, L. (1970). Amnesic syndrome: Consolidation or retrieval? *Nature, 228,* 629–630.

Wason, P. C. (1968). Reasoning about a rule. *Quarterly Journal of Experimental Psychology, 20*, 273–281.

Wason, P. C., & Johnson-Laird, P. N. (1972). *Psychology of reasoning: Structure and content*. Cambridge, MA: Harvard University Press.

Watson, J. B. (1913). Psychology as the behaviorist views it. *Psychological Review, 20*, 158–177.

Waxman, S. R. (2002). Early word-learning and conceptual development: Everything had a name and each name gave birth to a new thought. In U. Goswami (Ed.), *Blackwell handbook of child cognitive development* (pp. 102–126). Malden, MA: Blackwell.

Wegner, D. M. (1994). Ironic processes of mental control. *Psychological Review, 101*, 34–52.

Wegner, D. M. (1996). *Personal communication*.

Wegner, D. M. (1997a). When the antidote is the poison: Ironic mental control processes. *Psychological Science, 8*, 148–153.

Wegner, D. M. (1997b). Why the mind wanders. In J. D. Cohen & J. W. Schooler (Eds.), *Scientific approaches to consciousness* (pp. 295–315). Mahwah, NJ: Erlbaum.

Wegner, D. M. (2002). *The illusion of conscious will*. Cambridge, MA: MIT Press.

Wegner, D. M., Schneider, D. J., Carter, S. R., III, & White, T. L. (1987). Paradoxical effects of thought suppression. *Journal of Personality and Social Psychology, 53*, 5–13.

Weisberg, R. W. (1999). Creativity and knowledge: A challenge to theories. In R. J. Sternberg (Ed.), *Handbook of creativity* (pp. 226–250). New York: Cambridge University Press.

Weisberg, R, W. (2006). Modes of expertise in creative thinking: Evidence from case studies. In K. A. Ericsson, N. Charness, P. J. Feltovich, & R. R. Hoffman (Eds.), *The Cambridge handbook on expertise and expert performance* (pp. 761–787). New York: Cambridge University Press.

Weiskrantz, L. (1997). *Consciousness lost and found: A neuropsychological explanation*. New York: Oxford University Press.

Weiskrantz, L. (2000). To have but not to hold. In J. J. Bolhuis (Ed.), *Brain, perception, memory* (pp. 310–325). New York: Oxford University Press.

Weiskrantz, L. (2007). The case of blindsight. In M. Velmans & S. Schneider (Eds.), *The Blackwell companion to consciousness* (pp. 175–180). Malden, MA: Blackwell.

Weist, R. M. (1985). Cross-linguistic perspective on cognitive development. In T. M. Schlechter & M. P. Toglia (Eds.), *New directions in cognitive science* (pp. 191–216). Norwood, NJ: Ablex.

Welbourne, S. R., & Ralph, M. A. L. (2007). Using parallel distributed processing models to simulate phonological dyslexia: The key role of plasticity-related recovery. *Journal of Cognitive Neuroscience, 19*, 1125–1139.

Wellman, H. M. (2000). Early childhood: Cognitive and mental development. In A. E. Kazdin (Ed.), *The encyclopedia of psychology*. New York: Oxford University Press.

Wellman, H. M., & Gelman, S. A. (1992). Cognitive development: Foundational theories of core domains. *Annual Review of Psychology, 43*, 337–375.

Wells, A. (2005). Worry, intrusive thoughts, and generalized anxiety disorder: The metacognitive theory and treatment. In D. A. Clark (Ed.), *Intrusive thoughts in clinical disorders: Theory, research, and treatment* (pp. 119–144). New York: Guilford Press.

Wells, G. L., & Bradfield, A. L. (1999). Distortions in eyewitnesses' recollections: Can the postidentification-feedback effect be moderated? *Psychological Science, 10*, 138–144.

Wells, G. L., & Olson, E. A. (2003). Eyewitness testimony. *Annual Review of Psychology, 54,* 277–295.

Wells, G. L., et al. (2000). From the lab to the police station: A successful application of eyewitness research. *American Psychologist, 55,* 581–598.

Wenzel, A. (2005). Autobiographical memory tasks in clinical research. In A. Wenzel & D. C. Rubin (Eds.), *Cognitive methods and their application to clinical research* (pp. 243–264). Washington, DC: American Psychological Association.

Wenzlaff, R. M (2005). Seeking solace but finding despair: The persistence of intrusive thoughts in depression. In D. A. Clark (Ed.), *Intrusive thoughts in clinical disorders: Theory, research, and treatment* (pp. 55–85). New York: Guilford Press.

Werker, J. F., & Tees, R. C. (1984). Cross-language speech perception: Evidence for perceptual reorganization during the first year of life. *Infant Behavior and Development, 7,* 49–63.

Werker, J. F., & Tees, R. C. (1999). Influences on infant speech processing: Toward a new synthesis. *Annual Review of Psychology, 50,* 509–535.

West, R., Herndon, R. W., & Ross-Munroe, K. (2000). Event-related neural activity associated with prospective remembering. *Applied Cognitive Psychology, 14,* S115–S126.

West, R. L. (1995). Compensatory strategies for age-associated memory impairment. In A. D. Baddeley, B. A. Wilson, & F. N. Watts (Eds.), *Handbook of memory disorders* (pp. 481–500). Chichester, UK: Wiley.

Westling, E., Garcia, K., & Mann, T. (2007). Discovery of meaning and adherence to medications in HIV-infected women. *Journal of Health Psychology, 12,* 627–635.

Wexler, M., Kosslyn, S. M., & Berthoz, A. (1998). Motor processes in mental rotation. *Cognition, 68,* 77–94.

Wheeldon, L. (Ed.). (2000). *Aspects of language production.* Philadelphia: Psychology Press.

Wheeler, M. A. (2000). Episodic memory and autonoetic awareness. In E. Tulving & F. I. M. Craik (Eds.), *The Oxford handbook of memory* (pp. 597–608). New York: Oxford University Press.

Wheeler, M. E., & Treisman, A. M. (2002). Binding in short-term visual memory. *Journal of Experimental Psychology: General, 113,* 48–64.

Whitbourne, S. K. (2008). *Adult development and aging: Biopsychosocial perspectives* (3rd ed.). Hoboken, NJ: Wiley.

White, J. (2003). *Personal communication.*

White, S. J., & Liversedge, S. P. (2004). Orthographic familiarity influences initial eye fixation positions in reading. In R. Radach, A. Kennedy, & K. Rayner (Eds.), *Eye movements and information processing during reading* (pp. 52–78). Hove, UK: Psychology Press.

Whitley, B. E., Jr., & Kite, M. E. (2006). *The psychology of prejudice and discrimination.* Belmont, CA: Wadsworth.

Whitten, S., & Graesser, A. C. (2003). Comprehension of text in problem solving. In J. E. Davidson & R. J. Sternberg (Eds.), *The psychology of problem solving* (207–229). New York: Cambridge University Press.

Wickelgren, W. A. (1965). Acoustic similarity and intrusion errors in short-term memory. *Journal of Experimental Psychology, 70,* 102–108.

Wickens, D. D., Dalezman, R. E., & Eggemeier, F. T. (1976). Multiple encoding of word attributes in memory. *Memory & Cognition, 4,* 307–310.

Wiers, R. W., & Stacy, A. W. (Eds.). (2006). *Handbook of implicit cognition and addiction.* Thousand Oaks, CA: Sage.

Wikman, A., Nieminen, T., & Summala, H. (1998). Driving experience and time-sharing during in-car tasks on roads of different width. *Ergonomics, 41,* 358–372.

Wilding, J., & Valentine, E. (1997). *Superior memory.* Hove, UK: Psychology Press.

Wiley, E. W., Bialystok, E., & Hakuta, K. (2005). New approaches to using data to test the critical-period hypothesis for second-language acquisition. *Psychological Science, 16,* 341–343.

Wilhelm, O. (2005). Measuring reasoning ability. In O. Wilhelm & R. W. Engle (Eds.), *Handbook of understanding and measuring intelligence* (pp. 373–392). Thousand Oaks, CA: Sage.

Willcutt, E. G., et al. (2005). Validity of the executive function theory of attention-deficit/hyperactivity disorder: A meta-analytic review. *Biological Psychiatry, 57,* 1336–1346.

Williams, C. C., Perea, M., Pollatsek, A., & Rayner, K. (2006). Previewing the neighborhood: The role of orthographic neighbors as parafoveal previews in reading. *Journal of Experimental Psychology: Human Perception and Performance, 32,* 1072–1082.

Williams, J. D. (2005). *The teacher's grammar book* (2nd ed.). Mahwah, NJ: Erlbaum.

Williams, J. M. G., Mathews, A., & MacLeod, C. (1996). The emotional Stroop task and psychopathology. *Psychological Bulletin, 120,* 3–24.

Williams, L. M., & Banyard, V. L. (Eds.). (1999). *Trauma & memory.* Thousand Oaks, CA: Sage.

Wilson, B. A. (1995). Management and remediation of memory problems in brain-injured adults. In A. D. Baddeley, B. A. Wilson, & F. N. Watts (Eds.), *Handbook of memory disorders* (pp. 451–479). Chichester, UK: Wiley.

Wilson, M. (2002). Six views of embodied cognition. *Psychonomic Bulletin & Review, 9*, 625–636.

Wilson, T. D. (1997). The psychology of meta-psychology. In J. D. Cohen & J. W. Schooler (Eds.), *Scientific approaches to consciousness* (pp. 317–332). Mahwah, NJ: Erlbaum.

Winerman, L. (2006, January). Let's sleep on it. *APA Monitor*, 58–60.

Wingfield, A. (1993). Sentence processing. In J. B. Gleason & N. Bernstein Ratner (Eds.), *Psycholinguistics* (pp. 199–235). Fort Worth: Harcourt Brace.

Wingfield, A., & Kahana, M. J. (2002). The dynamics of memory retrieval in older adulthood. *Canadian Journal of Experimental Psychology, 56*, 187–199.

Winkler, I., & Cowan, N. (2005). From sensory to long-term memory: Evidence from auditory memory reactivation studies. *Experimental Psychology, 52*, 3–20.

Winston, J. S., Strange, B. A., O'Doherty, J., & Dolan, R. J. (2005). Automatic and intentional brain responses during evaluation of trustworthiness of faces. In J. T. Cacioppo & G. G. Berntson (Eds.), *Social neuroscience: Key readings* (pp. 199–210). New York: Psychology Press.

Wisniewski, E. J. (2002). Concepts and categorization. In D. Medin (Ed.), *Stevens' handbook of experimental psychology* (3rd ed., Vol. 2, pp. 467–531). New York: Wiley.

Wohlschläger, A. (2001). Mental object rotation and the planning of hand movements. *Perception & Psychophysics 63*, 709–718.

Wolfe, J. M. (1998). What can 1 million trials tell us about visual search? *Psychological Science, 9*, 33–39.

Wolfe, J. M. (2000). Visual attention. In K. K. De Valois (Ed.), *Seeing* (2nd ed., pp. 335–386). San Diego: Academic Press.

Wolfe, J. M. (2001). Asymmetries in visual search: An introduction. *Perception & Psychophysics, 63*, 381–389.

Wolfe, J. M., & Cave, K. R. (1999). The psychophysical evidence for a binding problem in human vision. *Neuron, 24*, 11–17.

Wolfe, J. M., Horowitz, T. S., & Kenner, N. M. (2005). Rare items often missed in visual searches. *Nature, 435*, 439–440.

Wolfe, J. M., et al. (2006). *Sensation and perception*. Sunderland, MA: Sinauer.

Wolfe, M. B. W. (2005). Memory for narrative and expository text: Independent influences of semantic associations and text organization. *Journal of Experimental Psychology: Learning, Memory, and Cognition, 31*, 359–364.

Wolfe, M. B. W., & Goldman, S. R. (2005). Relations between adolescents' text processing and reasoning. *Cognition and Instruction, 23*, 467–502.

Wolfe, M. B. W., Magliano, J. P., & Larsen, B. (2005). Causal and semantic relatedness in discourse understanding and representation. *Discourse Processes, 39*, 165–187.

Woll, S. (2002). *Everyday thinking: Memory, reasoning, and judgment in the real world*. Mahwah, NJ: Erlbaum.

Wood, N., & Cowan, N. (1995). The cocktail party phenomenon revisited: How frequent are attention shifts to one's name in an irrelevant auditory channel? *Journal of Experimental Psychology: Learning, Memory, and Cognition, 21*, 255–260.

Woodward, A. L., & Markman, E. M. (1998). Early word learning. In W. Damon (Ed.), *Handbook of child psychology: Cognition, perception, and language* (5th ed., Vol. 2, 371–420). New York: Wiley.

Workman Publishing Company. (2007). Bad President countdown 2008 calendar. New York: Author.

Worthen, J. B. (2006). Resolution of discrepant memory strengths: An explanation of the effects of bizarreness on memory. In R. R. Hunt & J. B. Worthen (Eds.), *Distinctiveness and memory* (pp. 133–156). New York: Oxford University Press.

World almanac and book of facts. (2005). New York: World Almanac Books.

Wraga, M., et al. (2005). Imagined rotations of self versus objects: An fMRI study. *Neuropsychologia, 43*, 1351–1361.

Wright, D. B., Boyd, C. E., & Tredoux, C. G. (2003). Inter-racial contact and the own-race bias for face recognition in South Africa and England. *Applied Cognitive Psychology, 17*, 365–373.

Wynn, V. E., & Logie, R. H. (1998). The veracity of long-term memories—Did Bartlett get it right? *Applied Cognitive Psychology, 12*, 1–20.

Yamauchi, T. (2005). Labeling bias and categorical induction: Generative aspects of category information. *Journal of Experimental Psychology: Learning, Memory, and Cognition, 31*, 538–553.

Yang, L.-X., & Lewandowsky, S. (2004). Knowledge partitioning in categorization: Constraints on exemplar models. *Journal of Experimental Psychology: Learning, Memory and Cognition, 30,* 1045–1064.

Yang, S.-N., & McConkie, G. W. (2004). Saccade generation during reading: Are words necessary? In R. Radach, A. Kennedy, & K. Rayner (Eds.), *Eye movements and information processing during reading* (pp. 226–261). Hove, UK: Psychology Press.

Yarmey, A. D. (2007). The psychology of speaker identification and earwitness memory. In R. C. L. Lindsay, D. F. Ross, J. D. Read, & M. P. Toglia (Eds.), *Handbook of eyewitness psychology* (Vol. 2, pp. 101–136). Mahwah, NJ: Erlbaum.

Yoder, J. D. (2007). *Women and gender: Making a difference.* Cornwall-on-Hudson, NY: Sloan.

Yoon, C., May, C. P., & Hasher, L. (2000). Aging, circadian arousal patterns, and cognition. In D. C. Park & N. Schwarz (Eds.), *Cognitive aging* (pp. 151–171). Philadelphia: Psychology Press.

Young, C. A. (2007, July 21). *Scientists endeavor to make humanoid robots more graceful.* Retrieved July 25, 2007, from http://news-service.stanford.edu/news/2007/July11/robots-071107.html

Young, C. J. (2004). Contributions of metaknowledge to retrieval of natural categories in semantic memory. *Journal of Experimental Psychology: Learning, Memory, and Cognition, 30,* 909–916.

Young, J. E., Klosko, J. S., & Weishaar, M. E. (2003). *Schema therapy: A practitioner's guide.* New York: Guilford.

Yussen, S. R., & Levy, V. M. (1975). Developmental changes in predicting one's own span of short-term memory. *Journal of Experimental Child Psychology, 19,* 502–508.

Zacks, J. M., Tversky, B., & Iyer, G. (2001). Perceiving, remembering, and communicating structure in events. *Journal of Experimental Psychology: General, 130,* 29–58.

Zacks, J. M., Vettel, J. M., & Michelon, P. (2003). Imagined viewer and object rotations dissociated with event-related fMRI. *Journal of Cognitive Neuroscience, 15,* 1002–1018.

Zacks, R. T., & Hasher, L. (2006). Aging and long-term memory: Deficits are not inevitable. In E. Bialystok & F. I. M. Craik (Eds.), *Lifespan cognition: Mechanisms of change* (pp. 162–177). New York: Oxford University Press.

Zajac, R., & Hayne, H. (2006). The negative effect of cross-examination style questioning on children's accuracy: Older children are not immune. *Applied Cognitive Psychology, 20,* 3–16.

Zangwill, O. L. (2004a). Ebbinghaus, H. In R. L. Gregory (Ed.), *The Oxford companion to the mind* (2nd ed., p. 276). New York: Oxford University Press.

Zangwill, O. L. (2004b). Wundt, Wilhelm Max. In R. L. Gregory (Ed.), *The Oxford companion to the mind* (2nd ed., pp. 951–952). New York: Oxford University Press.

Zauberman, G., & Lynch, J. G., Jr. (2005). Resource slack and propensity to discount delayed investments of time versus money. *Journal of Experimental Psychology: General, 134,* 23–37.

Zeman, A. (2004). *Consciousness: A user's guide.* New Haven: Yale University Press.

Zentella, A. C. (2006). Hablamos Spanish and English. In H. Luria, D. M. Seymour, & T. Smoke (Eds.), *Language and linguistics in context: Readings and applications for teachers* (pp. 85–89). Mahwah, NJ: Erlbaum.

Zimmerman, B. J. (2006). Developmental and adaptation of expertise: The role self-regulatory processes and beliefs. In K.A. Ericsson, N. Charness, P. J. Feltovich, & R. R. Hoffman (Eds.), *The Cambridge handbook of expertise and performance* (pp. 705–722). New York: Cambridge Press University.

Zoelch, C., Scitz, K., & Schumann-Hengsteler, R. (2005). From "rag(bag)s to riches" Measuring the developing central executive. In W. Schneider, R. Schumann-Hengsteler, & B. Sodian (Eds.), *Young children's cognitive development* (pp. 39–69). Mahwah, NJ: Erlbaum.

Zwaan, R. A., & Rapp, D. N. (2006). Discourse comprehension. In M. J. Traxler & M. A. Gernsbacher (Eds.), *Handbook of psycholinguistics* (2nd ed., pp. 249–283). Amsterdam: Elsevier.

Zwaan, R. A., & Singer, M. (2003). Text comprehension. In A. C. Graesser, M. A. Gernsbacher, & S. R. Goldman (Eds.), *Handbook of discourse processes* (pp. 83–121). Mahwah, NJ: Erlbaum.

◎ Literary Credits

Color Figure 2: (inside front cover) Photo by Arnold H. Matlin, M. D. Photo taken at Servicio Infantil Rural Nimian Ortiz, in El Sauce, Nicaragua, a school supported by the Matlin family.

Demonstration 5.2: Balch, W. R. (2006). Introducing psychology students to research methodology: A word-pleasantness experiment. *Teaching of Psychology*, 33, 132-134.

Figure 5.2: A perceptual discrimination investigation of the own-race effect and intergroup experience, Walker, P. M. & Hewstone, M. © 2006. Copyright John Wiley & Sons Limited. Reproduced with permission.

Figure 6.1: Roediger, H. L., III & Karpicke, J. D., Test-enhanced learning: Taking memory tests improves long-term retention, Psychological Science. © 2006 Blackwell Publishing.

Figure 6.6: Knouse, L. E., Paradise, M. E., & Dunlosky, J. Journal of Attention Disorders. © 2006 Sage Publications, Inc.

Figure 10.4: Reprinted from Journal of Memory and Language, 54, Christoffles, I.K., de Goot, A.M.B. & Kroll, J.F., Memory and language skills in simultaneous interpreters: The role of expertise and language proficiency. 324-345, 2006, with permission from Elsevier.

Table 10.1: Shin, H. B., & Bruno, R. (2003, October). Language use and English-speaking ability: 2000. Washington, DC: U.S. Census Bureau.

Table 10.2: Statistics Canada (2006). Population by mother tongue, provinces and territories. Retrieved May 7,2007 from http://www40.statcan.ca/l01/cst01/demo11a.htm

Figure 11.2: Journal of Cognition and Culture. © 2007. BRILL.

Demonstration 12.10: Schwartz, B., et al. Maximizing versus satisficing: Happiness is a matter of choice. *Journal of Personality and Social Psychology*. © 2002. American Psychological Association.

Table 13.1: Individual and developmental differences in eyewitness recall and suggestibility in children with intellectual disabilities, Henry, L. A. & Gudjonsson, G. H. © 2007. John Wiley & Sons Limited. Reproduced with permission.

Name Index

Abelson, R. P., 267, 277
Acenas, L.-A. R., 192
Adams, J., 407
Adeyemo, S. A., 363
Adler, J., 377
Adler, S. A., 446
Adler, T., 137
Agans, R. P., 432
Agassi, J., 294
Ainsworth, W., 33, 306
Alba, J. W., 281
Albert, M. L., 141
Alexander, J. M., 465
Allbritton, D. W., 307
Allen, G. L., 203, 205
Alloway, T. P., 447
Allport, A., 369
Alter, J., 152
Alvarez, G. A., 109
Amabile, T. M., 387–389
Ambady, N., 379
American Psychiatric Association, 87,
    114, 186
American Psychological Association, 296
Amir, N., 138, 140
Anastasi, J. S., 144
Anderson, J. R., 67, 255, 257–259, 364,
    370
Anderson, M. C., 158
Anderson, R. E., 206
Andrade, J., 211
Anglin, J. M., 474
Aristotle, 4
Arnold, J. E., 327
Aronson, E., 428, 438
Aronson, J., 378
Ashby, F. G., 83
Atkinson, D., 343
Atkinson, R. C., 9–11, 96, 99–101
Atran, S., 252
Awh, E., 111
Ayres, T. J., 101, 102

Baars, B. J., 85, 89
Baayen, H., 326
Bäckman, L., 456, 458
Baddeley, A. D., 10, 94, 96, 97, 101,
    104–113, 128, 167, 169, 175,
    176, 182, 211, 241, 264, 289,
    447, 473

Badgaiyan, R. D., 140
Baer, J., 385
Bahrick, H. P., 145, 170, 348
Baker, J. M. C., 195
Baker, K. D., 70
Baker, L., 318
Baker-Ward, L., 453
Balch, W., 130–131, 132, 170
Baldwin, D., 476
Baldwin, D. A., 49
Baldwin, M. W., 267, 280
Baltes, P. B., 441, 442
Bamberg, M., 312, 330
Banaji, M. R., 279, 455
Bangerter, A., 331
Banyard, V. L., 156
Barash, D., 85
Bardovi-Harlig, K., 343
Bargh, J., 6, 8
Barnes, J. B., 4
Barnett, R. C., 219
Barnett, S. M., 368, 374
Baron, J., 357, 370, 395, 419, 429, 430
Barr, D. J., 333, 334
Barr, R., 443, 444, 445, 446
Barrett, H. C., 377–378, 404
Barsalou, L. W., 245, 247,
    250–255, 263
Bartlett, F. C., 7, 267, 276–277, 281,
    312–313
Baruss, I., 85
Bassok, M., 367, 368
Bates, E., 291, 293, 300, 301, 471, 473,
    474, 476
Batt, V., 77, 305, 315
Bauer, B., 207
Bauer, P. J., 442, 448–449
Bayliss, D. M., 114
Bazerman, C., 353
Bazerman, M. H., 405
Bearce, K. H., 446
Beardsley, T., 112
Beattie, G., 288
Bechtel, W., 4, 8
Beck, M. R., 49
Bediou, B., 54
Beeman, M., 301
Behrmann, M., 73
Beilock, S. I., 380
Bellezza, F. S., 125, 126, 173, 174

Ben-Zeev, T., 243, 246, 255, 258, 260,
    315, 365, 370, 374, 385, 413
Beni, R. D., 208
Bennett, M. D., 405
Bentin, S., 52
Bereiter, C., 339, 364
Berg, T., 338
Berger, C. R., 330
Berkowits, D., 273
Berliner, L., 157
Bernstein, D. M., 157
Bernstein, S. E., 310
Berntson, G. G., 13, 14, 16, 303
Berrios, G. E., 264
Berry, S. L., 194, 195
Bersick, M., 278
Bessenoff, G. R., 281–282
Betsch, T., 405
Bevan, K. M., 46
Bialystok, E., 341, 343–347, 456
Biber, D., 335
Biederman, I., 34, 38, 41,
    41–42, 42
Bieman-Copland, S., 466
Billman, D., 241
Binder, J., 14
Binder, K. S., 297
Biorge, A. K., 335
Birdsong, D., 346, 348
Birnbaum, M. H., 409
Birren, J. E., 441, 456
Bisconti, T. L., 441
Bishop, M. A., 429
Bjork, E. L., 128, 145
Bjork, R. A., 128, 166, 169, 170, 172,
    183, 427, 464
Bjorklund, D. F., 447, 448, 450, 451,
    463, 465, 476, 479–480
Blades, M., 225
Blanc, M. H. A., 345
Blascovich, J., 380
Block, R. A., 423
Blodgett, A., 327
Bloom, L. C., 124
Bloom, P., 467, 468, 472, 473,
    474, 476
Bluck, S., 132, 145
Bock, K., 289, 294, 325, 326, 327
Boden, M., 16, 17
Boden, M. A., 385

Subject Index

Note: New terms appear in boldface print.

Absentmindedness, 178–179
Abstract reasoning problems, 400
Abstraction, 274–276
Accuracy. *See also* Theme 2 (efficiency and accuracy)
    autobiographical memory and, 144–145
    of experts versus novices, 375–376
    of eyewitness testimony, 154–156
    of metacomprehension, 194–195
    of prediction of memory performance, 183–187
    of recall for pleasant items, 131–132
Acoustic confusions, 107–108
ACT-R (Automatic Components of Thought-Rational), 257–259
Active processes. *See* Theme 1 (active processes)
ADHD, 114, 186, 188
Affirming the antecedent, 397, 399
Affirming the consequent, 397–398, 399
African Americans. *See* Blacks
Age of acquisition, 345–348
Aged. *See* Elderly people
AI. *See* Artificial intelligence (AI)
Alerting attention network, 79
Algorithms, 365–366
Alignment heuristic, 230–231
Alphabet
    pronunciation of letters of, 305
    recall of lists of letters, 107, 173
    recognition of letters of, 38–41, 75
Ambiguity in language, 56, 297–299
Ambiguous figure-ground relationship, 36–37
Ambiguous figures and imagery, 213–215
Ambiguous sentences, 294
American Sign Language (ASL), 208
Amnesia, 139–140, 448–449
Analog code, 205, 216–217
Analogy approach, 366–368
Anchor, 419

Anchoring and adjustment heuristic, 394, 419–424
Anchoring effect, 419–424
Anesthesia, 139
Angles and cognitive maps, 228
Animal research
    face recognition, 52
    single-cell recording technique, 16, 41, 52
    visual stimulus, 16, 41
Antecedent, 397–399
Anterograde amnesia, 140
Aphasia, 299–301
Approach social goals, 134–135
Artificial intelligence (AI)
    computer metaphor, 17
    computer simulation, 18
    definition of, 16–17
    parallel distributed processing approach, 19–20
    pure AI, 17–18
    reading and, 319–320
Asian Americans, 379
ASL (American Sign Language), 208
Association for Behavioral and Cognitive Therapies, 12
Atkinson-Shiffrin model, 9–11, 100–101
Attention
    bottleneck theories of, 81
    change blindness and, 48–49
    definition of, 67
    dichotic listening, 69–70
    distributed attention, 82
    divided attention, 66, 68–69, 165–166
    in elderly people, 459
    explanations for, 77–84
    feature-integration theory, 81–84
    focused attention, 82
    inattentional blindness, 48, 50–51, 68
    in infants, 442–443
    introduction to, 66–67
    neuroscience research on, 78–81
    problem solving and, 357, 359
    saccadic eye movement, 66, 75–77
    selective attention, 69–74
    Stroop effect, 70–72, 80
    theories of, 81–84

    visual search, 72–74
Attention-deficit/hyperactivity disorder (ADHD), 114, 186, 188
Attribute substitution, 434–435
Auditory imagery, 211
Autobiographical memory
    Betrayal trauma, 158
    characteristics of, 145
    of children, 448–449
    definition of, 121, 144
    ecological validity and, 145
    episodic memory compared with, 121n
    flashbulb memory, 148–151
    schemas and, 145, 146
    source monitoring and, 147–148, 449–450
Availability heuristic, 394, 413–419
Avoidance social goals, 135

Babbling, 417
Base rate, 408, 409–411
Base-rate fallacy, 409
Basic-level categories, 249–250
Bayes' theorem, 410
Behaviorist approach
    and behaviorism
    consciousness and, 85
    definition of, 6
    external events and, 97
    history of, 6
    imagery and, 203
    insight and, 382
    language behavior and, 293
    schema and, 267
Belgium, 341
Belief-bias effect, 401, 419
Betrayal trauma, 158
Biases
    belief-bias effect, 401, 419
    confirmation bias, 402–405, 419
    consistency bias, 146, 154
    experimenter expectancy, 208–209, 216
    foresight bias, 183
    hindsight bias, 430–432
    my-side bias, 430
    own-race bias, 142, 443
Bilingual, 341

Themes of This Textbook

Theme 1:   The cognitive processes are active, rather than passive.

Theme 2:   The cognitive processes are remarkably efficient and accurate.

Theme 3:   The cognitive processes handle positive information better than negative information.

Theme 4:   The cognitive processes are interrelated with one another; they do not operate in isolation.

Theme 5:   Many cognitive processes rely on both bottom-up and top-down processing.

Color Figure 2 (for Demonstration 2.4)

Color Figure 3 (for Demonstration 3.1)

Part A

RED	BLUE	GREEN	YELLOW	GREEN
RED	**BLUE**	YELLOW	BLUE	RED
YELLOW	GREEN	YELLOW	GREEN	**BLUE**
RED	RED	**GREEN**	YELLOW	**BLUE**

Part B

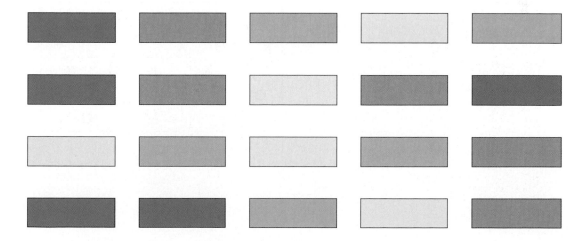

Color Figure 4 (for Demonstration 3.2)

Part A

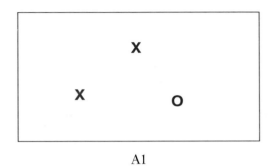

A1   A2

Part B

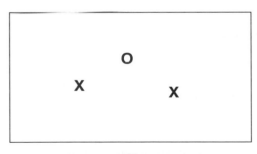

B1   B2